Mastering
Lotus Notes and Domino 6

Mastering™
Lotus® Notes® and Domino 6

Matt Riggsby

Cate McCoy

Scot Haberman

Andrew Falciani

SYBEX®

San Francisco   London

Associate Publisher: Joel Fugazzotto

Acquisitions Editor: Chris Denny

Developmental Editor: Brianne Hope Agatep

Editor: Kim Wimpsett

Production Editor: Liz Burke

Technical Editor: Tomkin Lee

Graphic Illustrator: Tony Jonick

Electronic Publishing Specialist: Judy Fung

Proofreaders: Erich Lach, Emily Hsuan, Sarah Tannehill, Nancy Riddiough, Yariv Rabinovitch, Laurie O'Connell, Monique van den Berg, Dave Na

Indexer: Ted Laux

Book Designer: Maureen Forys, Happenstance Type-O-Rama

Cover Designer: Design Site

Cover Illustrator: Tania Kac, Design Site

To Susan…a best friend who I owe to Notes…
amazing how bits and bytes can magically produce
friends.
—Cate McCoy

For Pliny the Elder and Isidore of Seville.
—Matt Riggsby

Acknowledgments

AT THE END OF a long and hard journey, one cannot help but feel simultaneously relieved and a bit sa
This book has been that type of journey, and as I return to a normal life once again, I'll both miss it an
be thankful that it is now in your hands and not mine. My family and friends are also thankful it is i
your hands since I can now pay them the attention that they deserve but have been denied for man
months. As I am constantly reminded by a dear man, I am truly blessed to be loved and called *friend* b
so many people, and I thank each of you for once again encouraging me on my chosen path.

Special thanks to the team at Sybex who take as much pride in their work as I take in mine. It's a wra

—*Cate McCoy*

For this edition, thanks are due (in approximate chronological order) to the following: Scot Haberma
and Andrew Falciani, for declining to work on this edition, thereby giving me the opportunity to do s
Chris Denny, for getting me involved; Brianne Agatep, for orchestrating the work; Liz Burke, for ridin
herd on two authors with wildly unpredictable schedules; Kim Wimpsett, for editing a morass of chang
into a readable text; Tomkin Lee, for making sure that what we wrote is true as well as readable; Jud
Fung, for laying out the book; and, of course, Stephanie, for putting up with my spending so much tim
at the computer working on this book instead of with her.

—*Matt Riggsby*

Contents at a Glance

Contents

Introduction

To make knowledge work more productive will be the great management task of this century, just as to make manual work productive was the great management task of the last century.

—Peter Drucker, *Landmarks of Tomorrow*, 1959

WHEN YOU WERE IN high school, did you check the box to say you wanted to be a knowledge worker when you grew up? Unlikely! The past 50 years has presented each of us with the challenge of mastering the information we need to do our best job, and we have, in the process, become the epitome of the knowledge worker. IBM's Lotus Notes and Domino 6 software supports the knowledge worker with the task-centered focus needed to acquire, store, organize, program, and distribute information in today's fast-paced world. With this exciting new version, the evolution that is Lotus Notes and Domino continues.

Mastering Lotus Notes and Domino 6 presents the Lotus Notes client and the Domino Designer client as they appear to the people who use them. We begin with an overview of Notes as it appears to the person who processes daily e-mails, checks their calendar, and interacts with company information. We then continue on to the Internet and look at how to do those same tasks using a web browser instead of the Notes client. Finally, we move to the power behind the scenes and learn how to program and deploy applications using Domino Designer. If you're new to Lotus Notes, this book will get you started using the remarkably powerful Notes client. If you're an advanced user, this book will help you get the most out of its many features. If you're ready to take control of your information from an application perspective, we'll get you going with the core concepts you need to start building your own applications.

New in Lotus Notes and Domino 6

The focus of the new release of Lotus Notes and Domino is productivity. IBM has added an enormous number of features to the Notes client to make processing daily work tasks easier. The Domino Designer client now includes new and powerful Internet development features to keep pace with and to stay ahead of other software development tools.

The Notes Client

The Notes client has a new look and feel to it, though its organization remains essentially the same as Release 5. Core applications have been refined and packed with more features as a result of feedback from users. The following are some of the most important improvements in the Notes client:

- Color-coded entries in the calendar

- A quick-access toolbar to see mail and the calendar with a single click
- Quicker updates to Notes and Internet passwords
- Internet-style e-mail replies
- Drag-and-drop shortcuts to the desktop
- Document locking
- An at-a-glance count of unread documents in folders
- Print spooling to speed printing in the background as you continue working
- Security settings summarized in the User Security screen
- A configuration wizard for fast setup of Notes
- Connection wizards to create Internet accounts and newsgroup readers
- Keyboard shortcuts for many tasks
- Drag-and-drop interactions with views

Domino Designer

The Domino Designer client and its capabilities have grown once again! This release of Designer also includes significant enhancements for Domino Designer:

- The ability to reuse shared resources across multiple databases
- Enhanced source code and object printing
- Better support for mobile devices
- Finer control over graphics with stored images
- The ability to add layers to pages and forms
- Better performance and more features in the formula language
- Built-in support for connections to external databases
- A new Hypertext Markup Language (HTML) editor
- Extensible Markup Language (XML) in the Designer and with Java and LotusScript, as well as support for Document Type Definitions (DTDs)
- Reusable shared JavaScript libraries

Most of the improvements in Designer 6 are fairly subtle, so no brief listing can really explain the changes adequately. Chapter 1 contains a somewhat more detailed listing of changes, and if you're familiar with Release 5, you'll be particularly excited as you discover the coding enhancements throughout the book.

How This Book Is Organized

This book is organized into four parts, making it easy for you to find the information you need.

Part I: Introducing Lotus Notes 6

Part I introduces Notes and how best to utilize the Notes client. It covers in detail the updated user interface and how you can be more productive using the Notes client as your source for both personal and enterprise information. It also covers the basic features of Notes, such as databases, views, and documents, along with the core functionality of personal information management.

CHAPTER 1: WHAT IS LOTUS NOTES?

Chapter 1 provides an overview of the Notes client—what it is and how you can use it as an effective personal information management tool. Also, several sections explain the structure of Notes databases and many of the new features specific to the Notes client.

CHAPTER 2: GETTING FAMILIAR WITH NOTES

Chapter 2 covers the main features of the client interface—everything from using the Welcome page (and configuring it) and the application window to using the integrated Notes Help facility.

CHAPTER 3: WORKING WITH DATABASES

In Chapter 3 you'll find an explanation of the basic Notes database concepts. We'll discuss navigating common Notes database features and dealing with Notes documents.

CHAPTER 4: TAILORING LOTUS NOTES 6

Chapter 4 discusses a variety of options for configuring the Notes client. This includes setting client preferences, managing network connections, and creating entries in your personal address book to manage your contacts.

Part II: Mastering the Basics with the Notes Client

Part II gives you an in-depth look at the powerful usability features in the Lotus Notes client. This part guides you through using the client to send and receive mail as well as to organize it, using the calendar to keep track of your commitments, interacting with other Notes users, and finding information easily. We also explain and demonstrate security and collaboration, two of Notes' strengths.

CHAPTER 5: COMMUNICATING WITH NOTES MAIL

In today's business world, the need to work with e-mail is as fundamental as the need to breathe air. This chapter takes you through the organization of the mail interface, shows you how to send and receive mail, describes how to filter out spam, and shows you how to keep yourself organized with folders. You'll learn how to address mail with minimum typing and configure the client so that you can send auto-responses when you're out of the office.

CHAPTER 6: CALENDARING AND SCHEDULING

Notes and Domino 6 includes major improvements in the area of calendaring and scheduling. In this chapter, you'll get to know the new user interface components, schedule different types of calendar activities, and send meeting notices. You'll learn how to navigate the calendar, set calendar preferences, allow other users to access your calendar, and use your calendar to work with others.

CHAPTER 7: COLLABORATING WITH NOTES

Chapter 7 shows you how to use the server-based collaborative applications such as forums (discussions), TeamRooms, and Document Libraries. We also demonstrate using workflow applications and signing off on approvals.

CHAPTER 8: SEARCHING FOR INFORMATION

Having lots of information is of no use to you unless you can find it when you need it. In Chapter 8, you'll look at how to search for information in views, solitary databases, and multiple databases. In addition, you can use the Notes client to search the Internet.

CHAPTER 9: COMMUNICATING WITH DOMINO SERVERS

In Chapter 9, you'll learn how to go mobile with the Notes client. Communicating with a Domino server requires a good understanding of Connection documents and Location documents used with the Notes client. In this chapter, you'll discover everything you need to connect to a Domino server whether you're in your office or on the road.

CHAPTER 10: REPLICATION

Replication is a core technology feature of Domino. In Chapter 10, you'll look at this powerful feature, learn what it is, and learn what you need to do to make it happen in your Notes client. We'll introduce the new user interface for the Replicator area of the Notes client and show how to organize it to send and receive Notes mail and Internet mail.

CHAPTER 11: LOTUS NOTES AND DOMINO SECURITY

Chapter 11 covers the security standards that protect your information in Lotus Notes and Domino. Since its inception, the security model behind Notes has been a feature that makes other products pale in comparison. In this chapter, we'll explain how to configure settings so that you can protect your data.

CHAPTER 12: INTEGRATING NOTES WITH OTHER APPLICATIONS

Chapter 12 demonstrates how you can import and export information to and from your Notes client. The information you need is not always accessible from within Notes, so there are quite a few options that allow you to move information freely, such as attaching files and using the Windows Clipboard. We'll also provide thoughts on how to use ODBC to integrate Notes with other applications.

Part III: Lotus Notes Domino and the Internet

Part III focuses on using Lotus Notes and Domino in the world of the Internet. You can use the Notes client to retrieve Internet mail or use a browser client to retrieve Notes mail. You can set up newsreaders to pull information from an Internet news server. You can also use the Lotus Notes built-in web browser to store Internet information inside a Notes database.

CHAPTER 13: ACCESSING THE INTERNET WITH A NOTES CLIENT

Chapter 13 explains how to configure the Notes client to be your portal to the Internet. You can use it to access web pages, search the Internet, and look up information in Internet directories.

CHAPTER 14: MANAGING NOTES E-MAIL WITH A BROWSER

In Chapter 14, you'll learn how to do all your familiar mail tasks using a web browser instead of a Notes client. You can create, address, send, and receive mail using a web browser connected to a Domino server.

CHAPTER 15: DOMINO OFF-LINE SERVICES AND INOTES

Chapter 15 introduces the Domino Off-Line Services (DOLS) product that lets you work with web-based information using a web browser client in offline mode. This chapter looks at what this service is and how you might put it to work for you.

Part IV: Developing Lotus Notes Applications with Domino Designer

Part V introduces you to the development side of Notes: using the Domino Designer client to develop Notes and web applications and recognizing the various design elements that make up a Notes database. This part includes chapters that demonstrate how to incorporate automation into your applications and how to use the various programming languages available for use in Notes.

CHAPTER 16: INTRODUCING DOMINO DESIGNER

Chapter 16 examines the various components of the integrated development environment (IDE) that a developer uses when creating an application. It also shows you how to navigate the Domino Designer development environment.

CHAPTER 17: DATABASE CREATION AND PROPERTIES

Chapter 17 explains how to create your first database and the various database options that can affect the performance of a Notes application. It includes tutorials on the different ways you can create a database and information to help you keep your databases secure.

CHAPTER 18: UNDERSTANDING THE FORMULA LANGUAGE

Chapter 18 introduces the formula language, the simplest and most pervasive language in most Notes databases. It demonstrates the syntax rules of the language and introduces some of the most useful commands.

CHAPTER 19: BASIC FORM DESIGN

Chapter 19 introduces you to Notes forms and how to create them. It also explains form properties and the fundamental elements necessary to make a useful form for editing and displaying data.

CHAPTER 20: ADVANCED FORM DESIGN

Chapter 20 details the more advanced design elements that you can use on a form (such as sections and layout regions). You'll also learn how to use actions and hotspots to provide automation and add graphics to your forms.

CHAPTER 21: USING VIEWS AND FOLDERS

Chapter 21 covers views. Specifically, you'll learn what elements make a view, and you'll see how to create a view. Also, this chapter describes the many view options available to an application designer.

CHAPTER 22: OUTLINES, PAGES, FRAMESETS, AND NAVIGATORS

Chapter 22 covers four design elements (outlines, pages, framesets, and navigators) and how you can use them to create an easily navigated database.

CHAPTER 23: SHARED RESOURCES AND OTHER FEATURES

Chapter 23 discusses shared resources, subsidiary objects such as graphics and downloadable files th
can be incorporated into a Notes database for central maintenance.

CHAPTER 24: LANGUAGE EXTENSIONS AND THE OBJECT MODEL

Chapter 24 outlines the use of two advanced languages in Notes: LotusScript and Java. It explain
LotusScript syntax rules and gives a brief overview of the Notes/Domino object model, the key
both LotusScript and Java programming. It also touches on the use of JavaScript.

CHAPTER 25: SHARED CODE OBJECTS

Chapter 25 discusses the use of centrally managed, shared objects that contain program code, inclu
ing agents, shared actions, and code libraries.

APPENDIX A: INSTALLING IBM LOTUS NOTES AND DOMINO 6 CLIENTS

Appendix A includes step-by-step instructions for installing the Notes client and Domino Design
on your computer. You'll learn about installation directories and how to set up the software.

ADDITIONAL RESOURCES

The website for this book (`www.sybex.com/SybexBooks.nsf/booklist/4053`) contains a number
databases that illustrate points and techniques throughout the book.

Conventions Used in This Book

This book implements a number of conventions to present information in as readable a manner a
possible. Tips, Notes, and Warnings appear from time to time in order to call attention to specif
information.

TIP *This is a Tip. Tips contain specific product information.*

NOTE *This is a Note. Notes contain important ancillary discussions.*

WARNING *This is a Warning. Warnings call attention to bugs, design omissions, and other trouble spots.*

This book takes advantage of several font styles. **Bold font** in text indicates something that the us
types. A `monospaced font` is used for code, output, Uniform Resource Locators (URLs), and file an
directory names.

How to Contact the Authors

Thanks for letting us be your guides through Lotus Notes and Domino 6. Feel free to share your tale
of success with us. You can reach Cate at `cate@alphapointsys.com` or through the AlphaPoint websi
at `www.alphapointsys.com`. Matt is equally accessible through e-mail at `mriggsbynotes@mindspring.co`
Enjoy this new release of Lotus Notes and Domino!

Part 1

Introducing
Lotus Notes 6

In this section:

Chapter 1

What Is Lotus Notes?

LOTUS NOTES IS A powerful, integrated information management client. It can help you manage your e-mail, business and personal contact information, schedule, and tasks, and it can act as a multipurpose Internet client. With Release 6, you can browse Internet or intranet websites while connected to a network or retrieve previously browsed information offline. You can search for information in Light Directory Access Protocol (LDAP)–based directories on the Internet or your company's intranet. Release 6 can integrate multiple Post Office Protocol (POP) and Internet Message Access Protocol (IMAP) mail accounts—the two dominant protocols for receiving e-mail—into a single, universal Inbox or, if you desire, into separate mailboxes that you can switch between with a menu option. It will even enable you to participate in Usenet discussions on the Internet, online and offline. Notes does all of this through a consistent, integrated interface, and it can do so on multiple platforms; the Notes client is available for both MacOS and Windows.

Notes is also the client-side software of the Lotus Notes/Domino family of products, which provide you with the most complete solution for effectively communicating and collaborating among teams, groups, and entire enterprises. Used to access Notes databases on the Domino server, Notes can provide immensely powerful applications tailored to the needs of an organization. Notes databases are particularly strong when it comes to workflow applications and document-centric applications such as online catalogs and discussions. Notes can also be used within environments entirely based on Internet-related services such as Hypertext Transfer Protocol (HTTP)/Hypertext Markup Language (HTML), LDAP, POP3/IMAP/Simple Mail Transfer Protocol (SMTP), and Network News Transfer Protocol (NNTP). It won't act as a fully featured File Transfer Protocol (FTP) client, but short of that kind of intensive file-transfer activity, Notes provides you with just about any communications protocol you'll need.

- ◆ Introducing Lotus Notes
- ◆ Uses of Notes
- ◆ What's new in Release 6?

Uses of Notes

You can use Notes in a variety of personal and business situations. For example, you can use Not with your Internet service provider (ISP) account to communicate with family and friends or to acce the full range of web-based information. As a tool for those involved with businesses, Notes can wo on a local area network (LAN) or with an ISP account to communicate with colleagues or custome keep up with changes affecting the industry, research business opportunities, and stay competitive Combined with Domino, Notes can unleash the full potential of teams, departments, and entir enterprises. Indeed, using Notes without Domino is like driving an 18-wheeler and never hauling more than a few bags of groceries.

The Core Functionality of Notes

No matter how you plan to use Notes—either as an Internet client or a Domino client—you can sta out by recording your personal information. Just "out of the box," without any attempt to communica with other computers via an ISP or LAN, Notes includes core functionality that lets you manage yo personal information as follows:

- ◆ Store contact information
- ◆ Manage your schedule using the built-in calendar
- ◆ Take control of your tasks by entering items in the to do list
- ◆ Keep a personal journal

You store and manage your Contact information using the Notes' built-in personal address boo You can think of this as your electronic Rolodex. Notes enables you to store a wide variety of info mation about each contact, including phone numbers, physical addresses, e-mail addresses, and s on. By recording your contact information in Notes, you eliminate the need for paper address bool

Notes includes a calendar for you to keep track of your schedule. You can enter appointments anniversaries, reminders, and events just as you can on a paper calendar. You can also use the calend group scheduling if you are participating in a Domino-based collaboration environment.

There is even a personal to do list in Notes. It contains personal task entries that can include, for example, priorities, status, and start/due dates. Your to do list also contains group to do items assigne to you if you are participating in a Domino-based collaboration environment.

Also, Notes includes a personal journal that can store other information. If you use Notes in co junction with a Palm handheld or IBM WorkPad personal digital assistant (PDA), your persona journal synchronizes with your PDA's memo pad application. This makes the personal journal a co venient place to store information, such as a travel itinerary, notes for a meeting, or directions, th you may need when you're away from your desk.

Notes as an Internet Information Client

If you plan to use Notes as an Internet client, you'll have the following added capability:

- ◆ You can receive e-mail from one or more POP/IMAP mail accounts and send mail to any SMTP server.
- ◆ You can access LDAP-based directories, such as Bigfoot and VeriSign, to search for peopl
- ◆ You can participate in Usenet-based discussions.
- ◆ You can browse Internet or intranet websites.

As a full-featured messaging client, Notes can be configured to retrieve POP mail and copy it to your local mail database. You can configure it to retrieve IMAP mail and copy it to your local mail database, access IMAP mail accounts online, and even replicate a copy of an IMAP mail account to a locally stored database for offline use. You can configure Notes to send outbound messages directly to an SMTP server. For message content, Notes supports a wide range of standards, including Multipurpose Internet Mail Extension (MIME), Secure Multipurpose Internet Mail Extension (S/MIME), HTML, and X.509 certificates.

Whether you are using Notes to access the Internet or an intranet, you can use LDAP directories to search for people or to address e-mail. On the Internet, you can configure Notes to access popular directories such as Bigfoot and VeriSign. On an intranet, you can use Notes to access your corporate directory, assuming it has been made available through LDAP.

You can also configure Notes as a newsreader, too. This means you can participate in Internet-based Usenet discussions in the same familiar interface you use with your e-mail. Also, Notes allows you to replicate newsgroups to a local database so you can interact offline or use Notes' powerful full-text search capabilities.

For browsing, Notes provides two integrated solutions. First, Notes includes a native browser. This native browser supports HTML 4 standards and can be used to access most sites. Second, Notes provides integrated browser services using the Microsoft Internet Explorer object linking and embedding (OLE) object. This means you get the all the features of Internet Explorer within the Notes interface and with Notes' capability to store pages for offline use, forward pages that are formatted exactly as they are in the browser, and so on.

Notes as a Domino Client

As useful as the Notes client can be as a personal information manager and Internet services client, using it as a Domino client is where its true power lies. In addition to all of the personal information management and Internet client capabilities mentioned, Notes is also the value-added client for Domino server environments. You can use Domino servers exclusively to provide messaging and application services to Internet clients such as web browsers, POP/IMAP mail clients, or newsreaders. This is a great way to provide capabilities to a wide range of client environments. The downside is that you are limiting the functionality to what these Internet clients can support. To go beyond that, you can use the Notes client to add the following functionality:

- The ability to natively access Notes/Domino database applications
- The ability to use Domino as your mail server
- The ability to use Domino for group scheduling
- The ability to replicate databases to your computer and work disconnected with full application functionality
- A greater range of application security, including encryption to the field level
- Full-text searching on all information stored in indexed databases, both locally and on remote servers
- The ability to read all major file formats using built-in file viewer technology
- Data integration and management services such as import/export and Open Database Connectivity (ODBC)

- ◆ Integration with network environments that are not based on TCP/IP
- ◆ Presentation of all information in a consistent, easy-to-use manner

You can even use Notes in conjunction with hosted Domino environments and receive all of t[]
benefits mentioned. Lotus has teamed with service providers to offer shared or hosted Domino s[]
vices. Shared Domino services enable organizations to take advantage of all the capabilities of Do[]
ino without the burden of deploying and managing the infrastructure. This extends the sophisticat[]
capabilities of Domino to a broader range of organizations.

NOTE *Just to make the relationship between Notes and Domino clear: Notes is client software. It runs on your com-*
puter and exchanges information with a server as you interact with it directly. Domino is server software. It runs on a
different computer, probably much bigger and faster than yours, and it serves as an administrative center and a centra[]
storehouse for data exchanged with any number of clients.

Flexible Configuration

In addition, Notes is installed on your computer in a way that enables you to start using it for one p[]
pose and easily change the configuration as your needs change. For example, you could start using Not[]
exclusively as an Internet client. If you later encounter a situation that requires access to a Domino serv[]
all that's required is a simple change in configuration. You would not be required to reinstall Notes[]

Notes can maintain multiple configurations, and these configurations are based on location. Thi[]
means you can use Notes with one configuration while you're in the office and another when you wo[]
from home, all on the same machine. With this feature, you can use Notes for a variety of purposes[]

Key Concepts

Behind all of Notes' features, there's a definite structure, and knowing how Notes works will help y[]
figure out how to use it. You should become familiar with a few key concepts before dealing with t[]
Notes client and Notes databases.

Databases

The Notes client is, at its heart, a client for using databases created with the Domino Designer cl[]
ent. The information Notes deals with and the tools for dealing with that information are co[]
tained within a single database file (Notes database files generally use the suffix .nsf). For examp[]
the configuration information that allows you to switch between using Notes as an Internet client []
and a Domino server client is stored in a database on your computer. Messages you receive, wheth[]
from the Internet or from within a Notes network mediated by a Domino server, and even web[]
pages you view if you use Notes as a web browser, are also stored in a database.

In addition to the data itself, a Notes database contains a number of design elements that provide us[]
interface features and automation. Every button, list of items, or page layout you see within a Notes da[]
base is given shape by a design element. The database may also contain a great deal of program code t[]
perform calculations and do other automated tasks. This program code can be in a number of differe[]
languages: the Notes formula language, a relatively simple language derived from a spreadsheet macr[]

language; LotusScript, a more complex, powerful language, similar to Visual Basic; and the cross-platform languages Java and JavaScript. There are advantages and limitations to each, and which language is used can be limited by the context in which the program code is to run. We'll get into the specifics of these languages in Part 4, "Developing Lotus Notes Applications with Domino Designer."

The data in Notes databases is held in structures called *documents*. Documents are discrete, semi-structured bundles of information. Like a table row in a relational database, a document consists of a number of items called *fields*. For example, a document might contain the following as separate, identifiable elements: a creator's name, a workflow status, lists of potential and future approvers, and a block of text discussing a proposal. However, unlike a relational database table row, a document in a Notes database is not limited to a specific set of fields. During its life cycle, a document can have any number of fields added or removed and their data changed. You can think of documents and databases as paper documents in a filing cabinet. Related documents may have things in common (for example, they could all be survey forms, with different answers to the same set of questions), but there's nothing to stop you from scribbling notes in the margins.

Still, even though documents aren't rigidly connected to one another like rows in a relational database table, they can be linked together. Documents can be linked in a parent-child relationship. That is, documents can carry with them information marking them as being related to a specific parent document. Other documents may in turn have those documents as parents.

To get to documents, you'll often use design elements called *views* and *folders*. Views and folders are elements that provide the user with lists of documents, a bit like a table in a relational database. Each row represents a single document, and each column represents data in the document (or, at least, information derived from data in the document). The Contacts view in your address book is a typical view (see Figure 1.1). Each row is a single contact. Each column shows some bit of information about that contact: the contact's name, phone number, and so on.

FIGURE 1.1

Contacts view

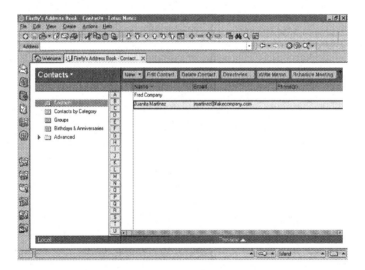

Views and folders are nearly identical. The only difference is in how documents are selected to appear in them. Views use a formula to automatically select documents; if you're familiar with relational databases, the contents of a view might be regarded as the results of a Structured Query Language (SQL) query. The user selects the contents of folders, on the other hand, on an ad-hoc basis. Rather than applying a formula, the user adds documents to a folder exactly like you might put several pieces of paper into a physical file folder.

You'll use *forms* for your main interaction with documents. A Notes form is a template that includes prompts and field interface objects that provide you with a means for entering information. You can think of a form as a shape into which the data is poured. A document, by itself, has no page layout information or controls; it's just a batch of data. The form designates where (if at all) each field appears, as well as its font, size, and color. It also includes any labels and other static, explanatory text, program code to validate input, computations, and code to perform automatic actions such as saving changes, creating responses, or sending update notifications. The Contact form is a commonly used form (see Figure 1.2). The document itself can't be displayed; it's just a bunch of data. The Contact form is what tells the computer where to display all the names and address information. The form design also includes the action buttons at the top as well as the program code behind them.

FIGURE 1.2

A document using the Contact form

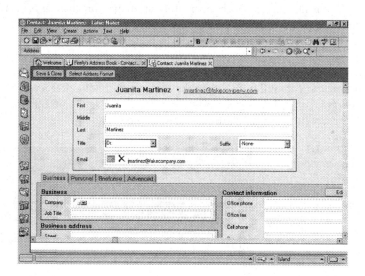

One point for experienced database users to keep in mind is that although Notes is a database, it is not a *relational* database. At first glance, you might think fields and documents are similar to columns and rows in relational databases, particularly because views and folders display them in a similar fashion. Although you can use Notes design elements to emulate columns and rows, they are different in many ways. Relational databases are repositories for highly structured information. They contain *tables*, which logically structure data into *rows* and *columns*. Every row in a given table has all of the columns defined in the table, no more and no less. This lends itself to collections of rows that are similar to one another. Most relational database tables also incorporate unique key values to identify individual rows. For example, a table containing a list of employees might have an employee ID number as a key. Each row would represent a single employee, so no two rows could have the same value in the employee ID field; the database will reject any attempt to duplicate an employee ID. No such constraints exist in Notes; there could be multiple documents with the same employee ID.

Another aspect of relational databases that is different from Notes databases is how data is manipulated in sets. The user or developer interacts with the relational database by using SQL, which is designed for working with sets of rows in tables. It's possible to select a group of documents with the Notes client's search functions or program code, but ultimately you manipulate the documents individually. There are many other differences, but another important one to note is that relational database servers are designed to manage concurrent access to the sets of rows in the database. Because of this, they are well suited for applications/systems in which many users must modify the same information. With new document-locking capabilities, Release 6 is better suited to such applications, but still not as well as many relational databases.

WHAT APPLICATIONS SHOULD AND SHOULD NOT BE DEVELOPED USING NOTES/ DOMINO?

The following types of applications are not generally well suited for Notes:

◆ Those involving a high degree of concurrent editing of the same data

◆ Those with highly structured data

◆ Those with high-volume data requirements

An airline reservation system is a clear example of an application that is not well suited for Notes. Thousands of travel agents will be accessing the system concurrently, trying to book reservations on a finite set of flights. It involves a high degree of concurrent edits and has high-volume data requirements.

On the other hand, a system to manage the process of conducting business travel would be a good application for a Notes database. Consider the following simplified process:

1. The employee completes a form to initiate the travel approval process.

2. The request is either approved or denied and communicated back to the employee.

3. If approved, the employee contacts the appropriate organization to make the travel arrangements.

4. The reservations are made and communicated back to the employee, along with maps, driving directions, and other relevant information.

5. The employee verifies that the arrangements were made properly.

6. The employee completes the trip.

7. After the trip, the employee initiates the expense-reporting process in a similar fashion.

8. If the travel request is denied, the employee completes the instructions provided with the denied request and resubmits it.

Continued on next page

In this example, the travel request is only relevant to a single user at a time. The employee creates the request and sends it to management for approval. The manager acts on the request and returns it to the employee. Also, the process involves communicating with nonstructured data, maps, and other relevant information along with the itinerary. Process-oriented applications such as this one are generally well suited for Notes databases. Notes databases are appropriate for many different types of applications, including:

- Process-oriented (as previously mentioned)

- Broadcast, where common information is widely disseminated to a large audience

- Discussion

- Library

- Mail/messaging

- Surveys or information collection

- Communities of interest

- Online publications

Replication

One of Notes' long-standing strengths is replication. A *replica* is a special kind of copy of a database. When presented with replicas of a database, Notes can synchronize them. When told to replicate the databases, Notes will quickly compile a list of changes made to both copies since the last time the two were synchronized and send the updated information in one or both directions, bringing both copies up-to-date with one another. This capability allows users to create and maintain mobile copies of databases without the time and trouble of creating complete new copies to replace out-of-date ones. Users can also work on a database while separated from their organization's main servers; when they connect to their network again, they can replicate, sending only their new information to the organization's servers and downloading only new information added by others.

Security

Notes has put considerable emphasis on storing data securely. It provides solid security at a number of different levels, allowing users and administrators to fine-tune access to databases and individual documents, even limiting permissions to sections of documents and individual fields. In addition to access permissions, individual items of data and entire copies of databases can be encrypted so that even if users get inappropriate permission, they won't be able to read the data. Users and groups of users can be prohibited from accessing Domino servers and running potentially dangerous program code in contexts where it can do real damage. Is it any wonder that Notes has been used as an internal mail client by the Central Intelligence Agency and National Security Agency?

One feature introduced in Release 5 and enhanced in Release 6 is that permissions can be set to selectively prevent program code from being executed within the Notes client itself. That may sound unspectacular, but it's actually an important security feature. A profound vulnerability of some e-mail clients is that they'll happily run program code written in appropriate languages. The problem with this is that it becomes easy for someone to write malicious code masquerading as a friendly e-mail message. The code executes when an unsuspecting recipient opens the message. Indeed, a great many computer viruses are spread that way these days. In Notes, however, every bit of program code carries with it a digital signature identifying the last person who modified it. When the code runs, Notes checks permissions that have been granted in the client to that person, and if there's something wrong with the digital signature or if the instructions in the code exceed the author's permissions, it will ask you how to proceed. In short, you can determine whose code you trust and whose you don't, making it hard to write viruses like those plaguing other e-mail clients.

Messaging

Because Notes is all about sharing information, another of its major functions is messaging. Notes makes it easy to send messages to others in the form of e-mail. *Others*, in this case, means individuals, groups, and even other database applications. Messages can be sent in an automated fashion, messages can be sent to potentially any database, and potentially any document can be mailed, quite possibly carrying its own user interface and automation with it. Messaging also permeates many of the Notes functions mentioned so far. For example, you can share and coordinate to do items and calendar events between groups of people via specially constructed e-mail messages.

What's New in Notes 6?

The change from the earlier family of Notes products to Release 5 could have been called revolutionary. There were fundamental changes to both the Notes client and Domino server. The move from Release 5 to Release 6 is more evolutionary, adding a number of smaller features and fine-tuning existing ones. However, for this kind of software, even small changes are significant. Included in this section is an overview of some of the most significant changes in Notes, including:

- Mobile user improvements
- Welcome page and navigation enhancements
- Mail enhancements
- Calendar enhancements
- Rich-text enhancements
- Security
- Other client interface enhancements

For Domino Designer, the highlights include the following:

- New design elements
- Revamped underpinnings for formula language
- Improved programming interface

- ◆ Easier integration with enterprise data
- ◆ Improved language support

As important as these changes are for the Notes/Domino product line, database design isn't som thing with which most users will ever deal. Details on the new and improved Domino Designer, ar what it means for building Notes databases, begin in Chapter 16, "Introducing Domino Designe

Mobile User Capabilities

Configuring Notes to work with standard Internet protocols has become much easier. Release 6 p vides a client configuration wizard, allowing you to quickly configure Notes for use in a new env ronment and quickly move from one batch of settings to another if your computer moves betwee environments.

Release 6 also introduces the idea of the "roaming user." A user who has been designated by adm istrators as a roaming user can move from one computer to another—say, a desktop connected to LAN at work, a laptop in the field using a modem, and a second desktop at home connected to the se ers via a digital subscriber line (DSL) or cable modem connection—keeping separate copies of a ma box, a calendar, and a personal address book synchronized.

Welcome Page and Navigation Enhancements

The Welcome page, the Notes client home page, is now more customizable. You can choose betwee information-dense framesets, providing links to just about any web page or database the client ca reach, and more ornate Personal Pages, combining web page/Notes database information, applet and personal touches such as pictures and background patterns.

Many Welcome page styles include a Quick Notes frame. Quick Notes gives you a place to wri a quick memo, take a note, create a reminder, or insert a contact entry into your address book witho having to go through all the steps to open the relevant databases and create new documents.

The new Bookmark launcher allows you to insert bookmarks into your Welcome page, letting yc launch favorite databases and web pages quickly.

The Welcome page is discussed in Chapter 2, "Getting Familiar with Notes."

Mail Enhancements

Release 6 has an improved addressing interface, making it easier for you to find names and addresse Not only can you search by full name, you can search by individual items such as first and last name address, and company name.

Mail folders have been greatly enhanced. Folders will now retain sorting orders, and users ca change the order in which columns appear. Folders also display how many unread documents the contain.

You can create replies in a broad range of styles, including Notes-native rich-text replies, streamlined replies with attachments stripped out, and Internet-style plain-text replies with bracket-commented text. In earlier releases of Notes, bracket-commented replies could only be created with additional programming.

Notes memos are now compatible with *v-cards*, a popular electronic business card format.

Most of these features are covered in Chapter 5, "Communicating with Notes Mail."

Calendar Enhancements

Calendar entries can now be individually color coded, allowing you to graphically distinguish between, for example, personal and business appointments, religious and company holidays, or events associated with different departments or projects.

Calendar navigation is now faster, with choices more visibly apparent. The layout of calendar documents has also been altered, making it easier to enter and find scheduling information. It's also easier to customize the chunk of time displayed by the calendar. You can go from showing arbitrary (or nearly so) numbers of days or weeks at a time and limit your calendar to displaying work weeks and work months, excluding weekends.

Calendar invitations are now more sensitive to time zones. That is, you can designate a specific time zone for the meeting regardless of what your time zone is. This makes it easier to coordinate meetings and teleconferencing in geographically widespread organizations.

It is also easier to view the status of meeting invitees. In earlier versions of Notes, it took additional steps to see who had replied to a meeting invitation. In Release 6, participant status is visible on the invitation itself.

Most of these features are discussed in Chapter 6, "Calendaring and Scheduling."

Rich-Text Enhancements

The bodies of memos, calendar entries, to do documents, and documents in discussion databases are almost always rich-text fields. The same rich-text capabilities are also used for designing some important database elements, so changes to Notes' rich-text capabilities have implications for both users and designers.

There are several new table capabilities. Tabbed tables can now have tabs on the side as well as on the top. Tables can also be built as a series of collapsible sections. Entire rows, columns, and tables can be selected without having to drag through them.

You can now rearrange text lists (for example, bulleted lists and numbered lists) by dragging and dropping selected lines.

You can give buttons in rich-text areas color, borders, and a fixed size regardless of their contents.

You can hide selected paragraphs from mobile devices, such as PDAs and text-enabled cell phones. In the previous version of Notes, it was possible to selectively hide bits of text if they were being viewed through a web browser or Notes client. This capability has been extended to mobile devices.

Security

You can now change passwords more easily. It's also much easier to synchronize the Notes client password and the Domino server password. The Notes client password is stored within a file on the Notes client machine, and the Domino user password is stored on the server. With Release 6, the server can mediate changes to either password to synchronize them.

Notes can use Smartcards, a credit-card-like electronic identification card, for login and locking the user identity. This requires a Smartcard reader, an additional bit of hardware.

All security settings, from automatic message encryption to code execution permissions, are now displayed together in a detailed User Security screen.

Most of these features are discussed in Chapter 12, "Integrating Notes with Other Applications."

Other Client Interface Enhancements

Long limited to adding documents to folders, drag-and-drop capabilities have been added to oth
places in the Notes interface. You can drag documents to the computer desktop to create shortcu
and you can drag databases in the Replicator page.

Spell checking is somewhat more flexible. It can now ignore words in all caps and words conta
ing numbers.

Printing is much improved. Notes can now do background printing, sending jobs to a printer witho
locking up the Notes client until the job is done. You can also print calendars in a variety of time rang
and time zones, address book contents as a mailing list, and framesets in their entirety rather than o
frame at a time.

Notes now features document locking without extensive additional programming. Relational da
bases usually have a feature called *record locking*, which prevents multiple users from attempting to edit t
same row of a table at the same time. Document locking provides similar safety.

Summary

In this chapter, we provided an overview of what the Lotus Notes client is and how it can be use
We also introduced some of the basic concepts underlying how Notes works and highlighted son
of the new features of Release 6.

In the next chapter, we'll begin exploring the basic features of the software. We'll introduce yc
to navigating and customizing the Welcome page. We'll also discuss the elements of the Notes app
cation window, personalizing Notes with bookmarks, and using Notes Help.

Chapter 2

Getting Familiar with Notes

NOW THAT YOU HAVE an understanding of what Lotus Notes is all about, it's time to explore the basics of using the software. Whether you are a new user or an existing user of a previous release, this chapter will quickly familiarize you with the features of the Notes client that you'll see or need to use when you first launch it.

◆ Navigating in and customizing the Welcome page

◆ Using the elements of the Notes application window

◆ Utilizing Notes Help

Starting Your Day in the Welcome Page

When you get into Notes, you'll see the Welcome page. You can think of the Welcome page as the Notes equivalent of a web browser's home page, but it's far more flexible and customizable than anything you can get out of a web browser. The default Welcome page, as shown in Figure 2.1, allows you to perform many common Notes functions, including reading your e-mail, viewing your calendar, viewing your to do items, searching for information (both in Notes databases and on the Web), and reviewing information about Release 6. You can even create your own customized Welcome pages with what Notes refers to as *styles*. The default Welcome page's style is called Basics.

NOTE *Actually, your Welcome page isn't what you'll see the very first time you launch Notes. Rather, you'll be presented with a screen that will give you the option to set up some preferences, learn a little about Notes, and make a Welcome page as described in this section. However, if you're not inclined to deal with that, there's also a button that will give you some default settings and take you to the default Welcome page.*

FIGURE 2.1

The default
Lotus Notes
Welcome page

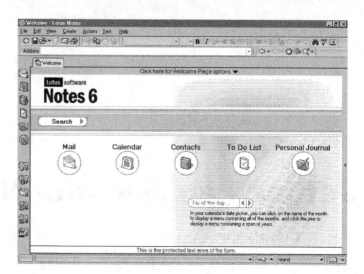

When you launch Notes, you will most likely be asked to enter your password in the Enter Pas‌word dialog box, shown here.

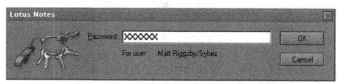

This is generally true if you are using Notes in a corporate environment in conjunction with Lot‌‌ Domino servers. If so, just type the password provided by your Notes/Domino administrators an‌ press Enter.

TIP   *As you type in your password, the keyring graphic will change. This is a little-known security feature. It should‌ be the same sequence of graphics every time you type in the correct password; Notes picks the images according to a complex‌ formula that looks at what you type and what your password is. If you happen to see a different sequence of graphics, there‌ may be a program emulating Notes trying to steal your password. It can also distract anybody looking over your shoulder.*

As you can see, the Basics style Welcome page is a task-oriented starting point for accessing th‌ most commonly used features of Lotus Notes. To show how you can begin to use the features of‌ Notes right from the Basics style Welcome page, let's view your electronic mail Inbox:

1. Move the mouse so it hovers over the image of an envelope with the caption Mail on the le‌ side of the Basics style Welcome page.

2. When the button highlights, click the left mouse button.

A screen similar to the one in Figure 2.2 appears. When it does, just press the Esc key to return to the Welcome page.

FIGURE 2.2
The Inbox

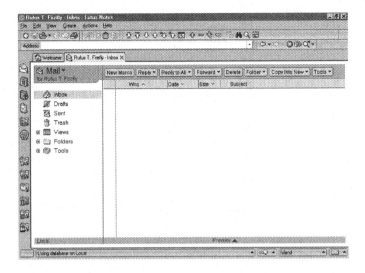

Even this basic design has hidden features. One of them is in the Search function. If you click the arrow next to the Search button, a drop-down menu will appear. With the menu, you can designate what you want to search: people in your Notes organization, Notes databases (looking through a catalog of Notes databases generated by your organization), web content (using Lycos or Hotbot as search engines), or Usenet posts (using AltaVista). Once you've selected a search method, you can enter text to search for and press the Search button to activate the search.

A more powerful hidden feature is the Quick Notes window, a hidden frame hiding tools to quickly jot down new mail messages, contacts, journal entries, and reminders. On the right edge of the screen, you'll see a left-pointing triangle. Clicking it will open the Quick Notes window (see Figure 2.3); if it's not big enough, you can click and drag the gray bar to resize it. It initially appears with the Memo section expanded. You can collapse it and expand any other section by clicking the expand/collapse box in the heading you desire.

The last hidden section is at the top, where you'll see the words *Click here for Welcome Page Options*. Clicking opens yet another hidden section with options for customizing your Welcome page (see Figure 2.4).

FIGURE 2.3
Basics style with
the Quick Notes
section expanded

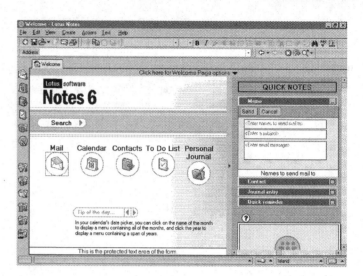

FIGURE 2.4
Basics with
the Welcome
page options
section open

Creating and Customizing Welcome Page Styles

Configured properly, the Welcome page is a single-screen snapshot of your most important infor
mation. Unlike a web browser home page, your Welcome page doesn't have to be a single page. It ca
be a frameset full of links, lists of documents, search tools, web pages, useful applets such as a cloc
or calendar, even pictures of your dog, if you so desire.

The easiest way to get a new Welcome page is to select one of the premade styles listed in the Welcome page options screen. You're already familiar with Basics. Basics with Calendar gives you the Basics screen plus a frame containing your Notes calendar. Basics Plus gives you frames for all the links from Basics plus your calendar, your Inbox, and a search tool. It also adds a new hidden tool off the bottom of the screen, the Launch Pad (see Figure 2.5). To open the Launch Pad, click the bottom border and drag it up. The Launch Pad allows you to put links onto your Welcome page. You can drag just about any kind of link or shortcut into the Launch Pad. For instance, you can put web links and Notes bookmarks there. More interestingly, you can drag applications and even individual documents from your desktop to create bookmarks for them within Notes.

FIGURE 2.5

The Launch Pad
with bookmarks
for applications

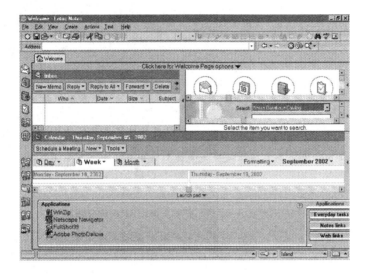

There are also a number of Headlines styles. These are Welcome page styles that incorporate your Inbox and your calendar on the left and a web page on the right. If your screen is large enough, these styles are good to keep an eye on your own information and keep a favorite web page ready to hand.

But these prepackaged styles may not be what you want, so Notes allows you to assemble your own Welcome page. To help you create your own Welcome pages (you can have several and switch between them as you desire), Notes provides you with a helpful wizard to walk you through the process.

To start the process, click the Create a New Welcome Page button. The wizard will start (see Figure 2.6). Pay no mind to the silly hat and give your Welcome page a name; then hit the Next button to get to where the real work begins.

At this point, the Welcome Page Display page, you'll need to choose between Frames and a Personal Page (see Figure 2.7). The Frames option gives you a number of frames into which you can put a variety of elements, such as Notes views and web pages. This is a good choice if you want maximum functionality and information on your Welcome page. A Personal Page is a bit more of a personal desktop. You can put many of the same elements on a Personal Page that you can in frames, but you can also place background patterns, applets, pictures, and other features to make your Welcome page perhaps not so functional, but certainly more welcoming.

FIGURE 2.6
New Welcome
Page Wizard

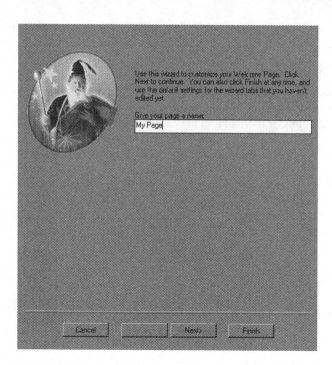

FIGURE 2.7
Welcome Page
Display page

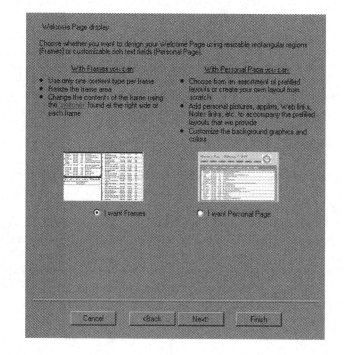

FRAMES

If you select the Frames option, you'll see a checklist of options you can have on your Welcome page. You can select up to six items of the following: Inbox, Calendar, To Do List, Database Subscriptions, Everyday Tasks, Database, File System, Web Page, and Search.

Once you've selected your options, you'll have the opportunity to select a layout, designate which frames hold each selection, and, depending on the content you select, fine-tune the content to specific web pages or databases.

Inbox

The Inbox option enables you to quickly see a listing of e-mail messages sent to you. Messages appearing in red text are ones you have not opened yet (Notes says that they're unread, but the computer doesn't actually know whether you've paid attention to them once you opened them), whereas those appearing in black letters are messages you have already opened. You can open the messages listed as well as open your mail database. To select a message, you only need to click it once. To open it you can select it and hit the Return key or just double-click it. To close the message and return to the Welcome page, press the Esc key or select the X on the right side of the message window's task button. You can open your Inbox by selecting the Inbox icon or the word *Inbox* in the bar at the top of the Inbox section; close it by pressing the Esc key or by selecting the X on the right side of the Inbox window's task button.

Calendar

Your calendar can also be displayed in a section of a Welcome page. This is a great tool for quickly seeing appointments scheduled for the current day. To select an appointment, you only need to click it, just as you would select a message in your Inbox. To close the appointment and return to the Welcome page, press the Esc key or select the X on the right side of the appointment window's task button. You can open your calendar by selecting the calendar icon or the word *Calendar* in the bar at the top of the Calendar section; close it by pressing the Esc key or by selecting the X on the right side of the Calendar window's task button.

To Do List

Your to do list can be included in another section of a Welcome page. The To Do section provides a convenient way to see a listing of your current tasks. To do documents can be manipulated like calendar documents and messages in your Inbox.

Database

The Database option lets you use a database subscription. Database subscriptions allow you to monitor Notes databases for documents that might be of interest. For example, you can create a subscription to monitor your mail database for messages containing the term *New Business* or to monitor a particular Notes database for documents containing the word *Java*. From the Database Subscriptions area of your Welcome page, you can see a listing of the matching documents and open them if you want. See Chapter 4, "Tailoring Lotus Notes 6" for more about creating and modifying subscriptions.

Everyday Tasks

An Everyday Tasks frame gives you one-button links to your mailbox, calendar, to dos, and person journal. It's essentially identical to the links provided by the Basics Welcome page.

Database

When you select Database, you can further select from one to six Notes databases. These can l locally stored databases, such as your personal address book, or databases on a Domino server. Ea database is displayed in its own frame as though you had opened it itself. This is an excellent way keeping track of databases you use frequently.

File System

This option allows you to display one to six directories in your computer's file system, much like t Windows Explorer. The directories you choose can be on your computer or accessible to your co puter via a network. You can use these frames to navigate around your file system, locate, and laun files.

Web Page

This option allows you to view web pages in frames in your Welcome page. Like the Database optio you can choose from one to six different web pages. To make this option work, you'll need to ha Notes or Notes with Internet Explorer designated as your web browser; other web browser optio aren't tightly enough tied into the Notes client.

Search

The Search option provides you with a tool for searching the Web and Notes databases. Again, th is identical to the function provided by the Basics Welcome page.

Optional and Hidden Features

There are a few incidental options connected to frameset Welcome pages. When you're selecting co tent for your frames, you also have the option of including a preview frame. The preview frame w appear at the bottom of your Welcome page. When you have a preview frame open (such as the Qui Notes frame, which is collapsible), any document you have selected in another frame is displayed in t preview frame. This lets you look at documents without opening them in separate windows.

If you don't choose the preview frame, you can choose to include the Launch Pad. This is the sam element as the Launch Pad already described for the Basics Welcome page. Unfortunately, the Launc Pad and the preview frame are mutually exclusive.

Finally, once you've created your frame-based Welcome page, you don't have to stick with the co tent you've selected. Each frame has a switcher, a collapsible menu that allows you to switch the frame content to something else. Click the triangle in the right margin of a frame to open its switcher men

The menu, shown here, allows you to switch the frame's content to any other kind of content you could have in your Welcome page. You could display your calendar, a web page, a database, and so on in the same frame. Finally, you can use the Restore option to reset the frame back to its original content.

Further Adjustments

You can make a few other changes after you've created your frameset. One of the most useful features is that you can adjust the size of the frames. If you move your mouse to the bars separating the frames, you can click and drag the frame-defining lines around, making a desired frame bigger at the expense of other frames.

Depending on the options selected when you created your frameset, you may have a preview window or the Launch Pad at the bottom of the screen in a collapsible frame. You can open or close this as you desire.

PERSONAL PAGE

When you select the Personal Page option, you'll see options for several premade page layouts (see Figure 2.8). You can get a closer look at each design and read about its features by selecting the one you want to see and clicking the Enlarge Selected Layout link. Unlike frames, Personal Page designs won't shrink to fit your screen. However, some of them are designed specifically for smaller screens using 800 × 600 resolution. The frame-like layouts aren't actually framesets. The "frames" simply indicate layout regions where you can place content when you go to customize the page. You'll also need to go through one more step with those layouts, selecting a background pattern.

Once you've selected a style, you can customize your page further. At the top of the page, you'll see an Edit button. Clicking it will switch the page into an editing mode (see Figure 2.9).

When you get the page into editing mode, you'll see the display across the top change. Instead of an Edit button, you'll see Save and Cancel buttons. Next to them is a drop-down menu from which you can select a different background pattern. The question mark button brings up a help page describing options for changing the page.

FIGURE 2.8

Personal Page
layouts

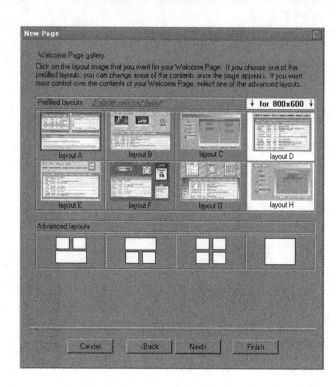

FIGURE 2.9

A Personal Page
in editing mode

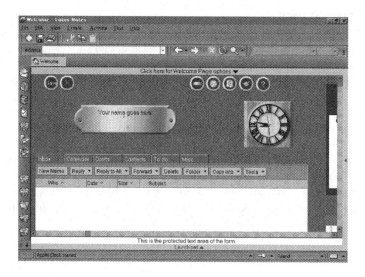

Personal Pages have a number of areas (called *fields*) where you can place content. Fields are usually marked by two squared-off half brackets.

One of the items you'll see associated with most fields on a Personal Page is the Field Helper, a drop-down menu that allows you to select the type of content that goes into the field. First, select the kind of content you want. In most cases, the next thing to do is to click the helper to bring up the following options:

Pictures   Clicking the Field Helper icon when Pictures is selected brings up a file navigation dialog box that will allow you to browse your computer and find a graphic image to bring into the field. At the moment, the field supports Windows bitmaps (.bmp), GIF, JPG, CGM, TIFF, PCX, and Lotus PIC images.

Shared Images   Clicking the Field Helper when Shared Images is selected brings up a dialog box allowing you to insert a shared image contained in a Notes database. The dialog box defaults to showing images from the current database, but you can browse through other Notes databases.

Attachments   The Attachments button opens a file navigation dialog box letting you embed a file in the field. The file will appear as an icon. Later, you'll be able to launch the file or view it. This operates like a file attachment in a mail message; see Chapter 5, "Communicating with Notes Mail," for more information.

Embedded View   The Embedded View option allows you to display a view or folder, such as your Inbox, in your Welcome page.

Date Picker   The Date Picker is a compact calendar that displays the current month with the current date highlighted. You can navigate back and forth between months. The primary purpose of a date picker is for navigation in conjunction with a full calendar, but it's a nice if not terribly versatile calendar on its own.

Applets   The Applet option lets you insert a Java applet in your Welcome page much like you'd put a Java applet into a web page. You can write your own or use prewritten Java applets. You might use this for a Java-based clock, a miniature slide show, or perhaps a small game of Space Invaders.

Text   The Text option lets you fill the field with…well, text. This is the one option that doesn't require that you click the Field Helper button after choosing an option. Click inside the field instead and start typing.

OLE Objects   This option allows you to select from a list of OLE Objects. The list of OLE objects contains a wide variety of elements from simple graphic images to Word and Excel documents, which you can edit while still inside Notes.

Calendar   This option, a specialized version of Embedded View, puts your calendar in the field.

Inbox   This option, also essentially a specialized Embedded View, makes your Inbox appear in the field.

Clear   This option removes whatever content is already in the field. If you're trying to replace the existing contents, you might go here first.

The Welcome Page as Your Home Page

The Welcome page is also the default home page for Lotus Notes. As such, it is automatically load
when you run Notes. Also, the task button associated with the Welcome page cannot be closed. If y
would rather have another database as the starting point for your environment, Notes gives you th
option. To change your home page—to your mail database, for example—do the following:

1. Right-click the mail icon on the Bookmark bar so the following context menu appears.

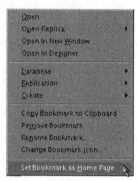

2. Choose Set Bookmark as Home Page from the menu. The Set Home Page dialog box appea
confirming your request to change the home page.

3. Click the OK button to confirm the change.

You'll notice that the task button for the Welcome page, labeled Welcome, disappears and yo
mail database's task button changes so there is no X on the right side. You can use this feature to s
any bookmark as your home page in Notes.

TIP *To change your home page back to the Welcome page, click the Bookmark button labeled Favorite Bookmarks, right-
click the icon labeled Welcome, and set that as your Welcome Page.*

Using the Application Window

Before going too much further into the actual functionality provided by Notes, it is important to
understand how the application is presented on the screen. When Notes is launched, it creates a w
dow on your screen known as the *application window*. The application window is made up of a numb
of elements. This section will explain what the major elements of the Notes application window a
and how they are used.

The application window is designed to be familiar to users of the platform on which it is runnin
The Microsoft Windows version of Lotus Notes has the familiar Windows-style interface. At th
top of the screen is a title bar, which includes the name of the application and the active task. On tl
left side of the title bar, there is an icon that allows the user to control the application. On the righ
there are controls for minimizing, maximizing/restoring, and closing the application. On the left si
below the title bar, there is a set of menu options that should be familiar to most Windows users.

The MacOS version of the software has a similar appearance, but with a definite Macintosh accent. The title bar has a box on the left side that closes the application and another on the right side that expands and collapses the window.

The remainder of the application window is specific to Lotus Notes and is detailed in the next section.

Everything you do with Notes requires you to be familiar with the basic elements of the application window. It is how you interact with Notes and how Notes presents itself to you.

The menus should be familiar if you are accustomed to graphical applications; they represent the traditional method for choosing actions to perform within Notes. The toolbars, task buttons, status bar, context menus, and pop-up keyboard access shortcuts are Notes-specific elements and are explained in the following sections (see Figure 2.10).

FIGURE 2.10

The Notes application window

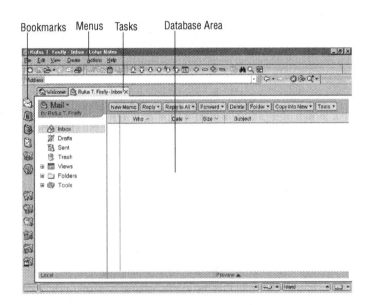

Toolbars

Immediately beneath the menu bar at the top of the application window, you'll find the toolbars, a group of context-sensitive palettes of buttons generally representing menu commands. Users familiar with previous releases of Notes will notice that the Navigation bar (a Release 5 innovation created to emulate web browser navigation buttons) and SmartIcons (a feature much like toolbars but with a slightly puzzling nonstandard name) have been combined into more flexible toolbars. By default, you'll usually see these toolbars:

Universal   Lets you save, print, and get the current database object's properties.

Editing   Lets you cut, copy, and paste.

Address Allows you to enter a URL as you would for a web browser. You can also open Not databases with this toolbar.

Navigation Allows you to navigate backward and forward among Notes documents and obje as you would pages you've viewed in a web browser.

Edit Document Provides editing tools for rich-text areas, with menus to select font and typ size, buttons to style text and attach files, and so on.

Toolbars and individual buttons that don't work in a particular context may disable themselves they aren't applicable. For example, when you're looking at the Welcome page, the Edit Docume toolbar will be grayed out and none of the buttons will do anything.

New toolbars may also appear and disappear, depending on the context. For example, if you op your Inbox, a Navigate View toolbar will appear. The Navigate View toolbar has buttons that let y scroll around the view, expand and collapse view entries, open or forward the currently selected d ument, and so on. If you open a document (that is, if your Inbox drops behind a Notes document the toolbar will disappear because it is no longer needed. Of course, it will appear again if you go ba to your Inbox.

You can move the toolbars around to customize your interface. For example, if you use a lot c fonts and text styles, you may want to move the Edit Document bar out of its corner where it can I compressed to near uselessness if you have a low screen resolution. To move a toolbar to a differe place, simply click the vertical bar at the left end of the toolbar and drag it to the desired location Other toolbars will shrink or move out of the way to let your toolbar fit in its new location. If a to bar shrinks to hide icons, they'll still be available through a submenu. A set of down-pointing arro will appear. Click the arrows, and the hidden items will appear in a pop-up menu.

You're also not limited to the toolbar area at the top of the page. If you drag the toolbar outsic of the toolbar area at the top of the application menu, it will become a floating window. Toolbars w always appear on top of anything else in Notes. This means they're always available, but they can g in the way of the documents you're trying to see. If you want to get it out of the way, you can jus move it back to the toolbar area, where it will regain its original shape.

You can even customize which toolbars appear and when, if you're feeling adventurous. If you select File ➤ Preferences ➤ Toolbar Preferences, you'll bring up dialog box for adjusting toolbars (s Figure 2.11).

The Toolbar Preferences screen has three parts. Basics allows you to set up some basic display options (including whether to display toolbars at all). Toolbars lets you determine which toolbar will appear. Finally, Customize lets you modify the contents of individual toolbars. You can add ar remove icons and even create new ones using the Notes formula language.

FIGURE 2.11

Toolbar
Preferences
dialog box

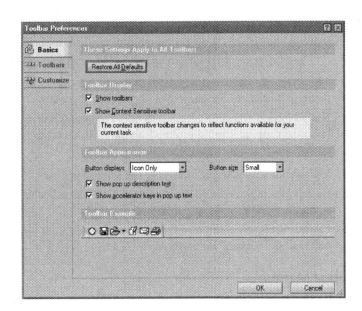

Task Buttons

Task buttons are tabs located below the menus and toolbars that represent open documents, views, and other database elements within Notes. Task buttons allow you to easily navigate between tasks and quickly close active tasks. The active task's task button is always highlighted and includes an *X* on the right side, as shown here.

The *X* on the right side quickly closes the active task. When you hover your mouse over the task button of a nonactive task, the button is highlighted and the *X* becomes visible. This allows you to quickly close nonactive tasks. Task buttons can also be used to create bookmarks. You can select a task button with the mouse and drag it to the Bookmark bar or one of your Bookmark pages. This is explained further in the section on bookmarks in Chapter 4.

DRAGGING TO THE DESKTOP

With previous versions of Notes, the closest you could get to a specific Notes element from the desktop was to create a shortcut to the Notes database file. If you were dealing with a database on a Domino server, you couldn't even do that because your local file system had no contact with databases on the server. But that has changed with Release 6. You may now drag-and-drop shortcuts to Notes elements to your computer's desktop.

To create a shortcut to a task window, simply click the window and drag it outside of the Notes application window to your desktop. If you quit Notes and double-click the shortcut, Notes will launch and open the item for which you created the bookmark.

The Status Bar

The status bar, shown here, is the bottommost area of the application window.

It has five separate sections that provide you with information and allow you to access frequent used functions. The status bar allows you to perform these tasks:

- See if Notes is accessing a local network (a lightning bolt appears), a remote network/serv (a modem appears), or no external computers (no icon appears)
- See a list of recently displayed system messages
- Quickly identify your access level to the active database
- Switch location or edit the current location document, which changes your Notes configu tion information
- Quickly access common mail functions, such as creating a mail message, opening your mai and sending outgoing messages

Context Menus

Context menus are menus that appear when you right-click your mouse inside the Notes applicatic window. These menus include choices that are relevant to the area of the application window tha your mouse was pointing to when you right-clicked it. For example, the following context menu w be displayed when you right-click any bookmark.

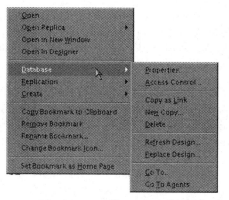

Context menus are a convenient means of accessing functions within Notes. Because they displa a limited set of menu choices, they focus your attention on functions most likely required for the tas you are performing. For example, using the context menu associated with the Bookmark page is a great way to quickly open a replica of a database. It also provides quick access to the Database, Re lica, and Create menus.

Pop-Up Keyboard Access Shortcuts

Pop-up keyboard access shortcuts are highlighted letters and numbers in the Notes application window. When the Alt key is pressed, these highlighted letters and numbers appear as small pop-up boxes that are similar to Balloon Help. Pop-up keyboard access shortcuts allow you to quickly perform navigation and task actions that would normally require the use of your mouse. The benefit, especially to those with good keyboard skills, is that you do not have to constantly switch back and forth between the keyboard and mouse when trying to accomplish common tasks. As shown here, the Create New Memo task actions are one keystroke away when you use pop-up keyboard access shortcuts.

NOTE   *Pop-up keyboard access shortcuts are a visual representation of keyboard shortcuts that existed in previous releases, with enhancements for the Bookmark bar and task buttons.*

The Properties Box

The Properties box is a special dialog box that allows you to access a Notes element's properties. Many elements in Notes—such as databases, documents, and forms—have properties. Although not all the elements have the same properties, they all use a Properties box. One of the more useful features of the Properties box is that when it is left open, it reflects the properties of the element on which you are currently working. When you change from one element to another element (for example, when you move from one task window to another), the Properties box reflects the properties of the new element.

The easiest way to open a Properties box is to first select or highlight the item whose properties you would like to view. To view the properties of your mail database, perform the following steps:

1. Open your mail database by selecting the Mail link on the Bookmark bar on the left side of the screen (top icon).
2. Choose File ➢ Database Properties. The Properties box is displayed, showing the database properties for your mail database, as shown in Figure 2.12.

You will use the Properties box to perform many common functions, including:

◆ Obtaining information about a database

◆ Performing maintenance tasks on a database, such as compacting and archiving

◆ Setting print settings for a database or document

◆ Manipulating text settings

FIGURE 2.12

A Properties box
showing database
properties

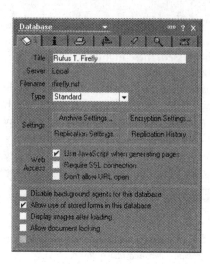

Also, you'll use many of the properties available in the Properties box when you are designing
Notes databases. Refer to Chapter 16, "Introducing Domino Designer," for more information o
how you use the Properties box while designing Notes databases.

Navigating around the Properties box is fairly easy. Try some of these methods just to get
comfortable:

- To switch to a different property page, click a tab.
- To move the Properties box, drag it by its title bar.
- To float the Properties box as a toolbar, click the toolbar icon.
- To get help for the element or options, click the question mark icon.
- To close the box, click the close icon.

Bookmarks

Bookmarks are the primary method of getting around inside Notes. The graphic in the margin shov
the default Bookmark bar.

The Database Area

The Database area is the heart of the Notes application window. It is the area where Notes databas
are presented to you.

Please refer to Chapter 3, "Working with Databases," for a complete discussion of Notes dat
bases and how you work with them.

Getting Help

Help is always a keystroke away in Notes. Just press F1 and Notes will open a new application window with the help database displayed. The help database is your online document for Notes. It looks similar to the screen shown here.

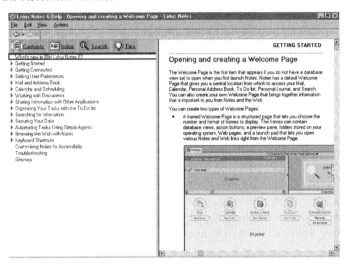

As you can see, the help database is presented in two frames. The left side displays topics and the right shows the content. There are three main views: Content, Index, and Search.

You can access these views by selecting the appropriate link at the top of the left frame.

The Content view displays the help information by topic (as a book is organized by chapters). This view makes it easy to read help information by area of interest. When you first start using Notes, you may want to read through the help information this way or print it from this view. Some of the high-level areas of interest include Getting Started, Mail and Address Book, and Calendar and Scheduling. Topics that have subtopics will have a right-pointing triangle icon to the left of them.

Clicking this triangle icon will expand the subtopics underneath the main topic. Clicking the triangle again will collapse them. Each subtopic may also have subtopics, creating an outline-type hierarchy. To display the contents of a particular topic, just click its title. A page will be displayed on the right side. If the page is longer than the frame, a scroll bar will appear on the right side, enabling you to scroll down the page. Pages can also have links to other pages. Links are displayed as blue, underlined text. When you move your mouse over the link, the cursor changes to a hand icon.

Just click the link to go to the page it represents. This is similar to browsing Web pages. You can also use the Go Back, Go Forward, and Stop buttons shown in the Navigation bar to navigate between pages you have viewed.

TIP *The left side of the help window displays a view, but there is no view selection area displayed. This is the area wher you would normally select multiple documents if you wanted to print more than one at a time. To select multiple document in this view, just click the title of the document you want to select and press the spacebar. Notes will display the view selectior area and will indicate that the document has been selected by showing a check mark icon. You can select other document by clicking in the view selection area. You can also choose Edit ➤ Select All to display the view selection area and hav all help documents selected. Choose Edit ➤ Deselect All to undo this.*

The Index view is similar to the index of a book. This view displays the help information in alph betical order by word or phrase. The view is useful when you know the topic for which you are loc ing. Like the Contents view, the Index view displays an outline-type hierarchy. Each word or phra has a right-pointing triangle to the left indicating there are either additional words/phrases or topi underneath. One difference between this and the Contents view is that no content will be display on the right when you click the hierarchy of words and phrases. You must click the title of a top to display the contents of that topic. Navigation is the same as it is in the Contents view.

TIP *You can use the Quick Search feature of Notes in the Index view to navigate to specific words or phrases with min imal effort. Just start typing the first few letters of the word or phrase you would like to find. The Starts With dialog box is displayed with the characters you've typed. Click the OK button and Notes will navigate to the first word or phrase in the view starting with the characters you've typed.*

The Search view displays all of the topics contained within the help database sorted by title. Th view is not organized like the Contents or Index views. There is no hierarchy and the topics are n categorized. Also, this view includes the Search bar at the top of the left frame. Because Notes He is contained in a Notes database, it can be searched by using the powerful, built-in full-text index f tures of Notes. You can use the Search bar to initiate a search through all topics in the help databa

1. Enter a word or phrase in the Search For field.
2. Click the Search button.

Notes will display topics that include the word or phrase you entered. The contents displayed in tl right frame will include highlights on the words or phrases for which you were searching. The Search b can also be used to form complex queries. For more information on using the Search bar, see Chapter "Searching for Information." You can use the Quick Search feature of Notes in this view, too.

Bookmarking Help Topics

You can bookmark help documents to make it easy to find topics of interest later. This is helpful f topics you may refer to over and over. Maybe you don't work with tables all the time and would lil to have easy access to the help topic without having to go find it. Follow these steps to bookmark help topic:

1. Right-click the topic and choose Bookmark from the context menu.
2. In the Add Bookmark dialog box, select an existing bookmark folder in the Add To field (click the New Folder button to create a new one.
3. Click the OK button.

A bookmark to the topic will be placed in the bookmark folder you selected.

Summary

You are now familiar with some of the basic aspects of Lotus Notes. The new Welcome page provides you with a single place to access your mail, calendar, and to do list. You can also customize the Welcome page to provide you with a single-page view of the information that is most important to you. We explored the Notes application window and identified the screen elements with which you will interact to manage your information.

The next chapter will introduce concepts of the Notes database. It will define what Notes databases are, how they are presented to you, and how to perform tasks common to all Notes databases.

Summary

Chapter 3

Working with Databases

UNLIKE OTHER GENERAL-PURPOSE communication and information management applications, Notes is really a runtime environment for databases created with the Domino Designer integrated development environment (IDE). In fact, the core functionality of Notes—including mail, calendar, to do lists, contacts, and so on—is provided through a set of databases included with the software. This is the main reason Notes is so powerful; it can be programmed to help you accomplish a wide range of tasks that involve communication, collaboration, or coordination of unstructured information. In this chapter, we'll explain how to get into and around Notes databases and how to deal with certain common Notes objects.

- Working in databases
- Working in views
- Using forms to create and modify documents
- Working with rich-text fields
- Checking your spelling
- Printing your information

Opening Databases

First, you need to open the database in which you need to work. There are a number ways to open databases in Notes. The most common ways include the following:

- Selecting a link from your Bookmark bar
- Selecting a link from one of your Bookmark pages
- Selecting File ➢ Database ➢ Open (or pressing Ctrl+O)
- Selecting a link embedded in a Notes document

If you use the File ➤ Database ➤ Open method, you will need to know where the database is stored (on your computer or on a Domino server) and in which directory it is located on the target computer. As shown here, there is a drop-down list, labeled Server, for selecting the server where the database resides.

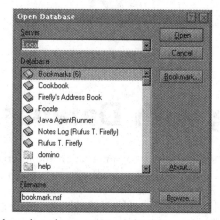

In the Server drop-down list, the entry Local doesn't actually represent a server. It represents your own computer. When Local is selected, the list of databases represents those stored locally on your computer. If you select the drop-down arrow on the right side of the field, a list of servers is displayed. The servers displayed are a combination of those you have previously browsed and those to which you have predefined connections. If you want to open a database on a server you haven't contacted before, just type the server's name. The Database field is a list box that lets you select from a list of databases on the selected server. It lists databases in alphabetical order by title, followed by a list of folders. The Filename field allows you to enter a filename directly.

NOTE   *In the Open Database dialog box, the list of databases available on a given target computer is relative to the computer's* Data *directory. When Local is selected, the list of databases displayed is relative to the* Data *directory of your local Notes environment, which by default is* C:\Program Files\Lotus\Notes\Data *on Windows computers.*

The Open button opens the database or folder currently selected in the Database list box or typed into the Filename field. You can also double-click a database or folder name listed in the Database list box to open it. If you choose to open a database, the Open Database dialog box will disappear and the selected database will be displayed in the application window. If you choose to open a folder, the contents of that folder will be displayed in the Database list box. When you navigate into a folder, the last entry in the Database list box will be an up arrow with two periods (shown here).

If you double-click this icon or highlight it and click the Open button, Notes will display the contents of the folder up one level in the folder hierarchy. Users familiar with Unix or DOS will recognize two periods as symbolizing the parent of the current directory.

The Bookmark button will allow you to create a bookmark to the database selected in the Database list box or typed into the Filename field. See Chapter 4, "Tailoring Lotus Notes 6," for more information on creating and using bookmarks. You can create any number of bookmarks without closing the Open Database dialog box. Just keep selecting databases and clicking the Bookmark button.

The Cancel button closes the Open Database dialog box without opening a database.

The About button displays the About Database document for the selected database. The developer of the database creates this document (shown here), which usually displays high-level information regarding the purpose and scope of the database. After viewing the About Database document, click the Close button to return to the Open Database dialog box.

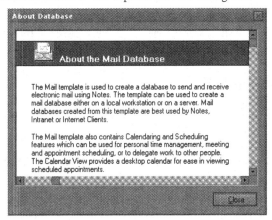

The Browse button allows you to browse your file system for Notes databases located outside your local Notes Data directory. This is handy if you are trying to open a database that you have downloaded from an Internet site or some other external source to a folder/directory on your computer. It can also be used to open database templates, but if you want to open a template, you'll probably use the Domino Designer client instead. Database templates are an advanced topic; see Chapter 17, "Database Creation and Properties." You can only browse your local file system (this includes any networked volumes you may be able to access as though they were local drives). However, you may not browse the directories of Domino servers this way. When the Browse button is selected, a File Open dialog box displays (shown here), allowing you to choose a file from your local computer's file system.

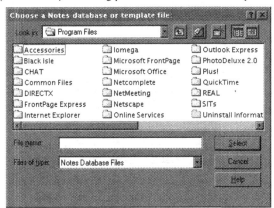

To close a database, press Esc or click the X on the right side of all task buttons associated with the database. The database isn't really closed until you've closed all documents, views, and other elements associated with it, so if you want to close a database, make sure there aren't any open windows lurking behind items from other open databases.

Working in Views

Once a database is opened, you are most likely to be presented with a *view*. A view is the main interfa
to a database and is generally designed to show you summary information about documents in th
database. This summary information is displayed in a row/column format where, usually, each do
ument is represented as a row. There are a few exceptions (for example, a single document can
made to occupy different rows and some rows can contain a category heading rather than a doc
ment), but we'll deal with those later. A view typically consists of three parts: the view action bar, t
view icons, and the view content area.

Using the View Action Bar

Many views will afford you the opportunity to perform other actions, such as creating a new doc
ment, forwarding a selected document or documents, or marking documents with a new status. Yo
typically perform these actions with the view action bar, shown here.

The view action bar is specific to each view in each database and contains buttons that enable yo
to perform application-specific functions. For example, the view action bar associated with the Inbo
folder of the mail database enables you to perform common functions associated with reading yo
e-mail, such as the following:

♦ Creating a new memo

♦ Replying to the message selected in the view

♦ Forwarding the message selected in the view to another mail user

♦ Deleting the currently selected message

♦ Moving the currently selected message to another folder or removing it from the Inbox

♦ Copying into another document in your mail database

♦ Accessing mail database tools

Buttons on the view action bar can execute a function directly or display a menu of function
from which to choose. For example, the Tools button on the mail database's Inbox folder displa
this minimenu of tools (shown here).

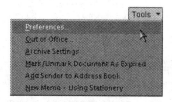

When the view action bar has too many buttons to fit on the screen, two opposed arrows are d
played on the far-right side of the view action bar.

You can use these arrows to shift the view action bar left and right to access buttons that don't f
on the screen.

Using the View Icons

View icons run along the left side of the View pane and indicate the status of a document in the view:

- Selected for an action (check mark); click in the margin next to a document to select it.
- Marked for deletion (x-mark).
- Unread (asterisk).
- Involved in a replication conflict (diamond).

Using the View Content Area

The view content area makes up the remainder of the View pane and consists of rows and columns in which selected data from documents is displayed. The documents included in the view are determined by the View Selection formula, a set of criteria the view uses to determine which documents it displays. The columns included in the view determine the actual data displayed. Each column has its own formula and properties that can be modified by the developer. See Chapter 21, "Using Views and Folders," for more information on designing views. At the top of each column, there is a header area. If small up or down arrows like those shown here are displayed in a column's header area, you can click the column header to sort the view by that column.

If the column header has vertical bars separating it from other columns, you can click and drag the horizontal bar to resize the column.

Options in the view definition determine whether these features are enabled.

Working with Documents and Views

The main point of views, of course, is to allow you to locate and deal with documents. From the view, you are able to perform many common actions on documents, such as the following:

- Opening and closing documents
- Deleting documents
- Organizing documents into folders
- Working with sets of documents
- Searching documents

Opening and Closing Documents

As previously mentioned, a view displays summary information about documents. This is great if you are trying to find a specific document or if you are only interested in seeing the summary information. If you want to see or edit the contents of a document, you need to open it from the view interface. Follow these steps to open an existing group document in your address book:

1. Open your address book by selecting the address book icon on the Bookmark bar (third from the top by default).
2. Select the Groups view from the view/folder list in the Navigation pane.
3. Select a row in the view content area representing the document you want to open. For this example, select the row displaying LocalDominoServers.
4. Either press Enter or double-click the row.

The document will be displayed in a new task window, using the appropriate form, of course. To close the document, either press Esc or click the X to the right of the form's task button.

If you're using a Windows computer, you can set an option allowing you to close documents and other task windows by double-clicking the right mouse button. To enable this feature, follow the steps:

1. Select File ➤ Preferences ➤ User Preferences to open the User Preferences dialog box.

2. Select the Basics icon on the left side (this is the default choice).

3. In the Additional options box, scroll up until you see the choice called Right Double-Click Closes Window.

4. Click to the left of this choice to enable it. A check mark appears to the left of it.

5. Click OK.

A warning message dialog box will appear with the text *Some preferences will not take effect until next time the program is started.* This is normal, but it means what it says. Double-clicking the right mouse button won't close windows until the next time you start Notes.

Deleting Documents

Another common action you will perform from the view interface is deleting documents from the database. Follow these steps to delete a document:

1. Select a row in the view content area representing the document you want to delete.

2. Either press Delete or select Edit ➤ Clear.

An x-shaped icon is displayed in the view icon area next to the deleted document. At this point, the document is not actually deleted from the database. Rather, it is marked for deletion. If you close the database or press F9 to refresh the view, a message box appears with a message asking if you want to delete the selected documents from the database.

Select the Yes button to permanently delete the documents. If you are refreshing the view, selecting No leaves the documents marked for deletion. If you are closing the database, selecting No removes the deletion mark and closes the database. Upon reentry, the documents are no longer marked for deletion.

This, at least, is how most databases will work. However, there are some important exceptions. First, deletions take place *immediately* in your mailbox database. This includes your Inbox, your calendar, and your to do items; all three functions are contained in the same database file. You should, therefore, be careful about what you delete from your mailbox.

Second, some databases have a feature called *soft deletion.* Soft deletes allow administrators a window of opportunity of several hours to recover documents after they are deleted by users. Soft deletion is a feature enabled on a database-by-database basis, so if you're thinking about deleting documents from a database, find out if soft deletion is enabled before you do.

Soft deletion is usually a feature enabled by a database developer. Fortunately, you can enable soft deletes in your own mail database. See Chapter 5, "Communicating with Notes Mail," for more information on how you can protect yourself on inadvertent deletions.

Organizing Documents into Folders

Folders enable you to organize documents in an ad-hoc manner. Folders can be personal, which allows you to individualize a Notes database. They can also be shared, which allows a group of people to manipulate the organization of documents in a Notes database. One common use for folders is organizing e-mail. You can create folders in your mail database and then file messages in them for future reference.

You can easily add folders to just about any Notes database, but you must have the appropriate authority. Because you should have the authority to create folders in your mail database, we will use it to demonstrate how to create a folder. To create a folder called Projects in your mail database, follow these steps:

1. Open your mail database by selecting the Mail icon from the Bookmark bar.

2. Select Create ➢ Folder. A Create Folder dialog box similar to the one shown here appears.

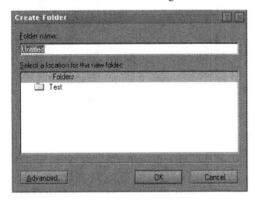

3. Enter a name for the folder in the Folder Name field. For this example, enter **Projects**.

4. Do not change anything in the other fields. By default, the new folder will be created at the top level of the view/folder hierarchy, and its design will be copied from the view/folder listed in the Copy Style From field, which appears beneath the list of existing folders on the left. For more information on designing folders, see Chapter 21. Click OK.

The Projects folder will be displayed at the top level of the folder hierarchy, and its design will be based on the All Documents view. You can also easily rename, redesign, move, and delete folders. To rename the Projects folder created in the preceding example to New Projects, follow these steps:

1. Select the Projects folder in the Navigation pane.

2. Select Actions ➢ Folder Options ➢ Rename. A Rename Folder dialog box will be displayed (shown here).

3. Type the new name for the folder in the Name field. In this example, type **New Projects**.

4. Click the OK button.

The Projects folder will now be displayed as New Projects. The process of moving a folder another location in the folder hierarchy is also fairly simple. It enables you to organize your folde into a hierarchy, even after they have been created. For example, you could create a folder nam Personal for personal correspondence, then create folders within that to hold messages from speci individuals. To demonstrate this feature, you'll need to create a new folder under which to organi an existing one. Follow the previous procedure for creating new folders to create a folder named Te: To move the New Projects folder under Test, follow these steps:

1. Select the New Projects folder in the Navigation pane.
2. Select Actions ➤ Folder Options ➤ Move. A Move dialog box appears (shown here).

3. Select Test in the Choose the Folder's New Location field.
4. Click the OK button.

The New Projects folder will now be displayed underneath the Test view. To move it back to tl top level of the folder hierarchy, perform the preceding steps without selecting anything in the Choo the Folder's New Location field. Also, you can easily remove folders when you no longer need them. I remove the New Projects folder, follow these steps:

1. Select the New Projects folder in the Navigation pane.
2. Select Actions ➤ Folder Options ➤ Delete Folder. A warning dialog box appears with a m sage that this delete action cannot be undone (shown here). This is normal.

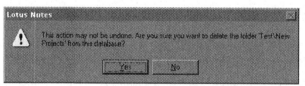

3. Click the Yes button to delete the folder.

The New Projects folder will no longer be displayed in the view/folder list. You can also redesi a folder after it has been created. You can access the folder design screen by selecting Actions ➤ Fold Options ➤ Design after selecting a folder. Folder design is an advanced topic; see Chapter 21 for mo information.

NOTE *If you remove a folder, the documents contained within it will not be removed, but the pointers to those documents will be deleted. Pointers are explained later in this section; see the "So What Do Folders Hold?" sidebar.*

Folders are visually similar to views. In fact, they are displayed alongside views in the database's view/folder list, which is generally displayed on the left side of the Database area. Views are shown with a report icon to the left of them, and folders are shown with a file folder icon.

Just as views do, folders display documents in rows and columns, and the rows can be grouped by data values contained within documents. The main difference between views and folders is that views show documents, meeting specific criteria, whereas folders show documents based on pointers that can be added and removed. The criteria by which documents are displayed in views are called the *View Selection formula*. It is defined when the view is created or modified by the developer using Domino Designer. In contrast, documents are displayed in folders if the folder contains a pointer to them. You can add document pointers to folders in a number of ways, including the following:

◆ Using the Actions menu

◆ Using a View Action button (if one exists)

◆ Direct manipulation using dragging and dropping

NOTE *The examples in this chapter will use* Mastering Lotus Notes 6 *Chapter 3 database (MasteringR6Ch3.*nsf*) provided on the Sybex website (*www.sybex.com*).*

So What Do Folders Hold?

With all this talk about pointers, some explanation is in order. Unlike folders and directories on your computer's hard drive, views and folders in Notes don't actually hold documents. Rather, they hold shortcuts, or *pointers*, to documents. When you add a document to a folder, you're actually just creating a pointer.

An important implication here is that a document can appear in any number of different views and folders, but because they're *all* just pointers to a single document, you can be assured of reaching the same document from anywhere it appears. This is a surprisingly powerful feature. For example, you can have a discussion database with views arranging the same data in different ways: one view sorting discussion documents by date, another by author, a third by subject, and so on. Likewise, you can have a calendar event appear in your calendar, in several calendar-related views, and your Inbox (in the form of an e-mailed invitation). A nice side effect is that if you're creating pointers rather than copies, all of those extra pointers take up a trivial amount of disk space. No matter how many folders a document appears in, it won't make the database bigger.

Still, it does take some getting used to. First-time Notes users often ask if the other copies of a document will be updated if they edit one of them. It's actually a nonquestion. There are no other copies; it's a single document that happens to appear in several different lists.

Using the Actions Menu

The most straightforward way to add document pointers to folders is to use the Actions menu. If a View Action button exists, it will operate the same way. Let's experiment by using the Chapter 3 database available at the Sybex website (www.sybex.com). Follow these steps to create a folder called *Important Topics*:

1. Open the Chapter 3 database (MasteringR6Ch3.nsf). If you've downloaded the databases from the website, it's in the MasterR6 directory within your Notes Data directory.

2. Select Create ➢ Folder.

3. Enter **Important Topics** into the Folder Name field.

4. Click the OK button.

The Chapter 3 database has some documents in the All Documents view. We'll use these documents to experiment with adding documents to folders. To add a document to the Important Topics folder, follow these steps:

1. Select the All Documents view.

2. Select a document in the View pane.

3. Choose Action ➤ Move to Folder. A Move to Folder dialog box appears.

4. Select the Important Topics folder from the Select a Folder field.

5. Click the Add button.

You won't see an indication that the document was added unless you select the Important Topics folder. If you perform this same procedure from inside a folder, you will notice that the Move to Folder dialog box has an additional button available, the Move button. This button is available because documents in folders represent pointers that can be moved or removed from the folder, whereas views show the actual documents, which can only be removed if the Selection formula is modified.

MANIPULATING USING DRAGGING AND DROPPING

Another way to add documents to folders or move them from one folder to another is to use dragging and dropping to manipulate them directly. Again, the document will not be removed from the view after this action is performed. To move documents from one folder to another folder, just select and drag the document from the folder to a folder icon in the Navigation pane. If you hold down the Ctrl key and then perform this action, the document will be added to the new folder without being removed from the source.

TIP   Remember how you can create shortcuts to task windows by dragging them to your desktop? You can do a similar thing with views. You can create shortcuts to documents from views by dragging the document from the view to the desktop.

WARNING   There's a subtle bit of terminology to keep in mind here. If you're moving a document out of a folder, you're not deleting the document, just removing it from the folder. Deleting a document deletes it from the database. If you would like to keep a document but remove it from a given folder, select the document in the folder and choose Action ➤ Remove from Folder.

Views and folders are design elements in a database. As such, they can be modified to suit your needs. You can use views and folders to display information in a variety of ways depending on the task you need to perform. To modify the structure of views or folders, you need to understand how to use Domino Designer to develop applications. Some changes may be simple, but other changes may be complex. Either way, a basic understanding of how databases are developed is important before starting. Please refer to Chapter 21 for more information on creating and modifying views and folders.

NOTE   Domino Designer 6 must be installed on your computer before you can create or modify design elements, such as views.

Working with Sets of Documents

Sometimes it's helpful to work on more than one document at a time. You can quickly delete, print, categorize, file in folders, mark read/unread, export to a file, and run agents against sets of selected documents. To select and deselect documents, you can use one of the following methods:

- Select the row of the document you want to select or deselect and press the spacebar.
- Click the view icon area next to the documents you want to select or deselect.
- Click and drag in the view icon area to select or deselect multiple, adjacent documents.
- Choose Edit ➢ Select All or Edit ➢ Deselect All to select or deselect all documents in the view.

Selected documents will have a check mark next to them in the view icon area.

Searching Documents

You can perform detailed searches on documents in a view by using the Search bar. You can toggle the Search bar on or off by selecting the Search button in the toolbar or by selecting View ➢ Search This View. When this option is first selected, the Search bar is collapsed and shows only the basic options, as shown here.

Selecting the More button on the lower-right side expands the Search bar to show all available options, as shown here.

Across the top is an indicator that tells you whether the database is indexed. The indicator's setting is based on whether the database currently has a full-text index created. A full-text index improves the performance of searches performed on Notes databases and adds functionality—such as searching attachments in Notes documents—but it requires additional disk space. At the bottom of the expanded Search bar is a button to create the full-text index if one does not already exist (the previous graphic is from a database that has already been indexed).

As you can see, there are many options available to you for searching Notes databases. You can specify various sets of conditions, use certain options, and even save searches for future use by you or your colleagues. See Chapter 8, "Searching for Information," for more on full-text indexes and searching.

TIP   Use the Quick Search feature of the Notes view by clicking in the View pane to make sure it has focus and typing characters on the keyboard. A Starts With dialog box will be displayed. Type the first few characters of the document you are trying to find. If the view is categorized, you will be positioned at the category matching the characters you typed. If it's not, you will be positioned at the first document containing the characters typed in the view's first column.

Creating and Modifying Documents

As discussed earlier, forms are used to create, modify, and display documents. Opening an existing document displays the contents of the document through its associated form. When the contents are displayed through the form but not available for changes, the form is in View mode. Many databases open documents to View mode by default. When the contents are displayed through the form and available for changes, the form is in Edit mode. When a new document is created, a blank form is opened in Edit mode. The main difference between the two modes is that you can make changes to the document only when it is in Edit mode.

Like their paper counterpart, forms in Notes are a collection of fields and field descriptions. Field descriptions provide a simple cue that helps you identify what information should be entered into a particular field. In the field shown here, the word *To* is a field description that tells you that the area next to it is for entering the name or names of recipients for this mail message.

To:

NOTE *There's a subtle distinction to be made here. When talking about documents, a field is a named piece of data. When talking about forms, as we are here, a field is a design element that holds, displays, and possibly computes data.*

Field descriptions are generally text elements, such as the word *To* in the preceding example. These text elements can also be formatted by font, size, style, and color.

Forms can also contain more complex elements, such as objects, pictures, tables, collapsible sections, hotspots, and Java applets.

Fields are represented either by distinct blocked-off areas of the screen or by a set of brackets on the screen. They are areas on the screen that accept your input; that is, where you would type information or select from a set of choices. When you enter a field, the cursor will be visible, signifying your position in the field. As you type, the cursor will change position as it does in other applications. There are many types of fields that can be presented on forms in Notes, including text, date/time, number, dialog list, check box, radio button, list box, rich-text list, color, combo box, rich-text, authors, names, readers, password, formula, and time zone. As a user, you only need to know that fields on a form accept user input and can include many types of information. Field descriptions provide you with cues that help identify what information should be entered into a particular field. If you are designing forms, see Chapter 19, "Basic Form Design," and Chapter 20, "Advanced Form Design," for a complete explanation of fields and how they can be used.

Creating New Documents

Most of the tasks you will perform in Notes—such as adding contacts to your personal address book, sending e-mail to an associate, and managing appointments in your calendar—involve creating documents. The basic process for creating documents is as follows:

1. Open a blank form.
2. Fill in the appropriate information.
3. Execute the Save function.
4. Close the form if necessary.

Generally, opening a blank form involves opening a database and clicking an appropriate action button. You may also open the appropriate form from the Create menu. In the case of common tasks, such as adding contacts, you can also create bookmarks to blank forms as shortcuts. For instructions on how to add blank forms as bookmarks, see Chapter 2, "Getting Familiar with Notes."

TIP *The Create menu also includes a special Mail submenu for documents created within your mail database, such as memos (mail messages), replies, tasks, and calendar entries. The Create ➤ Mail menu is available at all times within Notes so you can quickly access these forms.*

To demonstrate how new documents are created in Notes, let's create a new memo in your mail database. Follow these steps to create a new memo:

1. Open your mail database by selecting the Mail icon from the Bookmark bar.
2. Open the Drafts view by selecting Drafts in the Navigation pane.
3. Select Create ➤ Memo or click the New Memo button on the view action bar.

A blank memo form, like the one shown here, opens in Edit mode. You can tell the form has been opened in Edit mode because fields are available for entering information and the cursor is positioned in the first field.

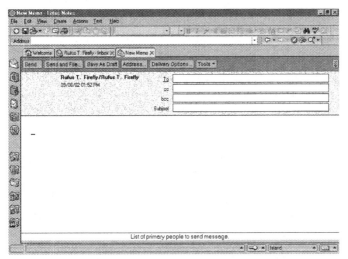

How you fill in the appropriate information on a blank form depends on how the form was designed. It involves navigating around the fields on the form and entering data in the proper places. To navigate around fields on a form, you can use the Tab and Shift+Tab keys or the mouse. Tab and Shift+Tab move the cursor forward and backward between fields until you encounter a rich-text field. Because rich-text fields can store formatted text, as well as many other types of data, Tab and Shift+Tab are interpreted as part of the text and not used to navigate fields. To navigate out of a rich-text field, use the mouse to select another field. When you use the Tab+Shift keys, your cursor will move from field to field based on the tab order defined by the form's designer. If you use the mouse, you can select any field on the screen in any order you choose. To fill in the blank memo form previously opened, follow these steps:

1. Press Tab to move your cursor to the Subject field, the blank space next to the word *Subject*.

2. Type **Test of creating new document** in the Subject field.

There are a few different ways to save a new document:

- Select File ➤ Save.
- Click the Save button on the Form Action bar if one exists.
- Press Esc and select the Save option in the dialog box that appears.
- Perform an action that causes form logic to save the document if the form is designed this w

Pressing Esc and selecting the appropriate Save option will also close the form. To close the fon yourself after saving the document, press Esc or click the X to the right of the form's task button. save the document you just created and close the form, click the Save as Draft button on the For Action bar. The form will be closed and you will be returned to the Drafts view, which should conta the document you just created.

Modifying Existing Documents

Editing documents is similar to creating new ones, except some of the fields may already have infe mation in them when you open the form. There are a number of ways to open a document for editi

- Select a document in a view and then click the Edit button on the view action bar if one exis
- Open the document and click the Edit button on the Form Action bar if one exists.
- Open a document and double-click anywhere in the Form Content area.
- Select a document in a view and press Ctrl+E.

Of course, a form could be designed to automatically open documents in Edit mode. If this the case, all you would have to do to edit a document would be to open it. Then, you can naviga around the form as if the document was just being created. After making whatever changes are n essary to the document, you can save it and close the form.

Using the Document Features

When you are viewing documents through forms, you can enable and disable a number of availab document features. The following options are available while the form is in View mode:

Show Page Breaks   Show Page Breaks can be toggled on and off. When it's enabled, a horizont line will be drawn across the form where page breaks will occur if the document is printed. Th is handy if you are trying to format text within a document so the document will paginate proper You can toggle the Show Page Breaks option on and off by selecting View ➤ Show ➤ Page Brea A check mark will appear to the left of the selection when the option is enabled.

NOTE   *To insert page breaks in a rich-text field, position your cursor where you want the page break and choose Create ➤ Pag Break.*

Show Pass-Thru HTML   Show Pass-Thru HTML can also be toggled on and off. This optic will display or hide text formatted as Pass-Thru HTML in the document. Text formatted as Pa Thru HTML is generally used for designing forms. You can toggle the Show Pass-Thru optic on and off by selecting View ➤ Show ➤ Pass-Thru HTML. A check mark will appear to the le of the selection when the option is enabled.

Show HTML Source   Show HTML Source is only activated when the form displayed contains HTML data, such as a web page that you are viewing through the native Notes browser or the integrated Internet Explorer browser supported by Notes. This function is similar to the View ➢ Source menu option common to web browsers. To view the HTML source of a web page, follow these steps:

1. Make sure you have a web page open as a form in Notes.

2. Select View ➢ Show ➢ HTML Source.

A new form will open within Notes displaying a page with the HTML source code of the web page you were viewing. In other browsers, the HTML source is displayed as plain text. In Notes, however, the HTML is actually formatted with tags highlighted in different colors.

In addition, the following document features are available when the form is in Edit mode:

Show Field Help   Show Field Help can be toggled on and off. When it's enabled, Notes displays the field help associated with fields on the form. Field help is a feature supported by Notes forms that enables a form designer to include text for each field to help the user fill in the proper information. The field help text is displayed in the system message area of the status bar if it is available and the Show Field Help option has been enabled. To toggle the Show Field Help option on and off, select View ➢ Show ➢ Field Help. A check mark will appear to the left of the selection when the option is enabled.

Show Hidden Characters   Show Hidden Characters can be toggled on and off. When it's enabled, Notes displays hidden characters contained within the document. Hidden characters include paragraph marks, tabs, and other formatting characters. To toggle the Show Hidden Characters option on and off, select View ➢ Show ➢ Hidden Characters. A check mark will appear to the left of the selection when the option is enabled.

Show Hidden from Notes   Show Hidden from Notes can be toggled on and off. When it's enabled, Notes displays elements that the designer of the form has designated as hidden to the Notes client. Choosing whether elements are hidden from the Notes client is a design topic and is covered in Chapter 18, "Understanding the Formula Language." To toggle the Show Hidden From Notes option on and off, select View ➢ Show ➢ Hidden from Notes. A check mark will appear to the left of the selection when the option is enabled.

Show Java Applets Running   Show Java Applets Running can be toggled on and off. When it's enabled, Notes displays Java applets currently running in the form. Java applets are software components generally associated with web-based applications, but Notes supports the execution of Java applets within the client. Java applets represent a sophisticated way to execute software on client computers and are outside the scope of this book. To toggle the Show Java Applets option on and off, select View ➢ Show ➢ Java Applets. A check mark will appear to the left of the selection when the option is enabled.

Entering Information into Fields

As previously mentioned, information is entered into Notes databases via fields on forms. These are called *editable* fields. Editable fields allow you to enter information. Other fields, such as computed or computed for display fields, show information and do not allow data entry. Each editable field type (discussed in the following sections) can be presented differently, and each allows you to enter certain information.

TEXT FIELDS

Text fields collect free-form but unformatted textual information, such as subjects for an e-mail m sage or a short description for a discussion topic. Text fields are very common. They can be present in a number of different ways on the form and in two different styles. The first style should be famil to anyone who has used Notes in the past. The text field is usually marked with brackets on the l and right sides.

Notes also supports text fields that use the native interface of the operating system (the secon style). Unlike Notes style fields, which grow or shrink to fit their content, operating system style fields have a fixed width and height.

DATE/TIME FIELDS

Date/time fields collect time-related information. The Notes database designer can customize the c play and edit format, but the actual data is stored as a special numeric value. This makes it possible perform calculations on dates stored in Notes databases. Storing date/time data as a special numer value is also efficient because it takes less space than data stored as text.

Just like text fields, date/time fields can be presented a number of different ways on the forr and in two different styles. With the first style, the field is marked with brackets on the left and right sides just like the text field. Notes also supports a special calendar control. The calendar con trol has a small icon at one end. If the field is set to want a date value, clicking the icon brings u a calendar set to the current date. You can scroll back and forth between months and click the da you want, as shown here.

If the field is set to want a time value, clicking the icon brings up a slider that you can use to sele a specific time, as shown here.

Date/time fields accept values from 01/01/0001 to 12/31/9999 (if you're trying to develop a Notes database to keep track of Hittite king lists, you've got problems). You will not be allowed to enter information if it's not a valid date or time value, although Notes has considerable ability to interpret questionable date and time data. They can also be programmed to require four-digit years. If a date/time field is not programmed to require four-digit years, Notes will interpret the date. If the year is entered as a two-digit number from 50 to 99, it will be entered as a year in the 20th century (1950 to 1999). If the year is entered as a two-digit number from 00 to 49, it will be entered as a year in the 21st century (2000 to 2049). Finally, date/time fields have a built-in ability to handle both Christian (AD/CE) and Muslim (AH) calendars.

*TIP   Don't want to type in today's date? Just type **today** into the date/time field. Notes will interpret it as the current date. The same applies to typing **tomorrow** and **yesterday**.*

NUMBER FIELDS

Number fields collect numeric information, including currency. They can be presented a number of different ways on the form and in two different styles. With the first style, the field is marked with brackets on the left and right sides just like the text field. Notes also supports operating system–style number fields; that is, data-entry fields shown in a style native to the operating system rather than the opposed-brackets style.

DIALOG LIST, LIST BOX, COMBO BOX, CHECK BOX, AND RADIO BUTTON FIELDS

Dialog list, list box, combo box, check box, and radio button fields collect information from pre-defined sets of choices called *keywords*. They make sure information entered is kept consistent. For example, you may have a database to keep track of products, and each product includes a value for the category field. If you made this a text field and let users enter values, there would probably be many variations of the same category. It would be much better to make it a dialog list or list box field.

With dialog list fields, the keywords are presented through a dialog box, as shown here.

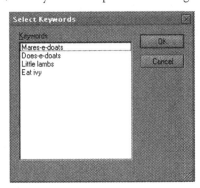

If dialog list fields are designed to allow multiple values, you will be able to choose multiple keywords. Selected keywords will have a check mark. If dialog list fields are designed to accept new values, you will be able to type new keywords into the dialog box. Dialog list fields may also be designed to present the Directories dialog box, the Access Control List dialog box, or a View dialog box. The

Directories dialog box is used to choose names instead of keywords, and the Access Control List d log box is used to choose names from the database's Access Control List (ACL). The View dialog b is used to display choices based on a view from a database.

List box fields present the keywords in a framed element in the Form Content area with arrow on the right side for scrolling through the choices, as shown here.

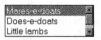

If list box fields are designed to allow multiple values, you will be able to choose multiple key words. Selected keywords will have a check mark. List box fields cannot be designed to accept ne values directly from user input, although a sufficiently clever developer can design fields that dra their choices dynamically from other data; Chapter 18 and Chapter 19 touch more on this.

Combo box fields present the keywords in a drop-down element in the Form Content area (show here). Combo box fields cannot be designed to allow multiple values or to accept new values direct from user input.

Check box fields present the keywords as a set of check box elements in the Form Content are (shown here). If check box fields are designed to accept multiple values, you can select multiple che boxes. Check box fields cannot be designed to accept new values directly from user input.

☐ Mares-e-doats
☐ Does-e-doats
☐ Little lambs
☐ Eat ivy

Radio button fields present the keywords as a set of radio button elements in the Form Conte area (shown here). Radio button fields cannot be designed to allow multiple values or to accept ne values directly from user input.

○ Mares-e-doats
○ Does-e-doats
○ Little lambs
○ Eat ivy

RICH-TEXT FIELDS

The rich-text field is a powerful feature of Notes. These fields are containers for storing many di ferent types of information. See the next section for more information on entering information in rich-text fields.

Rich-text lite fields are much the same as rich-text fields, but they're accompanied by a helper button. The button serves multiple purposes. It serves as a general helper to bring in graphics, attachments, applets, and other rich-text content.

The other field types—names, authors, readers, password, color, time zone, and formula—accommodate special requirements of certain applications. You can find more information on these fields types and the other ones briefly mentioned in Chapter 19 and Chapter 20.

Working with Rich-Text Fields

Rich-text fields contain formatted text and also act as a container for objects, attachments, pictures, tables, and other elements. They enable you to include data from a variety of sources in Notes documents. You can scan a document or picture and copy and paste it into a rich-text field. You can work with objects from other applications directly inside them; for example, you can create a Word document inside a rich-text field. You can also attach files from your computer to rich-text fields. Attachments can then be viewed or detached. Rich-text fields also provide a rich set of native formatting options for text created within them. You can tell you are in a rich-text field if the font, point size, and style areas of the status bar display values that are accessible.

Adding Formatted Text

It's easy to use rich-text fields to create documents that have formatted text. You just type the information into the rich-text field, use the mouse to highlight the area to be formatted, and then choose the desired formatting options. The following formatting options are among those available to you in rich-text fields:

- Font
- Point size
- Style (italic, bold, underline, strikethrough)
- Effects (shadow, emboss, extrude, superscript, subscript)
- Color
- Highlighting
- Paragraph alignment
- Paragraph margins
- List type (bullet, number, check mark, circle, square, uppercase and lowercase alphabetical, uppercase and lowercase Roman numeral)

TIP *Use the check mark list type to create lists in Notes rich-text fields that can have items checked or unchecked. You can use it to show which items have been completed or items that need emphasis.*

Formatting options can be selected from the menu, the context menu, and the Properties box. When your cursor is inside a rich-text field, a Text Properties menu appears in the menu bar.

If you right-click highlighted text in a rich-text field, a context menu similar to the one shown here will be displayed.

As you can see, the context menu provides you with some of the more common formatting options. You can also open the Text Properties box (shown here open to the Font tab) from this context menu by selecting Text Properties.

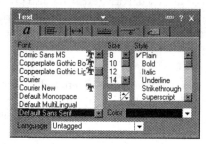

The first three tabs—Font, Paragraph Alignment, and Paragraph Margins—allow you to modify the most common options, such as:

◆ Font

◆ Size

◆ Style

◆ Color

◆ Paragraph alignment

◆ List style

◆ Paragraph spacing

◆ Margins

◆ Tab stops

◆ Pagination

You can also mark the text as being in a specific language, such as Tamil or Romanian, or even a specific dialect or national variant, such as British English or Bahrainian Arabic. Marking the text with a language does not change the font, but it does govern which dictionary Notes uses when spell checking the document.

The fourth tab, Paragraph Border, allows you to put a border around the paragraph. You can set the border style (single line, double line, dotted line, and so on) and color for the paragraph, and adjust the border's thickness on each side.

The fifth tab, Paragraph Hide-When, allows you to selectively hide paragraphs. Hiding paragraphs is a technique used most often when designing forms. See Chapter 18 for more information. The last tab, Paragraph Style, allows you to create and modify named styles based on the current paragraph's formatting options. Paragraph styles can then be applied to other paragraphs, simplifying formatting.

When you work in rich-text fields, Notes can also display a ruler across the top of the Form area. The ruler can be used to modify the left margin, the paragraph indent, and tab stops. To display the ruler, follow these steps:

1. Make sure you are in a rich-text field.
2. Select View ➢ Ruler. The ruler, shown here, appears at the top of the Form area.

To practice using rich-text fields, let's create a new mail message in your mail database. Here's how:

1. Open your mail database by selecting the Mail icon from the Bookmark bar.
2. Create a new mail message (document) by clicking the New Memo button on the view action bar or by selecting Create ➢ Memo.
3. Press Tab to move your cursor to the Body field, the blank area underneath the mail header information.
4. Type **Testing the features of rich text fields** in the Body field.
5. Highlight the text you just typed and play with formatting by selecting options from the Text menu or by using the Text Properties box as previously mentioned.

To close the form, press Esc or click the X to the right of the form's task button. A dialog box with save options will be presented.

Because we were just testing features of rich-text fields and don't need to save this document, select Discard Changes and then click the OK button.

TIP   If you select the Properties box toolbar icon while editing a rich-text field, the Text Properties box will minimize itself to show a set of common formatting icons. You can use it to quickly change the formatting of text without constantly going back to the menus.

You can also copy and paste formatted text into a rich-text field. If you copy information from an application that supports rich-text data (such as Microsoft Word) to the Clipboard, it can be pasted into a Notes rich-text field with its associated formatting. To see how this works, just follow these steps:

1. Create a memo document in your mail database as explained in the preceding example.
2. In Word (or another application that can copy rich-text to the Clipboard), highlight some text and select Edit ➢ Copy.
3. Go back to Notes and make sure your cursor is positioned in the body field, the blank area underneath the mail header information.

4. Select Edit ➤ Paste Special. The Paste Special dialog box appears (shown here).

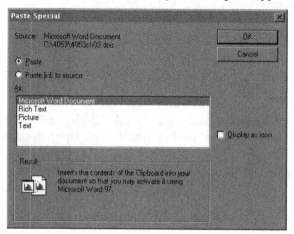

5. Select the Paste radio button, select Rich Text from the As field, and then click the OK butt

The text you copied to the Clipboard from Word should be displayed in the Notes rich-text fie
The text itself is editable within the rich-text field, just as if it were typed directly into the field. I
close the form, press Esc or click the X to the right of the form's task button. In the Close Windo
dialog box, select Discard Changes and then click the OK button.

WARNING   *This should be sufficient for most content, but many applications have advanced features that the Notes fla-
vor of rich-text can't reproduce. For example, revision marks in a Word document won't survive the migration to Notes.*

Adding Objects

OLE is a protocol built into Windows that enables applications to share data. It was Microsoft's
first foray into component software architectures and the precursor to programmatic interfac
such as ActiveX, COM/DCOM, and, now, Distributed InterNetwork Architecture. Objects li
ing and embedding (OLE) objects can be inserted into rich-text fields, making Notes a powerfu
OLE container application. Notes can control OLE objects programmatically, but it also provide
the interfaces required to let you link and embed objects into rich-text fields. See Chapter 1
"Integrating Notes with Other Applications," for more information on using object linking and
embedding in Notes.

Attaching Files

Rich-text fields can also contain attachments or computer files from other programs (for exampl
word processor documents, spreadsheets, images, and so on). You can insert attachments anywhe
in the rich-text field. Just position your cursor where you want the attachment inserted and selec
File ➤ Attach. A dialog box will be displayed that allows you to choose a file from your computer
disk drive. See Chapter 12 for more information on attaching file in Notes.

Adding Pictures

You can copy and paste graphic images into rich-text fields as well as import graphic files. This is useful for discussions in which a picture would help express an idea better than text alone. You can also include pictures in e-mail.

The Create Picture menu imports graphic files into rich-text fields. To import a graphic file, follow these steps:

1. Make sure you are in a rich-text field.

2. Select Create ➤ Picture. An Import dialog box appears (shown here).

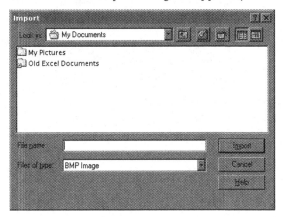

3. Using this dialog box, you can navigate around your computer's file system to locate the graphic file (JPG, GIF, or BMP formats) to import into the current rich-text field. The dialog box will only display files of the type selected.

4. Once you have chosen a graphic file to import, click the Import button.

The image will be displayed in the rich-text field.

NOTE   *You can use File ➤ Import instead of Create ➤ Picture, but although the latter limits you to a short, convenient list of image types, the former gives you a much longer list of file types you can import.*

You can also copy and paste graphics into rich-text fields. To do so, follow these steps:

1. Make sure you are in a rich-text field.

2. Launch the application containing the image you would like to copy and paste into Notes.

3. Select the image and copy it to the Clipboard by choosing Edit ➤ Copy (the Edit menu exists in most applications).

4. Go back to Notes and select Edit ➤ Paste.

The image will be displayed in the rich-text field. To manipulate the image inside the rich-text field, use the Picture Properties box. To display the Picture Properties box, use one of the following methods:

◆ Right-click the image and select Picture Properties from the context menu.

- Click the image and select Picture ➤ Picture Properties. Picture Properties box appears (shown here).

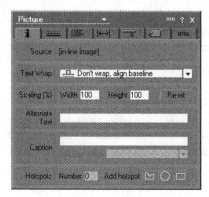

The Picture Properties box allows you to do the following:
- Determine how text should wrap around the image
- Change the image's scaling
- Add a caption to the image
- Add hotspots to the image
- Add a border to the image
- Add clickable hotspots to the image to perform actions or follow links
- Insert alternate text (similar to the ALT attribute for the HTML <IMG> tag)

Creating Tables

You can create tables in rich-text fields to structure text. Tables present information as a series of rows and columns. Each cell can contain rich-text elements such as formatted text, pictures, and so on. Cells can also contain other tables. Notes supports different types of tables including:
- Standard
- Tabbed
- Animated
- Caption
- Programmed

Generally, you will create standard tables when you are creating documents. The other table types are primarily used for designing forms and are discussed in Chapter 20. Follow these steps to create a standard table:

1. Make sure you are in a rich-text field.

2. Select Create ➤ Table. The Create Table dialog box appears (shown here).

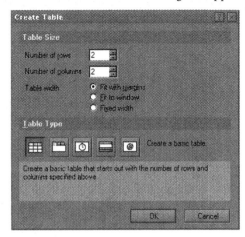

3. Select the standard table icon (the first icon on the left in the Table Type area).

4. Enter the number of rows and columns to include in the table. You can set some basic formatting here as well. A table can be fixed width or it can fit the available space, with or without margins.

5. Click the OK button.

A table like the one shown here will be displayed with the number of rows and columns you selected.

You can navigate between cells using the Tab key and the arrow keys. You can also use the mouse to position your cursor directly in a cell. Once the cursor is inside a cell, you can add formatted text and other rich-text elements as needed. This is a great way to structure information within a Notes document. A table can have formatted text in one cell, a picture in another, an attachment in a third, and any number of other rich-text elements in the remaining cells. You can also create another table in a cell. To create a table within a table, follow these steps:

1. Navigate to a cell within an existing table.

2. Select Create ➤ Table. The Create Table dialog box appears.

3. Select the standard table icon (the first icon on the left in the Table Type area).

4. Enter the number of rows and columns to include in the table.

5. Click the OK button.

Inside the cell where your cursor was positioned, a table will be displayed with the number of rows and columns selected. You can nest tables up to eight deep.

Once a table has been created, you can modify its formatting properties, including:

- Cell spacing
- Table border style
- Cell border style
- Row and column color/style
- Cell color
- Cell image
- Margins

You modify the formatting properties by selecting options on the Table Properties box. To c play the Table Properties box, follow these steps:

1. Navigate to a cell within an existing table.

2. Select Table ➢ Table Properties. The Table Properties box will be opened and the Table L out tab (shown here) will be displayed.

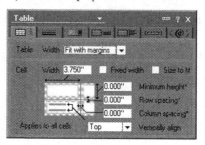

If you select the Properties box Toolbar button with the Table Properties box displayed, the Pro erties box will be reduced to a toolbar (shown here).

The Table toolbar provides a set of buttons that allow you to change the table in a number of wa

- Modify cell color
- Add and remove borders
- Merge and split cells
- Append, insert, and remove columns
- Append, insert, and remove rows

Also, from inside an existing table, a Table menu like the one shown here will be visible.

From the Table menu, you can open the Table Properties box to the Table Layout tab (as previously discussed), add rows and columns, merge cells, and size the table automatically.

Inserting Links

Another powerful feature of rich-text fields is that they can contain *links*, or pointers to other elements in Notes. You can create links from the following Notes elements: databases, views, documents, and anchors.

You can insert a link to direct another person to a specific Notes object. For example, you can mail someone a link to a database or a specific document in a database. This is a great way to share information that exists in a Notes database. Links are often used in workflow applications to alert users when they need to act on information. Links are represented as small icons inside the rich-text field (see Table 3.1).

TABLE 3.1: ICONS FOR LINK TYPES

LINK TYPE	ICON
Database	
View	
Document	
Anchor	

To insert a link, open the Notes object to which you would like to link, copy the link to the C
board, and paste the link into the target rich-text field. To demonstrate, let's create a database li
to your address book and insert it into a mail message:

1. Open your address book database by selecting the address book icon from the Bookmark
2. Select Edit ➤ Copy As Link ➤ Database Link.
3. Open your mail database by selecting the Mail icon from the Bookmark bar.
4. Create a new mail message by clicking the New Memo button on the view action bar or b
   selecting Create ➤ Memo.
5. Navigate to the body field, the blank area underneath the mail header information.
6. Select Edit ➤ Paste.

A database link will appear in the rich-text field. If you click the database link, your address bo
will open.

The only item on the list we haven't encountered before is an *anchor*. An anchor is a location ins
a rich-text area; users familiar with HTML will recognize this as similar to internal anchors in w
pages. Internal anchors are created in the process of copying as a link. To create an anchor, click
the point in the rich-text field where you want to link to and follow the previous instructions. You
be asked to name the anchor. Once the anchor has been created, you can Copy as Link, then paste
link elsewhere.

TIP *Speaking of web page links, Notes understands standard uniform resource locator (URL) syntax. It will auto
matically interpret any text in a rich-text field starting with* http://, ftp://, mailto://, *and* notes:// *as link
so you can send web and other links to other Notes users just by typing them. However, they only act as links when th
document is in Read mode. In Editing mode, they're just treated as text.*

Working with Other Rich-Text Elements

So far, we have explored formatted text, objects, attachments, pictures, tables, and links and how th
are used within rich-text fields. These are the most common elements you'll work with in rich-te
fields as you create Notes documents. Notes allows you to create a number of other elements
(although they are generally associated with designing forms), including the following:

Hotspots Text or graphic elements that pop up text, link to Notes objects, perform actions,
link to URLs. Hotspots can take on many guises. They may appear as raised buttons, graphic b
tons, and text links.

Sections Elements that enable you to collapse paragraphs to single lines within rich-text fiel
They can be used to hide large amounts of information contained within documents when it is
needed but allow it to be brought up quickly.

Java applets Software components that can be written to perform specific functions within
database.

Embedded elements Notes database design elements that can be embedded in rich-text fie

See Chapter 20 for more information on these elements.

Checking Your Spelling

Because much of what you do in Notes involves creating text—either in personal documents such as e-mail or in shared documents such as those in discussion databases—the need to check spelling is critical. Fortunately, Notes includes an integrated spell checker that enables you to check the spelling of individual words as well as the spelling in entire documents. It checks for misspelled words using the main dictionary and a secondary, customizable user dictionary. The default main dictionary for the North American version of Notes is English (United States) and is stored in a file (us.dic) in your Notes Data directory. The customizable user dictionary is stored in a separate file (user.dic) in your Notes Data directory.

Spell Checking a Document

To spell check an entire document, follow these steps:

1. Open the document you would like to spell check and switch to Edit mode (Ctrl+E).
2. Select Edit ➢ Check Spelling. The Spell Check dialog box will be displayed (shown here).

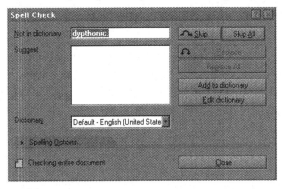

Clicking Spelling Options lets you set a number of basic spell checking functions as you go, such as avoiding words in uppercase or words with numbers in them.

The Spell Check dialog box gives you several choices for when it finds a word it doesn't have in its dictionaries:

- Fix the misspelled word by typing a replacement word or selecting a replacement from the list of possible guesses that Notes displays and then clicking the Replace button. If no word in the list of suggestions is suitable, you can type in a replacement of your own.
- Add the word to your customizable user dictionary by clicking the Add button.
- Skip the misspelled word by clicking the Skip button or skip all occurrences of the misspelled word by clicking the Skip All button.
- Manage your dictionary. The Edit Dictionary button lets you add, remove, and edit words in the user dictionary. See the "Managing Your User Dictionary" section for more information.

Spell Checking Selected Text

To spell check selected text, follow these steps:

1. Open the document containing the text you would like to spell check and switch to Edit mc (Ctrl+E).

2. Select the text you would like to spell check.

3. Select Edit ➤ Check Spelling. If the selected text has any misspellings, the Spell Check dia box will be displayed. If there are no misspellings, a message box will be displayed indicati that no misspellings were found, as shown here.

Managing Your User Dictionary

We have demonstrated how you can add words to your customizable user dictionary, but what if y accidentally added a word or you just want to see what words are included? Fortunately, Notes incluc a mechanism for viewing and changing the contents of your custom dictionary. Follow these steps access this tool:

1. Select File ➤ Preferences ➤ User Preferences.

2. Click the Basics button (square) in the upper-left corner of the User Preferences dialog bc

3. Click the User Dictionary button. The User Spell Dictionary dialog box will be displayec

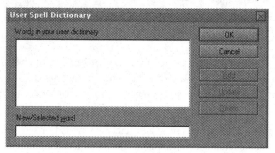

4. From the User Spell Dictionary dialog box, you can do the following:

   ◆ Add new words by typing the word in the field at the bottom of the dialog box and clicki the Add button

- Update words by selecting the word to be changed, typing the new word in the field at the bottom of the dialog box, and clicking the Update button

- Delete words by selecting the word to be removed and clicking the Delete button

When you are finished, click the OK button.

Changing Your Main Dictionary

As mentioned earlier, the default dictionary for the North American version of Notes is English (United States). If you would like to change the main dictionary Notes uses and you have a version of Notes that has installed alternate dictionaries, just follow these steps:

1. Select File ➤ Preferences ➤ User Preferences.
2. Click the International button (square) on the left side of the User Preferences dialog box.
3. Click the Spelling button, which will appear below the International button.
4. Click the Change button to the left of the Spelling Dictionary prompt (the third Change button from the top). The Spell Checking Options dialog box will be displayed (shown here).

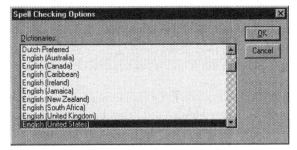

5. Select the dictionary to which you want to change and click the OK button. You may double-click a dictionary or select it and click the Set Default button to set it as the default dictionary.

Printing Your Information

Working with your information electronically is flexible and convenient if you happen to have a computer (and, in many cases, a network connection) handy, but there are times when you just have to have it printed. Notes allows you to print documents, views, and even framesets. In this section, we will introduce these three capabilities. Before discussing how to print documents and views, we will introduce the mechanisms Notes uses to control all printing.

Setting Up Your Page

Notes provides a set of page setup options to allow you to control how it formats output on the print page. These options are set using the Page Setup dialog box (shown here). You display the Page Set dialog box by selecting File ➤ Page Setup.

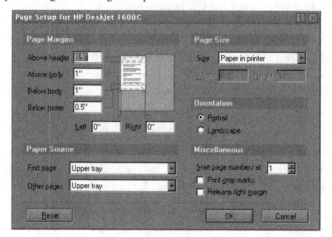

The Start Page Numbers At field allows you to define a starting number for page numbers includ in headers and footers. The default is one. If headers or footers include a page number, this value w be used to initialize the page counter.

The Page Margins fields allow you to set default margins for the printed output. The values f Above Body, Below Body, Above Header, and Below Footer insert extra space around the docume content and any headers or footers. When documents are printed, the Left and Right fields defir how much space will be added to the form's left and right margins. Left and right margins can al be set on individual paragraphs using the Paragraph Margins tab in the Text Properties box.

To accept the page setup values you have entered and close the Page Setup dialog box, click t OK button. To close the dialog box without saving your changes, click the Cancel button.

The Print Crop Marks check box inserts marks at the corners of the document content. The Relea Right Margin setting will override the printer's right margin settings, using Notes' own.

The values you set here will apply to any other documents you print from the same database. Ho ever, if you want to use the same settings in other databases, you'll have to set them again once for ea other database.

Defining Headers and Footers

Headers and footers can be set for the database as a whole or for individual documents. The databa header and footer are useful when printing views and to use as a default when documents do not ha their own headers and footers. Database headers and footers are set in the Printing tab in the Database Properties box (shown here).

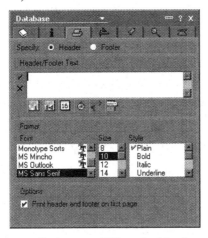

At the top, there are two radio buttons. When the Header radio button is selected, the header/footer text appears at the top of the printed page. When the Footer radio button is selected, the text appears at the bottom. As its name suggests, the Print Header and Footer on First Page check box at the bottom allows you to choose whether headers and footers are printed on the first page.

The field directly below the radio buttons is where you enter the value for the header or footer. It can be a combination of typed text and special codes. The special codes include:

◆ Page number

◆ Total number of pages

◆ Date

◆ Time

◆ Tab

◆ Database title

The special codes help you create a more descriptive header or footer for your output. You enter them by clicking their corresponding button directly below the header/footer entry field. Most of the time, these special codes are used in conjunction with text that describes the value that will be printed (for example, enter **Page:** before the special code for Page number). The special code for Tabs enables you to create sections in the header or footer. For example, you can create a footer with the database title on the left, date in the middle, and page number on the right as follows:

1. Open your mail database or another database for which you would like to set header and footer properties.

2. Open the Database Properties box by selecting File ➤ Database ➤ Properties.

3. Select the Printing tab.

4. Select the Footer radio button.

5. Click in the header/footer entry field directly below the radio buttons. Your cursor will b blinking in the upper-left corner of the field. The buttons for the special codes are directl below the header/footer entry field. They are, from left to right, Insert Page Number, Ins Total Number of Pages, Insert Date, Insert Time, Insert Tab, and Insert Title.

6. Click the Insert Title button. *&W* will be entered into the field.

7. Click the Insert Tab button. A vertical bar (|) will be inserted to the right of *&W*.

8. Click the Insert Date button. A *&D* will be inserted to the right of the vertical bar.

9. Click the Insert Tab button. A vertical bar will be inserted to the right of the *&D*.

10. Click in the header/footer entry field to the right of the vertical bar.

11. Type **Page** and click the Insert Page Number button. A *&P* will be inserted to the right of t vertical bar.

12. Type " **of** " and click the Insert Total Number of Pages button. A *&Q* will appear.

The next time you print views or documents from this database, the footer will be printed. T clear the footer, just highlight and delete the text entered into the header/footer entry field. To se the font, size, and style of header and footer text, use the settings on the Printing tab in the Data base Properties box.

This same mechanism defines document-specific headers and footers, too. The only difference is t Properties box in which they are set. You define database header and footer settings on the Printing t of the Database Properties box. For document-level headers and footers, you'll use the Printing tab the Document Properties InfoBox. Access the Properties box by following these steps:

1. Open the database for which you would like to set document-level header and footer propert

2. Select the document by clicking its row in the view.

3. Open the Document Properties box by selecting File ➢ Document Properties.

4. Select the Printing tab.

As you can see, the Printing tab is the same as the one in the Database Properties box. Each de ument in a Notes database can have its own header and footer settings. If established, these docume specific settings override the database header and footer settings.

Printing Views

The ability to print views in Notes is quite convenient. It is a quick way to get a listing of documen in a database. For example, you can use this feature to print a contact list from your personal addre book. If you participate in a tracking database, you can print views of active issues before a meetin By expanding or collapsing categories beforehand or selecting batches of documents, you can eve print customized lists of documents. To print views, just follow these steps:

1. Open the database for which you would like to print a view.

2. Highlight the view by clicking in the View pane.

3. Select File ➤ Print. The Print View dialog box will be displayed (shown here).

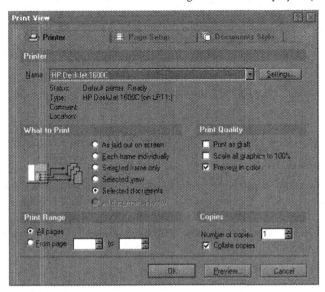

4. On the Printer tab under What to Print, select the Selected View radio button.

5. Adjust other print settings as you desire (number of copies, margins, and so on).

6. Click the OK button. The view will be printed on the current printer device.

Notes will print the view in a manner similar to the way it appears on the screen. Because views contain summary information about collections of documents, the printed view is like a summary report. One thing to keep in mind though is that Notes is not well suited to producing elaborately formatted summaries of data in individual documents. For more sophisticated reporting, you can have a report-writer application, such as Crystal Reports, access a Notes through an ODBC connection as though it were a relational database. For more information on connecting to Notes databases this way, see Chapter 12, "Integrating Notes with Other Applications."

If you want to change the settings for that device, remain in the Print View dialog box and click the Setup button. The printer device's Setup dialog box will appear, allowing you to change settings. Click the OK button on the printer device's Setup dialog box to return to the Print View dialog box. Click the OK button in the Print View dialog box to accept your changes and return to the Print dialog box.

NOTE *For calendar views, Release 6 includes special print formatting capabilities. When you print from a calendar view, there is a special Calendar Style tab in the Print dialog box. The Calendar Style tab allows you to select what information is printed and even allows you to print in Franklin Planer and Day-Timer formats. For more information about printing your calendar, see Chapter 6, "Calendaring and Scheduling."*

Printing Frames and Framesets

With Release 6, you can print individual frames and entire framesets. There are three options for printing frames under What to Print:

As Laid Out on Screen   This option prints out the entire frameset as it appears on the screen.

Each Frame Individually   This option also prints out the entire frameset, but it prints each frame as if it were a separate document.

Selected Frame Only   This option only prints out a single frame. To select a frame, click inside it before printing.

Printing Documents

When you need a hard copy of the contents of individual documents, you'll want to print the document. You can print e-mail messages that you might need while you are away from your computer or documents from a discussion database for reference in a meeting. Whatever the reason, Notes allows you to easily print documents in your Notes databases. To print one or more documents in a database, just follow these steps:

1. Open the database for which you would like to print document(s).
2. Select one or more documents in the view. If you select multiple documents in the view, each will have a check mark in the view icon area.
3. Select File ➢ Print. The Print dialog box will be displayed.
4. In the Content section, select the Print Selected Documents radio button.
5. Enter the number of copies to print in the Copies field.
6. Click the OK button.

Notes will print each document through its associated form. If the view from which you select the document(s) has a View Selection formula, it will be used to determine which form is used to print the documents. More information on View Selection formulas can be found in Chapter 21, "Using Views and Folders." You can also override the assigned form by using the Print dialog box. Here's how:

1. Open the database for which you would like to print document(s).
2. Select one or more documents in the view. If you select multiple documents in the view, each will have a check mark in the view icon area.
3. Select File ➢ Print. The Print dialog box will be displayed.
4. In the Content section, select the Print Selected Documents radio button.

5. Click the Documents Style tab, as shown here.

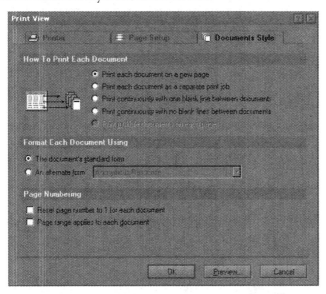

6. In the Format Each Document Using section, select the An Alternate Form radio button.

7. In the drop-down box, select the form you would like to use to print each document.

8. Click the OK button to return to the Print dialog box.

9. Enter the number of copies to print in the Copies field.

10. Click the OK button.

This time Notes prints each document, but it uses the form you selected to format the output. This is a powerful capability. You can use it to format documents just about any way you want. When you are developing solutions, you can use one form to accept input and another to print. For example, you might use a form with one font size on screen and a different form with another font size on paper. It is just one of the ways in which Notes separates content from structure.

When printing multiple documents, you can also customize how Notes separates the printed documents. By default, Notes prints each document on a separate page. You can instruct Notes to separate each printed document with a blank line or to print each adjacent document with no separation. You can even send the documents to the printer as separate print jobs. This can be useful to more closely monitor the status of your printing or to avoid overloading less capable printers with extremely large print jobs. These options can be set in the How to Print Each Document section of the Document Styles tab of the Print dialog box.

You can also print the active document (the document currently displayed in the Notes application window). In this case, the Print dialog box does not allow you to customize the output. Instead, you can choose to print all of the pages of the document or selected pages. The document is printed through its associated form.

In addition, Notes supports print preview. This allows you to review what you are printing befo sending it to the printer device. To preview one or more documents, just print as described earlier a click the Preview button in the Print dialog box when it is displayed.

Printing Attachments

Notes can also print the contents of attachments that can be displayed with the built-in file viewer. T is a quick way to print information contained within attachments without having to open the file usi the native application. It is also helpful when you don't have the application in which the attachment w created installed on your computer. To print the contents of an attachment, follow these steps:

1. Open the document containing the attachment you would like to print.

2. Scroll to the place in the document where the attachment's icon is displayed.

3. Right-click the attachment's icon and select View from the context menu. The file viewer ta window will be opened with the contents of the attachment displayed.

4. Select File ➤ Print. The Print dialog box will be displayed (shown here). There aren't nea as many options for printing attachments opened in the viewer, so the Print dialog box is mu simpler.

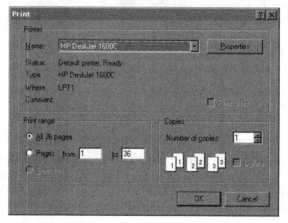

5. Select the print range and number of copies.

6. Click the OK button. Notes prints the contents of the attachment.

WARNING   *As with importing, printing attachments in Notes is sufficient for most purposes but can fall down when it comes to some advanced features. Many applications produce documents with features that Notes cannot display or can only approximate. For the best results, it is better to use the native application instead of the attachment viewing and print-ing capability of Notes.*

Summary

You're now familiar with what Notes databases are, how they are presented in the Notes application window, and how to perform common tasks within them. Everything explained in this chapter will be used throughout Notes (and the book). In fact, you may want refer to this chapter as you progress through the rest of the book.

In the next chapter, we'll introduce you to the Notes core databases that provide the basic Notes functionality, such as e-mail, contact management, and calendaring and scheduling.

Chapter 4

Tailoring Lotus Notes 6

NOTES IS A CLIENT for operating databases created with the Domino Designer integrated development environment (IDE). However, because of the range of uses to which it may be put, the Notes client itself can be customized in a number of ways to facilitate your work. In this chapter, we'll discuss how to customize the Notes environment to help you perform the tasks you want and more easily reach the information you need.

- ◆ Adding contacts to your personal address book
- ◆ Customizing user preferences
- ◆ Keeping organized with bookmarks
- ◆ Monitoring databases with subscriptions
- ◆ Keeping a personal journal

Adding Contacts to Your Personal Address Book

The first thing we'll discuss is the personal address book. You'll want to become familiar with this database because it is an important part of Notes. It is the place where you will store all of your personal contact information as well as a great deal of information about the configuration of Notes, particularly for mobile users.

NOTE   *In much earlier versions of Notes, a document containing contact/address information was called an address book entry. In the previous release, the sensible address book entry was changed to contact, perhaps because of length or perhaps because an address book contains items that have nothing to do with contact information.*

Importance of the Personal Address Book

The personal address book serves a number of purposes. On a day-to-day basis, it is most important as your place to keep track of personal contacts. These can include business associates, friends, family members, or whoever else you decide to include. For each contact, you can enter a wide variety of information, including:

- ◆ Name
- ◆ Company and title
- ◆ Phone numbers (up to six different numbers)
- ◆ E-mail address, web page address, and mail certificates
- ◆ Business and home addresses
- ◆ Spouse, children, and birthdays
- ◆ Rich text (comments, pictures, attached documents, and so on)
- ◆ Categorizations

With your personal contact information stored electronically in this database, you can take advantage of Notes to find information such as phone numbers or addresses. You can use Notes to print your contact information, or synchronize with your handheld device, or share the information with other applications using a number of different technologies. For more information on synchronizing Notes-based information with handheld devices, see Chapter 9, "Communicating with Domino Servers." For more information on integrating Notes-based information with other applications, see Chapter 12, "Integrating Notes with Other Applications."

The personal address book database may also be used for addressing e-mail messages. When sending an e-mail message to someone, you can either type in their e-mail address or select a name or address from a directory. One of the directories from which you can select addresses is your personal address book. If you make sure to enter your important contacts into your personal address book database, you won't have to remember their e-mail addresses. Also, you'll be able to address e-mail messages when you are disconnected from network-based directory servers, either your company's Domino server or Internet-based directory servers. Finally, your personal address book can contain personal distribution groups so you can use a single address to e-mail multiple people. This is convenient when you e-mail groups of people regularly, such as colleagues working on a project or close family members. For more information on using directory servers to address e-mail messages, see Chapter 5, "Communicating with Notes Mail."

Group entries in the personal address book also play a role in securing databases during replication. When the Notes client replicates with a Domino server, the Domino server must be given the appropriate authority to access databases stored locally on the client computer. This authority can be provided by adding the Domino server's name to the database's Access Control List, but it is more commonly provided by adding the Domino server to a group and adding the group to the database's Access Control List. For more information regarding replication, see Chapter 9.

Finally, the personal address book plays an important role in configuring Notes. Along with contact and group documents, the personal address book also contains documents for accounts, connections, locations, and so on. These documents control how Notes accesses Internet-based services, connects to Domino servers and dial-up networks, and maintains configuration information. For more information on configuring Notes, see Chapter 12.

Navigating Your Personal Address Book

To become comfortable with the capabilities of your personal address book, we'll show you how to open the database and navigate around the various views.

OPENING YOUR PERSONAL ADDRESS BOOK

You have a number of ways to open your personal address book database (your own comfort level will determine which method you choose):

◆ Selecting the address book icon from the Bookmark bar

◆ Selecting Open Address Book from the default Welcome page (or custom Welcome pages that include the Basic Tasks section)

◆ Selecting File ➤ Database ➤ Open (or pressing Ctrl+O), typing **names.nsf** in the Filename field, and clicking Open

You will notice that the personal address book has a frameset interface, as shown in Figure 4.1. The left side consists of two areas:

◆ A top area that displays the frame name and can be used to switch to advanced functions.

◆ A lower area that displays a Navigation pane for address book or configuration settings.

FIGURE 4.1

The personal
address book

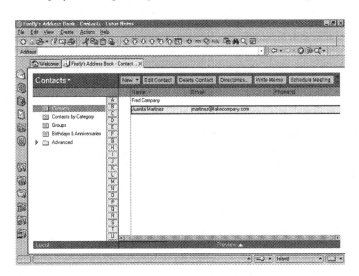

Also, the address book Navigation pane contains a Rolodex-style interface for selecting entries by the first letter of a person's last name. The frame on the right side contains the View pane.

NOTE   The Rolodex-style tabs display an affinity for the Contacts view. You can jump to entries in the Contact, Contacts by Category, or Groups views (using them in Contacts by Category jumps to the first entry in the first category matching the letter you click). If you click a letter in any other view, however, it will open the Contacts view and head for an appropriate entry.

If you click the word *Contacts* at the top of the left pane, you'll get a menu allowing you to swi
to the Advanced navigation pane. The Advanced pane, shown in Figure 4.2, shows only the Advanc
views. Those views deal with configuration information, such as location documents, which tell yc
computer what kind of environment to expect, and configuration documents, which tell your co
puter where to find servers.

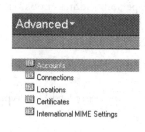

USING THE BASIC ADDRESS BOOK VIEWS

With the address book Navigation pane active, you will have four views available to you for navig
ing around contact and group entries:

♦ Contacts

♦ Contacts by Category

♦ Birthdays and Anniversaries

♦ Groups

The first three are for viewing contacts and the last is for viewing group entries. The Contacts vi
displays all contacts by last name or by company name if the last name is not entered. The Contac
by Category view displays all contact entries categorized. If you enter values in the Category field
each contact document, you can quickly locate entries. The Birthdays and Anniversaries view lists
birthdays and anniversaries for your contacts; each document can, potentially, appear twice.

As you can see, the Action bar for the Contacts view provides easy access to common tasks (s
Figure 4.3).

FIGURE 4.3

The Contacts
Action bar

The New button provides a menu of forms you can open to create new documents within your personal address book. The kinds of document you can create include the following:

- Contact
- Group
- Account
- Location
- Server Certifier
- Server Connection
- International MIME Setting

The Edit Contact button opens the currently selected contact document for editing. Delete Contact marks the currently selected contact for deletion. The Directories button opens the Directories dialog box. This dialog box lets you search for contact information in any directory your computer can reach, including your own address book and any other directories your computer has been configured to use. The Write Memo and Schedule Meeting buttons create new mail messages and new meeting documents, respectively, addressed to all currently selected contacts.

You can click the Tools button to display a menu with several options. The Tools ➤ Copy into Group option creates a new group document with the names of the selected contact or contacts already entered into the Members field. The Tools ➤ Categorize option brings up the Categorize dialog box (we'll talk about that next). The Tools ➤ Visit Web Page option brings up Notes' configured browser to display the contact's web page (see Chapter 10, "Replication," for more information on browsing the Web with Notes). The Tools ➤ Preferences option brings up the personal address book preferences document, allowing you to set configuration information for the personal address book.

The Categorize dialog box enables you to quickly categorize one or more contact entries without having to open each document. To categorize contacts, follow these steps:

1. Select the contact or contacts you want to categorize.

2. Select Tools ➤ Categorize. The Categorize dialog box will be displayed (shown here).

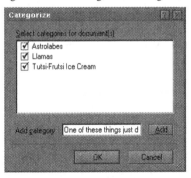

3. Check as many categories in the categories list as you want or enter one or more new categories in the Add Category field. To enter multiple new categories, separate each entry with a comma.

4. Click the OK button. The contacts you previously selected will be displayed under the appropriate categories in the Contacts by Category.

NOTE *Documents with fields that can contain multiple entries in a category field will be displayed in categorized view multiple times. It is the same document; it just shows up in several different places (this is similar to a single document being able to appear in several different views and folders at the same time).*

The Groups view displays all group documents contained within your personal address book. mentioned earlier, group entries create mail distribution lists and also provide security during re cation. By default, you will have two group entries: LocalDomainServers and OtherDomainServe These are generally used to provide security and can be ignored unless you are configuring Notes replicate with a Domino server. The Action bar for the Groups view provides easy access to comm tasks (shown here).

As you can see, the Group Action bar is nearly identical to the Contacts Action bar, except th its functions address groups rather than individual contacts and the Directories button is missin There's also a hidden difference: The Tools menu only has the Preferences option.

The Write Memo and Schedule Meeting buttons are similar to the ones on the Contacts Acti bar except the selected group or groups will be entered into the To and Invite fields.

Creating Contacts

You can either create new contact entries one by one or import contacts from another source. F information on importing and exporting information into Notes, see Chapter 12, "Integrating No with Other Applications." Also, Notes provides tools for migrating from a number of other e-m applications (Lotus regards this as an administrative issue; if you're feeling adventurous, you can re the administrative help file that comes with installation of the Domino Administrator client). As creating new contact entries, it is as easy as creating a new contact document and filling in the fiel With your personal address book open, you can create a new contact document in the followir two ways:

◆ Select Create ➢ Contact

◆ Select New ➢ Contact on the View Action bars of any of the contact-related views

You can also create contacts from the default Welcome page or any custom Welcome pages th include the Basic Tasks section. Whichever way you decide to create a new contact document, a bla Contact form will be displayed, as shown in Figure 4.4.

TIP *You can bookmark blank forms to make it easy to create new documents without having to open the database first In fact, there is a default bookmark folder for just this purpose called* **Create**. *This is a real convenience for contact because you will be adding them all the time. With your blank Contact form open, select and drag the blank Contact form task button to the* **Create** *folder on your Bookmark bar (or any other location on the Bookmark bar). Then select th New Contact icon from the* **Create** *folder on the Bookmark bar anytime you need to create a new contact.*

At the top of the Database area, you will see one button on the Form Action bar labeled Save a Close. After you are finished entering the information for your contact, you can click this button save the new entry in your personal address book. Next to that is a Select Address Format buttor

Clicking this button brings up a dialog box that allows you to select one of a number of address formats. Each format indicates in which countries the format is used. This lets Notes know which fields to select when constructing a mailing address (for example, the United States, Canada, and Australia include a state or province in addresses; most other countries do not) and in which order to use them.

At the top of the form, there is a section for basic identifying information:

◆ First name

◆ Middle name

◆ Last name

◆ Title (for example, Dr. and Mrs.)

◆ Suffix (for example, Jr. and Sr.)

◆ E-mail address

For most of these fields, you can either type the data or make a selection from a menu. But in the e-mail address field, you can type an address directly in the field, or you can click the button next to it to bring up the Mail Address Assistant dialog box (shown here).

When you open the Mail Address Assistant dialog box, you'll also be able to select the target m
system of the contact from the following choices: Fax, Internet Mail, Lotus cc:Mail, Lotus Note
Other, and X.400. Each choice has an associated dialog box that assists you in entering the requir
information.

NOTE *Today, most contacts you will store in your personal address book will have Internet mail addresses. These a*
normally formatted as name@domainname *(for example,* smith@acme.com*). With the other mail address types, it*
assumed you are using Notes in a Domino-based environment.

TIP *You can also enter Internet mail addresses using the following format:* "friendly   name
<name@domainname> *(for example,* "John Smith" <smith@acme.com>*). This is helpful when the Internet ma*
address does not include your contact's name or when multiple people share an address.

This information will be visible at all times when you have a contact document open. The ass
ciated dialog box has four tabs for different types of information: Business (shown here), Person
Briefcase, and Advanced.

The Business and Personal tabs allow you to enter physical address and phone information. The
Business tab has fields for job title, company name and location, four different phone numbers (pho
fax, cell, and pager), three alternate e-mail addresses, and a collapsible section for additional busines
information (website, department, and so on). If you enter a uniform resource locator (URL) in th
website field, you can open that web page from the Contacts view by selecting Tools ➤ View Web P;
If you need a different mix of phone number and e-mail address slots (for example, if someone h
one e-mail address but works at several different sites, each with its own phone numbers), you ca
relabel them by pressing the Edit Contact Labels button. This brings up a dialog box that lets yc
alter the visible labels (shown here).

The Personal tab also has fields for physical address and phone number, but they're explicitly marked as personal rather than business addresses (shown here). It also has fields for more personal information: the names of spouses and children, birthdays, and anniversaries. This tab also has an Edit Contact Labels button.

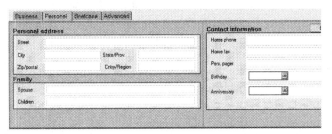

The Briefcase tab gives you a place to put rich-text content. It contains two fields: Contact Briefcase and Comments (shown here). There are no particular restrictions on how you use these fields, but Contact Briefcase is intended for complex digital content, such as file attachments and pictures. The Comments field is for your own notes.

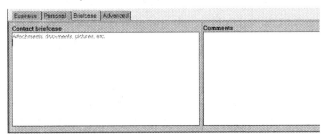

The Advanced tab (shown here) gives you a place for information that doesn't fit elsewhere: Notes and Internet certificates, full name, and phonetic spelling (useful if you find yourself with a client with a name such as, say, Mstislav Rostropovitch). You may also assign categories here, indicate whether to have the contact sorted by first name or last name in views, and whether to show business or personal information when previewing the document.

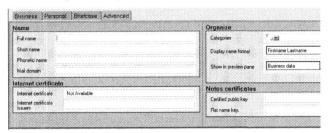

EXAMPLE CONTACT: PERSON

To create a contact entry for a person, perform the following steps:

1. Open your personal address book database.

2. Select New ➢ Contact on the View Action bar of the Contacts view.

3. In the First Name field, type **Juanita**.

4. Tab to the Last Name field and type **Martinez**.

5. Select **Dr.** from the Title field.

6. Click the E-Mail Address field and type "**Juanita Martinez**" <jmartinez@fakecompany.com

7. Click on the *X* to the right of the task button to close the Contact form.

EXAMPLE CONTACT: COMPANY

A contact doesn't have to be for a person. It can be for an organization as well. For example, if y
want to rent a car, you'll probably just call the rental agency, not a specific person at the compan
To create a contact entry for a company, perform the following steps:

1. Open your personal address book database.

2. Select New ➤ Contact on the View Action bar of the Contacts view.

3. Go to the Company field on the Business tab and type **John Company**.

4. Tab to the Office Phone field and type **111-555-1212**.

5. Tab to the Web Page field and type **www.johncompany.com**.

6. Select the *X* to the right of the task button to close the Contact form without saving the document.p

Creating Groups

Group documents in your personal address book are used as mail distribution lists and as Access Co
trol Lists. As mail distribution lists, they are a convenient way to address mail to a group of peop
As Access Control Lists, group entries control security when databases are replicated with Domin
servers.

Creating new group entries is similar to creating contacts. Again, it is as easy as creating a ne
group document and filling in the fields. With your personal address book open, you can create
new group document in the following two ways:

◆ Using a View Action bar, select New ➤ Group.

◆ Using a menu, select Create ➤ Group.

Whichever way you decide to create a new group document, a blank Group form will be display
(see Figure 4.5).

At the top of the Database area, you will see four buttons on the Form Action bar. The first, Sav
& Close, can save the new entry in your personal address book. The second, Refresh, will trigger for
mulas attached to some of the fields. Essentially, it performs some minor cleanup tasks. The third, So
Member List, will sort the entries typed in the Members field. The fourth, Cancel, closes the docume
without attempting to save it. Below that you will notice two tabs: Basics and Administration.

The Basics tab is selected by default when the blank Group form is displayed. It contains the f
lowing fields for information most likely to be filled in for your group entries: Group Name, Grou
Type, Category, Description, Members, and Mail Domain.

FIGURE 4.5

A blank
Group form

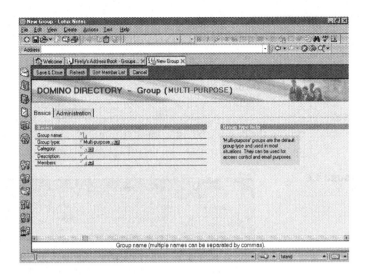

You must enter a group name and type. The group name should be something short but descriptive. For example, you could create a group named *Family* to use as a mail distribution list for family members. The type can be set to Mail Only if the group entry is only to be used as a mail distribution list. If it will also be used for replication security, you can set it to Multi-Purpose. The Categories and Description fields are optional, but they should be used to further describe the purpose of the group. The Members field is where you enter the names of the people you want listed in the group. The names can be separated by commas or entered on their own line. When the group document is saved or when you click the Refresh button, the entries will be formatted so each entry is on its own line.

To create a group entry, perform the following steps:

1. Open your personal address book database.
2. Click the Add Mailing List button on the View Action bar of the Groups view.
3. In the Group Name field, type **Brothers**.
4. Tab to the Category field and type **Family**.
5. Tab to the Description field and type **Immediate Family**.
6. Tab to the Members field and type **brotherlarry@bandb.com, brotherdaryl@bandb.com, otherbrotherdaryl@bandb.com**.
7. Click the Sort Member List button. You will notice that the three names are reformatted to display on their own lines and they are sorted (as simple strings).
8. Select the *X* to the right of the task button to close the Group form.

Customizing User Preferences

Notes gives you a broad range of personal preferences that customize how your Notes client runs. For the next several pages, we'll show how to set those preferences. You can reach just about everything we'll discuss by using the File menu, under File ➢ Preferences.

User Preferences

The first item under File ➤ Preferences is User Preferences. The User Preferences screen has five ta
Basic, International, Mail, Ports, and Replication.

You'll probably never have to use most of these options, but just to lay out the possibilities,
will discuss each of them in order.

BASIC

Unlike the others, the Basics tab has no basic theme unifying the options you'll find there (see Fi
ure 4.6). However, the options can be useful for modifying how Notes looks and acts.

FIGURE 4.6

The Basics tab

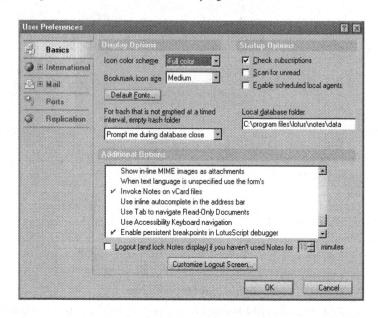

In the upper-left corner are the Display Options. Icon Color Scheme and Bookmark Icon Siz
modify the display of bookmark icons. Icon Color Scheme allows you to change the colors used
the icons, using anything from grayscale to full color. Bookmark Icon Size lets you change the o
screen size of the icons. By default, they're at their largest size, but you may want to switch to a smal
size if you're working with a small screen.

Default Fonts controls how Notes deals with text that may not have a font already assigned (f
example, for mail messages received from the Internet). Clicking the button brings up a screen th
allows you pick default serif, sans serif, monospace, and multilingual fonts. You'll often see "defa
sans serif" as the font in which mail messages appear; this is where the precise font used comes fr

The User Dictionary button allows you to bring up the User Spell Dictionary dialog box dis
cussed in Chapter 3, "Working with Databases." Its presence here may puzzle you at first becau
it has nothing to do with display options, or with anything else on the Basics tab, for that matter.
However, because the user dictionary is something that many users access frequently, it makes ser
to put it on the first tab of the User Preferences dialog box.

Below the Display Options section is a drop-down list that determines what happens to messages marked for deletion when you exit a database. By default, Notes will ask if you really want to delete them, but you can have Notes either delete them automatically or never delete them unless you do so manually.

In the upper-right corner are the Startup Options. By default, Notes will check your subscriptions but will not scan all databases for unread documents and will not allow scheduled agents to run locally, but you can change those options here. (Agents are like small programs within Notes that can automate processes for you; we'll be covering them in detail in Chapter 25, "Shared Code Objects.") Local Database Folder tells Notes where to start looking for Notes databases, including `names.nsf`. This is something you probably won't (and shouldn't) change, but if you need to move your Notes-related files to a new directory, changing this parameter will let Notes know where they've gone.

Most of the bottom of the Basics tab is taken up by the Additional Options list, which is a diverse but powerful list of options for customizing how Notes works. You can turn on an option by checking it or turn it off by unchecking it. The list is too long to explain in complete detail, but the following are some of the more useful or important items:

Mark documents read when viewed in preview pane   Notes can keep track of which documents you have or have not opened. This option marks as read any document that you've viewed in a preview pane, even if you haven't opened it from a view or folder.

Make Internet URLs into hotspots   As mentioned, Notes displays URLs as links, but you can turn that feature off.

Enable right double-click closes window   By default, Notes allows a lot of code to be run within it: JavaScript, Java applets, LotusScript, ActiveX components, and so on. If you think this makes Notes less secure, you can keep those items from running.

Make Notes the default web browser   Clicking this option makes Notes your default browser. If you launch a web page from your desktop, it will open in Notes.

Finally, as an added security feature, you can have Notes log you out if you don't use it after a specified period of time. This means that if you walk away from your computer for a long time, others won't be able to use your Notes client and appear to be you.

INTERNATIONAL

The International tab deals with languages and regional conventions. It has three subtabs whose functions overlap: General, Spell Check, and Calendar. On the General tab, you can set an overall language/region, such as American English or Canadian French (see Figure 4.7). You can also override individual aspects of that setting. For example, you could use American English but have your ruler use centimeters rather than inches.

Spell Check governs which dictionary (or dictionaries) is used. We've already discussed this tab in Chapter 3.

The Calendar tab governs how Notes deals with time (see Figure 4.8). You can indicate which day begins the week on different types of calendar. It's also possible to display your calendar in a secondary format and a secondary time zone. You can pick any time zone and display your calendar in the Hijri, Jewish, or Japanese formats.

FIGURE 4.7

International
(General) tab

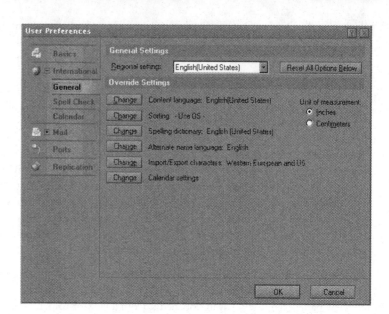

FIGURE 4.8

International
(Calendar) tab

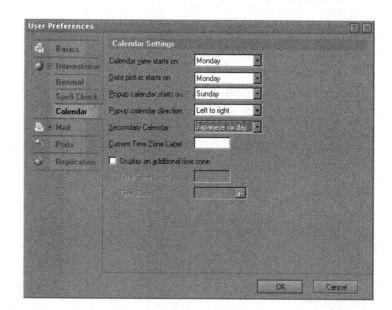

MAIL

This tab contains two subtabs, General and Internet, related to preparing, sending, and receiving ma
The General tab mostly deals with Notes' use as a mail client (see Figure 4.9).

FIGURE 4.9
Mail (General) tab

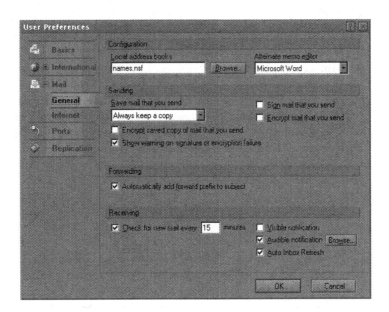

The Local Address Books field lists local databases your Notes client will search for e-mail addresses. By default, Notes will only search your personal address book, names.nsf. However, if you have other address book databases on your computer (for example, local replicas of your organization's address book), you could have Notes search them as well. Separate the names of address books with a comma, and enter either the full path (for example, **C:\Program Files\Lotus\Notes\Data\more.nsf**) or the path relative to the local database folder indicated in the Basic tab.

Alternate Memo Editor allows you to use the features of the word processor you have installed on your computer to write messages. If you select an alternate memo editor and the program you select is installed, you'll have the option of creating new mail messages with that word processor. You'll still be in Notes, but the menus and other editing features of your word processor will be available. This can give you a lot of power, but if your recipient doesn't have the same program, then some features may be displayed differently, if at all.

The Sending section sets options for what happens when you send a message. By default, Notes saves a copy of every message you can send, but you can turn that off as a space-saving measure. You can also encrypt and digitally sign the outgoing message and encrypt the saved copy for maximum security.

The Forwarding section lets you set an option when forwarding mail. By default, if you forward a message, Notes will add *Fw:* to the message subject, but that can be deactivated.

The Receiving section sets options for how Notes reacts when you get mail. If Notes is communicating with a Domino server, the client will check for mail and give notifications of new mail periodically. Post Office Protocol (POP) and Internet Message Access Protocol (IMAP) are different and aren't affected by these preferences. You can set the interval in minutes here. You can also tell Notes how to notify you: visibly (with a dialog box) or audibly (with a sound, which you can select with the Browse button). Finally, you can tell Notes to automatically refresh your Inbox. Sometimes

Notes will notify you of the arrival of a message, but you won't be able to see it because your Inb
display isn't automatically updated. The Auto Inbox Refresh setting makes that update automat

The Internet tab deals with some Internet-specific mail settings (see Figure 4.10). The Sending In
net Mail section determines how messages are configured when sent to the Internet. You can determ
whether outgoing messages use plain text, Hypertext Markup Language (HTML), or both, and wh
support to give to foreign language character sets. The Composing Internet-Style Replies section de
mines how text is quoted when you create an Internet-style reply. We discuss this in more detail in Ch
ter 5, "Communicating with Notes Mail," but to summarize: When replying to mail over the Interr
the convention is to use some kind of bracket or other character to indicate which text was contain
in the message being answered. If any text was in a previous reply, those brackets can pile up, so a mu
generation reply might look like this:

```
>>This was in the first message.
>This was in the second message.
This is new.
```

This tab allows you to determine which character is used to indicate a line of replied-to text. T
default value is a greater-than bracket (>), which is by far the most commonly used. However, so
organizations use different characters, such as pound signs (#) and curly braces ({}). You can also
the maximum line length.

FIGURE 4.10

Mail (Internet) tab

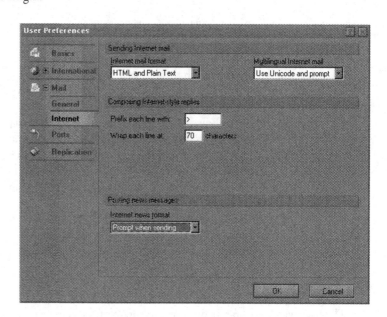

PORTS

Notes can communicate with servers over a broad range of network protocols: TCP/IP, NetBIC
NWSPX, and XPC. These settings should be set up automatically when Notes is installed and run
the first time, but if your network administrators need to change the way Notes talks to their servers, t

is where to go. It's also possible to encrypt traffic between the Notes client and Domino servers. This can have an impact on performance, so you shouldn't turn the option on unless you need to, but it can prevent eavesdropping on your local network.

REPLICATION

The Replication tab can be extremely useful for users who must operate remotely from their Domino servers (see Figure 4.11). The top section governs how much of large documents should be copied to the local replica. Document size can become a serious issue when replicating over dial-up lines. A document with a large attachment (say, a memo in which a friend has mailed you an MP3 file of his garage band's latest *magnum opus*) can increase the time it takes to replicate a database unacceptably long. You can, therefore, decide to replicate only limited size parts of long documents rather than their entire contents. The remainder of the message will stay safely in the source database, and you'll be able to do a full replication later if you happen to find the time or a better connection.

FIGURE 4.11

Replication tab

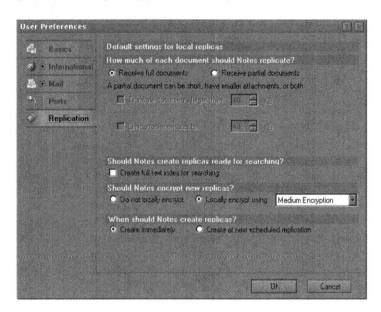

The bottom section of the tab governs how Notes works when you create a new replica. You can have Notes automatically create an index for searching and encrypt the new replica for added security. If you're pressed for time, you can have Notes wait for the next scheduled replication. If you select this option and create a new replica, Notes creates a sort of placeholder, a mostly empty file. If you've set up a replication schedule (see the next section, "Location Preferences," for more detail), Notes won't fill that placeholder up with data until the time for replication rolls around. We'll go into replication in more detail in Chapter 9, "Communicating with Domino Servers."

Location Preferences

Selecting File ➤ Preferences ➤ Location Preferences opens the current location document (see Figure 4.12 for an example). Location documents are important configuration documents in your personal address book. They tell your Notes client what kind of network connectivity environment expect. For example, they tell Notes where to look for a mail database, how if at all the compu is connected to the network (for example, through a dial-up connection or through a local area ne work, or LAN), and which browser to use when a Hypertext Transfer Protocol (HTTP) link clicked. If you want to have Notes connect to the outside world in a different way (for exampl if you temporarily want to get your mail from a POP server instead of a Domino server), you switch to using a different Location document.

FIGURE 4.12

A location document

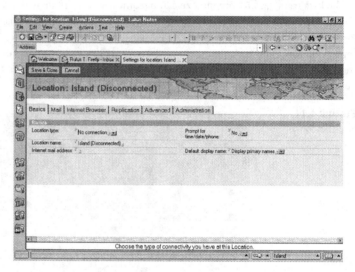

Not only do location documents provide important configuration information themselves, bu they also govern how a number of other important configuration documents are used. We'll consi how to manipulate location documents, then discuss how they interact with other configuration d uments in your personal address book.

USING AND EDITING LOCATION DOCUMENTS

Notes will always have a "current" location document. If it can't find one in your personal addre book, the Notes client will refuse to run! However, you can switch between locations at will. You c switch location documents in two ways. One is to select File ➤ Mobile ➤ Choose Location. You be given a list of location documents from which to choose. The other is to click the second-fro the-right button on the status bar (it displays the name of the current location). Clicking the butt brings up a menu listing location documents.

When Notes is installed, it comes with six location documents:

- Home (Network Dialup)
- Home (Notes Direct Dialup)
- Internet

- ◆ Island (Disconnected)
- ◆ Office (Network)
- ◆ Travel (Notes Direct Dialup)

You can find your location documents in the Locations view in the Advanced section of your personal address book. Each document outlines a set of circumstances in which Notes expects to operate. For example, the Island (Disconnected) document is for when the computer won't have any kind of external connection to any kind of server. The Internet connection, on the other hand, is for when the computer has already established an external connection.

Returning to individual documents, a location document can potentially have up to nine tabs: Basics, Servers, Ports, Mail, Internet Browser, Replication, Phone Settings, Advanced, and Administration.

However, not all of them will appear at once. The Location Type field on the Basics tab determines the general character of the location's expected connection and therefore which tabs are available. For example, a LAN connection doesn't need to call up an Internet service provider (ISP) with a modem, so there will be no Phone Settings tab. A No Connection location document doesn't need any kind of connection information, so it won't have Servers, Ports, or Phone settings tabs (you can still read mail locally and open locally stored web pages, so the Mail and Internet Browser tabs remain). We'll go into deeper detail in Chapters 9, "Communicating with Domino Servers" and 12, "Integrating Notes with Other Applications," but the following sections offer a brief overview of important settings you might change on each tab.

Basics

This tab holds the location name, the connection type, your address for Internet messages, and the address of a proxy server, if you need one.

Servers

This tab holds the names or addresses of different kinds of servers you might access, including your mail server. This is primarily for Domino servers. Configuration of other types of servers is covered by connection documents, discussed later in this chapter (under, surprisingly enough, "Connection Documents").

Ports

This tab lets you select the ports through which you attempt to talk to the servers. It uses the ports that are enabled in your user preferences. You'll probably never have reason to edit this tab.

Mail

This tab indicates where Notes should look for your mailbox database: on a server or locally, and the path to the file itself. If the location document is for a setting that isn't connected to a Domino server, the mail file location should be Local; otherwise, it may be either Local or a Domino server. This tab also determines where and how outgoing mail is routed.

Internet Browser

This tab determines which browser is used when you click on hypertext links in Notes. Your choi are Notes, Notes with Internet Explorer, Netscape Navigator, and Microsoft Internet Explorer. T first two choices open web pages within the Notes client; the last two use external applications.

Replication

This tab lets you enable and schedule automatic replication. If you've got local replicas of databa on a server, you can have Notes automatically update them by doing replication in the backgrou You can set a schedule for just about any interval and specific days of the week.

Phone Settings

This tab lets you designate a phone number for modem dialing. The fields include the number its area codes, international dialing codes, and special codes for outside lines.

Advanced

This tab has a great many subtabs, most of which you'll probably never touch, so we'll hit some hi lights. The Basics tab lets you designate alternate ID and other files; you can set up a location docum that lets you act as a completely different person. The SSL (Secure Sockets Layer) and Web Retrie tabs govern Notes' use as a web browser and for using SSL, the Internet encryption protocol. Second Servers lets you set up additional name servers for a variety of different network protocols.

Administrators

This tab lets you indicate the names of users who are allowed to make changes to the document. Bc default to the name of the creator. You'll probably never touch this tab either.

USING OTHER CONFIGURATION DOCUMENTS

An important aspect of location documents is that they govern the use of two other kinds of con uration documents in your personal address book: accounts and connections. You won't use the kinds of documents much if you're in a pure Notes LAN, but if you connect to non-Notes serv or deal with remote connections, they're vital.

Account Documents

Account documents define your identity for talking to remote servers. For example, if you use Notes get your mail from a POP account, you'll need to create an account document with the information t Notes needs to find the server and that the POP server needs to confirm your identity; you'll probal also need to create an account document for contacting a Simple Mail Transfer Protocol (SMTP) ser for outgoing mail. You'll find account documents in the Accounts view in the Advanced section in yc personal address book. You can create a new one, like the one shown here, by going to the Action bar and selecting New ➤ Account.

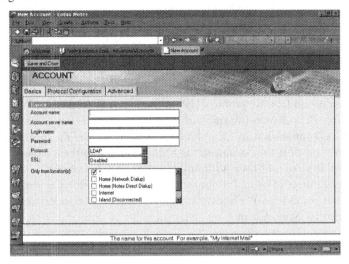

The Basics tab of the account document lets you determine for what kind of protocol the document's information is used:

- POP mail accounts
- IMAP mail accounts
- Light Directory Access Protocol (LDAP) directories
- Network News Transfer Protocol (NNTP) newsgroups
- SMTP servers
- HTTP servers (which is to say, web servers)

In addition, you'll be able to enter the location of the target server, your username, and your password. Depending on which protocol you select, there may be a Protocol Configuration tab that allows you to set further information for your account, and the Advanced tab always allows you to set the port.

So just how does all of this work? It varies from protocol to protocol, but we'll run through an example. We'll set up a fictional LDAP connection; LDAP connection documents you create will be visible as a source for searching for e-mail addresses, so you can check your work.

Notes comes with ready-made LDAP connection documents, but like the Yellow Pages, the LDAP servers to which they connect can be out-of-date. However, you don't have to settle for just the list of LDAP servers that Notes give you. You can communicate with as many LDAP servers as you like by setting up account documents in your personal address book. There are other LDAP directories

on the Internet, and many mail-serving programs, including Microsoft Exchange, Netscape Dire
tory, and of course, Domino, can act as LDAP servers as well. You can use account documents to c
nect to and search all kinds of address books. For this example, we'll imagine that a fictional comp;
has a publicly available LDAP server at `ldap.freedonia.com`.

To create an account, open your personal address book and go to the Accounts view. Click t
New ➤ Account button to create a new account. Fill in a descriptive name for the new server (f;
example, **Freedonia LDAP Server**) and fill in **ldap.freedonia.com** for the account server name. ,
fully qualified Internet address is necessary for Internet sites, but for sites on an internal corporate i
work, you can use an Internet protocol (IP) address (say, 174.121.23.49); you'll probably need
contact the Internet site owner to find out what the right server name is for Internet LDAP serv
and contact local administrators for in-house servers. Make sure the Protocol field is set to LD/
Once you save and close the document, the name you put into the Account Name field will app
in the Searchable section of your Address dialog box's Look In menu.

There's much more to be said about account documents, but we're just touching on some of t
most important points here. We'll cover account documents in more detail in Chapter 13, "Access:
the Internet with a Notes Client."

Connection Documents

Connection documents tell Notes where and how to talk to external servers. You can find connecti
documents in the Connections view in the Advanced section of your personal address book. You c
create new connection documents, like the one shown here, by selecting New ➤ Server Connecti;

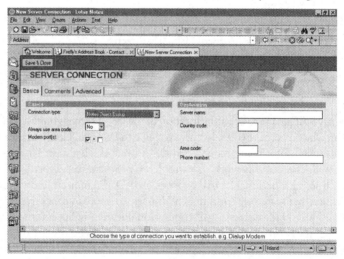

Connection documents give you a place to put a server name and, if it's a dial-up connection,
phone number. The Advanced tab allows you to indicate where login scripts for the server are co
nected, so if you need to perform specific tasks in order to get to the server properly, you can do :

By now, you're probably wondering what location, connection, and account documents have to do with one another. These three kinds of documents can and, indeed, must work together to allow the user to use Notes to contact any server or group of servers in any way. The key here is that any and all connection documents and account documents can be told to operate only for certain users and certain locations. The connection document you need to reach your mail server at work can be ignored at home and vice versa. This means that location documents can be used as a "master switch" to move between sets of configuration settings.

Consider this scenario: A user wants to use Notes on a single laptop computer to handle all of his mail. This includes both his work mail (on a Domino server) and his personal mail (on a POP server at his ISP). He'd have these sets of configurations:

◆ A location document for his office's LAN, indicating a copy of his mailbox database on the Domino server as his mail file. Using Notes in a LAN close to the Domino servers usually requires a minimum of configuration, so he might not need any connection or account documents.

◆ A location document for communicating with work while at home, indicating a local replica of his mailbox as the mail file. In addition, he'd probably need at least a connection document telling Notes where to dial for the Domino servers.

◆ A location document for communicating with the ISP, probably indicating a separate local mailbox database for storing personal mail. He'd probably use a set different connection documents for the ISP's POP, NNTP, and SMTP servers as well as account documents to properly identify himself.

It may sound complex, and in some cases it may be, but it's simpler if you think in terms of three elements: general conditions (location), specific servers to address (connection), and identification (account). Release 6 also has a powerful configuration wizard that will collect the information it needs and set up the documents for you. We'll be covering the specifics starting with Chapter 13, "Accessing the Internet with a Notes Client."

Toolbar Preferences

Chapter 2, "Getting Familiar with Notes," covers toolbar preferences.

Status Bar Preferences

File ➢ Preferences ➢ Status Bar Preferences gives you a dialog box that allows you to modify the status bar at the bottom of the Notes application window (see Figure 4.13). You have a choice of 10 status indicators (Communication, Font, Font Size, and so on). You can select a name and use the Move Up and Move Down buttons to change their order, and you can check the box next to the indicator's name to have it appear or uncheck it to have it not appear. There are two exceptions: Status and Progress. Those indicators cannot be removed from the status bar.

As you select different indicators, the width and height indicators may become active. You ca change the width of some but not all indicators. You can only change the height of the Status ir cator. Also, height doesn't actually mean how tall it is. Rather, it's a measure of how many previc lines of text it retains and will display when you click it.

Once you're done making changes, press the OK or Cancel button. If you press Cancel, the chan will go away. If you press OK, the changes will take place immediately.

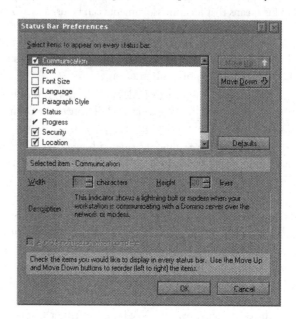

Personalizing Notes with Bookmarks

Your user preferences govern how Notes acts, but how can you get anywhere with it? One of the mary methods for opening databases and launching web links with Notes is the use of bookmar As the name implies, Notes' bookmarks are similar bookmarks in web browsers. They represent lir to Notes objects, as well as to Internet-based objects that can be referenced by using a URL. You bookmark views, documents, blank forms, web pages, and newsgroups.

Two visual elements make up bookmarks: the Bookmark bar and the Bookmark page. The Bo mark bar is located on the left side of the application window in a vertical column. The Bookma page is displayed directly to the right of the Bookmark bar, as shown in Figure 4.14, when you cli a bookmark folder.

FIGURE 4.14

The Bookmark bar and a Bookmark page

The Bookmark bar is stationary. It remains on the left side of the application window regardless of which task is active in Notes. The Bookmark page expands and collapses to display the contents of folders placed on the Bookmark bar. If you prefer to keep the Bookmark page expanded, you can "pin" it in place:

1. Select one of the Bookmark bar folder icons to expand it.

2. Select the page menu icon at the upper-left corner of the Bookmark page.

3. Choose the Pin Bookmark on Screen menu option.

The Database area will be adjusted to display the entire active task and the Bookmark page w now remain expanded. To manually close the Bookmark page, select the X on the upper-right side the Bookmark page. To have the Bookmark bar expand and collapse again, just repeat the preced procedure. While the Bookmark bar is pinned, you'll notice a check mark next to the Pin Bookm. on Screen menu selection.

There's another way of viewing the Bookmark page. Instead of viewing it as a list, you can vie them laid out on a page in a grid, much like icons on your computer's desktop. To view your bo marks as a page rather than a list, find the View menu at the top of the list and select View as Pa Your bookmarks will be displayed in a grid, like in Figure 4.15. To change it back, right-click t page to get the menu and select View as Slideout.

FIGURE 4.15
Bookmarks as
a page

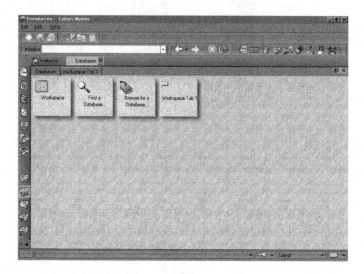

The default Bookmark bar contains two sets of links. The top section consists of links that direc access frequently used tasks, such as your mail and calendar. The bottom section contains folders other bookmarks. The default folders include Favorite Bookmarks, Databases, More Bookmarks, a History. In addition, you will see a folder for your Microsoft Internet Explorer and Netscape N igator bookmarks if Notes detects that these applications are installed during setup.

How Can You Create Bookmarks?

You can use the Open Database dialog box to create bookmarks, or you can use drag-and-drop te niques. Generally, you'll want to use the Open Database dialog box if you need to bookmark a p ticular database. Otherwise, you'll use drag-and-drop techniques.

CREATING BOOKMARKS TO DATABASES

It's easy to create a bookmark using the Open Database dialog box. First, you'll need to know wh the database is stored (locally or on a Domino server) and in which directory it is located on the tar computer. As you can see in the Open Database dialog box shown here, there is a drop-down list, labeled Server, for selecting the server where the database resides.

In the Server drop-down list, Local represents your local computer. When Local is selected, the list of databases includes those stored locally on your computer. If you select the drop-down arrow on the right side of the field, a list of servers is displayed. The servers displayed are a combination of those you have previously browsed and those to which you have predefined connections. The Database list box lets you select from a list of databases on the selected server. It also displays folders on the selected server where databases might be stored. The Filename field allows you to enter a filename directly.

NOTE   *In the Open Database dialog box, the list of databases available on a given target server is relative to the* Data *directory of the server. When Local is selected, the list of databases displayed is relative to the* Data *directory of your local Notes environment, which by default is* C:\Program Files\Lotus\Notes\Data.

The Open button opens the database or folder currently selected in the Database list box or typed into the Filename field. You can also open a database or folder listed in the Database list box by double-clicking its name. If you choose to open a database, the Open Database dialog box will disappear and the selected database will be displayed in the application window. If you choose to open a folder, the contents of that folder will be displayed in the Database list box, and the last entry will be an icon of an arrow pointing upward followed by two dots.

If you double-click the icon or highlight it and click the Open button, Notes will display the contents of the folder up one level in the folder hierarchy.

The Browse button allows you to browse your file system for Notes databases located outside your local Notes Data directory. This is handy if you are trying to open a database that you have downloaded from an Internet site or some other external source to a folder/directory on your computer. You can also use it to open database templates because the Open Database dialog box only displays database files. Database templates are an advanced topic; see Chapter 17, "Database Creation and

Properties." When you click the Browse button, a file open dialog box appears, allowing you to choose a file from your local computer's file system (shown here).

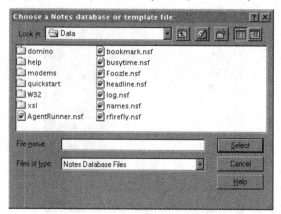

To use the Open Database dialog box to bookmark databases, follow these steps:

1. Select File ➢ Database ➢ Open or press Ctrl+O to open the Open Database dialog box.

2. Navigate to the database you would like to bookmark. For this example, use Local as the ser and select your address book.

3. Click the Bookmark button. The Add Bookmark dialog box appears.

4. Select the Favorite Bookmarks folder. The Favorite Bookmarks folder will be highlighted shown here.

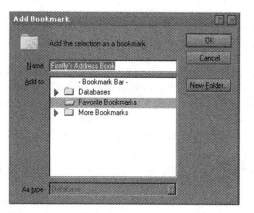

5. Click the OK button to create the bookmark.

The Add Bookmark dialog box closes and the Open Database dialog box redisplays. Just click t Cancel button to close the Open Database dialog box. To see if your bookmark was created, sele the Databases folder on the Bookmark bar. The new bookmark will show up in the list.

NOTE *You can also create new bookmark folders by clicking the New Folder button in the Add Bookmark dialog box. New bookmark folders are created in the folder highlighted in the Add To field.*

CREATING BOOKMARKS TO NOTES DOCUMENTS

It's easy to create bookmarks using drag-and-drop techniques. With a database open, just point to a particular document and drag and drop it on a bookmark folder icon on the Bookmark bar. You can place the link directly on the Bookmark bar by dropping it between existing icons.

CREATING BOOKMARKS TO BLANK FORMS, VIEWS, AND WEB PAGES

You can create bookmarks to blank forms, views, and Web pages by dragging and dropping their task buttons to the Bookmark bar. With the item you would like bookmarked open, just point to the task button and drag and drop it onto a bookmark folder icon on the Bookmark bar. You can place the link directly on the Bookmark bar by dropping it between existing icons.

How Can You Modify Bookmarks?

Once you have added bookmarks to the Bookmark bar or Bookmark page, you can also modify them. This is useful for changing the name displayed for the bookmark or changing the icon associated with a particular bookmark. You can also rearrange bookmarks on a Bookmark page or move them to other pages. Of course, you can delete bookmarks when you no longer need them.

MOVING BOOKMARKS

It's easy to move bookmarks by using drag-and-drop techniques. You can drag and drop existing bookmarks to a new location on the current Bookmark page. As you drag a bookmark around the Bookmark page, an indicator that shows you where the bookmark will be located after you drop it is displayed. If you drag a bookmark to the Bookmark bar, you can drop it directly on the bar or you can drop it on a folder icon. If you hover over a folder icon, the Bookmark page will open, allowing you to drop the bookmark in a particular location of the folder.

RENAMING BOOKMARKS

You can rename a bookmark by right-clicking it and selecting Rename from the context menu. A Rename dialog box will be presented, allowing you to change the name of the bookmark.

CHANGING A BOOKMARK'S ICON

You can also use the context menus to change a bookmark's icon. You can right-click a bookmark and select Change Icon to display the Insert Image Resource dialog box. From this dialog box, you can select alternate icons to use for the selected bookmark.

REMOVING BOOKMARKS

Removing bookmarks is another function that is performed by using context menus. Just right-click a bookmark and select Remove Bookmark from the context menu. A warning dialog box will appear. Click the Yes button to delete the bookmark or the No button to skip the delete.

How Can You Organize Bookmark Folders?

Notes is installed with a set of folders for organizing bookmarks. The top level of the hierarchy includes the following folders: Favorite Bookmarks, Databases, More Bookmarks, History, and Navigator/Internet Explorer Links.

You can add high-level folders, which will show up directly on the Bookmark bar, and you can a subfolders under existing folders. With this capability, you can use bookmarks to personalize y Notes environment.

Follow these steps to add bookmark folders:

1. Right-click any of the folder icons on the Bookmark bar.

2. Select Create New Folder to display the New Folder dialog box.

3. Type a name for the new folder in the Name field.

4. To have a folder created on the Bookmark bar, select the special entry labeled – Folders – the Select a Location field. To create a subfolder, navigate to the location in the Select a Lc tion field where you would like the folder created.

5. Click the OK button to create the folder.

The bookmark folder will show up in the location you selected. Folders can also be renamed a removed from the same context menu.

How Are Bookmarks for Replicas Presented?

In previous releases of Notes, you could display the server name on the Workspace page's datab. icon. This gave you an indication of the server on which the database was located, including the lo workstation. If you had selected the option to stack icons on the old Workspace page, you would h. seen a small arrow button on the upper-right side of the icon. This arrow was used to select whi replica of the database would be opened. With bookmarks, the interaction is slightly different. As y move your mouse over bookmarks, you will notice that the server where that database or Notes obj resides is displayed in the system message area of the status bar. If you select the bookmark, it w open from that location.

Bookmarks operate in a manner similar to the manner in which stacked icons operate. That is bookmark represents a link to a database regardless of the location of that database. Selecting a bo mark will open the replica last accessed. If you would like to open a different replica, located on a ferent server, just follow these steps:

1. Navigate to the bookmark of the database you are trying to open.

2. Right-click the bookmark. A context menu appears, as shown below.

3. Select Open Replica from the context menu.

4. Select the server of the replica you would like to open.

The database, or other Notes object, will be opened from the server you choose. This server will also be used the next time you select the bookmark. In the Open Replica submenu, you may have noticed the Manage List choice. Selecting Manage List will bring up a dialog box that allows you to pick a server.

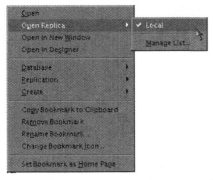

The Manage Replica Server List dialog box enables you to add additional servers where replicas of this database might reside. In previous versions, you had to open each replica to have it added to your stacked icons.

You can change which replica a bookmark points to without opening the actual database. Just hold down Shift when you choose the server from the Open Replica menu.

NOTE   *There's another, far older way of navigating Notes databases: the Notes workspace. Before Notes 5 and its web browser–like interface, Notes used a more desktop-like interface, called the workspace, which is still available in Release 6. The workspace strongly resembles bookmarks viewed as a page. Any database you open is automatically added to the workspace. The workspace isn't as flexible as bookmarks (only databases can appear in the workspace, not documents, views, or web links), but it can be useful if you have to navigate a large number of databases. To get to the workspace, go to the Databases bookmark folder; the Workspace bookmark should appear at the top. Selecting that bookmark will bring up the workspace, shown in Figure 4.16.*

FIGURE 4.16
The Notes
workspace

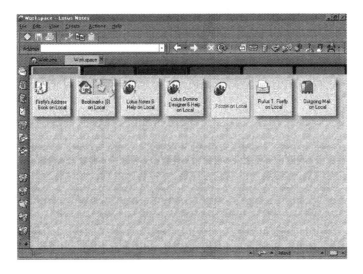

Creating Subscriptions to Monitor Databases

As mentioned when we were discussing the Welcome page, database subscriptions are monitors t
you can establish to keep current with the information that is most important to you. Once a su
scription is created, Notes will check the target database on a specific schedule for documents mat
ing the criteria you establish.

Subscriptions represent a great way to individualize Welcome page styles and have Notes work
you. For example, you can create a database subscription that monitors your mail database for n
sages from a particular person or for messages containing a certain string in the subject line. You
also create database subscriptions on discussion databases in which you participate. This way, No
informs you of responses to postings you may have entered or of new postings on a particular to

Let's create a database subscription on your mail database to monitor high-priority messages:

1. Open your mail database by selecting the Mail link on the Bookmark bar on the left side
   the screen (top icon).

2. Choose Create ➢ Subscription. A Mail Subscription form is displayed, as shown here. W
   just be dealing with the Basics tab. The Advanced tab doesn't contain any editable content a
   only displays information that might be useful to administrators trying to figure out any pr
   lems that might arise with your subscription.

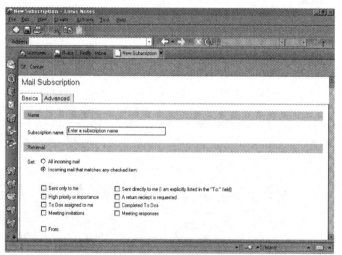

3. Clear any existing text and type **Monitor High Priority Mail** in the Subscription Name fi

4. In the Retrieval section, select the Incoming Mail That Matches Any Checked Item radio butt

5. Select the High Priority or Importance check box. This and most of the other options are si
   ply yes/no check boxes. However, if you check the From box, you'll be able to select addres
   to monitor.

6. Click the OK button at the top of the Database Subscription form.

To see the database subscription you just created, close your mail database by pressing Esc. Cli
the Favorite Bookmarks button and then click the Database Subscriptions button. In your Subscr
tions page, you will see a new entry, Monitor High Priority Mail. If you select any of the docume

titles listed under a particular database subscription in the left frame, Notes will display a preview of the document's contents in the right frame.

The Database Subscription form used in this example is formatted specifically for the Release 6 mail database. Other databases may have a different form, tailored for use by that database. Databases that do not have a specialized Database Subscription form will use a simpler default Database Subscription form.

NOTE *The Database Subscription section of custom Welcome page styles is similar to the Database page, except it only displays document titles. It also provides a quick way to access the Database page. Just click the Database Subscriptions button in the section's title bar and the Database page will be displayed.*

To manage existing database subscriptions, click Subscription Options in the upper-right corner of the Database Subscriptions page, shown below. The Subscription Options page opens.

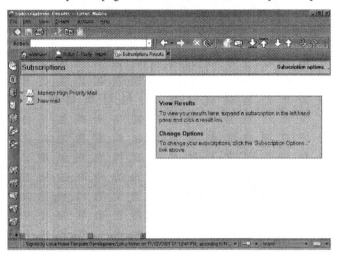

From the Subscription Options page, you can edit existing database subscriptions by clicking the Edit button. This lets you change parameters, such as the subscription's name, what documents to monitor, and the criteria for retrieving documents.

You can enable and disable subscriptions by clicking the Enabled/Disabled button. This is a good way to temporarily disable a subscription without losing its definition. To delete a subscription, follow these steps:

1. Select the subscription you would like to delete.
2. Press Delete to mark the subscription document for deletion.
3. Press F9 to permanently delete the subscription.

Keeping a Personal Journal

The personal journal is, like your personal address book, a database that is stored on your computer and that you maintain. It doesn't hold the wealth of configuration information that the personal address book does, but it does give you a place to make notes for yourself and write what you will, just like a paper journal.

Creating and Opening Your Journal

The best way to go to your journal the first time is by using a Welcome page style with the Basic Ta
button. When you click on the Personal Journal link, Notes will make sure you have a journal d
base. If it doesn't know where your journal is, it will ask you for a location, as shown here. If you do
have one, Notes will create one for you.

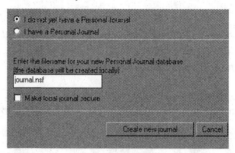

One option is to make your personal journal secure. Checking the Make Local Journal Secure
option will encrypt your copy of the database. This means that even if somebody manages to ma
a copy of your personal journal, they won't be able to read it.

The personal journal's design is dead simple: a navigation pane listing views and folders, and a c
tent pane displaying the selected view (see Figure 4.17).

FIGURE 4.17

The personal journal

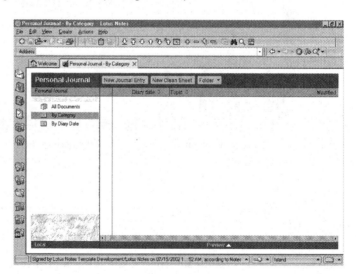

Making Journal Entries

From the View Action bar in Figure 4.17, you can probably deduce that you can create two kinds
documents with the personal journal database: journal entries and clean sheets. A journal entry allo
you to enter a title, a category, a date, and as much text as you want (see Figure 4.18). You don't ne
to enter any data, but a title and date are probably a good idea.

FIGURE 4.18

A new journal
entry

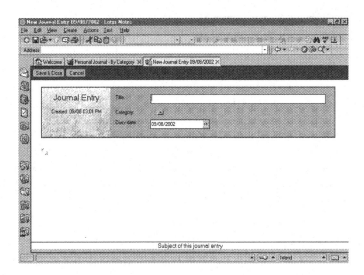

The text area of the Journal Entry form is a rich-text area, with all that that implies. You can style the text, import graphics, attach files, and so on.

A clean sheet is even simpler. When you first create a clean sheet, the form consists of a few action buttons at the top and a single rich-text field (see Figure 4.19). Clean sheets are good for scribbling. If you're inclined to keep and categorize your clean sheet documents, you can click the Title/Category button. This will make Title, Category, and Date buttons similar to those on a journal entry appear. You can fill them in and Notes will use that data to sort and categorize the documents, but if you choose to print your clean sheet documents, the title and category information won't print out.

FIGURE 4.19

A blank sheet

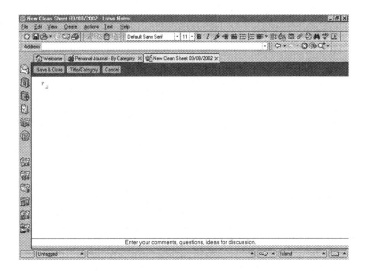

Organizing Your Journal

By default, the Personal Journal comes with three views: All Documents, By Category, and By D

All Documents lists all documents in the database in chronological order. By Category lists all c
uments by the categories you assign to them, just as in your personal address book's Contacts by C
egory view. The By Date view categorizes your documents by date of creation. This sounds sim
to what All Documents does, but All Documents simply lists the documents in order. By Date gi
you category headings, making it easy to isolate documents created on a given day.

However, what all these views have in common is that they show all of your documents at once. T
may not be sufficient to your needs. If you want to file away some but not all of your documents, y
can create folders. The Folders button in the View Action bar of each view gives you three options: C
ate Folder, Move to Folder, and Remove from Folder. These options allow you to create folders and .
and remove documents as discussed in Chapter 3, "Working with Databases."

Summary

You now have a good understanding of how to create and manage contacts and groups and how
configure your Notes client. You can modify how Notes works to suit local preferences, and you
tell Notes how to connect to available network resources.

In the next chapter, we'll discuss additional Notes mail topics, such as setting mail preferenc
navigating multiple address books, tracing sent messages, defining mail rules, archiving messages, a
using Notes Minder.

Part 2

Mastering the Basics with the Notes Client

Chapter 5

Communicating with Notes Mail

FROM THE BEGINNING, THE purpose of Notes has been to help people work together more effectively. As a software product, Lotus Notes Domino has three core strengths: security, application development, and mail (also referred to as *messaging*). The purpose of the product is geared toward better communication; it's a tool that helps organizations communicate. With Lotus Notes 6, IBM continues this focus with usability enhancements in its mail client. In today's electronic world, most business people start and end their day by managing their mail, and in this chapter you'll see how to use Notes and Domino 6 to stay on top of your daily communication tasks.

- ◆ New features in Notes Mail 6
- ◆ Understanding how mail works
- ◆ Processing incoming mail
- ◆ Addressing an outgoing e-mail
- ◆ Working with drafts
- ◆ Creating and using stationery
- ◆ Archiving the mail database
- ◆ Managing mail rules
- ◆ Setting mail preferences
- ◆ Using Notes Minder

What's New in Notes Mail?

Before diving into the day-to-day usage of the Lotus Notes mail client, let's review the new features and enhancements in Notes and Domino 6:

- ◆ Attachment context menu with Edit, Save and Remove, Remove, Save All, Save and Remove All, and Remove All options.

- Customizable color schemes to visually identify mail by different senders.
- Documents marked for deletion appear only in the Trash folder and not in other folders
- Drag-and-drop file attachment to detach from a mail message.
- Inbox automatically refreshes its contents when checking the server for mail.
- Inbox can be customized to change sort order of columns.
- Inbox shows the number of unread mail messages in parentheses.
- Out of Office notification can be run with a minimum of Editor access.
- New mail options such as Reply with Internet-Style History and Internet-Style Forward include text of original message prefixed with the > character.
- New mail options including Reply without Attachments and Forward without Attachme
- New mail rule, Send Copy To, forwards mail automatically that meets criteria specified by u in the mail rule.
- Progress bar appears when you save a file attachment.
- Soft deletions implemented in the mail database.
- Unread document marks can be tracked for folders as well as views.

NOTE *A view in Lotus Notes is a list of documents that meet a filter criteria specified by the view's design; the pro grammer sets this criteria. A* folder *is also a list of documents; however, the user adds each document to a folder inter actively or manually through dragging and dropping. Users can remove documents from folders, but deleting a documen from a folder deletes the actual document instead of just taking it out of the folder.*

How Notes Mail Works

The Lotus Notes client connects to the Domino server to send and receive mail. You can work w your mail while connected to the server or in stand-alone mode with plans to connect later to se and receive.

When you send mail, it leaves your Lotus Notes client, gets sent to the Domino server routing vice, and is forwarded to the intended recipient by the Domino server.

When you receive mail, it is received by the Domino server and then delivered to your mail d base and placed in your Inbox. Figure 5.1 depicts this store-and-forward mail mechanism.

FIGURE 5.1
Notes mail

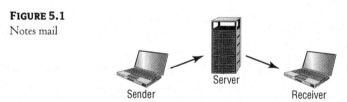

Sender   Server   Receiver

A core concept, therefore, is that you must be connected to a Domino server to send and rece Lotus Notes mail. When offline, you can process mail and connect later to send and receive.

Opening Your Mail Database

All of your incoming and outgoing mail messages are stored in your mail database on the Domino server. You can open the mail database in many ways, including the handy envelope icon on the bookmark area of the Notes workspace, as shown in Figure 5.2. This gives you quick access to your Inbox.

FIGURE 5.2

Mail bookmark

TIP *You can customize the Welcome page to display your Inbox as the first screen you see in Lotus Notes.*

If you don't have access to your mail database from a bookmark or the Welcome page, you can open it manually using the menu sequence File ➢ Database ➢ Open. Then, change the server name to the server that contains your mail database using the drop-down box, locate the mail folder as shown in Figure 5.3, open the folder, and find your individual mail database in the folder.

FIGURE 5.3

Navigating to the mail database

The nice thing about knowing this technique is that it will work for any database and from any computer. If you need to check your mail while using someone else's computer, you can switch to your user ID using File ➢ Security ➢ Switch ID and then use the File ➢ Database ➢ Open technique to navigate to your mail database.

Managing Your Mail

When the mail database is opened, it automatically displays your Inbox, as shown in Figure 5.4. You can think of your Inbox as the location for all mail messages that you haven't yet finished processing.

FIGURE 5.4

Inbox

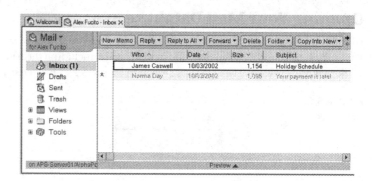

The screen is divided into three major parts known as *frames*. These frames help you do the th[ree] major tasks that comprise mail management: read, process, and navigate.

The right portion of the screen is devoted to reading the mail documents. To process the ma[il] there are action buttons along the top of the Inbox for managing the messages without opening th[e] additionally, similar buttons are located along the top of the actual mail message after you open i[t] that you can process it while you're reading it. To navigate the mail database, a set of system fold[er] and system views are anchored to the left side of the screen.

Reading the Mail

From the Inbox, which is shown in Figure 5.4, the right side of the screen displays all the read a[nd] unread messages in the Inbox by showing you a single line representing the mail message. This is w[hat] you'll use to decide if you want to read a particular e-mail. At this point, the mail message is not op[en] so you can't read its contents, but you can tell who sent the mail to you, the date it was sent, the s[ize] of the mail message, and the subject line. This is generally enough information to help you deci[de] whether to open the message immediately or push it off until later.

OPENING A MAIL MESSAGE

The technique used to open a mail message is the universal technique used in Notes to open a d[oc]ument: With the document selected, double-click any of its visible information. A black rectang[le] outlining the information is your signal that the message is currently selected.

TIP   You can also right-click the selected document to display a context menu with Open and Open in New Windo[w] options.

As you can see from Figure 5.5, once you've opened a mail message, action buttons to process t[he] message continue to be available along the top border area.

CLOSING A MAIL MESSAGE

A mail message is a *document* in Lotus Notes terminology, and several standard techniques close a document in any database in Lotus Notes. To close a document, you can do any of the followin[g:]

◆ Click the X button on the Inbox window tab located at the top right of the document's wind[ow]

- Right-click on the Inbox window tab and select Close Window from the context menu, as shown in Figure 5.6.
- Use the keyboard sequence Ctrl+W.
- Use the menu sequence File ➤ Close.
- Press Esc on the keyboard.

FIGURE 5.5

Inside a mail message

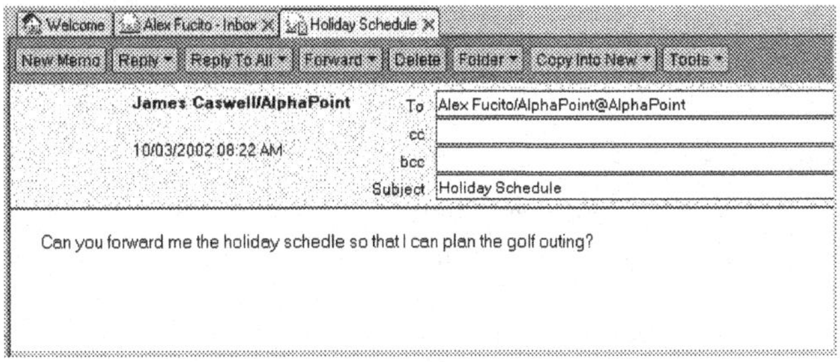

FIGURE 5.6

Context menu to close a window

PREVIEWING A MAIL MESSAGE

Located at the bottom of the main mail screen is an option labeled Preview that has an upward-pointing triangle. With an e-mail selected in the list (Inbox, Drafts, Sent, and so on), clicking the Preview button will display the contents of the e-mail, as shown in Figure 5.7, without actually opening the document. This can be handy; for instance, if you want to leave an e-mail marked as unread in the Inbox but actually peek inside and see what it says! Unread e-mails in an Inbox are denoted in red with a red star in the margin.

FIGURE 5.7

Preview mode

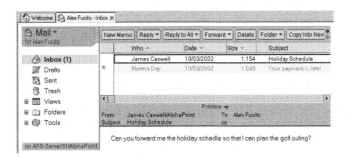

Processing the Mail

Processing your mail can be summed up as deciding what to do with existing mail messages and ating new mail messages. The buttons located along the top of the Inbox and along the top of an i vidual mail message provide the quickest way to process your mail. Let's work through each butt shown in Figure 5.8 and learn how to process the mail with the action buttons.

FIGURE 5.8

Mail action buttons

CREATING A NEW MEMO

When you click the New Memo button, you are creating a new e-mail and a new screen is present as shown in Figure 5.9. The screen has three parts: the action buttons at the top, the address inf mation below that, and the input area at the bottom. The action buttons process the e-mail aft you're written and addressed it, so let's begin with the writing and addressing tasks and finish w the buttons that apply to the individual e-mail.

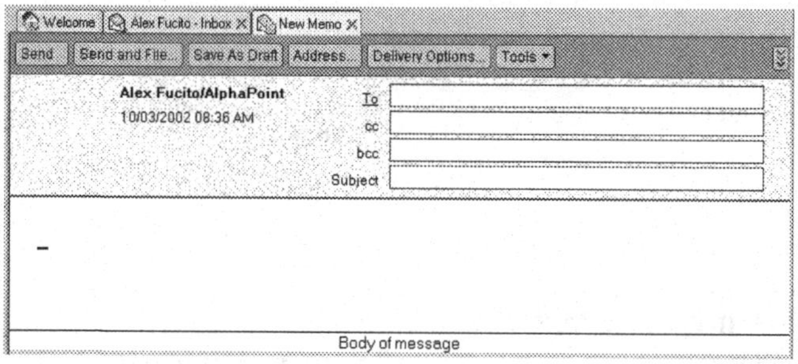

FIGURE 5.9

New memo

Writing an E-Mail

At the bottom of the New Memo area, Notes gives you a large area in which to write your messa The input area, or *message body*, is a rich-text area that allows you to set font sizes and colors, inse tables, and add graphics.

You can import the contents of many types of external files such as spreadsheets, audio files, a Hypertext Markup Language (HTML). Importing blends the contents of the external file direc with the e-mail. In other words, the contents of the external file appear in the input area.

TIP   *To import a file, use the menu sequence File ➤ Import.*

You can also attach files to an e-mail. The process of attaching a file adds an icon to the input a of the e-mail. When the recipient receives the e-mail, they double-click the icon to view the contents the attachment.

TIP   *To attach a file, use the menu sequence File ➤ Attach or the Attach toolbar icon that has an image of a paper cl on it.*

For people used to plain-text mail programs, the ability to format messages just as you would in a word processor is an exciting prospect. Just because you can do it, though, doesn't mean the person receiving it can see it, so consider a few things before getting too creative:

Font and color limitations   If the people you send mail to don't have the fonts you wrote your message with, their computers will substitute a different font and your message won't appear quite the way you wrote it. You're safe using common fonts such as Times and Helvetica, but restrain yourself from using odd fonts such as New Ottoman Hemi-Italic Sans Serif.

Size limitations   Notes formats its messages into 64KB blocks of information, meaning there is virtually no size limitation on how big you can make your e-mail. Your intended recipient, however, may have limits on the size of messages they're able to receive. This is especially true with attachments to e-mails; many systems reject messages that are large in addition to setting a limit on the size of a mailbox.

Format limitations   For mail sent outside of a Domino system—for instance, to an Internet mail system—an automatic conversion of a rich-text message to a plain-text format or an HTML format takes place on the Domino server. Colors, fonts, and some formatting will be lost in the conversion.

Addressing an E-Mail

There are two ways to address your Notes mail: using the Address button or typing the addressee information. If you know exactly who you're sending mail to, it's probably a little faster just to type in an e-mail address or, if you know that the recipient is in a local address book or Domino directory, a name. However, if you need to search for an address, it's a good idea to use the Address dialog box. With the Address dialog box, you can search local address books, Domino directories, and Light Directory Access Protocol (LDAP) servers over the Internet for just about any e-mail address in the world.

NOTE   *LDAP is an Internet standard for searchable e-mail address directories.*

Clicking the Address Button   With a new mail message open, click the Address button to bring up the Select Addresses dialog box, shown in Figure 5.10.

FIGURE 5.10

The Select Addresses dialog box

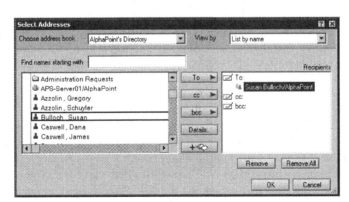

The first step is to choose the address book in which you want to search for a name. You will h at least two valid address books: one maintained by the Domino server, representing your compar address book and the other maintained by you, representing your personal address book. In additi you may have other directories including Internet directories.

To address your e-mail, you choose addressees from the list of names on the left side of the v dow and copy them to the To, Cc, Bcc recipients on the right side of the window using the butt between the two lists. When addressing an e-mail, be sure to choose either people or groups of peo from the list. Icons to the left of the name specify the difference: People are denoted with a single p ple person icon, and groups of people are denoted with a set of three person icons.

You can use the View By drop-down list at the top-right corner of the Select Addresses dialog b to sort the people listed on the left side of the window. By default, the list is uncategorized and so by last name (or, for groups, by group name). However, you can categorize it by Notes name hie chy (in large organization, users may be divided up among several layers of organizational units), porate hierarchy (your Domino administrators may assign users to a hierarchy separate from t Notes hierarchy), or by language (which subcategorizes by the first initial of the person's last nar

Domino directories can be very, very large. Depending on the size and hierarchy of your orga zation, your Domino directories could have thousands of entries. This, of course, can make it h. to find the name you're looking for or at least require you to scroll a long way down the list. To m. it easier, Notes gives you tools for quickly looking up names. If you type in the Find Names Start With area, Notes will jump down to the closest alphabetical fit to what you have typed.

If you select a person or group name, you can view the underlying document's contents by click the Details button to bring up more information about the person or group. It can be useful if y want to check an address, review the membership of a mailing list, or confirm that the John Sm you're about to send mail to is actually the correct John Smith.

Finally, if you're looking at the contents of an address book other than your personal address bo you can copy any person or group document into your personal address book by clicking the Cc button (with a picture of an open book) beneath the Details button, shown here.

This button can be useful for adding the names and addresses of people you want to send mai while you're disconnected from your Domino server, but use it with caution. Once you copy inf mation into your own local address book, you are responsible for keeping the information up-to-d in your personal address book. Your personal address book is manually managed by you and is ne updated by Domino automatically.

In addition to your personal address book, your company's address book, and other local addr books you may have, the drop-down list of available directories includes Bigfoot, Internet Directo and VeriSign. These are not Domino directories, but instead are LDAP directories on the Intern You can use Notes to search all of cyberspace in addition to your organization. To use Notes' p defined LDAP directories, all you need is a connection to the Internet through your computer.

The search dialog box for an Internet directory, shown in Figure 5.11, is displayed using the Sear button visible but grayed out in Figure 5.12.

The dialog box is slightly different than that used for a Domino directory search. When you choose a directory such as Bigfoot, the dialog box changes automatically to accommodate the diff ent types of information found in an Internet directory. Type a name or a partial name into the Sear

For area and click the Search button. Notes will send a request to the remote LDAP server and return a list of results in the area on the left. From this point, you can use the To, cc, bcc, Details, and Copy buttons just as you would for an entry in a Notes address book.

FIGURE 5.11

LDAP directory search

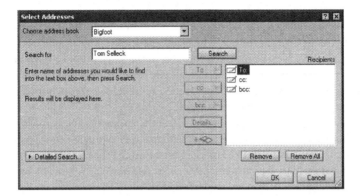

A simple search may not find the address you're looking for or may return too many results. You can refine your search by clicking the Detailed Search button, as shown in Figure 5.12. The areas at the top of the dialog box will then be grayed out, and a set of fields for more detailed searches will appear at the bottom. You can select a field name (Name, First Name, Street Address, and so on), select an operator (Begins With, Contains, and so on), and fill in data for which to search. You can add up to three conditions. You could, for example, search for addresses where the person's first name contains *Rob* (which would include Robby, Robert, Roberta, Robespierre, and so on), his last name is Jones, and he lives in Seattle. Once you have all the conditions in place, click the Search button.

FIGURE 5.12

Detailed search

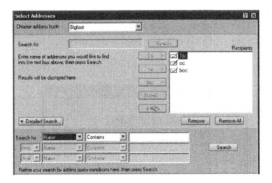

Typing Addresses   Typing may be the quickest way to address an e-mail, but it's also the most error prone, so type carefully! If your Notes client is connected to a mail server with access to the Internet, you can type any valid Internet e-mail address (an address in the format `somename@organization.domain`) into the address fields. If you're sending mail to several people, you can put multiple addresses separated by commas in the same line.

TIP   *Careful! This is a common trap for folks who use e-mail systems that treat aliases with a `lastname,firstnam` format and then separate multiple addresses by semicolons. Notes uses commas between multiple addresses.*

If you're sending mail to someone who is listed in one of your Notes address books, you can type the recipient's name (again, separated by commas if you're sending mail to multiple recipien If you're sending mail to someone in one of the address books you have access to, Notes can help with the type-ahead feature, which automatically completes names in address fields. If you type partial name, Notes can search through all the address books it has access to and fill in what it thi you're trying to type. For example, if you want to send mail to your colleague Chris Peterson, y could just type **Chris** or **Chris Pete**. Notes will look through its directories for names starting w *Chris* and fill in the first one it finds.

Although address type-ahead is faster than using the Select Addresses dialog box to search thro directories and can be more accurate than a user typing an entire name from memory, you should careful about using it. In a large organization that has hundreds or even thousands of people in i directories, there is a greater chance of people having the same or similar names. To return to the ceding example, if you try to send mail to Chris Peterson by typing in **Chris**, Notes might find name *Chris Petersen* instead; notice the different spelling. There's a chance of sending personal mai people you don't know or even, if your organization maintains directories of outside contacts, send sensitive information to people in other companies.

If you add a name by mistake, select it in the right pane and then click the Remove button. Wl you've added everybody you need to the address fields, click the Done button to close the Sele Addresses dialog box.

Sending, Filing, and Saving a Draft

Once you've written your e-mail and correctly addressed it, sending it is simply a matter of click the Send button at the top of the e-mail.

Another option is to click the Send and File button. With this option, the Folders dialog box, shown in Figure 5.13, is displayed and you can choose where you want the message you created be filed. You can choose from an existing folder or create a new one using the button at the bott of the dialog box.

FIGURE 5.13
Folders dialog box

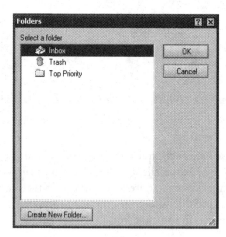

If you're not quite ready to send the e-mail yet but don't want to lose your work, you can save it as a draft so that you can come back to it later. To do this, click the Save as Draft button while creating a new memo (see Figure 5.9). Your unfinished e-mail will be added to the Drafts folder in the main mail database window, shown in Figure 5.14. You can go to this folder at any point, open the e-mail, and continue where you left off. Notice that the margin icon for the draft memo shows a piece of paper with a pencil; this identifies it as unfinished.

FIGURE 5.14

Drafts folder

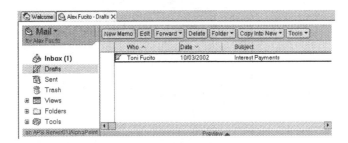

Setting the Delivery Options for an Individual E-Mail

Notes allows you to set a number of options that modify the way an individual message is treated, from encrypting its contents to marking its importance, both to the sender and intermediate mail servers. The Delivery Options button sets one-time-only settings for the current e-mail. There are two tabs of information: the Basic tab, shown in Figure 5.15, contains options for delivery, security, and mood stamps, and the Advanced tab, shown in Figure 5.16, contains options for workflow administration and Internet message formatting.

FIGURE 5.15

Basic delivery options

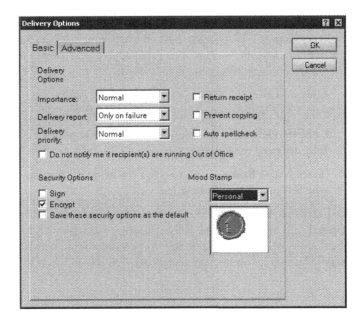

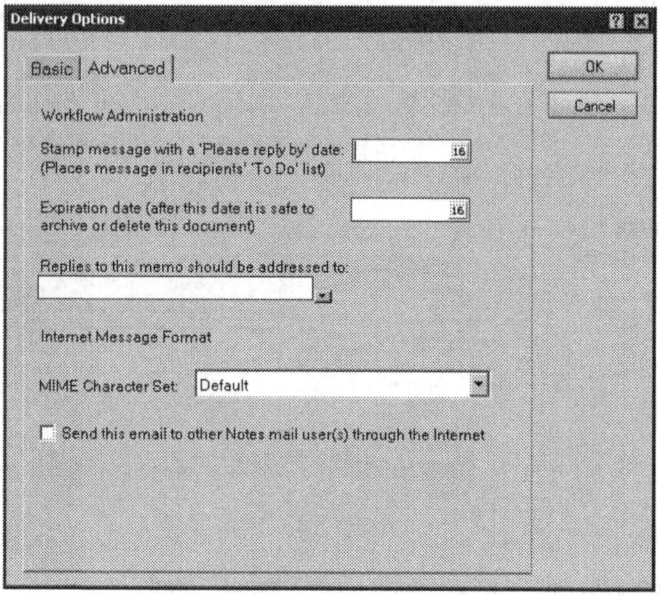

FIGURE 5.16

Advanced delivery
options

Delivery Options   After you compose your e-mail, you have the following options about how it w be delivered:

Importance   This is a marker for the recipient of the mail. You can mark your mail as hav High, Normal, or Low importance. Most mail clients, including Notes, have some visible sign the message's importance, so the recipient will see the significance you place on the message.

Delivery Report   Notes can report on where your messages go. This can be useful if you're h ing trouble getting messages to their destination or just want to figure out some things about yc network's topology. There are three options:

Only on Failure   You get a detailed message tracing the route your message takes if it fa to reach its destination.

Confirm Delivery   This option traces the route your message takes if the message is succe fully delivered to its destination.

Trace Entire Route   You receive a report on the route your message takes regardless of whether it reaches its destination.

Delivery Priority   This gives the message a priority that mail servers read. In general, messag marked with high priority are delivered before messages with lower priorities. This can speed the delivery of your mail, although the precise order in which messages are delivered depend heavily on settings on the mail servers between you and your message's destination.

Return Receipt   If this option is checked, you will receive a message when the recipient opens and reads your message. This option does not work with all mail systems.

Prevent Copying   If this option is checked and the recipient also uses Notes, the recipient will not be able to copy the contents of the message or forward it to others. Although this does not prevent the recipient from, for example, retyping the message or just telling other people about it, it does make it more difficult to inadvertently send sensitive messages to people who shouldn't see them.

WARNING   *This does not prevent the use of a screen capturing utility.*

Auto Spellcheck   If this option is checked, Notes will automatically check your spelling when you send the message. A Spell Check dialog box pops up after you click Send, and you have the opportunity to review misspelled words, add new words to your personal dictionary, and edit your personal dictionary. This is a useful feature when working with terms specific to a company or industry that might not be part of a traditional dictionary.

TIP   *You can also edit your personal dictionary using the menu sequence File* ➤ *Preferences* ➤ *User Preferences and selecting the International button and then the Spell Check option.*

Do Not Notify on Out of Office   With this option checked, if the recipient of the e-mail is using Lotus Notes and has enabled the Out of Office auto-reply option, you will not receive a return e-mail from the recipient when the mail is delivered.

Security Options   You can assign various levels of security to your e-mail. You may not care if someone reads a message to your boss stating that you'll review the files she left on your desk. However, you may want to ensure that the sensitive information about an invention cannot be read by anybody other than the intended recipient. The following options let you select the level of security for your messages:

Sign   If this box is checked, Notes will attach a digital signature to your message. When you open a signed message in Notes, the computer will compare the digital signature with information on a Domino server's address book and tell you whether the signature matches the sender's name. If it doesn't, the message may have been tampered with before it got to you.

Encrypt   If this box is checked, Notes will encrypt your message for the recipient. Only you and the recipient will be able to read the message, even if other people get permission to open your mailbox.

Save These Security Options as the Default   If you check this box, the options you have chosen will be sent to your mail profile and become the default options for all e-mail messages.

Notes encryption is excellent for securing data, particularly if the message never leaves the Notes system but it has its limits. The most important is that encryption will only work within a Notes system. If you attempt to send an encrypted message to an Internet address, Notes will let you know that the message cannot be encrypted and will ask you if it's OK to send an unencrypted copy. You can encrypt your messages with Secure Multipurpose Internet Mail Extension (S/MIME); however, not all mail servers and clients are S/MIME compliant. If you want to protect data sent to Internet addresses, you need to take steps outside of Notes. You could, for example, put the contents of your message into a password-protected document (not a great option; password-protected documents can be broken into by sufficiently determined crackers) or use third-party encryption software such as PGP to encrypt the message contents.

You may also encounter problems sending encrypted mail to some Domino servers. When you encrypt a message, Notes goes to the Domino server and looks up the public key of the person or people to which the message is addressed. However, if you're sending mail to a Notes user in a different Notes domain, you may not have access to the other domain's servers and directories. If you want to send encrypted mail to Notes users in a different domain, you'll need to create entries for them in your personal address book, request their public keys, and paste those into the Notes Certifiers fields in the appropriate Contact documents. If the person has a hierarchical ID (all Notes 4.5 and above users, as well as some earlier Notes users), the key will go into the Certified Public Key field. If the user has a flat file ID, the key will go into the Flat Name Key field. If you don't know what kind of ID your correspondent has (and you probably won't), enlist the aid of your Domino administrator.

Mood Stamp Mood stamps allow you to put a more expressive stamp on your message than the Importance option does. Your options are as follows: Normal, Personal, Confidential, Private, Thank You, Flame, Good Job, Joke, FYI, Question, and Reminder.

Each mood stamp has a picture that will appear in both the message and your Inbox. This feature is not available for mail sent outside of Domino.

Workflow Administration The options in the Workflow Administration section of the Advanced tab, shown in Figure 5.16, let you affect how others interact with your message:

Stamp Message with a Please Reply by Date You can set a date by which you would like a reply. In addition to letting the recipient know how quickly action must be taken on your message, it will also make the message appear in the recipient's To Do view.

Expiration Date You can also set a date after which the message becomes obsolete. Aside from being another way of letting the recipient know how much time there is to take action on your mail, archiving formulas can pay attention to expiration dates and immediately move expired documents from your mailbox database to an archive database.

Replies to This Memo Should Be Addressed To You can use this field to set a reply-to address. Although Notes allows you to choose addresses from available address books, you can type any valid Internet e-mail address instead. This option is useful if you want people to reply to a different address from the one you used to send the message (for example, if you're temporarily sending mail from somebody else's e-mail account but want to get the replies in your own mailbox). Most mail programs will automatically use the reply-to address, if there is one, when they set up a reply.

Internet Message Format   The Internet Message Format section lets you set options governing how the message is treated if it is sent over the Internet:

MIME Character Set   This option refines the character set used for MIME encoding for different operating systems and spoken languages around the world. This is one of those settings that if you don't know what these settings mean, ignore them.

Sending This E-Mail to Other Notes Mail User(s)   This option lets Notes know that even though your message is leaving your Notes system, it will eventually be read by a Notes user. Checking this option tells Notes to encode the message in such a way that it will appear as much like your original message as possible rather than stripping out most Notes features, as happens with most messages sent to the Internet.

Tools for an Individual E-Mail

There are four options available using the Tools button (shown previously in Figure 5.9) while creating an e-mail: Preferences, Out of Office, Insert Signature, and Save as Stationery.

The options for Preferences and Out of Office are identical to these same options available from the Tools button of the Inbox, which we'll cover in just a moment (see the "Tools" section). Let's focus on the signature and stationery options here because they apply just to the e-mail you're creating.

Insert Signature   A *signature* in a Notes e-mail is a small block of text appended to the end of outgoing messages giving identifying information such as a name and address, a standard company disclaimer, or a witty (or, as is often the case, not so witty) quotation. It is a way to personalize your outgoing e-mail, as shown in Figure 5.17. Your signature can be a few short lines of text, an HTML file, or an image file. One way to put this option to use is to sign your name on a piece of paper, use a digital scanner to capture it to an image file, and then use the image file as your Notes mail signature. Nifty!

WARNING   *Recipients of your e-mail may not be able to see embedded graphics in their systems because of size limitations, graphics support, or varying browser and software versions.*

FIGURE 5.17
Include Signature
dialog box

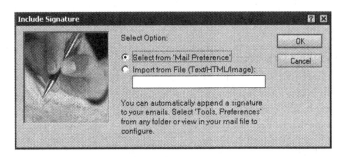

Save as Stationery   Do you have a memo that you send out every month? Is the gist of the letter essentially the same? Do you send it to the same people? If so, it might be a good candidate to be saved as a stationery memo. You can think of stationery as being similar in purpose to a form letter: something

you want to reuse time and time again. The Save as Stationery option lets you save the curre
e-mail you are working on under a name that describes the e-mail, as in Figure 5.18. Later, you
use this stationery when writing future memos.

FIGURE 5.18
Naming new
stationery

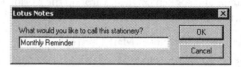

Creating Special Messages

In addition to traditional e-mail memos and replies, Notes gives you three special message types
work with from the Create ➤ Special menu in the Notes client (see Table 5.1).

TABLE 5.1: SPECIAL MESSAGE TYPES

MESSAGE TYPE	PURPOSE
Link Memo	This creates a document that, like a regular memo, has To, Cc, and Bcc fields. However, its body field holds a document link icon. The link is a connection to the currently open or selected Notes document. If you se a Link Memo to other Notes users, they will be able to click the icon to open the document.
Phone Message	In addition to the standard address fields, it has fields for the caller's name and organization, fields for phone and fax numbers, special-purpose check boxes (letting you mark the message as urgent, request a call back, and so on), and a space for a text message. This is useful for administrative assistants who need to keep a log of all phone calls received for a boss.
Memo to Database Manager	This will create a regular mail memo addressed to the people and grou with Manager access to the currently open or selected database.

REPLYING TO AN E-MAIL

You can reply to the sender of an e-mail from both the Inbox level or while reading the e-mail n
sage. In Notes and Domino 6, Notes distinguishes between replying to the sender of an e-mail ver
replying to all recipients of an e-mail. You do this with two different buttons: Reply and Reply
All, as shown in Figure 5.19.

FIGURE 5.19
Reply and Reply
to All

WARNING   *Be sure you use the correct button! The Reply button automatically addresses the e-mail to the sender of the original e-mail. The Reply to All button automatically addresses the e-mail to the sender as well as all recipients of the original e-mail.*

The two buttons each have four identical actions associated with them, as shown in Figure 5.20, and we'll describe each action here. The behavior of the buttons is the same whether you reply at the Inbox level or from inside an e-mail you are reading.

FIGURE 5.20

Reply actions

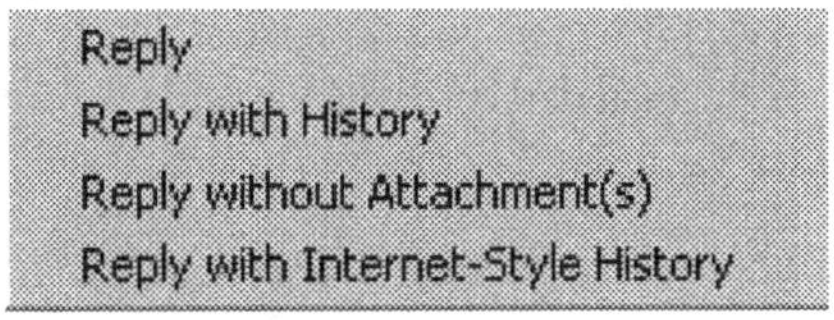

Reply
Reply with History
Reply without Attachment(s)
Reply with Internet-Style History

Reply   The Reply option creates a message with a subject of Re: (short for *Regarding*) plus the subject of the original message. The body of the e-mail is blank and allows free-form typing just like a new memo. When used from the Reply button, the reply is addressed to the sender of the original e-mail. When used from the Reply to All button, the reply is addressed to all recipients of the original e-mail.

Reply with History   Choosing Reply with History creates a message with the address and subject line set as it is in a reply, but it also brings the entire original message into the body of the reply. You can add your responses before or after the original message text or even insert your responses within the inherited message.

Reply without Attachment(s)   This option is the same as Reply with History but it does not forward any attachments that were a part of the original e-mail received.

Reply with Internet-Style History   The text portion of the original e-mail is included in the body of the reply e-mail, and each line is prefixed with a default character, generally the > symbol. No attachments or graphics are included with this option.

FORWARDING AN E-MAIL

You can use an e-mail you received as the basis for a new e-mail you want to send by forwarding it to somebody else. If you click the Forward button, Notes will create a new message containing the contents of an old one, just like using Reply with History. It will also inherit the original message's subject line. However, it won't inherit any addresses. Instead, you will need to provide new addresses. A forwarded message is treated as the start of a new discussion topic in the Mail Threads view.

As shown in Figure 5.21, you can choose to forward the mail message (which includes its attachments), forward it without the attachments, or forward it using the prefix character and style described in the Reply with Internet-Style History.

FIGURE 5.21

Forwarding options

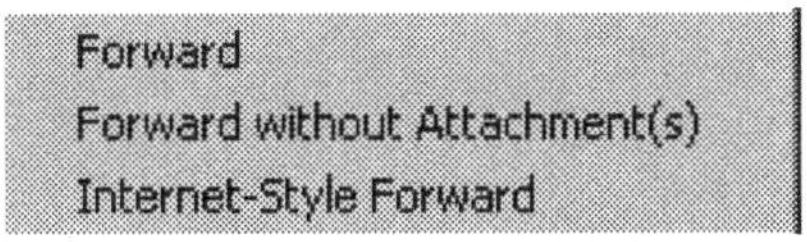

Forward
Forward without Attachment(s)
Internet-Style Forward

TIP   If you get a permission-related message while trying to forward a message, select File ➤ Mobile ➤ Edit Curre Location, click the Mail tab, and check the Mail File field. If the field is blank or doesn't have the location of the mail fi fill it in.

DELETING AN E-MAIL

Deleting an e-mail is alarmingly easy. With an e-mail selected in any of the mail database views or f ers, simply click the Delete button on the screen. You can also do this while reading an e-mail. Th are no "Are you sure?" messages. However, you do have a chance to retrieve the e-mail because i moved into the Trash folder of the mail database where it will stay until you permanently delete it fi the database. The Trash folder has a set of action buttons that will let you restore the item that marked for deletion.

FOLDER

You can manage folders in the mail database from several places. The Folder button at the top of mail database and at the top of any e-mail are two places to do this. You can create a new folder, m a document to a folder, and remove a document from a folder.

When you create a new folder, shown in Figure 5.22, you can give it any name that has mean to you. This is a personal folder that no one else will see (unless they peek over your shoulder wh you're reading your mail).

FIGURE 5.22

Creating a new
folder

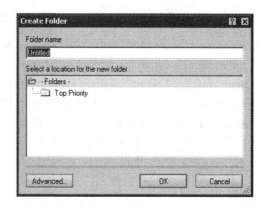

The purpose of folders is to help you organize your mail and other documents.

COPY INTO NEW

The Copy into New button is a time-saving feature that lets you easily integrate one mail messa; with a new one and with your Calendar and To Do lists. It provides three options:

New Memo   The entire contents of the message are placed into a new mail message, includi the addresses and subject. Like a forwarded message, a message created this way is treated as t start of a new mail thread.

New Calendar Entry   The contents of the message are copied into a new Calendar entry document. This is an excellent way of turning a proposed meeting into an actual meeting. The message body becomes the Details section of the new Calendar entry and the subject becomes its title. If your default Calendar entry is a meeting invitation, the names in the address fields become meeting invitees; the original's To field becomes the list of required invitees, the Cc field becomes the optional invitees, and the Bcc field becomes the FYI list.

New To Do   The subject of the message becomes the title of the new To Do, and its body becomes the Details section. If you make it a Group To Do, the message's To, Cc, and Bcc fields become the To Do's required, optional, and FYI participants.

TOOLS

The Tools button appears on all the views, folders, and e-mails in the mail database. It provides a way to customize the behavior of the mail database with a variety of task-oriented options. Depending on where you are in the mail database—for instance, in an e-mail as opposed to in the Trash folder—a context-appropriate subset of tool tasks may be available.

Add Sender to Address Book   This option allows you to quickly add the name and e-mail address of the sender of an e-mail to your personal address book.

Archive Settings   Use the Archive Settings options under the Tools button to modify the archiving options for the mail database. A full discussion on archiving can be found later in this chapter (see the "Archiving Mail" section).

Delivery Information   This option is available with an e-mail open on the screen. It provides you with information about who sent the e-mail, when it was sent, and when it was delivered, as shown in Figure 5.23. Additionally, you can inspect to see whether any delivery options or importance information was associated with the e-mail.

FIGURE 5.23

Delivery information

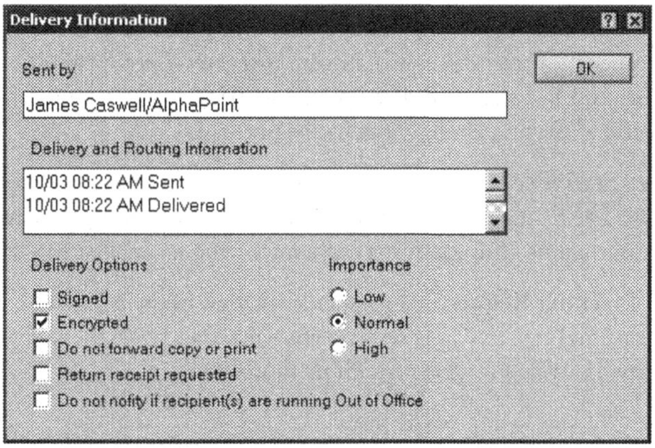

Insert Signature   The Insert Signature option lets you add a text phrase or image to the end an e-mail to personalize it.

Mark/Unmark Document as Expired   For archiving purposes, documents can have an exp tion data. Using this tool option will mark a document as expired or unmark it. The next time database is archived, the document is examined and if it is expired, it is archived.

New Memo–Using Stationery   This option lets you create a new memo and base it on an existing stationery memo. Stationery is similar to a form letter where a good deal of the infor tion is already filled out: You customize it, and send it as a new memo.

Out of Office   The Out of Office feature is a notification feature in the Notes mail database t will automatically respond to incoming mail when you're away from the office or wherever it is use Notes. The Out of Office feature is either in the enabled or disabled state. When you enable C of Office, people who send you mail in your absence will get a message telling them that their r sages have been received but you're away from the office and won't be able to respond until you back. Using the tabs on the Out of Office dialog box, you can set the contents of the outgoing r sage, tell Notes how long to send automatic responses, and even list people who should get spe message responses or no response at all (see Figure 5.24). At the bottom of the dialog box, a Disa or Enable button displays to change the state of the feature. To enable it, first set the Leaving a Returning dates using the calendar icons.

When you're finished filling in the fields, click the Enable button to start the Out of Office m itor on your mail database. When the Out of Office feature is active, it will run once a day. T monitor looks through all of the mail that has arrived since the last time it ran. If a sender has been informed that you're out of the office (and isn't on the list of exclusions), it will send th appropriate outgoing message and add that address to the list of people who have been inform That way, people you're corresponding with will only get a single message letting them knc you're gone. If they continue to send you mail, they won't be deluged with messages telling th something they already know.

Preferences   From the Tools button, you can set preferences for the mail database, the Calenc and the To Do list. A full discussion of setting mail preferences appears later in this chapter; the section "Setting Preferences for Mail."

Save as Stationery   While in a new e-mail, you can use the Tools option to save the e-mail as tionery. The recipient list, message text, and any formatting is saved with the name of your choi You can then use this stationery at a later time when creating new memos.

Send Tracking Request   From the Sent view in the mail database, you can use this Tools opti to trace a message that was sent by you. You can track the delivery status or trace the entire pa the e-mail traveled to get to reach its destination.

FIGURE 5.24
Out of Office

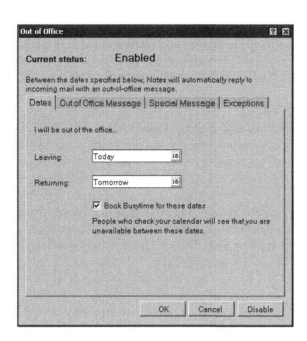

Navigating the Mail Client

Your mail database is organized in a way that makes it easy to navigate between the different types of information it contains. The folders and views anchored to the left side of the mail database, as shown in Figure 5.25, help you manage the mail by categorizing the items.

FIGURE 5.25
Mailbox navigation

Inbox

Your Inbox displays all unprocessed mail you've received from others. Although it's tempting to let system folder become the permanent storage location for all your mail, you'll find it easier to keep yourself organized if you process Inbox e-mails and make decisions to delete or file them appropriately

Drafts

The Drafts area of the mail database displays mail documents you create but have not yet sent. Y can temporarily store memos here that you come back and finish later. Once you double-click a dr to open it, it becomes an active e-mail that can be processed like a normal new e-mail.

Sent

By default, the Sent folder keeps and displays all mail documents you've sent to others. If you do want to keep a copy of mail you write or want to be prompted and decide on an individual basis, the menu sequence File ➤ Preferences ➤ User Preferences and set the Sending option on the Gene tab appropriately.

Trash

The Trash folder contains documents that have been marked for deletion from the database but t have not physically been deleted yet. When you close or refresh the database, you're prompted to if you're ready to permanently delete the documents. The action buttons in the Trash folder are s cific to tasks you carry out on soon-to-be-deleted messages.

Restore Moves the selected document out of the Trash folder and into the Inbox, marking i unread.

Restore All Moves all documents out of the Trash folder and into the Inbox, marking them unread.

Delete Selected Item Permanently deletes the selected document from the database.

Empty Trash Permanently deletes all the documents in the Trash folder from the database

Views

The Views area in the Mail area of the Notes client contains a combination of system views and perso views. Built into every mail client are the two views: All Documents and Mail Threads. If you have ated any personal views in the mail database, they will display directly below the Mail Threads view

All Documents The All Documents view displays all documents you have sent or have receiv This view is useful to search if you can't remember whether the e-mail you're thinking about a trying to find is one that you created or one that you received.

Mail Threads The Discussion Threads view displays mail messages grouped together if rela via the Reply action. This view is useful for managing a set of e-mails that refer to a single top showing all responses and the original e-mail.

TIP   *Use the menu sequence Create ➤ View to add personal views to your mail client. Personal views will appear after the Mail Threads view.*

Folders

Any personal folders you created in the Mail database are placed under the Folders category such as the Top Priority folder shown in Figure 5.25. You can create folders using the Folder button or the menu sequence Create ➤ Folder.

Tools

The Tools category in your mail gives you quick access to tasks you won't use every day but that tailor your mail to your needs. You can manage an archive of the mail file, create filtering rules on incoming mail messages, and customize reusable stationery for outgoing mail messages.

ARCHIVE

The Archive view appears in your mail file regardless of whether you have created an archive. If an archive does not exist, clicking the Archive view will have no effect. If an archive does exist, an indented entry appears so that you can easily access the archive, as shown in Figure 5.26. The archived database contains a Mail Archive title along the top left, and everything else is an identical copy of the structure of the primary mail database, including all folders and views. Figure 5.27 shows an open archive; notice the tab denoting the archived Inbox in parentheses and the separate tab simultaneously showing the actual Inbox.

FIGURE 5.26

Tools entry when an archive exists

FIGURE 5.27

Archived Inbox

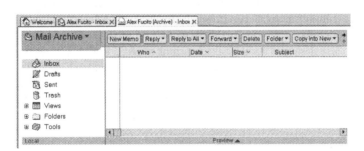

RULES

Rules are essentially filters that automatically move incoming mail into designated folders. Using rules, you can arrange your mailbox so that mail that meets certain conditions is handled automatically.

Example uses of rules are to file e-mails into folders automatically, delete unwanted mail automatically, and filter out spam mail from addresses that you provide.

The Rules view gives you tools for creating and editing rules. A rule consists of conditions and actions. When conditions are met, then the specified action is taken. When you click the New Rule button, you get the New Rule dialog box, shown in Figure 5.28, for creating new rules for moving or modifying incoming mail.

FIGURE 5.28

Mail rules

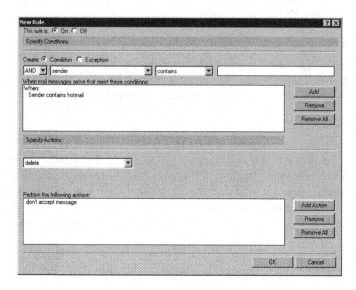

First, you need to set some conditions. A rule can search a number of fields in incoming mail: the To field, the Cc field, the message body, and several others. It can also examine the message's size or from where the message comes. When you have set the condition fields (say, the subject contains the phrase *make money fast*), click the Add button to add it to the list of conditions the rule follows. You can add a number of conditions to a single rule, connecting them with an AND or OR operator. If you connect multiple conditions with AND, the rule will act on messages for which all of the conditions are true. If you use OR, it will act on messages for which any of the conditions are true. You can also designate additional conditions as exceptions. If you want to remove a condition, just select it and click the Remove button. If you want to completely redo the conditions the rule follows, just click Remove All.

Once you've decided what your conditions are, you need to tell Notes what to do with the messages it finds; you specify this in the bottom part of the screen as actions. Your options are: Move to Folder, Copy to Folder, Send Copy To, Set Expire Date, Change Importance, and Delete.

If you choose the Move to Folder or Copy to Folder or option, click the Choose Folder button and designate the folder in which you want the message to end up. If you choose Change Importance, choose the importance you want it to have. Delete has no additional options.

After selecting an action, click the Add button to add the action to the list. As with the conditions, Remove gets rid of a selected action, and Remove All gets rid of all of them. You can add several actions to a rule, and they will be performed in order. You might start with a Move to Folder action to get the document out of your Inbox and then add a set of Add to Folder actions to distribute it around your mailbox.

There's no point in having more than one Move to Folder in a rule because the Move option removes the document from the folder. If you try to move a document into multiple folders, it will only appear in the last folder into which it was moved. There's also no reason to set a message's importance more than once because you'll only see the last importance the message is given. Finally, there's no reason to combine Delete with *anything*. If you have a rule that deletes a message, you'll never see it anywhere.

When you're done and ready to put the rule into action, set the rule to On or Off using the radio buttons at the top of the dialog box and then click the OK button to close the New Rule dialog box. Once you've saved and closed the rule, you can always come back later and disable it or even delete the rule altogether.

The logic you built using the New Rule dialog box is summarized as a WHEN-THEN statement that's fairly straightforward to read without opening the rule window, as shown in Figure 5.29. You can manage the list of existing rules using the buttons along the top of the rules window. You can edit or delete a rule, enable or disable a rule, or move a rule up or down in the list. The order that the rules appear in (top to bottom) represents the order in which they will be evaluated each time a new piece of mail comes into the Inbox.

FIGURE 5.29

A saved mail rule

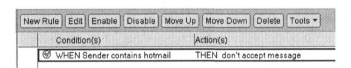

STATIONERY

Stationery is a reusable memo that can retain recipient lists, graphics, text messages, attachments, and any other formatting used in e-mails. You give the stationery a meaningful name and then use it the next time you have a similar e-mail to send. Stationery behaves much like a form letter in that it is reusable and customizable. Special buttons are provided to save a memo as stationery and to create a new memo using stationery. The Stationery view, shown in Figure 5.30, lets you manage any number of stationery pieces.

FIGURE 5.30

Stationery view

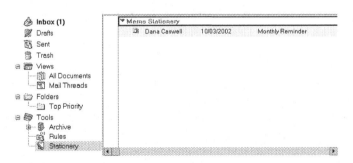

Archiving Mail

The process of archiving moves documents from one database to a separate database, usually out c server-based database to one stored on your personal computer. You can archive any database, not the mail database. In addition to changing the settings through the previously mentioned Tools optic you can also access the settings for the mail database or any database you happen to be in by using menu sequence File ➤ Database ➤ Properties to open the Database Properties InfoBox and use t Archive Settings button on the first tab. The Actions menu also contains an Archive option from wh you can choose Archive Now, Archive Selected Documents, Open Log, and Check Settings.

After you have set up the archive database, you can run the archiving process any time you want selecting File ➤ Database ➤ Archive. When you do, any documents that have come to meet your arc settings will be archived. The first time you archive the database, Notes will create a new database ba on the design of the database being archived. Then it will take old documents out of the original datak and put them in the archive. This means that documents that appeared in particular views in the orig database will appear in those views in the archive, making them easy to find. Archived documents sh up in the folders in which they were originally filed as well, a vital feature for finding messages in o full mail databases.

The Archive Settings has been completely updated for Notes and Domino 6 and now consists three screens of information: Basics, Settings, and Advanced.

Basics

On the Basics area of the Archive Settings dialog box you specify which computers will be invol in the archive activity. There is a FROM computer and a TO computer involved in the process. C erally, you archive FROM a server TO a LOCAL workstation. From the Basics tab, the Change l ton opens the Choose Archive Server dialog box, shown in Figure 5.31.

FIGURE 5.31
Choosing an archive
server

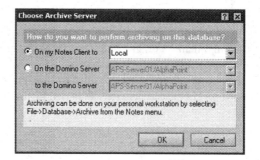

Settings

In the Settings area, shown in Figure 5.32, you are provided with two default archive profiles and ability to create new ones under meaningful names that you like. Also from the screen you can ena or disable scheduled archiving.

FIGURE 5.32

Archive profiles

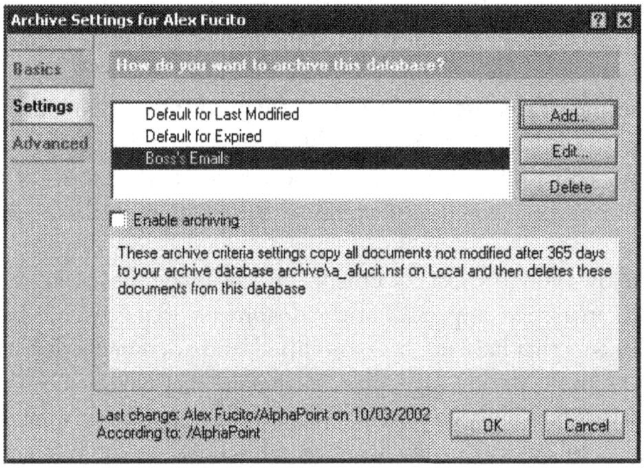

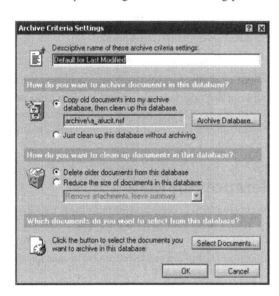

Clicking the Add button lets you configure a new archiving profile, shown in Figure 5.33.

FIGURE 5.33

Archive settings

On this screen, you can do the following:

◆ Set the location and name of the archive database.

◆ Specify whether to copy documents to another database and then delete them.

◆ Specify whether documents can just be deleted.

◆ Choose to delete older documents.

◆ Elect to reduce the size of the database by removing attachments.

The default location for archiving documents is an `Archive` directory in your local Notes `Data` di tory. By default, Notes bases the name of the archive database on the first six letters of the original d base's name, with *a_* added to the beginning to show the user that it's an archive database. For exam a database named `maindiscussion.nsf` would produce an archive database named `a_maindi.nsf`. H ever, the "initial *a* plus six letters" is only a convenient naming convention. You can rename your arch as you see fit. You can also create the archive in other subdirectories of your Notes `Data` directory or e on a Domino server (if you have permission to create new databases on the server; check with your D ino administrator).

Notes allows you to select documents by how long it has been since something has been done w them. You can archive any or all of the documents that have not been read after a given number days, documents that have not been modified, and documents that have been marked as expired. Y could, for example, decide to archive documents that haven't been modified in the past six mont documents that haven't been read in a year, or documents that were marked read more than a day a The default is to archive documents not modified in the past 365 days. Change this option by click the Select Documents button on the Archive Criteria Settings screen.

Advanced

The Advanced window lets you fine-tune the archiving process. You can specify:

- ◆ Not to delete documents that have responses.
- ◆ Log all archiving to a separate log database.
- ◆ Enable local archiving on a schedule.

With the option for not deleting documents that have responses, original messages won't be remo from your database until all of their responses are ready to be archived as well. You'll be able to foll an exchange of Reply documents all the way back to its origin, even if you haven't actually accessed original message in a long time.

Setting Preferences for Mail

Mail options give you considerable control over individual messages, but you need to set them o message-by-message basis. If you want to have some settings preset for all messages (say, you want encrypt or spell check all of your outgoing messages automatically), you need to set your mail pr erences. There are two areas of mail preferences for you to manage: systemwide settings and mail d base settings.

Systemwide Preferences

System settings apply to your entire Lotus Notes client. Some of the settings are specific to mail, a those are the ones we'll look at now. To open your system user preferences for mail, use the mer sequence File ➤ Preferences ➤ User Preferences and click the Mail option on the left side of the w dow. The mail preferences are split into two categories: General and Internet.

GENERAL

In the General settings area, shown in Figure 5.34, there are four categories of settings for user configuration, sending mail, forwarding mail, and receiving mail.

FIGURE 5.34

General mail preferences

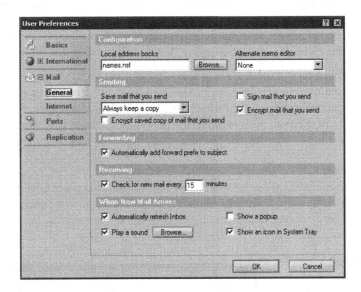

Configuration   You can configure the local address books used for looking up user addresses when addressing new e-mails. The default is names.nsf, the operating system file for your local address book. If you rename this file, then you'll need to update the name used in this configuration setting. You can also specify an alternate editor, such as Microsoft Word or Lotus Word Pro.

Sending   The options for sending let you specify whether Notes should automatically keep a copy of all mail you send, whether it should never keep a copy, or whether it should prompt you. Additionally, you can set options for signing and encrypting mail you send and mail you save.

NOTE   *Signing mail means Notes automatically attaches and manages a hidden digital sequence of characters that guarantee that the e-mail wasn't tampered with during transmission and that you actually sent it.*

NOTE   *Encrypting mail means to automatically scramble the contents of the mail message until the intended recipient safely receives it.*

Forwarding   When you forward a message to another person or database, the characters *Fw:* are put at the beginning of the document's title. To disable this option, uncheck the box in this part of the preferences.

Receiving   Several options in the Receiving section will affect what happens when your mail is received. Earlier in the chapter we described how all mail comes through the Domino server; so,

it makes sense that your Lotus Notes client must be checking the Domino server on a regular b
to see if there are any new messages for you. The default is to check for new mail every 15 minu
you can specify a higher or lower number here. Lowering the number, however, could put t
much demand on the server, so check with your system administrator before changing this opti
You also have options here to pop up a message box to visibly notify you when new mail arri
turn on a chime to audibly notify you when new mail arrives, and to automatically refresh yo
inbox whenever new mail arrives. This last option is a new Notes and Domino 6 feature.

When New Mail Arrives   This section of the user preferences configures settings for how
want to be notified when new mail arrives in your Inbox. You can play a sound, show a pop-
window, or change the icon in the system tray. The option to automatically refresh your Inb
means that mail will automatically show up as soon as it is delivered. When this option is disab
you'll see a blue circular refresh arrow; click it to manually refresh the Inbox.

INTERNET

We mentioned earlier that users who you send mail to may not be able to see all the rich text and fo
in the same way you see them. In this settings area of the user preferences, shown in Figure 5.35,
can specify conversion options for outbound Internet mail that can automatically convert outbot
mail for you.

FIGURE 5.35
Internet mail
settings

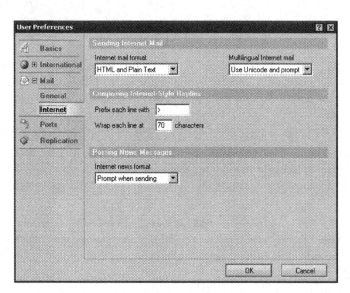

The options you have for outbound Internet mail are: HTML Only, Plain Text Only, HTML a
Plain Text (the default), and Prompt When Sending.

When you choose the Prompt When Sending option, a pop-up window will be presented wh
the mail is being sent to let you choose from the other three options.

This section also lets you specify how many characters each line can have before wrapping au
matically; the default is 70.

Another nice option is whether forwarded text in an e-mail should be prefixed with a > symbol or another symbol of your choice.

Mail Database Preferences

To call up your mail database preferences, click the Tools button in your Inbox and select Preferences or use the menu sequence Actions ➤ Tools ➤ Preferences. The Preferences dialog box defaults to the Mail tab, which contains four additional tabs: Basics, Letterhead, Signature, and Colors, shown in Figure 5.36. Also of interest are mail delegation preferences, which you can find on the Access & Delegation main tab.

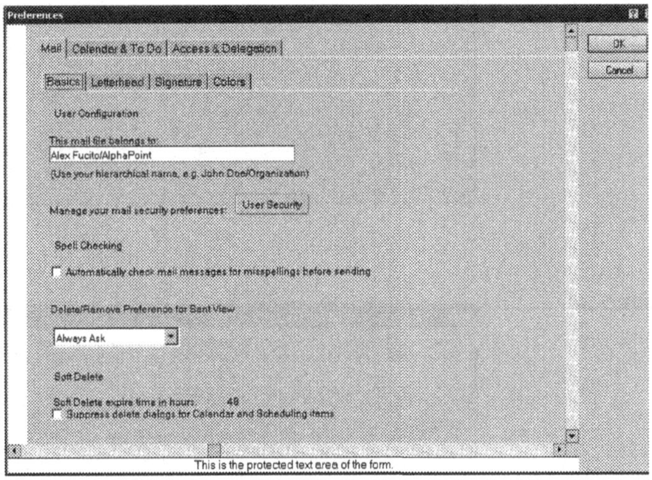

FIGURE 5.36

Mail database preferences

BASICS

The Basics tab contains the most important information and the options that require valid values for your mail to work properly.

Mail owner   This area should show your hierarchical username; if it shows anyone else's name, your mail is not configured properly! A hierarchical name will have at least two parts separated by a forward slash. The first part is your username; the second part is your organization's name. If you have a hierarchical name with more than two parts, your username will still be the first part and your organization name will be the last part. Additional parts between often specify suborganizations or departments within your larger organization.

User security   Clicking the User Security button (shown in Figure 5.36) prompts you for your Notes password and then allows you to set options for both Notes mail security and Internet mail security. Figure 5.37 shows these additional user security options. For Notes mail, you can enable check boxes to encrypt and sign mail with your Notes user ID for mail that you send or store.

For Internet mail, if you have Internet certificates, you can review them, send signed and encrypted Internet mail in MIME format, and receive Internet encrypted or signed mail. Clicking the

Internet-Style Mail Options button displays the dialog box shown in Figure 5.38; here, you can options specific to Internet mail to configure Notes to work like other popular Internet mail cli

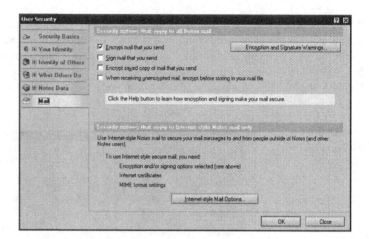

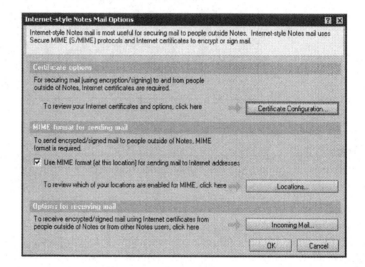

Spell checking   A check box is available to enable automatic spell checking on every e-mail y create. If this option is enabled, spell check takes place just before the e-mail is sent.

Sent view preferences   The Sent view in your mail database keeps track of all messages you ever sent to anyone. When a message is deleted, you may not want the message deleted automatica from the Sent view. These options allow you to specify what kind of notification and behavior y would like: Always Ask, Always Delete, and Always Remove.

Soft delete When you delete a message document from your mail database, it is temporarily placed in the Trash folder and then permanently deleted from the database when you close the database or refresh the database using F9 or the menu sequence View ➤ Refresh. You can override this behavior by using the Soft Delete Expire Time in Hours option. With this feature, you specify a specific number of hours that documents that have been marked for deletion will actually be available for before permanent deletion takes place. At the end of the time period you specify—say, 48 hours—the document is permanently deleted from the database.

Letterhead

The Letterhead tab lets you specify the graphic that appears at the top of your outgoing Domino mail messages. Your name and the current date/time information is also a part of the letterhead. Letterhead is not Internet mail compatible and will not appear for Internet mail recipients.

Signature

We mentioned earlier that a signature in a Notes e-mail is a small, personalized block of text or graphic appended to the end of outgoing messages. If you have a standard signature that you want automatically appended to all of your outgoing messages, enable the check box on this tab.

Colors

The Colors tab is a new Notes and Domino 6 feature that allows you to specify the background and text colors for e-mails received from specific users. You can set up three different color settings using the dialog box shown in Figure 5.39 and apply them to individual users and groups of mail senders. This gives you the ability to set e-mails from your boss to appear in red, e-mails from one friend in blue, and e-mail from another friend in green. There is also an option to restore the default mail colors if you tire of the ones you've chosen.

FIGURE 5.39

Setting background and text colors for groups of e-mail senders

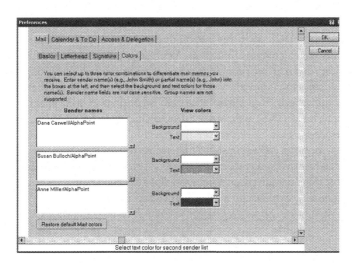

Setting Delegation Preferences

As part of the tools preferences, you can set options for mail delegation as well as calendar delegat
If you would like your assistant or supervisor to be able to read your mail, send it in your name
otherwise manage it, you can grant that permission from the Access & Delegation tab using the Ac
to Your Mail & Calendar subtab shown in Figure 5.40. You can navigate to this dialog box using
Tools ➤ Preferences buttons in the Inbox or while creating an e-mail.

FIGURE 5.40

Delegating mail

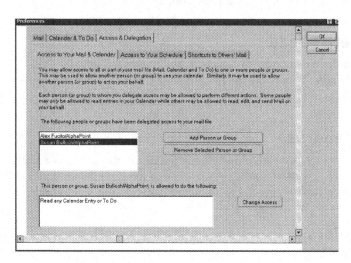

Access is granted to individuals and groups using two input box areas. The first input box a
shows a list of the people or groups who have access to your mail file. The second input box (at
bottom of the dialog box) shows the access granted to the currently highlighted person or grou
the first input box. In Figure 5.40, you can see that Susan Bulloch has been granted the ability to ▸
any calendar entry or to do list entry. Her access is limited to this; she has not been granted acces
read the mail. You can choose people to delegate to and set their access using the Add Person
Group button. Clicking this button displays the dialog box shown in Figure 5.41.

This screen contains four steps. With step 1, you choose either a user or a group to delegate
the drop-down arrow provides access to the list of users and groups in the Domino Directory. A
nately, you can choose the radio button to grant access to all users instead of specifying individ
users and groups. Step 2 lets you specify what parts of your mail file you want to allow other pec
to use. You can choose the mail, calendar, and to do list; just the calendar and to do list and no n
or no access at all.

The options you set in step 2 determine the options available in step 3 for choosing access p
ileges. The privileges you grant in step 3 display in the input box at the bottom of the Access to Y
Mail & Calendar tab (shown in Figure 5.40). If you grant access to your mail, calendar, and to do
the following options are available to you in step 3:

♦ Read Any document

- Read and Create Any Document, Send Mail on Your Behalf
- Read, Edit, and Create Any Document, Send Mail on Your Behalf
- Read, Edit, Create, and Delete Any Document, Send Mail on Your Behalf
- Read and Create Any Document, Delete Any Document They Created

FIGURE 5.41

Adding a person or group and specifying delegation privileges

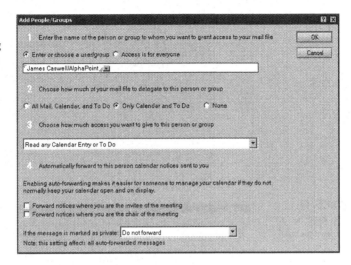

If you choose to grant access only for your calendar and to do list, the following options are available in step 3:

- Read Any Calendar Entry or To Do
- Read, Create, Edit, and Delete Any Calendar Entry or To Do

In step 4 of the Add People/Groups dialog box, you choose whether the person or group you're delegating to should automatically receive forwards of any calendar notices that come into your Inbox. Within this area, you can fine-tune the management of meeting notices by choosing to forward notices based on whether you are invited, whether you are the chair of the meeting, or whether it is marked as private.

To change the access of a group or person on your list, highlight the option in the first input box in Figure 5.40 and click the Change Access button. This displays the dialog box shown in Figure 5.42.

If someone has delegated privileges on their mail file to you, you can set up a shortcut to access their mail using the Shortcuts to Others' Mail subtab shown in Figure 5.43. The purpose of this dialog box is for you to add users to the drop-down list on the main Mail icon (above your Inbox) so that you can quickly switch to another user's mail files without needing to close your own first.

FIGURE 5.42
Changing delegation privileges

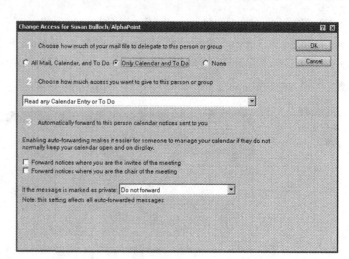

FIGURE 5.43
Setting shortcuts to other people's mail

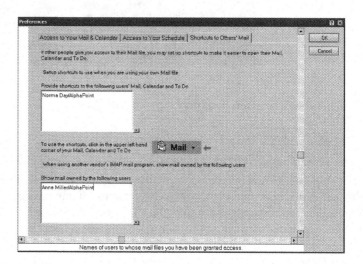

Using Word Processors with Notes Mail

Notes's capabilities for writing and formatting text are markedly more versatile than most e-mail packages. Because a message body is a rich-text field, you can play with a broad range of fonts, sizes, colors and other formatting features—but that's not good enough for some people. As versatile as Notes and other rich-text editors are, they still don't have the capacities of a full-fledged word processor. So, what if you need capabilities that even a standard Notes message won't give you, such as revision marking or footnotes? You have three choices. You could, if you wanted to invest the effort, hand-tool a Note message, changing font sizes, colors, and styles to make it look like you could easily produce numbered outlines or drop footnotes into the text—that clearly is the wrong way to go. You might write a document in your favorite word processor and attach it to a Notes message—better, but still clumsy because recipients would have to go through the extra steps of opening your attachment. Or, if you don't want you or your recipients to work that hard, you could just use your favorite word processor within the body of the Notes message itself. Notes supports the use of some popular word processors as message editors.

If you're interested in using a word processor to write your mail, open your user preferences (File ➢ Preferences ➢ User Preferences) and select the Mail option. In the area for Alternate Memo Editor, you can specify Microsoft Word or Lotus Word Pro as your editor of choice.

When you're done, you'll probably notice a new entry on your Create menu: either Word Memo or Word Pro Memo, depending on which word processor you chose. The new menu item will create a new memo with a word processor document as the message body. The memo will retain the Notes message header for the address and subject line as well as your bookmark buttons and tabs for other open documents and databases, but the body of the message will display your word processor's rulers and layout, and the word processor's toolbars will appear under the menu bar. Your word processor's menus will mostly replace Notes' menus; however, Notes will retain its File menu, and the Help menu will let you choose between two submenus: the Notes Help menu and the word processor's Help menu.

You will be able to use most of your word processor's features: page layout and outline views; customized toolbars; revision tracking; the word processor's native spell checking, table construction, and text formatting features; and even most macro-writing features. The features you won't be able to use are file related. For example, you can't save a word processor memo as an external document, although you could copy the contents and paste them into a new document created in your word processor.

At the same time, you can use Notes to store and mail your message. The address fields and addressing features function normally, and you can save your message as a draft if you need to go away and come back to it later.

There are, of course, potential drawbacks to using a word processor as your message editor. You won't be able to use attachments in your word processor messages. After all, you can't attach external files to word processor documents, so you won't be able to attach them to word processor documents that happen to be embedded in Notes documents.

Word processor messages are *much* larger than regular Notes messages. For example, a Word Memo is about 32KB bigger than a regular Notes Memo. If you take full advantage of Word's special capabilities, it will only get bigger. Word processor messages take up more room in your mailbox as well as in the recipient's mailbox, and they will correspondingly take longer to send. That won't make much of a difference if you're working on a good in-house network, but it can take a lot longer to send and receive word processor messages over a dial-up modem connection.

Using Mail Offline

With most of the features discussed in this chapter, it is assumed, or at least implied, that you're connected to some kind of server. However, you'll find that many Notes databases, including your mail, will allow you to work offline, not connected to any servers at all. This is particularly useful for laptop users, who may need to work with their mail while on a plane, on a train, or miles away from the nearest modem or network connection. However, even Notes users with a physical connection to a fast network might find some reason to disconnect from the servers.

The key to working offline is being in Island mode. You can switch to Island mode by select
File ➤ Mobile ➤ Choose Current Location and selecting Island from the list. Going into Island m
tells Notes that there are no external network connections of any kind, so it shouldn't try to inte
with any servers. You may actually have an active network or modem connection, and switchin
Island mode won't disconnect your computer from a network. While you're in Island mode, N
won't try to use that connection, but you and other programs you use still can.

Obviously, there are limitations to working offline. Most importantly, you can't use any datab
you don't have locally (that is, on your own computer). If you want to work with a database wl
offline, be sure you have a local replica. You also can't send mail. For mail to be delivered, it ne
to go to a mail server first; if Notes doesn't think it's connected to a server, the mail can't go anywl

However, you can still do a lot of work on your mail while offline. You can read existing messa
and write new ones. If you have a local copy of your mail database, you can use all of the docum
creation and document-editing tools you usually use. Notes even allows you to make *mobile* repl
of Directory Catalogs. The mobile replicas are compact summaries of the address books that live
the Domino servers, giving you access to your organization's address books in a fraction of the sp
they usually take.

You can even send mail...well, sort of. You can go so far as clicking the Send button. As alre
discussed, the mail can't actually go anywhere if Notes doesn't have a server to talk to. It can, thou
be stored away for later delivery. If you click the Send button while offline, Notes will create ne
databases to store the mail in: `mail.box` for Notes mail and `smtp.box` for Internet mail. You can w
and "send" as many messages as you want while offline, and they'll all be stored until you make a c
nection to a mail server. Once connected, you can tell Notes to send the queued mail, actually start
the messages on their way.

Using Notes Minder

Notes Minder is a small utility program that can check your mail and remind you of your appo
ments without actually running Lotus Notes. Notes Minder works behind the scenes to monitor y
mailbox for new mail and your Calendar for alarms, but it doesn't have any of the other features
the full Notes client. It will alert you to new mail and let you launch Notes when you want to, l
without the full Notes client's large memory requirements.

The Notes Minder is installed along with the Notes client and can be launched from the Sta
menu. When you launch the Notes Minder, it will ask for your Notes password and then sit quie
in memory, leaving a clickable icon in the system tray.

If you move your mouse over the system tray icon, you will see the last time the Minder check
your mailbox. If you double-click the icon, you'll jump directly to your mail, Notes will laun
and your Inbox will open. Right-clicking the icon brings up a menu you can use to control t
Minder with the following options:

Open Notes   Launches Notes immediately.

Check Now   Checks your mailbox for new mail. The Notes Minder doesn't keep a constant c
nection open to the Notes server; that would eat up too much memory and processor time. Inste
it checks your mailbox periodically for new messages. Selecting this option tells the Minder to ch
for mail immediately rather than waiting for the next interval.

View Mail Summary   This option lets you view a summary of new messages without having to launch Notes itself. It brings up a window listing the sender, date, and subject line of every unread message in your Inbox (see Figure 5.44). Using this option, you can see new messages that have arrived and then launch Notes if you decide one of them is important enough to read immediately. Double-clicking any of the items in the list will immediately launch Notes and open that document.

Properties   This option calls up the dialog box shown in Figure 5.45, which lets you set a number of options for the Notes Minder. You can tell the Minder whether to use audible notifications, whether it should pop up alerts to Notes messages, and how long it should wait between checks on your mailbox.

Enabled   You can temporarily disable the Minder by disabling this option.

Exit   Quits the Minder.

FIGURE 5.44
The Unread Mail
Summary window

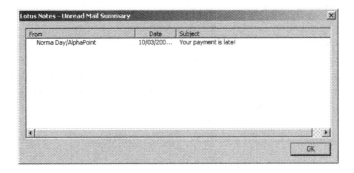

FIGURE 5.45
Properties for
Notes Minder

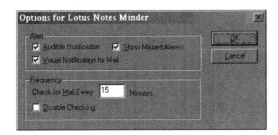

Closing Your Mail Database

All done with your mail? Here a four ways to quickly close the mail database from the Inbox screen. The techniques may be familiar to you because Notes uses the same approach for all databases:

◆ Click the X button on the Inbox window tab shown in Figure 5.46.

◆ Right-click on the Inbox window tab and select Close Window from the context menu.

- Use the menu sequence File ➤ Close.
- Press the Esc key on the keyboard to return to the Welcome page.

FIGURE 5.46

Closing a window

Summary

This chapter provided you with everything you need to know about Notes mail. Some of the conc
are straightforward, such as opening, reading, managing, and closing a mail document. Other
cepts give you insight into the complexity and power of Notes mail, such as using the Select Addre
dialog box to search Domino and LDAP servers, searching for addresses both within and outsid
your organization. You can control a number of settings to trace and secure your mail, make m
of those settings permanent by setting your mail preferences, sort and control incoming mail wi
rules, and keep the contents of your mailbox current by archiving old messages. Notes mail allows
to use some external programs such as your favorite word processor to edit mail messages, resp
automatically to incoming mail with the Out of Office feature, and keep track of incoming mail w
out having Notes running by using the Notes Minder.

In the next chapter we'll take a look at how Calendaring and Scheduling integrates with mail
cessing and see how the two work together in Notes.

Chapter 6

Calendaring and Scheduling

GROUPWARE-ORIENTED CALENDARING AND scheduling became a staple of the Lotus Notes world with version 4.5. With each new revision, ease of use has been improved and the integration with other mainline services in Notes, such as mail and the to do list, have continued.

Your Lotus Notes calendar is stored in your mail database. If you have a local replica of your mail database on your personal computer, you can use your calendar in stand-alone mode like other calendar software. The real power of a Notes calendar, however, becomes apparent when you connect to a Domino server. Using the server-based features of calendaring and scheduling, you can make your calendar available to other Notes users and work with other people's calendars as well.

Within a Domino network, your calendar is a flexible tool for organizing groups of people. You can schedule meetings, check on subordinates' and peers' free time, and coordinate group actions quickly and easily through your Notes calendar. In this chapter, we'll cover the basics of calendaring and scheduling in Notes, discuss how to navigate the user interface of the calendar, set up preferences and default values, add entries to your calendar, and use features such as group calendars and meeting invitations to get your calendar to work with others.

- ◆ Viewing the new calendar layout

- ◆ Creating calendar entries

- ◆ Customizing calendar preferences

- ◆ Managing the meeting process

- ◆ Working with a group calendar

- ◆ Printing calendar information

- ◆ Introducing the new to do list format

- ◆ Managing personal and assigned to do items

- ◆ Granting other users access to your calendar

- ◆ Accessing other people's calendars

What's New in Calendaring and Scheduling?

Let's take a quick look at the new features in calendaring and scheduling in Lotus Notes and Domir

- There are additional actions for the meeting chairperson.
- Entries are color coded.
- Conflicting documents can be configured to appear side by side.
- You can create and edit calendar entries at the view level.
- You can customize calendar entry information.
- You have the ability to delegate entire calendar management activity to another person.
- Notes displays a second non-Gregorian calendar customized to user preferences (Hinji, Jewish, Japanese six-day).
- You can display an alternate time zone.
- There are enhanced calendar printing options.
- A horizontal scroll bar displays at the bottom of view screen automatically.
- There's an improved interface for viewing availability of attendees when scheduling a meet
- New views include one work month, two work week, and summary.
- The resource reservation system has been revised.
- You can show time slots on calendar views.
- Notes now supports scheduling meetings that run past midnight (is this a good thing?).
- The tabbed interface makes it easier to switch between days, months, and years.
- Time zones can be added to meetings, appointments, and reminders.
- You can view and print the status of participants for a meeting.

In addition to explaining these new Lotus Notes and Domino 6 features, this chapter covers ev thing you need to know to maximize the capabilities of the calendar in your Lotus Notes client.

Getting Started with the Calendar

The default Welcome page, which uses the Basics style, is the easiest way to access your calen there is a clickable icon labeled Calendar directly on it. Because the calendar is a frequently us time-management tool, the goal was to be able to access it quickly from other places in Notes well. Try these to open your calendar:

- Select the Calendar icon on the Bookmark bar along the left edge of the Notes client.
- Customize the Welcome page to display the calendar directly.
- From within the Mail area, click the down-pointing arrow next to the word Mail on the m banner area at the top of the database; from there, choose Switch to Calendar.

Once open, the calendar area of the Notes mail client is arranged in two major parts: a left fra and a right frame, as shown in Figure 6.1. When information in the left frame is clicked or select the information shown in the right frame changes to correspond to what you've clicked on in the l frame.

FIGURE 6.1

The calendar

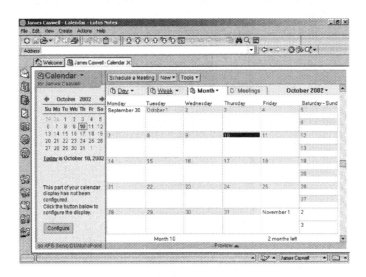

NOTE *Frames and framesets in Notes segment the screen into separate areas while maintaining a linked relationship between the areas. Clicking on one area of the screen generally changes content in a different area of the screen.*

On the top portion of the left frame, a small calendar in month format displays and helps you jump to a certain day, week, or month to work with in the larger calendar in the right frame. You can select a day simply by clicking it in either the small calendar or the large calendar. The day's calendar entries display in the larger calendar as a list. There are five types of calendar entries: appointments/meetings, reminders, events, anniversaries, and to do items. If the list of calendar entries for a given day is too long to fit on the screen in its entirety, a vertical scroll bar appears automatically.

The bottom portion of the left frame has been reserved for new notices or for your to do list. The first time you open your calendar, you'll want to configure this using the Configure button visible at the bottom left of Figure 6.1. When you click this button, a warning message will let you know that if you have a lot of notices or to do items in your existing calendar, creating the miniview area might take a bit of time (see Figure 6.2). When it's new and void of entries, however, miniview creation is very fast.

FIGURE 6.2

Preparing to
configure the
miniview

After the configuration completes, the Configure button is replaced with a switchable miniview (see Figure 6.3).

FIGURE 6.3

Miniview area
showing new
notices

You have two choices: New Notices or To Do. Switch between these two by clicking the do▮ pointing arrow to the right of the phrase *To Do* or *New Notices*, and choosing which miniview to sh▮ from the submenu that appears.

Changing the Calendar Layout

The look and feel of the calendar in Lotus Notes 6 has been completely reworked in this release. P▮ back at Figure 6.1 and note that there are four tabs that help you navigate the calendar: Day, We▮ Month, and Meetings. To change from one to the other, just click a tab.

On each of the Day, Week, and Month tabs , notice the drop-down arrow. These arrows give y▮ choices between how to display variations of the day, week, and month views of a calendar. For exam▮ as shown in Figure 6.4, the Week tab has the option to look at the calendar in increments of one we▮ one work week, two weeks, or two work weeks. You can view the Day tab in one- or two-day increme▮ and you can view months in one-month or one-work-month increments (which, by default, exclud▮ Saturday and Sunday).

In addition to the quick drop-down options for changing the format of what you see in the ▮ endar, the View ➤ Change Format menu options give you the ability to view one day, two days, ▮ week, one work week, two weeks, two work weeks, one month, and one work month. You can a▮ use the View ➤ Show menu item to show the calendar in Summary mode or Time Slots mode. T▮ idea here is that even if you're looking at your calendar a month at a time, it might be helpful to h▮ the time slots within a day appear so that you can easily see meeting times.

FIGURE 6.4
Tab drop-down
choices

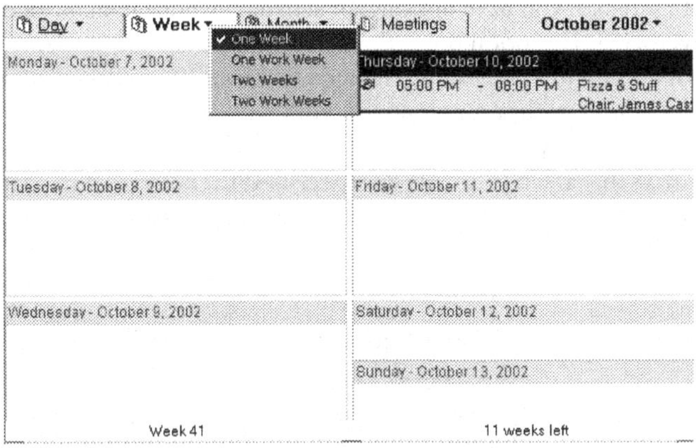

Setting Calendar Preferences

The option to use work weeks and work months is new in Lotus Notes and Domino 6. By default, a work week is Monday through Friday, and a work day begins at 7:00 A.M. and ends at 7:00 P.M. For those of you who don't like the idea of a 12-hour work day and take Wednesdays off, you can customize the definition of work weeks and work days. To do this, use the Tools button visible along the top of the calendar in Figure 6.1 and select the option beneath it for Preferences.

NOTE   Customized preferences for the mail database are set using this window. The mail database contains the mail, calendars, and to do lists.

CUSTOMIZING PREFERENCES

The Calendar & To Do preferences area has eight tabs to customize the behavior for your needs. As shown in Figure 6.5, there are three major tabs (Mail, Calendar & To Do, and Access & Delegation) that each contain tabs of their own. The subtabs specific to calendar management include Basics, Display, Scheduling, Alarms, To Do, Autoprocess, and Colors. Let's look at each of them in turn.

  Basics   This tab focuses on the behavior of the calendar when you add new entries. For instance, you can set the default type of calendar entry as meeting, appointment, all day event, anniversary, or reminder. When you double-click a time slot, the default calendar entry type automatically displays for you to configure its specific features. Additionally, you can set the default duration of an appointment or meeting to a set number of minutes; it defaults to 60. Anniversary entries also have a default to repeat for 10 years. Finally, you can define a list of default personal categories that will appear as choices on your calendar entries.

  Display   The Display tab below the Calendar & To Do tab is where you define your work week, which was mentioned a moment ago. The default work week excludes Saturdays and Sundays, but you can configure your own according to your work schedule. On the left, as shown

in Figure 6.5, you have options for setting the hour your work day begins and ends. Additio
ally, there is an option to set the default time that calendar entries should occupy; it starts o
with 60 minutes and can be changed to 15 or 30 minutes. On the right side of the screen, y
define the days that comprise the work week. Any day that has a check mark in it is conside
to be a part of your work week. Click the check box to turn the check mark on or off next
the days that are in your own work week. At the bottom of this tab, you set options to determi
how much or how little calendar information displays in your mail Inbox.

FIGURE 6.5
Defining a
work week

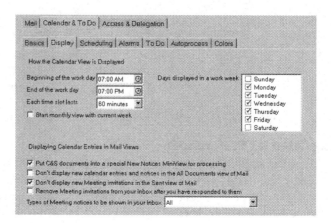

Scheduling   Domino uses this area to check the security of other users when they are attempt
to schedule meetings with you. Lotus Notes searches for available time slots (free time) in the
endars of anyone invited to the meeting. On this tab, you specify your work schedule, which
your availability. In addition, you can prevent meeting conflicts, and you can handle sched
details or best meeting times automatically. In Figure 6.6, you can see that this person works M
day through Friday from 9 a.m. to 5 p.m., with an hour for lunch, with Wednesday and Frid
afternoons off...lucky dog! Of course, it appears that they have to work on Saturday morning
well, so maybe they aren't so lucky after all.

The bottom half of the Scheduling tab determines Domino's behavior as entries are being ad
to your calendar (either by you or other people). The first option is a check box that will eit
enable or disable Notes' ability to check for conflicts as a meeting is being scheduled. The sec
option is a radio button choice to determine if the scheduler of a meeting should be able to see
schedule details for the people invited to the meeting or just the best times for scheduling a m
ing with those who are invited.

FIGURE 6.6
Availability

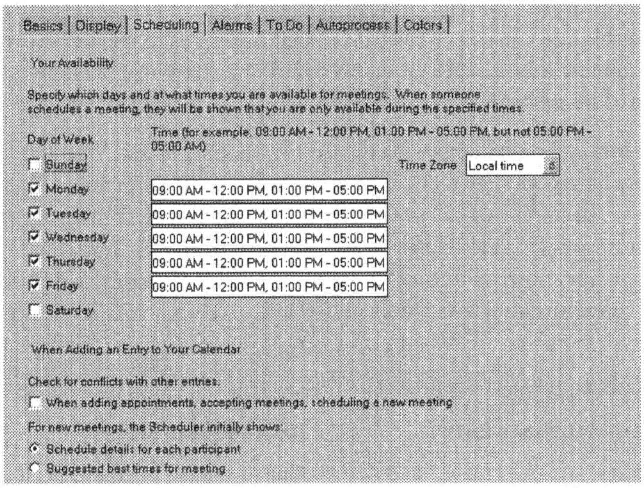

Alarms Lotus Notes will notify you with a prompt message box of items requiring your attention in the calendar. You can also set a sound to play as an alarm as well. By default, these notifications are turned on but may be disabled using this tab. Each type of calendar entry has associated warning times, which you can modify. Table 6.1 lists the default settings for each.

TABLE 6.1: ALARM SETTINGS

TYPE OF CALENDAR ENTRY	ADVANCE NOTIFICATION DEFAULT
Appointments/Meetings	30 minutes in advance
Reminders	0 minutes in advance, meaning the reminder simply pops up when you told it to do so
Events	1 day in advance
Anniversaries	1 day in advance
To Do	1 day in advance of due date

To Do To do items, discussed later in this chapter, automatically display in your calendar at the beginning of the day on which they come due. On this tab, you can disable this feature. Notes also automatically tracks a to do item's status, start date, and due date. This, too, can be disabled on this tab and Notes will simply treat to do items as a list of text items rather than time-managed items that come due and expire.

Autoprocess   As a groupware tool, the calendar is fully integrated with the Domino mail syst On this tab, you can enable automated responses to meeting invitations using the mail system automatic Inbox management to remove meeting invitations as you respond to them. This is a bit of housekeeping that will help you stay organized.

Colors   To go along with the new Lotus Notes and Domino 6 interface for the calendar, y now have complete control over the color coding of entries for both background color and t color. Each type of calendar entry is associated with its own set of colors, which helps them st out in your calendar. There is also a button to restore the default colors just in case you make sc bad color choices and want to start over! Table 6.2 lists the default background color for each t of calendar entry; text colors all default to black.

TABLE 6.2: DEFAULT CALENDAR ENTRY COLORS

TYPE OF CALENDAR ENTRY	BACKGROUND COLOR
Meetings	Blue
Appointments	Green
Reminders	Peach
Events	Yellow
Anniversaries	Pink
To do	Light blue

Adding Company Holidays to Your Calendar

Although the preferences area controls the look you like for your calendar, you might also want to t advantage of a nonpersonal setting that affects your calendar: company-recognized holidays. Many c panies specify holidays to be scheduled in the annual calendar. If your Lotus Notes Domino syst administrator has set up a master holiday calendar in Domino recording these company holidays, y can bring them into your personal calendar easily. Importing the holidays automatically reserves dates in your calendar and makes them unavailable for meetings. To add the holidays, use the Tools I ton (see Figure 6.1) and choose Import Holidays or select Actions ➤ Tools ➤ Import Holidays. Import Holidays dialog box groups the holidays by country and specialized purpose—from Austr. to Christian to Jewish and Vietnam.

Managing Calendar Entries

Earlier we noted that there are several types of entries that can be added the calendar. Depending which you choose, your entry may be integrated with the Domino mail system or it may just be stand-alone entry. The five types of calendar entries are appointment, anniversary, reminder, all-event, and meeting. Adding any of these types of entries to the calendar is straightforward. As sho in Figure 6.7, you can use the Schedule a Meeting button to add a meeting to the calendar or use

New button to add an appointment, anniversary, reminder, or all-day event. You can also use the menu sequence Create ➤ Calendar Entry or simply double-click the time slot in the calendar to create the default entry type.

FIGURE 6.7
Adding calendar entries

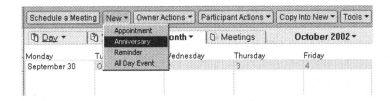

Once you choose an entry type, you can still change it to another type using the drop-down box next to the entry type to display the Change Calendar Entry Type window shown in Figure 6.8.

FIGURE 6.8
Changing entry types

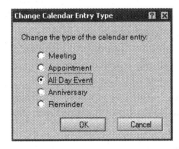

Each type of calendar entry has a different set of information requirements. Let's discuss each one in turn.

Making an Appointment

You add appointments to the calendar to reserve time so that other people can't schedule meetings on your calendar when you're not available. An appointment generally does not involve other people in your organization. You can use the appointment type of calendar entry for things such as a doctor's appointment, a carpool time, and time with your personal trainer. Figure 6.9 shows the appointment entry screen.

FIGURE 6.9
Making an appointment

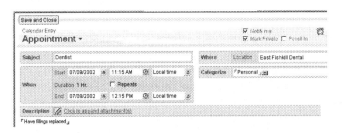

To create an appointment, Notes collects some standard information to use in the calend, including:

- Subject
- Start and end dates and times
- Duration of the appointment
- Whether this is a repeating calendar entry
- Location
- Category
- Description of the entry

It is important that you type a meaningful subject line so that you know what the entry is in calendar; whatever you type in this box is what will display on the calendar. You can fill in the s and end date/time fields using the time and date picker icons to the right of the input boxes. In Location area, type a description of where the appointment will be—for example, 1600 Pennsylv; Avenue if you happen to have an appointment with the President of the United States. The text L, tion area is also helpful if you need to enter something such as Joe's cubicle or the cafeteria. If y, enable the Repeats option, a dialog window appears and asks you how often you want to repeat calendar entry. The description area allows as much text as you want to type, as well as file atta, ments, tables, pictures, and links to Web addresses.

Many of the calendar entries include optional settings for setting alarms, keeping information vate, and allowing time to be double booked or scheduled over. These options are found at the right corner of a calendar entry:

Notify Me   When the Notify Me check box is marked, you can set alarm settings for this ticular calendar entry. Earlier, you saw that you can set the defaults in the Preferences area. H, you are overriding the defaults and setting alarms to behave differently than the defaults for t calendar entry only. Features you can change include disabling the alarm altogether, setting a ferent advance warning alarm period, setting the alarm to play a sound, or sending yourself e-mail with the event type and the description.

Mark Private   Enabling the Mark Private option has the effect of reserving the time slot on y calendar so that no one can schedule a meeting over the top of it; however, it does not display information about what you are doing during that time period.

Pencil In   When this option is enabled, the entry gets added to your calendar but other peo, can schedule meetings during the same block of time.

Adding an Anniversary

An anniversary is a calendar entry that marks a particular day as important but does not mark the ti, on your calendar unavailable. An anniversary is, by default, an annual event (good for birthdays, due dates, and actual anniversaries). However, you can also use it as a reminder for any event t recurs on a particular day but does not reserve calendar time—for instance, the day your monthly r is due. To add an anniversary, Notes collects the following information, shown in Figure 6.10:

- Subject

- ◆ Start date
- ◆ Whether this is a repeating calendar entry
- ◆ Location
- ◆ Category
- ◆ Description of the entry

FIGURE 6.10
Adding an
anniversary

The Notify Me, Mark Private, and Pencil In options are also available. In addition, you can add an attachment to the anniversary entry.

Setting a Reminder

Like an anniversary, a reminder is a calendar event that doesn't actually reserve time on the calendar. Instead, it serves an informational purpose to you. You might use this calendar entry to remind you to make a phone call at a particular time or remind yourself to leave an hour early to get to the airport. Figure 6.11 shows the window used to set a reminder. When created, a Reminder collects the following information from you:

- ◆ Subject
- ◆ Start date, time, and time zone
- ◆ Whether this is a repeating calendar entry
- ◆ Location
- ◆ Category
- ◆ Description of the entry

FIGURE 6.11
Setting a reminder

While the Notify Me and Mark Private options are available, the Pencil In option does not apply to reminders. Adding an attachment is also still possible.

Creating an All-Day Event

An all-day event reserves days at a time on your calendar. Your calendar appears unavailable to other people during the time the event runs. An event's time span covers full days and often multiple of days instead of just few hours. Figure 6.12 shows an all-day event scheduled for a Yankees game.

FIGURE 6.12

Scheduling an all-day event

Some standard information is collected to create an event:

◆ Subject

◆ Start date

◆ End date

◆ Location of event

◆ Category

Type a meaningful subject as this is the text that appears in the calendar. If you use a category Vacation, Notes will automatically ask you if you want to use the Out of Office notification while you're gone. At the bottom of the screen, you can type a brief or lengthy description of the event include attachments if you like.

As with anniversaries, appointments, and reminders, the Notify Me, Mark Private, and Pencil options are available as well as the ability to add an attachment.

Working with Meetings

The meeting calendar entry is the most interesting and sophisticated of the entry types. Because meetings involve other people, Notes has tied the scheduling of meetings directly into the Domino mail system to automate the process as much as possible. The process of meeting management in Lotus Notes can involve the following tasks:

◆ Scheduling a one-time-only meeting or a repeating meeting

◆ Sending meeting invitations to participants

◆ Responding to a meeting invitation (as a meeting participant)

◆ Managing the invitations (as the meeting initiator)

SCHEDULING A MEETING

As a calendar entry, Notes collects the expected types of information regarding the "who, what, what, where, and when" of a meeting. Like other calendar entries, Notify Me, Mark Private, and Pencil In are available, as well as a large text description area, attachment area, and a subject line that will appear in the calendar. Figure 6.13 shows a meeting form for a calendar entry. The fields that a meeting entry has in common with other calendar entries are the following:

◆ Subject

◆ Start and end dates, times, and time zone

◆ Whether the meeting should repeat

◆ Category

◆ Description

FIGURE 6.13

Meeting entry

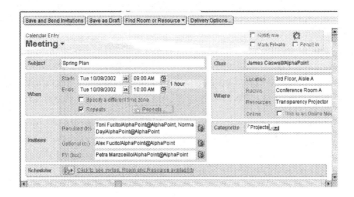

Setting Meeting Specifics

In addition to the standard pieces of calendar information, scheduling a meeting requires additional information that is unique to the meeting type of calendar entry: chairperson, meeting location, invitees, and scheduler options. Let's discuss these new types of information requirements and how you can work with them:

Chair　A chairperson is the person who sets up the meeting. The Lotus Notes username of the person creating the meeting entry is automatically added to this part of the form.

Where　The meeting location part of a meeting entry is a powerful component of meeting scheduling. When you choose a location, you can tie into the Resource Reservations system built into Domino if your system administrator has enabled it. Once enabled by an administrator, meeting rooms are listed in the Domino Directory address book so that a calendar can be maintained for each room. The location and media resources associated with the room fill in automatically after choosing or being assigned a room. Resources are most likely to include things such as overhead projectors and sound systems for meetings. However, your company may treat laptop computers for trips away from the office, company cars, and other portable pieces of company property as resources in the Domino Directory. If that is the case, you could "check out" a resource for away from the office by sending an invitation to the resource instead of to people and room

Invitees   Invitees are people you want to attend the meeting, or at least people who should informed of it. There are three levels of invitees, each with its own field:

- ◆ Required
- ◆ Optional
- ◆ FYI

The list of Required users are people who are vital to the meeting; their invitations will pror them to accept or decline the invitation. Optional invitees are people for whom the meeting is mandatory but who might want to attend; the invitation they receive will allow them to add entry to their calendars. The third set of invitees is FYI people; these are people who will rec an informational message letting them know that the meeting is taking place and allow them pencil the meeting into their own calendar. You could type names into each invitee field, but cl ing any of the buttons next to the fields will bring up a standard address dialog box, letting add people to the invitation lists with just a few clicks. People you add to the invitation in th Required area will end up in the To field, people added to the Optional list will appear in the field, and people added to the FYI area appear in the Bcc field of the address book dialog b

Scheduler   The meeting scheduler finds the best times for meetings by coordinating your ca dar with the free time calendar openings for the people you've invited to the meeting and avail meeting room resources. This is a powerful feature that is fully described in the "Reserving a M ing Room and Using the Scheduler" section.

Repeating Calendar Entries

The majority of meetings are scheduled as single-use or one-time-only entries, meaning that the m ing takes place as a unique event and doesn't recur. If you enable the Repeats check box (visible in When section of Figure 6.13), you can schedule the calendar entry multiple times on your calend The Repeat Options dialog box pops up when you click the Repeats button to the right of th Repeats check box (see Figure 6.14).

The first thing to decide is how frequently you want the calendar entry to repeat. After a give number of days? Every other Tuesday? The fifth day of every month? The first Monday in Octob every year? In the top portion of the window, you specify the repeat frequency. In the first drop down box, you select from Daily, Weekly, Monthly by Date, Monthly by Day, Yearly, or Custo However, just choosing, say, Weekly doesn't mean that the entry will repeat every week. Rath it means that the unit of time you choose is the unit of time on which the repeating entry is base For example, if you choose Daily, you can choose to repeat every day, every other day, every th day, and so on. If you choose Monthly by Day or Monthly by Date, you can repeat every mont every other month, and so on (quarterly meetings are simply held every third month, starting at th beginning of your fiscal year). The next step, then, is to refine the repeat conditions. The dro down list to the right of the first one allows you make the kind of refinements just discussed. Fo example, you could have an event repeat every second week, every third month, and so on.

FIGURE 6.14
Creating a
repeating
calendar entry

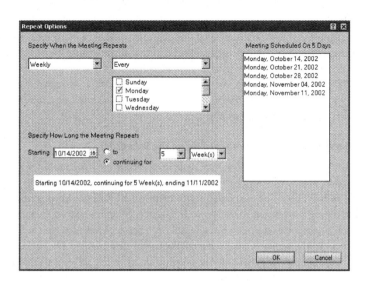

In the middle of the window, you specify a starting date for the calendar entry and an ending date. You can set a specific end date using the To radio button, or you can specify that the entry repeat for a set number of days, weeks, months, or years using the Continuing For radio button. Table 6.3 shows the available alarm settings.

TABLE 6.3: ALARM SETTINGS

FREQUENCY	DESCRIPTION
Daily	Every nth day, from daily to once every 31 days, with an option to skip or move the entry if it happens to occur on a weekend.
Weekly	Once or multiple times per week by choosing to repeat on Sunday, Monday…Saturday.
Monthly by Date	Once or multiple times per month by specifying 1st day, 2nd day…31st day with an option to count from the end of the month.
Monthly by Day	Similar to Monthly by Date, except you choose based on 1st Monday, 2nd Monday, 3rd Tuesday, Last Sunday, and so on.
Yearly	Every year, every other year, every 3rd year, through every 10th year.
Custom	If your event doesn't repeat according to rules, you can fill in your own set of dates using a date picker calendar.

On the right side of the window, a list of dates that meet your criteria displays. For custom repeats, the list becomes an input window letting you generate a specific list for your needs.

If the repeating event lands on a weekend, you can specify an exception to tell Notes what to choosing from options such as not moving it at all, moving it to a Friday or a Monday, or moving to the nearest weekday. You can also delete the item altogether if it falls on a weekend.

NOTE *If you need to change one of the calendar entries that was set as part of a repeating calendar entry, Notes w ask you what to do with the related entries. You can specify that the change should apply only to the entry you've edi. or choose to update all related entries.*

Reserving a Meeting Room and Using the Scheduler

In the calendar preferences area, discussed earlier in this chapter, you were able to specify your w schedule and to block out times that you wanted to be considered unavailable. The opposite of una able is free time. The scheduler component on a Domino server searches everyone's free time to tr find a time convenient to everyone. In essence, Domino is doing what the secretaries of yesteryear sp much of their day doing. The scheduler is a service that runs on the Domino server; therefore, a cc nection to the server is required to make use of this facility. The scheduler performs the hardest par scheduling a meeting: finding out whether the people you want to attend can and determining if a m ing room is available for you.

You can access the scheduler in two ways while creating a new meeting: find a room or resou by using the scheduler to search or display the availability of invited attendees.

The first way to use the scheduler is by performing a search. To use the scheduler to perform a sea click the Find Room or Resource button along the top of a meeting (see Figure 6.13). The drop-dc arrow on the button gives way to two menu options: Find Room(s) and Find Resource(s). Clicking Find Rooms button opens the Scheduler dialog box shown in Figure 6.15. To start the search fo available room, the start and end times of the meeting, number of attendees, and the meeting site pulled from the meeting notice and used by the scheduler when you click the Search button.

FIGURE 6.15

The scheduler

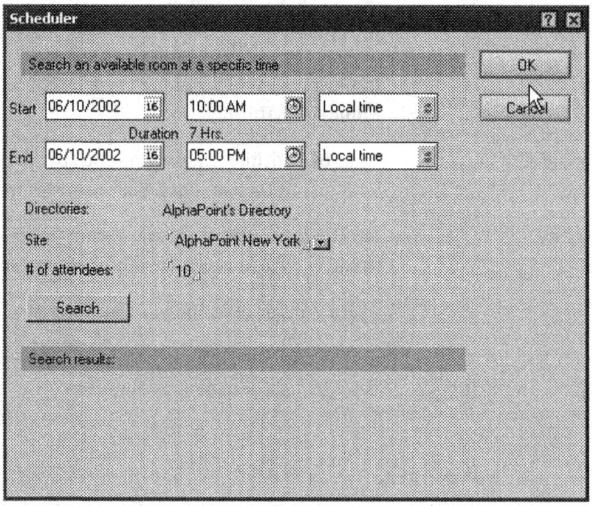

The scheduling system is dependent on the presence of sites, rooms, and resources. The Domino systems administrator creates these sites, rooms, and resources for the scheduler to use when fulfilling your meeting request. A few terms that are specific to scheduling are worth knowing:

Site   Company's location or address of a facility.

Room   Conference or meeting room identification and location; a room is located at a site.

Resource   A media requirement such as a transparency project, flip chart, speaker phone, and so on. Resources can be a part of a room or can be scheduled individually to be used in any room.

The second way to use the scheduler is by specifically using the Scheduler area when creating a new meeting to display availability. In Figure 6.16 you can see the following link: Click to see Invitee, Room and Resource Availability. Clicking this link or its associated Find Best Times for Meeting button to the left of the link starts the scheduler looking for an open time based on your meeting requirements and invitee list.

FIGURE 6.16

Using the Scheduler

Scheduler   Click to see Invitee, Room and Resource availability

As part of its search process for meeting times, the scheduler also displays the schedules involved in either Summary or Details mode. In Summary mode, shown in Figure 6.17, the Invitees list and scheduled rooms and resources displays with blocks of time marked as available or not for each invited person or resource. When looking at the Invitee list and their calendars in Details mode, shaded blocks of time in a column indicate when the person, room, or resource is busy, and the white blocks of time indicate when they're available (see Figure 6.18). The time you've chosen for the meeting will appear as a shaded block. The drop-down arrows to the right of Invitees and Scheduled Rooms display a menu listing what exactly to show: All, Available, or Unavailable. The default for both Invitees and Scheduled Rooms is to show All; change the option to refine the information you want to see at a given time.

FIGURE 6.17

Finding the
best time in
Summary mode

You can also query the scheduler for suggested meeting times using the drop-down arrow to the right of the Suggested Times heading, as shown in Figure 6.19.

FIGURE 6.18
Finding the
best time in
Details mode

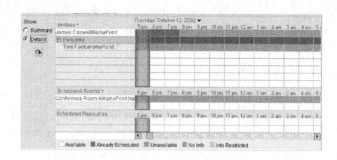

FIGURE 6.19
Suggested
meeting times

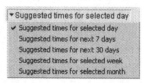

If you've chosen a bad time for a meeting, Notes will suggest a list of alternative times. You adjust the meeting time by using the same time-setting tools you used to set the original time or double-clicking one of the suggested alternate times to move the meeting to that time automatica If some invitees appear to be busy all the time, they may not have set up their free time profile; might want to send them a message telling them to check their user preferences and make their endars available.

The Delivery Options button will bring up a dialog box that will let you select options for th e-mail invitations your meeting invitation document will create. In the Delivery Options dialog b there is a Sign and Encrypt button that will do the same thing as the Sign and Encrypt options regular e-mail. Typically, you'll receive e-mail from the recipients of the invitation indicating whet they accept or decline. However, checking the I Do Not Want to Receive Replies from Participan option will prevent automatic e-mail responses. This is useful if you're inviting a large number of peo and don't want to be deluged by e-mail, but you won't be able to tell who has responded and who has Also, invitation recipients can usually delegate an invitation to somebody else or suggest an alterna time if they're not available for the meeting. This dialog box gives you options to prevent those ty of responses from being sent to you as well.

The ability to quickly and painlessly schedule meetings is a great feature. You can save hours j by eliminating the back-and-forth dialogue of scheduling a meeting between busy colleagues. H ever, the system does rely on users keeping their calendars up-to-date. It's important you keep tra of your time commitments, but you only need to create entries that will actually prevent you fro meeting with other people during a particular block of time.

SAVING AND SENDING INVITATIONS

When you've finished adding all the pertinent information to the meeting calendar entry and hav checked the schedules, you're ready to save the meeting notice and send it to the people you'd like attend. You can click the Save and Send Invitations button to send e-mail invitations to the invitees and attempt to reserve the meeting rooms and resources you want. Alternately, you can click Save as Draft to come back to this meeting notice later; no invitations are e-mailed using this button.

The meeting invitation is the document that transforms your calendar from a way of keeping track of your time into a major piece of groupware. Like an appointment, a meeting invitation takes up a block of time during which you're not available to other people. However, it also takes up other people's time. Sending a meeting invitation adds an entry in your calendar, as well as sending an e-mail to all invitees asking them to attend or informing them of the meeting.

RESPONDING TO INVITATIONS

When you send a meeting invitation to an invitee, it appears in the Inbox of their Notes mail client with a subject line that contains the word *Invitation* plus whatever subject you typed. When the invitation e-mail is opened, the meeting information displays together with a set of action buttons at the top of the invitation for processing it. Figure 6.20 shows a meeting invitation received and opened in the Inbox.

FIGURE 6.20

An inviting e-mail

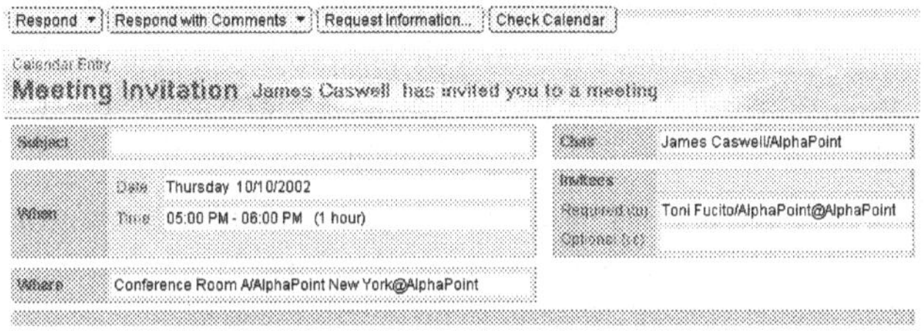

Respond ▾	Respond with Comments ▾	Request information...	Check Calendar

Calendar Entry

Meeting Invitation James Caswell has invited you to a meeting

Subject		Chair	James Caswell/AlphaPoint
When	Date Thursday 10/10/2002	Invitees	
	Time 05:00 PM - 06:00 PM (1 hour)	Required (to)	Toni Fucito/AlphaPoint@AlphaPoint
		Optional (cc)	
Where	Conference Room A/AlphaPoint New York@AlphaPoint		

When you receive an invitation, you should take action on it. You can respond to it, ask for additional information, and take a peek at your calendar to see what else you have on for that day. The drop-down box on each of the Respond buttons, visible in Figure 6.20, allows you to accept, decline, delegate, propose a new time, or tentatively accept the invitation:

Accept This is the option to select if you want to attend the meeting at the time proposed. It will make the meeting invitation appear in your calendar and reserve the meeting time on your calendar. Unless the meeting chairperson has set an option to forgo an acceptance, accepting the meeting automatically sends an e-mail back informing the chairperson that you will be attending the meeting. When you accept a meeting, it is added to your calendar and an e-mail with the subject of the meeting and the "accepted" notification is sent to the meeting chairperson, as shown in Figure 6.21.

FIGURE 6.21

An accepted
meeting invitation

Decline   Choose this option if you don't want to attend the meeting. Be sure to do this if you don't want to go to the meeting and you don't want to be informed of any changes in tim[e] or location. If you decline a meeting, you're permanently out of the loop. You won't receive [any] reschedule notices or meeting confirmations. If it's a meeting that you want to attend (or at le[ast] feel obligated to attend) but you can't attend at the scheduled time, choose Propose New Ti[me] instead.

Delegate   Use this option if you don't want to or can't attend the meeting but you want so[me]body to attend on your behalf. This option will give you a dialog box that allows you to dele[gate] the invitation to someone else. The person to whom you have delegated will receive an invitat[ion] and the chair will receive a notice. Normally, delegating a meeting invitation will take you ou[t of] the loop just like Decline will, but if you check the Keep Me Informed check box, you'll conti[nue] to receive reschedule notices and other messages the chairperson sends to invitees.

Propose New Time   If you want to attend the meeting but cannot attend at the chosen time, [you] can use the Propose New Time option. This option will give you a dialog box with time and d[ate] controls to select a new time. The dialog box also lets you check other invitees' free time sched[ules] so you can be sure the time you check isn't bad for other people. When you click the OK butt[on,] Notes will send the meeting chair a change proposal document. If the chair accepts the time cha[nge,] all participants will get a reschedule notice. If the chair declines the time change, you'll get a mess[age] letting you know.

Tentatively Accept   This option works much like the Accept option, but it will pencil in t[he] invitation, so the time won't be marked as busy in your calendar, giving you the opportunity [to] schedule something at the same time as this meeting.

The Respond with Comments button provides you with all of the same options, but in addit[ion] to taking the action, it will also give you a stripped-down memo form addressed to the meeting ch[air.] The Request Information button generates an e-mail back to the chairperson with the subject li[ne] copied from the meeting invitation. The Check Calendar button opens your calendar to the day [the] meeting is proposed for you to see if the meeting can be integrated into your other plans for the [day.]

MANAGING INVITATIONS

Creating a meeting invitation document and sending out e-mail invitations is just the first step in [the] meeting process. After the meeting has been set up, there are still management tasks involved. T[he] Domino meeting process involves the owner of a meeting, participants, and the Domino server, [as] illustrated in Figure 6.22. After a meeting has been scheduled, the owner of a meeting has tasks t[hat] can be performed, a participant has tasks, and the Domino server is the busy bee in the middle p[ro]cessing all meeting communication and scheduling.

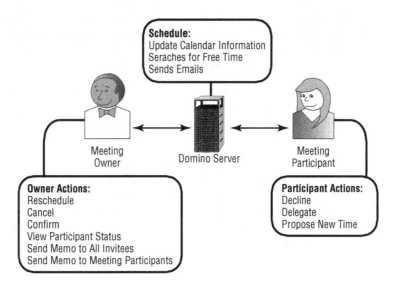

FIGURE 6.22

The Domino
meeting process

Schedule:
Update Calendar Information
Seraches for Free Time
Sends Emails

Meeting
Owner

Domino Server

Meeting
Participant

Owner Actions:
Reschedule
Cancel
Confirm
View Participant Status
Send Memo to All Invitees
Send Memo to Meeting Participants

Participant Actions:
Decline
Delegate
Propose New Time

Actions the Owner of a Meeting Can Take

Once you've set up a meeting, Notes provides you with a number of tools to help you monitor responses, reschedule or cancel the meeting, add and remove invitees and responses, and keep in touch with the invitees. Some management functions take care of themselves. For example, if you want to change a meeting time, all you have to do is open the meeting invitation, change the time, and save and close the document (you should, though, use the Reschedule option under Owner Actions; it's a little more elegant and gives you some extra options). If invitations have been sent out, Notes will send reschedule documents to all invitees. Likewise, if you reopen an existing invitation and add invitees or resources to a meeting after the first round of invitations, Notes will invite the new people. However, there are many other management tasks you might want to perform.

For a meeting you have scheduled, an Owner Actions button appears at the top of the meeting notice. All of the following options are available through the Owner Actions button on the calendar or through the Actions ➢ Owner Actions menu sequence. To perform an action on any meeting invitation, select the invitation by clicking it and then choose the menu option you desire:

Reschedule When you choose the Reschedule option, Notes will bring up a dialog box letting you select new dates and times using the same pop-up calendar and timeline tools you used to set the initial time. Once you set a time, you can use the scheduler to make sure all the participants are free. If you check the Include Additional check box, Notes will create a document you can use to add a message to the time change (for example, explaining why you've changed the meeting time). If you click the OK button, reschedule messages will be sent out to all participants and Notes will try to reserve the resources you invited.

Cancel   If you use the Cancel option, Notes will bring up a dialog box to confirm the cancelation. Like a reschedule, you can add a message to the cancellation e-mail, and if you check Delete All Responses check box, Notes will delete any e-mail responses you've already received for this meeting. Notes will also cancel any room and resource reservations you have made.

Confirm   If you select the Confirm option, Notes will send an e-mail reminding all participants of the meeting time and place. If you check the Include Additional Comments check box, Notes will allow you to add an additional message to the automatic reminder, perhaps updating the agenda or asking the invitees to bring special materials.

View Invitee Status   If you haven't selected the meeting option I Do Not Want to Receive Replies from Participants (the Delivery Options button when creating a new meeting), you receive e-mail responses from invitees telling you whether they can make it to the meeting. If you select View Participant Status, Notes will show you lists of who has accepted the invitation, who has declined, who has delegated, and so on. It will also show you whether the reservations you asked for have been made.

Send Memo to All Invitees   Selecting this option creates an e-mail to everyone who was initially invited to the meeting.

Send Memo to Invitees Who Have Responded   Selecting this option creates an e-mail to everyone who has confirmed their attendance at the meeting.

Send Memo to Invitees Who Have Not Responded   Selecting this option creates an e-mail to everyone who has not yet responded to your meeting invitation.

Actions a Participant to a Meeting Can Take

A meeting's owner must make any formal changes to the meeting as a whole, but if you accept an invitation, you may need to change or modify your original response. Notes gives you tools to change your initial response and request changes in the meeting. These options are available through the Participant Actions button on the calendar or the Actions ➤ Participant Actions menu. Keep in mind that the following are choices only when a meeting entry is modified, not the initial options when receiving an invitation:

Decline   If you are unable to go to a meeting you have already accepted, you can change your status by choosing the Decline option. Again, be sure to do this only if you don't want to attend the meeting. If you want to attend the meeting but can't attend at the proposed time, use Propose New Time instead.

Delegate   This option works like the Delegate option on the original invitation. Once you select a person to attend the meeting and click the OK button, Notes will send a response to the meeting chairperson saying that you have delegated somebody else to attend, and Notes will send a meeting invitation to the person to whom you are delegating.

Propose New Time   This option presents a dialog box that lets you choose a new time, and your proposed new time will be sent to the meeting chairperson for consideration and approval.

Creating Group Calendars

As scheduling a meeting has shown, Domino has the ability to go behind the scenes and look at everyone's calendars. This feature has been extended beyond scheduling into the group calendar area as well. A group calendar is a name you create to help you observe a set of individual calendars as a unit, looking at several calendars interactively and simultaneously. This can be a useful tool for keeping an eye on a department's activities or tentatively planning meeting times.

Group calendars are managed in a separate area from your regular calendar. Open the group calendar area using the Calendar drop-down list, as shown in Figure 6.23, and choose the View & Create Group Calendars option. Any existing group calendars would show up on this menu as well, letting you switch directly to it.

FIGURE 6.23

Switching to group calendars

Once in the group calendar area, you can use buttons to create a new group calendar, edit the membership of a group calendar, or delete a group calendar. Clicking a button for New Group Calendar opens the dialog box shown in Figure 6.24. Here, you give the calendar a title and add members using the Domino Directory address book. The people you add to a group calendar might include your employees, fellow members of a project team, department heads, or any other set of people you want to keep an eye on.

FIGURE 6.24

Creating a new group calendar

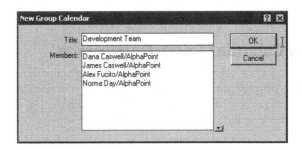

A group calendar, shown in Figure 6.25, lists the free time schedules of the people you have added to the group. Each person's information is represented on their own row.

The color legend below the group members gives you an idea who is available when. White is free time, red is busy time, orange is a person's scheduled busy time, gray indicates no information is available to the scheduler, and tan denotes restricted information that is marked private in a person's calendar. A row will be gray if the person has not set up their calendar preferences to allow it to be accessed by the scheduler. If you're looking at days in the past, Notes shows those in gray but it doesn't keep free time information for days in the past. The arrow buttons will move you back forth through time just as the arrow buttons on your personal calendar do. You can use the Mem button to adjust the group of people whose schedules you can view.

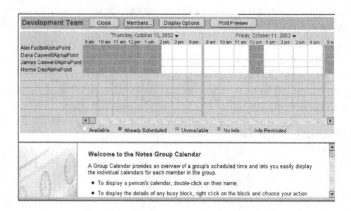

By default, the group calendar will show you an eight-hour slice of time for each day shown. You can use the Display Options button to adjust the starting time being displayed.

If you click a block of busy time for a person, you'll open the calendar document that takes up block of time in the other person's calendar. If you click a person's name rather than a block of b time, Notes will display that person's calendar. Be aware, however, that you can't use a group calen to view individual events in other people's calendars if you don't already have access to read their endars. The group calendar document only gives you an easy way to get to the data you have per sion to read.

Creating Calendar Entry Documents

When you create a new calendar entry, you are creating a new document in the mail database. Y can edit a calendar entry just as you would any other type of document. You can change the conte of a calendar entry at any time by opening it and making changes just as you would with any otl Notes document. You have the following options:

Opening a Calendar Entry With an entry selected, double-click to open the document. Ac tionally, a right-click displays the context menu for documents and from here you can choose Open menu item.

Editing the Entry With an entry selected, double-click to open the document and type an changes required. Additionally, a right-click displays the context menu for documents and fr here you can choose the Edit menu item.

Dragging and Dropping You can select and then drag and drop a calendar entry to a new d If time slots are visible, you can drag an entry into a specific time slot. When you move a calen entry, Notes will ask you to confirm the move.

You can also use calendar entries as the basis for other documents by using the Copy into New button in the calendar's button bar. Information from the calendar entry is copied into the new document you are creating. You can create a memo, another calendar entry, or a to do item using the copy into technique:

New Memo   Creates a new e-mail message with the subject from the calendar entry as the e-mail's subject and the description from the calendar entry as the text of the e-mail.

New Calendar Entry   Creates a new calendar entry of the same entry type, copying in all the fields. You can change the calendar entry type once the new calendar entry is created.

New To Do   Copies the subject from the calendar entry into the subject of the to do item.

Once you have created the new document, you can edit it at will without affecting the original.

You can use the Copy into New button without being inside the calendar entry document; select the item in the calendar and click the button.

Printing Your Calendar

Lotus Notes 6 sports a new interface for printing the calendar. To access the printing portion of the calendar, use any of the following methods with the calendar open:

◆   Print toolbar icon

◆   Ctrl+P keyboard shortcut

◆   File ➢ Print menu sequence

As you can see in Figure 6.26, the Print Calendar window is arranged using the tabbed interface that has been used in the rest of the calendar. There are three tabs: Printer, Page Setup, and Calendar Style.

FIGURE 6.26

Printing a calendar

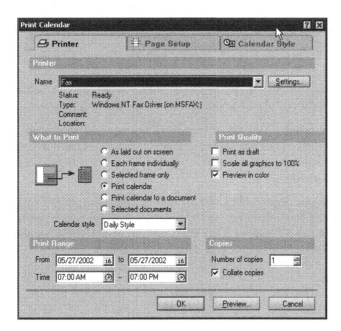

Printer   On the Printer tab, you can choose from a drop-down box of all accessible printers [] your computer. If a printer is installed for your operating system, it is included in this list in L[] Notes. In the middle of the screen, you can choose the printing quality, as well as what part of [] calendar you want to print and in what style. Table 6.4 describes the printing styles found on [] Printer tab of the Print Calendar dialog box.

NOTE   *The Calendar Style drop-down box on the Printer tab of the Print Calendar dialog box is different from [] Calendar Style tab, which deals with which information to visually lay out.*

TABLE 6.4: CALENDAR PRINTING STYLES

STYLE NAME	DESCRIPTION
Daily Style	One day per page, defaulting to the current day. Calendar entries are displaye[] a schedule format, with a row for each hour.
Weekly Style	One week per page, defaulting to the current week. Calendar entries are displa[] in a schedule format.
Work Week Style	A default five-day, Monday–Friday work week unless a different default has b[] setup to define the work week.
Monthly Style	One month per page, defaulting to the current month.
Rolling Style	Prints a range of weeks in week format inclusive of the start day and end day specified.
Calendar List	A simple list of all calendar entries for the specified period.
To Do List	Prints the to do list for the specified period.
Trifold Style	Daily, weekly, and monthly on one page in three panels; fits best on landscape[] paper.

At the bottom of the printing dialog box, you can choose a date and time range for which you w[] to print the calendar. You can also set the number of copies and collating option.

Page Setup   You can set page margins, page size, orientation, and paper source options on [] Page Setup tab. Page sizes range from the size of the paper in your printer to letter and legal, m[] envelope sizes, and a user-defined size. You also have the ability to start the printing at a partic[] page number.

Calendar Style   The Calendar Style tab lets you specify what information from your calen[] should be printed to paper and the styles that you want to apply. On this tab, you can specify [] print to a full page or 3 × 5 index cards or to one of the popular paper calendars on the mar[] including DayRunner, Day-Timer, and Franklin.

Using the To Do List

In addition to the mail area and the calendar area in the Notes mail client, one last piece of time-management information is stored in the mail database: the to do list. You can access the to do list from the default Welcome page (Basics) by clicking the To Do List icon. In addition, you can open it by doing one of the following:

◆ Select the To Do icon on the Bookmark bar along the left edge of the Notes client.

◆ Customize the Welcome page to display the to do list directly.

◆ From within the Mail area or the Calendar area, click the Mail or Calendar down-pointing arrow on the main banner at the top of the database; from there, choose Switch to To Do.

Once open, the to do list gives you a place to maintain a list of tasks you need to accomplish (see Figure 6.27).

FIGURE 6.27
To do list

To do items can be anything you want from something trivial that you simply don't want to forget to do down to something important such as filling out your time card. When you create a to do item, it is stored in the mail database as a document whose type and information is specific to a to do. So a to do item joins the ranks of the meeting documents and mail documents already stored in the mail database.

To do items contain the following types of information:

◆ Subject

◆ Person to which the task is assigned

◆ Due date

◆ Start date

◆ Whether the task repeats

◆ Priority

◆ Category

◆ Status ranging from not started, to in progress, to complete

◆ Text description that allows you to add file attachments

◆ Whether a dialog box should pop up to notify you of the item

◆ Whether the item should appear on your calendar or be kept private

Creating a To Do Item

If you're in the to do area, the easiest way to create a new to do is to use the New To Do Item bu
on the toolbar at the top of the screen. If you're in the mail area of the Notes client, the Copy
New button has a New To Do drop-down menu item that lets create a to do task based on an e-m
When you take this approach, the subject of the e-mail is copied to the subject of the to do item,
then the to do item opens for you to add any additional information.

When a to do item is created, it is added to the due date on your calendar so that you have a vi
reminder of the task. The tasks display in the calendar on the beginning of the day on their due c
as shown in Figure 6.28.

FIGURE 6.28

To do list in the
calendar

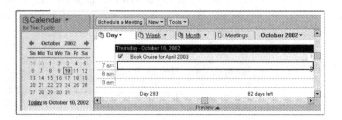

Like meeting and event documents, a to do item can be e-mailed to other people and added
their calendars as well. This is useful for to do items such as *Submit vacation schedules* that you might w
your staff to carry out at the beginning of the summer. This means there are really two types of to
items:

♦ Personal to do items for yourself

♦ To do items assigned to other people to accomplish

Personal To Do Items   A personal to do item is created when you choose the Myself radio but
in the Assign To area on the right side of the To Do Item screen, which is shown in Figure 6.2

FIGURE 6.29

A personal to do

Assigned To Do Items   You can assign a to do task to other people by selecting the Other
radio button visible (but not selected) in Figure 6.29. The list of participants includes those peo
who are required to do the task, those people for whom the task is optional, and those who a

receiving the task for informational purposes only (see Figure 6.30). On the right side of each of these fields, a clickable icon for the Domino Directory address book lookup is provided. Using the address book lookup, to do tasks map the To field to the Required field in a to do, the Cc field to the Optional field in a to do, and the Bcc field to FYI status. An assigned to do item appears in the All To Do's list with an icon showing multiple people, as well as the names of all people to which it was assigned.

FIGURE 6.30

Assigning a to do item

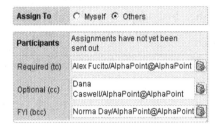

Managing To Do Items

The to do area consists of several views that will help make managing to do items easier. Each view shows a list of to do items that can be opened, edited, or deleted. A to do item also has an icon that appears to its left in the views indicating their priority: 1 is for high priority, 2 is for medium priority, and 3 is for low priority. A set of standard buttons displays at the top of every view when a to do item is selected. The Trash folder has buttons unique to its role in life: deleting to do items. Table 6.5 describes the standard views and folders. .

TABLE 6.5: VIEWS AND FOLDERS IN THE TO DO AREA

VIEW NAME	DESCRIPTION
All To Do's	Lists all to do items that have not been deleted whether they are complete or incomplete.
Personal	Shows a list of to do items you've assigned to yourself.
By Category	Using the Category field in the to do item itself, a categorized list of to do items is displayed; Category is a free-form text field, so you can type whatever you want as a category or pick from a list of provided categories.
Incomplete	A list of all items that do not have a status of Complete.
Completed	A list of all to do items that you've completed (but not deleted); an Unmark Completed button is available so that the status can be changed to reactivate the item.
Trash	Drag and drop to do items into this folder to delete them from the to do area; buttons in this area include Restore, Restore All, Delete Selected Item, Empty Trash, and Tools.

TIP *Click the view columns to resort the information according to how you would like to see it. For instance, to s[...] the Incomplete view by the Due Date column, click that column's header area. The items will resort themselves into ascer[...] ing or descending order depending on their starting sort order.*

As the last item in all of the views except Completed and Trash, a new feature of Lotus Not[...] is visible in Figure 6.27. The item is labeled *Ctrl-Click here to add a new document*. Doing this open[...] in-place editing to do item. This lets you create a new to do item without opening the To Do I[...] window and typing the specifics. Instead, you type the subject line of the To Do Item directly [...] the view itself and it is added to your to do list with a medium priority, a status of In Progress, a[...] assigned to yourself.

To process to do items, you use several standard buttons in the views:

◆ New To Do Item

◆ Mark Completed

◆ Delete

◆ Copy into New (memo, calendar entry, to do)

◆ Tools

WARNING *If you do not have a to do item selected, the only buttons that appear are New To Do Item and Tools*

Managing Assigned To Do Items

After you've selected the people you want to assign the task to using the Domino Directory add[...] book, you can save the task and send the assignments to the others with the click of a button. In y[...] list of to do items, tasks you've assigned to others appear in the All To Do's view. You can open th[...] do item and perform several item-management tasks using the options available in the Owner Acti[...] button: Reschedule, Cancel, Confirm, View Participant Status, and Send Memo to All Invitees.

When someone who you've assigned a task receives it in their Lotus Notes mail Inbox, it appe[...] with the To Do subject line preceded by the phrase *To do*, which distinguishes it from other type[...] e-mails. When opened, the document is labeled *Group To Do Item*, as shown in Figure 6.31, and [...] tains read-only information about the task, as well as action buttons to help them manage the t[...] you've assigned to them.

FIGURE 6.31

Receiving an assigned to do item

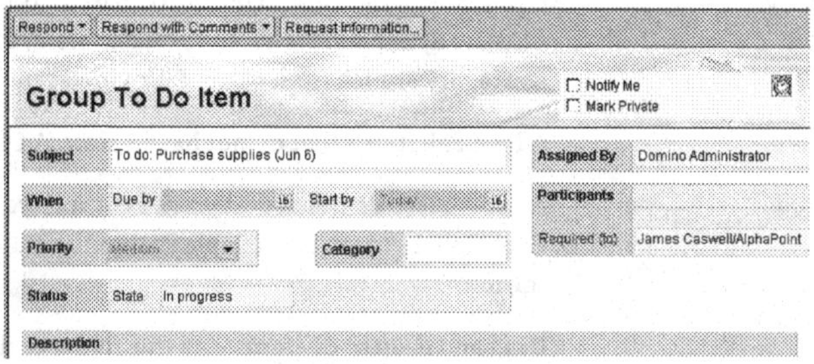

If you've had a task assigned to you, you can use the Respond button to accept the to do, decline it, delegate it to someone else, propose a new due date, or mark the item completed.

Similar actions are available with the Respond with Comments button, but it has the additional ability to let you type comments regarding the to do items that the sender will see. If you want more information about the to do task before using either the Respond or Respond with Comments button, use the Request Information button to send a prepared e-mail back to the person who assigned the task. This tight integration of the to do list with the e-mail system is one of Domino's strengths as a groupware product.

Granting Other Users Access to Your Calendar and Schedule

For the Domino scheduler and group calendars to work, you need to enable people to look at your calendar. You do this using the Access & Delegation tab of the Preferences area. You can get to this window using the buttons Tools ➤ Preferences and choosing the Access & Delegation tab. Beneath this tab, there are three other tabs: Access to Your Mail & Calendar, Access to Your Schedule, Shortcuts to Others' Mail. On the Access to Your Mail & Calendar tab, you specify the users and their privilege to your mail file and therefore your calendar. Figure 6.32 shows that the user Alex Fucito has been granted read, create, edit, and delete ability for any calendar entries or to do items. You can add people or groups to the list of authorized users with the Add Person or Group button. You set a user or group's access by using the Add Person or Group button or by using the Change Access button after setting the initial privileges.

FIGURE 6.32

Access to your mail and calendar

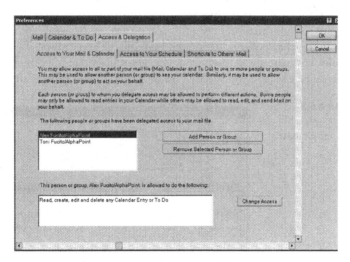

On the Access to Your Schedule tab, you specify who will be able to see the information on your schedule (see Figure 6.33).to see you calendar.

FIGURE 6.33

Allowing schedule access

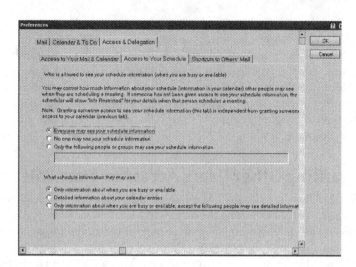

There are basically two levels of access you can grant to your calendar as well as to your to do

♦ Read Any Calendar Entry or To Do

♦ Read, Create, Edit and Delete Any Calendar Entry or To Do

The dialog box shown in Figure 6.34 opens when the Change Access button is clicked as well when a new person or group is initially granted access. In three steps, you choose how much acce to grant to your calendar, how much access to grant to a user within the file, and whether autom forwarding of calendar notices should take place. You can specify that meeting notices you rece should automatically go to someone else, you specify that responses for meetings you chair should to someone else, and you specify how to handle e-mails relating to private calendar entries.

FIGURE 6.34

Setting access to mail and calendar

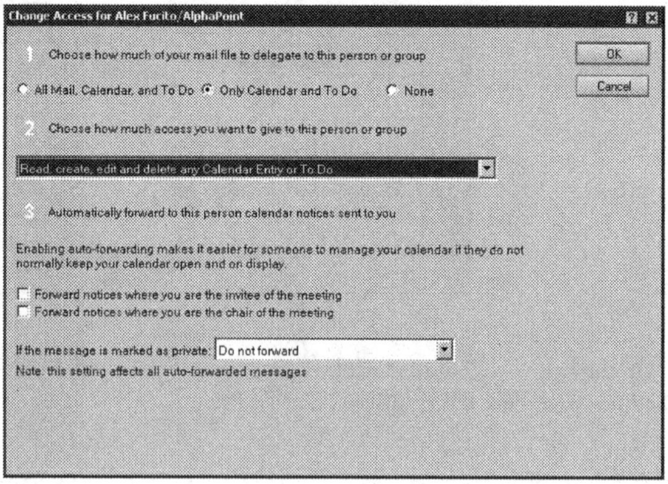

If a person has set up their calendar preferences in a way that allows you to work with their calendar, getting to their calendar is easy. From your own calendar, use the Calendar drop-down arrow and choose the option to open another person's calendar (see image below). When the calendar switches, the name of the person whose calendar it is will appear directly below the word *Calendar*. Because privileges on calendars are granted in pieces, you may find you can read the calendar but cannot add meetings to it or view items marked private.

WARNING   *Remember, you must be connected to a Domino server to switch to another person's calendar.*

Summary

Notes provides you with an appointment calendar that allows you to not only keep track of your own time commitments, but also to coordinate your time with others. Meeting invitations can be used to check on others' free time, invite them to meetings by e-mail, and reserve meeting rooms and other physical resources. Group calendars provide a means of keeping track of other people's individual calendars. To do items give you a method to construct lists of tasks that aren't bound to specific times but need to be tracked nonetheless; they also let you delegate tasks to other people. The tight integration of e-mail with calendaring, scheduling, and the To Do List showcases the power of Domino as a groupware tool. Coming up in the next chapter, we'll take a look at some of the other types of popular databases that can help you interact with the people on your team by sharing information in discussion databases and other collaborative databases.

Chapter 7

Collaborating with Notes

IN ADDITION TO BEING an integrated client for e-mail, personal and team scheduling, and web interaction, Notes is a runtime environment for collaborative applications. By definition, *collaboration* means working with other people and sharing information. These applications are represented as databases that have been created using the Domino Designer client. The pairing of collaboration and customized design is a powerful combination. It makes Lotus Notes a single, integrated environment for managing a wide range of information.

Notes ships with a set of off-the-shelf applications called *templates* for creating commonly used collaborative applications. For true collaboration, these applications are created on a Domino server, meaning that an application developer or a Domino administrator generally creates them. As a user, interactions with a collaborative application revolve around adding and sharing content with other people. In this chapter, we'll explore some of top collaborative databases that are based on Lotus Notes Domino technology.

- ◆ Collaborating through discussions
- ◆ Participating in a TeamRoom
- ◆ Managing a Document Library
- ◆ Using Microsoft Office Libraries
- ◆ Real-time interactions with Sametime
- ◆ QuickPlace collaboration
- ◆ Understanding mail-in databases
- ◆ Understanding collaboration issues

What's New in Notes 6 Collaboration?

Let's take a quick look at the new or enhanced features in Notes 6 collaboration:

- ◆ Updated color scheme in the discussion database
- ◆ Preview window for discussion database views

- Announcements page in the TeamRoom database
- TeamRoom security enhancements
- Ability to write individual status reports in the TeamRoom
- Ability to use the preview pane to peek at TeamRoom documents

Now that you have an idea of what's new, let's dive into collaborating through discussions.

Collaborating through Discussions

One of the most common applications for group collaboration is the threaded electronic discussion. Early examples of this were simple, text-based forums in bulletin board systems (BBSs). The Internet has its own version called *Usenet* (also known as *newsgroups*). Notes also has its own version referred to as *discussion databases*. A discussion database is a great application to roll out in an organization new to Lotus Notes because it shows the look and feel of a Notes application and showcases its collaborative ability.

The discussion database has been around since the inception of Notes. It provides an interface for creating new topics and responses to those topics (and responses to responses if needed). It is similar to other electronic discussions; one user posts questions or other information as a new topic, and other users respond with their input, or even their opinion. The Notes discussion also enables users to categorize topics, mark topics and responses as private, and include rich text.

NOTE   As a collaborative application, discussion databases should be created on a Domino server. After all, it would be a pretty lonely discussion if it were created on your personal computer and not accessible to anyone else!

The discussion database included with Notes is a fairly generic and free-form database, so it can be used for a variety of collaboration situations. Some of its more common uses include the following:

- Forums to discuss technical issues
- A repository for project-related communications
- A tool to brainstorm ideas
- A running commentary on a work-in-progress project

Opening a Discussion Database

You open a discussion database in the same way as other databases: using a bookmark, link, or menu. As a collaborative effort, a discussion database is normally stored on a server, so the only trick to opening this type of database is locating the correct server. In Figure 7.1, the Wine Tasting database on APS-Server01/AlphaPoint is selected and can be opened by clicking the Open button.

The first time you open a database, a single page of information displays describing the database. This is the About Database document. This document provides a quick overview of the purpose and intent of the database. All databases created using Lotus templates will have a completely filled out About Database document; custom databases created by other programmers may have one, as well.

In Figure 7.1, the About button is visible at the bottom-right corner of the Open Database dialog box. Clicking this button also opens the About Database document. Once the database is open, the document can be redisplayed using the menu sequence Help ➤ About This Database.

FIGURE 7.1

Opening a database

NOTE *A programmer can optionally set the About Database document to display every time a database is opened instead of just the first time.*

Navigating the Discussion Database

The discussion database is laid out with two primary frames, a frame on the left for navigating the information and a frame on the right for displaying the information. New in Notes 6 is the ability to click the Preview bar, visible at the bottom of the right frame in Figure 7.2, to peek inside the currently selected document without actually opening it.

FIGURE 7.2

Discussion database layout

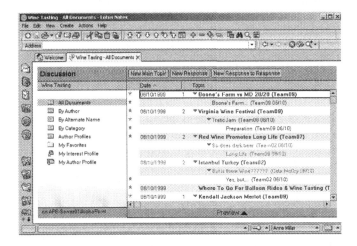

The left navigation pane contains a set of predefined views and folders:

◆   All Documents

◆   By Author

- ◆ By Alternate Name
- ◆ By Category
- ◆ Author Profiles
- ◆ My Favorites
- ◆ My Interest Profile
- ◆ My Author Profile

The All Documents view displays all the documents that have been created in the database and presents them in threaded format. The Notes terminology for a threaded discussion uses the phrase main topic documents and response documents.

RELATIONSHIPS BETWEEN DOCUMENTS

A threaded discussion view displays main documents aligned with one another and responses to main documents indented directly below the main document to show the relationship between two. This is also known as a *parent-child relationship* between documents, and the display hierarchy ally shows this relationship.

Refer back to Figure 7.2 and you can tell by inspection that the document with the subject *Wine Promotes Long Life* is a main document. The document with the subject *So does dark beer* is known as a response; below that, the document labeled *Long Life* is also a response—it just happens to a response to the previous response...what a mouthful! Along the top of the discussion database three buttons are visible corresponding to the types of related documents you can create. In Notes terminology, a discussion database (a threaded discussion) involves three types of documents

- ◆ Main document
- ◆ Response document
- ◆ Response to response document

The relationships between the documents are visible as a hierarchy in the All Documents view. This view displays the documents sorted in descending order by the date they were created. The most recent document created appears at the top of the list.

ICONS

A well-designed Notes view such as the All Documents view makes good use of colors, fonts, and ture icons to relay information and to trigger behavior. In the All Documents view in Figure 7.2, can see red stars in the view's margin area. The red star relays the information that you have not read this document. (The different color of the subject line also tells you this.) The red stars are called *unread marks*. For each person using the discussion database, Notes keeps track of whether they opened the document (one could suppose that you could open it and *still* not read it, but Notes is quite that good at tracking your behavior!). When you open the document, the red star disappears.

Another icon used in views, including the All Documents view, is the down-pointing triangle that appears on a document's subject line. This is a collapse/expand icon. When you click it, it will expand the list of documents to display all related documents. Click it again, and the list collapses. Meanwhile, the top-pointing caret in the Date column heading signals that you can click this column heading to sort the documents based on that column; if it started out in ascending order, clicking it would sort the documents into descending order, and vice versa.

You can use the toolbar to navigate between documents. Rolling your mouse over the toolbar will reveal the ToolTips for the navigation buttons (see Table 7.1).

TABLE 7.1: NAVIGATION USING THE TOOLBAR

BUTTON	TOOLTIP HINT	BEHAVIOR
⬇	Next Main	In a top-to-bottom technique, jumps to the next main document in the view list
⬆	Previous Main	In a bottom-to-top technique, jumps to the previous main document in the view list
⬇	Next	In a top-to-bottom technique, jumps to the next document in the view list
⬆	Previous	In a bottom-to-top technique, jumps to the previous document in the view list
⬇	Next Unread	In a top-to-bottom technique, jumps to the next document that has not yet been opened
⬆	Previous Unread	In a bottom-to-top technique, jumps to the previous document that has not yet been opened
✚	Expand	Expands a single category of collapsed documents
▬	Collapse	Collapses a single category of expanded documents
✚	Expand All	Expands all collapsed documents in the view
▬	Collapse All	Collapses all expanded documents in the view

In the All Documents view, additional information about the underlying documents is visible in the view without opening a document:

- Date the document was created.
- How many documents are in each hierarchy relationship.
- Subject of the document.
- Username of the person who created the document; this displays in parentheses at the end of the subject line.
- Date the response document was created; this also displays in parentheses at the end of the subject line.

NOTE *The designer or programmer chooses the information that displays in a view.*

You can determine how many documents are in a view by selecting all the documents. To do use the menu sequence Edit ➤ Select All; the number of documents that has been selected appea the status bar and reads something like *36 documents selected*. You want to turn off the selection r away, though, because you don't want to accidentally hit the Delete button! To reverse the selec process, use the menu sequence Edit ➤ Deselect All.

VIEW CATEGORIES

Each document in a discussion database contains a Category field. The person who creates the ument can type information in this field to help organize the documents around a category. As sh in Figure 7.3, a category can be a single word or several words. Each document that contains iden information in the Category field is what allows it to become grouped for display purposes.

FIGURE 7.3

Categories

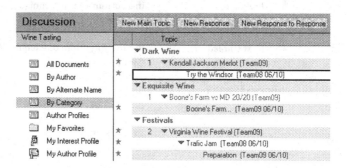

View categorization can happen in two ways. In the first way, a programmer can design a view t automatically creates a grouping based on any field in the document. The second way is using the ument's Category field, which is what the By Category view displays. In this view, you can change value of the Category field and therefore change how a document is grouped in this view. To change Category field, select a document and then choose Actions ➤ Categorize from the menu to disp the Categorize dialog box shown in Figure 7.4. A document can belong to multiple categories; it is p ically stored only once, but multiple category references can be added to it.

FIGURE 7.4

Categorizing a
document

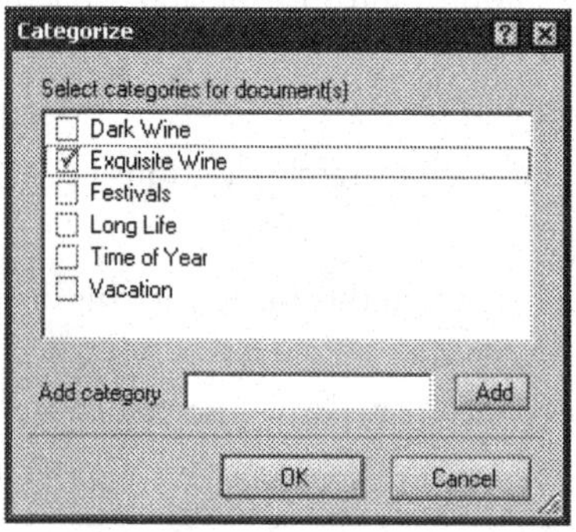

Using this dialog box, you can change the category to another that already exists in the Category field of one of the other documents, or you can add a new word or phrase to use as a category. You change the document's content by changing the Category field, and this updates the visual grouping.

The By Author view is an example of a view categorized based on a field chosen by the programmer (instead of the Category field). In this view, collapsible categories of documents are organized by the username of the person who first created or saved the document. This would be an easy way to see all the documents you have created in a discussion database. Similarly, the By Alternate Name view shows the author of a document using an alternate name if one was identified in the Domino Directory.

AUTHOR PROFILES

The Author Profiles view displays all Author Profile documents contained in the database. Author Profile documents are documents created by each author participating in the discussion to provide information about themselves; Figure 7.5 shows an author profile in edit mode. These documents help users determine who is participating in the discussion and their roles in the discussion. You should create an Author Profile document for yourself before participating in a discussion database. The special element, My Author Profile, links you directly to your own author profile. Author profiles also show up in the other views in the database.

FIGURE 7.5
Author profiles

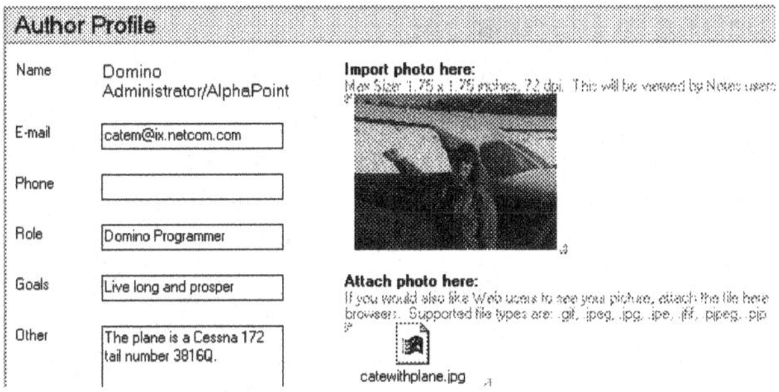

The My Interest Profile link brings up your interest profile for this database, which specifies the kinds of documents to notify you about when they are added; this is part of the newsletter service of the discussion database. Figure 7.6 shows an interest profile.

FIGURE 7.6
Interest profiles

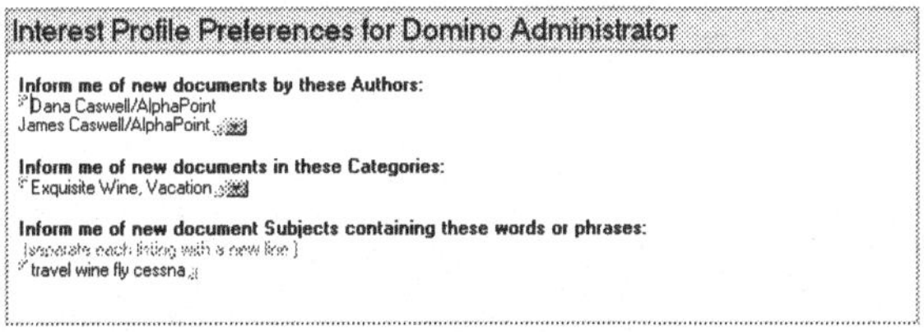

The newsletter process consists of automatic e-mails sent to notify you that documents of interest were added to the discussion that day. The newsletter service runs every night in a discussion database

and searches interest profiles for items to compile and mail as a newsletter. You can also take ad
tage of the subscription service that is part of Notes. Using the subscription service, you can subsc
to be updated of all changes to a database and receive the updates in your mail Inbox. You can
newsletters or subscriptions, not both.

TIP *If you use subscriptions, use the menu options Actions ➤ Convert My Interest Profile to a Subscription. This v
create the subscription profile and delete the interest profile.*

FOLDERS IN THE DISCUSSION DATABASE

The database template ships with one folder already created, the My Favorites folder. You can
it to keep track of specific documents in the database that you may want to quickly access later
you can with other folders in Notes, you can drag and drop documents into it or use the Action
Move to Folder menu.

WARNING *Remember, deleting an entry from the My Favorites folder actually deletes the document from the databa
To simply take it out of the folder and not delete it from the database, use Actions ➤ Remove from Folder instead.*

You can also create your own private folders in the database. To do this, use the Create
Folder menu.

Participating in Discussions

Just as we have demonstrated with mail messages, calendar entries, and to do list items, participa
in a discussion is a matter of creating documents. A discussion begins with the creation of a n
Main Topic document. From there, everyone joins in and responds to the topic. The forms for e
document provide the necessary fields to track the discussion. You can create new documents fr
the All Documents view, the By Author view, the By Alternate Name view, and the By Category vi
use the buttons at the top of the views. Figure 7.7 shows a New Main Topic document in edit mo
Main topics represent the central thread and major thought in a discussion. If you participate f
quently in a particular discussion, you might want to bookmark the Main Topic form so that you
quickly create new documents without even opening the database.

FIGURE 7.7

Main topic

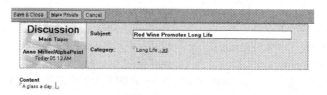

In the Subject area, you type something that meaningfully describes the topic of conversation. T
Category field, mentioned earlier, is a drop-down list of categories from existing documents, and you
add new ones on the fly. You can also specify more than one category for a document. The Content a
is an input area that you can add any type of information to : text, pictures, audio files, tables, Unifo
Resource Locators (URLs), and so on. Notes automatically generates the information about who
ated the document and when it was created and adds it to the top left.

When you're in edit mode, the buttons along the top let you save and exit the document, cancel the editing activity without saving, open the author's profile, or mark the topic private. The author's profile may not be very useful to you because you're the one creating the document! This button is intended more for documents that you read and you want to know more about the author.

If you click the Mark Private button, your Notes username is added to a special hidden field called a *Readers field*. Once the document is saved with the value of your user ID, that value in the Readers field will prevent anyone but you from accessing the document, which is one of the tightest security features offered in Domino.

WARNING   *If a document with a Readers field is stored in a database that replicates, the programmer and system administrator need to make sure the server's name appears in the Readers field as well so that the server can access the document in order to replicate it.*

When you are not editing or creating a new main topic but instead are reading one created by someone else, the buttons at the top of the document are different. They are Edit Document, New Response, and Cancel. The Edit Document may not appear if you do not have the appropriate security access to the database. Using the New Response button creates a parent-child relationship between the new document you are about to create (the child) and the one you are reading (the parent). By using this button, you are creating the relationship and therefore controlling the visual hierarchy that displays in the All Documents and By Category views.

Responding to Main Topics

When you are reading a main topic document or have one selected in one of the views but have not opened it yet, you can create a response to that document. This creates a parent-child relationship with the child being the document you are creating and the parent being the document you are reading or have selected. You can use either of the two response buttons to create a response document:

◆ New Response to Main

◆ New Response to Response

The difference between the two is which one will be the parent document. A main topic document can be a parent and so can a response document. Think of it as the grandchildren effect: You can be someone's father and someone else's child at the same time. This is the case with discussion documents. The button you choose determines the lineage as well as the visual hierarchy.

Once you are editing the response, the input form looks similar to the Main Topic form and contains a Subject field, a Category field, and a Content field. Like a Main Topic form, you can save and close the document, mark it private, check the author profile, or cancel out of it without saving.

One new field is added to a response document automatically. This is the Response To field. It contains a link to the parent document and the subject line of the parent document. This information will help you keep track of the threads of a discussion as you are creating new documents.

A new Response entry will be displayed in the discussion database's views. It will be located below the main topic for which it was created and indented slightly to show its place in the hierarchy. A small arrow displays next to the main topic, indicating that there are responses. Refer back to Figure 7.2 to see a complete document hierarchy again.

Archiving Discussion Documents

Any database can be archived. If an archive database has been created for a discussion database, vidual users can mark a document that they want archived. This will copy the document to the arc database and then remove it from the current discussion database. If the discussion database is hea used and generates many new documents every day, archiving will become a necessity to manage size and focus of the discussion.

To mark a document to be archived, you mark it as expired using the Actions menu. From h choose the Mark/Unmark Document as Expired option and set an expiration date. The marked ument will be archived the next time an archive runs. This means you can change your mind up the point the archive runs.

Participating in a TeamRoom

Discussion databases foster open, free-form interactions on a variety of topics, and a *TeamRoom* base takes a more focused approach to a topic. TeamRooms are for sharing the day-to-day prog regarding the goals and objectives of a group of people working together on a project.

Communication is key when multiple people are on a project. As the project takes on a life o own, the TeamRoom database becomes a living document of the progress of the team and the pro; The key benefit of using a TeamRoom database is that it becomes a repository for everyone invol in the project to share, store, and retrieve information about the project.

To create a new TeamRoom, use the TeamRoom template, `teamrm60.ntf`, which is located on server. The following steps will guide you in creating databases using templates:

1. Create a database using File ➤ Database ➤ New.

2. Choose the server with the template you want to use.

3. Select the appropriate template.

4. Click OK to create the new database.

Setting Up a TeamRoom

Creating a new database using the TeamRoom template automatically launches a setup routine, shown in Figure 7.8.

FIGURE 7.8
Kicking off
TeamRoom setup

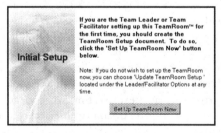

Clicking the Set Up TeamRoom Now button launches the TeamRoom setup document shown in Figure 7.9.

FIGURE 7.9
TeamRoom setup document

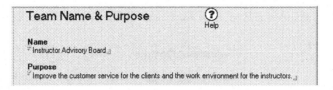

On the left side of Figure 7.9, a list of views or areas appears. Each of these is a component necessary to create the TeamRoom and support its approach to sharing information. To open the document associated with each, click a title. Let's look at the purpose of each of the documents.

Team name and purpose This document displays by default and allows you to define a name and purpose for the TeamRoom.

Team members Allows you to add and remove members for this TeamRoom. You can create a profile for each participant that includes a telephone number, an e-mail address, and other relevant information. You can also divide participants into subteams. For instance, in Figure 7.10, there are three team members. In a subteam, you might assign two of the three members to tackle a specific task. To be a member of a subteam, you must be a member of the team. After these teams are created, you can manage the team members using the Manage Lists button.

FIGURE 7.10
Team members

Categories Allows you to define categories for the documents that you post in the TeamRoom. For example, if the TeamRoom is for a marketing department, categories might include Sales, Public Relations, and Product Concepts.

Document Types Allows you to define the document types for documents in the TeamRoom. Document types determine the available fields on a TeamRoom document. The four default document types are Discussion, Action Item, Meeting, and Reference. A document may have reviewer information, priority settings, due dates, assigned to fields, meeting dates, and so on.

Milestones/Events   Allows you to define the important dates and events for the TeamRoom. This is building a timeline to measure the group's work.

Advanced Options   Allows you to activate monitoring agents to automatically send newsletters and reminders and to mark documents inactive based on an elapsed time (see Figure 7.11).

FIGURE 7.11
Advanced options

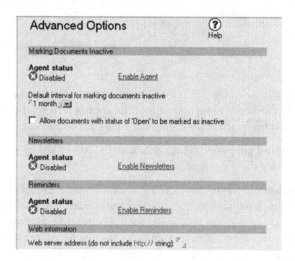

Participating in a TeamRoom

A TeamRoom consists of team documents created for sharing, as well as personal documents you create to keep yourself on track. When a TeamRoom is opened (every time except setup time), the announcements page displays. Figure 7.12 shows the navigation buttons on the left side of the TeamRoom announcements area and a list of announcements (only one for now) on the right. Announcements consist of a headline (like a subject line) and the content that should be read. The document is marked as either informational or must read. As documents lose their importance during the natural marching forward of time, it can be marked as active or inactive. Use the Set Status to Active button to change the status to Active.

FIGURE 7.12
TeamRoom
announcements

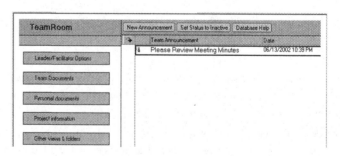

Use the buttons on the left side of the announcements page to get the best use out of the TeamRoom experience:

Leader/Facilitator Options   The task of leading a team involves organizing information as well as people. The options under this button, shown in Figure 7.13, include setting up the TeamRoom, creating status minutes, sending reminders, and controlling the security access for team members.

FIGURE 7.13
Leader/Facilitator
Options

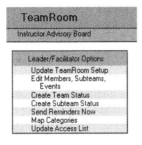

Team Documents   The heart of the TeamRoom is the information stored for the project at hand. The Team Documents button includes views of these documents, as shown in Figure 7.14, that sort them by date, category, subteam, author, due date, and status.

FIGURE 7.14
Team Documents

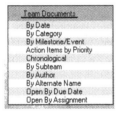

Personal Documents   As a member of team, you have tasks to do and items that get assigned to you. The Personal Documents button contains a set of views, shown in Figure 7.15, to help you stay on top of your assignments as they relate to the team.

FIGURE 7.15
Personal Documents

Project Information   Team announcements are a part of the overall project, and as such, they are the first item listed in the Project Information area (see Figure 7.16). Use the project area to get a feel for how the project as a whole is progressing by reading overviews, getting status reports, and accessing any document in the TeamRoom database.

FIGURE 7.16

Project Information

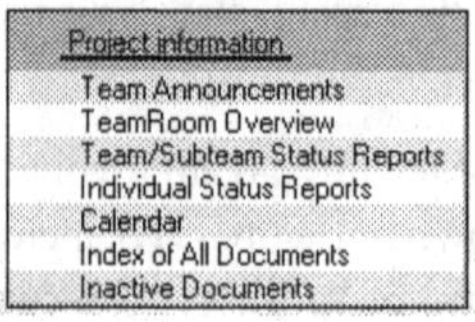

```
Project information
Team Announcements
TeamRoom Overview
Team/Subteam Status Reports
Individual Status Reports
Calendar
Index of All Documents
Inactive Documents
```

Other Views & Folders Personal views and folders that you create for your own use in
database.

Archiving TeamRoom Documents

Documents in a TeamRoom database can be archived just like those in a discussion database. If
TeamRoom is used over a period of years, this may be necessary. For projects whose lifespan is sho
than a year, archiving is usually not necessary and has the advantage that all the information regard
the project is stored in one database the entire time.

The process of marking documents as expired using the Actions menu and the Mark/Unma
Document as Expired option is identical to the discussion database. Set an expiration date, and
next time an archive runs, the marked document will be copied to the archive database and dele
from the active TeamRoom database.

Using Document Libraries

Notes 6 includes a prebuilt template called the *Document Library*. It is also referred to as the *I
Library—Notes & Web (R6)* database. The concept behind this application is that you can store d
uments in a central place so that others can use them as well as route them through Domino's e
tronic message system.

TIP *To create a new Document Library database, use the Doc Library—Notes & Web (R6) templa*
doclbw6.ntf.

The Document Library contains topics and responses in a similar manner as a discussion datab
The topics are the containers for documents stored in the Document Library, and the responses
vide comments or feedback. The Document Library also enables users to categorize topics and m
topics/responses as private. The Document Library, when hosted on a Domino server, can be u
by web clients as well.

The Document Library incorporates an optional generic review cycle for documents. When
ating new documents, you can choose who should be reviewers and how the process should oper
You can establish serial and parallel review cycles, set time limits for reviewers, and enable notificat
after each reviewer or after just the final reviewer. (Serial reviews occur when the document is
sented to each reviewer one at a time before being sent to the next reviewer. Parallel reviews oc
when the document is presented to all reviewers at the same time, they make their recommendatic
simultaneously, and the results are saved back to the database.) The review cycle provides a sim
workflow for documents added to the Document Library.

The look and feel of the Document Library is similar to the discussion database (see Figure 7.17). Use the navigation area in the left frame to choose documents to display in the right frame. Please review the section *Participating in Discussions* earlier in this chapter for more information on main topic documents, responses, and response to responses.

FIGURE 7.17
Document Library

Navigating the Document Library Database

The Navigation pane contains a set of predefined views and folders, including:

◆ All Documents

◆ By Author

◆ By Alternate Name

◆ By Category

◆ Review Status

◆ My Favorites

The All Documents, By Category, and Review Status views display documents and their associated responses the same way as a discussion database. The only difference between the views is the order in which the documents are sorted. These views also display responses as a hierarchy with each response positioned directly below its parent. The All Documents view displays the documents by the date they were entered, with the latest ones presented at the top of the view. The By Category view displays the documents categorized by the value(s) entered in the documents' Category field. Just as with the discussion database, a small arrow will be displayed to the left of each Category header, indicating that there are documents contained within that category. Within each category, the documents and their responses are displayed in the order they were entered.

The Review Status view displays the documents categorized by the document's current review status. A document can be in one of three review states:

◆ New

◆ In Review

◆ Review Complete

A small arrow to the left of each Review Status header indicates that this is a set of categorized documents. Within each Review Status category, the documents and their responses are displayed in the order they were entered and in a hierarchy showing a parent-child relationship.

The By Author view lists each document categorized by the author's name. The By Alternate Name view lists the document's authors' alternate names that are defined in the Domino Directory.

My Favorites is a folder included in the Document Library database. You can use it to keep t of specific documents in the database that you may want to quickly access later. As with other fol in Notes, you can drag and drop documents to it or use the Actions menus.

WARNING   *Remember, if you delete entries from the My Favorites folder, the actual document will be deleted from database. If you want to retain the document, select Actions ➤ Remove from Folder instead.*

Creating Document Library Entries

With the Document Library database open, you can create a new document in the following two v

- ◆ Select Create ➤ Document.
- ◆ Select the New Document button at the top of any view.

For frequently used Document Libraries, you can also create a bookmark to the new Docum form so you can create new documents without even opening the database. When you create a document, a blank new Document form will be displayed, as shown in Figure 7.18.

FIGURE 7.18

Document Library
document

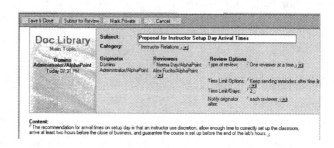

At the top of the database area, you'll see four buttons at the top of the form:

Save & Close   Saves the new document and closes the form after you are finished entering information.

Submit for Review   Initiates the review cycle for this document.

Mark Private   Adds your Notes username to a special hidden field called a Readers field. Once document is saved, the value of this field prevents anyone but you from accessing the documen

Cancel   Closes the form without saving the new document.

The new Document form contains the following fields:

- ◆ Subject
- ◆ Category
- ◆ Content
- ◆ Review Options

You can complete just the fields you need. Although it is not required, you should always ent subject so you know what the entry is for when it is displayed in the views. The Category field in new Document form is similar to the one in the new Main Topic form of a discussion database, wh was covered earlier in this chapter. This field can contain multiple values, which you can enter in the field or choose from the Select Keywords dialog box. To display the Select Keywords dialog box, click the arrow button to the right of the Category field. This Keywords list is generated from the current set of Document Library topics in the database. You can also add new categories in the New Keywords field. Just separate each value with a comma. The Content field is a rich-text field and can contain a wide variety of information, including formatted text, tables, pictures, objects, URLs, and attached files.

Creating Document Library Responses

You can create a response document with either the document open or the document selected in a view. You might create a response document if you wanted to comment on the content of the original document without changing that document. Because a review document becomes a child document to the original, you are guaranteed of being able to keep track of the document relationships. With the Document Library database open, you can create a new response or response to response document in the following two ways:

♦ Select Create ➤ Response.

♦ Click the New Response at the top of any of the views.

The information you need to supply for a response document includes a new subject and new content. An automatic reference is added to the parent document and the original category.

Setting Up the Review Cycle

The Document Library database includes a basic review cycle in the Document form. You can create a document in the Document Library database and have other individuals review and edit it. The review cycle can be serial or parallel. Serial reviews occur when the document is presented to each reviewer one at a time before being sent to the next reviewer. Parallel reviews occur when the document is presented to all reviewers at the same time, they make their recommendations simultaneously, and the results are saved back to the database. The cycle you should use depends on your needs. If you don't want to wait for any single reviewer, the parallel review may be more appropriate. When you want to be certain that a reviewer sees all cumulative reviews before responding, the serial review may be more appropriate. Refer back to Figure 7.18 to view the document review form.

This is a document intended to be mailed and processed by other people, so there are several fields on the document (see Table 7.2).

TABLE 7.2: DOCUMENT LIBRARY FIELDS

FIELD	PURPOSE
Subject	One-line description of document topic
Category	Brief grouping for document
Originator	The author of the document
Reviewers	Notes usernames of all people who will be reviewing the document

Continued on next page

TABLE 7.2: DOCUMENT LIBRARY FIELDS *(continued)*

FIELD	PURPOSE
Type of Review	One reviewer at a time or all reviewers simultaneously
Time Limit Options	No time limit; move to next reviewer if time is up regardless of approval status; s͏ reminders until status changes
Time Limit/Days	Number of days each reviewer is given without being harassed with e-mail remin͏
Notify Originator After	Send an e-mail to the originator after the final reviewer signs off or after each revie͏ signs off
Content	The document free-form input area

There are also special buttons included on the Document form for controlling the review cy͏ When a new document is being created, the Form Action bar will include the Submit for Rev͏ button, which you can click after entering the names of the reviewers and the review cycle optio͏ What happens next depends on the type of review cycle you chose. If you chose the review ty͏ One Reviewer at a Time, the following will occur:

1. An e-mail message is sent to the first reviewer, and a dialog box appears indicating that this occurred (see Figure 7.19).

FIGURE 7.19
Reviewer
confirmation

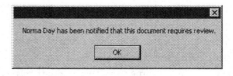

2. Another new document is created for review, and the original is saved as a response to the ͏ document. Only the originator can edit the original document saved as a response docum͏

3. The first reviewer is listed as the current reviewer.

4. The first reviewer opens the document to be reviewed either by clicking the document li͏ mailed to him or by opening the Document Library database and selecting the appropria͏ document.

5. The reviewer switches to edit mode to make changes to the document. At this point, only ͏ current reviewer and the originator have edit capability.

6. If the originator edits the document, a Clear Review Cycle button displays on the Form Act͏ bar. Clicking this button will clear the review cycle.

7. If the reviewer edits the document, a My Review Is Complete button displays on the For͏ Action bar. Clicking this button will initiate action that removes the reviewer from the Curr͏ Reviewer list, updates the review history maintained on the document, and closes the docume͏

At this point, this particular individual cannot edit the document. Notifications are sent via e-mail as follows:

- ◆ If there are more reviewers, the next reviewer is notified.

- ◆ If the document had the Notify Originator After option set to Each Reviewer, the originator is notified that this review has been completed.

- ◆ If this is the last reviewer, the originator is notified that the review cycle is complete.

8. Notification dialog boxes are displayed, indicating which e-mails were sent.

9. The next reviewer is listed as the current reviewer.

This continues until all reviewers have completed their review or the originator clears the review cycle. In either case, the document returns to a state where only the originator can edit it.

If you chose the review type All Reviewers Simultaneously, the following will occur:

1. An e-mail message is sent to all reviewers, and a dialog box appears for each individual, indicating that this has occurred.

2. Another new document is created for review, and the original is saved as a response to the new document. Only the originator can edit the original document saved as a response document.

3. All reviewers are listed as current reviewers.

4. Any of the reviewers can open the document to be reviewed by clicking the document link mailed to them or by opening the Document Library database and selecting the appropriate document.

5. The reviewer switches to edit mode to make changes to the document. At this point, all current reviewers and the originator have edit capability. Later, their changes will be merged.

6. If the originator edits the document, a Clear Review Cycle button displays on the Form Action bar. Clicking this button will clear the review cycle.

7. If the reviewer edits the document, a My Review Is Complete button displays on the Form Action bar. Clicking this button will initiate action that removes the reviewer from the Current Reviewer list, updates the review history maintained on the document, and closes the document. At this point, this particular individual cannot edit the document. Notifications are sent via e-mail as follows:

- ◆ If the document had the Notify Originator After option set to Each Reviewer, the originator is notified that this review has been completed.

- ◆ If this is the last reviewer, the originator is notified that the review cycle is complete.

8. Notification dialog boxes are displayed, indicating which e-mail notifications were sent.

This continues until all reviewers have completed their review or the originator clears the review cycle. In either case, the document returns to a state where only the originator can edit it.

Using a Microsoft Office Library

Do you use Microsoft Word, Excel, PowerPoint, or Paintbrush to create files? Do you save those someplace on your hard drive and hope to find them again someday? The goal of the Microsoft Office Library database is to help you get your Microsoft documents organized and apply a level security when accessing them.

TIP *To create a new Microsoft Office Library, use the Microsoft Office Library (R6) template,* doc1bm6.ntf.

The Microsoft Office Library database is similar to the Document Library database except includes additional integration with Microsoft Word, Excel, PowerPoint, and Paint. In fact, you create these types of documents from within Lotus Notes while in a Microsoft Document Libr This enables you to work with applications with which you are familiar and still take advantage Notes' ability to manage your data. Like the Document Library discussed earlier, the Micros Office Library supports document categorization, public/private documents, and document rev cycles. Also, you can take advantage of all of Notes' features because the Microsoft documents embedded within Notes documents.

You can perform the following tasks:

◆ Organize documents in folders.

◆ Find documents using Notes' built-in full-text search engine.

◆ Archive documents.

◆ Secure documents using Notes' database Access Control Lists (ACLs).

◆ Work offline with replicated databases.

In addition to the standard new document, new response, and new response-to-response ty of buttons we've seen in other collaborative databases, the Microsoft Office Library includes additional button to create a Microsoft Office document. The New MS Office Document butt includes a menu from which you can choose the type of Microsoft Office document you would l to create (see Figure 7.20).

FIGURE 7.20

Creating Microsoft
Office documents

You can also create new documents using the Create ➢ MS Office Document menu. As the N MS Office Document button does, this menu lets you choose which type of Microsoft Office c ument you would like to create. Having Microsoft Office installed on your machine is a requirem for this to work. When you create a new Microsoft Office document in the Microsoft Office Libr template, a Notes form is displayed with only an embedded object for the selected application. F ure 7.21 shows a Notes document with an embedded Microsoft Word document.

FIGURE 7.21

Embedded Word
document

There are no other fields displayed on the form; in this case it is simply an editing window for Microsoft Word. The buttons at the top allow the following processing of a Microsoft document that is embedded in a Notes document:

Save & Close   Saves the new document and closes the form after you are finished entering the information.

Mark Private   Adds your Notes username to a special hidden field called a Readers field. Once the document is saved, the value of this field prevents anyone but you from accessing the document.

Setup Review Cycle   Presents a form so that you can start a review cycle for this document by choosing a parallel or serial review, the number of days each reviewer should be given, and when the originator should be notified. Figure 7.22 displays the starting form for the review cycle.

FIGURE 7.22

Review cycle

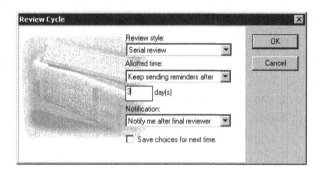

Properties   Create a subject line and categories for the document, as shown in Figure 7.23.

FIGURE 7.23

Document
properties

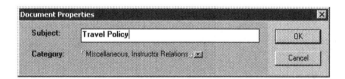

Cancel   Closes the form without saving the new document.

You can enter information in the embedded object the same way you would if the application running. The difference is that the Notes application window is still active, but the embedded obj menus and toolbars are displayed. The embedded object behaves the same way it does when you cr Object Linking and Embedding (OLE) objects in rich-text fields, which is explained in Chapte "Tailoring Lotus Notes 6."

The Microsoft Office Library template is designed for the Notes client only. If you are plann to collaborate with web browser users (using Domino server), use the Document Library templ instead. It is designed to support web browser users in addition to Notes users.

Real-Time Messaging with Sametime

If you have teenage children or know teenage children, the phrase *instant message* is probably a fam one. The concept of being able to send an instantaneous message to someone who is connected to Internet gained popularity with Netscape and AOL, but it's been given corporate respectability security from IBM and Lotus with the Sametime product.

Sametime allows real-time conversations with another Internet or Intranet user. This form of laboration tracks very closely with what we do in an office environment. If we have a question, walk down the hall and ask the guy or gal who knows the answer. With Sametime, the ability to s off a quick question or comment brings the workplace closer to the remote worker.

A variety of different messaging types can be transmitted between users on Sametime. This is done in a secure environment where users must log on to be seen by and interact with other use Types of information that can be shared in real-time mode include the following:

- ◆ Audio clips
- ◆ Chat sessions involving multiple select people but blocking other people
- ◆ Live documents that are currently being edited by Sametime users
- ◆ Online collaborative meetings
- ◆ Stored documents
- ◆ Text messaging
- ◆ Video files

When you're logged onto a Sametime server, you can see a list of other logged-on users and communicate with any of them. Sametime also offers the ability to temporarily control another us screen (if they allow it), which is useful to help-desk personnel trying to troubleshoot problems remote users.

NOTE *Sametime is an add-on product that integrates with Domino's address book. A separate server and licensing required.*

Collaborating with QuickPlace

QuickPlace is the enterprise edition of the TeamRoom database that is geared for secure web-ba collaboration. The concepts are the same, but the audience is larger and can encompass people in nal to a company, company suppliers, and outside individuals. The idea behind QuickPlace is th knowledge evolves from communication, and to have communication in a world where peop infrequently see each other, good online tools are needed. Communication is both structured and unstructured, including everything from the project agenda that someone agonized over creating down to the casual tidbit learned at the office water cooler. QuickPlace handles both types of communication. The goal of the tool is to share information and coordinate actions to make progress and decisions happen.

The features of QuickPlace include the following:

◆ Creating a secure place to collaborate, known as a *custom place*

◆ Discussion forums

◆ E-mailing members and groups

◆ Managing the numerous electronic documents produced in workgroups

◆ Movement of electronic documents between users for sequential or parallel approval and changes

◆ Sharing personal calendar information to coordinate schedules

You can use QuickPlace and Sametime together to combine the central repository nature of a stored database with the instantaneous conversations needed to interact most effectively.

NOTE   *QuickPlace is an add-on product that runs on its own server.*

Using Mail-in Databases

A Domino system administrator can assign an e-mail address to a Notes database so that it can receive mail. Any database that has been configured to do this can receive e-mail, making it a great collaboration tool as it acts as a receiver of central information. As a quick example of this, recall the last time you participated in an anonymous opinion survey. When you finished filling out the form and sent it on its way, it was e-mailed to a central location along with everyone else's response; it was *not* sent to an individual. The ability to send an e-mail or document to a database instead of a person is called a *mail-in database* in Domino.

With this feature, you can e-mail documents to discussion databases, Document Library databases, or other Notes databases that reside on a Domino server. This is a great way to collect information without a great deal of effort. Whatever you can e-mail can be sent to a mail-in database. The discussion database is commonly used as a mail-in database because it has a free-form structure. For example, you can use a discussion database as a mail-in database for collecting messages from Internet-based list servers.

List servers are automated mailers that send messages to individuals who subscribe to them. Usually, they are focused on specific topics, such as technologies, medical conditions, or political interests. There are also many news-oriented list servers. You can use the e-mail address of the mail-in database to subscribe to list servers. When the message is sent to the Domino server, it delivers the message to the mail-in database instead of to a mail database.

Issues with Collaboration Usability

Being able to share information with a wide audience is a good thing; the problem is that because you don't know who your audience is, there are several usability issues you should consider before creating or working with a collaboration database.

Security

When you use Notes databases on a Domino server for collaboration purposes, the rights and ~~priv~~ileges you have in the database will be dictated by the ACL you have been granted. If you created ~~a~~ database or are the owner of it, you would normally have Manager access, meaning you can do all t~~hings~~ in the database. If you're not the owner and you're just using or collaborating in a database you ~~did~~ not create, your access privileges will be limited. Usually, you will have Author access to a collab~~ora~~tion database. This means you can create new documents or topics and respond to existing ones, ~~but~~ you cannot modify content added by other users.

You can check to see what access privilege you have to a database that you are currently i~~n by~~ checking the status bar in the Notes client. The security icon is the third icon from the right on ~~the~~ status bar and looks like a key. Move your mouse over it to locate it, and then click the arrow to o~~pen~~ the Groups and Roles dialog box shown in Figure 7.24. From here, you can tell your access privi~~leges~~ and determine if you are a member of any special groups or roles in the database.

FIGURE 7.24

Checking the ACL

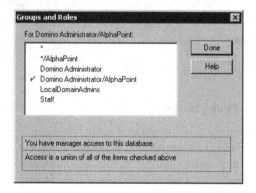

Web users cannot check their security level. They can, however, be issued user IDs and passwo~~rds~~ to log in to secure databases.

File Attachments

When collaboration databases are stored on a Domino server and configured to allow web brow~~ser~~ access, users with a web browser installed on their computer can create new documents, respond to e~~xist~~ing documents, and even participate in review cycles. Most of the functionality is the same betwee~~n a~~ Notes client and a browser client, but there are some differences that are primarily related to how att~~ach~~ment content displays.

If the information comes from an external source, such as a Word document, and is large or need~~s to~~ retain complex formatting, it can be attached to a document as a file. This way, the web browser users ~~can~~ save the file to their own computer in its native format. The downside is that all web browser users n~~eed~~ the application software in which the attachment was created to be present on their computer.

For this reason, be careful to attach only files saved in a popular file format or one you know y~~our~~ intended audience has. The discussion database and Document Library database allow both No~~tes~~ and web users to attach and detach (save) files. Microsoft Word format is a good type of file atta~~ch~~ment because most personal computers have a version of Word installed. There is even a Word ~~viewer~~

viewer that can be downloaded from the Microsoft website for users who don't have Word installed on their computer. Adobe Acrobat (PDF) is another good format; any web user can download a free Adobe file viewer. Documents created in Hypertext Markup Language (HTML) are also a good file attachment alternative because every web browser can view an HTML file.

Summary

Lotus ships its Domino product with several built-in applications to get any organization up and going quickly with collaborative groupware. In this chapter, we've looked at how to have discussions, participate in project-oriented team rooms, create document libraries for Notes documents and Microsoft documents, and send mail to mail-in databases. Key to all collaboration in Notes is the concept of main documents and response documents, as well as the review cycle process that is implemented in many of the Lotus templates. With the increasing amount of information Lotus Notes puts at your fingertips with collaborative databases, you'll need to be able to sift through it quickly to find what you need. In the next chapter, we'll learn about search techniques that can be used in any database including the ones we've learned about in this chapter.

Chapter 8

Searching for Information

COLLECTING AND STORING INFORMATION is great, but to be useful, you also need to be able to find the information with the touch of a few keys. Once you start using Notes to communicate via e-mail, organize your personal information, or participate in electronic discussions (and other collaborative applications), you will begin to accumulate a great deal of information in Notes databases. Notes includes powerful search features that enable you to find information stored in a view, in a single database, in multiple databases, in files on the file system, and on the Internet. Figure 8.1 illustrates the breadth of Domino's search capability.

- Searching for text in on-screen documents

- Searching for text in on-screen views

- Searching for documents in views

- Searching a domain

- Searching the Internet

Conducting On-Screen Searches

Notes can search for information from the smallest possible target, a single document, to the largest of targets, the Internet. Figure 8.1 depicts the scope of searching in Domino.

Notes can help you search the currently open document or view for text strings. If you're editing a document, you can also perform search-and-replace searches. Notes makes this feature available anytime you are looking at a document or view on the screen. You can also search for text strings within mail messages, to do list entries, discussion topics, web pages, newsgroup topics, and anything else that appears on a Notes' screen.

FIGURE 8.1
Search targets

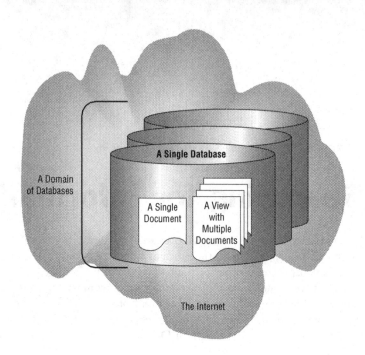

Searching Documents

To search for a text string within a document, follow these steps:

1. Open the document you want to search so that you're viewing it on the screen.
2. Use the menu sequence Edit ➤ Find/Replace to open the Find Text in Document dialog shown in Figure 8.2.

FIGURE 8.2
Finding text in a document

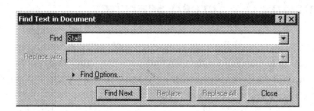

3. In the Find input box, type a word or phrase as the focus of the search.
4. Click the Find Next button.

If the text string is found, Notes will navigate to the area in the document where it was found and highlight the entire search string. You can click the Find Next button again to find additional occurrences of the text string, or you can click the Close button to close the Find Text in Document dialog box. If the text string is not found, a dialog box will be displayed indicating it was not found.

When a document is open for viewing, the Find Text in Document dialog box can also be opened in any one of the following ways:

- Click the Search button in the toolbar (its icon resembles a magnifying glass).
- Click the down-pointing arrow to the right of the Search button in the toolbar and use the Find Text option on the Search menu.
- Press the keyboard combination Ctrl+F.

You can also use the Find Text in Document dialog box to replace a single occurrence of a word or phrase as well as replacing all occurrences of the word or phrase; use the Replace or Replace All buttons as appropriate.

You can fine-tune your search using the Find Options toggle arrow (shown in Figure 8.2). When clicked once, the Find Text in Document dialog box expands to display additional search option check boxes; when clicked again, the area collapses and is hidden from view. To enable any or a combination of the options, click the appropriate check box:

Case Sensitive   Instructs Notes to search for text in which the capitalization matches the exact capitalization of the text you entered. If this option is not enabled, Notes will find all occurrences of the text you entered regardless of capitalization.

Accent Sensitive   Instructs Notes to search for extended or foreign characters when you enter criteria that include extended or foreign characters. If the Accent sensitive option is not enabled, Notes searches for extended or foreign characters even if the criteria only include regular characters.

Whole Words   Instructs Notes to search for the text you type with a blank space before and after the text. This forces the search to look for the words and phrases exactly as you typed them, and not embedded within other words or phrases. For example, a search for the word *cat* would not be found in the word *catalog*.

Direction   You can choose to search forward or backward in the document by selecting the Forward or the Backward in this drop-down box. Your direction choice remains in effect for the entire Notes session; options reset when a new Notes session is opened.

Wrap at Start/end   Instructs Notes to cycle back to the top of the document (or to the bottom of the document if you are searching backward) and continue searching after finding all occurrences of the text you entered. Disabling this option causes Notes to stop searching when it reaches the top or bottom of the document depending on the search direction.

Have you ever needed to search for a special character, like the ä (a German umlaut, whose pronunciation is similar to the English letter *a* in the word *cat*)? Special characters can be used in the Lotus Notes Find Text in Document dialog BOX with the help of the Character Map, a special Windows utility program. To use the Character Map in Windows 2000, do the following:

1. Use the menu sequence Start ➤ Programs ➤ Accessories ➤System Tools ➤ Character Map. If your operating system is not Windows 2000, the surest way to run the utility without needing to know the menu sequence is to use Start ➤ Run, enter **charmap**, and click the Open button.

2. From the grid presented, click the character you want to enter in the search, and then click the Select button to add the character to the input box.

3. Click the Copy button to copy the special character to the Windows Clipboard, and then close the Character Map.

4. Back in Lotus Notes, in the Find Text in Document dialog box, paste the character(s) into the Find field using the Ctrl+V keyboard sequence, and click the Find Next button to begin the search.

You can also type special characters using unique keyboard sequences. For instance, ä is identified with the keyboard sequence Alt+0228, meaning if you hold down the Alt key on the keyboard and then press the numbers 0228 sequentially on the numeric keypad, the ä will appear on your screen. You will need to have Num Lock on when typing the number. To find out what the keyboard sequence is for a special character, use the Windows Character Map utility; it displays the keystroke number in the lower-right corner of its dialog box after you select it from the grid. There is a caveat with this technique: if a document contains multiple font styles, say one which is Wingdings, a copy of the character when pasted in the Find edit box will show the ascii character. A search will yield all of the instances of the ascii character in addition to the special Wingding character you are seeking.

Searching Views

When you're displaying a view in Notes, you're limited to seeing a few words and phrases in column format with each row representing a document. You can use a variation of the Find Text in Document dialog box to find a word or phrase in the information displayed by the view. The menu sequence Edit ➤ Find/Replace opens the Find dialog box, as shown in Figure 8.3.

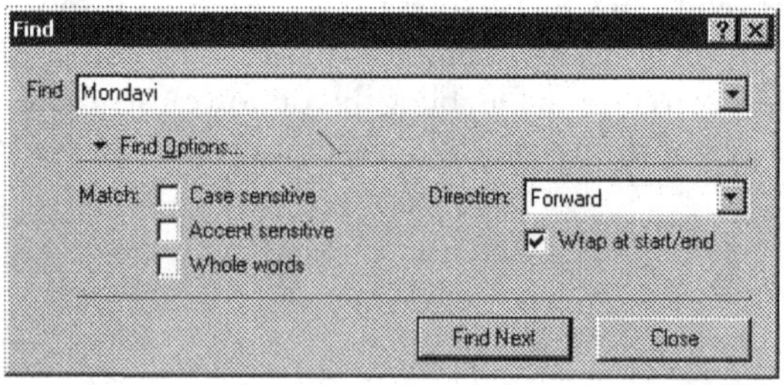

FIGURE 8.3
Finding text
in a view

All the options described previously in the Find Text in Document dialog box are identical, including the ability to search for special characters. The only difference is that you are searching the on-screen version of the view. For instance, Figure 8.3 is searching for the word *Mondavi*. Unless this word is included in the text displayed by the view, it will not be found by the search. Contents of documents are not searched with this technique.

WARNING *This technique does not search for information within the documents of the view; it searches only what is visible on the screen in the view.*

Searching the Contents of Documents

You can search the contents of multiple documents simultaneously using views and folders in Notes. Views and folders are collections of documents, and they can present all documents contained within a database or a subset of a documents in a database. They display collections of documents in an organized manner. Data from each document is presented in a row/column format, and the rows can be categorized for easier navigation. You can search for a word or phrase in a set of documents using views and folders.

A search of a view or folder is the equivalent of looking through the contents of the documents to return the set of documents that match your word or phrase criteria. The search can be based on simple criteria such as a single word or more sophisticated criteria that includes Boolean logic. All views in any Notes database can be searched, including the following:

- Your mail database (to find e-mail messages, calendar entries, or to do list entries)
- Your personal address book database (to find contacts or groups)
- Discussion databases (to find topics and responses)
- Document Library databases (to find documents)

A search of a view or folder searches only the documents referenced in that view or folder. If you need to search all documents in a database, you can create a view that includes all documents. Otherwise, you'll have to repeat your search in multiple views.

Performing Simple Searches

You can search for a text string contained anywhere in a document. We call this a *simple search*, and we use the search bar to perform the search. To open the search bar from within a database, open the view you want to search. Then, click the Search button on the toolbar or use the menu sequence View ➤ Search This View.

The search bar displays above the view you are about to search. Figure 8.4 shows the search bar at the top of the All Documents view.

FIGURE 8.4

Displaying the search bar

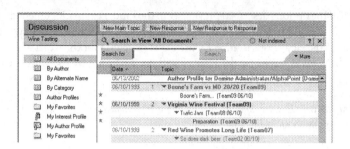

You start a simple search by typing the word or phrase you're looking for in the Search For on the search bar and clicking the Search button (or pressing the Enter key). In Figure 8.5, docum are searched for the word *Mondavi*, and a list of two documents is returned.

FIGURE 8.5

Searching documents

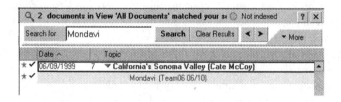

The result of the search is a list of all documents that match the criteria. Only the documents taining the text string you entered will be displayed in the search results. Each document will ha check mark to the left of it indicating that the search word or phrase was found in the docume Notice in Figure 8.5 that the word *Mondavi* appears on the view for one of the documents but not the other. Remember that using the search bar looks for the word or phrase in the content of the ument, not on the visible part of the view. The first document contains the word *Mondavi* in its tents but does not contain it as part of the visible view; the second document contains the word the document and on the view.

Search results are a temporary list of documents that meet your criteria. You can return to the v you were searching by clicking the Clear Results button to redisplay all documents in the view.

Full-Text Indexes

A database can be indexed to make a search both more comprehensive and more efficient. Note technique of indexing a database is called a *full-text index*.

DETERMINING WHETHER AN INDEX EXISTS

There are two ways to determine whether a database is full-text indexed. The first is to look for indicator on the top-right side of the search bar, as shown in Figure 8.5. If a database is not index the phrase *Not Indexed* appears and the circle is gray. If the database is indexed, the word *Indexed* app and a green circle appears. The second way to tell if a database is indexed is to inspect the datab properties; use the menu sequence File ➤ Database ➤ Properties and change to the Full Text tab tab icon looks like a magnifying glass). Here, the text will tell you whether the database has an inc as shown in Figure 8.6.

FIGURE 8.6
Database
Properties
InfoBox, not
indexed

The view searched in Figure 8.5 was not indexed; however, you were still able to find two documents. The absence of a full-text index does not prevent you from searching a database. However, when a view is indexed, you can use advanced search options and speed up the search process. Without a full-text index, Notes must search all words in all documents contained within the view. This is a slow process, especially on large databases. In addition, Notes can only return information in the order it found it in the view. To overcome these limitations, a full-text index is added to a Notes database. Figure 8.5 shows a down-pointing arrow with the word *More* to its right; this is a collapse/expand option. Expanding the More area displays advanced search options. Without the database indexed, the expanded More area looks like Figure 8.7.

FIGURE 8.7
More options
without an index

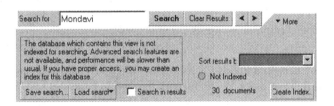

Without an index, the More area is limited in scope and does not provide any advanced search options. It tells you how many documents are in the view (30 in this one) and gives you a button to create an index.

CREATING A FULL-TEXT INDEX

To be able to create a full-text index on a Notes database, you must have at least Designer privileges in the database's Access Control List (ACL). For databases stored locally on your computer, you will generally have the appropriate access rights. For databases stored on a Domino server, there is a good chance you will not have the appropriate security level and will need to ask the system administrator to create the index for you.

To create a database index, use the Create Index button in the More area, visible in Figure 8.7, or the Create Index button on the Database Properties, visible in Figure 8.6. The options available when creating a Full-Text Index are shown in Figure 8.8.

FIGURE 8.8

Create Full-Text
Index dialog box

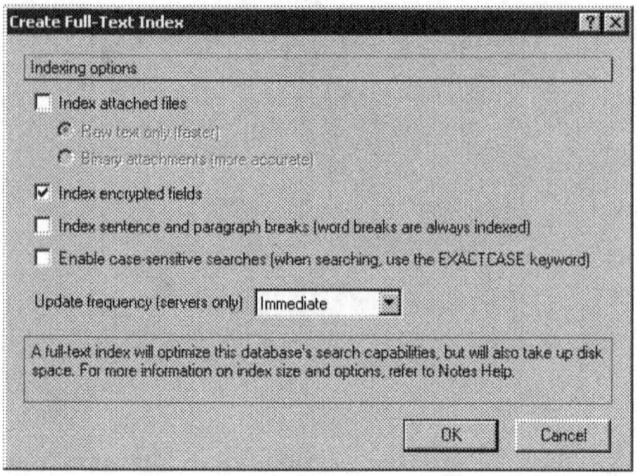

The size of the full-text index is determined by the options you choose on this dialog box. L
look at each one:

Index Attached Files   This option lets you choose whether to index attachments contained
Notes documents, for example, a Microsoft Word document attached to a Notes e-mail. If
enable this option, searches will return documents that contain your search word or phrase in
embedded attachment. Two suboptions are available if you choose to index attachments: R
Text Only or Binary Attachments. The Raw Text Only option limits the full-text index to sea
ing the alphabetic character (ASCII) portion of attached files. This makes searches faster beca
it excludes graphics, audio files, and images from the index, giving it less to search. The Bina
Attachments option includes more complex attachments, such as graphics, in the indexing crit

Index Encrypted Fields   This option instructs Notes to include the data from encrypted fi
in the full-text index. Be careful with this option because it will return documents that contain
encrypted word, which compromises the fact that the information was encrypted. Although
will not be able to see the item unless you have the correct security privilege, you will know t
it contains your search word or phrase.

Index Sentence and Paragraph Breaks   This option determines whether Notes stores informat
required for performing proximity searches using the PARAGRAPH and SENTENCE operat
These operators are useful if you want to find documents that contain two different words within
same paragraph or sentence in the document.

Enable Case-Sensitive Searches   This option determines whether Notes stores information
required for performing case-sensitive searches using the EXACTCASE operator.

Update Frequency   This option determines how often a full-text index on a database stored
a Domino server will be updated. This option has no effect on databases stored on your loca
machine.

After selecting appropriate options and clicking OK, the index is built. A message is displayed on the status bar indicating that your request to index the database has been noted and that you can search the database when it is complete. Once the index has been created, Notes automatically keeps it up-to-date.

You can manually manage a full-text index using the Database Properties InfoBox's Full Text tab, shown in Figure 8.9. The tab shows the options chosen when the full-text index was created and allows you to modify the frequency option.

FIGURE 8.9

Database Properties InfoBox, indexed

These options are useful when you know that documents have been added to the database and the automatic update has not yet taken place. To manually update an index, use the Update Index button on the Database Properties InfoBox's Full Text tab. From here, you can also delete an index. Clicking the Count Unindexed Documents button displays the number of unindexed documents.

When Notes creates a full-text index, it collects all of the data contained in all of the documents and stores the data in a separate structure outside of the database. This separate structure is optimized for searching and requires additional disk space on your computer or the Domino server. Typically, a full-text index will range in size from 20 to 50 percent of the size of the database being indexed.

Performing Full-Text Searches

Once a database has a full-text index, the options available in the More area are a bit more interesting. Figure 8.10 displays the additional options available to search an indexed database. Notice also that the phrase on the search bar now displays as *Indexed*.

FIGURE 8.10

More options with an index

Advanced full-text search features include the ability to find documents that meet certain se. conditions. You can type search conditions directly in the search bar or use the conditions but shown in Figure 8.10. The buttons provide access to input screens that collect information requ for each particular kind of search. You can do the following when a database has a full-text in

- ◆ Set search options for variants, fuzzy search, relevance, and maximum results
- ◆ Search for documents by typing search operators in the search for input area
- ◆ Search for documents by date
- ◆ Search for documents by author
- ◆ Search for documents by comparing a particular field to a specific value
- ◆ Search for documents created using a particular form
- ◆ Search for documents containing a set of multiple words
- ◆ Search for documents containing one of a set of words
- ◆ Search for documents by matching similarly filled-out documents
- ◆ Customize search options

SETTING SEARCH OPTIONS

Before performing a search, decide how you want to see your results and set the appropriate se options. After performing a search, be sure to use the Clear Results button to redisplay the orig view. You can set the following search options:

Use Word Variants   This option instructs Notes to find all documents containing the wo entered in the search bar as well as variations of it based on common prefixes and suffixes. F example, you can enter *cook* and Notes will find documents that contain the words *cooked*, *cooking*, *cookies*.

Fuzzy Search   This option instructs Notes to search for documents containing words and phr similar to the search string you typed and may compensate for some misspelled search words. F example, entering the word *Italan* would return documents containing reasonable likenesses like word *Italian*.

Search in Results   This new Lotus Notes 6 search option lets you execute an additional sea on the set of documents returned from the prior search. This option is only available after you run an initial search and are looking at a result set. Use it to refine and often reduce the num of documents returned by a search.

Sort Results by Relevance   This option tells Notes to sort the result set according to the n ber of times the search string was found in the document; documents with the highest number occurrences of the string appear at the top of the list.

Sort Results by Last Modified   This option instructs Notes to sort the result set by the da the documents were modified with documents having the most recent modification date appear at the top of the list.

Sort Results by First Modified   This option instructs Notes to sort the result set by the dates the documents were modified with documents having the least recent modification date appearing at the top of the list.

Sort Results by Keep Current Order (Sortable)   If the view you are searching is sorted, this option returns the search results using the view's primary sort order.

Sort Results by Show All Documents (Sortable)   This option tells Notes to display all documents in the view with the documents that match your search criteria marked with a check mark in the view margin. The view can be sorted in ascending and descending order by clicking the first column's heading.

Save Search   You can save your search criteria using the name of your choice for reuse and reexecution at a later point in time. In a database stored on a Domino server, you can also mark the search to be shared, which means other Notes' users can run the search query.

NOTE   *This option requires Designer privilege in the ACL.*

Load Search   This option allows you to open and execute previously saved searches. Shared searches are listed as (Shared).

Max Results   This option tells Notes how many documents to return from the search. Enter a decimal number between 1 and 5000; setting this number makes it a default for all Notes databases on your computer. The default is 0, which returns all documents.

OPERATORS FOR THE SEARCH FOR AREA

You can directly type operators into the Search For input box. For example, if you wanted to find documents that contained the words *Italy* and *lunch*, you would type the search as shown in Figure 8.11. Knowing the most popular combinations of operators will help you write effective searches. Notice that the More option does not have to be expanded to use the operators in the Search For area.

FIGURE 8.11
Searching with operators

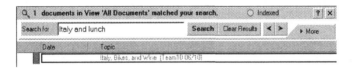

Operators are special words and characters that tell Notes how to perform a search. They are used in conjunction with values for which you are searching. For example, a search entered as *value AND value* will find all documents that contain at least one instance of each *value*. Entering a search criteria of *sales AND january* will find all documents that contain the words *sales* and *january* at least one time. Operators allow you to enter search criteria as you would on a typical web search engine.

Notes also includes operators that enable you to perform proximity searches if you created a full-text index using the Paragraph and Sentence options, these find documents that contain combinations of words in the same paragraph or sentence.

There is also an operator that enables you to specify weighting for words found so Notes can the result set. Wildcard operators are supported in addition to the basic conditional operators as AND, OR, NOT, = (equal to), < (less than), > (greater than), <= (less than or equal to), >= (greater than or equal to). Table 8.1 summarizes the available operators and the functiona they provide.

TABLE 8.1: SEARCH OPERATORS

OPERATOR	SYMBOL EQUIVALENT	DESCRIPTION	EXAMPLES
FIELD *fieldname*		Search a particular field in a document.	FIELD PERIOD January This example searches all document and finds only those with the word January stored in the Period field.
AND	&	Find all documents that contain all the values on either side of the operator.	sales AND January sales & FIE PERIOD January The first example finds all document that contain both the word sales and word January anywhere in a text fiel the document. The second example fi all documents that contain both the word sales anywhere in a text string the word January specifically in a fie named Period.
OR	|	Find all documents that contain either of the values on either side of the operator.	sales | January sales OR FIE PERIOD January The first example returns all docume that contain either the word sales or word January. The second example fi all documents that contain either the word sales or the word January in th Period field.
ACCRUE	,	Find all documents that contain either of the values on either side of the operator and report relevancy ranking.	sales ACCRUE January sales , FIELD PERIOD January The first example finds all document that contain either the word sales or t word January. The second example fi all documents that contain either the word sales or the word January in th Period field. Relevancy ranking is reported with this operator.

Continued on next p

TABLE 8.1: SEARCH OPERATORS *(continued)*

OPERATOR	SYMBOL EQUIVALENT	DESCRIPTION	EXAMPLES

NOT	!	Negate the statement.	`NOT (sales | January)`
			`!sales AND January`
			
			The first example finds all documents that do not contain the word sales or the word January. The second example finds documents that do not contain the word sales but do contain the word January.

SENTENCE		Find words located within a single sentence.	`Sales SENTENCE January` This example will find all documents that contain a sentence with both the word sales and `January`, e.g., `"The sales for January were abnormally low."` This operator is limited to searches of textual information.
PARAGRAPH		Find words located within a single paragraph.	`Sales PARAGRAPH` This example will find all documents that contain a paragraph with both the word sales and January located within it. This operator is limited to searches of textual information.
fieldname CONTAINS	=	Find fields that contain a specific value.	`Period CONTAINS January` This example searches all documents and finds only those where the field named Period contains the text word January.
EXACTCASE		Find a value matching the case to exactly what is typed.	`EXACTCASE January` This example searches all documents and finds only those that contain the text "January" spelled with initial caps; any other case would be ignored and not found by the search.

Continued on next page

OPERATOR	SYMBOL EQUIVALENT	DESCRIPTION	EXAMPLES
TERMWEIGHT *integer*		Assign a theoretical number to the frequency of which the search word appears in the document.	TERMWEIGHT 25 sales OR TERMWEIGHT 50 January OR TERMWEIGHT 75 Annual
			This example searches all document and finds documents that contain at least one of the words with the word "Annual" being the most important, then January, then sales. The results ranked (sorted) in this order.
Exact match	""	Find the words or phrases exactly as typed.	"OR" OR "AND" "full-text"
			The first example finds all document that contain either the word "OR" or word "AND" in the text of the docume without the double quotes, these wo cannot be included in a search becau they are operators. The second examp searches for the exact phrase "full-te: in documents.
Wildcards	? *	Do partial matches on text words.	Sa?e*
			This example will find all documents that contain words with the letters "in the first two positions, any letter in the third position, the letter "E" in th fourth position, and any combination and length of letters after the fourth position. The words "Safe", "Sales", "Safety" would all be found by this example's search.
Mathematical operators	= > < <= >=	Use with number and date fields to before, after, or between a range or exactly equal to a date.	FIELD PurchaseDate <= 11/12/:
			This example will find all documents where the date in the PurchaseDate fi is prior to or equal to November 12, 19 In order listed here, the symbols represent the operators *equal to, great than, less than, less than or equal to, greater than or equal to.*

DATE

The Date button in the More area allows you to search for documents created or modified in relation to a date. To search by date, you provide three pieces of information:

◆ Choice of whether to search by date created or date modified

◆ Choice of how to match the date

◆ Choice of date to match that can be visually chosen using the calendar icon

Figure 8.12 shows a search that will look for documents created before November 12, 2002. Table 8.2 describes the choices for how to match the date you provide.

FIGURE 8.12

Searching by date

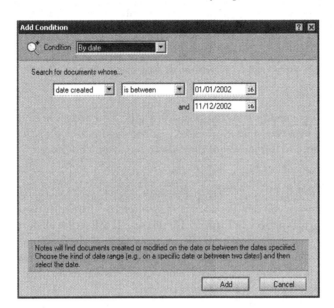

TABLE 8.2: BY DATE SEARCH CHOICES

BY DATE SEARCH CHOICE	ACCEPTABLE VALUE
is on	Valid date (eg. 11/12/2002)
is after	Valid date (eg. 11/12/2002)
is before	Valid date (eg. 11/12/2002)

Continued on next page

TABLE 8.2: BY DATE SEARCH CHOICES *(continued)*

BY DATE SEARCH CHOICE	ACCEPTABLE VALUE
is not on	Valid date (eg. 11/12/2002)
is in the last	Number of days
is in the next	Number of days
is older than	Number of days
is after the next	Number of days
is between	Two valid dates
is not between	Two valid dates

NOTE   *For is between and is not between, the dialog changes slightly to allow the input of two date values instead of o*

AUTHOR

The Author condition button visible in Figure 8.10 helps you find documents that were create
modified by a particular Notes user…or not! Figure 8.13 is the Add Condition dialog box for
Author option. In the Author drop-down box, your choices are:

- is any of
- is not any of

This means you can find documents written by a particular person or exclude documents wri
by a particular person. In Figure 8.13, this search will return all documents created by Dana Casw
The button to the right of the Name area is a link to the Domino Directory to help you look u
names in your organization's address book; this is the preferred way to place names in the input
just to help prevent those pesky typing errors. Place as many names in the input box as needed;
can separate them with a space or a comma.

When Domino searches for an author, it is looking inside a special hidden field and checking
value; this special field is a part of every Notes document created anywhere in Domino. The fie
name is $UpdatedBy. This field keeps track of the names of all users who have edited and saved a
ument. You can inspect the value of this field interactively for any document using a document
properties. When viewing a document or having it selected in a view, open its properties using t
menu sequence File ➢ Document Properties. The second tab is the Fields tab, and from here you
inspect the value of any of the fields in the document including hidden ones such as $UpdatedBy.
ure 8.14 shows the $UpdatedBy field highlighted on the left with its value displayed on the rig

FIGURE 8.13

Searching by author

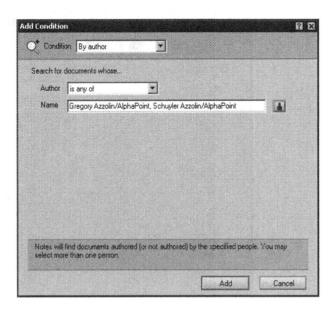

FIGURE 8.14

Document
Properties
InfoBox,
Fields tab

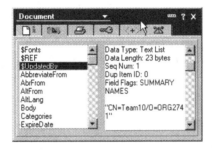

FIELD

Searching by field compares a field name you specify with a value you provide. The Fields tab in Figure 8.14 is a way to peek at a field's value interactively in a document as compared with the search tool, which does all the work for you. The value in the field is what is being checked during a full-text search. As shown in Figure 8.15, the drop-down boxes take some of the guesswork out of determining a field's name and help find a match condition that is appropriate to your needs and the field's data type.

FIGURE 8.15

Searching by
field value

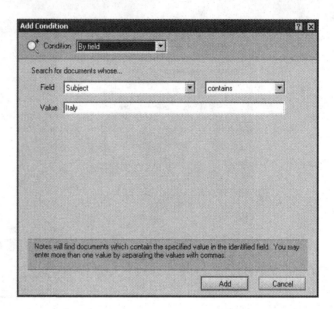

The Field drop-down list displays the names of all fields, hidden or visible, that are part of the document. To the right of the Field drop-down list is the match condition to use. The list of match conditions are wholly dependent on the type of data stored in the field you chose. For instance, you choose a number field, the list of match choices contains values such as *is equal to* or *is greater* if you choose a date, the list includes *is between*, and if you choose a string data type, you're sim looking for whether your search value is contained in the field's value. Table 8.3 lists the data ty and their condition comparison values.

TABLE 8.3: FIELD COMPARISONS

FIELD DATA TYPE	COMPARISON OPERATION	ACCEPTABLE VALUE
Number	is equal to	Valid number
Number	is greater than	Valid number
Number	is less than	Valid number
Number	is not equal to	Valid number
Number	is between	Two valid numbers
Number	is not between	Two valid numbers
Text	contains	A word or phrase
Text	does not contain	A word or phrase

Continued on next p

FIELD DATA TYPE	COMPARISON OPERATION	ACCEPTABLE VALUE
Date/Time	is on	A valid date
Date/Time	is after	A valid date
Date/Time	is before	A valid date
Date/Time	is not on	A valid date
Date/Time	is in the last	A valid date
Date/Time	is in the next	A valid date
Date/Time	is older than	A valid date
Date/Time	is after the next	A valid date
Date/Time	is between	Two valid dates
Date/Time	is not between	Two valid dates

FORM

If you want to locate documents created with a particular form in a database, use the Form condition button to open the Add Condition dialog box, as shown in Figure 8.16.

FIGURE 8.16

Searching by form

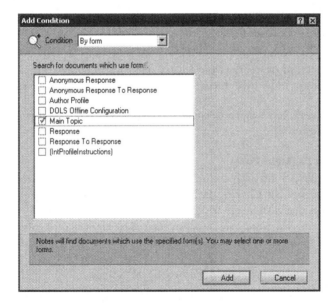

Choose one or multiple forms from the list, and a Notes search will return all documents crea using those forms. You can also use the Form option in combination with typing a word or phra on the search bar. Figure 8.17 shows the result of setting the form option from Figure 8.16 a. typing the word *Italy*. This search will result in documents created using the Main Topic form contain the word *Italy*.

FIGURE 8.17
Searching by form
with search string

TIP *When a condition button is used, a gray rectangle with a tag line representing the condition is added to the sea bar. You can edit the condition at any time by double-clicking the gray rectangle.*

MULTIPLE WORDS

If you want to search for documents involving multiple words, click the Multiple Words butto open the Add Condition box for multiple words, as shown in Figure 8.18. You can type indivic words or phrases in the numbered input boxes. The drop-down box above the input boxes spec which kind of search is performed:

♦ any of the terms below

♦ all of the terms below

Using the example of Italy and lunch with the "any" option, Notes will return documents th return the word *Italy* or the word *lunch* or that contain both words. If you choose the "all" option, search returns only those documents that contain both search words.

TIP *Using the "any" option is the equivalent of using the OR Boolean operator; using the "all" option is the equivale of the Boolean AND.*

FILL-OUT EXAMPLE FORM

This option is a nifty way to find documents created with a particular form that have value matc in a particular field. Clicking the Fill out example form button opens the dialog shown in Figure 8. this shows that documents created with the Main Topic form will be searched to see if the Sub field contains the word *Italy*. You can enter as much or as little information as you need, and you not need to provide values for all the fields.

FIGURE 8.18
Searching for
multiple words

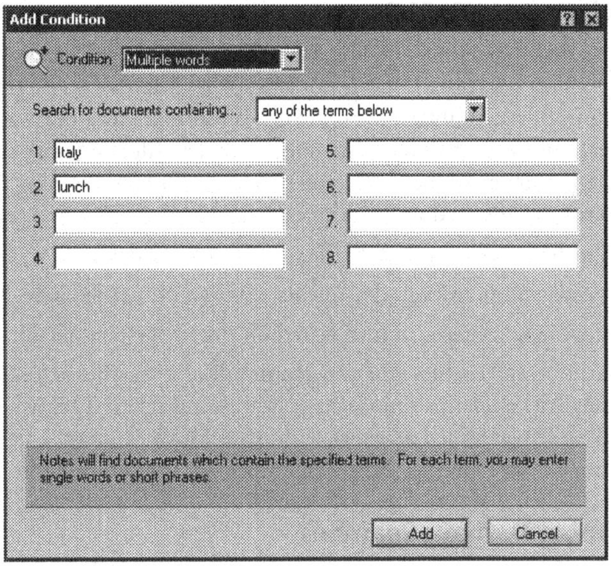

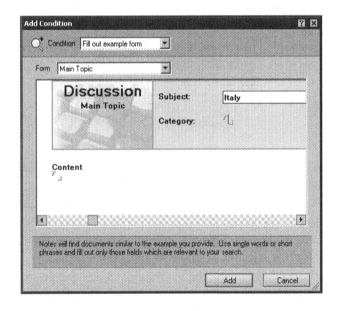

FIGURE 8.19
Searching by
filling out an
example form

This fill-in-the-blank approach to searching is one of the easiest ways to fine-tune a search.

Searching Domains

Are you ready for a definition? The dictionary defines *domain* as *a territory over which rule or control is* ~~cised~~. A Domino systems administrator can set up a domain in Notes as a territory in which you exert your search capabilities! In contrast to a full-text index that indexes a single database, a dor~~ index creates an index to multiple databases and to files outside of Notes.

You can use many of the techniques you learned when searching the contents of a document u~~ a view search to search a domain. You can search a domain to find the following types of informa~~

- ◆ Words and phrases in the title of a Notes database
- ◆ Words and phrases in documents within a Notes database
- ◆ Words and phrases in files stored on the file system outside of Notes

A domain search enables you to perform full-text searches across multiple databases in your D~~ ino domain. Although this sounds complicated, it is relatively easy because these full-text searche~~ similar to those performed on views. A domain search can even search files stored on server-based~~ systems outside of Domino. This enables you to find information regardless of where it is stor~~

Performing Domain Searches

To access a domain search, from the toolbar use the drop-down arrow to the right of the search ~~ nifying glass to reveal the search menu shown in Figure 8.20. From the menu, the Domain Sear~~ option can be used to search multiple databases.

FIGURE 8.20

Searching a domain

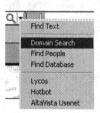

For this option to be available on the menu (meaning not grayed out) and for domain searche~~ work from your Notes client, two things must be true:

- ◆ The administrator of the Domino domain must have created a domain index.
- ◆ The location document in your address book must specify the name of the Catalog/Dor~~ Search server; you will have to manually add the name of your server here if the field is em~~

The Catalog/Domain Search server is defined on the Servers tab of your Location document shown in Figure 8.21.

FIGURE 8.21
Location document

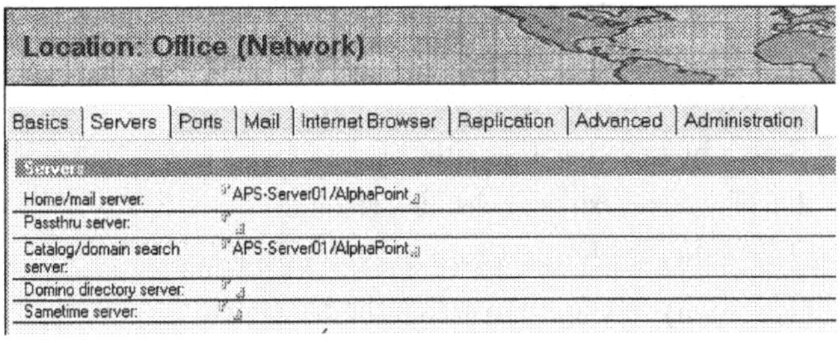

Location: Office (Network)

| Basics | Servers | Ports | Mail | Internet Browser | Replication | Advanced | Administration |

Servers

Home/mail server:	APS-Server01/AlphaPoint
Passthru server:	
Catalog/domain search server:	APS-Server01/AlphaPoint
Domino directory server:	
Sametime server:	

When you select the Domain Search option from the search submenu shown in Figure 8.20, the Domain Search form displays, as shown in Figure 8.22.

FIGURE 8.22
Domain
Search form

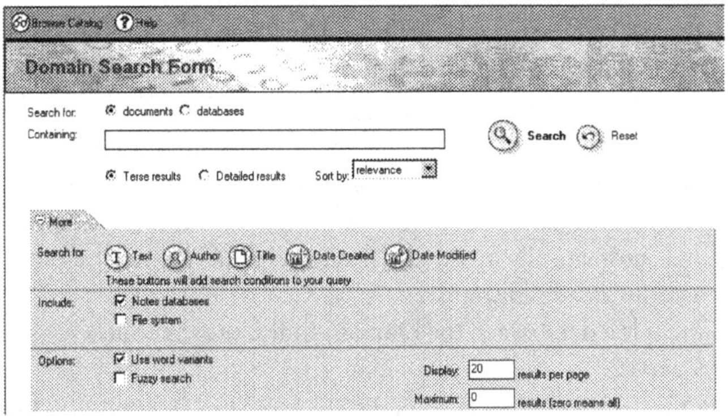

Domain Search Form

Search for: ⦿ documents ○ databases

Containing: [   ]   🔍 Search ↻ Reset

⦿ Terse results ○ Detailed results   Sort by: relevance ▾

▽ More

Search for: ⓘ Text ⓡ Author 🄳 Title Date Created Date Modified
These buttons will add search conditions to your query

Include: ☑ Notes databases
☐ File system

Options: ☑ Use word variants   Display: 20 results per page
☐ Fuzzy search   Maximum: 0 results (zero means all)

The Domain Search form is your interface for performing domain searches. At the top of the form, notice that there are two radio buttons: Documents and Databases. By selecting databases, you can search for words that appear in the title of a database. If you select documents, you can search for documents contained within the databases and file systems that are part of the domain search.

The following search options for locating documents in a domain are similar to those seen when searching for documents in a view; please review the description of these options by reading the "Searching the Contents of Documents" section earlier in this chapter:

◆ Use Word Variants

◆ Fuzzy Search

◆ Maximum Results (equivalent to Max Results in a view search)

◆ Sort By options (three choices here: Relevance, Oldest First, and Newest First)

◆ Search for Author

◆ Search for Date (limited to Date Created or Date Modified)

In addition to the standard options for searching the contents of a document, notice the follow additional options available for a domain search:

◆ Search by text (any text string)
◆ Search by title (database title)
◆ Display terse results or detailed results
◆ The ability to choose to search Notes databases
◆ The ability to choose to search the file system
◆ Specify the number of result lines to display per page

To perform simple searches of documents, select the Documents radio button, enter your cri in the Containing field, and click the Search button on the form. The search results display with title of each document that, when clicked, links you to and opens the database and document t contains the search text.

Adding Databases to the Domain Index

If you are the owner of a database that resides on a Domino server and you would like it included domain searches, you can ask the Domino system administrator to include your database or you ma able to do it yourself. The *Domain Index* is a full-text index maintained on a group of database on Domino server for use with a domain search. This index is created when a domain search is enable is updated automatically by the server on a schedule defined by the person who configures the dom search, usually an administrator.

To include a database in the Domain Index, use the following steps to set the multi-indexing c base property:

1. Open the database you would like added to the Domain Index.
2. Select File ➤ Database ➤ Properties.
3. Switch to the Design tab.
4. Enable the Include in Multi-Database Indexing option.

This will add this database to the Domain Index the next time the Domain Index process runs the Domino server.

NOTE *You must have Manager privileges in the ACL to enable this option.*

Viewing Catalogs

The Domino system typically contains two types of catalogs that contain information about da bases and that are used in searches:

◆ Database catalog
◆ Domain catalog

A *database catalog* contains information about the databases on a single Domino server. As new d bases are created on a Domino server, Domino automatically updates the database catalog.

You can view the contents of a database catalog directly by clicking the Browse Catalog button visible in the top-left corner of Figure 8.21. Clicking this button displays a categorized view of the catalog's content, as shown in Figure 8.23.

FIGURE 8.23

Database catalog

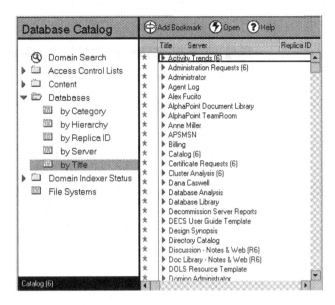

A *domain catalog* encompasses the information contained in multiple database catalogs and uses these in a domain search. This catalog is created by a Domino system administrator and can contain Domino databases as well as files on the file system.

TIP   You can use catalogs to locate a database and then add it to your Notes workspace.

Finding People

If you choose the Find People option visible on the search submenu in Figure 8.20, you can search for people information in the following types of data sources:

- Your personal address book
- Other locally stored address books
- Your organization's Domino Directory
- Bigfoot
- Internet Directory
- VeriSign

You search for information in your personal address book, other address books, or your company Domino Directory using the Find People dialog box, as shown in Figure 8.24. Here, the AlphaPo Directory will be searched for last names that start with the letters *CAS*. At the top-right of this di box, you can choose to search by name, by Notes name hierarchy, by corporate hierarchy, or categor by language.

FIGURE 8.24

Finding people

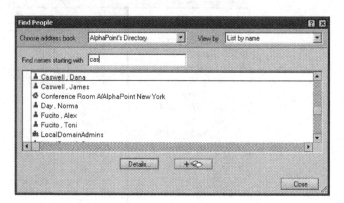

The options for Bigfoot, Internet Directory, and VeriSign all require that you are connected to Internet when you perform the search and that a Lightweight Directory Access Protocol (LDA account document exists in your personal address book. To configure an LDAP account docum use the menu sequence File ➤ Preferences ➤ Client Reconfiguration Wizard. This wizard, show Figure 8.25, creates the LDAP connection from your Notes client to a network LDAP server.

FIGURE 8.25

Configuring an
LDAP account

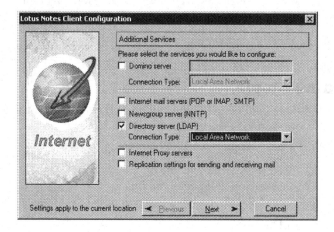

Searching the Internet

You can use your Notes client to search the Internet using popular search engines. If you look back to Figure 8.20, you'll see the search submenu lists the following direct Internet search engines:

- Lycos
- Hotbot
- Google Usenet

If you have a connection to the Internet, selecting any of these options will open that search engine's main search page. The search is carried out and the results are returned to you as a list of links in the Notes client. Just enter your search request as you would if you were using this search site outside of Notes. If your favorite search site is not listed on the Search button menu, you can add it to the menu by doing the following:

1. From inside the Notes client, open the search site's web page by entering the Uniform Resource Locator (URL) in the Address input box.
2. Drag the tab from the newly opened window into the More Bookmarks icon along the left side of the Notes client, and drop it into the Internet Search Sites folder.

Summary

You now understand how Notes can be used to find information stored in Notes databases. You can find text in individual documents or search for documents in views within specific databases. You can also use a domain search to find information in databases that are stored on any Domino server in a domain. You can even use a domain search to find data stored on file systems anywhere in the domain. We have also explained how Notes can be used as an interface for accessing Internet-based search sites and LDAP directories. In the next chapter, we'll learn how to configure the Notes client to communicate with a Domino server. Now that you know how to search for information, finding information on your home Domino server and other remote Domino servers is a next logical step.

Chapter 9

Communicating with Domino Servers

THE NOTES CLIENT IS a feature-rich environment that lets you independently manage a great deal of information. It is most powerful, though, when used to connect to a Domino server. At that point, the client becomes the tool that facilitates collaboration with other users and other information stored on remote servers. There are several key configuration tasks that must be performed correctly in order to communicate with a server; these configuration tasks generally result in a new document stored in the Notes client that is referenced internally any time the client connects to a server. The information stored in the configuration documents determine how you connect to a server; since Notes is a mobile client, you may have more than one way to get to your servers.

- ◆ Communications overview
- ◆ Connecting to a Domino server
- ◆ Dial-up communications
- ◆ Local area network connections
- ◆ Pass-thru connections
- ◆ Working in stand-alone mode
- ◆ Connection document wizards

A Communications Overview

One of the strengths of the Lotus Notes client is its ability to connect to a Domino server using a wide variety of communication and connection options. From network protocol to the physical connection method, the client can be configured to respond to most communication situations. From a high level, there are three things needed to make the communication happen:

- ◆ Telecommunications connection to a server

- ◆ Network-capable operating system for clients and server
- ◆ Network communications protocol between client and server

Telecommunications between a client and a server takes place by virtue of a network card inst: in the client machine or a modem with a telephone cable connection. The server must also have a work card or, in rarer cases, a modem and phone jack. This takes care of the physical medium.

An operating system is the software installed on a computer to talk to its hardware; it makes connection between when you physically press the A key on the keyboard to the digitized zeros ones that get stored in or displayed on your computer as a result of the keystroke. The operating tem must be capable of receiving bits (zeros and ones) of data from the network card or modem of the following operating systems can support a Domino server:

- ◆ HP-UX
- ◆ IBM AIX
- ◆ Microsoft Windows NT 4.0
- ◆ Microsoft Windows 2000
- ◆ Windows XP
- ◆ Sun Solaris/SPARC
- ◆ Linux

For the Notes client, which runs on a typical user's desktop computer, the following operati platforms can be used:

- ◆ Microsoft XP Professional
- ◆ Microsoft Windows 2000
- ◆ Microsoft Windows NT
- ◆ Microsoft Windows 98
- ◆ Microsoft Windows 95
- ◆ Macintosh PowerPC systems

A network communications protocol is a set of rules that two devices agree to use in order transfer bits and bytes of information between their operating systems. In Domino's case, t means transferring bits of information between a Domino server, running on one of the supporte operating systems, and a Lotus Notes client, also running on a supported platform. Table 9.1 li: the network protocols that can be used with Domino.

TABLE 9.1: DOMINO NETWORK PROTOCOLS

COMMUNICATION SCENARIO	NETWORK PROTOCOL
Local area network	TCP/IP
Local area network	IPX/SPX
Local area network	NetBIOS

Continued on next p

TABLE 9.1: DOMINO NETWORK PROTOCOLS *(continued)*	
COMMUNICATION SCENARIO	**NETWORK PROTOCOL**
Dialup connection	X.PC
Dialup connection	PPP

In a client/server networking configuration, the majority of information for a company is stored on a server. This is true in the Domino world as well. Information that needs to be shared between many users in Domino is stored on the server; information used only by a single user is generally stored on the client computer. Lotus Notes Domino is a distributed database system, with shared databases stored on a Domino server and local databases stored on the local computer and accessed with the Lotus Notes client.

Setting Up Dial-Up Communications

If you use Domino servers at work, you generally access them through a local area network (LAN). This is a communication mechanism that typically connects computers physically located in the same building. Most commonly, LANs are based on Ethernet networking technology and provide high-speed access to servers. Whenever your computer is on and connected to the server, the networking software maintains a permanent, always-available connection. This is known as a *persistent connection*, and is "always on." When you configure Notes for the appropriate LAN protocol—for instance, Transmission Control Protocol/Internet Protocol (TCP/IP)—the Notes client accesses the Domino server as needed using the network.

You may also connect to Domino servers through your company's wide area network (WAN). WANs typically connect computers that are physically located in different buildings, many times in different geographic areas. A WAN is usually a lower-speed communication mechanism than a LAN is, but it is generally associated with "always on" technologies. Again, you just configure Notes for the appropriate protocol, and it accesses the Domino server as needed. One of the nicest things about the TCP/IP network protocol is that it is transparent to you whether the remote server you're accessing is sitting in your office, in a different building, in a different city, or even a different country.

When accessing Domino servers remotely and not in your office with a LAN connection, you have several other connectivity options. You can use dial-up communication technologies with a modem attached to your computer and normal telephone lines. This includes accessing Domino servers from home, from a client's site, and from a hotel room while you are traveling. You can also use a digital subscriber line (DSL) or a cable modem that also uses TCP/IP to connect to a server as if it were on a LAN.

The major difference between dial-up communications and LAN communications is that with a dial-up connection, your computer must connect to the network using a phone line before Notes can access the Domino server. Notes supports two methods for making this connection:

- Notes Direct Dialup
- Network Dialup

Notes Direct Dialup occurs when Notes initiates the process of dialing through your compu modem directly to a modem attached to the Domino server. This is modem-to-modem comm cations; both machines, client and server, have a modem installed and all communications take through the modem.

Network Dialup occurs when Notes initiates the process of dialing through your computer's mo to a network dial-in server or Internet service provider (ISP) that in turn provides access to the Don server. This is modem to network card communications between the client and the server. Your cli modem dials a phone number that connects to a server using the server's network card.

Notes Direct Dialup

One scenario for dial-up communications in Notes is through Notes Direct Dialup. In this scenario modem on your computer dials a phone number that connects to the modem on a Domino server. N Direct Dialup is considered the "legacy" method of remotely connecting to Domino servers and is as heavily used as it once was. With network dial-up technology included in both Windows (95, 98, NT) and MacOS and the popularity of network dial-up solutions, the need for Notes Direct Dialup been reduced somewhat. In addition, Notes Direct Dialup is slightly more complicated when the ronment includes multiple Domino servers. Notes Direct Dialup is a solid solution for secure ren access by Notes clients. Notes Direct Dialup provides good value in the following areas:

- ◆ Higher security
- ◆ Integration with existing infrastructure

Notes Direct Dialup is somewhat more secure than network dial-up solutions because the D ino server only accepts calls from Notes clients. All of the inherent security of Domino is applie the dial-up connection. And a network administrator can take a server completely offline simpl disconnecting the phone cable. Notes Direct Dialup has been an integral part of Notes since its in tion, and it continues to be supported for Notes client communications.

SETTING UP NOTES DIRECT DIALUP

Notes Direct Dialup requires that the target Domino server have at least one modem and telephc line installed and be configured to accept dial-in calls. The Domino administrator performs t configuration necessary for a Domino server; if the server is not configured properly, Notes Dire Dialup will not work.

On your personal computer, a modem must be present, installed, and working correctly. A moc on a computer is assigned to a communications port, usually COM1 or COM2. In the Notes cli you need to configure three items to set up Notes Direct Dialup:

- ◆ A communications port
- ◆ A Location document
- ◆ A Connection document

The first item you need to configure is the Notes communications port. The port establishes an a ciation between Notes and the modem installed on your computer. This association allows Notes "talk" to the attached modem. To enable and set up a Notes communications port, follow these st

1. Use the menu sequence File ➢ Preferences ➢ User Preferences, which displays the User Pre ences dialog box.

2. In the User Preferences dialog box, click the Ports button along the left side to display the port information for the client (see Figure 9.1).

FIGURE 9.1
Communications ports

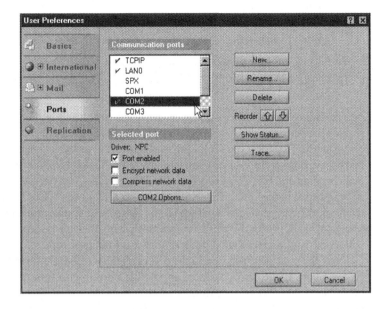

3. By default, a set of port entries (including COM2) will be displayed in the Communication Ports list box. Select the communications port associated with your modem; COM2 is fairly common.

4. Select the Port Enabled check box to enable this port.

5. Click the COM2 Options button to display the Additional Setup dialog box shown in Figure 9.2.

FIGURE 9.2
Modem options

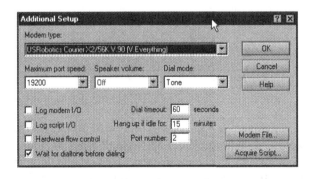

6. Select your modem from the list or select Auto Configure (for Unlisted Modems Only) if your modem is not listed.

7. Select a value from the Maximum Port Speed drop-down box. You can try a value that is t your modem's speed and then drop to lower speeds if you have problems. 19200 is a com choice.

8. Make sure that Port Number matches the port assigned to your modem (without the le COM). In our example, Port Number is set to 2, which is the same as saying COM2.

9. Change other dialing parameters as required.

10. Clicking OK in the User Preferences dialog box saves your changes and enables the port communications port is immediately available for use.

You can configure other options in the Additional Setup dialog box. When the check boxe enabled, Log Modem I/O and Log Script I/O will report activity to your Notes log. These are g debugging tools to use if you are having trouble with Notes Direct Dialup connections. The Modem button will display the Edit Modem Command File dialog box, in which you can make changes to modem command file. This file defines how Notes "talks" to your computer's modem. All modem are supplied as part of the Lotus Notes/Domino core product. The Acquire Script button will dis the Acquire Script dialog box, which allows you to select and optionally edit acquire scripts. Acq scripts define how Notes "talks" to modems that are available through a communication server, w is a device that provides shared pools of modems over a network.

Once the port is configured in the Notes client via User Preferences, you next need to tell t Notes client when to use it. You do this with a Location document stored in your personal add book, names.nsf. Location documents tell your Notes client about your communications envir ment, and it is common to have several different Location documents to handle a variety of comm ication environments. In a Location document, the Ports to Use check box determines which N communications ports are actually available to Notes. When you enable a Notes communication in the User Preferences dialog box as in the preceding steps, it is automatically enabled in the cur Location document's Ports to Use field. To access the current Location document and verify wl communications port is configured, do the following:

1. Use the menu sequence File ➤ Mobile ➤ Edit Current Location. Your current Location ument will be opened in edit mode.

2. Click the Ports tab. The Ports to Use check boxes display as shown in Figure 9.3.

FIGURE 9.3
Location document
ports

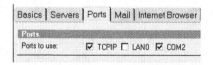

The last step in configuring your Notes client for Notes Direct Dialup is to create a Connection ument. Connection documents define what network communication protocol will be used to conr your Notes client to a specific Domino server. Like Location documents, Connection documents also stored in your personal address book. To create a Connection document to use with Notes Di Dialup, follow these steps:

1. Use the menu sequence File ➤ Mobile ➤ Server Phone Numbers; this opens your person address book and lists all existing Connection documents.

2. Click the New button at the top of the list and choose Server Connection from the menu; this displays a blank Server Connection document ready for you to fill in, as shown in Figure 9.4.

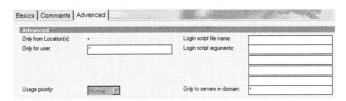

3. In the Connection Type drop-down list, select Notes Direct Dialup.

4. Fill in the following information: whether to use the area code, modem port (or * to have Notes try all ports), server name, area code, and phone number.

5. Click the Save and Close button at the top of the document.

The Notes Direct Dialup Connection document will be created and you will be returned to the Connections view of your personal address book, as shown in Figure 9.5. The telephone icon along the left edge for the APS-Server02 document identifies that Connection document as a Notes Direct Dialup connection.

New ▾	Edit Connection	Delete Connection	Tools.. ▾
	Server ▾	Port	Via
🖧	APS-Server01/AlphaPoint	TCPIP	APS-Server01
☎	APS-Server02/AlphaPoint	*	(914)2262200
🖧	home/notes/net	TCPIP	home.notes.net

You can further customize Notes Direct Dialup Connection documents using the Advanced tab on the Connection document, shown in Figure 9.6.

You have the following options:

Only from Location(s) Defaults to an asterisk, which enables Notes to use this Connection document regardless of your current location. If you would like to restrict a Connection document to specific locations, select them from this list box.

Only for User Restricts the Connection document to specific users. Enter an asterisk to r
this Connection document available to any user who uses Notes from this workstation.

Usage Priority Used by Notes to determine the order in which it uses Connection docum

Login Script File Name/Login Script Arguments Used to define login script informatio:
the connection.

Only to Servers in Domain Used to restrict the Connection document to a specific dom
Enter an asterisk to allow this Connection document to be used with any domain or ente:
domain name.

MANUALLY CONNECTING USING NOTES DIRECT DIALUP

With Notes Direct Dialup set up, you can connect to the Domino servers manually or automatic
Generally, you connect manually to the Domino server when you need to interact online. For exan
you would connect manually to create a replica of a server-based database on your computer's local
drive. You would also connect manually if you needed to open the server-based copy of a database w
you're away from the office.

Notes operates the same regardless of how you connect to the Domino server. Once the con
tion has been established, Notes performs as if you were connected through a LAN, albeit much n
slowly. To connect to a Domino server manually using Notes Direct Dialup, follow these steps

1. Use the menu sequence File ➤ Mobile ➤ Call Server. The Call Server dialog box will be
played, as shown in Figure 9.7. All servers available through Notes Direct Dialup and Netw
Dialup Connection documents will be displayed.

FIGURE 9.7
Preparing to call
a server

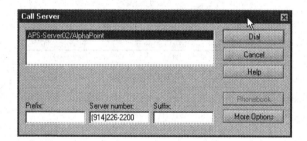

2. Select the server you want to call and click the Dial button.

NOTE *You can optionally change the connection information in the Call Server dialog box before dialing if necessar*
You can directly override the phone number, and the More Options lets you change the communications port, timeout se
tings, idle hang-up settings, and modem configuration details.

Notes will initiate dialing through your computer's modem. When the connection has been est
lished, a modem icon will appear in the activity indicator on the status bar. You can open and use ser
based databases as if you were connected locally, processing information as you normally would in
LAN environment just at a slower connection speed.

MANUALLY DISCONNECTING THE NOTES DIRECT DIALUP CONNECTION

By default, Notes will hang up Notes Direct Dialup connections after 15 minutes of inactivity. You can also manually hang up the connection using the menu sequence File ➤ Mobile ➤ Hang Up. The Hang Up dialog box, shown in Figure 9.8, displays with the active dial-up ports listed. From here, you can click the Hang Up button.

FIGURE 9.8
Disconnecting a
dial-up connection

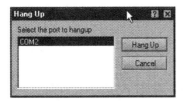

Network Dialup

A second scenario for dial-up communications in Notes is through Network Dialup. In this scenario, the modem on your computer allows the Notes client to dial a phone number using a remote access service (RAS) such as Windows Dialup Networking (DUN) to access Domino servers. If you already have dial-up networking installed on your computer and your Domino servers are accessible through a network dial-up solution or an ISP, this is the easiest way to connect remotely. All configuration related to your computer's modem is taken care of at the operating system level outside of Lotus Notes. All Notes needs is a properly configured Connection document specifying the use of Network Dialup, and it then uses the networking features of the operating system to access Domino servers.

SETTING UP NETWORK DIALUP

Notes Network Dialup only requires that your Domino servers are accessible through a network dial-up solution such as Windows NT Remote Access Server (RAS). In many companies, the information technology group provides this service. An outside service organization can also provide network dial-up. Recently, companies have even begun to use Internet-based virtual private network (VPN) solutions to provide secure network dial-up services.

To configure Notes to communicate with a Domino server using Notes Network Dialup, create a Network Dialup Connection document using the following steps:

1. Use the menu sequence File ➤ Mobile ➤ Server Phone Numbers. Your personal address book will be opened with the Connections view displayed. All existing Connection documents will be listed.

2. Click the New button at the top of the list of connections and select the Server Connection option from the menu.

3. When the new Connection document displays, select Network Dialup from the Connection Type drop-down box.

4. Select a port in the Use LAN Port field.

5. Fill in the Server Name field. The result will be a screen that looks similar to Figure 9.9.

FIGURE 9.9

Network dial-up

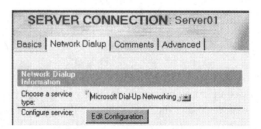

6. Click the Network Dialup tab.

7. Choose a service type of Microsoft Dial-Up Networking from the drop-down list. At th
point, the screen will look similar to Figure 9.10.

FIGURE 9.10

Service type

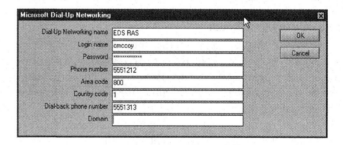

8. Click the Edit Configuration button and provide all the required information for the con
tion such as the DUN name, login name, password, phone number, and area code. The re
will be a screen similar to Figure 9.11.

FIGURE 9.11

Microsoft dial-up
settings

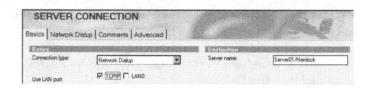

TIP *The DUN name needs to be identical to the one specified at the operating-system level. For Windows NT, you*
find this in Dial-Up Networking in My Computer; in Windows 2000, you'll find it in Network and Dial-Up Co
nections in the Control Panel of My Computer.

Once saved, the Network Dialup Connection document is added to the list of Connections in y
personal address book, as shown in Figure 9.12. Connection documents that use Network Dial
display with the electronic A symbol along the left margin.

FIGURE 9.12

Connection
documents

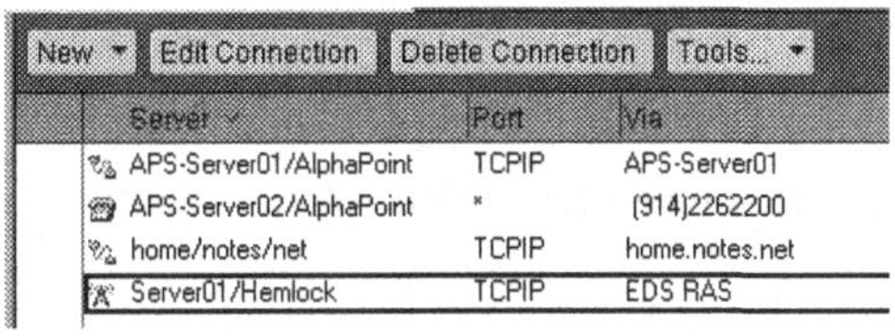

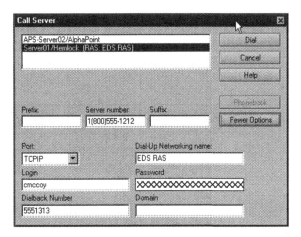

Server	Port	Via
APS-Server01/AlphaPoint	TCPIP	APS-Server01
APS-Server02/AlphaPoint	*	(914)2262200
home/notes/net	TCPIP	home.notes.net
Server01/Hemlock	TCPIP	EDS RAS

Network Dialup Connection documents can be further customized using the Advanced tab on the Connection form with the following information:

Only from Location(s)   Defaults to an asterisk, which enables Notes to use this Connection document regardless of your current location. If you would like to restrict a Connection document to specific locations, select them from this list box.

Only for User   Restricts the Connection document to specific users. Enter an asterisk to make this Connection document available to any user who uses Notes from this workstation.

Usage Priority   Used by Notes to determine the order in which it uses Connection documents.

Destination Server Address   Enter the TCP/IP networking address of the remote server here.

MANUALLY CONNECTING USING NETWORK DIALUP

With Network Dialup set up, you can connect to the Domino servers manually or automatically just as you do with Notes Direct Dialup. To use Network Dialup to connect to a Domino server manually, select File ➤ Mobile ➤ Call Server, select the server to call and away you go. The Call Server dialog box's More Options button reveals and allows the override of the port, networking name, login name, dial-back number, and domain (see Figure 9.13).

FIGURE 9.13

Calling a network
dial-up server

Notes will initiate dialing through your computer's modem. When the connection has been established, a modem icon will appear in the activity indicator on the status bar. Windows will also add a modem icon to the system tray. Just as you can with Notes Direct Dialup, you can open and server-based databases as if you were connected locally.

MANUALLY DISCONNECTING THE NETWORK DIALUP CONNECTION

By default, Notes will hang up Network Dialup inactive connections based on Windows moden tings for idle timeouts. You can also manually hang up the connection by selecting File ➤ Mobi Hang Up.

USING NETWORK DIALUP TO CONNECT TO THE INTERNET

You can also use Network Dialup to establish Internet connections for non-Domino services, in ing Post Office Protocol version 3 (POP3), Internet Message Access Protocol version 4 (IMA Simple Mail Transfer Protocol (SMTP), Network News Transfer Protocol (NNTP), and Lig weight Directory Access Protocol (LDAP). This feature is the equivalent of an auto-dialer in typ Internet clients.

Once it's configured, Notes can automatically dial your ISP account whenever you perform a f tion that requires Notes to be connected to the Internet. Notes will even dial your ISP account in background if the Notes Replicator is configured to send or receive Internet e-mail or to replic newsgroups and IMAP e-mail accounts.

The only difference between a Network Dialup connection configured to access a Domino se and one configured to access Internet services is the Server Name field. As demonstrated earlier, I work Dialup connections configured to access Domino servers require the Domino server name you want to create a Network Dialup connection for use with Internet services, just enter an aste in the Server Name field.

TIP   To access the Internet, use the Internet Location document together with a Network Dialup Connection docume

Setting Up Local Area Network Connections

The majority of communications between a Lotus Notes client and a Domino server take place a LAN connection. The Office Location document is preconfigured to use a LAN connection, shown in Figure 9.14.

FIGURE 9.14
Office Location document

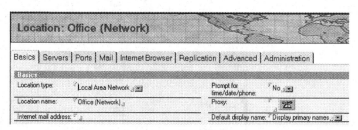

When this type of connection is chosen, Notes will attempt to use the network communicat protocol specified on the Ports tab to connect to a Domino server. Options include TCPIP, LAI COM1, COM2, and more.

If you have Notes dial an ISP using a local phone number, you establish a TCP/IP connection with that organization even though you are doing it through a phone line. In this type of scenario, you will be able to use Connection documents that specify local area networking. The ISP's connection to the Domino server in the Internet world would be of type TCP/IP and therefore allow your client to use this type of connection as well.

NOTE   *A LAN connection is by far the fastest type of connection.*

Setting Up Passthru Connections

Notes supports a feature called *Passthru*, which is provided by the Domino server. This feature allows you to connect to one Domino server and use its communications capabilities to connect to another Domino server. One common use of Passthru is in environments where you use Notes Direct Dialup communications to connect directly to Domino servers. After making the connection, you only have access to that one Domino server, so you cannot use databases residing on other Domino servers in your organization. Using Passthru, you can access databases residing on Domino servers other than the one you called.

Another common use of a Passthru connection is for accessing Internet-based Domino servers from within your organization's network infrastructure. At least one of your Domino servers must have either a permanent connection to the Internet or the capability to establish a dial-up connection to the Internet outside the company's security firewall. If this is the case, you can use Passthru to access the internal Domino server by going through, or passing through, the server outside the firewall to other Domino servers inside the firewall.

To configure Notes to use a Passthru Domino server, create a Passthru Connection document. To do so, follow these steps:

1. Use the menu sequence File ➢ Mobile ➢ Server Phone Numbers to display the list of existing Connection documents.

2. Click the New button and select Server Connection from the menu.

3. Select Passthru Server from the Connection Type drop-down box.

4. Enter the name of the Passthru Domino server.

5. In the Destination section, enter the name of the Domino server you want to access via Passthru.

When configured, the Passthru Connection document will be similar to the one shown in Figure 9.15.

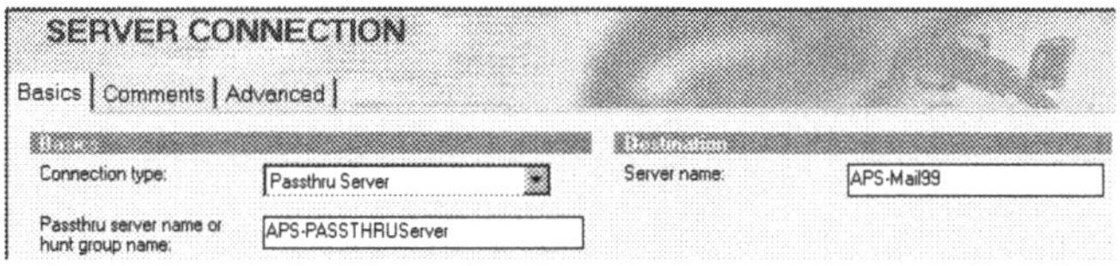

FIGURE 9.15
Passthru
Connection
document

The Passthru Connection document is added to the list of Connection documents in your personal address book. They appear with the icon of a server and a remote server along the left margin, as shown in Figure 9.16.

FIGURE 9.16
List of connections
with Passthru

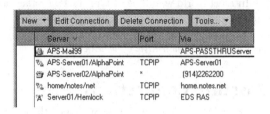

Server	Port	Via
APS-Mail99		APS-PASSTHRUServer
APS-Server01/AlphaPoint	TCPIP	APS-Server01
APS-Server02/AlphaPoint	*	(914)2262200
home/notes/net	TCPIP	home.notes.net
Server01/Hemlock	TCPIP	EDS RAS

You can further customize Passthru Connection documents using the Advanced tab on the Connection form to set the following options:

Only from Location(s)   Defaults to an asterisk, which enables Notes to use this Passthru Connection document regardless of your current location. If you would like to restrict a Passthru Connection document to specific locations, select them from this list box.

Only for User   Restricts the Connection document to specific users. Enter an asterisk to make this Connection document available to any user who uses Notes from this workstation.

Usage Priority   Used by Notes to determine the order in which it uses Passthru Connection documents.

Once a Passthru Connection document is created, Notes will automatically connect to the destination Domino server by first connecting to the Passthru Domino server. If the Passthru Domino server is only reachable via dial-up communications, Notes will establish the dial-up connection first and then passthrough to the remote Domino server.

Working in Stand-Alone Mode

A long time ago, the folks at Lotus envisioned the ability to work with the Lotus Notes client on a desert island without the need for a connection to a Domino server. Well, the island part is appealing, but bringing your laptop along might not make your significant other very happy. Still, you can indeed use Notes without the presence of a Domino server. To do this, you use the Island (Disconnected) location document stored in your personal address book. At the bottom-right of the Notes client, you can click the second area from the right to pop up a list of all existing Location documents, and then choose one from the list. Figure 9.17 displays a list of several Location documents and shows that the Island location is currently active.

FIGURE 9.17

Changing locations

In Island mode, the Location type is set to No Connection, and the location for the mail file on the Mail tab is set to the local server (see Figure 9.18).

FIGURE 9.18

No connection

Location: Island (Disconnected)

Basics | Mail | Internet Browser | Replication | Advanced | Administration |

Basics

Location type:	No connection	Prompt for time/date/phone:	No
Location name:	Island (Disconnected)		
Internet mail address:		Default display name:	Display primary names

When this Location document is active, the Notes client will not attempt to access any remote servers. Switch to this Location document when you have no access to a server—for instance, when you're working at 30,000 feet while traveling from New York to Los Angeles. Island mode is highly encouraged for road warriors when checking their e-mail. The intent is to minimize the time on the phone. It tells the e-mail program not to attempt sending or retrieving mail in the interim.

Using Setup Wizards

From the previous discussions in this chapter, you've no doubt gotten the feeling that Location and Connection documents are essential elements in getting a Lotus Notes client to communicate with a Domino server. In Release 6, Lotus has streamlined many of the steps involved in setting these documents up for your client through the use of the wizards. The Client Configuration Wizard and Connection Configuration Wizard help you easily create Connection documents.

Client Configuration Wizard

The Client Reconfiguration Wizard is accessible directly from the Notes client menu. To open the wizard, use the menu sequence File ➢ Preferences ➢ Client Reconfiguration Wizard to display the dialog box shown in Figure 9.19.

FIGURE 9.19
Client
Configuration
Wizard

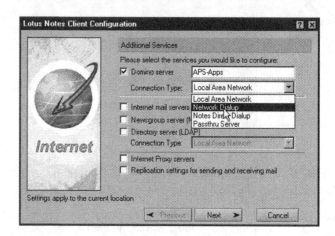

Depending on the type of connection chosen (Local Area Network, Network Dialup, Note Direct Dialup, Passthru Server), the remaining series of dialog boxes in the wizard ask you for required information to make the connection.

You can also use this wizard to make connections to non-Domino servers such as the follow

◆ Internet mail servers (POP, IMAP, SMTP)

◆ Newsgroup servers (NNTP)

◆ An Internet directory server (LDAP)

◆ Internet Proxy servers

Finally, you can also use this wizard to easily configure Domino replication settings for send and receiving Notes mail.

Connection Configuration Wizard

Inside a Location document, you'll find a button at the top that can help you create Connection uments using the Connection Configuration Wizard using an intro screen (shown in Figure 9.2 and one configuration screen (shown in Figure 9.21).

FIGURE 9.20
Connection
Configuration
Wizard

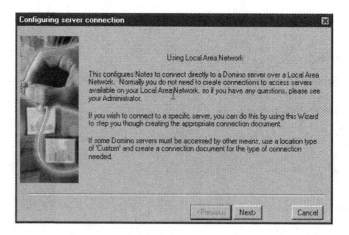

FIGURE 9.21
Configuration
settings

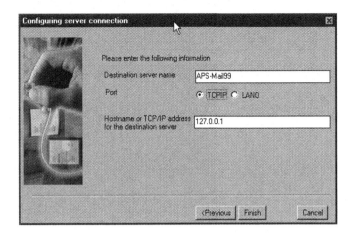

Summary

Connecting to a Domino server can be tricky. The secret to success lies in the Connection and Location documents stored in your personal address book. Dialing in to a server is certainly a valid connection methodology, and we've looked at how to dial up from one modem to another as well as from one modem to a TCP/IP server. Local area network connections are the fastest and most popular type of connection. Passthru connections let you connect to one server to access multiple servers behind a firewall. Using the Lotus Notes client in stand-alone, or Island, mode works well when there's no server at hand. All of these require good Location and Connection documents, and to help create them, Release 6 provides wizards to get you going quickly. In the next chapter, you'll see how to use your knowledge of server connectivity to maximize the benefits of Domino replication services.

Chapter 10

Replication

ONE OF THE MOST powerful features of the Lotus Notes client is that it can operate with full functionality whether connected to a Domino server or not. This is made possible by the distributed database technology that Lotus and IBM employ and by the replication technology that unites distributed databases. In Chapter 9, "Communicating with Domino Servers," we examined the various types of connections that a Notes client can make to a Domino server. In this chapter, we'll make use of the connection to a server to perform the process of replication.

- ◆ Defining replication
- ◆ Creating a database copy and a database replica
- ◆ The importance of the Replica ID
- ◆ Configuring replication settings
- ◆ Managing the Replication page
- ◆ Replicating a database interactively and in the background
- ◆ The relationship between replication to Location and Connection documents
- ◆ Setting Replication page options
- ◆ Being a roaming user
- ◆ Understanding replication save conflicts
- ◆ Replication security concerns

What Is Replication?

Replication is the process of synchronizing one copy of a database with another copy of the same database with the goal of making them identical in design elements and document contents. Replication allows you to interact with your mail and collaborative applications when you leave the office. Here are some of the more common uses:

- ◆ Reading and composing your e-mail

- Staying up-to-date in a Notes discussion database
- Referencing web pages offline
- Working with application databases on two different servers in different time zones

Replication is independent from the method you use to connect to your Domino server. Reption functions the same way whether you are connected through a local area network (LAN), area network (WAN), or remote access service. As long as Notes is configured to connect to a Dino server at some point in time, you will be able to replicate between the client and the server.

In order to replicate, three things must happen:

- Two database replicas must exist.
- A communications connection between the replicas must exist.
- The replication process must be initiated manually or through a schedule.

Notes can keep databases synchronized through replication, which can occur between two Domservers or between Notes workstations and a Domino server. Domino system administrators manseveral replication tasks on the Domino server as a part of their jobs. The focus of a Notes client is to replicate databases to your Notes client that you'll want to use when disconnected from a ser

Database Replicas and Copies

You can make two types of copies from a database: an ordinary copy and a replica copy. In an orary copy, the original database remains intact and the copy of it reflects the moment in time when copy is made. From that point forward, the two databases (the original and the copy) are distinct f one another; changes to each are made independently of one another and will never be shared betwthe two. Replica databases, on the other hand, can share changes made to them. A replica copy is n of an original database and maintains a relationship with the original database; these are referreas *replica copies*.

Between two replica databases, the replication process operates at the document level. During lication, Notes compares one database to another, determines any incremental changes by checkwhich documents are new, which have been modified, and which have been deleted in each, and t it sends and receives document additions, updates, and deletions between the databases. Whenument updates are sent (or received), Notes only copies data from fields whose values have chang Entire documents are not copied each time a change is made; only incremental changes are transfer This is called *field-level* replication, and it makes Notes replication efficient and fast.

Replication operates within the security model of Notes and Domino. If, as a user of a datab you only have the ability to read documents in a server-based replica, you will only be able to recnew and updated data from the server to your local replica. Any changes made on your end cango to the server because you have only read-access privileges.

Creating Database Copies

To create a snapshot copy of a database, you can use the menu sequence File ➢ Database ➢ NeCopy while inside the database. This will create a new (ordinary) copy of the database; however is not a replica copy.

The way Notes and Domino know whether a database is a replica or a copy is through the use of a unique identifier, the Replica ID, associated with every database. The Replica ID is a relatively long and hard to remember number. Even if a database is not a replica copy, it has a Replica ID. When a database is a replica, the original and the replica share the same Replica ID. When a database is a copy, its Replica ID is different from that of the original. If you're curious, you can check the Replica ID for a database. With the database open, display the database properties using the menu sequence File ➢ Database ➢ Properties, change to the Info tab, and observe the Replica ID number about halfway down the dialog box (see Figure 10.1).

FIGURE 10.1
You can find the Replica ID on the Info tab of the Database Properties InfoBox.

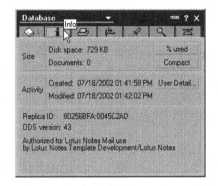

Creating Database Replicas

You can create database replicas on Notes workstations or on Domino servers. One common scenario in which you would create database replicas is when you use a notebook computer both in the office and away from the office. You can place replicas of key databases on your notebook computer's local disk drive so you can access them when you leave the office and without being connected to the Domino server. For example, you can place a replica of your mail database on your notebook computer so you can read messages or compose new ones while you are away from the office. You can also create a replica of an important discussion database so you can read topics others have posted, post new topics, or reply to existing topics, all without being connected to a Domino server. In this scenario, new documents that you create or existing documents that you modify while operating in a disconnected mode are stored locally in your replica copy of the database. When you connect to the Domino server, you need to replicate to synchronize any changes that were made.

Another common scenario for creating database replicas is when you use two computers. For example, you may use one computer at work and another at home. In this case, you probably connect to your office Domino server through dial-up communications, which are fairly slow. You could establish real-time access to the databases (which would be like opening them over the network in the office), but access would be sluggish. Alternatively, you could create replicas of key databases on your home computer's local disk drive so you can access them more quickly and without your dial-up communications connection active.

As a Lotus Notes user, you have two ways to create replicas:

♦ Through the Lotus Notes client
♦ Copying the operating system .nsf file that represents a database (which is done outside Lotus Notes)

NOTE *Copying the operating system file that represents a database is the same as creating a replica in Notes. If you conn to a Domino server's file system over a network—through Windows NT file/print services, for example—you can cop database file to your computer. We recommend you don't use this method, however, because you bypass Domino's securit*

Additionally, Domino administrators and Domino programmers can create replica database doing the following:

♦ Using the Domino Administration client
♦ Using the Domino Web Administration interface
♦ Using the Domino Designer client
♦ Using LotusScript to create them programmatically

To create a database replica, begin by being inside the open database that you want to use as y starting point. From the open database, use the menu sequence File ➤ Replication ➤ New Rep which displays a dialog box similar to the one shown in Figure 10.2. The Replica Settings tab is a lapsible area that has been expanded in the figure; it initially appears collapsed.

FIGURE 10.2

Create Replica
dialog box

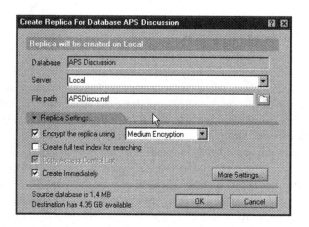

If a replica of the database already exists, you will see a slightly different dialog box, as showr Figure 10.3, warning you that a replica already exists.

FIGURE 10.3

Overwriting a
replica

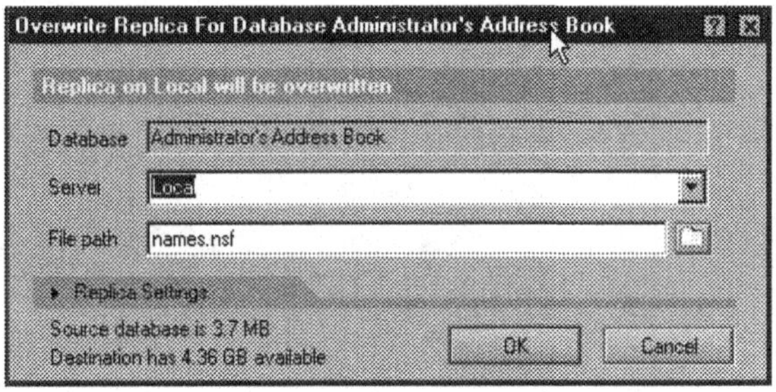

Let's focus on the information required when creating a replica and not overwriting an existing one:

Database   This is a read-only area that displays the title of the database; it will be identical for all replica copies of a database and cannot be changed.

Server   This drop-down list will display all servers to which you are presently connected. The default for the field is Local, meaning you want the replica copy to be created and stored on your local computer.

File Path   The file path and operating system name for the replica copy. You can change this to the unique name of your choosing. Notes databases generally have a three-character extension of .NSF (Notes Storage Facility); this is a good convention by which to abide. Use the yellow file folder to the right of the drop-down list to browse the file system to find the exact file path in which to store the file.

Encrypt the Replica Using   Encrypting a database, especially one stored on your local computer, is the best and most complete way to protect information. Encrypting means that only the person doing the encrypting will be able to open the database at a later time. Three strength levels of encryption are available: strong, medium, and simple. The differences between the three are reflected in the complexity of the algorithm used to encode the database as well as the time it takes to encrypt and decrypt the information.

Create Full Text Index for Searching   When a database has a full-text index, it can be quickly searched for information. Use this option to create a full-text index directly after creating the replica copy.

Copy Access Control List   The access control list (ACL) is the security mechanism that protects the database by listing users allowed to access the database and their privilege level once inside. Enabling this option copies the ACL from the original database and uses it for the replica copy of the database. For a full discussion of how an ACL protects a database, see Chapter 11, "Lotus Notes and Domino Security."

Create Immediately   Replicas can be created in the foreground interactively or in the background as part of Notes' multitasking capabilities. Choose Create Immediately to force the replica to be made in the foreground interactively.

More Settings   Clicking the More Settings button displays the replication settings area, shown in Figure 10.4, and allows you to set specific parameters to be used when doing a replication.

FIGURE 10.4

Replication Settings
window

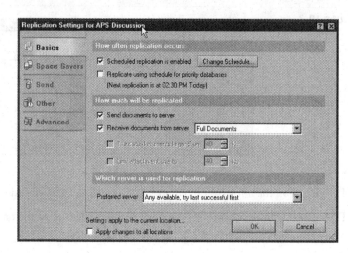

REPLICATION SETTINGS

Replicas can contain a subset of the information contained in the original or an exact duplicatio
the information. You can choose to include documents meeting a certain criteria. For example,
could create a replica of a database that tracks sales leads and only includes customers in your reg
You could also choose to include only documents added or modified in the last 30 days. If you
the criteria on the form name specified on documents, you can include certain types of documen
a replica. For example, you could create a replica of your mail database that only contains to do
entries.

The Replication Settings window helps you configure information about scheduling, choose
types and the amount of information that should be replicated, and set whether it should be sir
direction (send or receive) or bidirectional (send and receive).

*TIP   You can access the replication settings using other methods: either by selecting File ➤ Database ➤ Propert
and the Replication Settings button, by selecting File ➤ Replication ➤ Settings, or by right-clicking a database boc
mark and selecting Replication ➤ Settings.*

There are five replication configuration areas: Basics, Space Savers, Send, Other, and Advanc
Replication settings determine the characteristics of a database replica. You can use these setting
set up selective replication (or replication of subsets of documents). This is helpful when you n
to replicate a large database to your computer's local disk drive but you don't have space to store
entire database. You can also use selective replication to limit replication to recently added or n
ified documents. Let's look at each of the replication configuration areas:

Basics   The Basics area is what you see displayed automatically, as in Figure 10.4. Here, you
enable scheduled replication and set a schedule using the Change Schedule button, which displ
the Replication Schedule dialog box shown in Figure 10.5. In a very detailed manner, you can sp
ify the days and times that replication should take place and what kind of notification you wo
like regarding the process.

In the middle of the Replication Settings dialog box (Figure 10.4), you can specify whether this replica will send documents to other replicas. If you never want to send your updates to other databases, disable this option. Likewise, you can set constraints on the documents that this replica will receive from other replicas; you can specify to receive only:

◆ Full documents (the default)

◆ Partial documents

◆ Summary only

◆ Smallest first

If you choose to receive partial documents, you can set the size that documents should be truncated at (40KB default) and the maximum size attachments can be inside of documents (again, a 40KB default). This gives you a way to eliminate the replication of attachments altogether by setting the size limit to zero.

Finally, the Basics area lets you specify which servers to use for replication and which to try first. If you know you have a direct connection to a specific server, this is the place to set that server's name so that you can make the replication process go as fast as possible. You can also tie into the Location documents stored in your personal address book by marking the option to apply the replication settings to all locations.

FIGURE 10.5

Replication Schedule dialog box

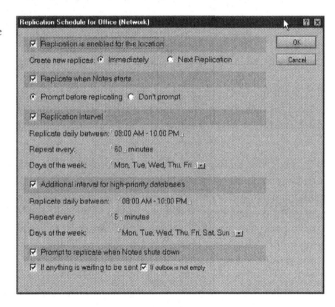

Space Savers   The Space Savers section allows you to choose to remove documents that have been modified within a period of time you specify in days; the number of days specified he related to the document purge interval discussed in the following section. You can fine-tune replication settings to reduce the number of documents transferred during a replication by cl ing to replicate documents in certain views or folders or by choosing documents that meet a ce criteria. You specify the criteria by writing a formula; the formula editing window becomes a when the Documents That Meet a Selection Formula box is enabled. Figure 10.6 is set to space by replicating only documents in the My Favorites folder.

FIGURE 10.6

Replicating subsets of information

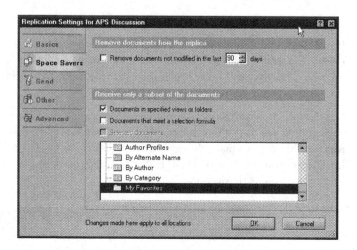

Send   You can prevent the sending of certain types of changes from one database to a repl database. This includes the ability to prevent deletions from replicating, changes in the title the database, the catalog information, and local security changes. Figure 10.7 shows the S options.

Other   The Other section allows you to temporarily disable replication, set a scheduled replica priority, limit incoming replication by date, and establish a CD-ROM publishing date. Tempora disabling replication is useful when you want to skip replication for a specific database with changing your configuration. When you enter a CD-ROM publishing date, Notes only scans documents created or modified since this date during the first replication. This is helpful when are using large databases that you receive the initial replica copy of via CD-ROM. Figure 10.8 sh the special limitations options.

FIGURE 10.7

Send options for
replication

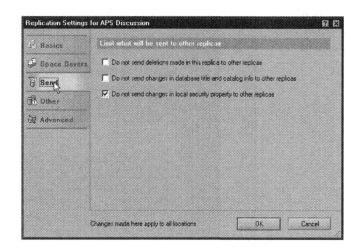

FIGURE 10.8

Special replication
limitations

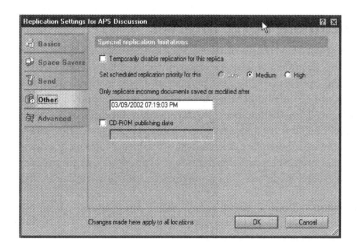

Advanced The Advanced section, shown in Figure 10.9, allows you to choose a specific computer to replicate with and a specific server from which it can receive changes. When this replica is located on a different computer or attempts to replicate with a different server, no replication will occur. You can also configure Notes to replicate subsets of documents in this section, such as the Space Savers section, except that you can also specify data at the design element level. The check boxes at the bottom allow you to choose specific design elements and fields to replicate.

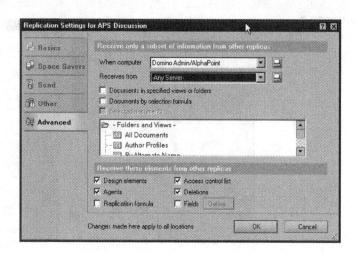

FIGURE 10.9
Server and element restrictions

Document Purge Interval

In the Space Savers area of the Replication Settings window, you can specify the number of day which a document will be automatically deleted if it has not been changed or modified. Whethe not this option is enabled, the number of days specified is used internally to the system; specific one-third of the number that appears here (see the top of Figure 10.6) is known as the *purge inte* In Figure 10.6, the number is 90 days (which is the default), making the purge interval 30 days. purge interval is used internally to Notes to manage deletion stubs.

When documents are deleted from a database, Notes retains a delete record, or *stub*, to track the ument. Lotus Notes uses this deletion stub to ensure that the document is removed from all replica the database. By default, Notes purges deletion stubs one day after the purge interval has taken pla

WARNING *Be sure to replicate at least one time during the purge interval in order to receive deletion stubs made other replicas; otherwise, one replica may contain documents that were deleted in other databases.*

Replicating a Database

Replication takes place between two replica databases at a time. If there is a replica copy on a server in N York and one on a server in Florida and one on a server in Virginia, the three do not replicate as a gro Instead, depending on how it's been configured, the New York database may replicate with the Flori database, and then the Florida database will replicate with the Virginia database. And then the process st all over again. Replication brings a database up-to-date, which means the second after it completes, tl databases are potentially out-of-date again—if there is activity in the database—until the next replica takes place.

One important aspect of database replicas is that they are on a peer level with the original datab Notes and Domino treat the databases the same regardless of which is the original and which is replica copy. In fact, they both are referred to as *replicas*. Replication, the process of synchronizing replicas, does not rely on which database was the original and which was the copy either. Replication depends only on the direction in which it was invoked (send, receive, or both), security, replication settings in each replica, and document changes contained in each replica.

So, given that two database replicas exist (meaning you created a database replica as discussed earlier) and a communications path between the replicas also exists, you can replicate a database. The replication process can take place based on the schedule specified in the Replication Settings window or manually.

Scheduled Replication

While you're working with your Notes client and have a connection to an appropriate server, replication will take place in the background according to the database's replication settings. You can check replication history to see the after-the-fact status of replication. Replication history is maintained in each database that contains a date-time stamped entry for each previous replication with specific servers. Notes uses this information to determine which documents need to be replicated.

You view replication history through the Replication History dialog box (see Figure 10.10). You have a number of ways to bring up this dialog box:

- Opening the database and selecting File ➤ Replication ➤ History
- Using File ➤ Database ➤ Properties and clicking the Replication History button
- Right-clicking a database bookmark and selecting Replication ➤ History from the context menu
- Right-clicking a database entry on the Replicator page and selecting Replication History

FIGURE 10.10

Replication History dialog box

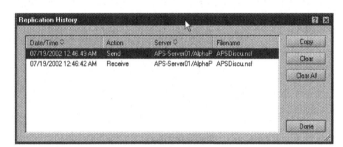

An entry is made to replication history for all replications, whether they are scheduled, carried out in the background, or interactively run.

Manually Replicating a Database

If you have a replica database open, the quickest way to replicate it is to use the menu option File ➤ Replication ➤ Replicate to display the Replicate dialog box, shown in Figure 10.11. The name of the database that is replicating appears in the title bar of the dialog box and is good to use as a visual sanity-check as you begin the process.

FIGURE 10.11

Menu-based
Replicate dialog box

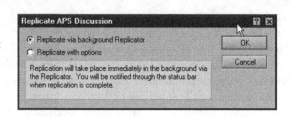

From here, you can choose to replicate in background mode (the default) or choose to repl
with options, which means to do it interactively immediately.

REPLICATE IN THE BACKGROUND

To replicate in the background, leave the default radio button checked and click OK. The replica
will take place with the current options set in the Replication Settings window for this replica. W
replication is performed in the background, you don't have to wait for it to complete to work on c
Notes tasks. You can read your e-mail, manage your to do list, or participate in a discussion data
while background replication is processing. The Notes Replicator also processes e-mail in the I
ground. It pulls e-mail messages from POP3 and IMAP4 mail servers, and it sends Domino
SMTP mail to remote servers. You just configure how you want background replication and e-
processing to occur and enable a schedule if necessary, and the Notes Replicator will automati
keep your local databases synchronized and your e-mail messages flowing.

The status bar at the bottom of the Notes client will display two successive messages telling
that the replication request was submitted and that it has completed (see Figure 10.12).

FIGURE 10.12

Status bar notices

That was easy! If there was a problem during the replication, that would also generate a mes
to the status bar.

REPLICATE WITH OPTIONS (INTERACTIVE)

Choosing the second radio button shown in Figure 10.11 lets you override the normal replicatio
tings for this run of the replicator process. Replication using this process will take place interacti
and you will watch its progress on your screen. When this option is chosen, the Replicate windov
plays as shown in Figure 10.13.

FIGURE 10.13

Replication options

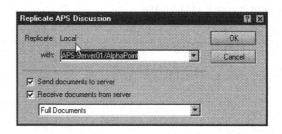

Once you've chosen the server to replicate with and decided on the send and receive options for this run of the replicator, clicking OK starts the replication process. A progress bar will display as the updates are being made, and the final result is a Replication Statistics dialog box (see Figure 10.14). This dialog box reports how many additions, deletions, and updates were sent or received as well as whether any errors were detected during the process.

FIGURE 10.14

Replication statistics

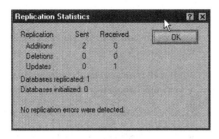

Interactive replication prevents you from doing anything else while the database is replicating. Because replication is an incremental process, sending and receiving only documents that change, the process itself goes fairly quickly for all but the first replication.

TIP   Manual interactive replication is also known as foreground replication.

The Replication Page

The Replication page in the Lotus Notes client centralizes replication activity for scheduled and regularly replicating databases. You can access it from the Replication bookmark. Figure 10.15 shows the page and bookmark. This page has been completely updated for Notes 6.

FIGURE 10.15

Replication page

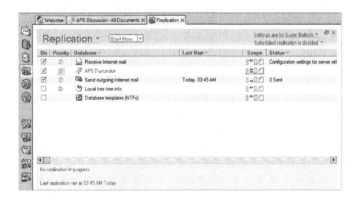

On the Replication page, you can configure how you want background replication and offline e-mail processing to occur. Each row in the main part of the screen represents types of entries and can be a replica database, an e-mail process, or a special action. Whenever you create a new replica, an entry is automatically added to this page. The order in which the entries appear is the order, top to bottom, in which Notes will replicate the databases.

Each entry in the list is associated with a type (see Table 10.1).

TABLE 10.1: TYPES OF REPLICATION ENTRIES

ENTRY TYPE	DESCRIPTION
Database	Application databases such as discussions and custom databases in your organization.
Send Outgoing Mail	Sends mail from your local Notes mail database (MAIL.BOX) to your home server's mail database; this entry cannot be deleted from the Replication p
Receive Internet Mail	Retrieves mail from POP and IMAP accounts.
Send Outgoing Internet Mail	Sends mail to SMTP accounts; this entry cannot be deleted from the Replication page.
Local Free Time Info	Updates calendar and scheduling entries; this entry cannot be deleted fro the Replication page.
Database Templates	Updates .NTF template database files; this entry cannot be deleted from t Replication page.
Call	Connects you to a Notes Direct Dialup location.
Hangup	Disconnects you from a Notes Direct Dialup location.

The Replicator page is related to and associated with the current Location document. Any sett you change on the Replication Page are saved with the current Location document. This is a powe feature, because you can establish multiple replication configurations and each is specific to a pa ular Notes configuration. Depending on the Location document currently in use, the list of ent on the Replication page will change. For instance, the option to Receive Internet Mail is only sho when the Location document in effect is associated with an Internet POP or IMAP mail accou

CONFIGURING A REPLICATION ENTRY

For each entry, you can control several configuration settings from the Replication page. The ch box located along the left side of each row determines whether the entry is enabled and curren active. Double-clicking this will either enable or disable the replication. The Priority setting is be read from the Replication Settings area (discussed earlier and shown in Figure 10.8) and is either h priority or not; one clock icon displays for normal priority, and two overlapping clock icons disp for high priority.

The Scope column shows you the direction of the replication using an arrow. Your local comp is on the left and the server is on the right. A right-pointing arrow tells you that the replication se information to the server but does not receive any information. Similarly, a left-pointing arrow t you that the replication receives information from the server but does not send any information two arrows are present, the replication both sends and receives. You can also click the Scope colu

When clicked for either the send mail or receive mail entries, a read-only dialog box displays that describes the direction and purpose of the replication entry. When clicked for the local free time information, the dialog box shown in Figure 10.16 displays and allows you to change the settings.

FIGURE 10.16

Free Time Replication Settings dialog box

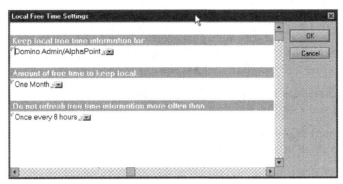

When the Scope button is clicked for database templates, the dialog box shown in Figure 10.17 displays and allows you to override the default of only receiving template changes.

FIGURE 10.17

Template defaults

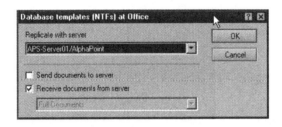

For application databases, such as discussions, TeamRooms, and custom applications in your company, clicking the Scope button opens the Replication Settings dialog box shown in Figure 10.4. From here, you can change any of the settings for the replication entry. For server selection, you can select a Domino server or you can select a choice that will enable Notes to try multiple servers. The first choice—Any Available, Try Last Successful First—will instruct Notes to use any server listed but to start by trying the server used in the last successful replication. For each Domino server listed, there will be a corresponding Any Available, Try *Servername* First option, which instructs Notes to use any server listed but to start by trying the corresponding Domino server.

TIP   *Double-clicking any of the non-action areas of the row (the check box and scope areas invoke an action) will open the local replica database.*

PERFORMING REPLICATION WITH THE REPLICATION PAGE

With the Notes Replicator configuration defined, you can now initiate background replication. It is considered background because it uses the Replication page and will not stop you from doing other tasks while the replication is running. So even though you will initiate it manually, it is known as

background replication. We'll call it *manual background replication.* Performing replication this way will a̶
you to update a specific database or send/receive e-mail without waiting for the next scheduled e̶
You can perform a variety of replication tasks depending on what is allowed for the Location ̶
ument you are using.

The Start Now button, visible near the top-left corner of the Replication page and shown in̶
ure 10.15, is a drop-down button with three choices:

Start Now When this option is selected, all databases with entries on the Replication page̶
with a check mark in the On column will begin replicating.

Start Mail Only Now When this option is selected, replication of mail will take place in̶
ing the sending and receiving of Notes mail and Internet mail.

Start High Priority Databases Now Only databases marked as high priority and enabled ̶
a check mark will be replicated.

With the Replication page displayed, the Actions menu in the Notes client gives you another ̶
to initiate variations of the replication process (see Figure 10.18).

FIGURE 10.18

Replication
Actions menu

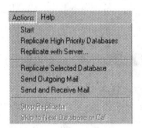

The following options are available from the Action menu:

Start When this option is selected, all databases with entries on the Replication page and ṿ̶
a check mark in the On column will begin replicating. This is the same as clicking the Start N̶
button on the Replication page.

Replicate High Priority Databases This option initiates replication for all databases marke̶
high priority. You can mark a database as high priority by modifying its replication settings.

Replicate with Server This option displays a dialog box that lets you choose a server with̶
which to replicate and initiates replication to the server selected for all enabled replication ent̶

Replicate Selected Database This option initiates replication for the database or set of da̶
bases highlighted (a solid blue background appears across the entire entry line) in the list of d̶
base replica entries. Use Ctrl+Shift and Ctrl+Alt to select multiple entries in the list.

Send Outgoing Mail This entry sends any pending messages stored on your local compute̶
the outgoing mailbox; the mail is sent to your home mail server by default or to a server that kn̶
how to deliver mail to your home mail server. If your current location document is set up for̶
Internet connection, Internet mail will be sent.

Send and Receive Mail This entry sends any pending messages stored on your local computer in the outgoing mailbox to your home mail server and receives incoming mail from your home mail server. If your current location document is set up for an Internet connection, Internet mail will be sent and received.

Stop Replicator This option interrupts and stops the replication process completely while it is in progress.

Skip to Next Database or Call This option stops the replication of the currently replicating database and moves to the next replication entry in the list.

REPLICATION AND THE RELATIONSHIP TO LOCATION AND CONNECTION DOCUMENTS

To perform a replication, the Replicator service establishes a connection to Domino servers in the same way Notes does when opening server-based databases. It uses the current Location document to determine what connection types are configured. If the server is not available directly, Connection documents visible to the current Location document establish the connection. The current Location document, combined with associated Account documents, is also used to determine how mail send and receive entries are processed. For a complete discussion of Location and Connection documents, refer to Chapter 9, "Communicating with Domino Servers."

You can edit or review the replication settings for the current Location document by using the menu sequence File ➤ Mobile ➤ Edit Current Location or by using the status bar pop-up for the Location area and choosing Edit Current. Both methods will directly display the Replication tab in the current Location document, as shown in Figure 10.19.

FIGURE 10.19

Location document replication settings

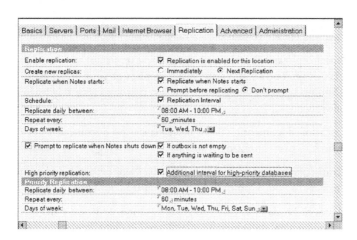

With the Location document open, you can enable replication, specify when to create new replicas, modify the replication schedule, and configure the prompts you receiving during the replication process. Defining a schedule involves entering values for the following fields:

Replicate Daily Between Defines the period or periods of time that the Replicator should initiate background replication. It is usually entered as a range (for example, 6:00 A.M. – 10:00 P.M.).

You can also enter individual times, which instructs the Replicator to initiate background lication at that time. If you want to replicate continuously, enter a range that covers a 24-h period (for example, 6:00 A.M.– 5:59 A.M.).

Repeat Every   Defines the repeat interval, in minutes, within the range of times defined ir Replicate Daily Between options. The Replicator will repeat background replication every t this interval of time passes.

Days of Week   Determines which days of the week are included in this schedule.

MAKING USE OF REPLICATION

In the daily process of doing your job, you will make use of replication whenever you disconnect f your office server and go mobile with Lotus Notes. Typical tasks that make use of replication inc the following:

- Reading and composing your e-mail
- Staying up-to-date in Notes databases
- Referencing web pages online or offline

Using Your Mail Database Remotely

The ability to read and compose e-mail offline is powerful. You can search your mail database loc if you need to refer to messages. You can catch up with new e-mail or organize existing messages folders when it is more convenient. You can even compose new messages as you think of sometl or respond to existing messages. When you have access to a phone line, you can use dial-up com nications to connect to your Domino server and synchronize your changes. To use your mail data remotely, there are certain requirements:

Local replicas   You must create a local replica of your mail database on your computer's lc disk drive. You should also create a replica of your organization's Domino Directory or Mc Domino Directory so you can address messages remotely by looking them up in company's address book.

Location document   You'll need a Location document to use while working remotely and n switch to this Location document when running Notes remotely.

Connection document   You'll need a Connection document to tell your Notes client how connect to your Domino server via dial-up communications.

Account Document   If you are using Internet-based e-mail remotely, you must create Acco documents to access Internet mail accounts. See Chapter 13, "Accessing the Internet with a N Client," for more information on Account documents.

Also, you should understand how Notes processes e-mail, including how it uses your person address book and locally stored Domino Directory replicas. See Chapter 5, "Communicating w Notes Mail," for more information on the mail capabilities of Notes.

Using Databases Remotely

In addition to mail, you can use the Lotus Notes client to work with *any* Notes database offline or remotely while dialing in. Let's say you use a lead-tracking database in the office. You can take a copy of this database with you when you make sales calls. Throughout the day, you can add new information to your local replica. When you get a minute, you can establish a dial-up communication with your Domino server and replicate all of your changes. At the same time, you can receive new information added to the database by your colleagues. To use a database remotely, there are certain requirements:

Local replica You must create a local replica of your database on your computer's local disk drive.

Location document You must have a Location document (or configure an existing one) to use while working remotely and must switch to this Location document when running Notes remotely.

Connection document You must create a Connection document to use when connecting to your Domino server via dial-up communications.

Group document If the database you are using remotely enforces security on all replicas, you may need to add Group documents to your personal address book. If this is the case, your Domino administrator should have the information you need to create these documents.

Referencing Web Pages Online or Offline

If you use Notes to browse the Web, you can also access previously visited web pages when you're away from the office. You can even search through previously visited web pages to find information. To access previously visited web pages, you'll need a few things:

Location document (for online browsing) You must create a Location document (or configure an existing one) to use for browsing the Web online using Notes. You can choose to use the native browser built into Notes or the Notes with Microsoft Internet Explorer feature. This allows you to use Microsoft Internet Explorer's familiar interface and Hypertext Markup Language (HTML) rendering engine and store web pages in a Notes database for offline use. You must switch to the Location document when you access the Web online via Notes. When you create the Location document, Notes will create your Personal Web Navigator database if it does not already exist.

Location document (for offline browsing) You must create another Location document (or configure an existing one) to use for browsing previously visited web pages offline using Notes. These pages are stored in your Personal Web Navigator database.

Connection document You must create a Connection document to use when you connect to the Internet remotely to update your Personal Web Navigator database.

ROAMING USERS

When the Domino system administrator registers you as a Lotus Notes user, he or she can designate that you have the ability to be a roaming user. If this is the case, some automatic replica databases are established for you on your home Domino server. These automatic replicas will allow you to a▪ key configuration features of your Lotus Notes client even when logged on from someone else's ▪ puter. Figure 10.20 shows the Enable Roaming for This Person option on the Basics tab that ▪ administrator chooses to mark a user as roaming.

NOTE   *The Roaming feature was not included as part of the initial version of 6.0 that was released on 9/26/▪ If you are not using a version that supports roaming, the Roaming category and its options will not be present. This feat▪ can be found in later releases of Lotus Notes and Domino.*

FIGURE 10.20

Allowing a person to roam

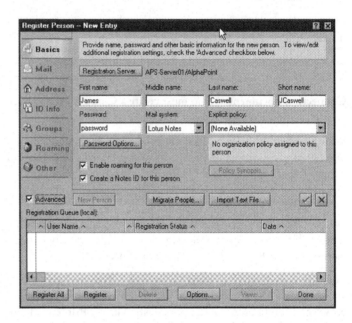

Additionally, there is an entire set of options that the administrator configures on the Roaming▪ when registering a new Lotus Notes user (see Figure 10.21).

The result of being set up as a roaming user is the creation of a special reserved Roaming subdirec▪ on your Domino mail server. Figure 10.22 shows these directories, which are stored in the directo▪ `C:\Lotus\Domino\Data\roaming`.

Within a roaming user's special roaming directory, an initial set of replicas on the server is a▪ matically created (see Figure 10.23). Table 10.2 describes the files.

FIGURE 10.21
Specifying roaming
options

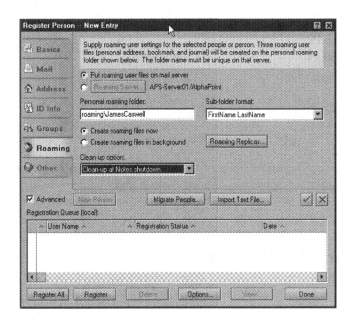

FIGURE 10.22
Roaming directories

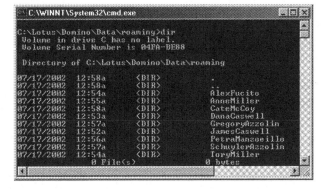

FIGURE 10.23
Roaming files

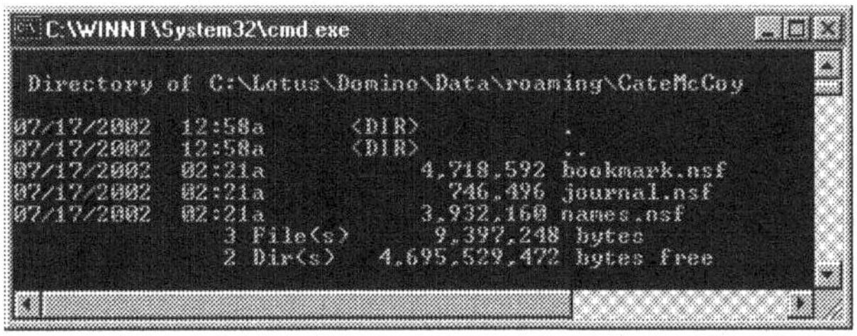

TABLE 10.2: INITIAL ROAMING FILES	
FILENAME	**PURPOSE**
Bookmark.nsf	The bookmarks that define what your Lotus Notes desktop looks like
Journal.nsf	Your personal journal
Names.nsf	Your personal address book

With the creation of these files, you can access your personal information even when you're sitting at your own computer. The result is that wherever you log on from, the screens you see Lotus Notes and your ability to replicate and use Location documents will be identical to how do it at your own computer.

Managing Replicas

The Replication page is your central place for managing replicas and the replication process. Toge with this page, there are other bookmarks and menu options that will help you stay on top of the lication process.

Bookmarks and Replicas

Bookmarks default to opening the newly created replica unless you specify otherwise. To find ou replica to which a bookmark points, right-click the bookmark and select Open Replica. A menu ing all replicas of the database and an option called Manage List will be displayed. The replica which the bookmark is currently pointing will have a check mark next to it (see Figure 10.24).

FIGURE 10.24
Replica bookmarks

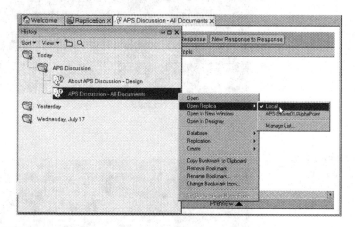

Notes will open the replica you select and change the bookmark so it will open by default from now on. You can change the replica to which a bookmark points. Without actually opening the replica, hold down Shift and click the server name of the replica in the submenu.

The Manage List selection will bring up a Manage Replica Server List dialog box. You can use it to add and remove replica servers for individual databases. To have Notes query your catalog server's Domain Catalog for replica servers, use the Discover button.

Removing an Entry from the Replication Page

There are several ways to remove a replication entry from the list on the Replicator page. If the replica is no longer valid, meaning it no longer exists, double-clicking the entry will pop up a message that asks you if you want to remove the bookmark (the entry listing) from the Replication page (see Figure 10.25).

FIGURE 10.25
Removing a
replication entry

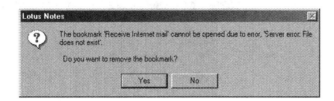

You can also directly remove any entry by using the submenu that appears when you right-click a replication entry. The submenu contains entries to do tasks like access the:

◆ View the Database Properties Infobox.

◆ Change the replication priority by clicking the High Priority entry.

◆ Check the replication history.

◆ Initiate the replication of the selected database.

The Visual Look of the Replication Page

At the top-left corner of the Replication page, the word *Replication* appears. This is a drop-down list of options that let you configure how the page is presented visually (see Figure 10.26).

FIGURE 10.26
Visual options for the
Replication page

You have your choice of icon sizes, with smaller icons allowing you to see more replication er
without needing to scroll. You can set the Replication page to be a slide-out window as well as cl
ing whether to display all replicas or only those that have a check mark in their "On" column.

Another nice feature to help you manage sets of database replicas is to put them in a folder.
is the Create Folder option visible in Figure 10.26. Using this option lets you name a folder wha
you want, drag and drop entries from the Replication page into the folder, and then replicate
folder entries as a group. Figure 10.27 shows a folder, Cates Replicas, with one entry, the APS
cussion database.

FIGURE 10.27
Replication folders

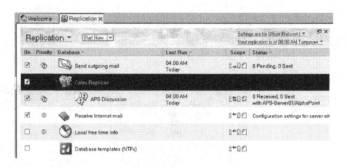

Replication Conflicts and Save Conflicts

Replication conflicts occur when multiple people change the same document in different repl
between replication cycles. Notes deals with these situations by designating one of the changed co
as a Main document and making the other a response to it in parent-child fashion. It determin
which document has been modified more times and designates it as the Main document. If both
been modified the same number of times, Notes determines which was saved most recently and
ignates this as the Main document. The child document is marked as a conflict internally to N
and displays in a view with a special gray diamond icon denoting it as a conflict (see Figure 10.

FIGURE 10.28
Replication or save
conflict

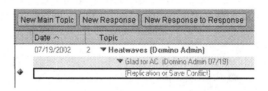

Resolving the conflict requires human intervention, and someone must open both document
inspect the changes, make the changes to the parent document, and then delete the child docum

The database designer can choose to enable a property that will allow Notes to merge some
lication conflicts into a single document. This instructs Notes to determine whether or not the sa
field was changed in each document, thus causing the conflict. If not, it will merge all changes int
single document. If the same field was changed in both documents, Notes saves the replication c
flict as described.

Save conflicts are similar to replication conflicts except they occur when multiple people change the same document in the same database on a Domino server. For save conflicts, Notes designates the first document saved as the Main document. When other users try to save their copy, Notes asks if they would like to save it as a save conflict, as shown in Figure 10.29.

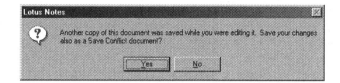

Choosing Yes saves the document as a response to the Main document and marks it with a diamond in the view in the same way as shown in Figure 10.29.

When replication conflicts and save conflicts occur, you have two choices:

◆ Save changes from conflict responses into the Main document and delete all conflict responses.

◆ Save changes from conflict responses and the Main document into a conflict response, save this conflict response as a Main document, and delete the original Main document and all conflict responses.

You can use copy/paste to save changes from one document to another. To save a conflict response as a Main document, you can follow this procedure:

1. Open the conflict Response document in editing mode.

2. Select File ➤ Save.

The Response document will be saved as a Main document. Deleting conflict responses is the same as deleting any other document; press the Delete key.

Replication and Security

Any database you create on your own personal computer is known as a *local database*. By default, you have Manager access to all local databases. This means you have manager-level access to replica databases stored locally on your computer unless the advanced ACL option, Enforce a Consistent Access Control List Across All Replicas of This Database, is in effect.

Without this option in effect, you are allowed to perform actions on local replicas that you would otherwise be unable to perform if the database was accessed from a Domino server. This sounds like a fairly large lapse in security, but don't worry. The replication process will ensure that access levels are observed. It will only allow changes back to the server-based copy that you are authorized to perform. For example, you could change the ACL of a locally stored replica because you have Manager access. But if you try to replicate this change back to the server-based copy, the replication process will fail. All other valid changes will be propagated.

With Manager access to locally stored replicas, you also have access to every document stored within those replicas. You could conceivably gain access to information that you would otherwise be unable to access on server-based copies. Again, this sounds like a lapse in security. In this case, there can be lapses in security if information controls are not properly implemented. At first glance, you might be inclined

to enable the advanced ACL option, Enforce a Consistent Access Control List Across All Replic[a]
This Database. This would provide some degree of security, but this option alone does not secure lo[cal]
stored replicas.

The only way to secure data in Notes databases is to mark them private, encrypt them, or res[trict]
databases that users can access to make replicas. Marking data private just means using Rea[der]
fields to restrict who can see what documents. Encrypted data is secure, but it also adds some c[om]
plexity. To restrict databases that users can access to make replicas, you have a number of opti[ons.]
One includes creating replicas that contain subsets of a database for specific groups of users. T[hen]
you can restrict access to the main (or master) database and the subset replicas on the Dom[ino]
server so users are forced to use only the subset replica that is appropriate for them. Using Read[er]
fields to mark documents private is probably the easiest way to ensure that users have appropr[iate]
access to information regardless of where databases reside.

Chapter 11, "Lotus Notes and Domino Security," examines the topic of security, and now [that]
you know what a replica database is, you can think about security in terms of local replicas.

Summary

Replicas are special types of Notes databases that you use just as you would any other Notes datab[ase.]
You can navigate through views, read and modify existing documents, and create new documents. [You]
can create full-text indexes on replicas so you can perform full-text searches. You can create subsc[rip-]
tions against them and set up archiving just as you can with any other database. The only differen[ce is]
that replicas are synchronized with other replica copies. You can make changes to a replica stored lo[cally]
on your computer and propagate the changes to server-based replicas of that database, and vice vers[a, so]
that changes made to server-based replicas can be propagated to your local replica. In this chapter yo[u]
learned how to create replicas and how to replicate them, as well as understanding a bit of the secu[rity]
involved.

In the next chapter, we'll continue looking at security by discussing all the security features a[vail-]
able in Lotus Notes and Domino.

Lotus Notes and Domino Security

SINCE ITS INCEPTION, LOTUS Notes has incorporated sophisticated security capabilities making it the single most secure client/server environment for your data. In large part, early adopters, government agencies, and corporate users were attracted to Notes because of its security features. The product was designed from the ground up to be used in a distributed yet secure environment. This means that good security features were planned and built into the product and not just tacked on later. In today's Internet and mobile workforce, the security features of Domino continue to impress and attract companies by protecting the increasingly important asset that information represents in today's businesses.

- Security layers
- Domino Directory
- Lotus Notes user ID files
- Public key infrastructure
- Securing databases
- Encryption

Understanding Security Layers

Domino and Lotus Notes take a layered approach to security, at the top level applying the most global level of security possible and at the bottom level providing granular protection. Figure 11.1 demonstrates eight layers of protection that can be mixed and matched to provide the type of security an application requires.

FIGURE 11.1

Layers of security

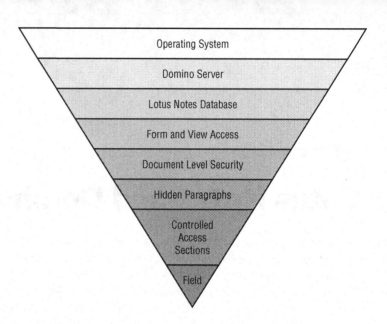

The eight levels depicted are as follows:

Operating system   The operating system on which Domino runs provides a measure of secu
because you need to log into it to use the software available on it. In addition, network administra
can assign read, write, and execute privileges on discretionary portions of an operating system se
to control what a network user can do once they are logged on to the operating system. If an opera
system user does not have the rights to interact with the directory on which Domino is installed,
operating system has effectively denied access at the highest possible point to Domino. Having ac
to an operating system does not automatically give you rights to use the Domino server.

Domino server   The Domino server software, which runs on operating system software, can
configured to allow or prevent individuals, groups, and servers in their quest to access Domino
Domino systems administrator manages the server configuration and controls who has access to
server. Having access to a Domino server does not automatically give you rights to use the datab
controlled by the Domino server.

Lotus Notes database   Every Lotus Notes database application has an access control list (AC
which determines the individuals, groups, and servers that are allowed to use that particular datab
The ACL specifies who may use the database and what privilege levels are initially given to the
of the database. Additionally, the entire contents of a local database can be encrypted, preventi
access by any users other than the user who encrypted it. Having access to a database application
not automatically give you full privileges within the database.

NOTE   *A local database is one that is stored on your computer's hard drive (as contrasted with a database stored on*
server's hard drive).

Form and view access   You can grant form access to control who can create new documents with a form as well as to control who can read documents with a particular form. At the view level, view access controls who can see a particular view. Additionally, views can be hidden from casual users. Having access to a form or view through its ACL does not automatically guarantee that you will be able to see or edit the information.

Document-level security   One of Notes' strongest security features is the ability to control at the user level who is allowed to see and edit documents. Programmers create this effect by using special fields called Authors, Readers, and Public Access fields. Having access to a document that uses any of these fields does not automatically guarantee that you will be able to see all the information contained within the document.

Hidden paragraphs   Programmers have the ability to completely or dynamically hide information inside of documents a paragraph at a time. A paragraph ends with a carriage return line feed character. Additionally, the ability to hide paragraphs from Notes users, web users, or both exists. Being able to see all the information in a document does not guarantee that you will be able to edit the information.

Controlled-access sections   Much like the area of a paper form labeled *For Accounting Use Only*, a programmer can specify a section of a document that is allowed to be edited by a specific set of users, groups, or servers. All other users are allowed to read the information but not modify it. Having edit access to all parts of a document list does not automatically guarantee that you will be able to see all the fields in the document.

Field   At the lowest level, Notes allows you to encrypt fields of information within a document, hiding it from users who do not have the proper encryption keys to decrypt the fields.

As administrators and programmers add increasing levels of security in the Lotus Notes and Domino system, the protection of the data stored in the system is increased.

The Technology of Domino Security

Security within Domino and Lotus Notes relies on two fundamental components:

♦ Domino Directory
♦ Lotus Notes user ID file

Every server has a Domino Directory that stores server configuration information and user information. You may know this as your company or organization's address book. The average user does not have access to the server configuration information but does have access to the user information. The user information is used to address and e-mail other Lotus Notes users.

Every Lotus Notes user working with the Lotus Notes client has a user ID file. Typically, the file has an .id file extension. It may take the form of user.id or the first initial of your first name and first seven characters of your last name, for instance, jjohnsto.id.

Security within Domino and Lotus Notes absolutely relies on the Domino Directory and a user's ID file.

Public Key Infrastructure

At the heart of security provided in the Domino Directory and a Lotus Notes ID file is public key structure (PKI). PKI uses *cryptography* to secure information. Cryptography is a method of scrambl data, passwords, and access paths to safeguard against malicious intent. In public key cryptography keys are used: a public key and a private key. These keys were created for you simultaneously or server when your Lotus Notes username was registered. A special encoding algorithm creates the Lotus and many other products use the RSA encoding algorithm.

NOTE   RSA is an acronym for the authors of the algorithm, Ron Rivest, Adi Shamir, and Leonard Adleman, developed it in 1977. It is the most popular type of encryption algorithm in use today and is a part of Notes as wel web browsers such as Microsoft Internet Explorer and Netscape Navigator.

UNDERSTANDING KEYS

In Lotus Notes, your unique private key is stored in your Notes ID file. The unique public key stored in two places: in the Domino Directory on the server and in your Lotus Notes ID file. public key is freely given to any Notes users who want it; it is publicly available through the Dom Directory. Your private key, on the other hand, is sacred and is never given to, used by, or maile anyone else. Your ID file is the only place it is stored.

How do these two keys work together? Much like going to the bank to open a safety-deposit your private key and your public key are required simultaneously to lock and unlock certain typ information in Lotus Notes. These keys are used to do tasks like the following:

- Authenticating a user
- Validating a user
- Encrypting an e-mail
- Decrypting an e-mail
- Adding an electronic digital signature to an e-mail
- Decrypting an electronic digital signature that was added to an e-mail
- Encrypting a database
- Decrypting a database
- Encrypting a field of information within a document
- Decrypting a field of information within a document

UNDERSTANDING CERTIFICATES

PKI is a certificate-based security solution that is ideal for a distributed computing environment; tralized computing environments do not need this type of security because a central control point be used to provide security. In a distributed environment, which is what Notes is, users are spread geographically and use different means of communicating with a server, making certificate-based se ity necessary.

You can think of a certificate as being similar to using a visa to visit another country; the visa allows you to access the country, but it does not control or grant privileges regarding what you're allowed to do in the country. Additionally, the visa is issued by a trusted and known source. . .generally a government entity. Similarly, a certificate identifies you to a server but does not control what you are allowed to do on that server and is issued by a trusted source. . .a certifier.

A certificate is a system-generated digital stamp that uniquely identifies a server. Servers give the certificates to other servers and to users to allow them to access the server. In Lotus Notes, both servers and users are issued certificates. The certificates are stored in the ID file; a server has an ID file as does a user. A certificate has a few attributes that make it unique:

◆ It derives from or is the root of a hierarchy.

◆ It has an expiration date.

◆ It has an identity (a name).

As an example of the hierarchy, examine Figure 11.2. Here, the Acme company is what is known as a *high-level certifier*. In Domino, it would be the certifier for the first Domino server created in an organization. Additional servers that were brought to life later have their own names but share the same certifier, known as the *root certifier*. In this depiction, the East and West servers derive from a common root certifier, as do all the users. Because they derive from the same certifier, they are said to inherently "trust" one another.

FIGURE 11.2
Certifier
relationships

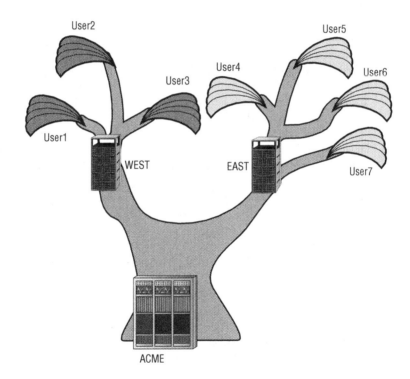

When you log into a Domino server, your Notes user ID is offered to the server for inspec
At that point, the server is looking for three things: a certifier it trusts, an unexpired certificate,
a verifiable identity. The process of verifying that the user has a trusted and unexpired certific
(meaning public keys) is known as *validation*.

At the same time your Notes client offers your ID to the server, your ID is looking for the s
three things! You want to know that the server you're trying to access is trusted, has an unexpirec
tificate, and has an identity you can verify.

So the trust relationship built into certificates is a two-way street. The server first validates th
ent, and in order to proceed, the client validates the server. At that point, the server uses a challe
response process to authenticate a user. *Authentication* is the process of providing the correct passw
to unlock the user's ID file.

TIP *Validation and authentication are often thought of as a unit.*

If you think of your ID file as being similar to your driver's license, certificates are like the s
placed on your license from the issuing state. Just as the seal verifies the authenticity of your lic
and your identity, certificates verify the authenticity of your user ID file and the information it
tains (name and public key).

Originally, Notes used a "flat" certificate structure. ID files contained a name and individua
tificates that validated that name to specific certifying entities. Validation and authentication betv
Notes clients and Notes servers (before they were called *Domino servers*) using flat certificates occu
when their associated ID files contained a certificate in common. Flat certificates were also use
sign and encrypt e-mail and to encrypt documents in databases. Since Release 3, Notes has also
ported a more sophisticated "hierarchical" certificate structure.

As described earlier, validation and authentication is the process performed when a Notes cl
attempts to connect to a Domino server. It is also used between Domino servers. This process ens
the identity of both participants. It is a two-way process. The server ensures the identity of the cl
and the client ensures the identity of the server.

With hierarchical certificates, ID files contain a name and a certificate that validates the name t
organizational certifying entity. In addition, they contain a hierarchy of certificates that validate the c
nizational certifying entity to intermediate organizational certifying entities and ultimately to the r
certifier (the certifying entity that validated all organizational certifying entities in the hierarchy).
idation and authentication between Notes clients and Domino servers using hierarchical certific
occurs when their associated ID files contain certificates generated from the same root certifier, mear
that they are in the same hierarchy.

If the client and server are in different hierarchies, Notes will attempt to use *cross certificates*. C
certificates provide a system of trust between hierarchies. For instance, in Figure 11.2, visualize a
ond, independent tree called ABC Company. In this case, Acme would grant ABC Company a cr
certificate, and vice versa, in order to allow the users of the two companies to trust information pas
between the two organizations. All users derived from a trusted root automatically trust all us
trusted by that root. So, if at the root level Acme trusts ABC Company, all the users below the r
automatically trust one another.

Domino Directory

Every Domino server has a Domino Directory, or address book. The operating system filename is usually `names.nsf`, and it is stored in the `c:\lotus\domino\data` directory of the server's machine. This is the file that contains both the server configuration information and the information about all the users of that particular Domino server. A server has an ID file. In addition, the organization's certifier has an ID file. It is the organization's certifier ID that is used to create all other IDs in the organization for both additional servers and users registered in the Domino Directory. Figure 11.3 shows the ID properties for a server's ID. This information is typically only available to administrators, but it is useful to see that the server is concerned with certificates as well as the user.

FIGURE 11.3

Server's
ID properties

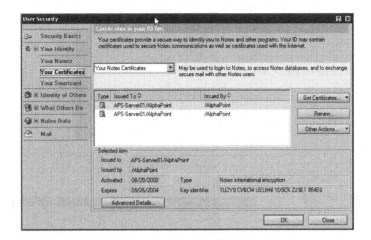

In the center, you'll see three entries for certificates issued to this server by a certifier. The server's name is APS-Server01. The certifier's name is AlphaPoint. In this case, the first entry represents the Notes international encryption certificate issued by the AlphaPoint certifier to APS-Server01. It expires April 4, 2102. This is a particularly long-range certification expiration date; most server certificates expire every two years. The second entry in the list of Notes certificates granted to APS-Server01 is the Notes multipurpose certificate; it also has an expiration date. Finally, the last entry in the list is a certificate issued by the AlphaPoint certifier to the AlphaPoint certifier designating this server as the root certifier. It too has an expiration date. One of the jobs of a Domino system administrator is to maintain the certificates on an ongoing basis because they are absolutely required to be valid for the day-to-day operation of the server.

Lotus Notes User ID Files

As you have surmised by now, your Lotus Notes user ID file is the key to security in your Lotus Notes client and is what allows you to access the safe and secure environment of the Domino server. The user ID file is a relatively small (approximately 3,500 bytes), special file created when your username was registered on the server. It is provided to you by your Domino administrator, or it may be stored in the Domino Directory.

Your ID tells Domino servers who you are. It contains the following information:

◆ Your identity (username)

◆ All certificates issued to you

◆ Your public key

◆ Your private key

◆ Any additional user-created secret encryption keys you created

◆ Any additional user-created secret encryption keys sent to you by other users

Your user ID generally has the file extension .id and is stored on your local computer or ⊂ shared network drive on the server. Because it is a small file, you may also store it on a disk. Your ID file is critically important to the operation of Notes; you cannot use the Lotus Notes client ▾ out it.

EXAMINING YOUR ID FILE

You can get an arm's-length view of the contents of your ID file using the Lotus Notes client ᵃ manage much of its content. The file is not a simple text or word processing file that can be opₑ or edited, but you can inspect and control a good bit of its contents through the Lotus Notes ₗ interface.

To access the contents of your ID file, use the menu sequence File ➢ Security ➢ User Secuᵣ After providing a password, the User Security dialog box displays (see Figure 11.4).

FIGURE 11.4
Lotus Notes
ID properties

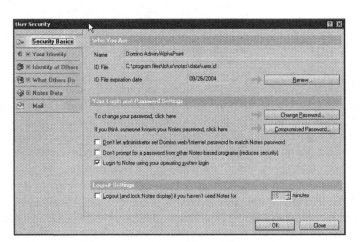

TIP   In Notes, passwords are case sensitive. This means you must type your password exactly as you typed it when yₑ set it.

The User Security interface has six component tabs that help you navigate through the ID's inf mation: Security Basics, Your Identity, Identity of Others, What Others Do, Notes Data, and Maᵢ Let's discuss each one in turn and take a look at the information that is visible by inspecting the ID

Security Basics

On this tab, shown in Figure 11.4, you can discern the user's identity (name), the name and storage location of the ID being examined, and its expiration date. From this tab, you can proactively manage your ID file using the following actions:

- Changing a password
- Walking through steps to troubleshoot a compromised password
- Requesting a certificate renewal

Your user ID never expires; what expires is the certificate that was issued to it. Domino administrators proactively manage the renewal process, so you may never have to request a renewal yourself, but it's nice to know where to do it should you ever need to request one. Changing your password, on the other hand, is something you should do frequently.

Another important feature on this tab is the automatic logout feature at the bottom of the screen. Here, it is enabled and timed at 15 minutes. What this means is that after 15 minutes of inactivity, your Lotus Notes client will log you out. You can also interactively log out of your Notes client at any time by using the menu sequence File ➤ Security ➤ Lock Display or by pressing the F5 key. Once logged out, the next action you take in the client will result in a prompt for your ID's password, as shown in Figure 11.5.

FIGURE 11.5

Password prompt

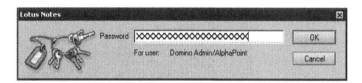

This is the same password prompt window you'll see whenever Lotus Notes and Domino want to challenge you for your password.

Your Identity

This tells you all the information that uniquely identifies you as a Lotus Notes user. Beneath the Your Identity tab are three options: Your Names, Your Certificates, and Your Smartcard.

Your Names   The information on the Your Names tab is primarily read-only and lists your username, any alternate usernames you use that make use of special characters such as the umlaut, any aliases, and your Internet e-mail name. Your Lotus Notes username might be a multiple-part name; it will always include your first and last names as well as the name of your certifier. For example, an ID on APS-Server01 might look like this:

```
James Caswell/AlphaPoint
```

or like this:

```
James Caswell/East/AlphaPoint/US
```

In the first case, the full username consists of just the first name and last name plus the cert name. In the second case, the full username consists of the first name and last name, a mid-leve tifier, plus the root certifier name. Both of these types of usernames represent hierarchical names have been standard in Lotus Notes and Domino since Release 4. Prior to Release 4, flat certific (meaning no hierarchy) were the default type of certificate.

On the Your Names tab, you can also proactively request a name change using the Name Cha button to generate an e-mail to the Domino administrator to perform the name change. After administrator changes your name (which may take several days due to the complexity involved), can decide if you want to be prompted to inspect and accept the name change prior to its taking e

Your Certificates   On the Your Certificates tab, you can examine the names and expiration dat the certificates stored in your ID file, as shown in Figure 11.6.

FIGURE 11.6

Your certificates

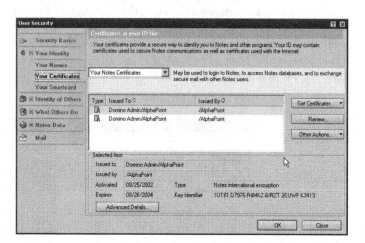

Like the server ID we examined in Figure 11.3, in the center, you'll see entries for certificates iss to this user by a certifier. In this case, the first entry represents the Notes international encryption tificate issued by the AlphaPoint certifier to the Domino Administrator user. It expires 8/26/20(You can tell that it was activated on 8/25/2002, so the default two-year certificate expiration inf mation was applied to this user ID. As the end of that time frame approaches, the Domino syst administrator will proactively renew certificates as a part of their job. The second entry in the lis Notes certificates granted to the user is the Notes multipurpose certificate; it also has an expiration

From this tab, you can proactively do many things to manage the certificates stored in your ID

♦   Get Certificates ➢ Import (Merge) Notes Certificates

♦   Get Certificates ➢ Request New Notes Flat Certificate

♦   Get Certificates ➢ Import Internet Certificates

♦   Get Certificates ➢ Request New Internet Certificates

♦   Renew

♦   Other Actions ➢ Export Notes ID (Safe Copy)

- Other Actions ➤ Respond to Cross Certificate Request
- Other Actions ➤ Mail, Copy Certificate (Public Key)
- Other Actions ➤ Create New Public Keys
- Other Actions ➤ Request Name Changes
- Other Actions ➤ Move Private Key to Smartcard
- Other Actions ➤ Delete from ID File

Your public key is stored in the Domino Directory and is available to other users in your Domino network. Colleagues outside of your Domino network can still securely communicate with you if they have a copy of your public key in their personal address book. Use the option Other Actions ➤ Mail, Copy Certificate (Public Key) to provide your key to Domino users who are outside your Domino system.

To request a certificate, you need to supply a user ID file to the certifying authority. A safe copy of your ID is a skeleton version of your ID file without the private keys that are stored in your real ID. The safe copy is what you will send to other systems that you want to be certified by and that request your ID for certification. You should never send your real ID to anyone.

WARNING *Sending your real ID is dangerous because it allows complete access to your system, your identity, and your encrypted information. When requested to provide an ID for certification purposes, always supply only a safe copy.*

When you create a safe copy of your ID, it is given the default name SAFE.ID and stored in the location of your choice. This may be to your hard drive, a network drive, a disk, or even a CD. From that point, you can mail it as an attachment to whomever requested it or send it via "snail mail" on a disk or CD. After SAFE.ID is certified, you'll receive it back (either through e-mail or physically). At that point, use the Get Certificates ➤ Import (Merge) Notes Certificates option on the Your Certificates tab to merge SAFE.ID into your real ID. This will copy the new certificates into your real ID. At that point, you can delete SAFE.ID. It is a file used only for transport purposes and is never used to log in to a Notes client.

Any certificate you obtain and store in your ID independent from certificates issued by your Domino server must be manually maintained by you. When they expire, they become invalid. Use the Other Actions ➤ Export Notes ID (Safe Copy) option to create a SAFE.ID file on disk that you can supply to the external certifier who originally issued the expiring certificate.

To successfully validate and authenticate with a Domino server whose ID was created from a different certificate hierarchy than your user ID, cross certificates must be issued. A cross certificate acts as a trust mechanism between two certificate hierarchies. The Domino administrator must issue a cross certificate to your ID, to the ID of any organizational certifying entities in your hierarchy, or to the ID of your hierarchy's root certifier. The level at which the Domino administrator issues the cross certificate determines the scope of the access being offered. Issuing the cross certificate to your ID is the most restrictive, and issuing it to your hierarchy's root certifier is the most open. As a user or database developer, you request a cross certificate from the Domino administrator who actually issues the cross certificate for your ID. If the Domino administrator to whom you are making the request is accessible via e-mail, you can request a cross certificate by sending an e-mail message. If not, you can request a certificate by mailing a disk through the postal service.

After a Domino administrator issues a cross certificate to your ID, you will need to accept a [...] certificate from the foreign hierarchy. This is required to complete the two-way process of verif[...] certificates. When you accept a cross certificate, it is stored in your personal address book. Accep[...] cross certificates is an automatic process that is initiated when any one of the following occurs[...]

- ◆ You attempt to access a Domino server in the foreign hierarchy.
- ◆ You attempt to read a signed or encrypted message from someone in a foreign hierarchy[...]
- ◆ You attempt to open a database signed by a person from a foreign hierarchy.

When the automatic process of accepting cross certificates is initiated, the Issue Cross Certificate[...] log box displays the certifier and server information and gives you the chance to interactively accep[...] decline the certificate. If you accept it, it is merged automatically into your information.

Your Smartcard   A new feature in Lotus Notes and Domino 6 is the ability to Smartcard-enab[...] Notes ID in your Lotus Notes client. A *Smartcard* is a physical electronic card, usually about the siz[...] a credit card, issued to system users in large organizations. The Smartcard generates a random, uni[...] alphanumeric personal ID number (PIN) known only to the card and to the systems that use it. W[...] you type in the PIN, it is checked algorithmically for accuracy, and only if the number is correct wil[...] logon succeed.

Identity of Others

Certificates identify people, services, and certification authorities. On this tab, you can enable or dis[...] (better known as *trust* or *not trust*) the certificate associated with a provider that is stored in your II[...]

People, Services   This tab contains a list of people and services that have been merged into you[...] file for the purpose of sending encrypted mail or other communications between you and another [...] son or service. From the list, you can check a box to trust or stop trusting the source. You can [...] view certificate details, trust details, and delete a certificate.

Authorities   You can configure your Notes ID to trust specific authorities. Some of these are se[...] for you automatically, for instance, the certifier that issued your Lotus Notes ID. In Figure 11.7, [...] can see that this user's ID trusts the certificate authority named AlphaPoint.

From Figure 11.7, you can also see that this ID trusts the certifier known as ORG2741. By click[...] the Trust Details button, you can tell that this ID issued a cross certificate to the certifier ORG2[...] (see Figure 11.8).

Cross certificates are stored in your personal address book and state that you will trust any c[...] munications with users and servers that have been certified by ORG2741. Because this certifier is [...] side your own hierarchy, it is known as a *cross certificate*.

The list of certificates changes based on your Certificate Authority View Type. In Figure 11.8,[...] Trusted Notes option is in effect, so those are the certificates being displayed. Other options incl[...] All Notes, All Internet, Notes Root Certificate Authorities, Internet Root Certificate Authoriti[...] Notes Intermediate Certificate Authorities (like East and West in Figure 11.2), Internet Intermed[...] Certificate Authorities, or All.

FIGURE 11.7
Certificate
authorities

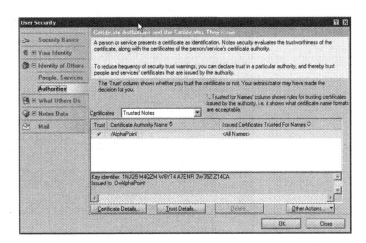

FIGURE 11.8
Trust details

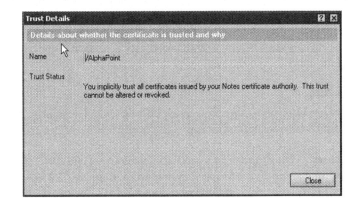

What Others Do

The What Others Do tab stores the execution control lists (ECLs) for your Lotus Notes client. There are three: Workstation ECL, Applet ECL, and JavaScript ECL.

An ECL is designed to protect the Notes client environment from malicious and misbehaving code. It can restrict the execution of Notes formula code, LotusScript code, Java applets, and JavaScript. Additionally, you can specify that only code signed by specific users should not be trusted. Figure 11.9 shows that Domino Administrator/AlphaPoint is allowed to do everything within this client. You can enable or disable the check boxes to the right to restrict individual users, set a default, or control users who do not have any kind of known signature.

FIGURE 11.9
Execution
control list

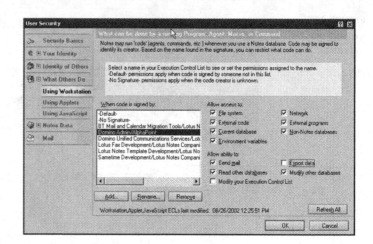

The ECL is similar in concept to the controls in a web browser that a user can enable to pre
cookies from being set or JavaScript code from being executed. In most systems, the Domino sys
administrator establishes your workstation's ECL to standardize security across an organization.
means you may not have access to change the ECL yourself; however, you can always view the sett
using this tab.

Notes Data

The Notes Data tab is where you encrypt databases and documents within a database. There are
subtabs: Databases and Documents.

Databases   Using this tab, you can set a default to automatically encrypt all new locally stored
bases. Database encryption is the best way to protect data on a laptop; if the laptop is stolen or
the data is inaccessible to anyone who does not have the user ID file and its current password.
encrypt a database, Notes scrambles the information in the database making it inaccessible to any
other than the user ID who encrypted it. The encryption is performed using the private key sto
in the ID file. Because this is the only place this key is stored, the ID is required to decrypt the
base. Access to encrypted databases is transparent if the correct user ID is used, meaning you'll n
be prompted with, "Hey, do you want to decrypt or not?" Instead, the information simply appe
unscrambled (decrypted). On the other hand, if you do not have the right ID and try to access
database, you receive a warning message telling you that you're not authorized to open the datal

Documents   Field-level encryption within documents can be accomplished with user-created secr
encryption keys. These keys are different from your public/private keys in that they are single-key ba
rather than dual-key based, meaning all you need to decrypt the data in the field is the same key that
used to encrypt it. Figure 11.10 shows the secret key management window where you can create a new
(giving a name and comment), mail the secret key, and other actions including exporting a secret key by
ing it to a file, deleting a secret key, and importing secret keys given to you by other Lotus Notes use

FIGURE 11.10

Managing secret
encryption keys

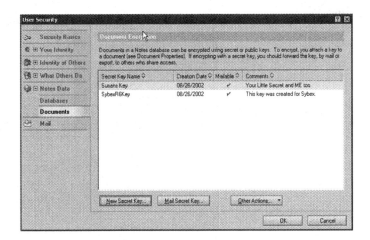

A secret key is applied to the entire document, and any encrypted fields in the document are automatically decrypted and displayed if the secret is present in the ID file when the document is opened. An example of when this might be used is for human resource information; all the information about a person's name and address might be public, but salary information is sensitive and might be stored in an encrypted field. When the document is saved, if the secret key is present, the data in the field is encrypted.

WARNING *Do not delete a secret encryption key from your ID file unless you are absolutely certain there are no documents requiring this key. You will not be able to access encrypted field data on these documents after deleting the associated secret encryption key.*

You can also encrypt data with public keys by selecting each person from the Domino Directory. This is a workable solution when there are only a few individuals who need access.

An individual only needs one of the selected encryption keys (either a secret encryption key or a public key) to access the encrypted field data. All fields designed to support encryption are encrypted using the selected public or secret encryption keys. Users with the appropriate keys will be able to access all encrypted field data on the document.

Mail

Using the Mail tab of the User Security dialog box, shown in Figure 11.11, you can set default actions that do the following:

◆ Automatically encrypt all mail you send

◆ Automatically add a digital signature to all mail you send

◆ Automatically encrypt a saved copy of all mail you send

◆ Automatically encrypt mail you receive that was unencrypted when sent

FIGURE 11.11

Mail encryption
defaults

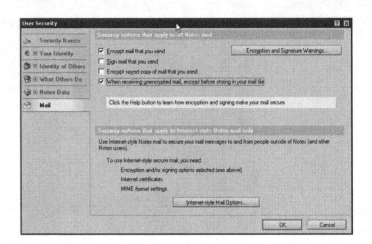

For mail encryption and digital signatures, a combination of your private and public keys is u
Notes handles all the encrypting and decrypting automatically and invisibly. It applies the approp
key at the appropriate time. As background information, Table 11.1 clarifies which key Notes
at a given action point.

TABLE 11.1: ENCRYPTION KEYS FOR SPECIFIC ACTIONS

ACTION	KEY USED
Send an encrypted e-mail	Receiver's public key
Digitally sign an e-mail	Sender's private key
Decrypt an encrypted e-mail	Receiver's private key
Decrypt a digitally signed e-mail	Sender's public key

Your public key is a special code contained within your ID and within the Domino Directo
As the name implies, it is the portion of your unique identity that is shared with others. With yo
public key, other Notes users can participate in secure Notes/Domino communication with
For example, other users can send you encrypted messages. These are messages that have b
scrambled so that other users, even administrators of the Domino environment, cannot read the
When other users send you encrypted messages, your public key is used to encrypt them. When
receive an encrypted message, Notes is able to decrypt it because your ID contains a private key t
can unlock encryption that was performed using your public key. Only your private key can decr
these messages.

NOTE *Your public key is also used to verify the validity of certificates and cross certificates.*

SETTING A PASSWORD ON YOUR ID FILE

Your ID file is your key to using Notes. Anyone who gains access to it can impersonate you in the system. For this reason, it is critically important that you protect this file. The most important security measure you can implement is a password. This ensures that no one can easily use your ID file if they happen to obtain a copy of it. The Domino administrator chooses the minimum level of password protection required for your ID file when it is created. ID file password protection ranges from no password to complex password patterns. If you are setting a password for the first time, you will have either no starting password or one established by your administrator.

To set or change the password on your ID file, use the menu sequence File ➤ Security ➤ User Security and, after providing your password to allow you to work with the ID file, use the Change Password button. Refer to Figure 11.4; the button is located on the right side of the dialog box about halfway down.

When your ID was first created, the Domino system administrator set a strength for it, meaning how good does the password have to be…one character? Two characters? Mixed case? Using numbers within words? If you do not enter a password meeting the minimum requirements set by the Domino administrator, you'll be continually prompted until you manage to appease the password gods with a complex-enough password. Complexity is based on length and the use of letters and numbers.

If your Domino administrator has configured your ID file so no password is required, you will also have the option of clearing the password from your ID file. In the Basics section of the user ID dialog box, click the Clear Password button.

BACKING UP YOUR ID FILE

Because your user ID file contains a private key that uniquely identifies you, there is no way to re-create it. This is quite different from systems that simply use name and password combinations centrally stored in a server. Take precautions to protect your ID file by making a backup copy of it. It is good practice to create multiple secure backups just in case one becomes corrupted. Consider copying your ID file to a disk that you can store in a locked cabinet or room.

WARNING   Your user ID contains a public/private key pair that is calculated when the ID is created. It cannot be re-created! If the file becomes damaged, if you forget the password, or if you lose the file, you will not be able to read data encrypted with that ID.

ID RECOVERY

Notes and Domino includes a method for recovering IDs when users have forgotten their passwords. This is an optional service that an administrator can use on a Domino server, so not all servers will have this feature enabled. ID recovery requires that the Domino administrator set up ID recovery for your ID file. This adds recovery information to your ID file and creates an encrypted copy in an ID repository database. Anytime you change your password or update your user ID, Notes prompts you with a dialog to back up your ID file, which will send it to the Domino server so that the most current copy is available if it needs to be recovered.

When you initially attempt to log in to Lotus Notes, if you provide an incorrect password or do not supply one at all, a dialog box informing you of a wrong password displays; this is shown in Figure 11.12. At this point, you can click the Recover Password to access recovery information for your password or click the Close button to stop trying to get into Notes.

FIGURE 11.12

Unsuccessful
Notes login

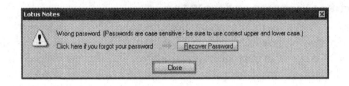

Recovery information is held by the Domino system administrator and, in some cases, mult
Domino system administrators. Each administrator might hold a piece of the complex recovery
word that is embedded into your user ID file. After retrieving the pieces of the recovery passwe
from the administrator(s), you'll choose an ID file to recover after clicking OK in the Unsucces
Notes Login dialog box. At this point, you will be required to enter the series of passwords prov
by your Domino administrator(s). Once your ID is recovered, change its password immediately
discard the recovery information.

TIP   *Remember to replace all copies of your ID file with the recovered ID file.*

SWITCHING ID FILES

When you launch Notes and access a Domino server (or perform any other action that requires y
user ID file), Notes opens the ID file that was most recently used by the Lotus Notes client. If
most recently used ID file is stored on the computer, Notes will attempt to open it. Notes prom
you for a password if one exists. If the most recently used ID file is stored on a disk or other exte
media, Notes prompts you to insert the appropriate media or select another ID file. Selecting ano
ID file is called *switching IDs*.

You may have multiple IDs that you use for different reasons, or your machine may be used
multiple people logging into one Notes client with different Ids, perhaps using location docume
configured to log in to a specific id. In either case, the process of switching to a different ID and u
it is simple. You can use the menu sequence File ➤ Security ➤ Switch ID to interactively change
at any time.

Notes logs out of the original user ID file and activates the newly selected user ID file. When
you switch IDs, you'll always be prompted for the password associated with the ID file you are tr
to activate.

Understanding Database Security

Your user ID establishes secure communication with Domino servers. After successfully validating
authenticating, the Domino server determines whether you are authorized for access based on additic
security configured for the server by the Domino administrator. Assuming you are authorized to ac
the server, the next hurdle your ID has to pass is database-level security to actually open and use d
bases. Database encryption, which was discussed earlier, is one way you might be prevented from acc
ing a database. Another way is through the restrictions identified in the database's ACL.

Access Control Lists

The database ACL acts as the front door into a Lotus Notes database. Depending on which key you have, you may or may not get in. The ACL determines who can access a given database and what level of authority or privileges they have inside the database. You can view the ACL for any database you have open using the menu sequence File ➢ Database ➢ Access Control, which opens the dialog box shown in Figure 11.13.

Access
control list

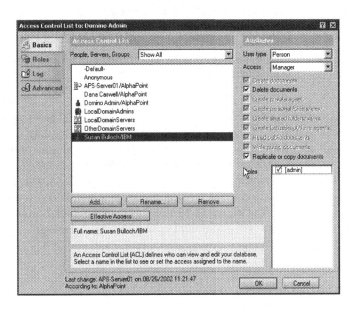

In the center of the dialog box on the Basics tab is a list of users, groups, and servers who are either granted or denied access to the database. The privilege level assigned to a user is visible in the top-right corner. In Figure 11.13, the user Dana Caswell/AlphaPoint is highlighted, and she has Author access to this database. Author access is one of seven possible privilege levels.

PRIVILEGE LEVELS

There are seven privilege levels that can be associated with a user, server, or group in a database's ACL. Groups listed in the ACL match group entries in the Domino Directory or your personal address book if the database is stored locally on your computer. Table 11.2 describes the seven levels in order of least privileged to most privileged.

TABLE 11.2: ACCESS CONTROL LIST PRIVILEGE LEVELS

LEVEL	DESCRIPTION
No Access	No authority to access a database
Depositor	Ability to create and save new documents

Continued on next page

LEVEL	DESCRIPTION
Reader	Ability to read content and navigate an application through hot links
Author	Reader privileges plus the ability to modify documents you created
Editor	Author privileges plus the ability to modify documents created by other users
Designer	Editor privileges plus the ability to make programming design changes
Manager	Designer privileges plus the ability to delete databases, change ACL security settings, and mo͏ replication settings

As you can tell from the descriptions, the Manager-level privilege is required to actually char͏ database's ACL. Although you have Manager access to all local databases on your machine, it is l͏ you will not have Manager access to any or few databases on your organization's server. This priv͏ level is generally granted only to Domino administrators and senior developers.

Once a user is granted one of the seven basic access privileges, there are several additional permiss͏ that can be applied within the privilege level to fine-tune what the user is able to do in the datal͏ Along the right side of Figure 11.13, optional privilege check boxes are visible that can be enable͏ disabled as required. The additional permissions are as follows:

- ◆ Ability to create documents
- ◆ Ability to delete documents
- ◆ Ability to create personal agents
- ◆ Ability to create personal folders/views
- ◆ Ability to create shared folders/views
- ◆ Ability to create LotusScript/Java agents
- ◆ Ability to read public access documents
- ◆ Ability to write public access documents

Each access level is given a combination of the additional permissions automatically. Some of͏ additional permissions can be enabled or disabled depending on the access control privilege assig͏

Default Entry

Every database ACL contains an entry listed as -Default-. If your user ID is not specifically liste͏ the ACL or your ID is not contained in any of the groups listed in the ACL, the privilege associa͏ with the default entry is granted when the Notes client is used to access a database.

Anonymous Entry

For databases that can be used from the Web without needing to log in, the Anonymous entry is required. The privilege associated with the Anonymous entry is granted when a web client is used to access a database and the user is not listed in any other way in the ACL.

Effective Access

A new feature in Lotus Notes and Domino 6 is the ability to check what your effective access is while using a database. Effective access is the actual privilege level you have on a given item while you are using it. Clicking the Effective Access button displays the dialog box shown in Figure 11.14. This screen will be useful when troubleshooting access and security problems in a database because it tells you exactly what privilege you have at the moment.

FIGURE 11.14

Effective
access

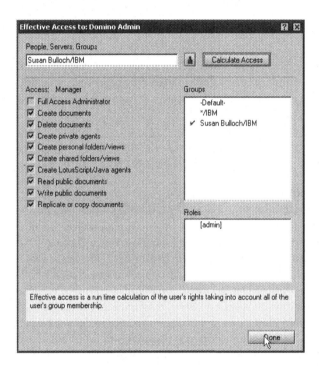

You can also use the Access Level indicator on the status bar to check your access level to the current database. This is the third area from the right on the status bar. It displays an icon corresponding to your access level to the current database. The key icon represents Manager access, which is typically the access level you will have to your mail database and other databases where you are the owner. If you click the icon on the status bar, the Groups and Roles dialog box shown in Figure 11.15 will be displayed. There will be a check mark next to all groups to which you belong.

FIGURE 11.15

Groups and roles

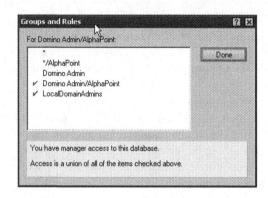

ROLES

The Roles section allows you to add, rename, or delete roles from the ACL. Roles are collectio
users created and maintained by a database manager inside the database. They are used to prog
matically grant or deny special privileges at runtime during processing.

LOG

The Log section displays an audit trail of changes made to the ACL. This is useful when you're t
to determine when, why, and who made a change to the ACL.

ADVANCED OPTIONS

The Advanced tab lets the manager of a database set the Administration Server, enforce a consi
ACL when databases replicate, and set a maximum Internet name and password privilege level.
administration server defines which Domino server will control the Admin Process for the data
(see the Domino 5 Administration help database). The Maximum Name & Password option de
the maximum access level allowed when this database is used with a web browser through a Doi
server. If this option is set to Editor, you would be restricted to Editor access when using this data
with a web browser even if you have Designer or Manager access.

The Domino Directory is intricately involved in database security. Because the Domino D
tory is located on a Domino server, it provides the best security coverage for server-based databa
For databases stored locally, a user's access defaults to Manager access. This lack of server-se
enforcement at the local level can lead to confusion when database replicas are involved. To pre
folks from thinking they are able to make changes at the local level, a special advanced datal
security option can be enabled. The Advanced option is the ability to enforce a consistent ac
control and is located in the Advanced area of a database's ACL. With this option enabled,
database will enforce the ACL at the local level rather than allowing Manager access to it. W
databases are replicated locally, the ACL is ignored unless the Enforce a Consistent Access Coi
List Across All Replicas of This Database option is enabled. Contrary to the wording of
option, though, it does not provide complete security to local replicas. All you have to do to g
access to the database is add a group that has higher authority (such as Manager rights) to your
sonal address book database and add your name to that group. The only way to truly ensure sec

of data on a local machine is to encrypt it. For server-based databases that you are replicating to your local machine, there is a good chance that this option has been turned on by the Domino system administrator, but be sure to check it before you go wild with the Delete key!

Database Encryption

Database encryption protects a database that is stored locally. It scrambles the database so only the authorized person can gain access. You generally do this to protect databases stored locally on your computer so others cannot access them. Database encryption is useful when you are sharing a computer with multiple users or when you are traveling with your notebook computer (it would protect your information if your notebook computer is stolen). Your user ID is used to perform database encryption. The only way to open an encrypted database is to use the ID with which it was encrypted. To encrypt an individual database, use the menu sequence File ➤ Database ➤ Properties and click the Encryption Settings button to display the Encryption window for the database, shown in Figure 11.16. From here, choose Strong Encryption, Medium Encryption, or Simple Encryption based on your speed performance requirements and security requirements.

FIGURE 11.16

Encrypting a database

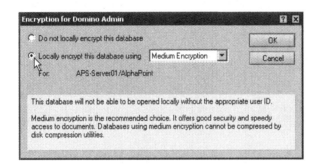

Summary

In this chapter, we presented an overview of the security system used in the Lotus Notes client and the Domino server. The Domino Directory and the Lotus Notes user ID are the foundation upon which all other security features are based. The technology behind the Lotus Notes user ID is PKI certificates and dual-key encryption. We explored the database security features of Notes including the access control list, database encryption, and mail encryption. In the next chapter, we'll move into the area of learning how to use Notes concurrently with other types of software including Microsoft OLE-capable products.

Chapter 12

Integrating Notes with Other Applications

WE HAVE DEMONSTRATED HOW you can use Notes to manage your e-mail, calendaring and scheduling, to do list, web browsing, and newsgroup interaction. It also has prebuilt templates, including an electronic discussion and a Document Library, that you can use to share information with colleagues. With all of these capabilities, Notes is a powerful information management tool. As such, you will need to share information with other applications. In this chapter, we'll discuss the Notes features that end users can use to integrate Notes with other applications.

◆ Using the Windows Clipboard

◆ Using Windows OLE

◆ Importing and exporting to and from Notes

◆ Attaching files

◆ Using NotesSQL

Using the Windows Clipboard

The most basic form of application integration that Notes supports is copying and pasting to and from the Windows Clipboard. When you are creating or editing documents, you can copy and paste information from another application to fields on the form. The data that is copied must match the data type of the field in which it is being pasted. For example, you can only paste a number into a numeric field.

You can also copy and paste formatted text into a rich-text field. If you copy information from an application that supports rich-text data (such as Microsoft Word) to the Windows Clipboard, you can paste it into a Notes rich-text field with its associated formatting. To see how this works, follow these steps:

1. Create a memo document in your mail database.

2. In Word (or another application that can copy rich text to the Clipboard), highlight some text and select Edit ➤ Copy.

3. Go back to Notes and make sure your cursor is positioned in the Body field.

4. Select Edit ➤ Paste Special. The Paste Special dialog box appears (see Figure 12.1).

5. Select the Paste radio button, select Rich Text from the As field, and then click the OK bu

The text you copied to the Clipboard from Word will be displayed in the Notes rich-text f The text itself is editable within the rich-text field just as if it were typed directly into the field close the form, press Esc or click the X to the right of the form's task button. In the Close Win dialog box, select Discard Changes and then click the OK button.

TIP   Notes 6 allows you to paste web pages copied from Microsoft Internet Explorer into rich-text fields. This is a g way to save a web page into a Notes document.

FIGURE 12.1

The Paste Special dialog box for a Word object

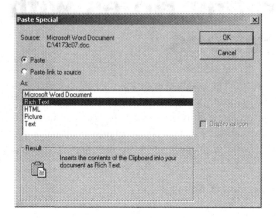

Using Windows Object Linking and Embedding (OLE)

You can insert Windows object linking and embedding (OLE) objects into rich-text fields (and forms), making Notes a powerful container application. OLE is a protocol built into Windows enables applications to share data. It is an outgrowth of the Dynamic Data Exchange (DDE) te nology, which was included in earlier versions of Windows. OLE is also Microsoft's first foray component software architecture and is the precursor to programmatic interfaces such as Active Common Object Model/Distributed Common Object Model (COM/DCOM), and Distribu InterNetwork Architecture (DNA). Notes can control OLE objects programmatically using Lo Script, but it also provides the interfaces required to let end users link and embed objects into r text fields. You can insert OLE objects into rich-text fields in two ways:

♦ Copying and pasting from an OLE-enabled application

♦ Using the Create menu

Let's say you want to include a Word document in a Notes document because you want to eit e-mail it to a colleague or share it with a group by adding it to a discussion. If the Word docum already exists, you can either copy and paste it into Notes or use the Create menu.

Copying and Pasting OLE Objects

The easiest way to insert OLE objects into a rich-text field is to copy and paste them. Follow these steps to copy and paste a Word or WordPad object into a rich-text field:

1. Create a memo document in your mail database.

2. Within Word or WordPad, select the text to be inserted into Notes and copy it to the Clipboard.

3. Return to Notes and make sure your cursor is positioned in the Body field.

4. Select Edit ➢ Paste Special. The Paste Special dialog box appears.

5. Select the Paste radio button, select Microsoft Word Document or WordPad from the As field, and click the OK button.

The text you highlighted in Word will appear in the Notes rich-text field. If you click the text pasted into Notes, a box will appear around it. This indicates that the text is an object. To close the form, press Esc or click the X to the right of the form's task button. In the Close Window dialog box, select Discard Changes and click the OK button. The alternative in the Paste Special dialog box is to choose the Paste Link to Source radio button. Selecting the Paste Link to Source radio button in the Paste Special dialog box creates a link to the object instead of embedding it into the rich-text field. The main difference is that links are kept synchronized and embedded objects are not. Links are also more fragile; anyone opening a document containing a link must have access to the object represented by the link. If you e-mail a message containing a link to a file on your computer, the recipient will most likely be unable to access it because he probably does not have access to your computer's hard drive.

Using the Create Menu to Insert OLE Objects

Another way to insert an OLE object into a rich-text field is to use the Create menu. You can insert Word text as follows:

1. Select Create ➢ Object from the Notes menu. A Create Object dialog box appears (see Figure 12.2).

FIGURE 12.2
Creating an embedded object

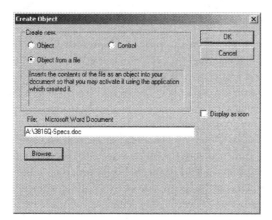

2. Select the Object from a File radio button in the Create New section.

3. Either type the filename of the Word document you want to insert or click the Browse bu[tton] to explore your computer's disk drive.

4. After entering the File field, click the OK button.

The text from your Word document will appear in the Notes rich-text field. Again, if you [click] the text pasted into Notes, a box will appear around it. This indicates the text is an object.

Editing Embedded Objects

You can edit an OLE object embedded in a rich-text field. Just double-click the Word object i[n the] rich-text field. You'll notice that Notes is still running, but the menus appear to be those of W[ord] (see Figure 12.3). This is called *in-place editing*, and it's part of the OLE specification.

FIGURE 12.3

In-place editing

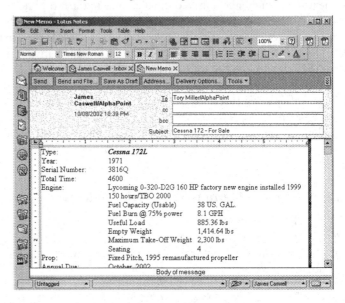

Some of the core applications shipped with Notes use OLE to integrate with popular deskt[op] applications. Notes mail provides the option of using Word or Lotus Word Pro. Also, the Docum[ent] Library for Microsoft Office template uses OLE to integrate Word, Excel, PowerPoint, and P[aint] with Notes. This particular Notes database never even displays a Notes form; it just launches [the] application from the view interface and automatically stores the data back to a Notes documen[t.]

You can also edit the object by opening it in the application in which it was created. You can ri[ght-] click the object and select Open from the context menu. If you have the application installed on y[our] computer, it will be launched with the object selected. You will notice that the launched applicat[ion] will have a few new options in the File menu. For Word, there will be a Close and Return to *Docu[ment] Title* option (where *Document Title* is the title of the Notes document in which the object is contain[ed]) and an Update option. If you select Update, changes you make to the object will be saved back to [the] Notes document. If you select the Close and Return to *Document Title* option, the object will be sa[ved] to the Notes document, the application will be closed, and you will be returned to Notes.

NOTE *The ability to insert OLE objects into Notes documents is a powerful feature, but it can cause some problems when the documents are also being shared with browser-only users through a Domino server. Some browsers are not designed to be OLE containers and may not render the object properly. Even when all of the users have Notes, OLE may not be the best way to store information. It requires that all users have the application that created the object installed locally on their computer.*

Notes Importing and Exporting

You can also import and export data to and from Notes. Notes supports two modes of import and export:

◆ View import/export

◆ Document import/export

View import allows you to take a set of records from an external data source and create a Notes document for each record. View export is just the opposite. It allows you to take a set of Notes documents displayed in a view and create a set of records that can be used by another application. For example, you may have a Notes-based time-entry database that you would like to use. Before you start entering your time, you would like to populate the database with data that you have been keeping in a spreadsheet for the last six months. Assuming the Notes database contains one document for each time entry, you could use view import to create time-entry documents from data stored in your spreadsheet.

Document import allows you to import picture files, word processing documents, and spreadsheet files from popular desktop applications into rich-text fields on Notes forms. Document export allows you to export a Notes document that is displayed through a form to either a word processing document or an image file.

View Import

View import allows you to create documents in a Notes database from records contained in an external file. Notes can perform view imports from three file formats:

◆ Lotus 1-2-3 worksheet files

◆ Structured text files

◆ Tabular text files

Regardless of the type of file you're importing, you must choose a form to use to create the documents. The form's field definitions are used in defining the fields on the documents. You must also choose to create either Main documents or Response documents from the external data. Optionally, you can choose to calculate fields on the form as documents are created. This option should be selected if you have computed fields on the form.

NOTE *If you choose to create Response documents, they will be created as responses to the currently selected document in the view. If no document is selected, you will not be able to create Response documents.*

Lotus 1-2-3 worksheet files are spreadsheet files generated by Lotus 1-2-3 (or other applications that can export to the WK1/WK2/WK3/WK4 format). The rows contained in the 1-2-3 file are translated to documents when imported by Notes. The columns represent the fields on the documents. When importing 1-2-3 files, you can enter a range name to import a subset of the spreadsheet or import the entire spreadsheet. In addition, you must choose how fields are defined on the documents created during import. The options are as follows:

- View Defined
- WKS Title Defined
- Format File Defined

View Defined instructs Notes to use the structure of the view to correlate columns from the spreadsheet to fields on the documents created during import. The data in the first column in the 1-2-3 will be copied to a field defined from the first column of the view and so on. WKS Title Defined instructs Notes to correlate column titles from the spreadsheet to fields on the documents created during import. Format File Defined instructs Notes to refer to the format defined in an external text file to relate columns in the spreadsheet to fields on the documents. This file is called a *Format file* (or COL because it is created using a `.col` extension). A Format file describes the layout of the data file. The following is an example of a Format file that uses a comma as a separator character:

```
;COL File for BUSNADDR.TXT
;Ignore leading quote
(") : width 1
Company: UNTIL '","'
Department: UNTIL '","'
Last: UNTIL '","'
First: UNTIL '","'
Middle: UNTIL '","'
Title: UNTIL '","'
Phone: UNTIL '","'
FAX: UNTIL '","'
DateActive: UNTIL '","'
Dateinactive: UNTIL '","'
Street1: UNTIL '","'
Street2: UNTIL '","'
City: UNTIL '","'
State: UNTIL '","'
Zip: UNTIL '","'
Notes: UNTIL '","'
```

Structured text files are text files that contain data formatted so that each field from each record is listed with its field name, value, and a carriage return/line feed character. Each record is separated with either a form feed character or some other special character code (chosen when the data is exported). This format is used to export documents from Notes database views. When importing structured text files, Notes uses field names contained in the file to correlate data values to fields on the documents created during import.

Tabular text files are text files that contain data formatted so that each field from each record is listed in the same position on the line and records are separated by a carriage return/line feed; this is also known as a fixed length record. This format is generic and can be exported from most applications. When importing tabular text files, Notes correlates fields from the tabular text file to columns in the view. If you choose to use a Format file, Notes refers to this file to correlate fields in the import file to fields on the documents. Below, we have an example of a COL file and the data file it describes.

```
;COL file for WINE.TXT
ProdCode: type text start 1 end 5
WineType: type text start 7 end 19
Vineyard: type text start 20 end 49
WineColor: type text start 50 end 60

;Data file WINE.TXT
3100  Zinfandel     Fucito Family Wines      Red
3101  Pinot Noir    Fucito Family Wines      Red
3102  Pinot Grigio  Fucito Family Wines      White
```

Again, view import is used to create documents in a Notes database from records contained in an external file. To perform a view import, follow these steps:

1. Open the database in which you would like to perform the view import.
2. Open the view to use for the view import.
3. Select File ➤ Import. The Import dialog box will be displayed (see Figure 12.4).

FIGURE 12.4

Importing a file to a view

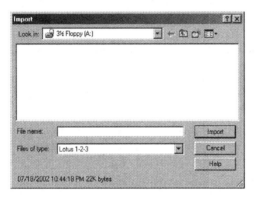

4. Select the type of file you would like to import from the Files of Type drop-down box.
5. Select a file from your computer's file system or enter a filename.
6. Click the Import button. An import settings dialog box specific to the type of file being imported will be displayed. Figure 12.5 shows the import settings dialog box for 1-2-3 worksheet files.
7. Select the appropriate import settings. See the information previously discussed in this section.
8. Click the OK button.

Notes will process the file you selected. A document will be created for each of the records in the external file.

FIGURE 12.5
Import settings
for 1-2-3
worksheet files

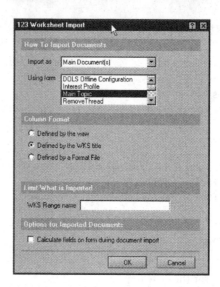

View Export

View export allows you to create an external file containing records for documents selected from Notes database. Notes can export data to the same formats mentioned in the preceding section

◆ Lotus 1-2-3 worksheet files

◆ Structured text files

◆ Tabular text files

When performing a view export, Notes creates a record in the output file for each document selected in the view. You can also choose to export all documents. To perform a view export, follow these steps:

1. Open the database in which you would like to perform the view export.

2. Open the view to use for the view export.

3. Select File ➢ Export. The Export dialog box will be displayed (see Figure 12.6).

FIGURE 12.6
Exporting from
a view

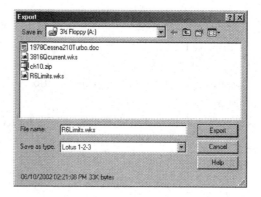

4. Select the type of file you would like to export from the Save as Type drop-down box.

5. Select a file from your computer's file system or enter a filename.

6. Click the Export button. An export dialog box specific to the type of file being exported will be displayed. Figure 12.7 shows the export dialog box for 1-2-3 worksheet files.

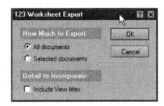

7. Select All Documents or Selected Documents, depending on what you want to export.

8. Select the other options as necessary.

9. Click the OK button.

Notes will process the export. The file created will contain rows for all documents or a row for each of the documents selected.

NOTE *If the export file exists, Notes will prompt you to replace the file or cancel the export. If you are exporting to a tabular text file, you will also be given the choice of appending records to the existing export file.*

Document Import

Document import allows you to copy data from an external file to a rich-text field on a Notes form. Notes can import a number of files into rich-text fields:

♦ ASCII text files

♦ Binary files with text

♦ BMP, CGM, GIF, and JPEG images

♦ HTML files

♦ Lotus 1-2-3, Lotus PIC, and Lotus Word Pro files

♦ Microsoft Excel, RTF, and Word files

♦ PCX and TIFF 5.0 images

♦ WordPerfect 5.x and WordPerfect 6.0/6.1 files

NOTE *When importing graphics files, Notes will import only the first image contained in the graphics file.*

When importing word processing files, Notes translates the formatting contained in the document to equivalent rich-text field attributes. (See the Notes help file for information about which formatting Notes translates during import.) When importing spreadsheet files, Notes supports named ranges for 1-2-3 and Symphony files. It does not support named ranges for Excel spreadsheets. When importing Hypertext Markup Language (HTML) files, Notes does not copy graphics images into the rich-text field. A red square appears where a graphics image is supposed to be placed.

To import an external file into a rich-text field on a form, follow these steps:

1. Open the database in which you would like to perform the document import.
2. Open the Notes document containing the rich-text field to which you would like the ext file imported.
3. If the Notes document is not already in editing mode, press Ctrl+E or double-click the
4. Position your cursor in the Notes rich-text field into which you want the file imported.
5. Select File ➤ Import. The Import dialog box will be displayed.
6. Select the type of file you would like to import from the Files of Type drop-down box.
7. Select a file from your computer's file system or enter a filename.
8. Click the Import button.

If a particular file type includes import options, Notes will present a dialog box for selecti options. The file you selected will be imported into the rich-text field at the point where the curs was positioned.

Document Export

Document export allows you to create an external file containing data from a Notes document displayed through a Notes form. Notes can export to a number of file formats:

- ASCII text
- CGM image
- Microsoft Word RTF
- TIFF 5 image

To export a document to an external file, follow these steps:

1. Open the database that contains the document you want to export.
2. Open the Notes document you want to export.
3. Select File ➤ Export. The Export dialog box will be displayed.
4. Select the type of file you would like to export from the Save as Type drop-down box.
5. Select a file from your computer's file system or enter a filename.
6. Click the Export button.

If a particular file type includes export options, Notes will present a dialog box for selecting options. The document you selected will be exported to an external file.

Attaching Files in Notes

Another way to include information from other applications in Notes documents is to use file att ments. You can attach any file from your computer's file system, so there are no limitations on wh types of data you can share.

In a view, a document with an attachment is usually displayed with a paper clip icon. When you open the document, the attachment will be displayed as an icon in the rich-text field of the document.

From within the document, you can do the following:

- Attach files.
- Obtain information about the attachment.
- View the attachment.
- Open the attachment.
- Edit the attachment.
- Save the attachment outside of Notes.
- Remove the attachment from the Notes document.

Attaching Files

You attach files from within rich-text fields. It is simply a matter of choosing the file or files from your computer's file system. To try this, let's create another new memo (document) in your mail database and attach a file as follows:

1. Create a memo document in your mail database.
2. Make sure your cursor is positioned in the Body field, the blank area underneath the mail header information.
3. Select File ➢ Attach. The Create Attachment(s) dialog box appears (see Figure 12.8).

FIGURE 12.8

Creating an attachment

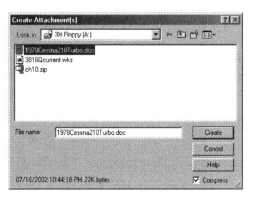

4. Select a file from your computer's file system. Try to select a document or some other data file (such as a Word document). Notice that the Compress check box is selected by default.
5. Click the Create button after choosing a file.

An icon representing the file you chose will be displayed. The file will be compressed and attached to the document. To close the form, press Esc or click the X to the right of the form's task button. In the Close Window dialog box, select Discard Changes and then click the OK button.

Obtaining Information about Attachments

You can obtain information about attachments by viewing the attachment's properties. For inst:
you might want to find out the size of the attached file before opening it or saving to your compu
file system. There are a couple of ways to view the attachment's properties:

◆ Double-clicking the icon representing the attachment

◆ Right-clicking the icon representing the attachment and selecting Attachment Propertie

Either way, the Attachment Properties InfoBox will open (see Figure 12.9).

FIGURE 12.9

Attachment
Properties
InfoBox

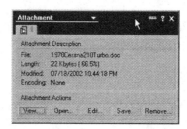

Saving Attachments to Disk

Saving attachments is another common practice. If you come across a document in a discussion of
base or if someone mails you a message with an attachment, you may want to save that file to y
computer's file system. This is called *saving* or *detaching*. You can detach files by using one of the
methods:

◆ Right-click the attachment icon and select Save or Save and Remove from the context m
Save puts the file on your hard drive and leaves it in the Notes document. Save and Rem
puts the file on your hard drive and removes it from the Notes document.

◆ Double-click the attachment and click the Save button on the Attachment Info tab of th
Attachment Properties InfoBox. The Save and Remove option is not available using this
method.

A Save Attachment dialog box will be presented, and you can choose the location in which to :
the attachment on your computer's file system.

TIP *If a document has multiple attachments and you need to detach all of them, right-click one of the attachment ic*
and select Save All, Save and Remove All, or Remove All from the context menu.

Viewing Attachments

Notes has built-in file viewers so you can view files of certain types even though the software is
installed on your computer. You can use the built-in viewers to view attachments in Notes. Th
enable you to quickly preview an attached file without having to load the application in which it
created. This is a great feature when you don't have the application that created an attachment loa
on your computer. To view attachments, you can use several methods:

◆ Right-click the attachment's icon and select View from the context menu.

- Double-click the attachment's icon and click the View button on the Attachment Info tab.
- Use the Attachment menu in the Notes client, which is only visible when an attachment is selected; from the menu, select View.

A File Viewer window opens in your Notes application window and the attachment is displayed. With the attachment displayed in the File Viewer window, you can do any of the following:

- Navigate around the attached file.
- Select rich text from the attached file and copy it to the Clipboard (for pasting into a Notes rich-text field or another application).
- Print the information displayed by the file viewer.

When you are finished viewing the attached file, press Esc or click the X to the right of the File Viewer window's task button. Notes 6 uses the KeyView software from Verity to view attachments. The help file contains the following list of supported file formats; if a file cannot be viewed, an error message will explain this in a dialog box.

Ami Pro 3.x (SAM)	AmiDraw (SDW)
AVI and MOV files	Bitmap (BMP)
CCITT Group 3 Fax (TIF)	CompuServe (GIF)
Computer Graphics Metafile (CGM)	DIB and EPS files
Executable files (EXE)	HTML (HTM)
JPEG files (JPEG, JPG)	Lotus 1-2-3 3.0, 4.0, 5.0, 6.x, R9 (WK*, 123)
Lotus 1-2-3 97 and 98, R9 (123)	Lotus 1-2-3 for Macintosh
Lotus 1-2-3 for OS/2 (WG2)	Lotus Freelance for OS/2 (PRS)
Lotus Freelance (PRE, PRZ)	Lotus PIC
Lotus SmartSuite Release 9 file formats	Lotus WordPro 96/97, R9 (LWP)
Microsoft Excel 2.x, 3.0, 4.0, 5.0, 7.0, 97, Office 2000 (XLS)	Microsoft PowerPoint 4.x, 7.0, 97 (PPT)
Microsoft Word for Macintosh 2.0, 3.0	Microsoft Word for Windows 6.0, 7.0, 97, Office 2000 (DOC)
Paintbrush/DCX (multipage PCX) (PCX)	PICT and PICT2 Graphics (PCT)
Revisable Form Text (RFT)	Rich Text Format (RTF)
Tagged Image File Format (TIF and EPS)	Text file (TXT)

Windows Metafile Graphic (WMF)	WordPerfect 5.x, 6.x, 7.x, 8.0
WordPerfect for Macintosh 2.0, 3.0	WordPerfect Graphics (WPG)
XyWrite	ZIP files (ZIP)

TIP   *If you view an attached Zip file, the file viewer will display its contents and let you extract the files contained within*

WARNING   *You may get unexpected results when you print files from a viewer. If possible, print files from their na applications.*

Opening or Editing an Attachment

If you open or edit an attachment from within Notes, you can load the application in which t attachment was created and open the attached file in one step. This option is useful if you need modify the attached information. To open or edit an attachment from within Notes, use one the following methods:

◆ Right-click the attachment's icon and select Open or Edit from the context menu.

◆ Double-click the attachment's icon and click one of the Open or Edit buttons.

NOTE   *Edits made to files launched from attachments are not automatically saved back to the attachment. You must s the file to disk, make the edits, and then reattach the file.*

Going Relational with NotesSQL

Another way to integrate Notes with other applications is a technology called NotesSQL, whi turns Notes databases into relational-like databases through the use of Open Database Conr tivity (ODBC) data sources. SQL stands for Structured Query Language; this is the programm language used to interact with relational databases. ODBC is relational, and SQL is used to inter with the data in an ODBC data source. These data sources are then available to other Windc applications that support ODBC. For example, you can use Crystal Reports to build reports bas on Lotus Notes data or perform a mail merge in Word by using your Notes personal address bo database and NotesSQL. Other Microsoft Office applications support ODBC as well. You Microsoft Access to read (and modify) Notes databases or use Microsoft Excel to perform anal This is a powerful and relatively easy way to integrate other applications with Notes.

Configuring a Notes database as an ODBC source is done using the ODBC manager in Windc To open it in Windows 2000, use Start ➤ Settings ➤ Control Panel ➤ Administrative Tools ➤ L Sources (ODBC). Each Notes .nsf database that will be used as an ODBC data source is identi with its own data source name. Figure 12.10 shows how to associate the Data Source Name of y choice with an .NSF file. Figure 12.11 shows this new data source in the ODBC Data Source Adr istrator as a System DSN (data source name). Since System DSNs are available to all users on a c puter, they are preferred over User DSNs which are specific to one logged in user.

FIGURE 12.10
Configuring Notes as an ODBC data source

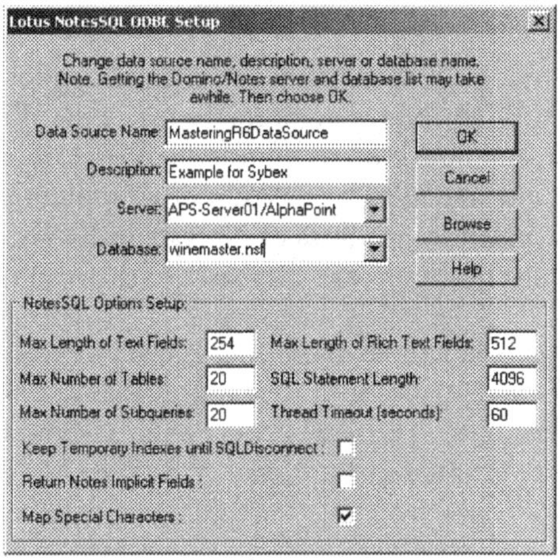

FIGURE 12.11
ODBC Data Source Administrator

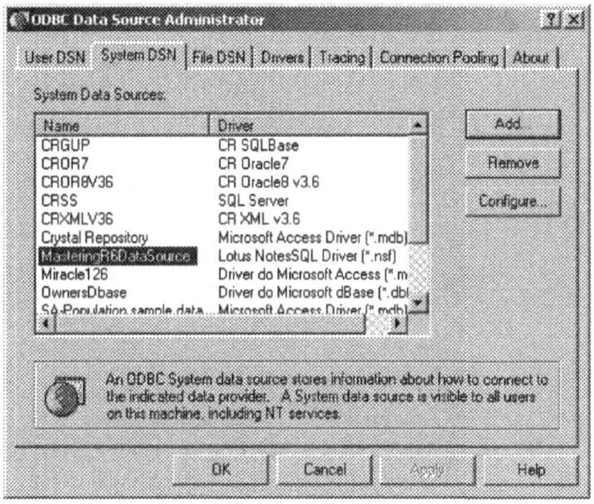

To use a Notes database as an ODBC source, the data source has to exist on the machine that has the .NSF stored. In other words, ODBC configuration is a client-side step and is unique to each computer. The example we've used shows how to configure an ODBC System DSN for Windows 2000, and its worth noting that each operating system will have slightly different window dialogs for ODBC (Windows 98 and Windows XP, for example). Any Windows operating system, however, will support creating an ODBC data source to an NSF file as long as you have the NotesSQL driver.

Once configured as an ODBC data source, the forms and views within the NSF are treated as relational tables with the fields representing columns of data. To obtain NotesSQL, visit the IBM Lotus site at **www.lotus.com** and search for *NotesSQL*. Many products, like Crystal Reports 9, install the driver for you.

NOTE *The link as of this writing is* **http://lotus.com/developers/devbase.nsf/HomeData/ K20010112044839** *but as with all Internet links, things may move by the time you read this!*

Summary

In this chapter, we explored various methods for integrating Notes and Notes data with oth applications. We explained how Notes supports the use of the Windows Clipboard for copy and pasting information and how Notes supports the Windows object linking and embeddi (OLE) specification for integrating with other Windows applications. We also demonstrated t import/export and attachment capabilities of Notes. Finally, we introduced NotesSQL, wh turns Notes databases into relational-like databases so that you can integrate Notes with ot applications.

In the next chapter, we look at how to use your Lotus Notes client to interact with informa on the Internet.

Part 3

Lotus Notes Domino and the Internet

Chapter 13

Accessing the Internet with a Notes Client

THERE IS NO DOUBT that the Internet has influenced every major area of technology in the past decade. Lotus Notes Domino is no exception, and Lotus Notes and Domino 6 continues the strong integration of Internet standards and capability with the rich functionality of the Lotus Notes client. Notes weaves Internet-based protocols, content standards, and security standards into its proven collaborative computing model. For web browsing within Notes, you can choose between the built-in native browser and the integrated Microsoft Internet Explorer browser control. Using either of these two browsing modes, you can save web pages to a database for offline use. Notes is also a powerful newsreader application and can replicate entire newsgroups to your computer for offline reading and posting. Access to Internet mail accounts is easy to configure and creates a central repository in the Notes client for all your Internet mail needs.

- ◆ Notes support for Internet standards

- ◆ Browsing the Web

- ◆ Participating in newsgroups

- ◆ Setting Internet-only user preferences

- ◆ Configuring Internet-only personal address book settings

- ◆ Setting up an Internet-only Location document

- ◆ Sending and receiving Internet mail

Notes Support for Internet Standards

Internet standards are the rules that software vendors agree to abide by to have a maximum amount of compatibility for all users. This means being able to use any web browser to access a website and having the majority of sites provide a level of support (some are text only) regardless of browser type or version. It also means creating content in a format that can be easily read by others. Hypertext Markup Language (HTML) is the formatting language of web pages. Standards also provide a way to send rich text in e-mail messages to users of any Internet mail system and having a way to post text messages to newsgroups. Finally, Internet security standards enable you to securely access sites, mail servers, and news servers including the sending and receiving of encrypted mail acros public Internet. In the following sections, we'll explore the Internet standards supported by Lo Notes and Domino.

Internet Protocols

Protocols are the mechanisms that enable computers to communicate with each other and enab applications to interact with one another. Notes supports the following Internet protocols:

- ◆ Transmission Control Protocol/Internet Protocol (TCP/IP)
- ◆ Hypertext Transfer Protocol (HTTP)
- ◆ Post Office Protocol (POP)
- ◆ Internet Message Access Protocol (IMAP)
- ◆ Simple Mail Transfer Protocol (SMTP)
- ◆ Lightweight Directory Access Protocol (LDAP)
- ◆ Network News Transfer Protocol (NNTP)

TRANSMISSION CONTROL PROTOCOL/INTERNET PROTOCOL (TCP/IP)

TCP/IP is the standard communication protocol of the Internet. It is actually a suite of protoc Most often, TCP/IP is associated with the networking aspects of computer-to-computer comm nications. An operating system, such as Windows NT or Windows 2000, provides the actual sup for TCP/IP networking. It also provides the user interfaces for programs such as Lotus Notes to TCP/IP as a method to transmit data. In this respect, Notes can be considered a TCP/IP app tion. You can configure it to communicate with Domino servers and Internet servers using TCP

HYPERTEXT TRANSFER PROTOCOL (HTTP)

HTTP is the protocol used by web browsers to communicate with web servers. Notes supports use of HTTP in its native web browser capability.

POST OFFICE PROTOCOL (POP)

POP (or POP3) is the common protocol for retrieving e-mail messages from an Internet mail se (POP server). It is considered an offline protocol because it is used to download (or copy) mess from the POP server to a local client application for storing, viewing, replying, and other routine processing. Notes supports the use of POP to retrieve messages from POP servers and copy then your mail database. You can then read, reply to, or delete POP messages as you can any other mes

INTERNET MESSAGE ACCESS PROTOCOL (IMAP)

IMAP (or IMAP4) is another protocol for retrieving e-mail messages from an Internet mail ser (IMAP server). It is more sophisticated than POP because it can be used when you're online as as when you're offline. For use online, it operates in much the same way client/server mail syste such as Microsoft Outlook/Exchange and Notes/Domino operate. The IMAP server contains y message store, or repository. The IMAP client reads and writes to this message store online; mess are not stored locally on your computer. Notes supports this mode by creating a new type of database called a *proxy database*. It looks like your mail database and you interact with it the same way, but no messages are actually stored in it. In addition, there is another option for interacting with IMAP servers that is distinctly a Notes feature. You can create a replica of your IMAP proxy database and work offline. Notes then uses replication to synchronize your local replica with your IMAP server-based message store. Finally, Notes also supports the use of IMAP to retrieve messages from IMAP servers to your mail database; this is similar to POP.

SIMPLE MAIL TRANSFER PROTOCOL (SMTP)

SMTP is the common protocol used for sending e-mail messages to Internet mail servers (SMTP servers). Notes supports the use of SMTP to send outbound messages from Notes directly to the Internet. The Lotus Notes client provides direct support for SMTP, allowing the Notes client to send Internet mail on its own to an SMTP server without the need to go through a Domino server first. This, combined with the POP and IMAP support previously discussed, make Notes a stand-alone Internet mail client. Domino servers also support SMTP and can use the protocol to both send and receive Internet mail at the server level.

LIGHT DIRECTORY ACCESS PROTOCOL (LDAP)

LDAP (LDAP 3) is a common protocol for accessing directories on Internet directory servers (LDAP servers). Directories are storehouses for information such as e-mail addresses and usernames. LDAP provides a way to quickly look up and retrieve information from directories. Internet LDAP-capable directories store contact information for people and groups. They are similar to the Domino Directory in this regard. Some popular LDAP directories are Four11, Bigfoot, and Yahoo. They contain contact information they get from phone books and other sources as well as from individuals who enter their contact information. You can use Notes to search LDAP directories for a person's e-mail address when you send Internet mail or for other contact information (for example, phone number, address, and so on) when you are trying to locate someone.

NETWORK NEWS TRANSFER PROTOCOL (NNTP)

NNTP is the common protocol for Internet-based discussion groups or electronic forums called *newsgroups* (or Usenet). It is used to read and post messages on news servers (NNTP servers). Newsgroups are similar to bulletin board systems (BBSs), which were popular before the widespread use of the Internet. They are a standards-based version of the Notes discussion database. NNTP and IMAP operate in a similar manner; the NNTP server contains a message store, and the NNTP client reads and writes messages to this repository. Notes supports NNTP by using a proxy database as it does with IMAP.

Internet Content Standards

Content standards are predefined or widely accepted methods for storing information. They are defined by international standards organizations or by market presence. Content standards enable an application to read and write data so the data can be easily read and written by other programs. Notes supports the following Internet content standards:

- Hypertext Markup Language (HTML)
- Extensible Markup Language (XML)

- Multipurpose Internet Mail Extension (MIME)
- Java
- JavaScript
- Native image formats

HYPERTEXT MARKUP LANGUAGE (HTML)

HTML is the formatting language used to create and present web pages in a browser. It is the ubiquitous common layer that all web browsers understand and use. Notes supports HTML in a number of ways, including:

- Mail message format
- Newsgroup posting format
- Native browser
- Copy/paste to rich-text fields
- Programming (in Domino Designer)

EXTENSIBLE MARKUP LANGUAGE (XML)

XML is a superset of the HTML formatting language; however, it is not used to format or present information. Instead, it is used to package and describe data. It is a text-based standard that is compatible with newer web browsers and is attractive as a middle layer of data transfer. Like HTML, XML is a tag-based language where a set of starting and ending tags describe the data in the field. For instance, a tag `<firstname>` and its ending tag `</firstname>` would surround a piece of data thereby providing the data and its meaning in a simple format. The following line is representative of a typical XML tag:

```
<firstname>James</firstname>
```

MULTIPURPOSE INTERNET MAIL EXTENSION (MIME)

MIME is a method for packaging complex messages for transport across a communications protocol such as TCP/IP. A complex message might include embedded graphics, audio clips, messages with file attachments, messages in Japanese or Russian, or digitally signed messages. It is used to form data into individual elements (similar to fields) so it can be easily read by other applications. When combined with standard encoding mechanisms (for example, uuencode) that can translate binary data into a text format, MIME provides a powerful mechanism for sharing information. Notes supports MIME for sending and receiving Internet mail, for reading and posting newsgroup topics, and for rich-text fields exposed to browser users through Domino.

NOTE *uuencode is a set of algorithms that convert files to a 7-bit ASCII format. It is a protocol that can be used to send e-mail attachments between different operating systems (Unix, Windows, and Macintosh).*

JAVA

Java is a programming language that executes in a special Java runtime environment called the Java Virtual Machine (JVM). Java can be considered content in the sense that Java applets (small, stand-alone programs written in Java) can be embedded in Notes documents, pages, and in Notes rich-fields. The Notes browser also supports Java applets on web pages. All this is made possible because Notes contains an integrated JVM that interprets the Java byte code at runtime; web browsers also have a built-in JVM. Domino Designer includes a Java integrated development environment (IDE) for developing and compiling Java agents in Notes applications.

JAVASCRIPT

JavaScript is a scripting language used to integrate objects on web pages and other front-end-oriented screens. Web clients and the Lotus Notes client both support JavaScript as a processing language, with full support in a browser and a reasonable level of support in a Notes client. Like Java, JavaScript is content in the sense that the native browser can interpret web pages containing JavaScript. Domino Designer also allows JavaScript to be used in developing Notes/Domino applications.

NATIVE IMAGE FORMATS

Images are a major element of web pages. The formats most commonly used by web page designers are Graphic Interchange Format (GIF) and Joint Photographic Experts Group (JPEG). Notes stores images based on these formats in their native form in the Notes database. Other image types are supported in Notes, but are converted to and stored as bitmaps.

Support for Internet Security Standards

Security standards are mechanisms for ensuring that information is accessible only to the individual or group of individuals for which it was intended. They can apply to data communications or actual content. Again, international standards organizations or market presence define these standards. Notes supports the following Internet security standards:

- Secure Sockets Layer (SSL)
- X.509 certificates (Internet certificates)
- Secure Multipurpose Internet Mail Extension (S/MIME)

SECURE SOCKETS LAYER (SSL)

SSL is a data communications protocol for TCP/IP. It is used to encrypt network transmission so information is not sent over the Internet in clear text. Web vendors commonly use it for securing credit card information entered in web pages and sent over the Internet. Notes supports SSL in its native web browser and in its protocol support for POP, IMAP, SMTP, NNTP, and LDAP. You can tell that SSL is being used in a browser communication by the presence of the HTTPS prefix instead of HTTP where the *S* denotes secure.

X.509 CERTIFICATES (INTERNET CERTIFICATES)

X.509 certificates are part of a standards-based Public Key Infrastructure (PKI), which is a mechanism for ensuring that users are who they say they are. A third-party certifying authority validates the identity of a user and issues that person a key. This key is then used to access the system. It provides a higher degree of security than just a user ID and password provide. Notes supports X.509 certificates for web browsing and sending/receiving secure e-mail.

SECURE MULTIPURPOSE INTERNET MAIL EXTENSION (S/MIME)

S/MIME is a standard for sending and receiving secure e-mail. It is used in conjunction with X certificates. Notes supports S/MIME for sending/receiving signed and encrypted Internet e-r

NOTE *From an end-users point of view, all of these protocols represent acronym soup. If Notes works, hurray! Otherv call tech support!*

Browsing the Web from within Notes

It's fair to say that web browsing is commonplace today. Whether for personal or business nee there are many valuable sites. You can research products and services, or you can purchase them. can search for information and research topics. You can read news from around the world. Co nies use websites internally as intranets to communicate with employees and as extranets to con nicate with their business partners. Web browsing has become an integral part of everyday life.

There are two ways to use Notes to browse the Web:

◆ Using the Lotus Notes browser

◆ Using the Lotus Notes browser–integrated Microsoft Internet Explorer (IE)

The Lotus Notes browser is a fairly robust browser that supports most features used on com websites including HTML 4, Java applets, JavaScript, cookies, ActiveX controls, and plug-ins. rendering engine runs as a background task, and web pages are displayed as a Domino docun through a Domino form. When you open a Uniform Resource Locator (URL), a task windov opened for the browser form (unless one is already opened) and the page is displayed. Behind scenes, Notes is using a database called Personal Web Navigator (`perweb.nsf`). This database tains the form used to display web pages and acts as a repository for storing web pages offline.

You can also use the Notes browser in conjunction with the Microsoft IE browser control. is a powerful combination. You get the familiar interface and robust rendering engine of IE in a tion to the web-page sharing and offline features of Notes. Browsing with the Notes browser an is the same as browsing with the native browser except the form displayed contains the IE brov control as an object. This means that Notes is allowing the IE control to retrieve pages and dis them. Other browsing functions, such as forwarding a URL or saving a web page for offline us performed by Notes using special forms and programs in the Personal Web Navigator databas

NOTE *The Personal Web Navigator (6) database is not initially created for you when Notes is first installed. database is, however, created automatically for you the first time you choose to preview a web page in the Notes brow or the Notes browser with Microsoft Internet Explorer (these are a location document setting). The templ* `perweb50.ntf` *is used to create the Personal Web Navigator (6) database.*

Configuring Integrated Internet Browsing

You can configure integrated Internet browsing (meaning, using Notes to browse the Web) by ting specific user preferences, Location document settings, and Personal Web Navigator databa options.

USER PREFERENCES

You can set several Internet-related settings for the Lotus Notes client in the User Preferences area. You can access the User Preferences area of the Lotus Notes client (shown in Figure 13.1) using the menu sequence File ➤ Preferences ➤ User Preferences.

FIGURE 13.1

User Preferences dialog box

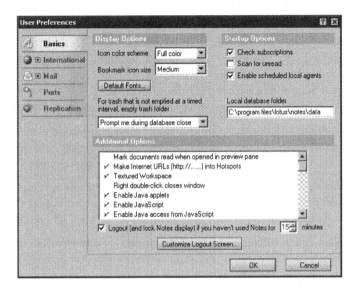

Several settings in the scrollable Additional Options area at the bottom of the Basics window determine how Notes operates with respect to integrated Internet browsing and the behavior of Notes itself. To activate an option, single click it so that a check mark appears to the left of the option; to deactivate the option, click it again. You have the following options:

Make Internet URLs into Hotspots You can enable this option to instruct Notes to convert URLs listed in rich-text fields to links. When this option is enabled, you can click URLs listed in e-mail messages, newsgroup postings, or any other database in Notes.

Enable Java Applets You can enable this option to instruct Notes to execute Java applets referenced by web pages. This also has an impact on Java applets contained in Notes documents. Enabling Java applets may expose your computer to security risks; check with your administrator before letting applets run on your machine.

Enable JavaScript You can enable this option to instruct Notes to execute JavaScript code that it encounters on web pages. This also has an impact on JavaScript contained in Notes documents.

Enable Java Access from JavaScript When this option is enabled, Notes will execute Java applets called from JavaScript code that it encounters on web pages. This also has an impact on Java applets called from JavaScript contained in Notes documents.

Enable JavaScript Error dialogs When this option is enabled, Notes will display a dialog box when JavaScript errors are encountered.

Enable Plugins in Notes Browser   When this option is enabled, Notes will support plug-

Enable ActiveX in Notes Browser   When this option is enabled, Notes will support Act: controls called from web pages.

Accept Cookies   When this option is enabled, Notes will support cookies. Website desig use cookies to save information on your computer.

Make Notes My Default Web Browser   You can enable this option to instruct Window use the Lotus Notes browser for all URL requests. When it's enabled, you will be able to open pages in Notes by entering URLs in the Windows Start ➤ Run box or by selecting shortcuts your Start ➤ Favorites.

Use Web Palette   The Use Web Palette option instructs Notes to use the color palette su ported by web browsers. This provides a more seamless interface for viewing both Notes datal and web pages; however, it has the effect of reducing the total number of colors visible within Lotus Notes client so that it has compatibility with web browsers.

Enable MIME Save Warning   If this warning appears, it means there is a Notes feature does not have a MIME equivalent, and therefore it may not appear to the MIME user in the s way that it appears in your Notes client.

Show Inline MIME Images as Attachments   When this option is enabled, when a MIME ir is received in an e-mail in the Notes client, it will appear in the Notes mail message as an attachm

LOCATION DOCUMENT SETTINGS

On the Basics tab of the Location document, there is a Proxy field. You can enter a proxy server name port in this field or you can set proxy options directly. Proxy options are used when you connect to Internet through a firewall and determine which communications port to use to access a web server

Every Location document has a tab devoted to Internet browsing settings (see Figure 13. Here, you tell Notes how to browse the Internet from the current location and how to retrieve open web pages. For more information on Location documents, refer to Chapter 9, "Comm cating with Domino Servers."

FIGURE 13.2

Location document Internet settings

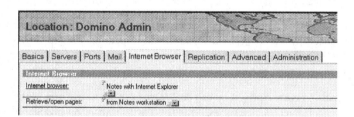

The Internet Browsing tab contains the following options:

Internet Browser   The Internet Browser field provides choices for how you want Notes to cess uniform resource locator (URL) requests. It provides a drop-down list of choices, as sho in Figure 13.3.

You can choose Netscape Navigator, Microsoft Internet Explorer, or Other to instruct Notes to pass URL requests to a separately running instance of the selected browser. In addition, the Other option lets you select the path for the browser's executable file. The Notes and Notes with Internet Explorer options configure Notes for integrated browsing. The Notes option instructs Notes to use its native browser, and the Notes with Internet Explorer option instructs Notes to use the IE browser control.

FIGURE 13.3
Integrated browsing options

Retrieve/Open Pages　From the Retrieve/Open Pages field, you can choose how Notes should retrieve web pages using one of two options:

◆ From Notes Workstation

◆ Work Offline

The From Notes Workstation option instructs Notes to perform page retrieval locally. When this option is chosen, Notes stores retrieved pages in your Personal Web Navigator database. The Work Offline option instructs Notes to disable interactive page retrieval.

There is a second area in a Location document devoted to web browsing activities. This is the Web Retriever tab, which can be found beneath the Advanced tab (see Figure 13.4).

FIGURE 13.4
Advanced location settings

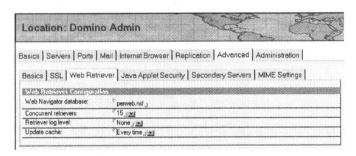

The Web Retriever tab has the following options:

Web Navigator Database   This field contains the name of the Personal Web Navigator ⟨ base and defaults to `perweb.nsf`. You can use different Personal Web Navigator databases fo ferent Location documents.

Concurrent Retrievers   This field defines the number of simultaneous requests allowed to be ⟨ of a Web server and created by the Web Retriever process running on your computer. A high nu⟩ will improve performance, but more resources will be required from your computer. The default

Retriever Log Level   The Web Retriever process can log its activity to your Notes log data⟩ There are three options:

- None
- Terse
- Verbose

Terse provides minimal logging, Verbose provides more complete logging, and None disable⟨ ging altogether.

Update Cache   This field defines how the Web Retriever process maintains its cache of w⟩ pages. There are three options:

- Never
- Once per session
- Every time

If you use the Notes with the IE-integrated browser mode, the Update Cache setting will corresp to the Windows operating system setting Check for Newer Versions of Stored Pages. You can c⟩ the latter by selecting Start ➤ Settings ➤ Control Panel and opening the Internet Options fo⟩ On the General tab there is a Settings button in the Temporary Internet Files area that will dis⟩ the operating system settings for checking for newer versions of stored pages (see Figure 13.5)

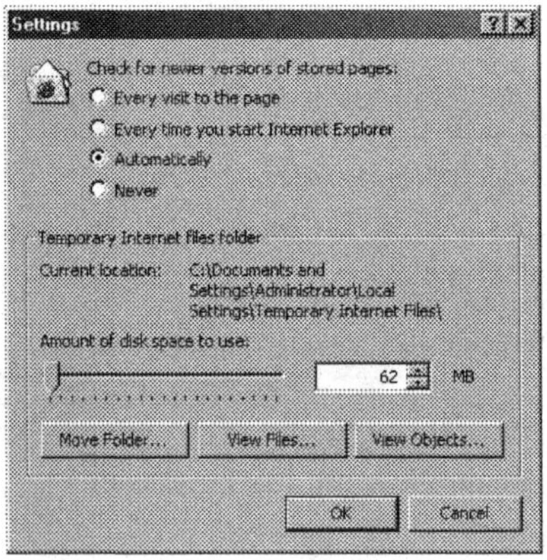

FIGURE 13.5

Operating system
stored page settings

Using Integrated Browsing

Browsing the Web using Lotus Notes means you're going to need to use a Notes database. Indeed, the integrated Internet web browser in Lotus Notes is a Notes database. The database will not only help you browse the Web, it will also bookmark and store links to pages you want to revisit. You can initiate a browser session within Notes using this database in a number of different ways:

Bookmarks You can bookmark web pages just as you can any other Notes form; just drag the browser page's tab to the Bookmark bar after it displays in Notes. Then, you can click a web page bookmark, and the Notes browser will display the page.

TIP *On install, Notes will also automatically display your IE Favorites and Navigator bookmarks on the Bookmark bar.*

URL links Notes can present URLs as active links when they are placed on forms or included in rich-text fields. This enables you to click links in mail messages, discussion database topics, or any other document in Notes as if it were a web page. When you click a link, Notes will open a browser form and display the page.

Open URLs You can type URLs directly into the Navigation bar's Address area (shown in Figure 13.6) and then press Enter. Notes will open a browser form and retrieve the page represented by the URL you entered.

FIGURE 13.6
Notes URL
Address area

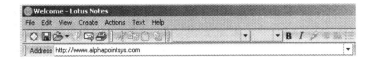

Internet searches Just click the Navigator bar's Search button and select a search site. Notes will open a browser form and display the search site you selected. Figure 13.7 shows the Lycos search site. Notice that the web page is being displayed inside the Lotus Notes window.

Welcome page Web browsing is also incorporated on the Welcome page. You can create a style that includes one or more web page sections. This can be used to display a news site or portal from which you can launch a browser task.

Personal Web Navigator You can browse Web pages by opening the Personal Web Navigator database.

Regardless of how integrated browsing is initiated, the operation is the same. A browser form is opened and the requested Web page is displayed. The Navigation bar goes back or forward, refreshes pages, and stops pages from loading. If you click any web page bookmarks, click any web page links, or perform other actions that request web page retrieval, Notes will display the page in the current browser form.

Because browsing is integrated into a Notes form, it is presented with the normal Notes ι interfaces. You can print the active web page as if it were another document. You can create b marks to active web pages that are just like any other bookmark. As mentioned earlier, to cre bookmark to a web page, drag the browser form's task button to the Bookmark bar or any bo mark folder.

FIGURE 13.7

Internet searching through Notes

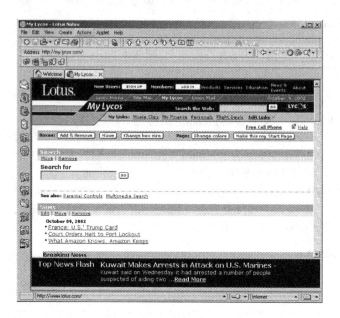

NOTE *You will not be able to drag the browser form's task button to the IE or Netscape Navigator bookmark folde The bookmarks in these folders can only be used for opening web pages.*

TIP *If you are using Notes with IE, you can add the active web page to your IE Favorites. Just right-click in the brow form and the IE browser object will display its context menu. This menu contains an option for adding the current p to your Favorites.*

Along with the normal features associated with web browsing, Notes provides a few extras. can forward a web page as a URL or as a page. When you forward a web page as a page, the cont of the web page are copied into a mail message so you can send it to another person or save it f future reference. Because it is stored in its native format in a rich-text field, the web page has the s look and functionality as the actual page on the web server. Select Actions ➢ Forward to initiate process, which opens the dialog box shown in Figure 13.8.

FIGURE 13.8

Forwarding a
web page

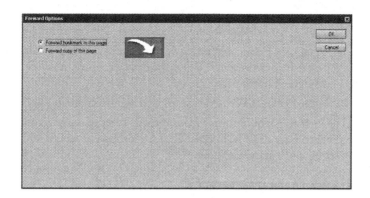

If you have your Personal Web Navigator database configured to save all pages you've visited, you have the option of deleting individual pages using the menu sequence Actions ➤ Delete. If you have it configured to save only pages that you specify, you will have the option of saving the current web page using Actions ➤ Keep Page.

BROWSING THE WEB SECURELY

You can use integrated browsing to access secure websites. With the native Notes browser option enabled, secure access is controlled by Notes. If the Notes with IE option is enabled, secure access is controlled by IE. For more information on using IE to browse secure websites, see the Microsoft IE help file. The native Notes browser supports SSL for encrypting the HTTP communications, and it supports X.509 certificates (Internet certificates) for accessing secure websites. SSL is discussed earlier in this chapter in reference to the NNTP protocol, but it is similar for HTTP.

Using the Personal Web Navigator Database

When you configure Notes for integrated browsing, it automatically creates a Personal Web Navigator database for you. This database is used as a repository for web pages that you visit when you're using integrated browsing. You can then view the pages offline. Your Personal Web Navigator database also provides two advanced web browsing features called Web Ahead and Page Minder.

Web Ahead is a process that runs on your computer to retrieve web pages from links that are on pages one or more levels down from the pages you visit. This is helpful when you're browsing offline because many of the web pages you visit will have links to other pages.

Page Minder is a process that runs on your computer to check specific web pages for changes. If changes are found, it sends either the page or a summary of the page to you via e-mail.

Configuring the Personal Web Navigator Database

The Personal Web Navigator database also contains configuration information. You can set a home page that is opened when you open the Personal Web Navigator database. You can set database size options so that pages are automatically removed based on criteria you define. You can instruct Notes

to save all visited pages or just those you specify. We'll discuss a few of the more advanced opt
To open the Personal Web Navigator's Internet Options form, follow these steps:

1. Open your Personal Web Navigator database. If it is not already bookmarked, open the base named `perweb.nsf`. When the database opens, it will open a separate form to displa configured home page.

2. In the Personal Web Navigator database, select Action ➤ Internet Options.

The Internet Options form will be opened. You can use it to configure Web Ahead, Page Mi and other preferences. The Internet Options form uses a tabbed interface, and each tab contains a cific set of configuration options.

WEB AHEAD AGENT PREFERENCES

You can select the number of levels that Web Ahead should retrieve (up to four), and you can er the Web Ahead Agent from the Web Ahead tab of this form (see Figure 13.9).

FIGURE 13.9
Personal Web
Navigator options

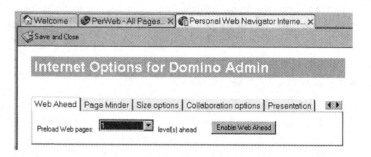

On the Web Ahead tab, enable the Web Ahead process using the following steps:

1. Click the Enable Web Ahead button.

2. A dialog box instructing you to verify or enable background agents will be displayed. Th required for Web Ahead to function properly.

You will be returned to the Internet Options form. The Enable Web Ahead button will be cha to Disable Web Ahead. If you need to enable background agents, select File ➤ Preferences ➤ User erences and select the Enable Scheduled Local Agents check box at the top-right corner of the dia box. (This option is visible in the Startup Options section of Figure 13.1.)

PAGE MINDER AGENT PREFERENCES

On the Page Minder tab, you can select how often Page Minder should check for updates, whe to send the page or a summary, and the e-mail address that should be used (see Figure 13.10).

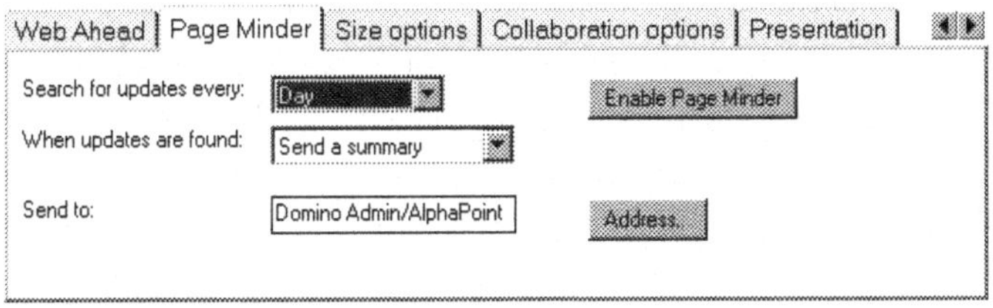

FIGURE 13.10

Page Minder
options

To enable the Page Minder agent, click the Page Minder tab and follow these steps:

1. Choose the frequency that Page Minder should check for updates: every hour, every 4 hours, once per day, or once per week.

2. Choose the action to be taken when an updated web page is found: mailing the actual page or sending a summary of the changes via an e-mail.

3. Type the Notes mail address to which updates should be forwarded. An Address button is provided to help you look up an address in the Domino Directory or your personal address book.

4. Click the Enable Page Minder button.

5. A dialog box instructing you to verify or enable background agents will be displayed. This is required for Page Minder to function properly.

After clicking OK, you will be returned to the Internet Options form. The Enable Page Minder button will be changed to Disable Page Minder.

Using Web Ahead

Once Web Ahead is configured and enabled, it will run every half hour. To have Web Ahead retrieve pages from links on web pages you have visited, follow this procedure:

1. With the Personal Web Navigator database open, open the All Pages view.

2. Find the page for which you would like Web Ahead to retrieve referenced pages.

3. Copy the page into the Web Bots/Web Ahead folder.

Web Ahead will include this page in its next scheduled retrieval. To remove a page from the Web Ahead schedule, remove it from the Web Bots/Web Ahead folder. Do not delete the page unless you intend to remove it permanently from the database. Instead, select Actions ➤ Remove from Folder.

NOTE *Web Ahead will retrieve web pages that require name and password authentication as long as you have successfully visited the page online. Notes stores this information in your Personal Web Navigator database, so make sure this database is encrypted if you want to ensure the security of this information. Web Ahead will also function properly through firewalls as long as you have successfully logged in to the firewall in the current Notes session.*

Using Page Minder

Once Page Minder is configured and enabled, it will run as defined in the configuration. To have Page Minder check pages for changes, follow this procedure:

1. With the Personal Web Navigator database open, open the All Pages view.

2. Find the page on which you would like Page Minder to check for changes.

3. Copy the page into the Web Bots/Page Minder folder.

Page Minder will include this page in its next scheduled execution. To remove a page from the Minder schedule, remove it from the Web Bots/Page Minder folder. Again, do not delete the page unless you intend to remove it permanently from the database. Instead, select Actions ➤ Remove Folder.

Browsing Pages Offline

Browsing web pages offline is just a matter of reading documents that are already stored in your sonal Web Navigator database. The key is to make sure your current Location document specif location type of No Connection. One convenient way to do this is to create a Location documer use while you are not connected to the Internet. By default, Notes creates a Location document a location name of Island for this purpose. It should also be configured to use the same integra browser mode your online Location document uses. If you normally use the native Notes brov configure your Island Location document to use the native Notes browser.

Participating in Newsgroups

Newsgroups are the Internet equivalent of discussion databases in Notes. They allow you to post ics and responses that are just like the topics and responses in the discussion database. There are of thousands of public newsgroups in existence and more are added every day; this is also know *Usenet*. Internet service providers (ISPs) maintain news servers (or NNTP servers) to host pub newsgroups for their customers, and they synchronize their copies with those from other ISPs continual basis. All you need is an NNTP client or newsreader application; your Lotus Notes cl can be configured to be an NNTP client. Figure 13.11 shows a typical newsreader web page.

FIGURE 13.11

An NNTP page

Newsgroups for Free Demo User
Demo Account Time Left: 24 hours
Sun 21 Jul 2002 2:10 AM

| Next Article | Junk All | Help |

New	Newsgroup	Description
41	newsreader.general	NewsReader.Com general issues and questions.
	newsreader.test	NewsReader.Com test postings.
9	news.announce.newusers	Explanatory postings for new users. (Moderated)
339	news.newusers.questions	Q & A for new users of Usenet. (Moderated)
2244	news.answers	Repository for periodic USENET articles. (Moderated)
1484	alt.binaries.clip-art	Distribution of DOS, Mac and Unix clipart.
743	alt.binaries.pictures.animals	Pictures of all types of animals.
3445	alt.binaries.pictures.animated.gifs	Animated GIFs.
671	alt.ascii-art	Pictures composed of ASCII characters.
1276	talk.bizarre	The unusual, bizarre, curious, and often interesting.
22	rec.humor.funny	Jokes that are funny (in the moderator's opinion). (Moderated)
10274	Total New Articles	

| Change Groups | Account Status | User Info | Display Options | Switch User | NewsReader.Com |

The way Notes implements NNTP support is fairly unique. Instead of just presenting an enti different interface in a helper application, Notes presents newsgroups in the form of a Notes d base. Because this database is designed like a discussion database, it will already be familiar to

Under the covers, this database is different from other Notes databases that we have discussed. It is called a *proxy database*, and it does not actually contain any documents. It retrieves documents from a news server and presents them through views and forms as if they were stored locally.

You can then create a local replica of your newsgroup proxy database, which will allow you to read and post offline. It will also allow you to use the powerful searching capabilities of Notes to find the information for which you are looking.

Configuring Notes as Your Newsreader

To configure Notes to be your newsreader application, you need to create an NNTP Account document in your personal address book. This Account document will define the news server and protocol information that Notes needs to create the proxy database. When you save the Account document, Notes will automatically create the proxy database for you.

To create an NNTP Account document, follow these steps:

1. Open your personal address book database.

2. Click the New button.

3. Select the Account option from the submenu, as shown in Figure 13.12.

FIGURE 13.12
Creating a New
Account Document

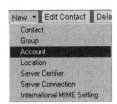

4. When the new Account document displays, select NNTP from the Protocol drop-down box. This is the protocol used to communicate with the news server. Figure 13.13 shows the document in read-only mode, but it is in editing mode when first created.

FIGURE 13.13
Choosing the
NNTP protocol

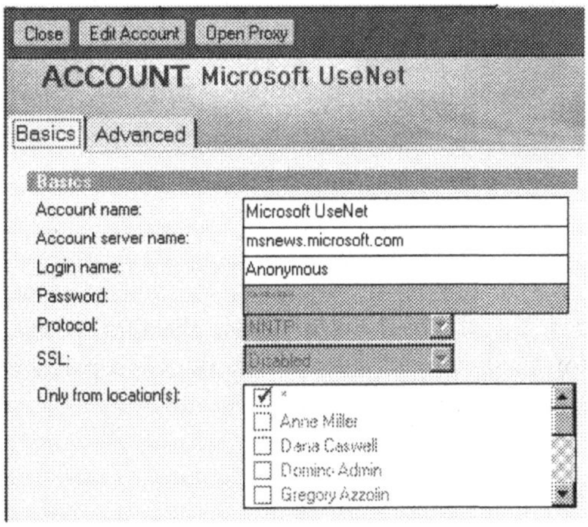

5. Enter a descriptive name in the Account Name field. This name generates the filename o proxy database. Because Notes automatically generates this name based on 8.3 file-na conventions, make sure the beginning characters are descriptive.

6. In the Account Server Name field, enter the name of your news server. Your ISP will pro the server name. If you are configuring Notes to connect to a corporate news server, your nization's internal information systems (IS) group will provide it.

7. Enter a login name and password if your ISP (or internal IS group) requires them.

8. Select Enabled from the SSL drop-down box if you want to encrypt the network comm cations between your computer and the news server. For some news servers, you must er SSL. Again, check with your ISP or IS group.

9. Select the check box for * (asterisk) from the Only from Location(s) list box to make t Account document available to all locations or select individual locations through whicl should be available.

10. Click the Advanced tab if you need to change the TCP/IP port or if you want to disa the use of replication history with this proxy database. By default, the NNTP service ι port 119.

When you save the Account document, Notes will automatically create a news server proxy base if one does not already exist. A bookmark to the proxy database will also be added to the L bases folder of your Bookmark bar. To open the proxy database, you can either use the bookmar open the Account document and click the Open Proxy button at the top of the document (whi visible in Figure 13.13).

CONFIGURING SSL

SSL encrypts communications in the Internet world. If you choose to enable SSL, you need to some Location document options. In the Location document on the Advanced tab, there is an subtab, as shown in Figure 13.14.

FIGURE 13.14

Location document
SSL settings

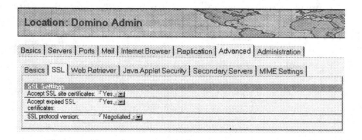

Notes supports SSL 2 and 3 or it can negotiate the appropriate version with the server. You set which version Notes will support by selecting the appropriate value from the SSL Protocol sion field. The choices are as follows:

- V2.0 Only
- V3.0 Handshake

- V3.0 Only
- V3.0 with V2.0 Handshake
- Negotiated

If you select a value that involves SSL 3, you will also need to obtain an Internet cross certificate for the server you want to access. To obtain an Internet cross certificate, follow these steps:

1. Select File ➢ Security ➢ User Security.

2. Select the Identity of Others tab and choose People, Services.

3. Select the radio button for Find More about People/Services to display the dialog box shown in Figure 13.15.

FIGURE 13.15

People and services

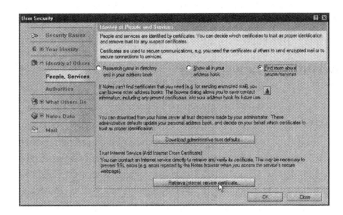

4. Click the Retrieve Internet Service Certificate button at the bottom of the dialog box to display the Retrieve Internet Service Certificate dialog box, as shown in Figure 13.16.

FIGURE 13.16

Retrieve Internet
Service Certificate
dialog box

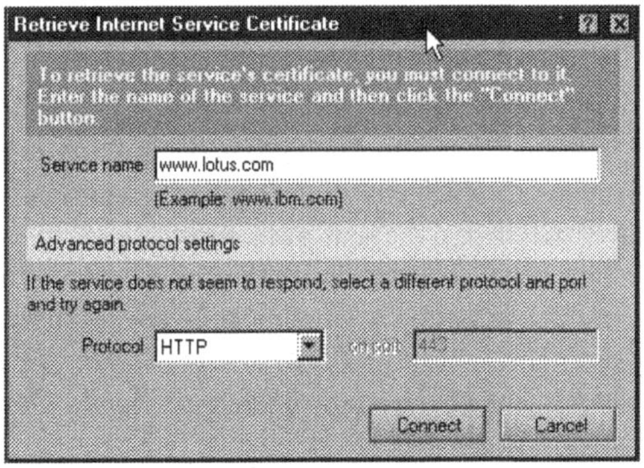

5. In the Service Name area, type the URL address of the certificate authority from whom need a cross certificate.

6. Choose the communications protocol to use from the drop-down box, which in turn wi the port number.

7. Select the protocol you want to use when you connect to the server.

8. Click the Connect button.

If Notes can connect to the server you entered using the protocol selected, an Issue Cross C icate dialog box will be displayed and you can cross certify at that point. The cross certificate w added to the Certificates view of your personal address book.

TIP   You can also create Internet cross certificates from existing Internet Certifier documents in your personal add book database in the Advanced ➤ Certificates view by opening an Internet Certifier document and selecting Actions Create Cross Certificate.

Subscribing to Newsgroups

Once you create an Account document and its associated news server proxy database, you need to scribe to specific newsgroups provided by your ISP's news server. To subscribe to newsgroups, fo these steps:

1. Open your news server proxy database. You can either click the appropriate bookmark or c the associated Account document and click the Open Proxy button (refer to Figure 13.

2. Click the Newsgroups button shown in Figure 13.17, and Notes will begin retrieving the of newsgroups provided by the news server. Be patient. Most ISP's news servers support full set of public newsgroups, which is currently in the tens of thousands.

FIGURE 13.17

Using the proxy database

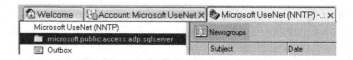

3. When the list of newsgroups displays, as shown in Figure 13.18, choose a radio button show all newsgroups, show only subscribed newsgroups, or show only text newsgroups.

4. Select the newsgroup to which you want to subscribe and click the Subscribe button. A folder will be displayed to the left of the newsgroup entry (see Microsoft.public.access.adp.sqlserver), the Subscribe button will be replaced with the Unsubscribe button when that item is selected. can use the Unsubscribe button at any time to remove yourself from the newsgroup.

NOTE   The list of newsgroups provided by a news server changes frequently. Click the Refresh button in the Newsgrou box to reload the list of newsgroups provided by the news server.

FIGURE 13.18

List of newsgroups

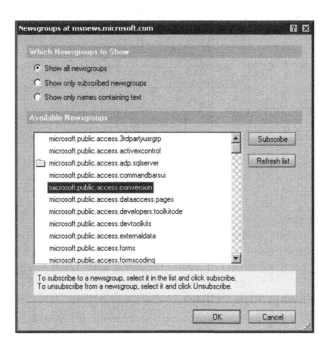

Reading and Posting to Newsgroups

Once you have subscribed to newsgroups provided by your news server, you are ready to read and post entries. Notes displays each newsgroup to which you subscribed as a view. To see the messages in the newsgroup, just click the newsgroup name on the left side of the proxy database. Notes will display the message summaries previously retrieved from the news server. If the view refresh indicator is displayed, there are additional message summaries to be retrieved. Notes retrieves message summaries in blocks or sets of messages. To retrieve a block of message summaries from the news server, press F9 or click the Refresh button on the Navigation bar. Notes will display a dialog box showing the progress of the retrieval and will then display the message summaries in a view list, as shown in Figure 13.19.

FIGURE 13.19

Summary of newsgroup messages

The Notes view shows message summaries. When you open a message document, it is at that point that Notes actually goes out and retrieves the full message from the news server and displays it through the form. To open a message, double-click its row in the view. The message will be displayed through the Main Topic form, as shown in Figure 13.20.

FIGURE 13.20

A Newsgroup Message

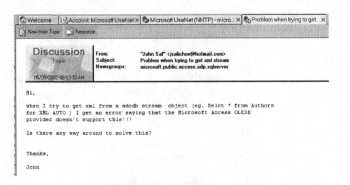

Reading and posting to newsgroups is similar to working in a Notes discussion database. W
reading a newsgroup message, you can post a response using the Response button or add a new t
using the New Main Topic button. While editing a new topic or a response, a Post Response bu
will appear, and when clicked, your information will be sent directly to the news server.

Using Newsgroups Offline

In true Notes fashion, newsgroups can also be replicated to your computer for offline use. This
great way to speed up interaction if you connect to the Internet via dial-up communications. It
provides additional functionality in that the local newsgroup replica can be full-text indexed f
sophisticated searching.

CREATING A REPLICA

The first task is to create a replica of your news server proxy database. The process is the same
is for creating a replica of any other database. See Chapter 10, "Replication," for more informa
on creating replicas.

SYNCHRONIZING THROUGH REPLICATION

After you create a replica of your news server proxy database, an entry is added to the Replicator
for the new replica. This entry controls how the Notes Replicator keeps the local replica synch
nized with the news server. It is the same as other replication entries in that it can be enabled or
abled and you can set replication options. The Notes Replicator will synchronize your local rep
with the news server in the background, as it does with Domino servers. You can work on other N
tasks while it is synchronizing, and you can schedule replication.

NOTE   *The only way to search newsgroups in Notes is to create a local replica. You can then create a full-text ind
and perform sophisticated searches as you can with any other database. See Chapter 8, "Searching for Information,"
more information on searching Notes databases.*

Sending and Receiving Internet Mail

One of the major reasons people use the Internet is to send and receive mail. It is still the most popular form of electronic collaboration and widely used by all types of users. Notes 6 integrates Internet messaging the same way it integrates other Internet services—by wrapping the Notes interface around the appropriate protocols and standards. Using Notes as an Internet mail client is just a variation of using Notes as a Domino Mail client and the Lotus Notes client Location and Connection documents.

NOTE *See Chapter 5, "Communicating with Notes Mail," for a complete discussion of Notes messaging. Because Location and Connection documents are at the core of being able to send and receive Internet mail, it might also be useful to refer to Chapter 9, "Communicating with Domino Servers," which is where Location and Connection documents are discussed.*

Internet Location Document

In an Internet-only configuration, a Location document defines how Notes connects to the Internet, processes Internet e-mail, schedules replication of newsgroups, and so on. You can create multiple Location documents in your personal address book database for different configuration scenarios. Figure 13.21 shows a typical Internet Location document in a Lotus Notes client.

FIGURE 13.21

Internet Location document

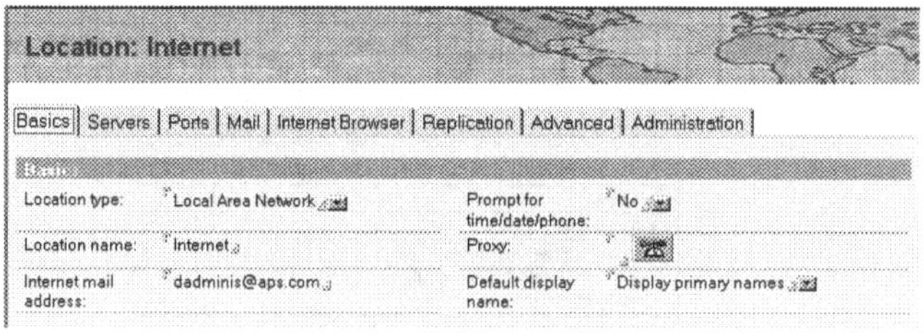

BASICS

The following options on the Basics tab affect an Internet-only configuration:

Location Type Local Area Network is the default setting and generally means that TCP/IP is the communications protocol being used.

WARNING *The Notes Direct Dialup option is not valid for Internet locations because it is used exclusively for connecting Notes to Domino servers.*

Internet Mail Address The Internet Mail Address field is required in Internet-only configurations. It defines your return address when you send outgoing messages directly to SMTP servers. This field should have no effect when using Notes in an Internet-only configuration, but it requires a value. Just enter your ISP domain name.

Proxy   This field defines proxy servers to use for web browsing and for accessing Domino sethrough firewalls. Because they are used for accessing Domino servers, do not enter values i
HTTP Tunnel and SOCKS fields.

SERVERS

The entire Servers tab is devoted to identifying Domino servers for the Notes client to use. Al
these fields should be left blank for an Internet-only Location document.

PORTS

TCP/IP should be the only communication port enabled in the User Preferences dialog box.
should also select the TCP/IP port to configure this Location document to connect to the Inte

MAIL

Settings on the Mail tab determine how mail will be routed. For an Internet location, there shou
no reference to a Domino server in any of these fields. Figure 13.22 shows the Mail tab in the Inte
Location document.

FIGURE 13.22

Internet Location
document Mail tab

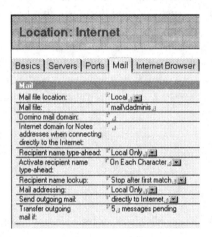

The following options on the Mail tab affect Internet-only configuration:

Mail File Location   Because you will be using Notes without Domino servers, this field sho
always be set to Local. This instructs Notes to look on your local computer for your mail datab

Mail File   This field is used in conjunction with the Mail File Location field. It contains the]
and filename of your mail database.

Notes Mail Domain   Because you are using Internet mail and not using Notes mail, this fi
should be left blank.

Internet Domain for Notes Addresses   Because you are not using Notes mail, this field sho
be left blank.

Recipient Name Type-Ahead   Because you will be using Notes without Domino servers, this field should be set to Disabled or Local Only.

Mail Addressing   Because you will be using Notes without Domino servers, this field should be set to Local Only.

Send Outgoing Mail   Because you will be using Notes without Domino servers, this field should be set to Directly to Internet.

Transfer Outgoing Mail If   Set this field to the number of outgoing messages you want queued before the Notes Replicator forces a connection to the SMTP server.

INTERNET BROWSER

The options on the Internet Browser tab work the same way whether or not Domino servers are used. You can choose to use the integrated web browser features of Notes, or you can configure Notes to pass URL requests to an external web browser.

REPLICATION

The options on the Replication tab work the same way whether or not Domino servers are used. In an Internet-only configuration, the Replicator receives messages from POP and IMAP servers, sends messages to SMTP servers, and manages replication with Network News Transfer Protocol (NNTP) and IMAP servers. You can enable or disable scheduled background replication. If you enable it, you can further define the scheduling parameters.

ADVANCED

The Advanced tab in a Location document, shown in Figure 13.23, has several subtabs and many of them affect Internet-only configuration.

FIGURE 13.23

Location document
Advanced tab

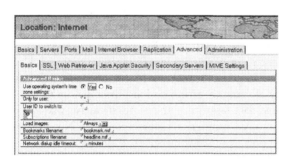

Basics   You can use the Network Dialup Idle Timeout field to force Notes to hang up Network Dialup connections after a predefined period of inactivity. All other fields function the same whether or not Domino servers are used.

SSL   The fields on the SSL subtab determine how Notes supports SSL communication with Internet servers. This is also true in Internet-only configurations.

Web Retriever   The fields on the Web Retriever subtab affect integrated web browsing i Notes. This is also true in Internet-only configurations.

Java Applet Security   The fields on the Java Applet Security subtab define security aspects o Java Virtual Machine (JVM) built into Notes. This is also true in Internet-only configuratior

Secondary Servers   The fields on the Secondary Servers subtab are only used to access Dor servers. All of these fields should be left blank.

MIME Settings   The fields on the MIME Settings subtab define what encoding method N uses when formatting MIME data. This is also true in Internet-only configurations.

Setting Up Accounts to Access Internet Servers

Account documents are used the same whether or not Domino servers are used. They determine Notes accesses Internet servers for mail, news, and directory services. In an Internet-only confi; tion, you must create Account documents for each Internet service you need to access. Also, remer that Account documents are linked to Location documents. You establish this link by selecting tions in the Only From Location(s) field on the Advanced tab of the Account document.

Receiving Internet Mail

Notes supports a variety of options for operating with Internet mail servers, including:

- Receiving POP messages into your Notes mail database
- Receiving IMAP messages into your Notes mail database
- Interacting live with an IMAP mail server
- Replicating your IMAP message store to a local Notes database

Notes can also support all of these options simultaneously, making the Lotus Notes client a versal mail client.

RECEIVING POP MESSAGES INTO YOUR NOTES MAIL DATABASE

Post Office Protocol (POP) is considered an offline protocol. It is used to access a mail server copy messages to a local data repository. Notes is actually well suited for this type of operation includes a variety of communication options, from dial-up to wide area networks (WANs). It : has a sophisticated data repository, the Notes database, that can be full-text searched, replicat secured, and customized, just to name a few capabilities. Notes provides support for POP mail ser through Account documents in your personal address book. You can create a POP Account do ment for each POP account you want pulled into your mail database. You can define as many as need and associate them with Location documents as desired. You can make them available te Location documents or just a subset. The Account document also includes a choice for leaving sages on the mail server.

When you create a new POP Account document, Notes adds an entry to the Replicator p This entry controls how Notes accesses your POP account on the POP server. Clicking the Se and Receive Mail button on the Replicator page or the Receive Mail button in your mail datab will instruct Notes to connect to your POP mail server and retrieve your messages in the ba ground. Mail retrieval will also be initiated if you have background replication scheduled.

IMAP Support

IMAP is more sophisticated than POP. It can be used to provide interactive sessions with the server, or it can be used as an offline protocol. Notes supports both of these scenarios and adds one unique to Notes—creating a local replica of your IMAP message store.

Receiving IMAP Messages into Your Notes Mail Database

When IMAP is used to receive messages into your Notes mail database, it operates the same way POP operates. Notes provides support for offline IMAP through Account documents in your personal address book. You can create an IMAP Offline Account document for each IMAP account you want pulled into your mail database. You can define as many as you need and associate them with Location documents as desired. You can make them available to all Location documents or just a subset.

When you create a new IMAP Offline Account document, Notes adds an entry to the Replicator page just as it does for POP accounts. This entry controls how Notes accesses your IMAP account on the IMAP server and can be used to interactively send and receive IMAP mail on demand. Mail retrieval will also be initiated if you have background replication scheduled.

Interacting Live with an IMAP Mail Server

When IMAP is used interactively, Notes operates in a manner similar to that described for newsgroups. You create an IMAP Online Account document, and Notes creates an IMAP server proxy database. This database is designed like a normal Notes mail database, so using it is similar to using Notes mail. When you open the IMAP server proxy database, Notes retrieves message summaries from the IMAP server and displays them as documents in a view. If you open one of these documents, Notes retrieves the full message from the server and uses a form to display it. You can then create a reply and Notes will send it through the currently configured outbound mail path, most likely an SMTP mail server. Notes even presents folders from your IMAP account as folders in the IMAP server proxy database.

Replicating Your IMAP Message Store to a Local Notes Database

The process for creating a replica of an IMAP server proxy database is similar to the process for creating a replica of a news server proxy database. This enables you to work interactively offline and adds powerful capabilities (such as full-text searching) to standard IMAP messaging. The first task is to create a replica of your IMAP server proxy database. This is the same as creating a replica of any other database. See Chapter 9, "Communicating with Domino Servers," for more information on creating replicas.

After you create a replica of your IMAP server proxy database, an entry is added to the Replicator page for the new replica. This entry is used to control how the Notes Replicator keeps the local replica synchronized with the IMAP server. It is the same as other replication entries in that it can be enabled or disabled and you can set replication options. Double-clicking this entry will also open the local replica. The Notes Replicator will synchronize your local replica with the IMAP server in the background the same way it does with Domino servers. You can work on other Notes tasks while it is synchronizing, and you can schedule replication.

You can also manually replicate your local replica with the IMAP server in the foreground. You generally use this to perform one-time synchronization between scheduled events. This is also the same as foreground replication with Domino servers. For more information on foreground and [ground replication, see Chapter 9, "Communicating with Domino Servers."

Sending Internet Mail

Regardless of how you receive mail, through POP or IMAP, Notes provides two methods for ser[outbound mail:

- Directly to the Internet
- Through a Domino server

If you are using Notes in an environment that includes Domino servers, you will most likely outbound mail through a Domino server. If the Domino server is properly configured, it can be to send messages to Internet recipients. All you do is enter a properly formatted Internet mail add and Domino will take care of the rest. This requires setting the Internet mail address in your cu[Location document, as shown in Figure 13.24.

FIGURE 13.24

Send outgoing mail

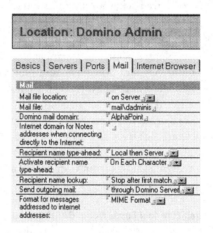

There are two options for sending outgoing mail (the option is the second-to-last entry on [Location document). You can choose to send outgoing mail:

- Through Domino Server
- Directly to Internet

To configure Notes to send outbound messages through a Domino server, just select Throu[Domino Server in the Send Outgoing Mail field on the Mail tab of your current Location docum[

CONFIGURING NOTES FOR SMTP

You can also configure the Notes client to use SMTP to send outbound messages directly to [Internet. You do this by selecting Directly to Internet in the Send Outgoing Mail field on the N tab of your current Location document. After this change is saved to your current Location doc ment, Notes will create an `smtp.box` database in your Notes `Data` directory. This database queues bound messages sent directly to the Internet.

In addition, you need to create at least one SMTP Account document in your personal address book database. The document defines the SMTP server to which Notes will send outbound messages. The SMTP Account document is similar to NNTP, POP, and IMAP Account documents in that it can be made available to all Location documents or just those selected. Once you create an SMTP Account document, Notes adds an entry to the Replicator page just as it does for POP and IMAP offline accounts. This entry is used to control how Notes accesses the SMTP server. You can click the Send and Receive Mail button on the Replicator page to instruct Notes to connect to the SMTP server and deliver any messages queued in smtp.box in the background. Notes can also be configured to connect to the SMTP server when the number of messages queued reaches a predefined threshold. Notes also delivers queued mail if you have background replication scheduled.

USING INTERNET DIRECTORIES TO ADDRESS MESSAGES

You can enter Internet mail addresses of recipients directly in the Mail Memo form. This is useful when you know the recipient's Internet mail address or can reference it quickly. You can also add frequently used Internet mail addresses to your personal address book. Notes can even use Contact entries in your personal address book for type-ahead addressing, where Notes translates names as you enter them in the To, Cc, or Bcc field of the Memo form. If you are using Notes as an Internet mail client, there is another option.

You can access LDAP directories on the Internet to search for Internet mail addresses of people you are trying to contact. Notes provides support for LDAP directories through Account documents in your personal address book. You can create an LDAP Account document for each LDAP directory you want to search for Internet mail addresses. You can define as many as you need and associate them with Location documents as desired. You can make them available to all Location documents or just a subset.

For each new LDAP Account document you create, Notes adds an entry to the Look In dropdown box on the Select Addresses, Directories, and other dialog boxes used to search address books. You just select this entry and enter search criteria as you normally would, and Notes passes the request to the LDAP server. The results of your search are presented in the dialog box as usual. This is a great way to search Internet directories such as Bigfoot, Four11, and Yahoo!

Secure Internet Mail

Notes supports S/MIME for secure Internet mail. S/MIME uses X.509 certificates (Internet certificates), which make up a system of trusted certificates to ensure the validity of signatures and encryption of messages. The sender and recipient each have a certificate issued by a certifying authority (CA) or an organization that can be trusted. This is the same as states issuing driver's licenses. Because people trust the state's system, they trust that licenses issued by the state are valid. Domino can be used as the CA within your company, but third-party CA service providers are commonly used to ensure validity of certificates outside individual organizations. Individual users can also obtain certificates from these third-party CAs. For example, you can obtain a personal certificate from VeriSign. The process is explained at its website (www.verisign.com/client/index.html), but it basically follows the same procedure as other CAs. The process is as follows:

1. Go to the CA's website and request an Internet certificate. If the CA does not have specific instructions for Notes 6, follow the process for Netscape Navigator. (If your Notes ID is based on International security, select the LowSecurity option.)

2. Wait for the CA to e-mail you a key or PIN.

3. Open the URL e-mailed back to you from the CA. Copy and paste the key or PIN e-m
   to you where requested. Submit the form.

4. Notes will display a dialog box stating that an Internet certificate is available and asking i
   want to install it. Click the Yes button.

5. Check your Notes ID file to verify that the Internet certificate was installed. Select File
   Security ➤ User Security, go to the Identity of Others area, and choose the Authorities op
   Your new Internet certificate will be listed in the Certificates Issued To area at the botto
   the screen.

NOTE   *To obtain Internet certificates, Notes must be configured to use its native browser. See "Browsing the Web f*
within Notes" earlier in this chapter for more information on configuring Notes this way. Also, you must have a tru
certificate and an Internet cross certificate for the CA from which you would like to obtain an Internet certificate.

The only way to ensure that a certificate issued by a particular CA is valid is to obtain the CA's tru
certificate, usually the root. Trusted certificates are stored in your personal address book database.
default personal address book database contains a set of trusted certificates for popular CAs. If the
not already an Internet certificate document for the CA you are using to obtain your Internet certifi
you must add one. To add an Internet certificate for a particular CA, follow these steps:

1. Make sure you have configured Notes to use the native Notes browser. This is explaine
   "Using Integrated Browsing" earlier in this chapter.

2. Go to the website of the CA for which you would like to obtain the trusted certificate and
   the link to the root certificate. If the root certificate is in Raw X.509 BER format or Bas
   Encoded format, you will be prompted to install it.

If you choose to install the root certificate, it will be added to your personal address book.
will also be prompted to create an Internet cross certificate to this root certificate. This is simila
manually creating Internet cross certificates, which was discussed in "Configuring SSL" earlier in
chapter.

After you go through the process of requesting and picking up your Internet certificate, it wi
added to your Notes ID file with your Notes certificates. See Chapter 11, "Lotus Notes and Don
Security," for more information about your Notes ID file.

SENDING SECURE INTERNET E-MAIL

You must install an Internet certificate in your Notes ID file to send secure Internet e-mail messa
explained in the preceding section. To send a signed e-mail message to another Internet e-mail u
just compose a message as you normally would and select the Sign delivery options before sending
message.

To send encrypted e-mail, you must have the recipient's Internet certificate in the Contact e
in your personal address book. With a signed e-mail opened, select Actions ➤ Tools ➤ Add Ser
to Address Book to add the sender's Internet certificate to your personal address book. To ser
encrypted e-mail messages, just select the Encrypt deliver option before sending.

If you receive an S/MIME signed e-mail message, Notes will recognize the digital signature by displaying signature information in the message area of the status bar when you open the message. If Notes is not already configured to trust the CA of the digital certificate used to sign the message, you will be prompted to create a cross certificate. This is similar to manually creating Internet cross certificates, which was discussed in "Configuring SSL" earlier in this chapter.

Summary

In this chapter, we discussed how Lotus Notes Domino provides support for the wide variety and ever-evolving Internet standards. With the Lotus Notes client, you can browse the Internet, use Notes as a newsreader, and send and receive Internet mail.

In the next chapter, we'll continue our Internet focus and show you how to use a web browser to process your Lotus Notes Domino mail.

Chapter 14

Managing Notes E-Mail with a Browser

IN CHAPTER 5, "COMMUNICATING with Notes Mail," we looked at how to manage your Notes mail while using the Lotus Notes client. That's not the only way to get to your mail! In this chapter, we'll review the functionality of mail and tell you how to use all the popular features from a web browser. The Domino server doubles as an application server for things such as mail and a web server. This duality lets Domino administrators provide access to your mail through a web interface. This is not a separate mail system. Instead, it's the same system being accessed from a different method. Consider your mail to be like your house; you can get into your house from the front door, the back door, the garage door, the windows, and for really tiny people, the dog's door in the kitchen. These are multiple access paths for different kinds of traffic. Web mail is the same idea. Your mail file is sitting in the same place on the Domino server that it always does. It makes no difference to your mail file whether you fetch your mail with the web client or with the Lotus Notes client; either way, you're still accessing the same mail file stored on the Domino server.

- Overview of web mail technology
- Logging in for web access
- Opening your mail file from a web client
- Reading and responding to mail
- Creating, addressing, and sending web mail
- Differences between web mail and Lotus Notes access

Overview of Web Mail

Like traditional Domino and Lotus Notes mail, web mail involves the Domino server in all transactions. In Chapter 5, the picture was fairly straightforward; a Domino server stores and forwards mail in conjunction with the Lotus Notes client. Domino web mail makes use of the same server, but

the picture is a bit more complicated because of the inherent security issues surrounding public
net access and private company information. Figure 14.1 depicts the access paths to a Domino s
for web access.

FIGURE 14.1
Web mail access

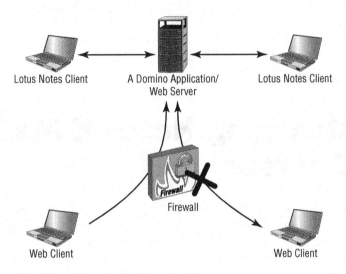

Lotus Notes Client   A Domino Application/
Web Server   Lotus Notes Client

Firewall

Web Client   Web Client

Security Firewalls

While Lotus Notes clients continue to have access to the Domino server, web access for web br
clients is added and generally goes through a security *firewall*. A firewall is either a piece of sof
or a piece of hardware that works with a web server and filters out or allows traffic to pass thr
based on business criteria. Information flows to and from a computer using ports (which are
highways); there are many ports into a computer and each port is identified by a unique nur
(which are like highway numbers).

A Notes client communicates with a Domino server using a dedicated port (1352) for all
missions. When a web client communicates with a Domino server, which is also the web serve
communicating over a public web port (usually 80). For a web client to be able to communicate
a Domino web server, the system administrator must allow traffic to come through the firewall
port 80. An administrator can configure the firewall so that anyone can send messages to the
server, but to retrieve messages, you must log in to authenticate yourself (as shown in Figure 1
You do not have to be a Domino user to send mail to a Lotus Notes client or Domino web c

The most important point, however, is that not all Domino systems are configured to allo
to connect from the Internet. The Domino system administrator must allow it and configure
Domino server to provide web browser client access for the Internet, for intranets, or for extr
If you do not have access to your mail from a web browser and would like to, you will have to
with your company's system administrator to learn the policies and mechanisms in place for y
organization.

Domino Web Users

The Domino Directory, the central configuration database on a Domino server and which is stored on the Domino server, contains a person document for each user associated with that server. When the Domino system administrator registered you as a Lotus Notes user, she or he had the opportunity to configure your person document for web access as well. Figure 14.2 shows a typical Person document in the Domino Directory.

FIGURE 14.2
Person document

NOTE *The Roaming feature (and therefore the tab) was not included as part of the initial version of 6.0 which was released on 9/26/02. This feature can be found in later releases of Lotus Notes and Domino.*

Notice the Internet mail address that appears at the top of the document, DanaCaswell@aps.com in Figure 14.2. This person document and the server itself have been configured for Internet access. If Lotus Notes users or non-Notes users send mail to the Internet address DanaCaswell@aps.com, that mail is sent to the Domino server. Mail sent from a web user passes through the firewall for storage on the Domino server; mail sent from a Lotus Notes client does not go through the firewall and is likewise stored on the Domino server.

The person document identifies the mail server as well as the location and name of mail file. Here, the mail file is stored in the `MAIL` subdirectory in the operating system file `dcaswell.nsf`. The `.nsf` extension is assumed with Lotus Notes Domino mail systems.

To access your mail from a browser, you will need to know the Uniform Resource Locator (URL) address for your mail; your Domino administrator can provide this to you. Your company may have set up a portal or home page with links from which everyone accesses their mail, or you may just be given a direct URL to type into your browser's address window. Figure 14.3 shows a typical URL to access a Domino mail file. Table 14.1 explains the pieces of the URL.

FIGURE 14.3
URL for a
Domino mail file

URL COMPONENT	DESCRIPTION
`http://`	Tells the web browser to use Hypertext Transfer Protocol (HTTP) to talk to the ▮ server.
`aps-server01`	This piece of the URL is the address of the Domino server. It may simply be the n▮ of the web server for the company if you're on an intranet and formatted as sh▮ here, or it may be formatted as a web address, such as www.aps-server01.co▮ as a four-part Transmission Control Protocol/Internet Protocol (TCP/IP) addre▮ such as 10.0.0.100.
`mail`	This is a subdirectory on the Domino server; it is the default subdirectory name ▮ for all mail files.
`dcaswell.nsf`	This is the operating system name of the Notes mail database for this person.

Logging In for Web Access

The person document in the Domino Directory, shown in Figure 14.2, specifies an Internet pa▮ word. It is the password entered into this field that is required when you log into Domino from a browser. This field is encrypted in the person document and is not visible to anyone. The passw▮ typed into this field may be different from the password associated with your Lotus Notes user▮ Web access does not make use of the Lotus Notes ID file in any way. After typing the URL to ac▮ your mail file or using the portal or home page link to get to your mail, you'll be prompted by▮ Domino web server to log into your mail file. Because your mail file is a Lotus Notes database, is the same login screen you would see when accessing any secure Lotus Notes database, not just ▮ mail. The login screen you see may resemble the one shown in Figure 14.4; however, your orga▮ tion may use custom login screens, and in that case, it would override this default login dialog ▮

FIGURE 14.4

Logging into a database

You can log in with the first name and last name specified in your person document or with a sl▮ name, also specified in the person document. The password you type is the one that matches wh▮ stored in the person document. It will not display on login and is instead replaced with asterisk▮

If the login is unsuccessful, any of the following things may be the cause:

◆ First name typed incorrectly.

◆ Last name typed incorrectly.

◆ Password typed incorrectly.

◆ URL for mail file location is not correct.

◆ Domino server is not allowing access.

◆ You are not connected to the Internet/intranet/extranet.

A typical error screen on login returns a number identifying the error and a short, generally not very helpful, error message. Your organization may also use custom error screens that may provide information on whom to contact regarding the error. Figure 14.5 shows a typical login error after a failed attempt to access a mail file.

FIGURE 14.5

Authentication error

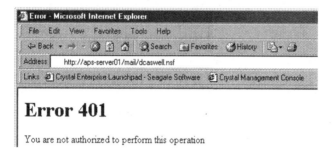

Exploring the Web Mail User Interface

Upon successfully logging in to your mail file on the Domino server, the mail file opens and displays in a browser. Figure 14.6 displays a mail file directly after a successful login.

FIGURE 14.6

Web mail file

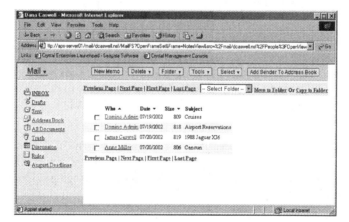

The screen design closely parallels that of its Notes client counterpart. Along the left are views folders. If you have created any personal folders or views in the mail database, they display dir below the Rules entry. In Figure 14.6, the August Deadlines entry is a personal folder.

Using a web browser to access a Notes view automatically adds two navigation bars to your sc one at the top of every view and one at the bottom of every view (as shown in Figure 14.6). Table describes the navigation links.

TABLE 14.2: Web Navigation Links

LINK NAME	DESCRIPTION
Previous Page	In a long list of documents, clicking this link will move you to the set of docume that appears before the current set of documents; this has no effect when you' currently viewing the first page.
Next Page	In a long list of documents, clicking this link will move you to the set of docume that appears after the current set of documents; this has no effect when you're currently viewing the last page.
First Page	In a long list of documents, clicking this link will move you to the set of docume that appears at the top of the list; this has no effect when you're currently view the first page.
Last Page	In a long list of documents, clicking this link will move you to the set of docume that appears at the end of the list; this has no effect when you're currently view the last page.

Additionally, a drop-down dialog box appears at the top of the mail file containing the name all folders in the database. Links to move a document to a folder or copy a document to a fold appear to the right of the drop-down box.

Along the top of the views and folders are buttons used to process the messages the view or fo is displaying. The center of the screen is devoted to showing lists of messages corresponding to view or folder you are currently using as well as displaying the text and editing areas for the mes itself.

The default views and folders are as follows:

Inbox   The Inbox displays all unprocessed mail you've received. From here, you can process mail using the button links along the top of the view. The Select button adds check marks to of the messages, or you can select them individually to process them for deletion or other ta One useful task is selecting an e-mail and using the Add Sender to Address Book button at the of the Inbox view.

Drafts   The Drafts area of the mail database displays mail documents you create but have not sent. You can temporarily store memos here that you come back and finish later. Once you c a draft to display it, an Edit button lets you start changing it. Once in editing mode, all the nor mail processing actions are valid.

Sent   The Sent folder keeps and displays all mail documents you've sent to others.

Address Book   This link displays a list of contacts and groups that are private to the current user.

All Documents   The All Documents view displays all documents you have sent or received. This view is useful to search if you can't remember whether the e-mail you're thinking about and trying to find is one that you created or one that you received.

Trash   The Trash folder contains documents that have been marked for deletion from the database but that have not physically been deleted yet. To delete a message, select the check box to the left of the message and then use the Delete ➤ Delete link, as shown in Figure 14.7. A blue trash can icon appears to the left of documents marked for deletion, as shown in Figure 14.8. To delete the documents from the mail file, use the Empty Trash button from the Trash folder or the Delete ➤ Empty Trash link from inside a memo. The Restore button moves the selected document out of the Trash folder and into the Inbox.

FIGURE 14.7

Deleting a message

FIGURE 14.8

Documents
oed for
deletion

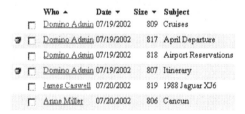

Discussion   The Discussion view displays mail messages grouped together if related via the Reply action. This view is useful for managing a set of e-mails that refer to a single topic, showing all responses and the original e-mail.

Rules   This view displays a list of all mail rule filters defined in the mail file as well as provides access to creating new rules and editing existing rules. Figure 14.9 shows one mail rule defined for this mail file.

FIGURE 14.9
List of mail rules

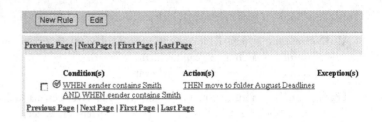

Condition(s)	Action(s)	Exception(s)
WHEN sender contains Smith AND WHEN sender contains Smith	THEN move to folder August Deadlines	

Defining Mail Filter Rules

Are you annoyed by spam emails? You can get control of them in your mail file using the browser
like you can in a Notes clients. Mail rules are filters that can process incoming mail and sort it
designated folders or directly into Trash. Incoming mail that meets a set of conditions is route
otherwise handled automatically.

The Rules view gives you tools for creating and editing rules. A *rule* consists of conditions a
actions. When conditions are met, then the specified action is taken. When you click the New F
button, a window displays for creating new rules for moving or modifying incoming mail (see F
ure 14.10). The screen is split into two basic parts:

◆ An area to specify conditions to meet or exceptions to filter out

◆ An area to specify the action to take if the conditions and exceptions are met

FIGURE 14.10
Creating a
mail rule

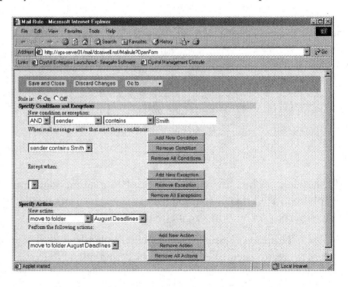

First, you need to set some conditions. You can tell a rule to search a number of fields in incom
mail: the To field, the Cc field, the message body itself, and several others. It can also examine t
message's size or from where the message comes. When you have set the condition fields (say,

subject contains the phrase *make money fast*), click the Add button to add it to the list of conditions the rule follows. You can add a number of conditions to a single rule, connecting them with an AND or OR operator. If you connect multiple conditions with AND, the rule will act on messages for which all of the conditions are true. If you use OR, it will act on messages for which any of the conditions are true. You can also designate additional conditions as exceptions. If you want to remove a condition, just click it and click the Remove button. If you want to completely redo the conditions the rule follows, just click Remove All.

Once you've decided what your conditions are, you need to tell Notes what to do with the messages it finds; you specify this in the bottom part of the screen as actions. Your options are as follows:

- Move to Folder
- Copy to Folder
- Set Expire Date To
- Change Importance To
- Delete

If you choose the Move to Folder or Copy to Folder or option, click the Choose Folder button and designate the folder in which you want the message to end up. If you choose Change Importance, choose the importance you want it to have. Delete has no additional options.

After selecting an action, click the Add New Condition button to add the action to the list. As with the conditions, Remove Condition gets rid of a selected action, and Remove All Conditions gets rid of all of them. You can add several actions to a rule, and they will be performed in order. You might start with a Move to Folder action to get the document out of your Inbox and then add a set of Add to Folder actions to distribute it around your mailbox.

There's no point in having more than one Move to Folder in a rule because the Move option removes the document from the folder. If you try to move a document into multiple folders, it will only appear in the last folder into which it was moved. There's also no reason to set a message's importance more than once because you'll only see the last importance the message is given. Finally, there's no reason to combine Delete with *anything*. If you have a rule that deletes a message, you'll never see it anywhere.

When you're done and ready to put the rule into action, set the rule to On or Off using the radio buttons at the top of the window box then click the Save and Close button to close the rules window. Once you've saved and closed the rule, you can always come back later and disable it or even delete the rule altogether.

Managing Your Mail

The web client interface to your mail file on the Domino server gives you the same kind of control over managing your mail as you would have from a Notes client.

Opening a Mail Message

In the list of messages, the first column always displays as a link. The information in the first column may change from one view to another, but the first column will always be a link. Clicking the link opens the message. You can also open the message in a new window by right-clicking the link to display the submenu; choose the option to Open in New Window, as shown in Figure 14.11.

FIGURE 14.11

Opening a
document in
a new web
window

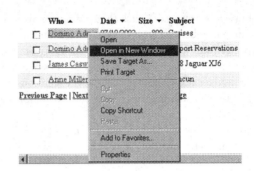

Closing a Mail Message

After reading and viewing a message, use the browser's Back button to return to the list of messa⟶
Alternately, simply clicking one of the other views or folders will also change the screen and dis⟶
the open message. If you opened the message in its own new browser window, close the browser ⟶
dow using the X at the top-right corner of the browser.

NOTE   There is no mechanism for previewing (viewing without opening) a message or document through a web brows⟶

Working with New Memos

From a web client, you have full capability to create, address, and send new memos to other peo⟶

WRITING AN E-MAIL

The New Memo button, visible in Figure 14.6, creates a blank e-mail, as shown in Figure 14.1⟶

FIGURE 14.12

A new e-mail

The area at the top of the e-mail is the header information; it displays the sender of the e-mail and its date and time as well as the addressing information of whom will receive the e-mail directly (To), who will receive a courtesy copy of it (Cc), and who will be on blind copy to it (Bcc). The subject line is a free-form text area where you can type a one-line description of the e-mail's contents. The link for attachment(s) and the Browse button associated with the link lets you search for and add files as attachments to the e-mail.

The message input area is the bottom half of the screen. It is a plain-text area, and it defaults to a system font in black. For full-function editing including font control, color control, and special text formatting, click the link to use the rich-text applet. Doing so changes the text area to the one shown in Figure 14.13.

FIGURE 14.13
Rich-text editing

WARNING *Whenever Domino uses an applet to provide functionality, you will notice a delay in initially downloading the applet to your browser.*

ADDRESSING AN E-MAIL

The Address button at the top of the e-mail area helps you to fill in the To, Cc, and Bcc fields. Typing the addresses directly is certainly an option, but looking them up and pasting them in generally results in fewer addressing errors. When you click the Address button, Domino opens an addressing dialog box in a new window (see Figure 14.14).

FIGURE 14.14
Addressing a web e-mail

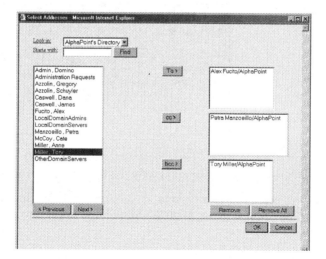

The Look In drop-down box gives you access to your company's address book on the Dom
server as well as your personal address book. The list on the left side of the screen displays all the u
in the address book directory. The Previous and Next buttons at the bottom of the list are used w
the list of names is longer than what the window can display at one time. By selecting one and t
clicking the To>, Cc>, and Bcc> buttons, you copy the address into the areas on the right side
the screen.

You can use the Starts With option and the Find button to search for a user's name in the lis
names in the directory. At the bottom of the addressing fields, the Remove and Remove All butt
can clear one selected name from a field or clear all the names from the addressing fields.

When you're done addressing the e-mail, clicking OK transfers the information into the e-m
that you are writing and closes the addressing window.

FINISHING AN E-MAIL

Once an e-mail is properly addressed, you have three options for finishing up your editing process.
Send button at the top of the screen (see Figure 14.12) and its submenu allow you to do the follow

Send   This option sends the e-mail to the people in the To, Cc, and Bcc fields. When this op
is selected, the e-mail is sent but no copy of it is kept in your mail file.

Send and Save   This option sends the e-mail to the people in the To, Cc, and Bcc fields an
saves a copy of the e-mail in your Sent view.

Save as Draft   This option does not send the e-mail to anyone; instead it saves it to your D
view for later editing and sending.

SETTING DELIVERY OPTIONS

When your e-mail is sent, you can set several options that will affect how it will be delivered and h
it will display in the recipient's mailbox. The Delivery Options button opens a new web client w
dow, as shown in Figure 14.15.

FIGURE 14.15
Delivery options

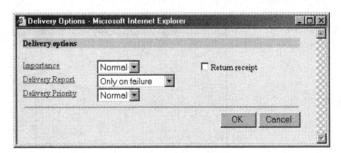

You can set the following options for the delivery of the current e-mail:

Importance   Using this option sets an icon as a marker for the recipient of the mail. You c
mark your mail as having High, Middle, or Low importance; an icon will convey this meaning
the mail recipient.

Delivery Report   Domino can track your message during its delivery process and send an e-mail to you listing the path it took to its destination. This can be useful if you're having trouble getting messages to their destination. There are four options:

Only on Failure   You get a detailed message tracing the route your message takes if it fails to reach its destination.

Confirm Delivery   This option traces the route your message takes if the message is successfully delivered to its destination.

Trace Entire Route   This option gives you a report on the route your message takes regardless of whether it reaches its destination.

None   No tracing will be performed.

Delivery Priority   This gives the message a priority that the Domino and other mail servers can read. In general, messages marked with high priority are delivered before messages with lower priorities. This can speed up the delivery of your mail, although the precise order in which messages are delivered depends heavily on settings on the mail servers between you and your message's destination. There are three settings: High, Normal, and Low. Normal is the default.

Return Receipt   If this option is checked, you will receive a message when the recipient opens and reads your message. This option is not supported by all mail systems and therefore may not return any results to you.

COPY INTO NEW

A new e-mail can be copied into a new to do item or a new calendar entry. The Copy into New button at the top of the screen (see Figure 14.12) will allow you to do either action.

GO TO

The Go To button is a quick way to jump to the Inbox, calendar, or your to do list.

Processing E-Mails in Your Inbox

When you open an e-mail through the web interface, you have the opportunity to reply to it while you're reading it. The Reply button at the top of an open e-mail gives you several options to reply to the sender of the e-mail as well as other people associated with the e-mail. Figure 14.16 shows your options, and Table 14.3 describes their behavior.

FIGURE 14.16

Replying to an e-mail

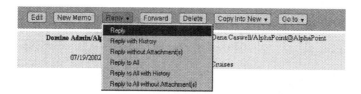

TABLE 14.3: REPLY ACTIONS

ACTION NAME	DESCRIPTION
Reply	This option creates a message addressed to the sender of the origi e-mail with a subject of Re: (short for *Regarding*) plus the subject the original message. The body of the new e-mail is blank and allo free-form typing just like a new memo.
Reply with History	This option creates a message with the address and subject line as it is in a reply, but it also brings the entire original message i the body of the reply.
Reply without Attachment(s)	This option is the same as Reply with History, but it does not forward any attachments that were part of the original e-mail.
Reply to All	This option automatically addresses a new e-mail to the origina sender as well as all recipients of the original e-mail including C and Bcc addresses.
Reply to All with History	This option creates a new message as with Reply to All, and it additionally brings the content of the entire original message into the body of the reply.
Reply to All without Attachment(s)	This option creates a new message as with Reply to All but will forward any attached files.

The Forward button (visible in Figure 14.16) is available when you are reading an open e-m This option creates a new mail memo with a blank address area and the entire text and contents the original e-mail copied into the body of the new e-mail.

You can copy an e-mail you are reading into a new to do item or a new calendar entry. The Co into New button at the top of the screen (visible in Figure 14.16) will allow you to do either act

You can also use the Go To button when reading an e-mail as a quick way to jump to the Inb calendar, or your to do list.

Working with Folders

You can create and remove folders while navigating most of the views in the mail file. A Folder but and a submenu appear at the top of many of the views, as shown in Figure 14.17.

FIGURE 14.17
Creating a folder
in the Sent view

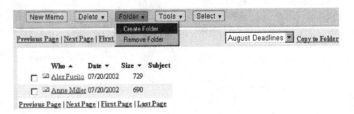

Using the Create Folder option opens a new web browser window. From here, you can assign a name to the folder and add the folder to a hierarchy within your other folders. Creating a folder within a hierarchy is known as *nesting*, and you can use the Current Folders option to nest the new folder below a current folder, or you can type the name of the folder with a backslash. For instance, August Deadlines \ Cessna Project would create a new folder called Cessna Project beneath the existing folder August Deadlines.

The Remove Folder menu option in Figure 14.17 also opens a separate web client window, as shown in Figure 14.18. This dialog window gives you the opportunity to remove a folder by choosing its name from a drop-down list. This does not delete documents; it just removes the folder. If you remove a folder that contains other folders, all folders within the folder being removed are also removed. Again, no documents are deleted, only the folders are destroyed.

FIGURE 14.18
Removing a folder

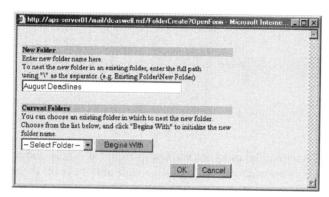

At the top-right corner of many of the views is a drop-down list that lets you select the folder of your choice. This drop-down arrow is visible in Figure 14.17, and the folder August Deadlines is selected. The Copy to Folder link to the right of the selected folder gives you a quick way to add documents selected in the view to the folder selected in the drop-down box.

The Select button, which has the submenu options Select All and Deselect All, allows you to add check marks to the check boxes next to documents. This is handy as a way to select documents to copy to folders.

Using Tools

A subset of all the tool actions in the Notes client are available to you in the web client interface for your mail file. The Tools button in your mailbox gives you the ability to set preferences for your mail, calendar, and delegation activity as well as performing a search and getting to web mail help.

NOTE   Some of the options that require a Lotus Notes client instead of a web client are archiving mail, creating and using letterhead, creating and using stationery, and encrypting and digitally signing e-mail.

PREFERENCES

You can use the web client to configure basic mail, calendar, and delegation preferences for your Lotus Notes Domino mail. Remember, any changes you make through the web interface are being

made to your mail file on the Domino server, so you will see the changes in your Lotus Notes clie[...]
as well. Figure 14.19 shows the Preferences link navigator.

FIGURE 14.19
Setting mail
preferences

The preferences set using this window will affect all e-mails and calendar entries created. Do not [...]
this area if your intention is a one-time override of features for the current e-mail or calendar entry.

Mail

There are three links for the Mail preferences to set options for mail you send:

Basics   The Basics window displays by default. From here, you can set the owner of the mail [...]
as well as choose whether to put an offset character such as an angle bracket (>) as a prefix on m[...]
sage replies.

Signature   The Signature area lets you define a text byline (phrase) that can be added to e-m[...]
and provides a check box that will automatically add the signature to the end of every message y[...]
create and send.

Address Book   The Address Book option lets you add new categories that are used when yo[...]
create new contacts.

Calendar

There are three links for the Calendar preferences to let you configure time available on your calen[...]
and how entries are made:

Freetime   The Freetime settings, shown in Figure 14.20, let you define the availability you wa[...]
other users to see when they access your calendar. The check boxes let you choose the day of the we[...]
and then you must type the hours of availability for each day. The default is 9 A.M. to 12 P.M. a[...]

1 P.M. to 5 P.M. Be careful to type the time format using leading zeros on all hours and double digits for all minutes as follows:

```
09:00 AM - 12:00 PM, 01:00 PM - 05:00 PM
```

FIGURE 14.20

Defining calendar free time

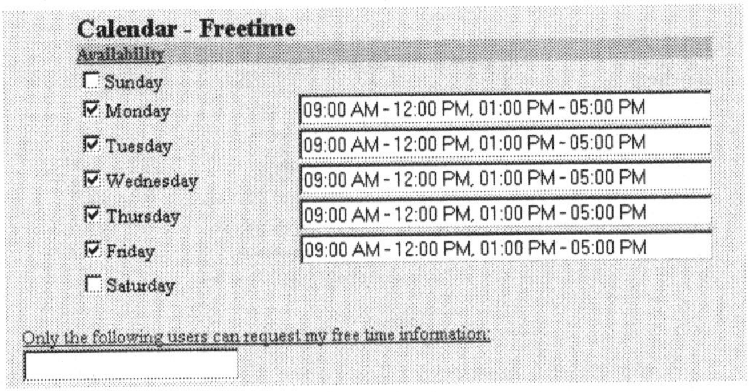

Calendar - Freetime

Availability

☐ Sunday	
☑ Monday	09:00 AM - 12:00 PM, 01:00 PM - 05:00 PM
☑ Tuesday	09:00 AM - 12:00 PM, 01:00 PM - 05:00 PM
☑ Wednesday	09:00 AM - 12:00 PM, 01:00 PM - 05:00 PM
☑ Thursday	09:00 AM - 12:00 PM, 01:00 PM - 05:00 PM
☑ Friday	09:00 AM - 12:00 PM, 01:00 PM - 05:00 PM
☐ Saturday	

Only the following users can request my free time information:

Entries   Using the Entries area of the Calendar preferences, you can set the default length of time in minutes for appointments and meetings as well as how many years to repeat anniversary entries. Additionally, you can specify that calendar entries be excluded from your All Documents view and whether meeting invitations should appear in the Sent view.

Autoprocess   The Calendar Autoprocess area will determine how to handle meeting invitations received in your Inbox. You can automatically add them to your calendar, automatically add meetings received from only specific users, or delegate meeting invitations to another person. You can also specify that meeting invitations be removed from your Inbox after you respond to them and whether the meeting replies should appear in your Inbox at all.

Delegation

You can delegate tasks in your mailbox using the two tabs for Delegation preferences:

Mail   Using the Mail delegation area, you can specify the names of users and groups who are allowed to do each of the following mail and calendar management tasks:

◆ Read the mail and read calendar.

◆ Read and send mail on my behalf and read the calendar.

◆ Read, send, and edit any document in the mail file.

◆ Delete mail and calendar entries.

Calendar   Using the Calendar delegation area, you can set read and edit privileges on your calendar. You can specify a global setting to allow everyone to read your calendar or specify the names of specific users and groups who can read it. Likewise, you allow everyone to create new calendar entries or edit existing entries, or you can specify the names of specific users and groups to whom you'd like to extend this privilege.

SEARCH

If a full-text index has been created on the Domino server for your mail file database, you can use the Search option to find information in the mail file. Figure 14.21 shows the generic search window. Your organization may be using a customized search screen instead of this one.

FIGURE 14.21
Searching the mail file

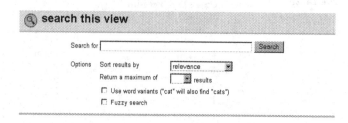

For a complete discussion on how to use the search facility, refer to Chapter 8, "Searching for Information."

HELP

Built into the Lotus Notes Domino web mail facility is help specific to the web interface. Figure 14.22 shows the help options that are set up as links in your browser.

FIGURE 14.22
Getting help

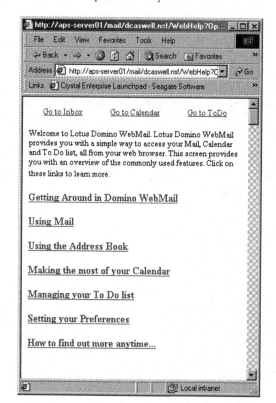

Logging Out

When you logged in to your mail file through the web browser, your username and password were stored in the browser's cache (temporary storage in memory) so that you could easily move from screen to screen in your mail file. You will stay logged in to your mail file until you close the browser. As a security precaution, it is a good idea to close your browser when you're done with your mail and whenever you walk away from your computer.

Summary

Domino is both a web server and an application. This powerful combination makes it possible for your Lotus Notes mail file database to be accessible from either a Lotus Notes client or a web browser client. A large subset of the tasks you can do in a Notes client can be performed in a web client, and this chapter gives you the information you need to use the web client.

In the next chapter, we'll look at another approach to working with your mail from a browser through the use of a Lotus product called iNotes.

Chapter 15

Domino Off-Line Services and iNotes

THE RELEASE OF LOTUS Notes and Domino 6 has focused attention on the Domino server's core strength: delivering information securely to a client. One of the new and exciting pieces of this is that the word *client* now means much more than just the Notes client. As we explained in Chapter 14, "Managing Notes-Mail Using a Browser," the client types that interact with a Domino server include the web browser client as well as the Notes client. Hand-held devices (mobile devices) and an iNotes client (a specialized Web client) are all additional types of clients. These clients have the ability to communicate in real-time, or connected, mode or in disconnected, or offline, mode. For the Notes client, working in disconnected mode requires configuring the Location and Connection documents correctly and then using the replication process when connected to synchronize information. For web clients, the offline capabilities of Domino are provided by Domino Off-Line Services (DOLS). This feature allows disconnected use of Notes databases for clients such as iNotes. In addition to offline capabilities, iNotes provides a more feature-rich web interface than traditional WebMail in Domino. In this chapter, you'll learn more about both of these two interrelated technologies.

- ◆ What is Domino Off-Line Services?
- ◆ Understanding the role of DOLS
- ◆ Working with DOLS as a client to a Domino server
- ◆ What is iNotes?
- ◆ How do iNotes and DOLS work together?
- ◆ Using collaboration applications with iNotes

Using Domino Off-Line Services

Lotus Notes and Domino have always represented the best of client/server technology. In today business world, however, there is not always a persistent connection between a client and a server DOLS gives you a way to work with Domino databases in disconnected, or offline, mode. DOLS an add-on service for Domino 6 that can be configured to run on a Domino server. For users to ta advantage of DOLS, no additional licensing is required beyond the Client Access License that gc erns web browser clients.

As a service, DOLS provides replication and security while allowing users to interact with DOL enabled Domino applications in offline mode through a web browser. DOLS can also be useful f reducing the demand for network resources during peak times; it does this by reducing the number users connected to the server and allowing remote users to work offline using local computer resourc until they need to reconnect. DOLS can be approached from three perspectives:

- Using DOLS
- Developing DOLS-enabled databases
- Administering DOLS in the server environment

A User's Perspective on DOLS

The point of entry for the DOLS experience begins with a web client. When connected to a database th allows the use of DOLS, a Go Offline link will be present. If you're in the mail file, this link appea at the bottom-left corner of the screen. This link switches you to offline mode. Once in offline mod the user experience when working with a DOLS-enabled database is similar to that of a Notes clier. Databases work as they do in the Notes client, and when reconnected to the Domino server, any changes to the content are synchronized between the offline copy and the server-based copy throug a replication process. DOLS provides support for five basic service areas:

- Managing the creation, modification, and deletion of documents.
- Replicating information from a local machine to a server. In DOLS, replication is referred t as *synchronization*.
- Searching for information in a database using a full-text index.
- Triggering agents to run offline without access to a Domino server; this includes LotusScri and Java agents.
- Working within Domino's security framework.

Although many of the Notes client features work in a DOLS environment, a few features do no

- Rich text (although rich-text lite is available if a programmer chooses to enable it)
- Group calendar and scheduling
- Local database encryption
- Scheduled agents

FIRST TIME SYNCHRONIZATION

You manage the synchronization process for DOLS with iNotes Sync Manager. A DOLS-enable database is called an *offline subscription*, and it needs to be enabled by the Domino administrator or th programmer of the database. Once the subscription is enabled, a user accesses it using a web browse that reads information from the server. A list presents the set of subscriptions available on the server, and from that point, the users can choose to install individual subscriptions locally on their machines.

When the Go Offline link is clicked for the first time, some one-time initial processing and setup takes place to install the subscription. The subscription itself may include just one database, or in the case that the database being taken offline involves interactions with other resources and databases, a subscription may include any related databases as well. If Lotus iNotes Sync Manager is not already installed on your machine, this software will download automatically from the Domino server via your Web browser. Several routine dialog boxes will display, including a verification to continue, the iNotes license agreement, and the Lotus iNotes Installer (see Figure 15.1).

FIGURE 15.1
Lotus iNotes
Installer

As the installer does its job of gathering the necessary databases to install, as well as any of the iNotes software itself, a DOLS informational message may appear in the background (see Figure 15.2).

FIGURE 15.2
General
information
on DOLS

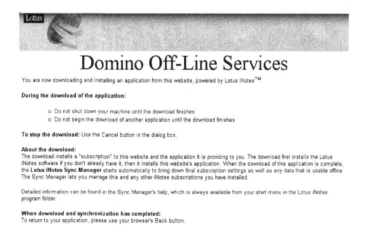

When the subscription is successfully downloaded to your machine, the Lotus iNotes Sync M ager opens to show a list of subscriptions (see Figure 15.3). If the Sync Manager did not already ex on your computer, the software for it is installed during the download of the first subscription. T also installs a new menu item in the Start ➤ Programs path called Lotus iNotes.

FIGURE 15.3

Lotus iNotes
Sync Manager

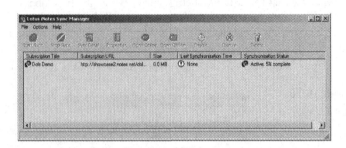

MAINTAINING SUBSCRIPTIONS

The Sync Manager interacts with a subscription. When you create a new subscription, Sync Ma ager opens automatically. To access Sync Manager at other times, use Start ➤ Programs ➤ Lot iNotes ➤ Lotus iNotes. You can also access the Sync Manager help using a similar path, Start Programs ➤ Lotus iNotes ➤ Lotus iNotes Help. To close Sync Manager, use File ➤ Exit; any scheduled synchronizations will not take place when Sync Manager is closed.

Table 15.1 describes the tasks that take place in the normal process of working with a DOLS subscr tion using Sync Manager. The majority of the options are also available by selecting the subscription a right-clicking it to display a submenu of the choices. The Properties icon controls all details regarding t individual subscription, including the schedule on which it synchronizes, how much information synch nizes, and the synchronization user ID and password to use for the particular subscription.

TABLE 15.1: SYNC MANAGER BUTTONS

BUTTON ICON	TASK DESCRIPTION
Start Sync	Starts synchronization for selected subscription(s)
Stop Sync	Stops synchronization for selected subscription(s)
Sync Detail	Displays details on current synchronization process including a progress bar with percen complete
Properties	Displays a tabbed dialog box containing subscription name, schedule, security, and synchronization options to control specifics regarding the individual subscription.
Open Online	Opens a subscription online, connected to a Domino server

Continued on next pag

TABLE 15.1: SYNC MANAGER BUTTONS *(continued)*

BUTTON ICON	TASK DESCRIPTION
	Opens a subscription offline, disconnected from a Domino server
	Enables the synchronization of a subscription that has been previously disabled
	Disables the synchronization of a subscription that has been previously disabled
	Deletes the selected subscription from Sync Manager

When you choose to interact with a database in either offline or online mode, DOLS will open the subscription (database) in the appropriate place. There should be little difference between how an application looks offline and how it looks online. In Figure 15.4, a discussion database has been opened in disconnected offline mode. You can tell this from the URL; it references 127.0.0.1, which is the default Transmission Control Protocol/Internet Protocol (TCP/IP) address for a local machine in the Windows operating system environment. The 89 after 127.0.0.1 is an internal port address used for DOLS. Figure 15.5, on the other hand, references the same discussion database in online mode; the URL references a live web address. Notice how similar the two figures look.

FIGURE 15.4
An offline
discussion
database

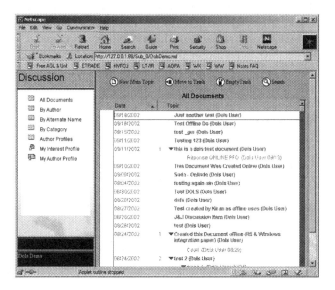

FIGURE 15.5
An online
discussion
database

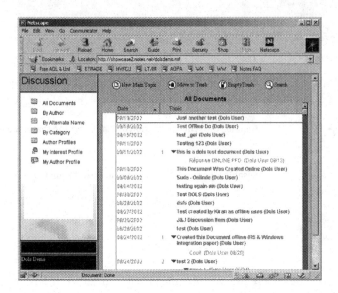

SECURITY AND DOLS

DOLS works within the framework of the existing Domino security model. DOLS requires a syn chronization password before it begins its offline synchronization process; security is paramount the Domino security model and is always respected. Figure 15.6 shows the Security tab of the su scription properties. This tab specifies the user ID and password to use for the subscription. Whe ever a subscription is accessed in offline or online mode, you'll be prompted for the user ID and password associated with the subscription; Figure 15.7 shows this login prompt. The full first nam and last name are required for login, not the Notes shortname.

On its initial synchronization, the password is read from and set to the Internet Password field your Person document on the server. However, all synchronizations after the initial one require you Notes password as the synchronization password. You'll need to manually update the synchroniz tion password if your Internet password is different from your Notes ID password by using the fo lowing steps in DOLS:

1. Choose the mail file subscription entry.

2. From the menu in Sync Manager, choose Properties ➤ Security.

3. Update the synchronization password to be identical to your Notes password.

NOTE *If the correct password is not supplied during synchronization, a Web HTTP 500 error will occur and the database will not be accessed.*

FIGURE 15.6
Logging in to a
DOLS subscription

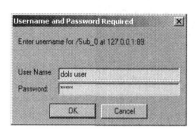

FIGURE 15.7
DOLS security
settings

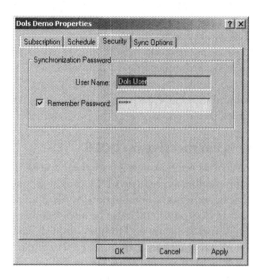

TRYING OUT DOLS

You can try out the offline and online features of the DOLS products in a quick and easy demo found
on the www.notes.net site. Figure 15.8 shows a list of demos you'll find, including DOLS.

FIGURE 15.8
DOLS demo

A Programmer's Perspective on DOLS

A Domino programmer can enable any Notes database, custom or IBM Lotus–supplied, to use DO[?] technology. To do this, you must add specific design objects to the database to support the offline [?] vices. Lotus ships DOLS to developers in the DOLS template, `dolres.ntf`; the template name is DO[?] Resource. You must interactively copy all the design elements in this database from the template in[?] the custom application; be sure to do a one-time copy and not a link to the original source.

The design elements consist of three pages, one form, four subforms, three image resources (gra[?] ics), and two agents. One of the pages is the DOLS Load Download page; this page is the one us[?] will use to access DOLS with the Go Offline link. After copying the design elements, you shoul[?] remove any template name associated with the element. Open the properties for each design eleme[?] and on the Design tab, clear the Inherit from the Design Template field and clear the check boxes f[?] prohibiting design refresh and propagating design changes.

Once all the design elements are in place in the custom database, one last step is required to ma[?] it available to the iNotes Sync Manager subscription service. The last step is to configure a Prof[?] document on the server to identify the database as a DOLS-enabled database. You can create an[?] change this Offline Subscription Configuration Profile document using the agent design element[?] that were manually copied into the database by the programmer.

An Administrator's Perspective on DOLS

The administrator's role in the DOLS process is critical because DOLS is a service that must run on t[?] server. The administrator installs and configures DOLS by setting security options, setting up agen[?] and managing the Offline Subscription Configuration Profile documents (if the programmer does no[?] The administrator or a help desk person may also be involved in helping users install subscriptions.

Software for DOLS is installed with the Domino server. It can be triggered to initialize when[?] building the first server in an organization, or it can be set to start via a setting in the server conf[?] uration document later. The DOLS service runs on port 89.

Every database that is DOLS-enabled must have an associated Profile document (this is the Offli[?] Subscription Configuration Profile document), which tells the server that the database should be ma[?] available to users for offline work. The Profile documents for the databases are centrally stored on t[?] Domino server in the DOLS Administration database. This database is not created automatically fo[?] server! An administrator uses the DOLS Administration database template (`doladmin.ntf`) to manua[?] create `DOLAdmin.nsf`. In the Profile document, the following types of settings govern the synchroniz[?] tion features provided in the specified application:

- ◆ Full-text indexing
- ◆ LotusScript and unscheduled agents
- ◆ Java classes and applets
- ◆ Automation schedule to apply to initial synchronization; user controlled after that point
- ◆ Required database files to replicate
- ◆ Optional database files to replicate
- ◆ Date filtering controls to synchronize a subset of documents
- ◆ Maximum database size that the database can be to synchronize

- Maximum size of the subscription as a whole (because a subscription may include more than one database)
- Option to be notified when synchronization is complete
- Option to route mail when client closes
- Option to replicate information when client closes

With the ability to take applications offline, users are free to move about the organization, the country, and the world. When combined with iNotes technology, the experience from a web client almost matches that provided by the Notes client experience.

Using iNotes

iNotes takes a fresh look at accessing your mail and calendar using a web client. Although the Notes client shines when it comes to connected access to a Domino server, using the iNotes Web Access client gives you many of the same features as a Notes client but from within a web browser environment. You can send and receive mail, work with your calendar, manage your to do list, and add new people to your contact list. When combined with DOLS, you can do these tasks offline as well. Figure 15.9 shows the iNotes user interface.

FIGURE 15.9

iNotes user interface

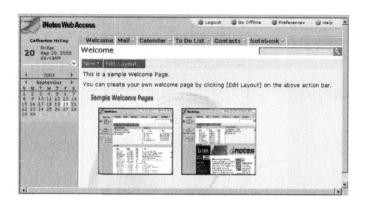

Traditional web-based access to your mail file on a Domino server (known as WebMail) is good, but iNotes provides a better interface to the workday applications such as mail, calendaring, and task management. iNotes is a closer match to the functionality of the native Notes client than ordinary web access. The goal of this client was intuitive navigation and easy-to-use screen controls.

Because both iNotes Web Access and WebMail use a web browser to interact with a Domino server, a uniform resource locator (URL) is the mechanism used to activate both types of access. Many organizations provide a portal application to navigate directly to a person's mail. You can also invoke both iNotes and WebMail directly in a browser by typing an appropriate URL:

iNotes Web Access `http://www.yoursite.com/mail/yourmail.nsf?OpenDatabase&ui=inotes`

WebMail `http://www.yoursite.com/mail/yourmail.nsf?OpenDatabase&ui=webmail`

The keyword ui designates that you want to switch web user interfaces into the mail applicatic The keywords inotes and webmail designate which of the two web interfaces you want to use to access the Domino server.

A User's Perspective on iNotes

To access mail, a user can employ the Notes client, the iNotes Web Access client, or the browse WebMail. All three access the single mail file for the user stored on the Domino server, just throu; slightly different user interfaces. The tasks available with iNotes Web Access are as follows:

- Mail Inbox
- Calendar
- To do list
- Contact list
- Notebook

For iNotes to be available in an organization, the Domino server must be enabled to run iNote a task that is carried out by the Domino system administrator. Figure 15.10 shows the iNotes W Access interface for mail; the folders in the mail application appear along the left side as links. Noti that the screen layout and options offered closely mirror that in the traditional Notes client.

FIGURE 15.10
iNotes mail Inbox

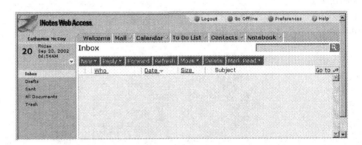

Figure 15.11 shows the interface for the calendar; a variety of day, week, and month views are ava able. When you use the iNotes calendar interface to schedule meetings, iNotes will prompt you t invite and address meeting notices to other people (known as invitees). If you receive a meeting in tation in your InBox, it will automatically appear on your iNotes calendar.

FIGURE 15.11
iNotes calendar

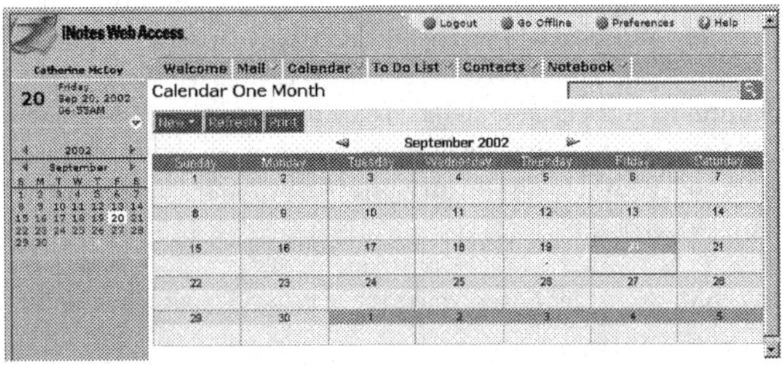

Figure 15.12 shows your personal to do list. You can manage and prioritize tasks for personal or business purposes. When you create a new to do task, it becomes an entry on your list that includes a start date, description, and information on whether the task repeats periodically and how frequently.

FIGURE 15.12
iNotes to do list

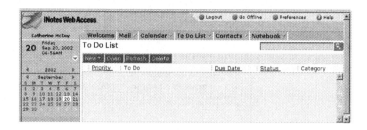

Figure 15.13 shows the iNotes Web Access contact list. Using this tool, you can manage and track people you keep in touch with frequently. The tabbed interface lets you quickly move between alphabetized groups of people, their e-mail addresses, and their company information.

FIGURE 15.13
iNotes contact list

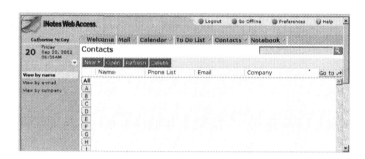

Figure 15.14 shows the iNotes Notebook, which is similar to the personal journal in the Notes client. Use this tool to keep track of your thoughts by topic and the date entered or modified.

FIGURE 15.14
iNotes Notebook

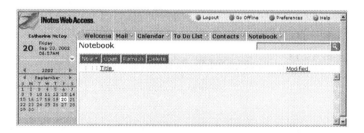

Just as in the Notes client, you can personalize the Welcome page layout and set mail and calendar preferences. Figure 15.15 shows the user interface for setting preferences. It is important to know that changing any settings affects the entire mail file; iNotes Web Access is simply one way to view the mail file; WebMail and the Lotus Notes clients are two other ways.

FIGURE 15.15

Setting preferences

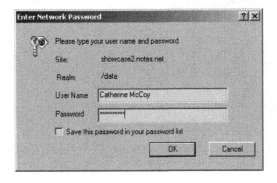

You can use DOLS to "go offline" with the iNotes Web Access client; the top-right corner of the iNotes Web Access client contains a direct link to do this. When you do this, certain server-based functionality will not be available. For instance, you cannot address a mail message to someone listed in the iNotes directory or use the Directory Catalog. Folders will work; however, you'll need to use your browser's Refresh button after going back into online mode to see any new or modified folders or the absence of a deleted folder.

SECURITY AND INOTES

iNotes uses the first name and last name from the Person document on the Domino server to authenticate your access to a mail file. The password is the Internet password. Figure 15.16 shows the login screen to access mail.

FIGURE 15.16

Logging into iNotes

Like DOLS, iNotes is available as a demo directly from the www.notes.net site. You can create a temporary user ID and password and take a look at the iNotes user interface. (Refer to Figure 15.8 to see the option to access the iNotes demo.)

A Programmer's Perspective on iNotes

There is not really a programmer aspect to working with iNotes; it's a stand-alone, ready-to-use client from a web browser. iNotes Web Access can be integrated with Lotus Sametime as well as any DOLS-enabled custom applications, but this integration happens by virtue of administrator efforts rather than programmer efforts.

An Administrator's Perspective on iNotes

You do all administration of the iNotes service centrally on the server for all users... sounds like the old-fashioned world of mainframes with the updated twist of the web browser interface. There is no deployment or client rollout required because the databases are stored centrally on the server and the web client connects directly to that server. You implement iNotes for Domino through the iNotes template, iNOTES6.ntf.

iNotes Web Access installs on user machines by downloading files from the server. This is what makes deployment easy; the server is the single point of maintenance and control. If configuration or executable files change on the server, users who have previously installed iNotes automatically receive incremental changes the next time they use iNotes.

To enable users to work with iNotes, the administrator must replace the mail template used on the server with the iNotes-specific template. The administrator does this conversion by loading the convert task, specifying the mail files to convert, specifying the template currently being used, and specifying the new iNotes template to start using. While the conversion is taking place, the user's mail is unavailable, so consider doing the conversion during off-hours.

Summary

Web browsers have become one of the ubiquitous client types for accessing information anywhere and any time. iNotes is this type of client. It provides a feature-rich environment for collaboration with the Domino server. When combined with DOLS, iNotes can be used in stand-alone mode and can synchronize updates when once again connected to a server. There are Domino Designer (programmer) and Domino Administrator (administrator) components to configuring both of these two technologies to work effectively on a Domino server. In the next part of the book, we'll take a closer look at more Domino Designer features as you move forward into the world of programming in Lotus Notes and Domino.

Part 4

Developing Lotus Notes Applications with Domino Designer

In this section:

Chapter 16

Introducing Domino Designer

MOST PEOPLE WILL ONLY see the Notes client we've been dealing with so far, or perhaps some combination of the Notes client, Notes databases accessed through a web browser, and iNotes. However, database designers get an additional client of their own, the Domino Designer, which is a development tool for building Notes/Domino databases.

And although Domino Designer allows you to build only Notes databases and their related objects—and not, for example, individual, freestanding Hypertext Markup Language (HTML) pages or Java applets—it does allow you to build web-enabled applications, sometimes without having to do any additional work to make the database web-capable. Domino technologies have been integrated with web technologies, which brings the native web technologies to the Notes environment and extends the native Domino technologies to the web environment. You can now write your application once, and it will run both in the Notes client and on the Web. You can use HTML tags in your applications if you want, but Domino design elements can automatically render themselves as HTML or Java applets to provide more robust functionality to the web browser.

◆ Opening Domino Designer

◆ Navigating Domino Designer

◆ Introducing the design elements

Entering the World of Designer

You can launch the Domino Designer client in three ways:

◆ Select the Designer icon from the Notes client.

◆ Launch Designer from an open database in the Notes client.

◆ Use the Start menu.

To use these options, Domino Designer must be installed when Notes is initially installed. If you do not see any of the following options, review Appendix A, "Installing IBM Lotus Notes and Domino 6 Clients."

Using the Designer Icon

When you start the Notes client, the Designer icon is located on the vertical Bookmark bar, wh is displayed on the left side of the application window. Click the icon to automatically launch D ino Designer. Once it is launched, one of the databases will be automatically opened for you. You be positioned on the opening splash screen.

NOTE *If you don't see the Designer icon in the Bookmark bar, you did not install the Domino Designer program duri the installation process. Please review the Appendix.*

Launching Designer from a Database

To open Domino Designer from within a database in the Notes client, choose View ➤ Design a Domino Designer will be automatically launched (this option won't be available in an open docum or page, but you will be able to see it if you're in a view, folder, or frameset). One nice side effect using this method is that the database will also be opened in Designer, positioning you in the Des list on the Forms element. The Work pane for all of the forms will also be displayed.

NOTE *If you don't see the menu option for Design within the View menu structure, you may not have installe Designer or you may not have Designer or Manager access to the database.*

Using the Start Menu

The final option for launching Domino Designer is to use the icon placed in the Start menu. Th placement of the Domino Designer icon depends on how you defined your installation. By defau the program icon will be placed in a program group called Lotus Applications. The title for th Designer icon is Lotus Domino Designer. When you select this option, Designer will be automa cally launched and you will be positioned on the splash screen (just as if you clicked the Designer ic from within the Notes client).

NOTE *If you don't see the Designer icon in the Lotus Applications group, you did not install the Domino Designer pro gram during the installation process. Please review the Appendix.*

Navigating Domino Designer

Throughout the remaining chapters of this book, we'll be referring to the various areas of the Domi Designer user interface. So before we embark on exploring what Designer has to offer, let's first go ov the different areas that make up the user interface. To open Domino Designer, just select the Design icon from the Notes client. Once opened, Domino Designer will look similar to Figure 16.1.

The overall look of Designer is similar to that of the Notes client. Let's take a closer look at t individual elements that make up the general Designer user interface.

FIGURE 16.1

The Domino
Designer interface

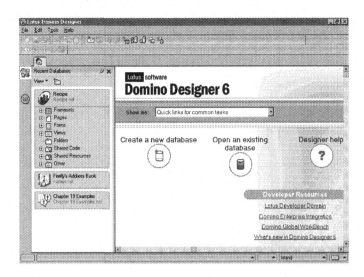

The Designer User Interface

As shown in Figure 16.1, there is a context-sensitive menu bar along the top of the Domino Designer interface. The available options displayed are determined by what actions are available for the active window. In Figure 16.1, only the File, Edit, Create, Tools, Text, and Help menus are available. This is not to say that these are the only menus available in Designer, but rather that these are the only options available for the currently active element (the Welcome screen).

NOTE *Depending on your preferences, the toolbars may or may not display in Domino Designer. As in the Notes client, you can change which toolbars are available by choosing File ➤ Preferences ➤ Toolbar Settings.*

Below the menu bar (in the upper-left corner of the window) are the Properties box icons and preview icons, or buttons (*icons* and *buttons* are used interchangeably for the Properties box and preview icons). The Properties box icon allows you to quickly display the Properties box for the active design element. The preview icons allow you to quickly preview your design in either the Notes client or a currently installed web browser (you can also preview via the menu bar). In Figure 16.1, there are four preview icons. The first icon will launch the design element in the Notes client, and the remaining icons will launch the element in the Notes browser, Internet Explorer, and Netscape Navigator, respectively.

NOTE *The number of browsers you have installed on your machine will determine the various preview icons that will be displayed.*

Vertically aligned along the left side of Designer is the Bookmark bar, which contains a list of icons known as *Design bookmark folders*. The first icon is reserved for a special folder and is automatically created for you. This is the Recent Databases folder, which will always display the databases you've opened in the order they were opened, with the most recently opened first. When you add a database to the Bookmark bar, it appears in a semicollapsed form. You'll be able to see the database title, icon, and a list of classes of design elements. Clicking on the database title area will collapse it, hiding the design element list (or expand it if it's already collapsed). You can expand or collapse most of the design element entries by clicking them.

Any remaining icons are completely configurable. To create a new Design bookmark folder, right-click the Bookmark bar and choose Create New Folder from the pop-up menu or click the folder icon at the top of the `Recent Databases` folder. A new folder icon will display in the Bookmark bar. You can change the icon and also rename the folder by right-clicking the actual icon and selecting either the Change Icon or Rename option from the pop-up menu. Each of these folders will contain a bookmark to the actual design of a database.

NOTE *As soon as you change the design of any element in a database, the database will be added to the* `Recent Databases` *folder at the top of the list.*

If you open multiple objects, tabbed windows will be seen just below the menu bar, just as in the Notes client (if you have the toolbars turned on, the tabbed windows are just below them). Whenever a database or design element is opened, a corresponding tabbed window will also be displayed. Tabbed windows allow you to quickly navigate among open windows on your workspace. When you place your cursor over the button, an *X* that will close the corresponding window will appear.

NOTE *By default, Domino Designer will always have one open tabbed window, known as the* home window. *Selecting this tab will always display the Welcome to Domino Designer page shown in Figure 16.1.*

TIP *You can press Ctrl+Tab to move between the tabbed windows. You can also press Alt+W to display a number for each tabbed window. Pressing the number will take you to the corresponding window.*

THE DESIGN AND WORK PANES

To open the Design pane, click one of the Design bookmark folder icons. The Design pane, shown in Figure 16.2, is a sliding window that displays whenever a Design bookmark folder icon is clicked. It operates much like a bookmark folder in the Notes client. You can keep the Design pane open by clicking the icon located in the upper-left corner of the pane (this icon is known as a *pushpin*; hence you are "pinning" the Design pane open). You can close the Design pane by clicking the *X* in the upper-right corner of the pane. If you have not pinned the Design pane open, the Design pane will automatically slide shut when the cursor is removed. The Design pane contains a list of all the databases and templates that have been bookmarked. Each database or template is displayed by its respective application icon, database title, and database path and filename.

TIP *If the Design pane cuts off the database title, you can hover the mouse over the application icon and the entire title will be displayed.*

The application icon can be selected to expand/contract the Design list, which contains a list of all the design elements for the database. Once a type of design element is selected from the Design list, the Work pane will be displayed with all the elements listed.

The Work pane provides a somewhat more detailed listing of everything in the database for the currently selected design element. Don't confuse the Work pane with the work area, which we will examine next. The Work pane is a selection window, as shown in Figure 16.2. To open a specific element from the list, double-click the entry (you can also right-click the element and choose Edit from the pop-up menu) and the Designer workspace will display.

TIP   *A quick way to create design elements is to select the Design Action button from the Work pane. Every design element from the Design list has a Design Action button to create a new element.*

FIGURE 16.2

The Design pane in Domino Designer

THE DESIGNER WORKSPACE

The Designer workspace is composed of the work area and the programmer's pane (although the programmer's pane is actually more than one pane). The work area and programmer's pane can be displayed simultaneously, as shown in Figure 16.3, but you can also use the pane separator bars to resize either area to your liking. The upper pane is the work area, and the lower pane is the programmer's pane.

When you first open a design element from the Work pane, you will be automatically placed in the work area for that element. In Figure 16.3, a form has been opened and the work area is displaying the individual design elements that make up the form. The work area is where the actual design work for an element is done.

The programmer's pane is composed of two parts, the Info list and the script area. To make matters even more confusing, the Info list contains two tabs, the Objects tab and the Reference tab.

FIGURE 16.3
The Designer
workspace

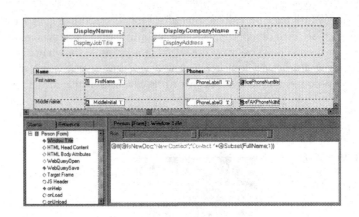

The Objects Tab

The Objects tab gives you access to any individual design element and the associated events and attributes for the opened element (the opened element in Figure 16.3 is the form). You can scroll down through the list and see that each design element has various events or attributes, which are discussed in more detail in later chapters. You can navigate through the list by clicking on the plus (+) or minus (−) signs to expand or collapse the events and attributes for a design element.

The Reference Tab

The Reference tab is a context-sensitive list displaying the information about each programming language recognized in the programmer's pane. From the Reference drop-down list box, select the language you would like information about, and the Reference tab will display a list of events, properties, or methods for that language. You can paste the information from this list directly into the script area. Table 16.1 shows a complete list of information available in the Reference list for each programming language.

TABLE 16.1: PROGRAMMING LANGUAGE AND REFERENCE LIST COMPONENTS

PROGRAMMING LANGUAGE	REFERENCE TAB COMPONENTS
Formula language	Database fields, formula @commands, formula @functions
Java	Core Java, Notes Java, third-party Java
JavaScript	Web document object model, Notes document object model
LotusScript	LotusScript language, Domino: classes, Domino: constants, Domino: subs and functions, Domino: variables, object linking and embedding (OLE) classes

The Reference tab can be extremely handy when you're trying to master a new language. It is also quite an asset for databases that contain a large number of fields. Instead of having to remember all the names, you can just select them from the list of database fields.

The Script Area

The script area is also context sensitive. It will determine the programming language allowed for the element you select from the Objects tab. Unless you've chosen an element that allows only one type of programming language, you can select different programming languages from the drop-down list box (the languages you can choose are listed in Table 16.1). Likewise, you can also, in some cases, use a drop-down box to determine whether your code will run on the Web or in the Notes client. You may even be able to set a different language for each context. For example, you could use the formula language for a button in the Notes client and a completely separate JavaScript function for the same button on the Web. Most of your programming will be performed in the script area. Keeping that in mind, Lotus has put a lot of effort into making the script area more robust for the developer.

You can adjust the various attributes from the programmer pane's Properties Box, which can be displayed by right-clicking in the script area and choosing Programmer Pane Properties from the pop-up menu (see Figure 16.4). Depending on the programming language, your code will be displayed in various colors, allowing you to easily identify the constants and the commands. With the first (Font) tab, you can also change the font and font size to make it easier to read. With the second (Format) tab, you can alter certain aspects of the way the Designer formats code. By default, long formulas wrap and nested LotusScript statements are automatically indented, but you can turn those settings off. You can also choose to have "Option Declare" automatically inserted in your LotusScript programs (we'll explain this in Chapter 24, "Language Extensions and the Object Model," but it's useful).

FIGURE 16.4

Programmer pane properties

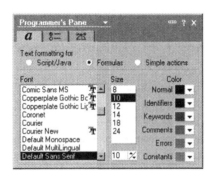

TIP   *You can turn off formula wrapping and LotusScript auto-indent, but if you don't already have very, very strong feelings on the subject, don't. Letting Notes indent your code makes it more readable with little effort on your part.*

The third (Auto Complete) tab gives you control over one of Release 6's most useful properties: auto-completion of code. As you type in formula or LotusScript, Designer can follow along with you and give you useful pointers for what to type next. If you're working in the formula language and s typing in a formula, a list of formulas will pop up (shown here).

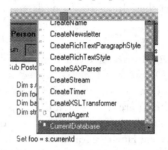

You can keep typing or pick the one you want off the list, automatically completing your typi Once you're into the formula, you'll be given useful prompts demonstrating the syntax of the form with which you're working (shown here). Likewise, if you're typing in LotusScript, you'll get lists objects, their methods, and their properties as appropriate.

Because we refer to them quite frequently, it's important you understand the various design el ments of Designer, covered next.

Domino Design Elements

To access the database design elements, you need to understand the Design list for each database d played in the Design pane. Finding most of the design elements is an easy task, but a few are somewh hidden. The Work pane is also quite a valuable tool for displaying information about each design e ment. With that in mind, let's go over the design elements with a brief synopsis of each. We'll st from the top of the Design list and make our way down to the last element.

THE FRAMESET DESIGN ELEMENT

Framesets became known as a web development tool; they are used to break up a window into se tions, or *frames*. However, you can use framesets in applications designed for the Notes client as we You can easily create a multipane interface for the user. The panes can be used to access different are of the application or even different applications or websites. Domino Designer includes a wizard th allows you to quickly generate a frameset without having to write one line of code.

THE PAGE DESIGN ELEMENT

Pages resemble web pages created with a WYSIWYG (what you see is what you get) editor. You use a rich text-like layout interface to construct them. Pages are used to display static information. you want to collect data, use a form instead. Pages are typically used as containers for outlines an embedded views, or for unique elements such as home and help pages in a database.

NOTE *A page is used for display purposes only. If you would like to capture information as well, you need to use a form*

THE FORM DESIGN ELEMENT

Forms are the most common design element used within a Notes database. A form is used as the basis for entering and viewing document information. If you want a user to enter information, you must use a form (don't confuse this design element with a page).

A form is the most flexible of all the design elements in that it can contain fields, text labels, sub-forms, layout regions, graphics, tables, objects (such as OLE objects), file attachments, Uniform Resource Locators (URLs), links, Action buttons, and background colors and graphics. Other design element can contain some of these things, but a form can contain *all* of them. See Chapter 19, "Basic Form Design," and Chapter 20, "Advanced Form Design," for detailed discussions of understanding and utilizing forms in applications.

THE VIEW DESIGN ELEMENT

Views are the second most common design element used within a Notes database. Views list the documents in a database. The designer has total control over what documents—and what information from each document—to list. A view has a selection formula, usually written in the formula language, which it uses to pick documents when it is accessed. It is through views that users access documents (they are sometimes accessed through folders).

NOTE *The view design element can be displayed on the web as a Java applet.*

You can sort and group (categorize) documents based on their contents. Typically, you will display information about documents so users can easily identify each one. You can also use views as reports by displaying the important information from each document so the user has no need to actually open the document.

THE FOLDER DESIGN ELEMENT

A folder is almost exactly like a view. The only major difference is that the programmer cannot specify which documents to list in a folder. Documents are moved to a folder, usually from a view, but they can also be programmatically placed into a folder (not, however, from within the folder design element). A folder is usually created as a repository into which the user places documents.

SHARED CODE

This is a category of design elements that can include program code or provide automation. Rather than being used directly by users, as the previous objects are, shared code objects are usually incorporated into other design elements.

The Agent Design Element

Agents automate tasks within a Notes database. You can use them to perform a specific task in the database for the user. You can program them to perform tasks as simple as changing a field value or as complex as interacting with external applications. Agents can run in either the foreground or the background. For web applications, an agent is similar to a Common Gateway Interface (CGI) program.

The Work pane for an agent is slightly different than it is for the previous design elements. There are two additional columns called Trigger and Owner. The Trigger column displays how the agent is executed (or triggered). This column might display values such as Menu, Scheduled, or Hidden.

The Owner column displays the name of the owner of the agent. For all nonprivate agents, the va
is Shared. For private agents, the name of the actual user who created the agent will be displayed

The Outline Design Element

Outlines allow you to visually lay out the design of your application. Using outlines, you can cre
and manage all types of element links within your database and links to external sources as well. Y
can use the outline to create a visual map that the end user can use to navigate to the various pie
of your application.

If you select the outline design element, the Work pane will open and display all the outlines c
rently defined for the database (note that all of the elements discussed in the following sections cont.
the same type of information in the Work pane unless explicitly stated). The Work pane is broken do
into six columns, as shown in Figure 16.5. The Name/Comment column displays the common elem.
name and any associated comments that the designer has typed in for the element. The Alias colum
exactly that, an alias for the element. This name is typically used internally by the designer when acc
ing this design element. Because the name can change, programming to the alias name may save y
maintenance in the future. The Last Modified and Last Modified By columns show when and who v
the last person to change this design element. The last two columns, Notes and Web, tell you whet
this design element can be displayed in either the Notes client or a web application.

FIGURE 16.5
The Work pane
for the outline
design element

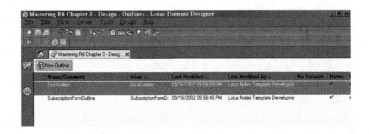

The Subform Element

A *subform* is a design element that contains fields, text, and so on. The subform can be shared amo
multiple forms. Although you cannot use subforms by themselves, you can insert them into forms
save time on maintenance. For example, if you display the same information as a footer in multip
forms, you can create one subform and place it on the forms you need instead of rebuilding each in
vidual object for each form. If that information needs to be changed, you only need to update it
one place, the subform.

NOTE   *A subform can contain the same elements as a form.*

The Shared Field Element

A *shared field* is another type of shared resource. You can define a field once and share it across multip
forms and subforms. For example, if you want each of your forms to have an authors field calle
From, just define a shared field called From, set it to an authors field, and insert it into any form
subform within the database.

The Work pane for shared field resources does not contain the Notes or Web columns.

NOTE   *It's important to remember that a shared field is really a shared field definition, not a shared piece of data.*

The Shared Action Element

You've seen actions before in the form of Form and View Action buttons. With shared actions, you can create a button for common actions, such as opening a form or closing a document, and use that one in a number of different places.

TIP   *When you start creating a database, one of the first things you should do is to create Close Document and Save and Close buttons as shared actions. Just about every form you create will have one or both, so get them out of the way early.*

The Script Library Element

The script library is a shared resource that allows you to define a set of LotusScript, JavaScript, or Java routines that can be used by any other element within the database that uses the same language. As with other shared resources, by using a common script library, the time spent on maintaining an application can be reduced.

The Work pane for script library resources does not contain the Notes or the Web columns.

SHARED RESOURCES

These elements are mostly files generated with other programs, such as graphic images and word processor documents. Shared Resources provide a place to put such elements inside a Notes database, making them readily available to the application.

The Image Element

A common problem with previous releases of Notes was the inability to store images in a central location. Now, using an image resource, you can place graphic files (GIF and JPEG) in one common location, and they can be used throughout your application. This will save on maintenance time because you only need to update the image resource in one place. Any references to that image resource will automatically be updated. You can use an image resource on pages, forms, Action buttons, and outline entries and as background images on forms, documents, pages, table cells, and Action buttons.

The Work pane for an image resource does not contain the Notes or Web columns.

The Files Element

New to Notes 6 is the ability to store other files as resources in the database. Using a file resource, you can place any kind of file, such as a spreadsheet, text document, compressed archive, or sound file, in the database. Like image resources, file resources allow you to centrally manage and maintain your files.

The Applet Element

You now have the ability to save Java applets as a shared resource for the database. For large applets, you can also store some of the related files as a shared applet resource. The Resources section is used as a "shared" or common pool. Suppose you have a file that several Java applets use (a set of error m̲essages, for example). This file could change. You have the option of including this file as part of e̲ach individual applet. You could also store this file in the shared applet resource. Then, instead of hav̲ing to change the file in every applet, you only need to go to one place to make the change.

The Work pane for applet resources does not contain the Notes or Web columns. A detailed d̲iscussion of Java applets is beyond the scope of this book. The purpose of this discussion is to in̲troduce you to the use of Java applets as elements in Notes databases.

The Style Sheet Element

This new design element, which is exclusively for web use, allows you to keep a list of Cascading St̲yle Sheets (CSS). A major item in the HTML 4 standard, style sheets allow you to define consistent t̲ext styles for HTML documents. With this element, you can incorporate the same capabilities into y̲our web-based Notes applications.

The Data Connection Element

New in Release 6, the data connection element allows you to define a connection to an external r̲elational database. You can use this element to automatically import data from other databases and u̲se that information in your Notes applications.

THE OTHER ELEMENT

Like the shared elements previously discussed, the Other element is not actually a resource; rather i̲t is a catchall for resources that don't fit any other category. When you select the Other element, t̲he Work pane will expose the following design elements:

Database Resources

This is, if such a thing can be believed, the miscellaneous category of the Other resources. It contai̲ns these items:

Icon   An icon that, when selected, brings up the Design Icon dialog box, which allows you t̲o directly edit the current database icon for a database.

The Using Database document   A document in which you can tell users how to use this application.

The About Database document   A document in which you can explain the purpose of this application.

The database script   A script into which you can enter LotusScript or formula code for event̲s that occur at the database level, such as when the database is opened or closed.

The Work pane for displaying these elements is a bit different as well. There are only four colum̲ns displayed: Name, Defined, Last Modified, and Last Modified By. The Defined column is the oddb̲all in the group and, if checked, tells you that something has been defined for that element.

The Navigator Design Element

A Navigator is a graphical design element that allows the user to easily access other database elements, such as views, folders, and documents. If you're a web designer, you can think of it as something like a clickable image map. Navigators can include graphical buttons and hotspots that, when clicked, execute some action. They can be attractive and fairly flexible, but they can be slow and take up a lot of memory.

The Synopsis Element

The synopsis element is not really a design element; it's a tool that can gather information about all the design elements within the database and generate a report. When you select the synopsis element, the Design Synopsis dialog box is displayed (see Figure 16.6). You can gather information about any combination of design elements. You can also elect to have the report generated to the screen or to a database.

FIGURE 16.6

The Design Synopsis
dialog box

The synopsis is quite flexible in that it allows you to pick and choose the design elements for which you want a report generated and also what you want the report to include. By filtering the data, you can control the length of the report. This is a useful tool for gathering information about the design of a database. It can also be helpful when you're trying to locate information within a database. For example, if you want to see if a field is still being used, you can generate a report containing all the design elements, save it to a database, and then search the database for the particular field.

Summary

In this chapter, we discussed the various components that make up the Domino Designer application. We identified and explained the various panes and windows a developer needs to use to create applications for either a Notes or a web environment. Although there are quite a few similarities between the Notes client and Domino Designer, there are also quite a few areas that make Domino Designer distinctly different. Lotus has made every effort to standardize the look and feel of both programs to lower the learning curve.

Those of you who are seasoned Notes programmers will find that the design has changed drasti-
cally. Although the changes are significant, the overall structure is still intact. The new Designer interface has new capabilities that should improve the environment for rapid application development.
Some of the major advantages are that most properties are available via point and click and that the
addition of Java applets eases the burden of trying to create both a Notes client and Web application.

In the next chapter, we'll discuss how to begin creating new databases. We'll also cover the basics
for database security and the various options that can affect database design and performance.

Chapter 17

Database Creation and Properties

NOW THAT YOU HAVE a basic understanding of navigating the Domino Designer workspace, it's time to get to the nitty-gritty: creating a database. In this chapter, we will describe the three ways you can create a database: from scratch, from a database template, or by copying an existing database.

Although there is no right or wrong way to create a database, the following sections will help explain each database creation method and allow you to decide which method best fits your needs. Whichever method you decide to use, creating a database is the first step in the design process.

This chapter will also cover options for creating databases, database properties in the Properties Box, and database-level security (later chapters will cover options for security on individual documents).

- Creating a database from scratch
- Creating a database from an existing template
- Copying an existing database
- Database creation options
- Database properties using the Properties Box
- Ensuring database security

Creating a Database from Scratch

Although it's easy to create a database in Notes, creating one from scratch (which is the default option) is the most difficult of the three options presented. You start with an empty database and manually create all the elements (forms, pages, views, and so on) that will eventually make up the completed database design. The completed application can be as simple as a few linked pages or as complex as a complete multidatabase Internet site with links to external data sources.

To design a database from scratch, first you need to create an empty database. To create a new database using Domino Designer, follow these steps:

1. Choose File ➤ Database ➤ New (or press Ctrl+N). The New Database dialog box appears (see Figure 17.1).

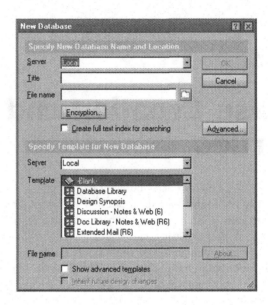

2. From the Server drop-down list, select an appropriate server name, just as you would for opening a database:

   ◆ Selecting Local will store the database on your computer's hard drive (for now, you should select this option).

   ◆ Selecting or entering a server name will store the database on that server. This will allow multiple people to work on the same database design.

3. Enter a short descriptive title for the database. For this example, type **Blank Mastering R6**. The database title is the "human-readable" name of the database (as opposed to the filename, which is more for the computer's consumption), so the title is important for identification by your end users. It will be used in conjunction with bookmarks and all subsequent Open Database dialog boxes. Make sure the title is meaningful enough for users to recognize the function of the database.

TIP   The maximum length of a database title is 96 bytes. For most purposes, that means 96 characters, although it can be fewer if your operating system uses multibyte characters. That's a contingency we don't cover.

4. Enter the filename for the database (note that the default filename will be the title with an .nsf extension). For this example, type **R6Book/Blank_Mastering_R6.nsf**. R6Book will become a subdirectory within the Notes data directory.

5. Click the OK button.

Once you have completed the database creation process, the database will automatically open, displaying the types of design elements in the Design pane. Because the database you have just created is empty, the Work pane will not display any design elements. Also, a bookmark for the new database will be placed at the top of the Recent Databases portfolio list in the Design pane.

Where Does My Database Get Saved?

When you create a new database, you'll notice that there's a file folder button next to the File Name field. If you click this button, the database file can be saved into a different directory. By default, all new databases are saved to the Notes root Data directory (that is, the Data directory of the Domino server or the Notes Data directory of your local machine). Clicking the file folder button will open the Choose a Folder dialog box. For a local server, this dialog box is nothing more than a directory tree of your hard disk, as shown in Figure 17.2. Selecting a directory and clicking the OK button will prefix the database filename with the drive and directory selected. If you selected or entered a server name, a different dialog box will appear when you click the file folder button. Selecting a subdirectory and clicking the Select button will still prefix the database filename with the directory, but the directory will be relative to the Notes data directory residing on the server.

FIGURE 17.2
The Choose a Folder dialog box for the Local machine

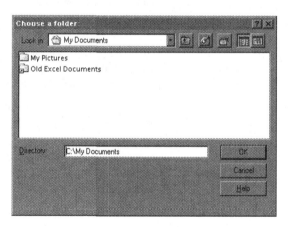

Another shortcut to placing database files into subdirectories is to type the subdirectory name manually as you did earlier. If the directory you name does not already exist, using the name will automatically create the subdirectory underneath the Notes root Data directory whether the server selected is Local or an actual Notes server. For example, if you type **MyDir\MyDatabase.nsf**, the database MyDatabase.nsf will be placed into the MyDir subdirectory within the Notes root Data directory.

Creating a Database from a Template

Notes provides you with *templates*, database designs that are ready to use right out of the box with modifications necessary. For example, the discussion template, Discussion–Notes & Web (R6.0 contains all the design elements for a complete application for both the Notes client and the W forms, views, framesets, and so on. It's easier to create a database from a template than it is to cre one from scratch. Indeed, one nice feature of the Domino Designer is the many templates that ha already been created for you (commonly referred to as *master templates*). Table 17.1 lists the most co monly used master templates included with Notes 6.

TABLE 17.1: THE MASTER TEMPLATES INCLUDED WITH NOTES 6

TEMPLATE TITLE	DESCRIPTION
Discussion–Notes & Web (R6)	An electronic conference room that allows threaded discussions wit built-in author profiles and automatic mailing for topics of interest. Designed for both Notes clients and web browsers.
Doc Library–Notes & Web (R6)	General document storage with built-in review workflow (both seri. and parallel) and archiving. Designed for both Notes clients and wel browsers.
Microsoft Office Library (R6)	Just like the Doc Library template except designed specifically for th Microsoft Office suite; loads the OLE object and sizes it to the windov Designed only for the Notes client.
Mail (R6)	Combined mailbox, personal calendar, and to do list. This is the template used for the Notes mailbox that we discussed in Part II, "Mastering the Basics with the Notes Client," of this book.
Personal Journal (R6)	Electronic diary where a user can write and organize thoughts and ideas. Designed only for the Notes client. This template creates the personal journal discussed in Chapter 4, "Tailoring Lotus Notes 6."
Site Registration 6.0*	A sample database showing how to register web users for a Domino-based application. Designed only for web browsers.
TeamRoom (6.0)*	A database for team collaboration; allows several different types of document communication that represent meetings, discussions, an Action items. Built-in parallel review and archiving. Designed for bot the Notes client and web browsers.

* The Site Registration and TeamRoom templates reside on the server and are not installed with Domino Designer.

Although no template may fit the requirements for the application you want to build, a templa that has some of the features you want can give you a helpful head start. Rather than building an app cation from the ground up, you can use the template to give you a basic skeleton and then add or mo ify the other features you need.

To use Domino Designer to create a database from an existing template, follow these steps:

1. Choose File ➤ Database ➤ New (or press Ctrl+N). The New Database dialog box appears.

2. From the Server drop-down list, select the appropriate server name as you did in the previous example (again, you should probably select Local).

3. Enter a short descriptive title for the database. For this example, type **Mastering R6 Discussion**.

4. Enter the filename for the database. For this example, type **R6Book/Mastering_R6_Disc.nsf**. The new database will be saved within the **R6Book** subdirectory along with the database from the preceding example.

5. Select the Discussion–Notes & Web (R6) template from the list (see Figure 17.3). To display additional templates, do one of the following:

   ◆ Check the Show Advanced Templates box, which will display all the basic and advanced templates for the selected server. Most of the advanced templates are designs to support administrative tasks rather than end users. As such, they won't be widely applicable, but it's good to know from where these things come.

   ◆ If you have access to a Domino server, click the Template Server button, which will display the Template Servers dialog box and allow you to select a different server. Once a server is selected, the list of templates that reside only on the selected server will be shown.

FIGURE 17.3
Selecting a template

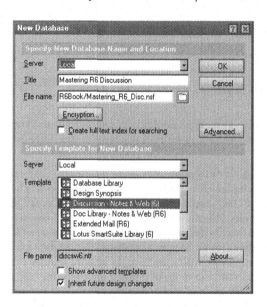

NOTE *When a template is selected (except for Blank), the Inherit Future Design Changes option will be enabled automatically. If you're planning to modify your new database, uncheck the box.*

6. Click the OK button.

Once you have completed the database creation process, the database will automatically open and display the various design elements in the Work pane. Because the database was based on an existing template that already contained quite a few design items (unlike in the preceding example), the Work pane will display all of the defined design elements, as shown in Figure 17.4.

FIGURE 17.4

A new database created from a template; note all the design elements visible in the Work and Design panes

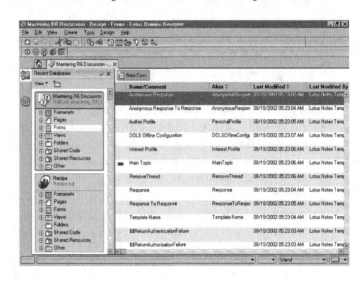

TEMPLATES AND DATABASES (.*NTF* AND .*NSF* FILES)

Before we go any further, a quick review of the differences between databases and templates is in order to ensure that there is no confusion about these two types of files. Although they are similar, there are some basic differences.

A template file uses the .ntf extension. A database file uses the .nsf extension. A template is a database skeleton that contains design elements but, usually, no documents (a template file can, technically, contain documents, but it's bad practice to create them that way). A database contains both the design elements and the documents. The confusion arises because both file types are essentially databases. You can create documents and execute design elements within a template just as you would inside a database. So what really distinguishes a template from a database? The difference is actually a property located in the Database Properties Box, which will be discussed later in the chapter. Both the template and the database have this property available, and to make things more confusing, you can set this option for both. The important thing to know is that the .ntf and .nsf extensions do not determine if the file is a template or a database; the property does. Although it may seem like the extension is the determining factor, it isn't. Using two different file type extensions is simply a convention that makes it easier to distinguish databases and templates at the operating system level. It is a good practice to keep the property set for the appropriate extension, but Notes will not inform you if you have a database (.nsf) set as a template, nor will it inform you if you have a template (.ntf) set as a database.

Continued on next page

Why use a template? This is a good question because both a database and a template seem to be the same. The main reason is that, in a template, all of the design elements can modified and maintained separately from the database file. There is an option that allows a database design to be either replaced or refreshed from a template (the refresh can be done manually or automatically on a schedule if it's on a Domino server). If a database design is replaced, all the design elements will be blindly copied from a template into the database. This is actually a powerful tool for controlling database design and managing changes. If a developer is making changes directly to the database itself as others are using it, the users will be inconvenienced by running into design elements in a state of flux. Formulas and program code may try to run on objects that do not yet or no longer exist. However, if a template is used, changes can be made and tested away from the production environment. Then, once the design changes have been completed satisfactorily, they can be "pushed" to the production database en masse during a scheduled lull in activity (say, overnight, when nobody will be using the database anyway). Having a template ready at hand also makes it possible to rapidly fix malicious or ill-advised changes to the database design.

Those aren't the only advantages of using a template. Anyone can use a template to quickly and easily create a new database. For example, you created the Mastering R6 Discussion database in a few seconds using the template. You will also save design time by using templates. Common agents or forms that do not require any additional work can be copied from a template. If the common agent changes, the change can be refreshed to all the databases without any interaction from the designer.

There are quite a few combinations that you can use when you are refreshing a database. The simplest example refreshes all of the design elements. In Figure 17.4, an option called Inherit Future Design Changes is selected. This option sets a database property for the database you are creating so the entire design will always be refreshed from the template. This is a global (or database-wide) setting. In other words, an exact copy of all the template's design elements will be placed into your database. You can also set the Refresh option so that individual design elements are refreshed from a template and other design elements are never refreshed. And you can update different design elements from other templates. This is quite useful when you want to include some design elements from one template and other design elements from another template. Obviously, there is quite a bit of flexibility when using templates.

As you can see, a template is an integral part of the application design process. It's a good idea to use a template for each database you create. You can also create a "toolbox" template that contains all sorts of agents, forms, views, and other objects that you seem to create repeatedly. Keep in mind that, when a database is refreshed, the Access Control List (ACL) never changes. The only components that get refreshed are forms, fields, form Actions, event scripts, views, folders, view Actions, agents, outlines, pages, framesets, Navigators, shared fields, and some of the Database Property selections.

Copying an Existing Database

Finally, you can create a new database by making a new copy of an existing database. This option is usually the preferred choice if you have found an existing application that contains the majority of the functionality you desire (if the database does *everything* you want your new application to do, you should make sure your original database is based on a template and create the new database from the same template). Before copying the database, make sure the designer of the database has not hidden the design elements. This will prevent you from being able to modify any of them. To determine if the design is hidden, open the Database Properties Box for the database and select the Design tab. If the design is hidden, you will see the message *No design information available*.

To create a database by using Domino Designer and copying from an existing database, follo these steps:

1. Open the Mastering R6 Discussion database you created in the preceding section.

2. Choose File ➤ Database ➤ New Copy. The Copy Database dialog box appears (see Figure 17

NOTE   *You can also right-click the database's design bookmark icon in the Design pane and choose Database ➤ New Cop*

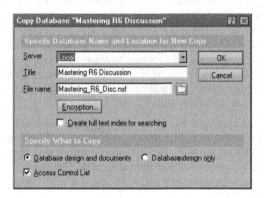

FIGURE 17.5
The Copy
Database
dialog box

3. From the Server drop-down list, select a server name to indicate where you want your new co to appear (again, using Local is a good thing at this point).

4. Enter the title **Copy of Mastering R6 Discussion** for the new database. The default is to use t same title as the original database. To eliminate any possible confusion, you should change the t

5. Enter the filename **R6Book/Copy_Mastering_R6_Discussion.nsf** for the new database. default, the title and filename are filled in with the same title and filename as the database bei copied. If you forget to change the filename, you run the risk of attempting to overwrite t database you're copying, which will naturally result in an error message.

6. Unless you really want to copy both the database and its documents, select the Database Design Only radio button.

7. For these purposes, deselect the Access Control List check box. By default, this option is select and will copy over the current ACL settings, which may render you powerless. Deselecting th option will ensure that you will be placed as the Manager of the database. However, if you ha Manager access to the source database and want to retain a similar permissions scheme, keepi this box checked can be a time saver.

8. Leave the Create Full Text Index option blank. You are not copying over any data documen so there is not much to index anyway.

9. Click the OK button.

Again, once the new database has been created, it will be opened in the workspace and an entry w appear at the top of the Design pane.

Once you open your newly copied database, there is no difference from the original. All of the design elements are intact, and if they are based on a template, the relationship will still be intact as well. The only big differences are the title, the location, and the actual name of the database (assuming you changed them at all).

Other Options You Can Choose

Up to this point, you may have noticed that there are quite a number of options for creating databases that were not mentioned. In the previous examples, the defaults were used so you could get comfortable with the entire creation process. Now that you have a better understanding of how databases are created, we can inundate you with the various options, including:

- Local database encryption
- Advanced database options
- About the template

Encrypting a Local Database

Once you begin to get comfortable with Notes and using local copies of the databases, security becomes a major concern. With the advent of notebook computers and personal digital assistants (PDAs), data can be replicated from a server and carried around by the user. Because notebooks are popular targets of theft, your corporate data can be carried away by the thief as well. This is where locally encrypting the database comes in handy.

Local database encryption will prevent prying eyes from getting at your data. When encryption is enabled, the physical database file is encrypted or scrambled using the public key of the designated ID. This "scrambling" prevents anyone from browsing the data unless they have the corresponding Notes key (the appropriate Notes ID, which in turn requires an appropriate password). Keep in mind that this added security (or, indeed, any and all added security for any computer system or application) does have a price—performance. Because the data needs to be scrambled when it is written and unscrambled when it is read, it will take a bit longer for data to be transferred to and from the file. However, the encryption/decryption process is often too rapid to slow you down significantly, and a few fractions of a second here and there are a small price to pay for the added security.

When creating a new database, you will notice that there is an Encryption button on the New Database dialog box (refer to Figures 17.1 or 17.3). To encrypt the Mastering R6 Discussion database, just click the Encryption button and the Encryption dialog box appears (see Figure 17.6).

To remove encryption from a database, select the Do Not Locally Encrypt This Database option (this is the default encryption option). To encrypt the database, select the Locally Encrypt This Database Using option. There are three levels of encryption that you can select for a database. Let's examine each a bit more closely.

TIP   *Don't worry if you can't remember the details for each encryption option. A brief description of each selected option displays in the Encryption dialog box.*

FIGURE 17.6

The Encryption
dialog box

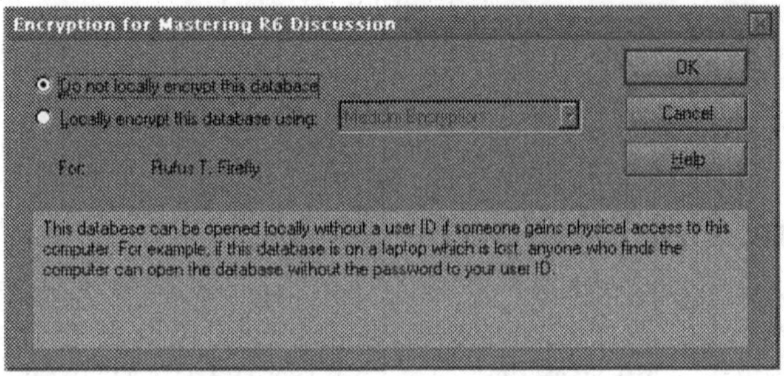

Simple Encryption Simple encryption provides some limited security. This type of security w
not keep out most hackers, but it will give you the best performance and keep out casual thiev
You can also use disk compression utilities on a database with this level of encryption.

Medium Encryption Medium encryption is the best choice for most databases. This type c
security is strong enough to give most hackers a lot of trouble but still give you acceptable perf
mance. Keep in mind that you cannot use this level of encryption if you use a disk compressic
utility.

Strong Encryption Strong encryption is the highest level of security and will stop almost a
hackers from getting at the data. There is a definite performance degradation when accessing t
data. Keep in mind that you cannot use a disk compression utility with this level of encryptio.

NOTE *You can change the encryption on an existing database. To encrypt a local database, choose File ➤ Database ➤
Properties and click the Encryption button on the Basics tab.*

WARNING *When you encrypt a database locally, you will notice that there is a For button and a username. This determines the user ID that has access to the locally encrypted database. If you change the user to someone other than yourself
make sure you have a replica copy of the database or access to the alternate ID file or you will deny yourself access.*

Setting Database Advanced Options

Some other options available when you create a new database are listed under the Advanced butt
(see Figures 17.1 or 17.3). These options don't need to be specified at the time the database is create
You can also access the options from the Database Properties Box under the Advanced tab (discuss
later in this chapter under "Using the Database Properties Box"). There are a number of setting
where you'll want to do exactly that. For example, some options increase the amount of internal trac
ing Notes performs, keeping a list of people who access documents. You might turn it on temporari
to monitor database use, then turn it off once you've collected enough data to reduce the load on yo
servers. Keep in mind that, if you change an option, you may need to compact the database for th
setting to take effect.

To display the Advanced Database Options dialog box (shown in Figure 17.7) when you are creating a new database, just click the Advanced button.

FIGURE 17.7

Advanced Database Options dialog box

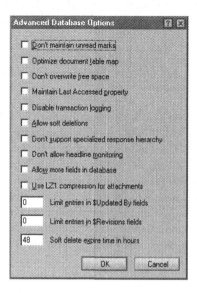

Some of these options may give your databases a significant performance boost, whereas others may actually degrade performance or disable functions you want. By default, none of the options are selected. Although some of the options are beyond the scope of this book, the more important options are listed in the following sections.

Don't Maintain Unread Marks   System resources are required to maintain unread marks in a database, which can slow down performance. This option should only be selected for databases in which unread marks on a document are not useful, such as log files or the help files. Do not confuse this database option with views that do not display unread marks. If this option is not selected, the overhead required to maintain unread marks is still in effect regardless of what the views options specify. On the flip side, if you aren't getting unread marks for any of your view in a database, you may want to check to see if this option has been selected. For this option to take effect after database creation, you will need to compact the database.

Maintain LastAccessed Property   For every document, there is an internal LastAccessed field that maintains the date when the document was last modified. Selecting this option will change the default behavior so that the internal LastAccessed field will be updated every time a document is *read*, regardless of whether any changes are made or even if documents are put into editing mode. Because documents are usually read more often than they are edited, this increases the amount of work the computer has to do, particularly for applications such as online catalogs and discussion

databases. On the other hand, this option is great if you want see when and how often your d
uments are opened. To view the contents of this internal field, select any document in the databa
open the Document Properties Box, and select the Info tab. You'll see an Accessed field and
date when the document was last accessed (read or modified, depending on the status of the d.
base option).

WARNING   *You must select the Maintain LastAccessed Property option if you use the Database Properties archive to*
that deletes documents based on days of inactivity.

Allow Soft Deletions   Chapter 2, "Getting Familiar with Notes," briefly discussed soft del
tions; if soft deletions are allowed, there's a window of time during which deleted documents c
be recovered. It's a useful feature, and it doesn't have an appreciable effect on performance, but s
deletions are not allowed by default. They must be enabled here. When Allow Soft Deletions
used in conjunction with the Soft Delete Expire Time in Hours option, you can specify how ma
hours a deleted document will remain in the database. You can also create a special view that w
display the deleted documents. Within the Shared, Contains Deleted Documents view type, n
takenly deleted documents can be retrieved simply and easily. Once the specified number of hou
has passed, the documents are permanently deleted from the database.

WARNING   *The Shared, Contains Deleted Documents view will not show the deleted documents unless the Allow Sof*
Deletions property is selected.

Don't Support Specialized Response Hierarchy   You can select this option to improve perfo
mance. Every document in a database stores information that associates it to a parent or response d
ument. This information is only used by the @functions @AllChildren and @AllDescendants. The
two @functions are commonly used in view selection or replication formulas. If you don't plan to u
either of these two commands, select this option. Selecting this option does *not* disable the response h
archy information in the database, so it will not affect views or replication formulas. It only prohibi
the use of certain functions that allow you to elaborate on basic response hierarchies. If you are creati
a view or replication formula that uses @AllChildren or @AllDescendants and it is not working co
rectly, check the status of this option. By default, this option is not selected.

Don't Allow Headline Monitoring   Using this option will also help performance on your da
base, but it should only be used for databases to which users are unlikely to subscribe. Enable th
option to prevent users from creating subscriptions to the database (this can also be set up at th
server level). If this option is enabled, users will get the message *Subscriptions are disabled for this datab*
if they try to set up a subscription. Subscriptions are stored in the Headlines database for a use
which is most likely how this option got its name. By default, this option is not selected.

Limit Entries in $Updated By Fields   Each document contains a hidden field called $Updat
By; each time the document is edited, the $Updated By field stores, by default, the name of the us
who edited it. After numerous edits, this field can become quite large, consuming disk space an
more importantly, slowing view updates and replication. Use this option to limit the number
entries maintained in the $Updated By field. Once the number of entries is reached, the oldes
entry is removed to make room for the newest entry. By default, this option is set to 0, signifyi
no limit to the number of entries stored in the field.

TIP *A special variety of form called* anonymous forms *do not have the $Updated By field.*

Limit Entries in $Revisions Fields   This option is similar to the Limit Entries in $Updated By Fields option. The only difference is that the $Revisions field tracks the date and time for each document editing session. This field is primarily used by Domino to resolve replication or save conflicts that can occur between two users editing the document. By default, the $Revisions field saves 500 entries, consuming 8 bytes of disk space for each entry. Again, this field can grow, slowing down view updates and replications. Use this field to limit the number of entries maintained in the $Revisions field. Once the number of entries is reached, the oldest entry is removed to make room for the newest entry. Also keep in mind that a setting that is too low may increase replication and save conflicts. A suggested limit is 10.

Clicking the About Button

Although it's not really an option, the About button (see Figures 17.1 or 17.3) for database templates is worth mentioning. When you are scrolling through the list of templates (both basic and advanced templates), it's difficult to determine what the template really contains unless the designer gives the template a descriptive title. If you click the About button in the New Database dialog box, the About document for the highlighted template will display. If the designer of the template did a thorough job, the About document should tell you everything that you need to know about the template. As shown in Figure 17.8, the Discussion–Notes & Web (R6.0) template's About document gives a brief overview about what the database does, the recommended ACL settings, and so on.

FIGURE 17.8

The About document from the Discussion–Notes & Web (R6) template, viewed via the About button

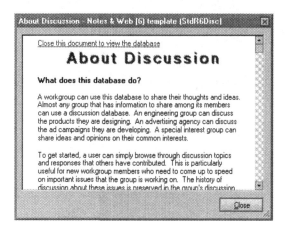

Using the Database Properties Box

Now that you have a basic understanding of the database creation process and the database creation options, it's time to explain how to modify database properties on an existing database. But before we get into more detail about the database properties, we'll return to the concept of Property Boxes.

What Is a Properties Box?

A Property Box is a special dialog box in Notes that gives the user and the designer access to an ment's properties. You've already seen Properties Boxes in the Notes client (for example, for rich t or tables), but they take on an increased importance when you start working with Domino Desigr Many elements in Notes—such as databases, documents, and forms—have properties. Although all the elements have the same properties, they all use a Property Box to access them, and you'll that Box extensively to modify the objects' properties.

One of the useful properties of a Properties Box is that when it is left open, it reflects the proper of the element on which you are currently working. When you change from one element to anotl the Properties Box reflects the properties of the new element. The Properties Box also reflects chan without requiring that you select an OK or Done button. Changes to the property settings are ma as soon as you click somewhere else in the Properties Box.

The easiest way to open a Properties Box is to first select or highlight the item whose propert you would like to view. Open one of the databases you've created earlier in this chapter. To disp a Properties Box (see Figure 17.9), click the Properties button on the toolbar.

NOTE *You can also open the Properties Box by right-clicking an element (such as a database, document, or form) an choosing the Properties menu item.*

FIGURE 17.9

The Properties box for a form in a database

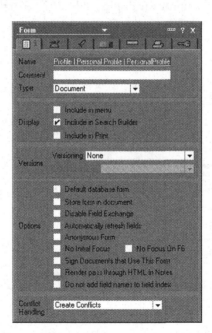

The tabbed pages allow you to choose many different options for the selected element:

◆ To switch to a different property page, click a tab.

◆ To move the Properties Box, drag it by the title bar.

- To float the dialog box as a toolbar, click the toolbar icon in the upper right corner of the properties box.

- To get help for the element or options, click the question mark icon.

- To close the box, click the close icon.

The Properties Box also has a drop-down menu that allows you to select a different element. The element values change depending on the element currently being viewed, but you can easily have a range of several elements to choose from in any one location. For example, say you're working on a field in an elaborate form. The field on the form might be inside a table, which could be inside a collapsible section, which is on the form, which is contained by the database. Each of those has a separate set of properties. If you click the menu, you can choose between seeing the properties of the field, the table, the section, the form, and the database, and you can switch back and forth between them at will.

Now that you have the basic understanding of what a Properties Box contains, let's move on to a working example.

Open one of the databases you've created. Display the Properties Box for the database by either clicking the Properties button in the toolbar or right-clicking and selecting Database ➤ Properties from the pop-up menu. The drop-down menu at the top of the Properties Box should say Database. If this is not the case, select Database from the menu, but this time with the Properties Box visible.

The Basics Tab

The Basics tab displays the general database information (see Figure 17.10). The title of the database can be changed, but note that the server and filename cannot. They simply reflect information about the file that can't be changed from within Notes. The database title is the text that the end user always sees in the Open Database dialog box. The database title is also the default label when new database bookmarks are created.

FIGURE 17.10
Database
Properties box

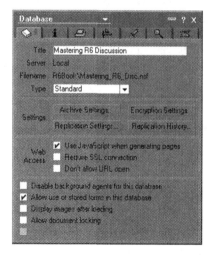

DATABASE TYPE

The database type, which is located in the Type drop-down list box, can be one of the following

- Standard
- Library
- Personal Journal
- Domino Directory
- Directory Catalog
- Multi DB Search
- Portfolio
- IMAP Server Proxy
- News Server Proxy
- Subscriptions
- Mailbox
- Mail File

Although it is not necessary for you to know the details of each database type, you should know that a type is used in conjunction with one of the predefined Notes master templates. For example the Personal Journal database type is automatically assigned to a database created from the Personal Journal template. The Personal Journal type, when applied to a database, will not offer the option creating shared views, agents, or folders because it is designed for your personal use. We do not adv changing the database type. The Standard type will fit 99 percent of your needs.

ARCHIVE SETTINGS

The Archive Settings button is a bit deceiving. Clicking it brings up the Archive Settings dialog box which *does* govern how documents are archived, but it also governs what happens to original documer after they are archived, which means that it's also a document deletion tool. When documents are archived, they are removed from the current database, hence the mention of deletion. The Archive S tings dialog box is broken down into three sections: Basics, Settings, and Advanced (see Figure 17.1 Archiving saves space, makes it easier for users to search for information, and improves overall databa performance. It's often a good idea, but you may not want to set it up if your application requires a re tively static set of documents or if older documents must still be accessed.

The Basics tab of the Archive Settings dialog box displays where archiving will take place, bot where the source database is expected to be and where the archive database will be added. Pressing t Change button brings up a dialog box that allows you to change those settings.

The Settings tab has a check box that actually activates archiving and allows you to set up criter determining which documents are archived (see Figure 17.12). The How Do You Want to Archi This Database section lets you set up multiple criteria for archiving different kinds of documents. F example, you might want to archive some documents immediately after they are marked as expire and all other documents after a year. To create a new set of criteria, click the Add button.

FIGURE 17.11
Archiving basics

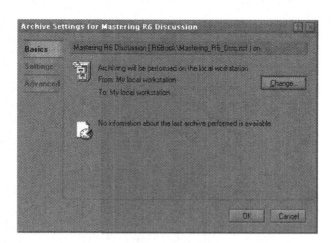

FIGURE 17.12
Archiving settings

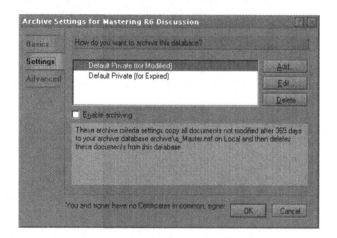

The Add button brings up the Archive Criteria Settings dialog box (see Figure 17.13). You'll be able to determine where old documents go (archive them to a specific database or just clean them out of the current one), what happens to the originals (delete them or keep an abbreviated summary in the database), and which documents to archive. Clicking the Select Documents button brings up the Archive Document Selection dialog box. You can archive documents that have expired in a designated time range, documents that have not been modified in a designated time range, or documents that are in specific views and folders.

FIGURE 17.13

Archive Criteria
Settings dialog box

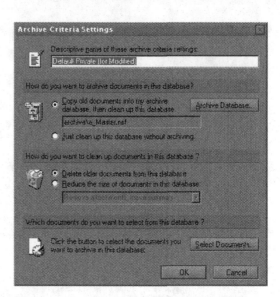

The Advanced tab gives you options to fine-tune archiving (see Figure 17.14). You may avoid deleting documents with responses (deleting parent documents plays merry havoc with displaying their responses), maintain a log of archiving activity, and ensure that local archiving only takes place if specific Location documents are in use.

FIGURE 17.14

Advanced archiving
options

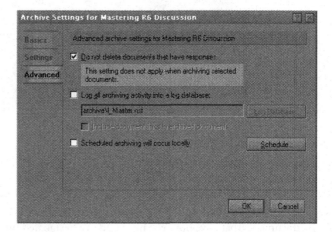

ENCRYPTION

The Encryption button allows you to encrypt local databases to prevent those without the proper Notes ID from accessing the local data. This was covered in detail in "Encrypting a Local Database" earlier in the chapter.

REPLICATION SETTINGS

The Replication Settings button allows you to set the various replication options for the database. Clicking this button will display the Replication Settings dialog box (see Figure 17.15). You don't have to use the Database Properties Box to access the Replication Settings dialog box. This dialog box can also be displayed via the Replication page or by choosing File ➤ Replication ➤ Settings. If you have databases that reside on multiple servers and there seem to be some irregular problems, this is a good place to look to ensure that all the settings are correct.

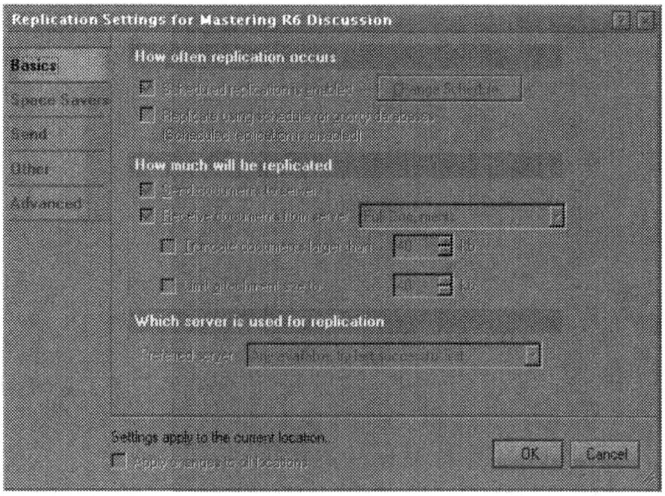

FIGURE 17.15

Replication
Settings
dialog box

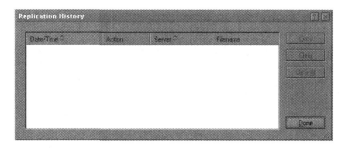

REPLICATION HISTORY

This isn't a design setting so much as it is a logging tool. Notes maintains a history of replication events for any database that has been replicated at least once. The replication history determines which documents to include in the next replication. This ensures that only added, modified, or deleted documents are replicated, which saves both time and bandwidth. Figure 17.16 displays a typical example of a replication history. Keep in mind that clearing the replication history will make the next replication take much longer because the servers will have nothing to compare against to determine which documents have been added, modified, or deleted.

FIGURE 17.16

Replication
History
dialog box

WEB ACCESS: USE JAVASCRIPT WHEN GENERATING PAGES

With this option selected, Domino can convert formula-language hotspots and Action buttons into JavaScript functions when viewed through the Web. This option is extremely important, especially when used with databases designed for older versions of Notes. Selecting this option for version 4 databases could cause unexpected behavior on Actions, buttons, and hotspots. Deselecting this option does not preclude you, the designer, from using JavaScript in the database. You can code JavaScript wherever you like regardless of the setting of this option. Selecting this option determines how Domino will interpret and render the web pages for your application. That is all the option does. If you select this option:

- Web documents and Navigators display faster because the hotspot formulas are not evaluated until a user clicks each hotspot.
- You can design forms with multiple buttons.
- Domino will not automatically generate a Submit button.
- You can use additional @commands.

If you deselect this option:

- Hotspot formulas in documents and Navigators are evaluated at display time, slowing down the initial page rendered to the browser.
- Domino will only recognize the first button on a form and automatically convert it to a Submit button (if no buttons are defined, Domino will automatically create one).
- All formulas and commands are evaluated before the page is displayed and any nonsupported @functions or @commands will not be displayed.
- Many of the @commands, such as @Command([FileSave]), are not supported on the Web.

For most web applications, you'll want to select this option. We use this option just for the @Command([ViewRefreshFields]) command. This allows you to recompute a web page without actually saving the document. This may not sound like a useful feature, but it saves time and can be done unless the Use JavaScript When Generating Pages option is set.

WEB ACCESS: REQUIRE SSL CONNECTION

Secure Sockets Layer (SSL) is a security protocol that protects data by encrypting it as it passes from the client to the server. SSL can be set up at the web server level, but this would require that all web applications be running SSL. This option, when selected, protects all data that uses SSL and resides only within the database. Only select this option when you need a secure connection between the client and the data residing on the web server because it will affect performance.

WEB ACCESS: DON'T ALLOW URL OPEN

It is possible to open and manipulate Notes objects through commands in URLs. Selecting this option prevents that from happening. This will allow you to mediate database interaction on the Web with servlets, keeping users from directly manipulating your database objects.

DISABLE BACKGROUND AGENTS FOR THIS DATABASE

Selecting the Disable Background Agents for This Database option will prevent automated tasks from executing on or changing any of the database documents. Be careful about using this option; it will prevent you and users from automating many tasks.

ALLOW USE OF STORED FORMS IN THIS DATABASE

Select the Allow Use of Stored Forms in This Database option to allow documents within the database to store the form along with the actual data. Having the form inside the document ensures that the document will display properly. This feature is typically implemented when documents will be mailed to other databases or mailed to other users and you are not sure if the form will be available. Without the correct form, you have no idea what data will display.

WARNING *The Allow Use of Stored Forms in This Database option requires a lot of disk space. Every document stores the document data along with a copy of the form.*

DISPLAY IMAGES AFTER LOADING

This option modifies how the database presents form data to the user. By default, form data goes to the user in the order it appears on the form, from the top down. This can cause a noticeable pause if the form has a large graphic in it; Notes must get the image data before it can continue. With this option checked, Notes waits to send the image data until after the rest of the data has been sent. That is, all the form information can be drawn on screen, becoming available to the user much sooner, and the graphics are filled in afterward.

ALLOW DOCUMENT LOCKING

A chronic problem with Notes databases has been the problem of save conflicts. Two users can edit the same document at the same time, eventually providing the database with two different changed documents. The documents are presented as save conflicts, and unless there's already a mechanism in place for dealing with such problems, they must be reconciled by a human. With this box checked, document locking is imposed: If one user starts editing a document, other users are not allowed to edit it. Moreover, if the database has an Administrative Server indicated in its ACL, that server acts as a master lock server, so users working with replicas of the database on other servers will also be unable to edit the document as long as it is locked. This feature won't prevent replication conflicts, which occur when two users using unconnected replicas of a database (for example, two local replicas on computers in Island mode) make changes to the same documents, but it can cut down markedly on save conflicts.

ALLOW CONNECTIONS TO EXTERNAL DATABASES USING DCRs

A new feature of Release 6 is the Data Connection Resource (DCR), a ready-made, easily used connection to external databases. To make use of DCRs, this option must be checked. A peculiar aspect of this setting is that you can't select it until you have created at least one DCR. To check this option, create a DCR, close the database, then reopen it; the option should then be available.

The Info Tab

The Info tab provides file-related information about the database, such as the size, time, and date ated or modified; the number of documents; and space utilization (see Figure 17.17). The Size fi shows the total amount of space the database has allocated, and the Documents field is the total n ber of data documents for the database. The actual design elements are not counted as documer (even though a design element is, in a technical sense, a document). Therefore, when you are rep cating a database, you may see a much higher number of documents being transferred than this n ber reflects.

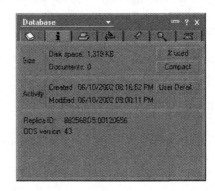

% USED

Clicking the % Used button displays the percentage of space in the database that isn't white spa The number will display to the left of the button. This number is not automatically displayed; y must click the button. *Whitespace*, in this context, means space that is taken up on disk by the datab: but does not contain documents or design elements. Whitespace is generally created from deletio in the database, especially if some of the deleted documents contain large attachments.

COMPACT

Click the Compact button to compact the database, which removes the whitespace, thereby reduci: the amount of space the database takes up on disk. If the % Used number falls below 90 percent, y may want to compact the database. To start the compacting process, just click the Compact butto which is conveniently located to the right of the percentage number.

WARNING *If medium or strong encryption is in use, you cannot compact the database.*

ACTIVITY

The Activity area displays the time and date the database was created and the last time it was modifi

USER DETAIL

The User Detail button brings up the User Activity dialog box, which is a useful feature for analyzi: user reads and writes. As shown in Figure 17.18, an audit trail shows what happens every time a us accesses a document. To begin recording the user activity for the database, you must activate tl

Record Activity option. Turning the Record Activity option on does not affect the results recorded to the Notes log, but it does require an additional 64KB for recording the information. Also, you can select the Activity Is Confidential option. There may be times when you don't want users to be able to see who has been doing what inside the database. Enabling this option prevents those without Manager or Designer access from seeing this dialog box.

FIGURE 17.18
User Activity
dialog box

NOTE *If you elect to disable the Record Activity option for a database, the Statlog task running on the server will turn it back on.*

REPLICA ID

We've discussed database replicas in several places through this book. The way Notes keeps track of replicas is by the replica ID, a read-only property of the database. Each replica has the same replica ID as the original database. This ID is also used in many different functions that refer to a database within Notes. The replica ID is displayed on the Info tab as a read-only field.

Replica ID is the *only* bit of data that Notes uses to identify which database is a replica of which. This means you can create a replica copy that has a completely different database title *and* a completely different filename from the original, and Notes will still be able to correctly identify it as a replica.

TIP *You may have noticed that the replica ID for a database is rather long and can be an easy target for a typo. To prevent this from happening, use the design synopsis to copy and paste the replica ID into your code. From the Design pane, select the Synopsis option. Click the Database Information tab and select the Replication check box. When the synopsis is displayed, simply highlight the replica ID and copy it to your code.*

The Printing Tab

The Printing tab specifies headers and footers when you print information from the database (see Figure 17.19). This is the one tab that is exactly the same for many of the Properties Boxes (such as those for a document and for a form). From this tab, you can change the header and footer text, the font, the point size, or the style.

We discussed headers and footers for printing back in Chapter 3, "Working with Databases." This tab works in the same fashion. There are actually three types of headers and footers that you can specify when printing data: headers and footers for a document, for a form, and for a database. With that in mind, there is also a type of hierarchy associated with the three different types of headers and footers.

Just remember that document headers and footers override form and database headers and footers and that form headers and footers override database headers and footers.

FIGURE 17.19

Database properties, Printing tab

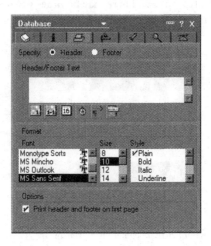

The Design Tab

The Design tab is one of the more important tabs for the designer. It allows you to set important properties for design inheritance and how the database behaves in a server environment. As shown Figure 17.20, you can specify whether a database is a template, inherits from a template, or gets displayed in an Open Database dialog box. Let's step through each option one at a time.

FIGURE 17.20

Database properties, Design tab

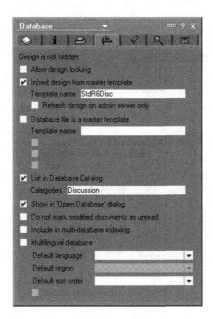

DESIGN IS NOT HIDDEN

Although not really an option, this line lets you know whether you will have access to the design elements of the database. As mentioned earlier, you can create a copy of a database and "hide" the actual database design. This will allow you to protect your code from accidental changes or from prying eyes. If the design is hidden, you will see the message *No design information available.*

HOW TO HIDE THE TEMPLATE DESIGN

Before we tell you how to hide the design of the database, we must warn you that, once this process has been completed on a database, there is no way to make the design visible again. This means you will not be able to change the database design directly. Please make sure that you always have a copy of the design stored someplace in case you need to make a change to it.

To hide the design, your entire database design should be supplied by a template. This template must be in the root directory of either your local workstation or the Domino server (the list of available templates is only pulled from the root directory, but when a template is refreshed, it can be anywhere within the data directory structure). With your master copy of the design safely tucked away, you are ready to hide the design of the individual database.

Assuming that the database already exists, you will need to replace the database design with the design residing in a template. To replace the design, follow these steps:

1. Open your database from your portfolio bookmark folder.

2. Choose File ➢ Database ➢ Replace Design. (You can also right-click the database design icon in the Design pane and select Database ➢ Replace Design.)

3. From the Replace Database Design dialog box, select the server location of the template by clicking the Template Server button.

4. In the template list, highlight the template that will replace the database design.

5. If you are not sure which template to use, highlight the template and click the About button. The About This Database document will display (this step is optional).

6. If your template is not listed, select the Show Advanced Templates option; the template may have been marked as an advanced template (this step is optional).

7. Select the Hide Formulas and LotusScript option. This is the key to hiding the design.

8. Click the Replace button.

9. A warning message box will display, asking if you really want to do this. Click Yes to proceed or No to abort the replace.

10. A progress dialog box will display and update as each element is replaced. Once the replace is completed, your design is hidden.

To verify that the design of the database is hidden, open the Design tab of the Database Properties Box. You should see that no design information is available. If you open the database in Designer, you will see that none of the design elements are visible.

ALLOW DESIGN LOCKING

We discussed document locking earlier in the chapter; this is the Designer version of it. With th
enabled, it is possible to lock individual design elements, keeping other developers from attempt
to modify them at the same time.

INHERIT DESIGN FROM MASTER TEMPLATE

This option will be automatically selected if you created a database from a template and select
Inherit Future Design Changes. When a design refresh is initiated, the Inherit Design from the Mas
Template option tells the database to use the template (whose name is in the Template Name fie
to refresh the entire database. The template name is not the actual filename of the template; it's the na
you have assigned to the template (this is the next option we will discuss). In this example, the te
plate name is StdR60Disc and the entire database design will be inherited from that template. Ma
sure design changes are performed in the template, or, when the next refresh is initiated, your chan
will miraculously disappear. You may, if you desire, check the box and fill in a template name af
the database has been created, but keep in mind that if you refresh the design of your existing datab.
from a template, any design elements you have created may be replaced or deleted.

WARNING   *Databases can be automatically refreshed on the server from a template if the Design task is initiated o*
the server. The Design task is a server-initiated program that will refresh all databases from their templates. This can b
good and bad. It's good if you need to refresh a lot of databases and do not want to do it manually. It's bad if your template
are residing on the same machine as your application and you want to update them manually.

REFRESH DESIGN ON ADMIN SERVER ONLY

With this option checked, the database's design will only be automatically refreshed on the admi
istrative server indicated in the database's ACL. Checking this option will save a bit of load on yo
servers if you operate in a multiserver environment, because only one of them will be performing t
update.

DATABASE IS A TEMPLATE

Setting this option determines whether the database is a template. Please keep in mind that *any da*
base can be marked as a template. The extension .nsf or .ntf does not determine whether a file is
template; the extension is used for displaying files in dialog boxes such as the Open Database dial
box. If you select this option, you must also enter a Template Name. Type a name that is descripti
of the template, up to 128 characters. This is the name that will be used in the Template Name fie
for the Inherit Design from Template option. Do not confuse the template name with the databa
title displayed in the template lists (such as in the New Database dialog box or the Replace Desig
dialog box). The template name is only used for inheritance when design elements are refreshed
replaced.

NOTE   *The Inherit Design from Template and Database Is a Template options are not mutually exclusive. You can*
select both for a database.

WARNING *Notes does not automatically check to see if the template name you type is already in use. It only checks when a refresh is initiated, and if the name is already in use, an error message will be displayed in the status bar and also written to the Notes log.*

LIST AS ADVANCED TEMPLATE IN NEW DATABASE DIALOG

As we've already shown, some specialized templates will only appear on a list of template choices when you check an Advanced Templates box. This is where you can set that property.

COPY PROFILE DOCUMENTS WITH DESIGN

Databases can contain documents called Profile documents, unique documents often used to contain basic settings (important file locations, names of process administrators, and so on). Setting this option allows you to include already-filled-out Profile documents along with the design elements, providing the database with ready-made default values.

SINGLE COPY TEMPLATE

This setting allows you to create links to design elements in databases that use the template.

LIST IN DATABASE CATALOG

A special database resides on the server called the Database Catalog. A task that runs on the server (the Catalog task) can automatically place any database that resides on the server into this catalog. The end user can review the Database Catalog for databases that interest them or use the catalog as a central point for listing all the databases on the server. Selecting this option allows the Domino server to create a document for the database inside the Database Catalog. You can also use the optional Categories field to group similar databases. For example, all of the sample databases for this book will be under the Mastering R6 category. If you look in the Database Catalog using the Databases by Category view, you'll see a list of all the sample databases grouped under the heading Mastering R6.

TIP *If you would like to assign a database to multiple categories, just separate each entry with a semicolon (;).*

SHOW IN OPEN DATABASE DIALOG

If you find that a database will just not show up in any of the Open Database dialog boxes, this is the option to check. If Show in Open Database Dialog is not selected, the database will never show up in any of the database lists. This does not mean that the database cannot be opened, just that it cannot be seen by the "casual" user. If Notes users know the path and filename of the database, they can maneuver to the right directory and type in the filename in the Open Database dialog box and the database will open right up. This option should not be used as a security measure because it is not secure. It should only be used to keep your directories from looking cluttered and ease navigation to your more commonly used databases.

DO NOT MARK MODIFIED DOCUMENTS AS UNREAD

If you select this option, documents won't be marked as unread if you modify them. By default, when a document is updated, it is automatically marked as unread. This way, a user can open a database and scan for all the documents that are new or modified. This technique is an extremely efficient way to make sure you have read all the documents in a database. Imagine your users' surprise if one day th open the database and all the documents are marked as unread! This can easily occur if an agent written to update each document and this option is not selected. In some cases, letting the users kn that the data in all the documents has changed is beneficial. But if you write an agent to update hidc data and forget to select this option, your e-mail Inbox is going to be quite full of questions and cc plaints. So keep that in mind the next time you need to write an agent that could possibly affect a la number of documents.

INCLUDE IN MULTI DATABASE INDEXING

The Include in Multi Database Indexing option marks a database for inclusion in the Domair Search. The Domain Search allows a user to search for information across all databases within t Notes domain. This is an extremely powerful tool, yet once some basic administrative tasks are p formed, it only takes a few seconds to include a database in it. All you need to do is enable th Include in Multi Database Indexing option and your database will be searchable via the Doma Search.

MULTILINGUAL DATABASE

This option is used primarily for applications that will have different language versions. This fal outside the scope of this book, but keep in mind that the language and region options work in c junction with a user's web browser. If the user's browser is set to a language and you have a databa set to the same language, the web server will automatically display it to the user appropriately.

The Launch Tab

The Launch tab controls what a user will see when your application is opened (launched) in eithe Notes client or a Web browser. There is a separate launch option for each, as shown in Figure 17.2 This gives you the flexibility of launching one application on a workstation and another applicati on the Web.

FIGURE 17.21
Database properties,
Launch tab

WHEN OPENED IN THE NOTES CLIENT

This option will allow you to specify what should happen when the database is opened from the Notes client. There are quite a few launch options available for the Notes client, as can be seen when the drop-down list is selected. Keep in mind that, depending on the launch selection, other fields and options may display. The following list includes all the current Notes launch options available:

Restore as Last Viewed by User This is usually the default for new databases and will return users to the same place in a database they were when they left the application. You also have the option of selecting whether to show the About document for the database if it has been modified and/or to show the About document for each user the first time they open the database (for clarity, in the remaining launch options, we will refer to these options for the About document as the About document options). If you select either of these options, the About document may display first and then the user will be returned to the same place in the database they were when they left the application.

Open About Database Document This option will launch the About document every time the user opens the database. Please keep in mind that unless your About document contains useful navigational tools, many people find this quite annoying.

Open Designated Frameset If this option is selected, a specific frameset must be selected from the Name list box. The Name list box contains a list of all the framesets currently defined in the database. This is the option selected for the current example database. The About document options are also available.

Open Designated Navigator This option will allow you to select which type of Navigator to display in the Navigation pane of the application. There are three types of Navigators that can be selected (and the About document options are available for all three as well):

Folders This option displays a "tree" style navigation, showing all the views and folders available to the user.

Standard Navigator This option requires that a Navigator (the graphical kind) be selected from the Name list box, which displays all the current Navigator design elements defined to the database.

Page This option requires that a page be selected from the Name list box, which displays all the current Page design elements defined in the database.

Open Designated Navigator in Its Own Window This option will allow you to select which type of Navigator to use as well, but there are only two selections: Standard Navigator and Page. This option is typically selected when a full-page Navigator will be used as the main portal for the application (such as a home page). The About document options are not available.

Launch First Attachment in About Database This option will automatically launch the first attachment contained within the About document. It is useful when another application will be used as the main portal for the application. The About document options are not available.

Launch First Doclink in About Database   This option will send the user to a database, element, or document (depending on the type of doclink used). It is useful when you would like send the user to a specific place within your Notes application. The About document options not available.

If you select the Preview Pane option (View ➤ Document Preview ➤ Show Preview), the docum Preview pane will be displayed according to this setting. This option is not available if the Note launch option is set to Open Designated Frameset.

This drop-down list is exactly the same as the When Opened in the Notes Client option except t it only affects the users accessing the application via a web browser. Note that the About docum settings do not have any bearing for web users. The following options appear in the When Oper in the Notes Client drop-down list:

Use Notes Launch Option   This option tells Notes to use the same launch option specified the When Opened in the Notes Client option.

Open About Database Document, Open Designated Frameset, and Launch First Doclink About Database   These are the same as the options described for the When Opened in th Notes Client option.

Open Designated Page   This option will allow you to select from a list of pages currently defined in the database.

Open Designated Navigator in Its Own Window   This option will allow you to select from list of standard Navigators that are currently defined in the database.

Launch Designated Doclink   This option allows you to paste a doclink to jump to when th database is opened. When you use this option, you'll notice that two new buttons appear und neath the list box: Paste Doclink and Go to Doclink. The doclink to be pasted can be a valid da base, an element, or a document. You must first copy the link to the Clipboard (Edit ➤ Copy Link) or you will receive an error message when the Paste Doclink button is selected. To paste t doclink, click the Paste Doclink button. To test your link, click the Go to Doclink button.

Launch First Document in a View   This can be quite an interesting option. At first glance, may not seem useful, but this option can dynamically display a different document each time a us opens the database. It all depends on how often the first document in a view changes. Before pa ing over this option quickly, make sure you give it a little thought.

The Full Text Tab

One of Domino's most powerful features is its ability to locate information through the built-in searching facility. Although a full-text index is not required for a Notes client user to have the abili to search documents, the lack of one makes searching extremely slow and takes up valuable comput resources. Also, a full-text index is required to enable searches over the Web. Without a full-tex index, the search options available to the user are also limited. You can use the Full Text tab to determine if the database has a full-text index and also to determine what settings were selected when the index was created.

As shown in Figure 17.22, the example database has already been indexed. The Full Text tab shows the date and time the index was last updated and the current amount of space the index has used. Keep in mind that, if the database resides on a Domino server, the index will automatically be updated on a schedule based on the value in the Update Frequency field. Also shown on this tab are the options used when the index was created. In the example database, the index included attachments (Index Attachments: On) and word breaks (Index Breaks: Words Only). If the database has not been indexed, you'll see the message *Database is not full text indexed* in place of *Last index time* across the top of the tab.

FIGURE 17.22
Database properties,
Full Text tab

One last thing to consider when performing full-text indexing on a database is the amount of space that will be required. This varies widely and depends on both the database contents and the options selected, but it will typically be about 60 to 70 percent of the total database size. With that in mind, let's find out how to index your database.

CREATE INDEX

This button starts it all. Clicking this button will display the Create Full-Text Index dialog box (see Figure 17.23). From this window, you can select the combination of options that you would like the full-text index to include. Once you make all of your selections for the index, click the OK button and your request will be queued on the server for processing. When the creation process is completed, you can look in the directory that contains the database and see a new directory with the .ft extension. This directory contains all the files that the full-text index uses. Let's take a look at the index options in more detail:

Index Attached Files   One feature of the full-text index is the ability to index attached files. This allows the user to search for text not only in the Notes documents but also in any of the attachments. For example, if the Notes document has a Microsoft Word file or an Adobe Acrobat PDF file attached and the attachment contains the word *testing*, when the user searches for *testing*, the full-text index will find a match and display the document in the results to the user. By default, this option is not selected.

Index Encrypted Fields   This option allows encrypted fields to be placed in the full-text inde for searching as well. Selecting this option will compromise the security of encrypted fields beca contents of encrypted fields will end up in the nonencrypted index files. Also, searches will tu up documents that contain the searched-for text in encrypted fields. By default, this option i selected.

Index Sentence and Paragraph Breaks   This option allows the user to apply proximity para eters to searches within the text. A *proximity parameter* is a special keyword in the search text th allows two words in the same proximity to be found. For example, if you use the search text *car tence tire*, the full-text index will return the document if the words *car* and *tire* are contained in same sentence. By default, this option is not selected.

Enable Case Sensitive Searches   This option is self-explanatory. The only catch is that user may not know that this option is enabled, which can cause quite a problem because a search on C will not find a match on the text *car*. By default, this option is not selected.

Update Frequency   This option applies to databases that reside on the server only. This is described in more detail later in this section.

FIGURE 17.23
Create Full-Text
Index dialog box

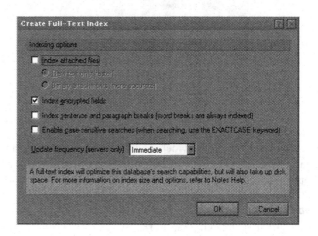

NOTE   *A database must have at least one document before you can index it.*

DELETE INDEX

The Delete Index option deletes the current full-text index and removes all the files that the index c ated. If you need to change any of the index options, make sure you delete the index first and the create the index again.

UPDATE INDEX

Selecting this option will queue a request to the server to update the full-text index immediately regardless of the Update Frequency setting. To determine if the index needs to be updated, click t Count Unindexed Documents button to see how many documents are not included in the curren index.

UPDATE FREQUENCY

This option determines how often the full-text index will be updated. To determine the frequency, look at the size of the database, how often data is updated, and how soon users will need the information. The process of updating full-text indexing can be quite time consuming and resource intensive. See Table 17.2 for a description of each option and when the updates to the index will occur.

TABLE 17.2: FULL-TEXT INDEX FREQUENCY OPTIONS AND TRIGGERS

FREQUENCY OPTION	UPDATE TRIGGER
Immediate	As soon as possible after the database is closed
Hourly	Every hour as scheduled by the Chronos server task
Daily	Every night when the Updall server task is executed
Scheduled	As scheduled by a program document for the Updall server task located in the Domino directory (if the program document is not in the Domino directory, the update to the full-text index will not be performed)

The Advanced Tab

Does the Advanced tab shown in Figure 17.24 look familiar? Although the options are the same, this is actually a different dialog box than the Advanced Database Options dialog box (shown in Figure 17.7) that is displayed by clicking the Advanced button in the Create Database dialog box. The Advanced tab is a bit smaller, and everything on the screen has been described earlier in the chapter. We mention this tab to let you know where you can change the advanced options if necessary. If you do decide to change any of the options listed in the dialog box, it is a good idea to compact the database to ensure that the options will take effect.

FIGURE 17.24
Database properties, Advanced tab

Protecting the Data Using the ACL

As the designer of the database, it is your responsibility to decide who will have access to what. Do confuse this responsibility with that of the administrator. You will not maintain the security for database; you are responsible for *defining* the security, determining who, potentially, can have access which objects and actions. You should work closely with your administrator to determine the secur requirements for your database. By defining the database security, you can provide access to the inf mation to some users and deny access to others.

What Is the ACL?

ACL stands for Access Control List. Every database includes an ACL, which controls the overall le of access to the database for users and servers. When you are determining the security for a databa keep in mind that setting up security for a Notes client overlaps with setting up security for a w based or Internet client but requires somewhat different steps. Because the web-based client does r use the Notes ID as does the Notes client, the web server is more limited in enforcing the security the application.

Open one of the databases you've created so far and choose File ➤ Database ➤ Access Control access its ACL (see Figure 17.25). In the People, Servers, Groups drop-down list, you can see the defa entries that are created each time a new database is created on the server. There is one special grou Default, that cannot be removed. This is the default access to the database if a user or server is not list If Anonymous is not listed, any users accessing the database from the Web will be granted the Defa access.

FIGURE 17.25

The ACL

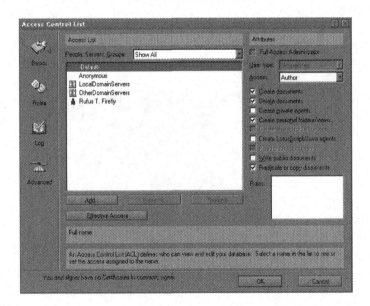

Understanding Access Levels

Notes allows you to assign one of seven different access levels to users in your database. To assign an access level to a group, server, or person, select the Access drop-down box on the right side of the Access Control List dialog box. Generally speaking, these levels of permission define the most a user can do. It's often possible to limit what a user can do to a subset of documents, not the entire database. The Access levels are as follows (from least to most restrictive):

Manager Can perform just about any operation within a Notes database. Users with Manager-level access can modify the ACL, encrypt the database, modify replication settings, and delete the database. A manager can also perform all the tasks of the lower access levels.

Designer Can modify all design elements, modify replication formulas, create a full-text index, and perform all the tasks of the lower access levels.

Editor Can create documents and edit all documents, even if the documents were created by another user. This is highest level of access that should be granted to end users. If a user will never use the Domino Designer client or the Domino Administrator client, they should never have anything higher than Editor. An editor can also perform all the tasks of the lower access levels.

Author Can create documents. Can also edit documents, but only those they created or have been granted specific permission to edit. This is solely dependent on the existence of an authors field (a data field with specific properties) within the document; the user's name or the name of a group to which he belongs must be in an authors field.

Reader Can only read documents. It's possible to limit the range of documents a reader (or anybody else, for that matter) can access with another special type of field.

Depositor Can create documents but can never read them (this is typically used for survey-type applications).

No Access Can do nothing at all under normal circumstances, although it's possible to create public-access documents that even users with No Access can read and even write.

You may limit the display of users and groups to a particular level of access using the drop-down menu above the list. To modify the list of servers, people, or groups from the ACL, just use the Add, Rename, or Remove buttons located under the access list. The Effective Access button brings up a dialog box that shows the complete range of permissions granted to a user or group (see Figure 17.26). A user belongs to a group or role, or if a group belongs to another group, they may have more permissions in the database than are apparent in the ACL listing. This dialog box will work its way through all group memberships and sum up the user's permissions.

FIGURE 17.26

Effective access

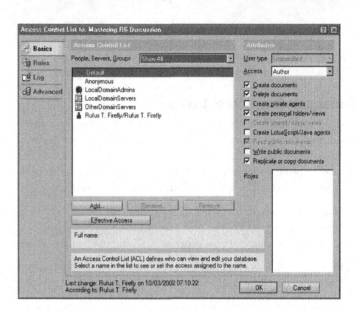

The Full Access Administrator check box can't be edited. Rather, it reflects a setting on the serv Users and servers may be designated on the server as Full Access Administrators. Full Access Adm istrators have certain wide-ranging permissions even to databases to which they have not explicit been granted permissions. If a user selected in the ACL is a Full Access Administrator, the box w be checked.

WARNING   *When creating a web application, be sure to check the Maximum Internet Name & Password Access optio (accessed by clicking the Advanced icon in the Access Control List dialog box). This may save you from many frustratin moments. You can limit the maximum level of access to a database via the Web, which is probably a good idea. For example you may allow Notes users permission to edit documents related to their department or a specific job task, but allow no editin whatsoever through a web interface.*

ACCESS PRIVILEGES

Also note that, for each access level, there are access-level privileges that can be assigned as well, reflect by the check boxes down the right side of the ACL dialog box. The access privileges give you the fl ibility of further refining data access. For example, you could grant users Author access yet not allo them to delete any documents they created.

The Read Public Documents and Write Public Documents access privileges are a bit differe from the others. You will notice that you can select these privileges for the various access level which will allow the reading or writing of documents that have been created with a form marke as Available to Public Access Users. You can also mark folders and views as Public Access, mak them available as well. Using the Public Access privilege, you can allow those with no access o Depositor access to read and write specific documents.

ROLES

One last tool available to you that allows further refinement of the security process is the Roles tool. Roles are a bit like groups, but they only exist within a database. You can create roles, assign users and groups to roles, and use the names of roles as you would the names of groups or users within individual document permissions. The main peculiarity to using roles is that if you use a role (say, in a list of document authors), you must put brackets around it. For example, if you put DocAuthors in any kind of security settings, Notes will think it's a username or group. If you use [DocAuthors] instead, Notes will think it's a role.

There are no hard and fast rules for using roles. You decide how they would work best for you and your application. You can assign roles to any entity defined in the ACL. A typical use for roles is to further refine a specific access level—for example, if you need to differentiate between groups of people who have the same access level.

A good example of using roles is displayed in the Public Name and Address book. Most users are granted Author access. This allows them to maintain their own Person record. But you would also like a specific group of individuals to be able to create groups. If you assign this group the GroupCreator role, the application can differentiate between the two groups of people who both have Author access.

To create a role, open the Access Control List dialog box and select the roles icon, which will display the Roles list box and the Add, Rename, and Remove buttons.

Just enter as many roles as you need (up to 75). Each role name is limited to 15 characters.

WARNING *There's one other major drawback to using roles: They essentially don't work if the database is accessed locally. They're great if the database will always be accessed from a server, but try to avoid them if the database will be accessed as a local replica.*

Summary

In this chapter, you gained a better understanding of how to create a database. You can create a database from scratch, from a template, or by copying over an existing database. We also discussed all the database creation options available. Finally, we went into detail about the database properties and the importance of setting security for your database.

To better understand the various design elements that make up a database application, you should first look at the basic formula language that Notes supports. The next chapter will describe what formulas are, how to create a formula, and where they can be used.

Chapter 18

Understanding the Formula Language

LIKE MOST OTHER DEVELOPMENT environments, Notes has its own internal language for enhancing and automating applications. Actually, Notes gives you a choice of up to four, depending on context, but we'll start with what is arguably both the easiest and most pervasive: the formula language. The formula language is a simple yet powerful language used heavily throughout Notes applications. Formulas broaden the flexibility of an application and automate everyday tasks into a few simple commands. Because only Notes and Domino understand it, the language takes advantage of the internal structure and processes. It's important you have at least a working knowledge of the formula language before going any further. Even though Notes allows you to use several languages, it's easier to use the formula language for many tasks, and in some important contexts, it's the *only* language available to you. In some cases, it's possible to have individual items or even entire sections of data-entry forms appear or not appear depending on conditions you set (for example, if a document has been submitted for approval, you can make the Submit for Approval button vanish). However, you must use the formula language to describe those conditions.

In the examples throughout this chapter, we'll be referring to the Formula Examples database (`Formula_Examples.nsf`) provided on the Sybex website (www.sybex.com).

- The definition of a formula
- The components of a formula
- Result formulas
- Action formulas
- Formula editors

What Is a Formula?

A *formula* is a series of one or more expressions that comprise one or more constants, variables, op[?] ators, keywords, @functions, and @commands. The Notes formula language began its life as a [?] guage for doing spreadsheet calculations. At its heart, therefore, a formula is an expression th[?] produces a value, such as a date, a batch of text, or a number. Certain commands don't produce usa[?] values (those commands are called, conveniently, *@commands*), but at the end of most complex fo[?] mulas, the whole expression will end up computing a value. If your purpose in writing the form[?] is to, say, set field values or send mail, you will probably end up ignoring the final value, but it's th[?] nevertheless.

The formula language has evolved far from its roots in Lotus 1-2-3. In Release 6, the engi[?] underlying the formula language has been completely rewritten from the ground up. Many featu[?] that were tacked on in past releases have been better incorporated, making the language run faste[?] More importantly for the programmer, the formula language has at long last acquired some featu[?] sought after by the development community, including true looping capability. The list, a struct[?] that contains multiple values in a single variable, has been restructured so that it's easy to address in[?] vidual values like arrays in other programming languages. The formula language has also acqui[?] fundamentally important commands for iteration and flow control (if you know any old-time No[?] developers, go tell them that; you're likely to see them do a happy little dance on their desks).

NOTE *@Functions and @commands get their names from a convention of the language's spreadsheet heritage. Specia[?] formulas and commands in the formula language have an at (@) symbol at the beginning to distinguish them from word[?] that aren't commands. For example, the formula @UserName computes the name of the current Notes user. Typically[?] @functions get data, @commands do something (for example, open a document or send mail). This is a bit like Microso[?] Excel, where an equal (=) sign at the beginning of a cell's contents indicates that the contents are a formula, not a litera[?] value.*

Figure 18.1 is typical of a formula returning some type of result. This formula can be found [?] opening the Computed Field Example form in Domino Designer and clicking the CurrentDateTi[?] field. In this example, the formula is only one command, @Now. So how does this return a result? T[?] @Now formula returns a time-date value representing the current date and the current time. By placi[?] this command in a computed field, the date and time—at the moment the form is opened and the f[?] mula is executed—will be displayed to the user. Because the CurrentDateTime field is a comput[?] field, you need to place the formula whose value is to be displayed in the Value event for the fiel[?] As you can see, this formula does not perform an action; it just returns some value. It executes on[?] when you open the form. If you press the F9 key, the formula will be executed again, and the val[?] of the field will display a new value.

In Figure 18.2, the formula is a bit different because it can be seen performing an action. You c[?] find this example in the same form by clicking the Close Document Action button. To view the f[?] mula behind the Action button, open the form in the Domino Designer, choose View ➤ Action Pa[?] and select Close Document (see Figure 18.3). @Command([FileCloseWindow]) will close the docu[?] ment for the user. Because this is an Action command, nothing is returned, but an action takes pla[?] (the closing of the document).

FIGURE 18.1
Setting a formula
to return a
result for the
CurrentDateTime
field

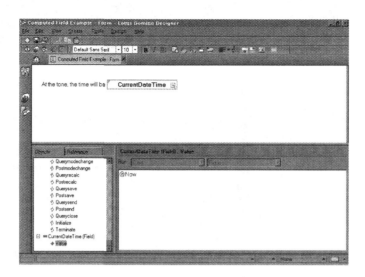

FIGURE 18.2
The Current-
DateTime field in
action

To see the form in action, select the Notes preview icon located in the upper-right corner of the screen.

When the icon is clicked, the form will automatically launch in the Notes client. As you can see, the current time and date is automatically displayed. Now click the Close Document button and the document will automatically close.

FIGURE 18.3

Setting a formula
to perform an
action

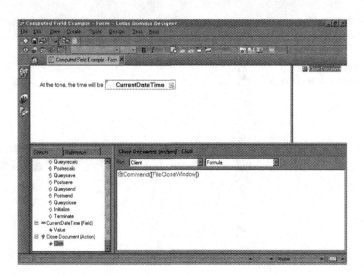

Anatomy of a Formula

A formula is not just a compilation of statements thrown together in an indiscriminate manner. The
is a general syntax, a set of basic rules, that must be followed.

Top-Down Left-Right Processing Each statement expression in a formula is executed in sequen
from top to bottom, left to right. For example, if a formula contained the following statements, sta
ment 2 will execute after statement 1, and statement 3 will execute after statement 2:

```
Statement expression 1;
Statement expression 2;
Statement expression 3;
```

Statements are generally executed from the top down, but with new commands in Release 6, i
possible to conditionally repeat blocks of code.

Statement Separator If the formula contains multiple statements, a semicolon (;) must separa
each statement, for example:

```
FIELD FullName := @UserName;
FIELD FirstName := @Left(FullName;" ");
```

A semicolon is the only necessary separator. You could put all of our code on a single line of te
if you wanted, as in the following example, but it would be much harder to read:

```
FIELD FullName := @UserName;FIELD FirstName := @Left(FullName;" ");
```

TIP   *The formula language doesn't require it, but you should put each instruction on a separate line. If you have a particularly complex instruction, you might want to chop it into separate lines of text. You can spread a formula out over as many lines as you want; the only separator it recognizes is the semicolon.*

Spaces   The amount of spaces you use in a formula is solely up to you. The only requirement is that a keyword must be bordered by at least one space. In the following two lines, the first statement is as valid as the second one:

```
FIELD temp:="1";
FIELD temp := "1";
```

Case   The formula language is not case sensitive, so you don't have to worry about proper capitalization. When a formula is saved, Notes will automatically convert the @functions, @commands, and keywords to their proper case. In general, keywords are in all caps, and the @functions and @commands are mixed uppercase and lowercase. Any text constants you define will not be altered. Likewise, the case of variable names will not be altered, and variables with the same name but different capitalization are treated as equivalent. That is, a MyField variable and a MYFIELD variable will be treated as the same variable.

TIP   *Notes will automatically color code your formulas based on text expressions, keywords, and @functions/ @commands. This makes it easier to read a formula.*

Main or Selection Expression   Most formulas must have a main or selection expression. A *selection expression* is an expression using the SELECT keyword, which we'll discuss in Chapter 21, "Using Views and Folders." This sort of expression is usually used to select documents for views or agents. A *main expression* is one that returns a value. For example, this formula sets the value of a few variables but has no main expression:

```
X := 1;
Y := 2;
Z := X + Y
```

Despite setting variables, the formula does not return a single value. This formula, however, has a main expression:

```
X := 1;
Y := 2;
X > Y;
Z := X + Y
```

This is a tricky example, but it's worth examining. The main expression here is X > Y. X > Y performs a logical test. If X is greater than Y, the value of the expression is true. If not, the expression is false. The formula goes on to set another variable, but that's ultimately irrelevant to whether the formula is legal. All that matters to Notes is that somewhere along the line, a value is produced.

In this case, the value returned is zero, which means false. The line X > Y is the only line that actually produces a value; the other lines set the values of variables.

It's possible to have more than one expression return a value in a formula. If this is the case, the value of the formula comes from the last expression returning a value. Consider this example:

```
X := 1;
Y := 2;
X > Y;
Z := X + Y;
Z
```

Here, we have two expressions producing values. The third line produces a true/false value. The fifth line produces a numeric value (3, the sum of the variables X and Y). The fifth line, as the last line returning a value, produces the ultimate value for the formula.

A formula is composed from a collection of one or more statements that fall into one or more of the following categories: constants, variables, operators, keywords, and @functions. The following sections discuss each of these categories.

Formula Constants

In the formula language, a *constant* is simply a literally stated value rather than a computed quantity. For example, if you wrote code that has the name of your organization written into it, you'd probably use a constant expression. The date of the beginning of the fiscal year, however, is something that changes depending on the circumstances of the formula, so that would not use a constant expression.

A constant used in formulas is always one of three data types: text, numeric, or time-date. To declare a constant, just assign a value to a variable. You don't have to worry about case, but remember to use the assignment operator (:=) instead of the equality operator (=). Both of these operators are discussed later in the chapter, under "Formula Operators." An example form, Constant Variable Example, has been set up to give a working example for each type of constant. Each of the following sections will refer to a field contained on that form. To follow along, open the Constant Variable Example form in Designer.

TEXT CONSTANTS

A text constant is composed of any character surrounded by quotation marks ("") or curly braces ({}). Which you choose depends on how much other programming you do. Most other programming languages use quotation marks for the same thing but use braces for different purposes. With the weight of tradition behind them, if you plan to do other programming, cultivate the use of quotation marks. However, if you use quotation marks *and* you need to include quotation marks as part of the constant value, you must use the backslash (\) followed by the quote ("). Table 18.1 shows a few examples of constants and their values.

TIP *The backslash is also known as the* escape character *in the formula language. Keep this in mind because it is used quite frequently when formulas are created in Notes.*

CONSTANT DECLARATION	VALUE OF CONSTANT
X := "My Name"	My Name
X := {My Name}	My Name
X := ""My Name""	Generates an error when saving
X := "\"My Name\""	"My Name"
X := {"My Name"}	"My Name"
X := "c:\temp"	c:temp
X := "c:\\temp"	c:\temp
X := "12"	12 (this is text, not numeric)

On the example form, the TextConstant field has been set up using text constants to display a message to the users, as shown in Figure 18.4. In the programmer's pane, select the Objects tab and then select the Value event for the TextConstant field. If you select the TextConstant field directly on the form, the Value event will be highlighted by default.

FIGURE 18.4

Using a text constant in a formula

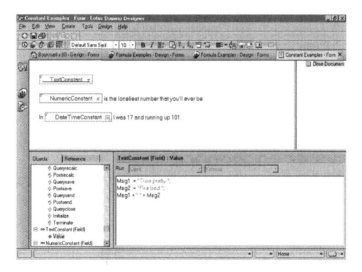

NUMERIC CONSTANTS

A *numeric constant* is composed of a combination of numbers from 0 to 9 and any other special numeric punctuation (such as the period, scientific notation, negative sign). Table 18.2 shows a few examples of numeric constants and their formats.

TABLE 18.2: EXAMPLES OF NUMERIC CONSTANTS

CONSTANT DECLARATION	VALUE OF CONSTANT
X := 123	123
X := 12e3	12000
X := 12E3	12000
X := -23	-23
X := -1234.5	-1234.5

On the example form, the NumericConstant field uses numeric constants for some pointless varables to do some trivial math, as shown in Figure 18.5. In the programmer's pane, select the Objects and then select the Value event for the NumericConstants field. If you select the NumericConstant field on the form directly, the Value event will be highlighted by default.

FIGURE 18.5

Using a numeric constant in a formula

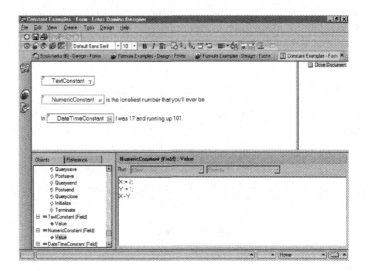

TIME-DATE CONSTANTS

A *time-date constant* is composed of a date, a time, or a date and a time enclosed in square brackets ([]). F constants containing both the time and date components, it doesn't matter if you specify the time fir and then the date or the date first and then the time. You can specify time in a 24-hour format (milita time) or a 12-hour format (you must use the A.M./P.M. designation for the 12-hour format). When y enter a date, the year is optional; it will default to the current year. If you decide to specify a year wi two digits, 50 or more will default to the 1900s, and less than 50 will default to the 2000s. You can al specify a year with four digits. Table 18.3 shows a few examples of time-date constants and their valu

TABLE 18.3: EXAMPLES OF TIME-DATE CONSTANTS

CONSTANT DECLARATION	VALUE OF CONSTANT
X := [1/1]	1/1/2003
X := [1/1/45]	1/1/2045
X := [1/1/55]	1/1/1955
X := [05:00]	05:00:00 A.M.
X := [13:00]	01:00:00 P.M.
X := [13:00 1/1]	1/1/1998 01:00:00 P.M.
X := [1/1 13:00]	1/1/1998 01:00:00 P.M.
X := [13:00 AM]	Generates an error when saving

TIP   In "true" military time, the time does not include a colon (:). In Notes, the 24-hour format must contain the colon or the formula will not save.

On the example form, the DateTimeConstant field has been set up using a time-date constant to display a line from a really cool song, as shown in Figure 18.6 (the field has been formatted to display only the year). In the programmer's pane, select the Objects tab and then select the Value event for the DateTimeConstant field. If you select the DateTimeConstant field on the form directly, the Value event will be highlighted by default.

To see the form in action, click the Notes preview icon located in the upper-right corner of the screen. When the icon is clicked, the form will automatically launch in the Notes client, as shown in Figure 18.7. Now click the Close Document button, and the document will automatically close.

FIGURE 18.6

Using a time-date constant in a formula

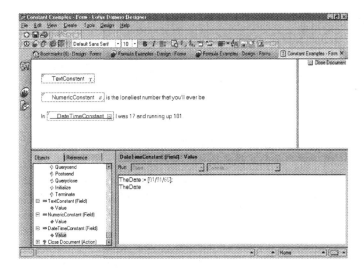

FIGURE 18.7

Viewing the form in the Notes client

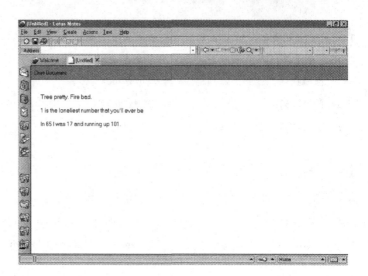

WARNING   *Date values can't be any earlier than 1 A.D.*

Formula Variables

When you use a formula, you really need to be concerned with only two types of variables: temporary variables and field variables.

TEMPORARY VARIABLES

A *temporary variable* is nothing more than a temporary storage area. It sounds silly, but the life for this type of variable is no longer than the life of the formula. This type of variable is usually used for holding values that will only be needed later in the formula.

NOTE   *If you're an experienced Notes/Domino developer, you'll be happy to know that you can now reassign values of temporary variables as many times as you want.*

For example, Figure 18.8 shows a formula in the Value event for the UserMessage field. Open the Formula Variable Example form and click the UserMessage field. In the programmer's pane, select the Objects tab and then select the Value event for the UserMessage field. If you select the UserMessage field directly on the form, the Value event will be highlighted by default. The second line of the formula is using a temporary variable called *CurrentUser*, which is set to the first name of the current user. Following that there are a few other temporary variables being declared. The *MorningMsg*, *AfternoonMsg*, and *NightMsg* variables are storing some text message values. All of the variables will be needed only in the @ function on the next line where the code is trying to determine the time of day and display a personalized message to the user. Once the comparison is over, there is no reason to hold the temporary variables any longer.

FIGURE 18.8

The WelcomeMsg
Value event uses
temporary variables.

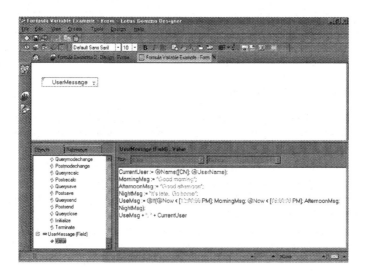

You can see the results of this field in Figure 18.9. To see the form in action, select the Notes preview icon located in the upper-right corner of the screen. When the icon is clicked, the form will automatically launch in the Notes client. Notice how the welcome message reflects the time of day and who the user is.

FIGURE 18.9

The welcome
message as seen in
the Notes client

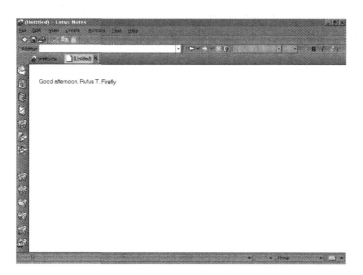

If for some reason you need to hold a value after the formula has completed, there are a couple of options. You can save the value to the current document and then delete the variable later, but this is not a clean solution (it uses a field variable, which is discussed in the next section). Another option is to save the value into a Profile document (a special kind of document that we'll discuss in Chapter 19, "Basic

Form Design"), which poses similar problems. A third option is to use environment variables. An e: ronment variable is not an actual variable type, but it does allow field values to be saved for later use. 1 method you choose depends on why you want to save the value and what you want to do with it.

ENVIRONMENT VARIABLES

A perennial problem with writing code in Notes is the inability to pass parameters from one set of instruc tions to another. In most cases, this does not pose a problem, but the need eventually arises. There are a number of workarounds for this problem. One of them is to use environment variables.

An environment variable has special @functions and keywords available to assist the developer. Each envi ronment variable is written and read from the notes.ini file. Every Notes client must have this file defined The Domino server has one as well. These functions allow one function to write a value to the file so the nex one can pick it up when needed.

This seems great, but there is one catch: Which notes.ini file is updated, the user workstation file or the server file? This is an important question. If the formula is in a database that resides on a server and it's a replication formula, scheduled agent, selection formula, or column formula, it will be stored on the server.

When you use environment variables, prefix the actual name with a dollar sign ($) within the notes.ini file. For example, if you set an environment variable called CompanyName in your formula, it would show up in the notes.ini file as $CompanyName (this is more important when you are using LotusScript because it does not prefix variables with $).

Setting and retrieving the variables is easy. To set the value of variable CompanyName, use the @SetEnvironment @function (although you can also use @Environment or the ENVIRONMENT keyword). For example, to set the CompanyName variable to EDS, code one of the following lines:

```
@SetEnvironment("CompanyName";"EDS")
ENVIRONMENT CompanyName := "EDS"
@Environment("CompanyName";"EDS")
```

To retrieve the value of a variable, use @Environment (yes, it both sets and retrieves values). Here is an example to retrieve the previous value:

```
SCompanyName := @Environment("CompanyName")
```

There are two final points to keep in mind when you use environment variables. First, you can only set and retrieve text values to notes.ini. If you want to save a numeric value, you must first convert it to text. Second, when you are done with the environment variable, you can remove it from notes.ini by setting the variable to null, as in this example:

```
@SetEnvironment("CompanyName";"")
```

FIELD VARIABLES

Field variables either retrieve or store a value on the current document. They are used in the same fas ion as temporary variables are used except the value will not disappear when the formula terminate instead, the value will be stored in the current document *if* the document is saved. You can also u a field variable to create a field on a document even if there is no field element on the form. If you store a value to a field variable and the field you create by doing so doesn't exist on the current document, it will be created. To create a field variable, you only need to prefix your variable with the FIELD keyword. For example, this formula sets the value of a document field named President to Jefferson.

```
FIELD President := "Jefferson"
```

Figure 18.10 shows the formula for the Save and Close Document button of the Formula Variable Example form. Open the Formula Variable Example form, and click the Save and Close Document button. The first line of the formula is using a field variable by placing the value of 1 into the SaveOptions field. If you look closely at the form, you may notice that a field definition for the SaveOptions field exists at the bottom of the form. In this case, the formula is modifying the field for the current document. The purpose of this formula is to save the document. The default value for the SaveOptions field is 0, which tells Notes to never save the document. Changing this value to 1 will allow the document to be saved. SaveOptions is a reserved field name in Notes; if you have a field by that name in a document, it will have special properties.

FIGURE 18.10
Using a FIELD variable in the Save and Close Document button formula

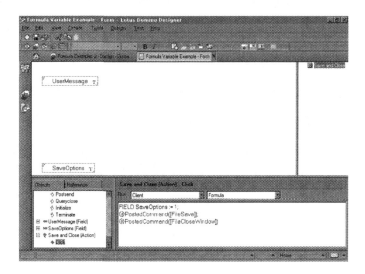

When you access fields on a document, make sure your formula understands what type of field you are using. An error will result if your formula treats the contents of a numeric field as though they were text or time-date, text as though they were numbers or time-date, or time-date as though they were text or numbers.

You can access any field on a Notes document regardless of the actual field type with one exception: a rich-text field. Rich-text fields can contain complex data, far more complex than formulas are capable of handling, so they cannot be accessed directly. You can, though, get a simplified version of the contents of rich-text fields indirectly with the @Abstract formula.

Forgetting to prefix the variable with the FIELD keyword is another mistake commonly made when creating formulas that access field documents. This is a common mistake because your formula will actually execute properly but will not return the expected results. You see, a variable without the FIELD keyword is nothing more than a temporary variable, which was discussed in the preceding section.

Formula Operators

Operators carry out some type of action within a Notes formula. These actions can include assigning, modifying, and combining values. The following sections list the operators (and explain their precedence) and discuss each of the seven categories of operators: arithmetic, assignment, comparison, list, logical, text, and unary.

OPERATORS AND PRECEDENCE

Table 18.4 lists all the operators in their order of precedence. Those grouped together are of equal precedence.

TABLE 18.4: OPERATORS IN ORDER OF PRECEDENCE

OPERATOR	OPERATION
:=	Assignment (precedence is not applicable)
:	List concatenation
[]	List subscript
+	Positive
–	Negative
*	Multiplication
**	Permuted multiplication
/	Division
*/	Permuted division
+	Addition
*+	Permuted addition
–	Subtraction

Continued on next page

OPERATOR	OPERATION
*_	Permuted subtraction
=	Equal
*=	Permuted equal
<>, !=, =!, ><	Not equal
*<>	Permuted not equal
<	Less than
*<	Permuted less than
>	Greater than
*>	Permuted greater than
<=	Less than or equal
*<=	Permuted less than or equal
>=	Greater than or equal
*>=	Permuted greater than or equal
!	Logical NOT
&	Logical AND
|	Logical OR

Operations occur in the following order:

Parentheses   Operations enclosed within parentheses are always evaluated first.

Precedence   Operations not enclosed within parentheses are always evaluated based on the order specified in Table 18.4.

Left to right   Operations of equal precedence are always evaluated from left to right.

ARITHMETIC OPERATORS

The arithmetic operators are *, /, +, and –, and they perform multiplication, division, addition, and subtraction, respectively.

ASSIGNMENT OPERATOR

The assignment operator (:=) is responsible for setting the value of a field variable on the left side of the operator to the value on the right. The value on the left side of the assignment operator always assumes the type (such as text or numeric) from the right side. Any variable on the left side that is not preceded by the FIELD keyword will be a temporary variable. Do not confuse the equal (=) sign the assignment operator because it will not work. The equal sign (=) is only used for comparison. example, the first statement is not the same as the second:

```
MyVar := "Are these the same?"
MyVar = "Are these the same?"
```

The first statement tells Notes to set the value of MyVar to "Are these the same?" The secon statement asks if the value of MyVar is "Are these the same?" This is a common mistake and easy make. It will not generate a syntax error, but it will cause a lot of hair pulling.

NOTE   *The most common mistake developers make when they try to use formulas is using the equal sign (=) instee of the assignment operator (:=) when assigning values.*

COMPARISON OPERATORS

The comparison operators (=, <>, !=, =!, ><, >, <, <=, and >=) compare values of the same type an return either true (1) or false (0).

TEXT OPERATOR

In addition to its use as a mathematical operator, the plus sign (+) concatenates text. For example, expression "Port" + "manteau" produces the value Portmanteau.

LIST CONCATENATION OPERATOR

The list concatenation operator (:) allows you to combine values (of the same data type) into a li If you've programmed before, a list is essentially the same as an array. For example, to build of list cities into a temporary variable called *Cities*, just do the following:

```
Cities := "Atlanta":"Baltimore":"Seattle"
```

There are also quite a few @functions designed just for processing lists. Some functions, such @Subset and @Replace, are designed specifically for processing lists of data.

But using the *Cities* variable from the previous example, how would you write a formula that retur a list where all the cities are in their proper case? You could write some code to perform @Properca (a formula that changes the case of a text string) on each member of the list, but we haven't gott to dealing with individual list members yet. Besides, that's more complex than it needs to be. Rath you can hand a list to a formula and have that formula act on every member of the list all at once

```
@Propercase( Cities )
```

That is all that is required. @Propercase is applied to each element of the list individually, whi is pretty snazzy. This can be used by a wide variety of @functions. It may not seem like much, b with a bit of imagination, you can perform some amazing tasks.

WARNING   *When you operate on lists, make sure all negative numbers are enclosed in parentheses or you may no get the result you expect (remember that the list operator has the highest precedence). If a negative is not enclosed ir parentheses, the negative is carried through the rest of the list. For example, if* ListA := 1:-2:3 *were added tc* ListB := 1:1:1:, *the result would be* 2:-1:-2, *not* 2:-1:4.

You can also perform operations on lists. There are two types of operators: pair-wise and permuted.

Pair-wise operators act on lists just as the name suggests, in pairs. When two lists are processed, the first element of list 1 is paired with the first element of list 2, the second element of list 1 is paired with the second element of list 2, and so on. Pair-wise operators are exactly the same as permuted except pair-wise operators don't have the asterisk (*).

Permuted operators pair each element in one list with each element in the second list. When two lists are processed, the first element of list 1 is paired with each and every element in list 2, the second element of list 1 is paired with each and every element in list 2, and so on.

You may be confused by now, so we'll give you an example of each type performed on the same lists. If you have two numeric lists, 2:4 and 6:8, and you multiply the two lists together using a pair-wise operator, such as 2:4*6:8, the result would be the list 12:32. If you use a permuted operator, such as 2:4**6:8, to multiply the same lists, the result would be the list 12:16:24:32.

LIST SUBSCRIPT OPERATOR

A desperately needed new feature of the formula language in Release 6 is the ability to get the values of individual items within a list. In earlier versions of Notes, this was an onerous task. For example, let's say you wanted to know what the second member of the previous Cities list was. You'd have to use a formula like this:

```
PartialList := @Subset(Cities; 2);
@Subset(PartialList; -1)
```

The first line breaks off the start of the list up to the second item, and the second takes the last item off of the end of the list. This was painfully inelegant, and it greatly irked programmers who were used to languages where it was easy to get specific items in arrays.

Now, though, Notes can do that as well. The list subscript operator is two brackets ([]). To get a specific member of a list, use the list name and the number with brackets. We can now get the second item in Cities with a single expression, thusly:

```
Cities[2]
```

When using list subscripts in creating other lists, put each list item expression in parentheses, like this:

```
WesternCities := "Sacramento":{Portland}: (Cities[3])
```

LOGICAL OPERATORS

The logical operators (!, &, and |) allow you to combine logical values that will return true (1) or false (0). This may sound easy, but it can get quite complicated. Table 18.5 shows you a few examples using all three of the logical operators. Pay special attention to the last three because the OR (|) logical operator behaves a bit differently than you may think.

TABLE 18.5: EXAMPLES OF LOGICAL OPERATORS

EXAMPLE	LOGICAL VALUES	RESULT (TRUE OR FALSE)
(1=1) & (1=1)	(True) and (True)	True
! 1=1	Not True	False
1=1 | 1=1	True or True	True
1=2 | 1=1	False or True	True
1=2 | 1=2	False or False	False

TEXT OPERATOR AND UNARY OPERATORS

The text operator (+) allows you to combine two or more text variables. The unary operators (+, - allow you to specify the sign of a numeric variable.

CONVERTING DATA TYPES

One of the annoying things about the formula language and its interaction with document field values is that there is little control over data typing. Let's say you've got a formula producing the value FieldA * FieldB. If FieldA and FieldB happen to contain numeric values, you're in good shape. However, because any field in a Notes document can contain any kind of value, either of them might be a text or time-date value, which will cause an error when you try to perform your multiplication.

It is, therefore, a good idea to force your data into the correct data types before you perform further operations on them, and Notes gives you functions to do just that. If you want to create a text value, use the @Text function. @Text(fieldvalue) yields a text value, regardless of what type of data fieldvalue may be. @Text can also take a special second parameter that will produce special date and numeric formats (for example, month/day/year or currency formats). However, to use those properly, you will have to know the data type of the value you're processing. Processing a time value with a date format or a date value with a number format can cause problems. Release 6 has two new functions to produce number and time-date values: @ToNumber and @ToTime. You can use these in preference to the older functions, such as @TextToTime, which require you know the format of the incoming data. Both @ToNumber and @ToTime turn a value into a numeric or time-date value, respectively. So, if you're worried about getting an error from FieldA * FieldB, you can use @ToNumber(FieldA) * @ToNumber(FieldB) and sleep soundly at night.

Formula Keywords

Luckily, there aren't many keywords for formulas you need to memorize. Table 18.6 describes all t keywords. Remember that a keyword is always the first word in a formula statement. They will alwa be in uppercase because the formula editor automatically converts them when the formula is save

TABLE 18.6: FORMULA KEYWORD VALUES AND DESCRIPTIONS

KEYWORD	DESCRIPTION
DEFAULT	Applies a default value to a field. If the field exists on the current document, the current value of the field is used. If the field does not exist, the field is created with the default value. For example: `DEFAULT MyVar := "Some default value"`
ENVIRONMENT	Assigns a value to an environment variable in the notes.ini file. For example: `ENVIRONMENT MyVar := "Some text value"`
FIELD	Assigns a value to a field for the current document. If the field exists on the current document, the contents are replaced. If the field does not exist, the field is created with the value assigned. For example: `FIELD MyVar := "Some value"`
REM	Inserts comments into the formula. For example: `REM "These are my comments"`
SELECT	Determines if the current document is valid for processing in the formula (must return a logical value). For example: `SELECT Form = "Main Topic"`

If you're new to programming, you cultivate the use of REM. A REM statement is ignored when the formula is executed. It might sound mildly absurd at first, but a keyword that renders a line of code inoperative is useful for a number of reasons. First, and most importantly, it's a way for you to make comments about the purpose and inner workings of the formula within the formula itself. If you're dealing with a complex formula you haven't seen for six months, a few hints about why you did what you did can be invaluable. Second, when you're debugging a formula, you can temporarily disable individual lines of code with REM statements as you go. This capability can be useful for isolating problematic statements.

@Functions

Notes contains hundreds of @functions used in a wide variety of ways. Each @function always returns some type of value. When returning a value, the function essentially replaces itself with the value. These functions can be used anywhere within a formula and can also be nested within themselves. For example, the following piece of code is a valid nested formula:

```
FIELD Readers := @Trim( @Unique( From : @UserName ) )
```

Breaking down the formula, you can see that the contents of the From field are being combined with the result of the @Username function to form a text list. The @Unique function then removes any duplicates from the list. The @Trim function then removes any beginning or trailing blanks from each entry in the text list, and the results are stored in the document field called Readers.

@FUNCTION SYNTAX

The general format for an @function is as follows:

```
@functionname( argument1; argument2; ....argumentn)
```

An @function always starts with the @ symbol followed by the name of the function. Not all fu[nc]
tions require arguments. For those that don't, the parentheses are not required. Parentheses are o[nly]
required for functions that have arguments.

If the @function has multiple arguments, each argument must be separated by a semicolo[n.]
Each argument's data type must match that of the @function's description. @Functions may a[lso]
require special keywords, which are always surrounded by brackets ([]) and are *not* placed in quo[tes]
as a text literal is. The keyword must match those described in the function's help description. Th[is]
is a slightly different use of brackets than the list subscript operator; when used as a keyword, th[e]
brackets are not used in a conjunction with a variable. `Countries[2]` uses a subscript; `@Name([CN`[;]
`@UserName)` uses a keyword.

VARIOUS FUNCTIONS AND COMMANDS

@functions can be commonly grouped or associated based on their intended usage. What you m[ay]
find even a bit more confusing is that many of the @functions can also have more than one synt[ax.]
Identifying and explaining all the various uses and syntax is outside the scope of this book. The he[lp]
files, which you should already have if you're thinking about designing a database, already descri[be]
them all in detail. However, to get you oriented in the language and give you a general idea of so[me]
of the things formulas can do, we will discuss a few of the more common @functions and how th[ey]
are applied. We'll also return to some of these in examples in the rest of the book, so you can see the[m]
in context. For full descriptions, see the Domino Designer help files.

Error @Functions

There are basically six @functions that we would classify as error related. They are most com[-]
monly used in fields for user data entry. `@Failure()` and `@Success` are typically used within Inp[ut]
Validation formulas. If the data input by the user is incorrect, `@Failure()` will display an error me[s-]
sage to the user and stop the current process of saving the document. `@Success` is returned fro[m]
the formula if everything is OK. `@IsError()` is a quick-and-dirty way of checking for errors. I[t]
takes two statements as parameters. It evaluates the first statement. If the first statement does no[t]
produce an error, `@IsError` returns the value of the first statement; if it does produce an error, th[e]
value of the second statement is returned. `@IsError()` does something similar, but you'll need t[o]
do a bit more programming to use it. The formula tests a field or variable to see if it contains a[n]

error. When an error occurs, the contents of the variable are set to `@Error`. Whether you check for an error is completely up to you. If a field contains an error and is left undetected, the field will display an error statement to the end user. The last function, `@Return()`, allows you the option of terminating a formula and returning a value.

String/Text Functions

Notes is a document-based programming language and repository. Keeping that theme in mind, you can imagine that there are quite a few text-oriented functions. Notes has @functions for converting all data types to text, concatenating and comparing text, and locating and extracting strings and substrings of text. The most common function you will probably use is the `@Text()` function, which will take any data type and convert it to text. For example, `@Text( @DocumentUniqueID )` is commonly used in a view column; this can be quite useful for web views, where document IDs can be used to construct links to individual documents. Another common text function combination that we use is `@Right( "00000" +` `@Trim( field ); 5 )`. This will take an ordinary alphanumeric field and return a zero-padded value (the value of 52 would be transformed to 00052). This may not appear terribly useful, but for sorting alphanumeric values, it becomes quite useful. There are also formulas that massage text strings into more tractable values. For example, `@Left` and `@Right` take the leftmost and rightmost characters from a string, `@Length` returns the length of a string, and `@Replace` and `@ReplaceSubstring` can substitute one string for another.

Arithmetic Functions

There are some basic number and mathematical functions as well. `@Sum()` is an interesting function in that it sums numbers and number lists and returns the total value. There are also `@Round()`, `@Min()`, `@Max()`, and `@Random()` for other numeric manipulation. Notes also contains the simple mathematical functions such as `@Abs()` and `@Sign()` and trigonometry functions such as `@Sin()` and `@Tan()`.

Time-Date Functions

Notes has a multitude of functions for processing the time-date fields and variables. There are functions that are document specific, such as `@Created()` and `@Modified()`, and some that are date oriented, such as `@Month()` and `@Year()`. One interesting function is `@Adjust()`, which will allow you to adjust a time-date value (either forward or backward) by years, months, days, hours, minutes, or seconds—quite flexible indeed. For example, the formula to compute a date and time one year and a day and a second from right now would be `@Adjust(@Now; 1; 0; 1; 0; 0; 1);`.

List Functions

Because the formula language sets up the special list structure, it also provides functions for manipulating and analyzing them. `@Count` and `@Elements` give the number of members a list contains. `@Min` and `@Max` return the smallest and largest members of a list, respectively. The charmingly named `@Explode` chops a string up into a list, and `@Implode` joins the members of a list into a string. `@Unique` removes duplicate values in a list. `@IsMember` and `@IsNotMember` indicate whether a given value is a member of a list. Finally, `@Sort` puts list members into an order indicated by a keyword.

NOTE *Why both* `@Count` *and* `@Elements`*? They react slightly differently to empty lists.* `@Count` *returns 1, and* `@Elements` *returns 0.*

@If

@If, the formula language's decision-making function, is possibly the single most used function in language. @If is invaluable for deciding whether to perform actions, which of a number of values assign to a field or variable, and so on. You'll provide @If with pairs of conditions and results, p one additional result expression. When executed, the @If statement evaluates the first conditi expression. If the expression produces a true value, the formula returns the first result. If not, Nc moves on to evaluate the second condition. If that condition is true, the formula returns the seco value. If the condition is true, the second value is returned, and so on. If none of the conditions is tr the final result (which does not have a corresponding condition expression) is returned. You ca include up to 99 condition-result pairs. Here's an example:

```
@If(JamDate > @Now; "Jam Tomorrow"; JamDate < @Now; "Jam Yesterday"; "Jam Today"
```

When the formula executes, Notes compares the value of the variable JamDate to the current d and time. If JamDate is in the future, the formula stops there and returns the value "Jam Tomorrov If not, it goes on to the next condition. If JamDate is in the past, the formula returns the value "Ja Yesterday." If neither condition is true, the formula returns the value "Jam Today." Because @Now (give time values down to hundredths of a second, it's almost always "Jam Yesterday" or "Jam Tom row," but almost never "Jam Today."

When working with @If, it is important to remember that the formula keywords discussed in t previous section must come at the beginning of a statement. That means you can't set a field val within an @If statement. Rather, you must set the field value to the results of an @If statement. F example, this is not a legal statement:

```
@If(JamDate > @Now; FIELD JamStatus := "Jam Tomorrow"; JamDate < @Now;
    FIELD JamStatus := "Jam Yesterday"; FIELD JamStatus := "Jam Today")
```

This, however, is a legal statement:

```
FIELD JamStatus := @If(JamDate > @Now; "Jam Tomorrow"; JamDate < @Now;
    "Jam Yesterday"; "Jam Today")
```

User Functions

Some of the functions are directed solely at identifying the user and the environment. The most comm in this area are @Name() and @UserName. @UserName returns the current username (or server name), a @Name() allows you to format the results in many different ways. For example, the results of an @Name statement might look like CN=Benjamin Disraeli/OU=Torries/O=Parliament—not a very legible expr sion. To return just Benjamin Disraeli, the late Prime Minister's common name, use @Name() as in th example @Name([CN]; @UserName). Several other functions are useful for determining a user's place in t general scheme of things. @UserRoles returns a list of roles to which the user has been assigned. The ne function @UserNamesList returns even more information. It returns a list containing the user's full hi archical name, all the roles to which the user has been assigned, and all the groups of which the user a member. That last item, the user's group memberships, is only returned if the function runs on a serv so be careful using it if your application is to be used in local replicas.

Database and View Functions

There is also a set of functions designed for accessing information about the current view or database. The most common functions are @DBName and @ViewTitle, which return the database name and view name, respectively.

Lookup Functions

Lookup functions are designed for accessing groups of data both inside and outside the current database. The @DBColumn() function will return all the values for a column in a view. @DBLookup() will search for a specific value in a view and, when a match is found, return a specific field or column value. These two functions are commonly used in formulas for dialog box–style fields (such as a list box or check box) or to retrieve values from one document into another. Both require a sorted view in which to look up values. The formula must be provided with a target server, database, and view, a key value to find, and a column name or number from which to retrieve a value (it may also take some optional keywords at the end). The first sorted column in the target view is used as a key column in which values are looked up. Consider this example:

```
@DbLookup("" ; "" ; "Llamasaries" ; "Lhasa" ; 3 ; [FAILSILENT])
```

The first two parameters, server and database, are null, which means the formula will look at the current database on the current server. It looks at a view named Lamasaries and searches for the first entry in the view where the value in the first sorted column is Lhasa. It will return the value from the third column, whatever that may be. By default, if there is no value (for example, if the key value is not to be found in the key column), @DBLookup produces an error. However, the [FAILSILENT] keyword will make it return a null value instead.

NOTE *Another lookup @function is @DBCommand, which is used by web applications. For example, if you want to display the next set of documents, you can issue @DBCommand("Domino";"ViewNextPage"). This command is typically associated with Open Database Connectivity (ODBC) except in this context.*

Looping Formulas

A long-awaited enhancement to the formula language in Release 6 is the addition of looping functions. There are three: @While, @DoWhile, and @For. Each of these functions performs an action repeatedly while or until a set of conditions is met. This is enormously useful for processing lists of data, such as those in multivalue fields.

We'll demonstrate just one of the looping formulas. @For takes at least four parameters: an initial condition, a condition for completion, an increment statement, and a number of formula language statements (up to 252) to execute. Here's an example:

```
Fnames := "Bob": "Carol": "Ted": "Alice";
Lnames := "Meryll": "Lynch": "Pierce": "Fenner": "Smith";
@For(x :=1; x<=@Elements(Fnames); x:= x + 1;
y := @Elements(Lnames) - x;
Fullnames : (Fnames[x] + " " + LNames[y]);
);
Fullnames
```

The first two lines set up lists of names. The @For statement sets up an initial condition: x = The second statement sets up a condition that will cause the @For loop to continue as long as it is tr As long as x is less than or equal to the number of elements in the list Fnames, the loop will contin Until then, the remaining code is executed each time the function repeats. The third statement t what happens to x each time through: One is added to the current value of x. The next two stateme are executed in order each time through the loop. The first statement computes a value counti down from the number of elements in the list Lnames. The second statement adds items onto the e of the list Fullnames. Each item composed of a member of the first list (starting at the beginning the list and moving forward) and a member of the second list (starting at the *end* of the list and mov *backward*). At the end, the formula produces a list of names: Bob Fenner, Carol Pierce, Ted Lynch, a Alice Meryll.

@Mailsend

As mentioned before, one of the cornerstone features of Notes is e-mail messaging. Not surprising the formula language has a command that allows you to send mail messages: @Mailsend.

There are two ways of using @Mailsend, both of which are usually used in Action buttons, hotspe and agents rather than in formulas for form field or view column values. If it is used by itself, with any parameters at all, @Mailsend will mail the current document to everybody listed in a field nam SendTo. Used with parameters (there are, by the way, a lot of parameters and possible values for ther @Mailsend even allows you to construct messages on the fly without having an underlying document send. You can specify send to, cc, and bcc values, subject lines, and many aspects of the message bo

@Command/@PostedCommand Functions

These two commands are a special form of @functions. They are used to emulate menu command hence, they can only be used in the context of the user interface. Almost every menu command can mimicked by these commands. There are some "specialty" commands available as well. For exampl @Command([Compose];"Formula Variable Example") opens a new Formula Variable Example docu ment. The only difference between the two command functions is when they are executed. @Command executed immediately, whereas @PostedCommand is executed at the end of the formula regardless of whe it is actually located in the formula. The two most-used @commands are probably @Command([FileSave and @Command([FileCloseWindow]). The former saves the current document, and the latter closes it Almost every form you create will have Close and Save and Close buttons using those commands.

WEB APPLICATIONS AND FORMULAS

When delivering web applications, you will soon learn that formulas are extremely important. LotusScript, the next most widely usable language in Notes, will not be rendered to the Web for any of the elements or events on a form. In fact, the only place LotusScript can be used for a web application is in an agent (either the WebQuerySave or WebQueryOpen event); Java has its own, and quite considerable, complications. On the other hand, most formulas can be understood and translated by the web browser (assuming that the Use JavaScript option is enabled).

Continued on next page

For example, you can use formulas in the Input Translation event, the Input Validation event, Action buttons, and hotspots. One powerful feature is the ability to refresh the fields on the web form. This gives you the ability to recompute fields based on the values the user entered. If you have drop-down lists based on the value of an input field, they will be recomputed as well.

Now there are limitations as to which formulas you can use on the Web. You will not be able to issue @Prompt() to display a pop-up dialog box, but all the @functions that cannot be used are listed in the Notes help database. Another not-so-obvious feature of using formulas is using them along with pass-thru Hypertext Markup Language (HTML). There is no reason you cannot place a field on the form right in the middle of the pass-thru HTML. This field can use formulas to grab and format the data, which will be used by the HTML. For example, you could use @DbLookup in conjunction with the contents of a drop-down list to grab a list of document ID numbers from a view (using @Text in the view column to turn them into plain text first, of course) and turn that list into a dynamic list of related documents by incorporating them into pass-thru HTML. This technique is an extremely powerful combination utilizing the power of Notes along with JavaScript or native HTML.

So the next time you need to complete a task in Notes, evaluate the task to determine if it is possible to complete it with a formula. If not, look at some of the other tools available, such as JavaScript, LotusScript, and Java. For more information on the other languages available for Notes programming, refer to Chapter 24, "Language Extensions and the Object Model."

Database Objects That Expect a Formula Result

The formula language appears throughout Notes databases, providing important criteria and values. Table 18.7 describes the database objects and events that expect a result from a formula and what range of evaluated results is expected.

TABLE 18.7: FORMULAS EXPECTING A RESULT

OBJECT	FORMULA TYPE	EXPECTED RESULT/ACTIVATED	HOW TO ACCESS
Database	Replication	Evaluates to true (1) or false (0) and is applied to each document in the database. Activated when replication occurs.	Open the database and choose File ➤ Replication ➤ Settings or right-click the database design bookmark icon and choose Replication ➤ Settings. Click Space Savers, then select Documents That Meet a Selection Formula.
View/Folder	Form	Evaluates to the name of a form. Activated when a document is opened from the view.	Open the view/folder and click the Objects tab in the programmer's pane. Expand the View object and select the Form Formula event.

Continued on next page

TABLE 18.7: FORMULAS EXPECTING A RESULT *(continued)*

OBJECT	FORMULA TYPE	EXPECTED RESULT/ACTIVATED	HOW TO ACCESS
	Selection	Uses the SELECT keyword, evaluates to true (1) or false (0) and is applied to each document in the view. Activated when the view or folder is opened.	Open the view/folder and click the Objects tab in the programmer's pane. Expand the View object and select the View Selection event. In the script area, select Formula from the drop-down box.
	Column	Evaluates a text, numeric, or time-date value. Activated when the view or folder is opened.	Open the view/folder and click the Objects tab in the programmer's pane. Expand the Column object and select the Column Value event (you can also just click the column header). In the script area, select the Formula radio button.
	Show Action	Evaluates to true (1) or false (0). Activated when the view or folder is opened.	Open the view/folder and choose View ➤ Action Pane (you can also slide the Action pane slider bar). Double-click the action to display the Action Properties InfoBox and select the Action Hide-When tab. Enable the Hide Action If Formula Is True option. Type the formula in the text area or click the Formula Window button.
Form	Window title	Evaluates to a text or numeric value. Activated when a document based on the form is opened.	Open the form and click the Objects tab in the programmer's pane. Expand the Form object and select the Window Title event.
	Section title	Evaluates to a text or numeric value. Activated when a document based on the form is opened.	Open the form and select the section. Choose Section ➤ Section Properties to open the Section Properties InfoBox (you can also right-click the section and choose Section Properties). Select the Section Title and Border tab. Select the Formula radio button. Type the formula in the text area or click the Formula Window button.

Continued on next page

OBJECT	FORMULA TYPE	EXPECTED RESULT/ACTIVATED	HOW TO ACCESS
	Section access	Evaluates to a name or list of names. Activated when the section is accessed.	Open the form and select the section. Choose Section ➤ Section Properties to open the Section Properties InfoBox (you can also right-click the section and choose Section Properties). Select the Formula tab. Type the formula in the text area or click the Formula Window button.
	Show Action	Evaluates to true (1) or false (0). Activated when a document based on the form is opened.	Open the form and choose View ➤ Action Pane (you can also slide the Action pane slider bar). Double-click the action to display the Action Properties InfoBox and select the Action Hide-When tab. Enable the Hide Action If Formula Is True option. Type the formula in the text area or click the Formula Window button.
	Computed subform	Evaluates to a text value that is the name of a subform. Activated when a document based on the form is opened.	Open the form and click the Objects tab in the programmer's pane. Expand the Computed Subform object (you can also select the subform directly from the form) and select the Default Value event.
	Hide paragraph	Evaluates to true (1) or false (0). Activated when the text is accessed.	Open the form and place the cursor in the paragraph you want to hide. Choose Text ➤ Text Properties and Enable the Hide Paragraph If Formula Is True option. Type the formula in the text area or click the Formula Window button.
	Hotspot formula pop-up	Evaluates to a text value that is displayed in the pop-up box. Activated when the hotspot text is selected.	Open the form and click the Objects tab in the programmer's pane. Expand the Hotspot object (you can also select the hotspot directly from the form) and select the Click event.

Continued on next page

OBJECT	FORMULA TYPE	EXPECTED RESULT/ACTIVATED	HOW TO ACCESS
Field	Default value (editable field)	Evaluates to a text value that is displayed in the pop-up box. Activated when the hotspot text is selected. Evaluates to a value that matches the current field type. Activated when the document is created.	Open the form and click the Objects tab in the programme pane. Expand the Field object (you can also select the field directly from the form) and select the Default Value event
	Input translation (editable field)	Evaluates to a value that matches the current field type. Activated when the document is saved or recalculated.	Open the form and click the Objects tab in the programme pane. Expand the Field object (you can also select the field directly from the form) and select the Input Translation event.
	Input validation (editable field)	Evaluates to true (1) or false (0). Activated after the input translation.	Open the form and click the Objects tab in the programme pane. Expand the Field object (you can also select the field directly from the form) and select the Input Validation event.
	Value (computed field)	Evaluates to a value that matches the current field type. Activated when the document is created, saved, or recalculated.	Open the form and click the Objects tab in the programme pane. Expand the Field object (you can also select the field directly from the form) and select the Value event.
	Dialog list, check box, radio button, list box, or combo box field choices	Evaluates to a text value or a list of text values. Activated when the field is edited.	Open the form and select the field directly on the form. Choose Design ➢ Field Properties and select the Contr tab (you can also right-click the field and select Field Properties Type the formula in the text are or click the Formula Window button.

Continued on next pa

OBJECT	FORMULA TYPE	EXPECTED RESULT/ACTIVATED	HOW TO ACCESS
Rich Text Field	Section title	Evaluates to a text or numeric value. Activated when a document based on the form is opened.	Enter a rich-text field in editing mode from the Notes client. Select the section and choose Section ➤ Section Properties (you can also right-click the section and select Section Properties). Select the Section Title and Border tab. Select the Formula radio button. Type the formula in the text area or click the Formula Window button.
	Hide paragraph	Evaluates to true (1) or false (0). Activated when the text is accessed.	Enter a rich-text field in editing mode from the Notes client. Place the cursor in the paragraph to hide and choose Text ➤ Text Properties (you can also right-click on the paragraph and select Text Properties). Select the Paragraph Hide-When tab. Enable the Hide Paragraph If Formula Is True option. Type the formula in the text area or click the Formula Window button.
	Hotspot formula pop-up	Evaluates to a text value that is displayed in the pop-up box. Activated when the hotspot text is selected.	Enter a rich-text field in editing mode in the Notes client. Select the hotspot and chooseHotspot ➤ Edit Hotspot. Click the Objects tab in the programmer's pane. Expand the Hotspot object (you can also select the hotspot directly from the form) and select the Click event.

The formulas that return a result may be as simple as a one-line @function or as complex as a multiline compilation of variables, constants, and @functions. In either case, the final statement of the formula must return a value that the object container understands.

You may have noticed that a number of database objects require true or false values. In general, a numeri
value of zero is the same thing as false, and a value of one is the same thing as true. However, in the formul
language, as in a great many other programming languages, "true" is actually much more broadly defined. I
fact, *any* nonzero value is regarded as true by the formula language. That means any positive number, an
negative number, any string (including, and this can be tricky, 0, or zero as a text value), and any time-dat
value. If you're building formulas to provide true or false values, it's good form to make the formula retur
a one or zero, but so far as the formula language is concerned, the distinction is really zero and not zero.

Formulas That Perform an Action

A number of other items in Notes databases perform actions, which must be driven by formula
guage expressions. Table 18.8 describes the objects that require an action formula.

TABLE 18.8: FORMULAS THAT PERFORM AN ACTION

OBJECT	FORMULA TYPE	EXPECTED RESULT/ ACTIVATED	HOW TO ACCESS
Workspace	Toolbar button	Executes when the Toolbar button.	Choose File ➤ Preferences Toolbar Preferences. Click Edit Icon button and selec an icon from the list to edi Click the Formula button display the formula editor
Database	Agent	Executes on the database when triggered. Will process those documents determined by the selection criteria specified in the UI and the SELECT keyword in the formula.	Open the Agent and click the Objects tab in the programmer's pane. Expa the Agent object and select the Action event. If Action event is not shown the event list, make sure Formula is selected from drop-down list box in the script area.
View/ Folder	Action	Executes on the view when selected. Activated when Actions ➤ NameofAction is selected or when the button is clicked.	Open the view/folder and click the Objects tab in the programmer's pane. Selec the Action object from the list. From the script area, select Formula from the d down list box (you can als select the Click event fron the expanded Action obje in the Objects tab).

Continued on next p

OBJECT	FORMULA TYPE	EXPECTED RESULT/ ACTIVATED	HOW TO ACCESS
	Event	Executes on the view when triggered. Activated when the event occurs.	Open the view/folder and click the Objects tab in the programmer's pane. Expand the View object and select one of the following events: QueryOpen, PostOpen, RegionDoubleClick, QueryOpenDocument, QueryRecalc, QueryAddtoFolder, QueryPaste, PostPaste, QueryDragDrop, PostDragDrop, QueryClose. In the script area, select Formula from the drop-down list box.
Form	Action	Executes on the form when selected. Activated when Actions ➤ NameofAction is selected or when the button is clicked.	Open the form and click the Objects tab in the programmer's pane. Select the Action object from the list. In the script area, select Formula from the drop-down list box (you can also select the Click event from the expanded Action object in the Objects tab).
	Event	Executes on the form when triggered. Activated when the event occurs.	Open the view/folder and click the Objects tab in the programmer's pane. Expand the View object and select one of the following events: QueryOpen, PostOpen, QueryModeChange, PostModeChange, PostRecalc, QuerySave, PostSave, QueryClose. In the script area, select Formula from the drop-down list box.

Continued on next page

OBJECT	FORMULA TYPE	EXPECTED RESULT/ ACTIVATED	HOW TO ACCESS
	Hotspot button	Executes on the form when selected. Activated when the button is selected.	Open the form and click the Objects tab in the programmer's pane. Select the Button object from the list. In the script area, select Formula from the drop-down list box (you can also select the Click event from the expanded Action object in the Objects tab).
	Hotspot action	Executes on the form when selected. Activated when the hotspot text is selected.	Open the form and click the Objects tab in the programmer's pane. Select the Hotspot object from the list. In the script area, select Formula from the drop-down list box (you can also select the Click event from the expanded Action object in the Objects tab).
Standard Navigator	Hotspot	Activated when the user clicks the hotspot.	Open the Navigator and click the Objects tab in the programmer's pane. Select one of the following Hotspot elements from the list: Hotspot Rectangle, Hotspot Polygon, Hotspot Circle, Graphic Button, Button, Text, Rectangle, Rounded Rectangle, Ellipse, Polygon, Polyline. In the script area, select Formula from the drop-down list box (you can also select the Click event from the expanded Action object in the Objects tab).

Continued on next page

OBJECT	FORMULA TYPE	EXPECTED RESULT/ ACTIVATED	HOW TO ACCESS
Layout Region	Hotspot button	Executes on the form when selected. Activated when the button is selected.	Open the form and click the Objects tab in the programmer's pane. Select the Button object from the list. In the script area, select Formula from the drop-down list box (you can also select the Click event from the expanded Action object in the Objects tab).
Rich Text Field	Hotspot button	Executes on the form when selected. Activated when the button is selected.	Enter a rich-text field in editing mode from the Notes client. Select the button and choose Button ➢ Edit Button. In the script area, select Formula from the drop-down list box (you can also select the Click event from the expanded Action object in the Objects tab).
	Hotspot action	Executes on the form when selected. Activated when the hotspot text is selected.	Enter a rich-text field in editing mode from the Notes client. Select the hotspot and choose Hotspot ➢ Edit Hotspot. In the script area, select Formula from the drop-down list box (you can also select the Click event from the expanded Action object in the Objects tab).

These formulas do not necessarily depend on the return of an actual result, but with them, you can manipulate existing objects and execute different commands for various results.

Within Notes, every action performed by a user is known as an *event*. An event can be such things as opening a form, closing a form, clicking a button, or deleting a document. Certain objects within Notes are "event aware," meaning that the object can be programmed to respond to specific events with code related to that event. This is known as *event-driven programming*.

Not all objects within Notes can be programmed to act on all events. Each object is only aware of its own set of events. For example, the view and the form can both respond to the QueryOpen event, but a form cannot respond to the view's QueryOpen event, nor can the view respond to the form's QueryOpen event. Events may have the same name, but that is all they have in common.

As a programmer, you can use events to alter the default behavior of an object's event. This flexibility allows you to develop applications that are more robust and responsive to the needs of the users. Event driven programming is not limited to just formulas either (see Chapter 24, which discusses LotusScript and JavaScript).

Using the Formula Editors

Now that you have a basic understanding of what a formula is and how some important bits of the language work, let's look at how to define formulas and how to debug them. You can define formulas in many different places in the Notes environment, as described in the previous tables. To make matters a bit more confusing, there are also three different formula editors: the Edit Formula window, the script area formula editor, and the Toolbar formula editor.

Although each editor interprets the formulas exactly the same, they all have different options available to aid in the development process.

The Edit Formula Window

The Edit Formula window is displayed when the Formula Window button is clicked. Typically, the button resides in dialog boxes such as the Paragraph Hide-When tab of a Properties InfoBox for an element. Open the Formula Examples database and create a new blank form. Right-click the form to get the Text Properties InfoBox and select the Paragraph Hide-When tab.

You will see the formula text box (see Figure 18.11). You can type in the formula directly on the dialog box, but the space is rather limited, so for a complex formula, it can be downright confusing.

FIGURE 18.11

Using the formula text box on the Hide-When tab of the Text Properties InfoBox for a form

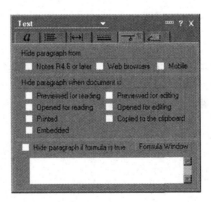

For a bit more room, you can select the Formula Window button to display a larger formula-editing window, as shown in Figure 18.12. The added space will allow you to type in and format your formula for easier reading.

FIGURE 18.12
The Edit Formula
dialog box

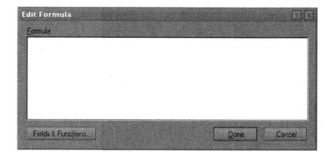

You will also note a Fields & Functions button in the Edit Formula dialog box. This button saves you from having to memorize every @function or database field. Selecting this button will display the Fields and Functions dialog box, as shown in Figure 18.13.

FIGURE 18.13
The Fields
and Functions
dialog box

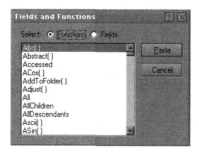

Select the Functions radio button to list all the available @functions. One small limitation of this list is the lack of a complete @command listing. The @command is listed as one of the functions, but all the keywords (of which there are many) used with the @command function are not on the list. Although this may seem like a severe limitation at first glance, you might soon realize that because @commands don't return values, you won't need them when setting hide-when conditions or for other contexts where you can use this box.

Select the Fields radio button to list all the current fields defined for the database. This is an extremely helpful option; it may help you eliminate many field name typos.

Once you have typed your formula in the Formula area, just click the Done button. If you have made any syntax errors, the Formula Error message box will display, explaining your error. Clicking the OK button will close the Formula Error message box and highlight the line in which the error occurs within the formula. Once the entire formula is correct, the formula editor will close and your code will be displayed in the small formula window, as shown in Figure 18.11. If for any reason you want to cancel your code changes, just click the Cancel button in the Edit Formula window.

The Script Area Formula Editor

The script area editor in the programmer's pane is a bit different than the Edit Formula window that it is a multipurpose editor. Not only can you define formulas, you may also be able to defin LotusScript, define JavaScript, or select a Simple action for an object (these selections are determin by the type of event). In a few objects, you can even write Java. Because this chapter only deals w formulas, when we make a reference to the script area, we are assuming that the Formula option been selected (sometimes this option may be in the form of a radio button or a drop-down list b in the script area.

Figure 18.14 displays the programmer's pane for the UserComments field on the Formula Edi Example form in the Formula Examples database. If you look closely at the pane on the left, you see that the Input Translation event has been selected for the UserComments field (also known a Field object). In the script area, the actual formula is displayed for the Input Translation event of UserComments field.

FIGURE 18.14

The programmer's pane of the Designer workspace displaying the Input Translation formula in the script area

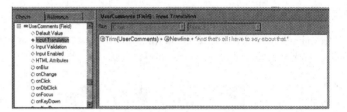

One thing in particular to note is that only a formula can be specified for an Input Translatio event because the drop-down list of the script area is grayed out. Likewise, you can't specify separ Input Translation formulae for the Web and the Notes client. When you use the script area for dev oping, there are many cases in which only one type of programming is allowed. We mention this point out how the Reference tab of the programmer's pane is "aware" of the programming langua too. Because the Input Translation event can only contain a formula, the Reference tab will only play or make reference to those statements that can be used inside a formula. The Reference tab data aware. In Figure 18.15, notice that the only valid selections for the Reference tab are databa fields, @functions, and @commands.

FIGURE 18.15

List box choices for the Reference tab

Once you make a selection from the Reference tab's drop-down list box, the list will populate with all the various commands or fields for your selection. If you would like to have the command or field automatically populated into your script, just highlight the command and click the Paste button. The code will be inserted into the script area where you last positioned your cursor in the script code. Once you have completed making all your changes, click the Accept icon to accept the changes. If you make a mistake, do not worry. Just click the Cancel icon to cancel all your changes.

One nice thing about the script area editor is the color syntax. Notice that keywords, functions, errors, and other text are highlighted in various colors as you type. This helps you track down errors and makes it easier to read. The colors are also configurable. To configure the properties, right-click in the script area and select Design Pane Properties from the menu. From the Design Pane Properties InfoBox, you can define the colors and the size of the text. Change the options to those that fit you best.

NOTE *Before you decide to use a formula, check first to see if a Simple action may do the job. Simple actions do not require any programming and are supported for some of the elements. Refer to the script area of the programmer's pane to see if the Simple action is a valid selection for any element in question.*

The Toolbar Formula Editor

The Toolbar formula editor is used in only one place within all of Notes. We are mentioning it only because it is a bit different from the other two. To access the editor, follow these steps:

1. Choose File ➤ Preferences ➤ Toolbar Preferences.

2. Choose the Customize tab.

3. Click the New button and select Button. This brings up the Edit Toolbar Button dialog box (see Figure 18.16).

FIGURE 18.16
The Toolbar
formula editor

4. Type your formula for the toolbar button or use the Commands & Functions button to paste in your favorite function. The Commands and Functions dialog box looks much like the Functions and Fields dialog box that you saw with hide-when formulas, but it lists @commands

instead of document fields (see Figure 18.17). Again, the lack of one of the three major components of a formula is a bit of a limitation, but this is a context in which you're more likely to use @commands than fields, so it's not a particularly severe limitation.

FIGURE 18.17
Commands
and Functions
dialog box

5. To save the formula, click the OK button. If you have typed in an invalid formula command, an error message dialog box will display.

Debugging Formulas

One major flaw to using formulas is the lack of a good debugging tool, which tends to create some rather creative ways to debug a formula. The formula editor will trap any syntax errors for you. The default setting is to highlight the error in red and place the cursor on the line in error. If a runtime error occurs, a cryptic message may display in the Notes client. A web application may just ignore the code or display an error message page. There are, however, a few tricks available for debugging a formula.

@Prompt   Use the @prompt function as much as you can to debug a formula in the Notes client environment. This @function will allow you to display a pop-up dialog box and display the contents of various fields. For example, if you want to see the contents of a field called MyName, just code @Prompt([OK];"Contents of MyName";MyName), and when the code is executed, a dialog box will appear displaying the contents of the MyName field.

Environment Variables   If displaying a dialog box is out of the question, another alternative is to save the contents of each field in question to the notes.ini file. Use the command @SetEnvironment("WhatIsTheName",MyName) to save the contents of the variable *MyName* to a variable in the notes.ini file called $WhatIsTheName. To see the contents of the variable, open the notes.ini file.

Document Fields   If neither of the two previous options is acceptable, the last alternative is to save the contents of the variables to a document. For example, suppose you need to run an agent for a web application. Displaying a dialog box is not possible because the program is run via the Web. Saving the values to the notes.ini file is not acceptable because the values would be written to the server's notes.ini and not your workstation's. The last alternative is to use the FIELD keyword and save all the temporary variables to the current document. Once you have completed your debugging sessions, either delete the fields from the document or delete the whole document.

Summary

In this chapter, we covered the various elements that a formula comprises. We also discussed where a formula can be used and how to use the different formula editors. Formulas are an important piece of the Notes application structure and should not be ignored. There are other alternative languages available, but none are as simple or as efficient as the formula language.

In the next chapter, we will discuss how to create document forms and the basic elements that can be placed on a form. We'll cover the document response or parent-child relationship and how a form is used to retrieve and save document data.

Chapter 19

Basic Form Design

THE FORM IS THE backbone of the Notes database. It is the structure used for entering and viewing data in all documents you'll work with in Notes. As a developer, you will most likely spend most of your time working with forms because end users will spend most of their time using your forms to interact with the databases.

A form's *design*, its look and feel, is a subjective issue that we won't presume to address in this chapter. Each developer has his own ideas about what looks good and what doesn't (or, perhaps, standards imposed on him by his organization, rendering his, and our, opinions moot). What this chapter will do is give you a basic understanding of forms, their properties, and how to create them. We'll also point out how form design for Notes and form design for the Web differ. Simple forms will often operate equally well in the Notes client and on the Web, but more complex designs and tasks will require slightly different design for each environment.

- ◆ Understanding Notes forms
- ◆ Creating a form
- ◆ Setting form properties
- ◆ Using simple form design elements

What Is a Form?

Most people are already comfortable with the concept of a paper form. Some simple examples are a credit card application, a fax cover sheet, and a personal check. Whatever kind of form it is, you are responsible for placing pieces of information in the areas provided. Once you have placed information on a form, you tend to think of it as a document rather than a form. That is exactly what a Notes form is, except it is an electronic document instead of a paper document.

A Notes form provides the areas for the end user to enter information, or at least view information entered by a user or an automatic process. Of course, you can jazz up the form to look nice and include helpful text, but the end result is that information is gathered from a form and saved into a Notes document. The first time you create a Notes database, you may wonder where to de[fine] its fields. This is another difference between Notes databases and relational databases. In a No[tes] database, there is no way to define fields separately from where they'll appear on a form. The fo[rm,] which is usually used to enter data, is also used to define the fields for a document. In other wo[rds,] when you create a form, you are defining both the data and the user interface at the same time.

Understanding the Form/Document Relationship

The relationship between a form and a document can be a difficult concept to understand at first, [but] it just takes getting used to it. As we've said earlier, a form is used to enter data into a document. [But] this is not the only way data can be defined on a document. Remember the FIELD keyword discus[sed] in Chapter 18, "Understanding the Formula Language"? If the field exists, the contents of the fi[eld] would be updated; otherwise, a field would be created. In other words, you can create a new field us[ing] a formula, regardless of what fields you've placed on the form.

NOTE *It gets better. Using the programming languages we'll discuss in a few later chapters, it's possible to create do[c]uments and populate them with all the fields you want without ever using a form.*

So, how can the data on a document be viewed if the field doesn't exist on the form? Briefly p[ut,] it can't. A form and its fields don't necessarily have any relationship to the data document. A fo[rm] is nothing more than a template you use to view the underlying data in the document. You might a[lso] think of it as a filter, showing you selected fields in the underlying document and perhaps allow[ing] you to edit them. If there aren't appropriate fields in the form design, some data in the documen[t] won't appear. This is where a Notes form is different from (and has significant advantages over[)] a paper form. On a paper form, there's no way to separate "presentation" elements (for example, t[he] labels on a check telling you where to sign and even the spatial arrangement of the places to write your information) and the data (your signature, the amount of the check, and so on). Notes, on t[he] other hand, takes the data and bundles it up separately from the form that was used to produce it. [A] document stores the data with their associated field names. The form is then applied to the docume[nt] and requests to see only certain fields from that underlying document.

Here's an example of how it all works: Suppose there are three forms defined for a databas[e.] FormA has a two fields defined: FieldA1 and FieldA2. FormB has two fields defined: FieldB1 a[nd] FieldB2. FormC has four fields defined: FieldA1, FieldA2, FieldB1, and FieldB2.

Now create a document using FormA. Type **A1** in the first field and **A2** in the second field ([see] Figure 19.1). Save the document. Now open the same document but use FormB (yes, you can use a[ny] form to open any document; use the menu command View ➤ Switch Form). What would you exp[ect] to see in the fields? You won't see anything because there are no FieldB1 or FieldB2 fields with da[ta] on the document. The document only contains data for fields FieldA1 and FieldA2 (see Figure 19.[2]). Now type **B1** and **B2** in the fields and save the document. Open the same document one last time b[ut] use FormC. All four fields would contain data where each field maps to its respective field name ([see] Figure 19.3).

FIGURE 19.1

A form is actually a template for the document and the data. This is FormA.

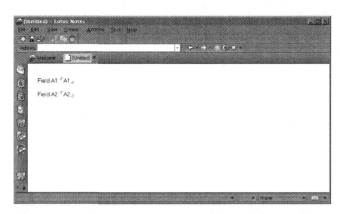

FIGURE 19.2

This is the same document in FormB.

FIGURE 19.3

This is the same document in FormC.

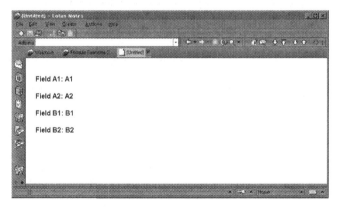

What this example shows is that a data document can contain any number of fields, and a fc can choose to show any number of fields from a document. This allows you to pick and choose wh fields to show a user.

How does Notes know when to pull up which form? There is a set of rules that Notes uses determine which form to use; they are as follows (in order of priority):

- If a form is stored with the document, that form is used to display the document.
- If a view has a form formula, the formula determines which form to use to display the docum
- The form used to create the document (this value is stored in the internal field called For is used to display the document.
- The default form for the database is used to display the document.

TIP   It's worth remembering that Form is a field containing a form name. It's just a field in a document, which mea: you can use program code to change its value just as you would any other document field. That gives you yet another we to determine which form a document will use.

You can design various forms for specific processes. For example, you can design one form for data input and another for reading the document, or you can have one form for printing and anotl form for accessing data from a web application.

Understanding the Document Hierarchy

So far, we've been discussing data documents, which are created when information is saved into fie on a form. Now we'll discuss the document hierarchy. The designer determines the hierarchical ty a data document will have when it is created with a form. Just as databases have a specific type (St dard, Library, Journal, and so on), there are also different types of documents for determining h archical relationships. In this case, there are only three:

Document   The high-level document (commonly referred to as the *main document*) that cann respond to any other document type.

Response   Created in response to a main document. There are special internal fields that ke track of this parent-child relationship. This type of document can inherit data from the main d ument. Within a view, the response document will appear indented under the main documen

Response to Response   Created in response to a main, a response, or another response to respoi document. They are similar to response documents in that there are special internal fields that ke track of the document relationship. Response To Response documents also appear indented und the documents to which they respond.

NOTE   Response and Response To Response documents don't have a fundamentally different kind of structure from on another. Responses just have one or two fields marking them as such.

These types will determine where a document resides within the Notes document hierarchy. One of the most common databases in Notes is the discussion database. A discussion database is similar to a forum or newsgroup discussion. Someone will post a question or general comment, and others can respond to either the original question or any response while maintaining the relationship between the main question and the responses.

A user will create a main topic, which is of the Document form type (the highest level of documents). Other users can respond to the main topic with a response document or to a response with a response to response document. These types of documents carry special meaning in Notes. Notes realizes the relationship between the documents and maintains that relationship for you. There are many special @functions and view options that take advantage of this special document relationship. Figure 19.4 shows an example of a discussion in a database using a document hierarchy.

WARNING *Be careful of orphaned documents. An orphan occurs when a parent document is deleted while its response documents are not. The response documents become orphans, still taking up space in the database while becoming hard to find in views and folders. Make sure there are not any child (response) documents before removing the parent.*

FIGURE 19.4
A Discussion view with the document, response, and response to response type documents

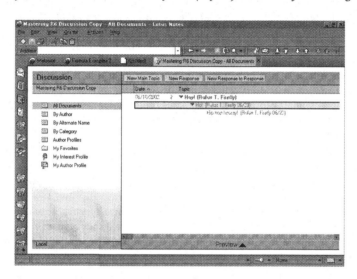

That being said, it's entirely possible that you'll create many applications without using response and response to response documents. For some applications, they make sense. Discussion databases are just one possibility. You might also create a database of project descriptions that spawn a number of individual task documents, a customer service database that logs incidents as Document-type documents and records of individual steps taken to remedy the problem as responses. However, in a workflow database where each document goes through its own independent approval cycle, or in a catalog or employee manual database where all documents are likewise fairly self-contained, everything will probably be a Document-type document.

There is another type of document that has not been mentioned, but it is quite powerful: the profile document. Profile documents are special because they will never show up in a view, yet they can be accessed anywhere and at any time.

One of the most useful aspects of profile documents is that there can be one and only one profile document of a given type in the database at any time. This gives you a single, easily found place to park important data. Say, for example, that you have an application that automatically routes requests from a requester to an approver to a fulfiller. There's only one approver and perhaps a small group of fulfillers at any one time, but most organizations have a certain amount of turnover, so people will move through those positions. So how do you determine who gets requests? When submitted for approval, your form would refer to the profile document to find the name of the current approver. This arrangement also lets the designer put more power to configure the database into the hands of day-to-day users instead of keeping himself busy by hard-coding data into formulas and agents. When the current approver moves on to another job, a manager can edit the profile document and replace the name of the old approver with a new one.

Because they're easily addressed by program code, you can also use profile documents as a sort of "parking lot" for temporary data. For example, you may have two agents that depend on data from one another. Unfortunately, it's sometimes hard to pass data from one agent to another. If you've got a profile document ready to hand over, you can send the data there with one agent and retrieve it with the other. You can also use a profile document to store data or preferences for an individual. Using the individual's username as the key to the profile, you can store any type of user-specific preferences. This can have a big impact on web applications. Users can set their preferences, and each time they return, their preferences can be looked up and restored. This eliminates the need for JavaScript cookies and is a lot easier to program because you can use simple Notes elements (usually, just some forms and @functions) to collect and use the data.

How do you create a profile document? There are special commands for both formulas and scripts (@functions and LotusScript) that create and modify these documents. You can create profile documents specific to a database or specific to individual users. If you use these commands, Notes will automatically create the document as a profile document. No special form is required. Use the same forms you use to create any other type of document (but don't use a form that is a type response or response to response). To demonstrate how easy it is to use a profile document, we'll show you an example using an @function. Assume that the form to use is called UserData and the field to use is called NickName. Grabbing the contents of that field from a profile for an individual is as easy as writing the following line of code:

```
@GetProfileField("UserData";"NickName")
```

If you need to store data or save the state of either an application or an individual's preferences, consider using a profile document. There is one caveat, however. As mentioned earlier, a view will not display a profile document. Remember too that profile documents don't get replicated. Keep that in mind if you plan to store information that needs to reside on multiple servers.

Designing a Form

A form is the basic interface for viewing and entering information in a database. It can include fields (which can either display data in a read-only form or present it for editing), static text, graphics, and actions. Particularly elaborate forms can contain more active objects, such as Java applets and embedded views. On any form, items may hide or be displayed again depending on the data in the underlying document. Although it's possible (and sometimes desirable) to separate web and Notes presentation, a single form can also be used for both a Notes client and a web application. Let's see how the entire process starts.

Creating a Form

There are two ways to create a form. You can either copy an existing form or create a new form from scratch.

COPYING AN EXISTING FORM

When deciding whether to copy an existing form, look for one that closely represents your intended functionality. You don't have to copy a form from the current database only. You can look at other databases and even templates. A good place to begin looking for a form is in the master templates, which are the templates included with Notes.

We'll guide you through the process of making a copy of the Main Topic form. To copy a form from Domino Designer, do the following:

1. Create a discussion database using the Discussion–Notes & Web (R6) template and name it *Chapter 19 Examples*.

2. In the Design pane, select the Forms design element from the Design list. This will display all the forms in the Work pane in a view-like list.

3. In the Work pane, click the Main Topic form to select it.

4. Choose Edit ➤ Copy (you can also right-click the Main Topic form and choose Copy).

5. Open the database that will contain the new form. To keep navigation simple, we'll make a copy of the form in the same database.

6. With the Forms design element selected from the Design list of the database, choose Edit ➤ Paste (you can also right-click the Work pane and choose Paste).

This process places a copy of the Main Topic form in the Work pane, as shown in Figure 19.5. The copy is called Copy of Main Topic (because a form of the same name already exists, Notes will automatically add *Copy of* to the beginning of the new form's name; if you made more copies, each additional copy would be named Another Copy of Main Topic). Now you can open the copied form and change it to fit your needs.

CREATING A FORM FROM SCRATCH

It's even easier to create a blank form because you don't have to find anything to copy, but it will mean more work down the line because you have little on which to build. In the beginning, you'll probably create blank forms to learn the basics. As you get more experienced, you'll most likely copy more forms to use as your starting point. To create a new blank form, follow these steps:

1. Open the Recipes database, available from the Sybex website (actually, you may want to do your work in your own blank database; the Recipes database contains finished examples).

2. Click the New Form button in the Work pane or select Create ➤ Design ➤ Form.

A blank form will display in the Work pane of the Designer workspace, as shown in Figure 19.6.

FIGURE 19.5

A list of form
design elements in
the Work pane

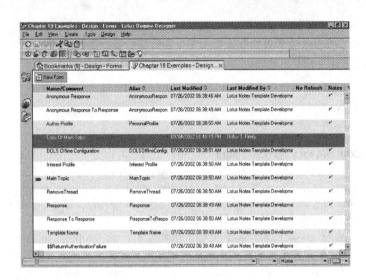

FIGURE 19.6

A blank form in the
Work pane of the
Designer workspace

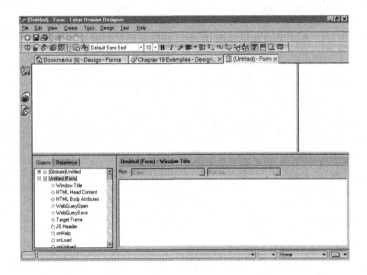

As you can see, the form is entirely blank, which means you'll need to create everything you want to appear. This can be quite tedious at times, and copying a form is sometimes a better option. If there are only a few things you want on an existing form and a great many that you *don't*, you may want to just copy individual elements. With the blank form still displayed, let's step through some of the highlights of the form properties.

Setting the Form Properties

Just like the database, a form has a set of properties that control its overall behavior. To open the Form Properties Box, choose Design ➤ Form Properties. The Box contains seven tabs: Form Info, Defaults, Launch, Form Background, Header, Printing, and Security. Because the Printing tab is the same as it is in the Database Properties Box (described in Chapter 3, "Working with Databases"), it will be skipped in this section.

THE FORM INFO TAB

The Form Info tab stores fundamental information about the form (see Figure 19.7). The following sections discuss these properties.

FIGURE 19.7

The Form Info tab of the Form Properties Box

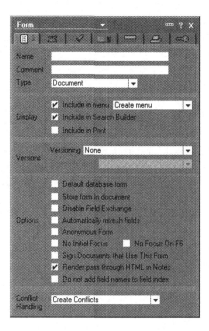

Name

When you create a form, you must assign a name to it. For our example, type **Recipe** in the form. If you save the form at this point, the form's name will be Recipe and that will be that. But now try something a little different: Clear the Name field and type **Recipe | Recipe**. Now the name of the form is Recipe and the name following the vertical bar (|) is the form's *alias* (in this case, it is the same name as the form, but often it won't be). Sometimes an end user won't like the name you selected for the form; many programmers have a tendency to use terse titles that users won't necessarily understand or remember. The name of the form will appear in various places in the Notes client (the Create menu, the Search Builder, and so on), and you may have to change it if the users don't like it. Unfortunately, by the time the users see your application, you probably will have hard-coded the form name in various places throughout your application. This is where aliases come into play. With an alias, can assign a name to the form that is separate from the name the user sees. If you rename the fo or simply name it something more descriptive to the end user, the alias remains the same. You can erence any design element by either its true name or its alias.

Comment

Although dreaded by most developers, it is a good idea to add some basic comments for every des element. In six months, when you no longer quite remember how the database works because yo haven't looked at the design since it was deployed, you'll be happy you did. For our example, ty **Original recipe form** in the Comment field.

Type

As mentioned previously, there are three document types. This form is a Document as opposed t Response or Response to Response.

Display

The Include in Menu check box and drop-down list box determine if an option to create the Rec document will be included in the Create menu in the Notes client and, if so, if it will appear in menu itself or in a subsidiary Create Other dialog box. The Include in Search Builder check box de mines if the recipe form can be used for entering search criteria when you use the By Form butto which is one of the advanced properties of the search bar. Selecting this option will not have any eff on a web application. The Include in Print check box determines whether the form is available as alternate form for printing.

Versioning

Versioning is a powerful option that allows you to determine if the original, unmodified version o document should be maintained separately when the document is modified. It is similar to taking a sn shot of the original document, saving the snapshot, and then allowing changes to be made to a work copy. You can decide if the new version should become a response to the document, if the prior versi should become a response to the document, or if the new version should become a sibling docume You can also specify whether versioning is automatic or manual. Selecting this option will not have a effect on a web application.

Default Database Form

The Default Database Form option designates the form as the default for the database. There m be cases when the form for a document is not available (if someone deleted it, for example). If th happens, the default form is used. You should always specify a default form for a database; obvious there can only be one. For our example, select this option.

Store Form in Document

If the Store Form in Document option is selected, Notes keeps a copy of the form within the do ment. Not only will the data be stored in the document, but the entire definition for the form w be stored as well. This is a useful option if you want documents created with your application to travel between databases (say, around users' mailboxes). However, there are a number of disadvantages. First, it makes the form static. The form definition is stored in the document, and changes made to the form design will not be reflected in any document created before the form was changed. Second, this option also makes the documents take up a lot of space. Form definitions are not tiny. For our example, do not select this option.

Disable Field Exchange

The Disable Field Exchange option disables Notes Field Exchange (F/X) for the form. F/X allows you to design forms so the field contents of an object linking and embedding (OLE) server application (such as Microsoft Word) will automatically appear in the corresponding fields of a Notes document. Depending on the types of fields involved, changing the contents of a field in Notes may automatically update the field in the OLE application or vice versa. Selecting this option will not have any effect on a web application. For our example, do not select this option.

Automatically Refresh Fields

The Automatically Refresh Fields option could have a dramatic impact on performance when it is selected for forms that contain a large number of computed fields. This option will force the form to recalculate when each data-entry field is exited. It has the same effect as pressing the F9 key or choosing the View ➤ Refresh menu option. This option can be quite helpful on forms that require the user to see how changing various field entries affects other fields; indeed, your users may expect it and be puzzled if it doesn't happen. When this option is selected, however, field validation occurs on each field as it is exited, which can sometimes be distracting to users. Selecting this option will not have any effect on a web application. For our example, do not select this option.

Anonymous Form

When Anonymous Form is selected, the $UpdatedBy field (which usually stores information about who last updated the document) will not be created. Instead, the $Anonymous field will be created with a value of 1 to try to hide the name of the user. What this means is that the form itself does not track user activity. This does not, however, make it impossible for you to do so. You can still capture usernames via the @UserName function and store it in a field, hence eliminating the anonymity of the user. Selecting this option does not automatically remove any reference to a user, nor will it have any effect on a web application. For our example, do not select this option.

WARNING *You can also use the User Activity log to determine who an anonymous user is. Just look at the date and time a document was created and compare that to the date, time, and users in the activity log.*

No Initial Focus

When you first open a form or put a document into editing mode, one field has "focus." The field is selected with a cursor in it, and if you start typing, what you enter will appear in that field. If you check this option, no field gets focus when you open the form or edit the document. Instead, the user must click a field in order to start entering data. For our example, do not select this option.

No Focus on F6

The F6 key and Shift+F6 are usually used to move focus between frames of a frameset. Selecting option disables that function for this form. For our example, do not select this option.

Sign Documents That Use This Form

Notes is capable of creating a digital signature identifying the last person who edited a documer. With this option selected, Notes will automatically sign the document when it is saved. This will prevent others from seeing or editing the document, but it will identify those who do. This opt: has no effect on web browsers. For our example, do not select this option.

Render Passthru HTML in Notes

One endlessly useful feature of Notes design for the Web, which we'll come to later, is called *Pass HTML.* You can mark any elements in a form, usually text or a field that computes text, to be trea: as Hypertext Markup Language (HTML) when sent to the browser instead of being translated appear as they do in Notes. This lets you custom-build HTML to achieve special effects, such instantly computed links or selected images, using Notes tools. Historically, the one significant dr. back to Passthru HTML was that if you used it, it essentially required that you create separate for for web and Notes use. The HTML you prepared for interpretation by the web browser appeared raw HTML in the Notes client. This setting allows you to work around that. Checking this be causes the Notes clients to interpret Passthru HTML on Notes forms as though it were being view with a web browser. Text marked as Passthru HTML is interpreted and rendered by the Notes clie So, if you've got programmatically created HTML links or image tags on your form, you can still what it looks like in the Notes client. The setting, not surprisingly, has no effect in web browsers. default, this item is checked, and we'll keep it that way.

Do Not Add Field Names to Field Index

Usually, when you create a field on a form, the field name is added to a "field index," a list of fi names (just names, no data types or other definitions) used in the database. Checking this box kee fields on the form from being added to the index. This is a setting you can usually ignore, as we v in this case.

Conflict Handling

This drop-down menu lets you decide what happens if Save or Replication Conflicts occur. Th default behavior is to create a Conflict document. A human will have to compare and reconcile conflicts. If you select Merge Conflicts, Notes will instead try to reconcile problem documents. presented with two documents with different sets of changes, Notes will try to merge all change into a single document. However, this only works if users change different sets of fields. If tv users have edited the same field, Notes will not be able to reconcile the conflict and will create Conflict document. If No Conflicts is selected, Notes will take a draconian approach to resolvir conflicts. In this case, no Conflict document is created, and there isn't any attempt to reconci them. The first-changed document is saved, and later sets of changes are discarded. Unfortunate: this setting does not affect web browsers. We'll keep the default setting of Create Conflicts.

THE DEFAULTS TAB

The Defaults tab defines the overall form defaults when the form is used to either open or close a document. Figure 19.8 shows an example of the Defaults tab of the Form Properties Box.

FIGURE 19.8

The Defaults tab of the Form Properties Box

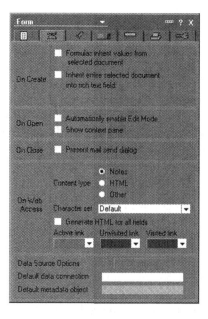

On Create

The On Create options only affect a document when it is being created. One nice feature is the ability to "inherit" values from a selected document. You can use this to bring values from a parent document into a response or simply to make it easier to copy values from one document into another. Select the Formulas Inherit Values from Selected Documents option to allow fields on a form to inherit the values from the selected document (this can be a document highlighted on a view or the document that is currently open). A small bit of programming using a formula is required for each inheriting field (more about this later when we discuss computed fields under "Field Type").

The Inherit Entire Selected Document into Rich Text Field option is similar but is both easier to use and less flexible. When this option is selected, two new drop-down list boxes are displayed. The first will list all of the rich-text fields (but not rich-text lite) on the form. You can select any of them to contain the inherited document. The second allows you to specify how the inherited document will be displayed on the form. You have three options to choose from: as a link, as collapsible rich text, or as regular rich text. The first option just places a link to the inherited document into the rich-text field. The second and third options make a copy of the inherited document and place the contents into the rich-text field. The main difference between the second and third options is that one will be collapsible (a mail memo Reply with History uses this option). What you inherit is essentially an image of the visible contents without any of the underlying machinery. You'll be able to edit text, but

Action buttons won't perform any actions, computed fields won't recompute if you change text, so on. Although you can inherit values from a document for a web application, you cannot inheri entire document into a rich-text field as a link. For our example, do not select any of the On Cr options.

On Open

The On Open options affect the behavior of the document when it is opened. When Automatic Enable Edit Mode is selected, the selected document is opened in editing mode in both the Notes ent and a web application. If the user has only Read access, the document will open in editing m within the Notes client but cannot be saved (the user will get an "authorization failure" message the Show Context Pane option is selected, the screen automatically splits in half when the docum is opened in the Notes client (this option is not supported on the Web). The upper pane will alw show the opened document. The lower pane will display either the parent document (for respon documents) or the document for the first doclink found in the text. For our example, do not sel either of these options.

On Close

The On Close option affects the behavior of the document when it is closed. Present Mail Send I log is a bit of a misnomer. When a document is closed in the Notes client, a special Close Wind dialog box displays. This dialog box does not allow users to address mail; it only allows them to s the document as a mail message or discard it. It is up to you, the designer, to make sure there is a t field named SendTo that will contain a mail address (the name SendTo has a special purpose Notes; if you attempt to mail a document, Notes will look for a field named SendTo for address Without this field, the user will get an error message stating that the SendTo field does not exis

Because it's difficult to present special dialog boxes on the Web, this option works differentl the form is used through a web browser. Instead of the Close Window dialog box displaying, a attempt to send the document is automatically made (if the SendTo field is not set up correctly, an er will be generated). This option doesn't actually trigger every time a document is closed. The fu tion is smart enough to determine if a field has changed. The mail message will be sent only if a fi has changed. For our example, do not select this option.

On Web Access

This section contains options that apply essentially to web applications, although there are som applications to Extensible Markup Language (XML). Content Type allows you to set what kind content a document using the form is treated as if used with XML interpreters. You may choose treat it as Notes, HTML, or some other type you enter yourself. The HTML option can be regard as an extreme version of pass-thru HTML, mentioned previously. When this option is selected, t Domino server doesn't attempt to render the form content into HTML. Instead, it just passes it o the browser. This option is helpful for pasting HTML files directly into a Notes database, but i should be used with extreme care.

Character Set allows you to designate a character set for web use (for example, Arabic or Cyrilli

It's common practice to hide fields on forms. You can have any number of fields to generate t final data or to identify the document, but ultimately they might clutter up the document if they w displayed. However, when the fields are hidden, programmatic tools on a web page can't access those fields. So, if you select Generate HTML for All Fields, you can keep access to that data. When the document is opened on the Web, it will contain hidden fields (<FIELD TYPE=HIDDEN> tags for all fields not visible on the form). It can, though, make the document somewhat larger, which will make it slower to access.

The last three options allow the developer to change the default active link, unvisited link, and visited link colors. For our example, do not select any of these options and leave the colors set to the default.

Data Source Options

This section enables you to use data connections (Notes objects that allow you to access external databases) on your form. Clicking the Browse button lets you look through available data connections and choose one. The one you choose will appear in Default Data Connection.

THE LAUNCH TAB

In the Launch tab, you can specify that various options automatically launch when an event occurs (see Figure 19.9). The Auto Launch options will automatically launch the first attachment, document link, or OLE object in the document when it is opened, depending on which property you select. These options do not work for a web application. The site to which the URL points will also launch when the document is opened (this option does work on the Web). The remaining Auto Launch options are somewhat dependent on what applications you have defined on your workstation. For example, if you select the WordPad Document Auto Launch option and keep all the defaults, an empty WordPad window is presented when the user is creating a new document. After the user creates the document and closes WordPad, the information is saved in the Notes document as well. You can design a form specifically for these options and create a powerful combination of Notes and other software packages. For our example, leave the default setting.

The Auto Frame options allow you to specify whether the form should use frames. If a frameset and frame are selected, the form will always be displayed in the selected frame within the frameset.

FIGURE 19.9

The Launch tab of the Form Properties InfoBox

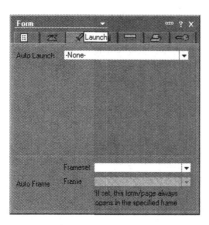

THE FORM BACKGROUND TAB

The options on the Form Background tab are for those who don't like the generic white backgro[und] of the form (see Figure 19.10). Click the arrow next to the Color drop-down list box to display [the] Color Picker, from which you can choose a color for the background.

FIGURE 19.10

The Form
Background tab
of the Form
Properties Box

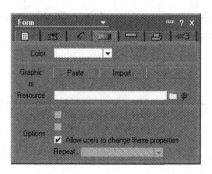

You can also paste or import a custom image by using the buttons in the Graphic or Resource [sec]tion. To paste an image, you must first copy it from another source (say, Photoshop or Paintbrush[) to] the Clipboard. When importing an image, you'll be presented with the Import dialog box. You [can] select from BMP, GIF, JPEG, PCX, or TIF image files. If you want to remove your image, just click [the] Remove button (this button is not selectable unless an image is already present as the background[)].

TIP If you want to insert high-quality graphics onto your form, don't use the Paste button because it will decrease the col[or] fidelity. Instead, either import the image or use an image resource. It is also more work to copy an image to the Clipboard an[d] then paste it than it is to just select an image.

You can also select an image from the Insert Image Resource dialog box, as shown in Figure 19.[?]. You can select these images, which have been saved as image resources (discussed in more detail in Ch[ap]ter 23, "Shared Resources and Other Features") in the database from a dialog box and paste them direc[tly] on the form. You can also use a formula to dynamically change the background image on a form. Ju[st] base the formula on the value of a field and have it return the name of an image resource. For examp[le,] `@If(Status="Problem"; "RedAlertBG"; "JustFineBG")` will use the image resource RedAlertBG if [the] value of the Status field is Problem, but otherwise it uses JustFineBG. When the formula is recalculat[ed,] the image changes. All of these options work on the Web.

There are also a few selections available to you in the Options section of the Form Background t[ab.] When selected, Hide Graphic in Design Mode allows you to prevent the graphic from being di[s]played while you are working on the form (it is sometimes distracting to display the graphic while y[ou] are trying to lay out the form). You also have the ability to hide the graphic from users whose m[on]itors can only display 16 colors by selecting the Hide Graphic on 16 Color Displays option; this [is] a fast-disappearing set of computers, but you may need to use it if your Notes/Domino installati[on] still supports old, old machines. Allow Users to Change These Properties enables users to overri[de] the background properties. The Repeat menu determines how, if at all, the background graphic [is] tiled, and it only becomes active if there is a background image. The options are as follows:

Repeat Once   Hardly repeating, the image appears once in the upper-left corner.

Repeat Vertically   The image is repeated across the top of the form for the width of the document.

Repeat Horizontally   The image is repeated down the left side of the form to the bottom of the document.

Tile   The image is repeated across and down to cover the entire background.

Size to Fit   The image appears once and is stretched or shrunk to fit the visible area.

Center   The image appears once in the center of the form.

For our example, leave the default settings.

FIGURE 19.11
The Insert Image Resource dialog box

THE HEADER TAB

Domino Designer allows you to create a header section simulating the look of having two frames within a form. With this option, you can slice the form into two parts. You can freeze the header so that certain key pieces of information are always visible as a user scrolls through a document. One drawback is that this option is only available for users in the Notes client.

Getting this option to work is a bit tricky. You must select the Add Header to Form check box to enable the other options on the tab (see Figure 19.12). However, you must first select the text the header should contain, so if you don't have any text or fields on your form, you won't be able to select the Add Header to Form check box (it will be grayed out). This means you must have at least one line containing either a field or text to select. Once you select the text, the Add Header to Form check box option will be enabled, allowing you to select it. You can also change the height, the scrolling, and how the header separator line will display (the Border option). For a good example of how to use this option, refer to your mail file and the Memo form. For our example, leave the default settings (because we don't yet have any text or fields on our form).

FIGURE 19.12
The Header tab
of the Form
Properties Box

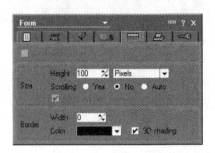

THE SECURITY TAB

Security is everywhere in Notes, and the form is no exception. As a designer, you can use the Secur~~~
tab to decide who can read and create all documents created with the form. As shown in Figure 19.~
there are two security options for reading and creating documents.

WARNING   *This tab is important if you want your security settings to apply uniformly to all documents created wi~*
this form. However, if you want security settings to apply to some documents but not to others or to change as the docume~
goes through its life cycle, you should use the special-purpose security fields we'll describe later under "The Authors Field"
and "The Readers Field."

FIGURE 19.13
The Security tab
of the Form
Properties Box

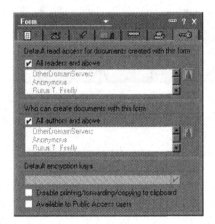

Default Read Access   With this option, you can allow or deny Read access for any docume~
created with this form. By default, the All Readers and Above option is selected, so all users w~
have Read access (dependent on the database Access Control List, or ACL) will be able to re~
the document. You can override this by deselecting the option, which will open up the list box f~
selecting individuals, groups, or servers who can read the document. The list box displays a co~
bination of all users and groups currently in the ACL and all roles that currently exist. If the en~
you would like to select doesn't exist in the list, you can click the address book icon, which displa~

the Names dialog box and allows you to "pick and choose" from the Domino Directory. When a document is created, Notes will automatically insert a readers field called $Readers, which includes all the entries selected from the Security tab. Because the security uses a readers field, if a user is not listed in the readers field, the document will never display in a view in the Notes client or a web application. (Readers fields will be discussed in more detail in their own section.)

WARNING   *Deselecting the All Readers and Above option only affects documents created after the change. Everyone will still be able to read documents created prior to the change.*

Who Can Create Documents with This Form   With the Who Can Create Documents list, you can decide who can use this form to create documents. By default, the All Authors and Above option is selected, so all users who have Create access (dependent on the database ACL) will be allowed to create documents. You can override this by deselecting the option, which works the same as the All Readers and Above option. Users who are denied access to create documents using the form won't be able to create a document from the Create menu. If they try to create a new document via the form, they will see the error message "You have insufficient access to perform this operation." If the user tries to create a document using the form via a web application, they will see the error message "You are not authorized to perform that operation." Don't get this option confused with authors fields. It does not use an authors field to prevent document changes; it blocks the user from using this form to create a document.

The Default Encryption Keys section throws another layer of individual security on the form. If you have specially created encryption keys, you can tell the form to use them by default, encrypting all documents created with the form. As with encrypting a database, this can give your database additional security that can't be bypassed by most tricks users may attempt, but it can also cause performance problems because each document accessed must be individually decrypted.

There are two other options on the Security tab: Disable Printing/Forwarding/Copying to Clipboard and Available to Public Access Users. Neither is selected by default. The Disable Printing/Forwarding/Copying to Clipboard prevents the user from performing those actions; the document may not be printed or forwarded and none of its contents can be copied to the clipboard. Although it prevents casual copying, this option is not really a *secure* way to prevent users from moving the data around electronically. A sufficiently clever user can find ways around it. It is more of a convenience for the developer to disable this function; instead of having to mark each element as not printable, for example, the developer can just mark it at a high level. This option works by creating a special-purpose field name $KeepPrivate and setting its value to 1 (that's 1 as a text value, not 1 as a number; setting it to the numeric value won't work). Notes will treat any document with a $KeepPrivate field with a value of 1 in the same way; checking this option just makes it automatic for the form.

On the other hand, the Available to Public Access Users option is quite handy and powerful. It works in conjunction with the database ACL and lets you allow those with No Access or Depositor access to view specific documents without having to grant them Reader access to the entire database (you should also grant this access to at least one view or folder). All you need to do to make this work is select the option and create a field on the form called $PublicAccess. Set the value of this field to 1 to grant public access for viewing (set it to 0 to block access to the public users). This works for both the Notes client and web applications.

Commands for Creating a Document

Before continuing with the creation of our form, let's digress for a moment and look at how a u creates documents. Earlier in this chapter, we mentioned allowing a user access to create a docum via the Create menu. Although this method is simple, there are quite a few variations for allowii user to create documents.

CASCADING MENUS

If you have a number of forms available, it may be a bit overwhelming to the end user if they're listed after another under the Create menu. If nothing else, sooner or later the Create menu will run out of ro To organize the list, you can group related forms so they cascade from a submenu. To create a cascac menu, all you need to do is use the backslash (\) character in the name of the form. For example, supp you have created three forms called Form 1, Form 2, and Form 3. To group all three together under Create menu option, add a group name followed by the \ to the name of each form. In this example, would name them Related Forms\Form 1, Related Forms\Form 2, and Related Forms\Form 3. Se the Create Menu option from the Include in Menu drop-down list box in the Form Info tab, and all tl forms will display in the Notes client, as shown in Figure 19.14.

FIGURE 19.14

Grouping common forms on the Create menu

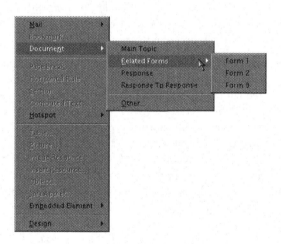

NOTE   We'll be using this technique to create hierarchies with everything from views to actions.

THE OTHER MENU

If the Create menu is beginning to get a bit crowded or confusing, another option is to place sor of the less important forms under the Other submenu. When this option is selected in the Notes ent, the Other dialog box will display. To place a form on the Other submenu, select the Create Otl Dialog option from the Include in Menu drop-down list box on the Form Info tab.

ACTION BUTTONS

Grandly cascading menu choices are all well and good, but what it ultimately comes down to is that users like buttons. Even if the new form is the first option on the Create menu, the user still has to click the menu to get a list of choices. Take a tip from the Action bars of just about every template Notes provides for end users and create Action buttons to build new documents wherever feasible. Because it requires writing a formula, albeit a simple one (@Command([Compose];"Your form name here")), it takes a little more work for you than just letting forms fall into the Create menu. Still, it ultimately means a lot less total time taken by your user community.

Even if it weren't a superior solution for use in the Notes client, the Action button solution also has the virtue of being the only solution for use on the Web. Web browsers don't have access to the Notes client's Create menu, so there's simply no other way to open a form and create a new document.

Using the Design Document Properties Box

We'll discuss one last topic before we proceed further. By now, you probably realize that every element within a Notes database has an associated Properties Box. There is another type of Box that is available for all of the design elements: the Design Document Properties Box. Every element accessible from the work area of the programmer's pane has one. This Box governs properties that all design elements have in common; we're presenting those properties here in the context of forms, but they're common to all design elements. To see this Box in action, follow these steps:

1. Open the Chapter 19 Examples database.

2. In the Design pane, select the Forms design element from the Design list (all the forms in the Work pane will display).

3. In the Work pane, highlight the Main Topic form.

4. Choose Design ➢ Design Properties (you can also right-click the Main Topic form and choose Design Properties).

The Design Document Properties Box consists of four tabs: the Info tab, the Fields tab, the Design tab, and the Document ID's tab.

NOTE   *There is another similar Box, the Document Properties Box. You can access it by selecting a document from a view and choosing Edit ➢ Properties, pressing Alt+Enter, or right-clicking the document and selecting Document Properties.*

THE INFO TAB

The Info tab is a display-only tab (see Figure 19.15). It displays various dates and times related to the design element; you cannot modify any fields directly, although they may change as you alter the design element. The Created field displays the date and time the design element was initially created. The Modified field displays the date and time the design element was modified in the original file (remember that there could be replicas). The Added field displays the date and time the design element was originally added to this database. The second Modified field displays the date and time the design element was last modified in this database. The Modified By field displays who was the last person to change the document. The Accessed field displays the date on which the design element was last read. The Size field displays the size (in bytes) of the entire design element. If you're wondering how much extra space a document will take up if you use the Store Form in Document option, this will tell you.

FIGURE 19.15
The Info tab for a design element

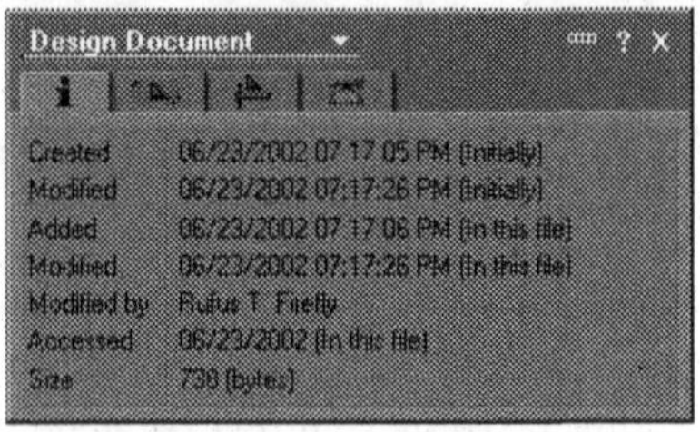

THE FIELDS TAB

The Fields tab contains a list of every field in the design document; this is another pane where n of the properties can be manipulated directly (see Figure 19.16). The left pane lists all the fields, the right pane lists the highlighted field's properties, such as field name, data type, length, and so The right pane will also show the contents of the highlighted field.

FIGURE 19.16
The Fields tab for a design element

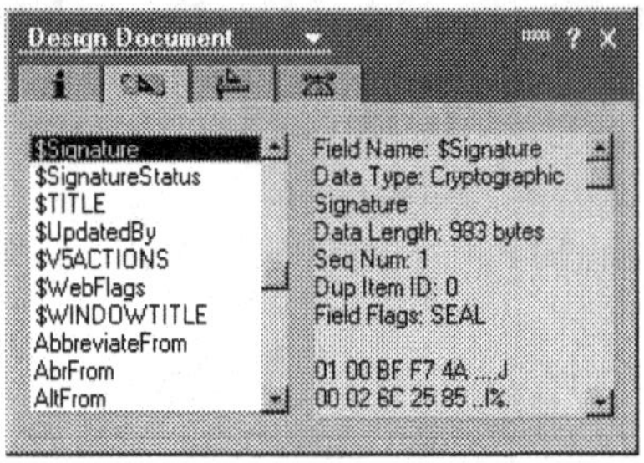

THE DESIGN TAB

In Chapter 17, "Database Creation and Properties," we discussed using a template to create a da base. When a database is refreshed (either manually or automatically via the Domino Design tas the template designated for the database will automatically update the design elements. This is gr when you only have one template, but sometimes a database uses more than one template, and th may be elements in the database that the various templates should refresh. For this purpose, you c use the Inherit from the Design Template field on the Design tab (see Figure 19.17). For each in vidual element, you can specify whether the design should be refreshed from a template. This opti overrides using the template designated for an entire database, but only for the individual element. F example, if you put something into the Inherit from the Design Template field for, say, a particu form or view in a database that inherits from some other template, that form or view will then inhe from the named template rather than the database template.

FIGURE 19.17

The Design tab for
an individual design
element

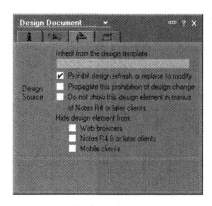

TIP   Properly using this feature takes foresight and planning, but it can pay off in a big way. You may eventually create a batch of design elements you want to reuse in a number of databases (say, standard functions for parsing web input or a standard workflow mechanism). If you do, you can create a single template that holds your reusable code. You won't base any databases directly on that template, but you can use it as the source for your standardized elements, maintaining them and updating them centrally rather than making changes in several different templates.

Select the Prohibit Design Refresh or Replace to Modify option to prevent either a refresh or replace from removing or modifying the design element. This feature can be extremely handy when you have modified a design element and want to keep your changes, yet you are also inheriting the database design from a template.

Another option that also deals with design elements inheriting changes is Propagate This Prohibition of Design Change. Enabling this option will prevent the Prohibit Design Refresh or Replace to Modify setting from being sent along when a database is refreshed. This option can be quite helpful in specific situations. For example, suppose you have a template and you don't want any of the design elements to be refreshed or replaced, so you enable the Prohibit Design Refresh or Replace to Modify option. When a database is refreshed from this template, it will also inherit this setting. The problem is that none of the database design elements will ever get refreshed. If you enable the Propagate This Prohibition of Design Change option, the Prohibit Design Refresh or Replace to Modify option will not be enabled on the database, but it will stay intact on the template.

Do Not Show This Design Element in Menus of R4 or Later Clients keeps the design element from appearing in menus. Its primary use is to keep forms from appearing in the Create menu and perhaps to keep agents from appearing in the Actions menu, although there are many other ways of hiding agents. Why Release 4 or later? Release 3 and earlier versions of Notes (yes, there are still a few out there, and Lotus is deeply committed to backward compatibility) simply lack the machinery to hide items in this fashion.

WARNING   When a design element is copied, the Prohibit Design Element Refresh or Replace to Modify option is automatically enabled unless the design element inherits from a template.

The options in the Hide Design Element From section are quite powerful yet not immediately dent to the designer. You can choose to hide an element from web browsers, Notes Release 4.6 later clients, mobile devices (that is, palmtop computers), or some combination of the three. This be important for design elements to which you don't want a particular environment to have acc and it gives you surprising flexibility in design for each environment. With a simple trick of nam you can automatically use a different form in each environment.

For example, assume that an application will be in all three environments. For design reasons, a fc needs to be specifically designed for each environment. The Notes client version of the form will all editing and a slate of other automated features. The web version will only allow viewing but with a of attractive graphics. The mobile device version will be as bare-bones as possible, keeping memory bandwidth requirements as low as possible. The Notes client form's name is Form Client | MyFo the web form's name is Form Web | MyForm, and the mobile device's name is Form Mobile MyForm. There are three forms with the same alias, so how will Notes know which to use? This is wl hiding the design element comes in handy. For Form Client, select the Web Browsers and Mobile ents options so Form Client cannot be viewed from a web browser or mobile device. For Form W select the Notes R4.6 or Later Clients and Mobile Clients options so Form Web cannot be viewed fr the Notes client and mobile devices. For the mobile device version, select the Notes R4.6 or Later ents and Web Browsers settings, hiding the form in those environments. Any document created w the Form Client will store the form alias MyForm internally in the Form field. Because Form Web a Form Mobile also have the alias MyForm, there won't be any problem displaying the document cc rectly. When creating an application that will be accessed in multiple environments, it's generally a gc idea to create multiple forms and hide them from the appropriate environments. This may duplic some maintenance, but it allows you to design your form specifically for a particular environment.

NOTE   *Why is the option Notes R4.6 or Later Clients and not just Notes Clients? Again, older Notes clients aren equipped to pay attention to this setting. There aren't many 4.5x or older installations still active, and those versions a no longer officially supported, but because Lotus is serious about backward compatibility, they are exact about what wi work in older versions and what won't.*

THE DOCUMENT ID'S TAB

The Document ID's tab is also a display-only tab. It includes the internal identification informati for the design document, as shown in Figure 19.18. Remember that everything in a Notes datab. is a document and design elements are no exception. Therefore, what is described in this section v also apply to the actual data documents themselves.

FIGURE 19.18

The Document ID's tab

The combination of letters and numbers actually do have some meaning. Contained within the ID section are the following:

Originator ID (OID)   Consists of the Originator ID File (*OF* followed by 16 digits), the Originator ID Note (*ON* followed by 16 digits), the Sequence Time (*SD* followed by 16 digits), and the Sequence Number (8 digits following *SN*). The OID identifies a particular revision of a note regardless of the location (remember that documents can reside in multiple replicas).

Universal Note ID (UNID)   Consists of the Originator ID File (*OF* followed by 16 digits) and the Originator ID Note (*ON* followed by 16 digits). The UNID identifies all copies of a note regardless of location or time it was modified.

Global Note ID (GNID)   Consists of the Database ID (*DB* followed by 16 digits) and the Note ID (*NT* followed by 8 digits). The GNID identifies a specific note in a specific database.

Database ID   The database ID, as identified in the GNID, is actually the replica ID for the database.

Note ID (NID)   The NID, as identified in the GNID, identifies a note in a database. The NID is the actual file position of the note.

Understanding the Form Events

In Chapter 18, we briefly mentioned some form events when discussing areas in which formulas can be used. In this section, we'll expand a bit further.

To get started, refer back to your empty Recipe form (if the form is not open, select it from the Work pane). When a form is first opened, the Form object is always highlighted in the Objects tab of the programmer's pane, as shown in Figure 19.19. The Form object is shown by its alias name, if it has one (that may not be immediately apparent because our form name and alias name are the same). The type of object is in parentheses next to the name. For our example, it is Recipe (Form). Each object in the Objects tab is expandable by clicking the plus (+) sign. This will reveal all the events available for the selected object.

FIGURE 19.19

The Form object for the Recipe form in the Objects tab

Each event in the list of events for the object has a symbol next to it. This symbol has two meani
First, it can designate what type of programming language was used to create the event. Second, if
symbol is filled in (used), you know there is an Action associated to the corresponding event. The c
can tell you for which environment the code is meant. If the symbol is yellow, the code is for use on
Web. If the symbol is blue, the code is for use in Notes (this is a black and white book, so we're c
showing one used symbol). Some events can take two different sets of code, one for use on the Web,
other for use in the Notes client. The web code must be JavaScript, but the Notes code can be anyth
from a Simple action to LotusScript. If it has two different sets of code, the half-yellow/half-blue c
code symbol is used. If there is not an Action associated to the event, the symbol is unused. Table 1
displays the programming language, the unused symbol, and the used symbol.

TABLE 19.1: EVENTS SYMBOL LIST

PROGRAMMING LANGUAGE	UNUSED SYMBOL	USED SYMBOL	DUAL CODE SYMBOL
Formula language	◇	◆	◆
JavaScript	○	○	●
LotusScript	◆	◈	◆

NOTE *Exactly which dual code symbol is used depends on which set of code was last viewed. If you last looked at t*
web version of the event, which must be JavaScript, you'll see the JavaScript symbol. If you last looked at the Notes versic
of the event, you'll see the appropriate symbol for the language it uses.

Specifying a Window Title

The Window Title event allows you to decide what should display in the title bar for the form. T
works for both Notes client and web applications. With this particular event, you can only use a f
mula to specify the title, and you can't chose different sets of code for Notes and the Web. You n
notice that the drop-down list boxes are grayed out.

To add a title for our form, follow these steps:

1. Highlight the Window Title event in the Objects tab. This will display the script area in
   programmer's pane.

2. Type **@If(@IsNewDoc;"New Recipe";NameOfRecipe)** for the title to be displayed.

NOTE *Pay special attention to the commands you use in the Window Title event if the application is to be used on t*
Web. Some commands that work in the Notes client don't work on the Web. The Designer Help for each command wi
tell you whether it works on the Web.

You've already seen the @If formula, but you'll probably use formulas built along these lines for most of your window titles, so let's run through the whole thing to see how it works: The formula first checks to see if the document is new or if the document already exists; @IsNewDoc is true if the document has not yet been saved, false if it has been saved. For a new document, the title will be New Recipe. For an existing document, the title will display the contents of the NameOfRecipe field, which we will be creating under "Adding Fields to Your Form."

Formatting Documents with HTML

There are two specific events that let the designer manipulate some of the HTML generated by the Domino server and give the developer access to important, if hidden, parts of an HTML document. Both of these events are recognized regardless of how Treat Document Contents as HTML is set on the Defaults tab of the Form Properties Box. The HTML Head Content event allows you to specify a formula that will modify the <HEAD> tag attributes for a web page. None of the contents within a <HEAD> tag are actually displayed, but you can specify things such as keywords for search engines. You could even, if you wanted to, generate JavaScript functions, just as you'd include Java-Script formulas in the <HEAD> section of a conventional web page. However, unless you want to dynamically generate your JavaScript (and there are cases where you may), you're better off using the JS Header event, which we'll explain in its own section. The other event, HTML Body Attributes, allows you to modify the <BODY> tag attributes. These tags can include the different link colors, the form background images, or margin sizes for the web page. Both of these events only affect web applications. For example, if you wanted visited links to appear black, you could put this formula in HTML Body Attributes:

```
{vlink="#000000"}
```

NOTE *There's another, older way to set up <HEAD> attributes. You can use another special field name: $$HTMLHead. The contents of a field named $$HTMLHead will be added to the <HEAD> section of the document, not the body. However, using the HTML Head Content event is generally a far superior way of creating header content.*

The Web Query Agents

One major drawback to web applications is that many of the events related to a document are not recognized, most notably, the QueryOpen and QuerySave events (these will be discussed later). This is not because of any fault of the Notes software; it's caused by a fundamental differences between how browsers interact with the server and how the Notes client interacts with databases. This limitation brought about a need to trap an event for web applications just before a document is displayed and just before a document is saved.

Hence, the WebQueryOpen and the WebQuerySave events were created. When displayed, both contain the following command in the script area:

```
@Command([ToolsRunMacro]; "<Your agent goes here>")
```

By replacing the text *<Your agent goes here>* with the name of your agent, you can easily access a web document just before it opens or just before it is saved. The actual semantics of how this is accomplished will be discussed in Chapter 24, "Language Extensions and the Object Model," which covers agents specifically. You just need to be aware that it is possible to accomplish either of these task using the two events. Indeed, if you develop applications for the Web, you may make heavy use these events to process documents when they are saved. These two events only pertain to web ap cations because the Notes client has many more events specific to its environment and allow designer programmatic access to the document.

Target Frame

If you're using a frameset, you can use this event to dictate which frame is used as the target for li and actions in the document. This can only take formulas—not JavaScript, LotusScript, or any ot language.

JS Header

This isn't an event so much as it is a place to park all of your JavaScript code. You can use it define JavaScript functions and variables that will be used in other places on the form. Now yc can type and maintain all of your JavaScript in one place. This may seem a bit trivial, but in p vious releases, JavaScript would have a tendency to be scattered and hidden in various elements packed messily into the $$HTMLHead. This event gives you separate options for web and Nor client JavaScript code.

"JavaScript" Events

The events we've looked at so far have some peculiarities attached to them. For example, Windc Title isn't an event so much as it is a bit of computed text, and the WebQuery events don't hold ev related code so much as they point to other code held elsewhere. But now we come to events that look to experienced programmers more like "real" events: The user takes an action and somethi happens.

Most of these events are related to events in the JavaScript document object model. Indeed, a nu ber of them *are* events from the JavaScript model. They've been incorporated into the form, giving a place to put code to be triggered when they happen, both on the Web and in Notes.

Table 19.2 describes the first set of document events and where they work. All are available to w clients, but some are available to Notes clients as well.

TABLE 19.2: THE JAVASCRIPT EVENTS

EVENT	DESCRIPTION	CONTEXT
onHelp	Triggered when the F1 key is pressed in the Notes client or when the onHelp event is triggered in the web browser. In Notes, this event usually uses the command @Command([OpenHelpDocument]).	Web and Notes
onLoad	Triggered after a document is loaded in web applications or opened in the Notes client. This is a good place to perform any type of initialization for a document. This event is similar to the PostOpen event.	Web and Notes

Continued on next pa

EVENT	DESCRIPTION	CONTEXT
onUnload	Triggered after a document is unloaded in web applications or closed in the Notes client. This is a good place to perform any type of cleanup for a document. This event is similar to the QueryClose event.	Web and Notes
onClick	Triggered when the mouse is clicked in the window.	Web only
onDblClick	Triggered when the mouse is double-clicked in the window (this event will yield unpredictable results if you also specify an onClick action because the onClick event will always occur before the onDblClick event).	Web only
onKeyDown, onKeyPress, onKeyUp	Triggered when the user depresses a key (onKeyDown), presses or holds down a key (onKeyPress), and releases a key (onKeyUp).	Web only
onMouseDown, onMouseMove, onMouseOut, onMouseOver, onMouseUp	Triggered when a user depresses the mouse button (onMouseDown), when a user moves the cursor (onMouseMove), when the mouse pointer leaves the client area (onMouseOut), when the mouse pointer moves over the client area from outside the client area (onMouseOver), and when the user releases the mouse button (onMouseUp).	Web only
onReset	Triggered when a user resets a form via a Reset button.	Web only
onSubmit	Triggered when a document is submitted in web applications or when a document is saved in the Notes client. This event is similar to the QuerySave event.	Web and Notes

The UI Events

The remaining events on the form are commonly referred to as the *LotusScript UI events*. This is a bit of a misnomer because you can use formulas, JavaScript, or LotusScript in all but four of the events. However, all of the events are only recognized by the Notes client user interface (UI) and do not apply to web applications.

Why would you need to know about all these events? They can come in quite handy for an application. A good place to initialize a wizard that would guide a user through a specific set of steps would be from one of these events (such as the PostOpen). Knowing about these events is extremely helpful if you ever need to understand or dissect one of the master templates. Table 19.3 explains the UI events.

TABLE 19.3: THE UI EVENTS

EVENT	DESCRIPTION
(Options), (Declarations), Initialize, Terminate	These events only recognize LotusScript. The (Options) and (Declaration events define the options and variables that are global in nature to the for Once set, all events of the form will recognize these settings. The Initializ event is executed only once when the form is opened. The Terminate even also executed only once, when the form is closed.
QueryOpen	This event is triggered when a document is opened in the Notes client, bu it's triggered before the document is actually opened. You may not be able access all of the document fields because the document has not been full initialized.
PostOpen	This event is triggered when a document is opened and fully initialized in t Notes client. All fields are available for querying.
QueryModeChange	This event is triggered before a document is changed to reading or editing mode in the Notes client.
PostModeChange	This event is triggered after a document is changed to reading or editing mode in the Notes client.
PostRecalc	This event is triggered after a document has been refreshed in the Notes client. All of the values on the document have been recalculated.
QuerySave	This event is triggered before a document is saved in the Notes client.
PostSave	This event is triggered after a document is saved in the Notes client.
QuerySend	This event is triggered before a document is sent as mail.
PostSend	This event is triggered after the document is sent as mail.
QueryClose	This event is triggered before a document is closed in the Notes client.

TIP *If you need to declare LotusScript variables and functions/subroutines that are global to all elements of a form use the (Globals) object of the form. The (Globals) section has (Options), (Declarations), Initialize, and Terminal sections of its own.*

Using Form Design Elements

So far, we've been dancing around the various parts of a form and its general attributes, but now we actually going to put things on the form itself. You can think of a Notes form as a big rich-text fie That is, you can put elements on it as though you were typing on it, putting objects into spaces usua defined as lines of text within margins set by rulers. This is not unlike web page design, which is li wise largely defined by lines of text or at least rows and columns of tables; it's different from for design for applications such as Microsoft Access or report writers such as Crystal Reports, where y can place elements to the pixel within a large area.

NOTE *There are always exceptions. In Chapter 25, "Shared Code Objects," we'll discuss the design elements—Layout regions and Navigators—that do allow you to freely lay out certain kinds of design elements.*

Creating Static Text

We'll start with the simplest thing you can put on a form: text. Also referred to as a *label,* static text is not a field, it cannot be called on in formula calculations, and it is not stored in the document. It's just text. Placing static text on a form is as simple as typing. Static text typically explains or helps a user determine what each field should contain.

Let's start shaping our example Recipe form so it can be more useful for the end user. To add static text to the form, follow these steps:

1. Create a blank database named Recipes.

2. In the Design pane, expand the Forms design element in the Design list by clicking the plus (+) sign (this will display all the forms in the Work pane).

3. Create a new form and name it Recipe.

4. With cursor at the top of the form, type **My Favorite Recipe**, which will be used as a title for the form.

5. On the next line (press the Enter key to move the cursor to the next line), type **Name of Recipe:**.

6. Type the following text, each on a separate line: **Recipe Instructions:**, **Comments:**, **Categories:**, **Created By:**, **Created On:**, **Last Updated By:**, and **Last Updated On:**.

When you have finished, your Recipe form should look similar to Figure 19.20. You can see that there is really nothing separating the title and the other static text. We need to make some formatting changes to make the text stand out a bit better. To change the size of the static text, you'll use the Text Properties Box.

FIGURE 19.20

The Recipe Form containing static text

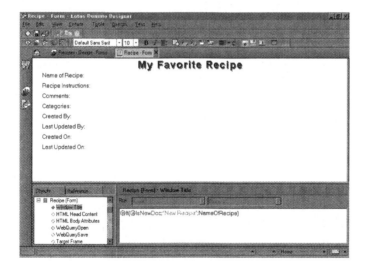

This Box should look familiar; we looked at it briefly in Chapter 3. We'll go over it again here more detail.

THE FONT TAB

You can use the Font tab to change text characteristics such as size, color, style, and font type (guage, an option for rich-text fields in the Notes client, isn't available here), as shown in Figure 19 The fonts you can choose from are the fonts currently installed on your workstation. The choices styles are plain, bold, italic, underline, strikethrough, superscript, subscript, shadow, emboss, a extrude. Note that certain combinations can be selected together, and others cannot; superscript, s script, shadow, emboss, and extrude are mutually exclusive.

FIGURE 19.21

Text Properties
Box, Font tab

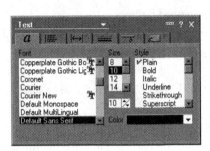

NOTE Be careful when choosing fonts for web applications. If the user doesn't have a font you've chosen on his machin it will not display properly. If you use a default font (for example, Default Sans Serif), the Domino server won't attem to set a font when it renders the form as HTML, except for Default Monospace, which it renders with <TT> tags. you use a nondefault font (say, Helvetica or Geneva), the Domino server will use <FONT> tags with a FAC attribute, using the name of the font you have selected.

For our Recipe form, let's go ahead and change the font characteristics for the static text:

1. Open the Text Properties Box by choosing Text ➤ Text Properties (you can also right-cl the static text and choose Text Properties). Select the Font tab.
2. Highlight the form title, My Favorite Recipe.
3. Choose Arial from the Font list box.
4. Select 18 from the Size list box (you can also type **18** directly in the Size field).
5. Select both the Bold and Shadow options from the Style list box (if you cannot see the Shad option, scroll down in the list box). A check mark will be displayed next to each option y select.
6. From the Color drop-down list box, select Navy.
7. Leave the remaining text labels as they are (the default font options are Default Sans Serif, Plain, and Black).

THE PARAGRAPH ALIGNMENT TAB

The Paragraph Alignment tab lets you format entire paragraphs of text (see Figure 19.22). A paragraph of text can be left justified, right justified, centered, or formatted with equal spacing or no justification. You also have the ability to create hanging indents on the first line of each paragraph. Another handy tool for lists of text is the ability to create list identifiers. There are 10 choices:

- None
- Bullet
- Circle
- Square
- Checkbox
- Number
- Alphabet (uppercase)
- Alphabet (lowercase)
- Roman (uppercase)
- Roman (lowercase)

FIGURE 19.22

Text Properties Box, Paragraph Alignment tab

Each style of list indents its text after a specially shaped bullet character, not unlike the list you've just read. The differences between the lists are in how the bullets appear. The first five use simple shapes. The last five use numbers or letters, incrementing as they go. For example, the first item in a Number list starts with a 1, the second with a 2, and so on.

There are also spacing options available for lines within the paragraph (interline), after the paragraph, and before the paragraph. All of the options on the Paragraph Alignment tab translate quite well in web applications except the spacing options for within, before, and after a paragraph.

To make a few modifications to the paragraph alignment in our Recipe form, follow these steps:

1. Open the Text Properties Box by choosing Text ➤ Text Properties (you can also right-click the static text and choose Text Properties). Select the Paragraph Alignment tab.

2. Place the cursor on the same line as the form title, My Favorite Recipe.

3. Center the alignment of the paragraph by clicking the centered button. Select 11/2 from Spacing drop-down list box.

4. Place the cursor on the Name of Recipe line.

5. Select 11/2 from the Spacing drop-down list box.

6. Place your cursor at the beginning of the Comments line. Select all the text to the botton the form.

7. Select 11/2 from the Spacing drop-down list box (because more than one paragraph is selec this setting will apply to all of them in one shot, saving you a few steps).

THE PARAGRAPH MARGINS TAB

On the Paragraph Margins tab, you can specify both left and right margins for the selected text an absolute size in inches or a relative size in percentage). See Figure 19.23. You can also specify ious individual tab stops and pagination options. Other than the options for margins, these opti do not necessarily work well in web applications. For our Recipe form, we'll just use the default

FIGURE 19.23
Paragraph
Margins tab

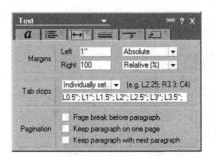

TIP   The relative percentage option for margins works extremely well if you have users who may be using different scree resolutions for your application. Instead of hard-coding a value, you can just specify that the right and left margins ha a gap that is 5 percent of the screen size.

THE PARAGRAPH BORDER TAB

On the Paragraph Border tab, you can specify a border for the paragraph (see Figure 19.24). You specify one of a number of border styles: None, Solid, Double, Dotted, Dashed, Inset, Outset, Ri Groove, Picture, and Image. You can also specify color, thickness on each side (as well as thickn specifically inside or outside of the paragraph border), and presence and size of drop shadow. T feature does not translate to the Web.

FIGURE 19.24

Text Properties
Box, Paragraph
Border tab

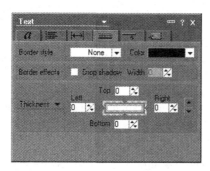

THE PARAGRAPH HIDE-WHEN TAB

We ignored this tab back in Chapter 3, but now that you know formulas, we'll be coming back to this over and over again. The Paragraph Hide-When tab is probably the most widely used tab for most form elements. The Paragraph Hide-When tab will allow you to display or hide text (and, once we get to them, other form elements) based on a broad range of options, as shown in Figure 19.25. The Hide Paragraph From section allows you to hide the text from Notes clients, web browsers, or mobile devices. You can also hide text depending on the mode in which the document is opened (reading, editing, and so on), during printing, during copying, and if the text is embedded in another document. Finally (and this is where the power lies), you can use a formula to hide paragraphs. The options on this tab work equally well in all environments. For our example, leave the default settings (that is, nothing should be selected).

FIGURE 19.25

Text Properties
Box, Paragraph
Hide-When tab

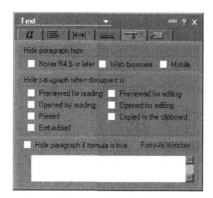

*TIP   If you always want to hide certain text, such as comments about the design of the form, you can select the Notes R4.6 or Later, Web Browsers, and Mobile options. You could also select all the options in the Hide Paragraph When Document Is section or select the Hide Paragraph if Formula Is True option and type **1** for the formula (1 means true in the formula language). However, checking the boxes in the top section gives better performance.*

You've seen bits of the formula language and you know where the hide-when conditions are, so theoret[...] cally we could go on to the next topic, but hiding design elements is an extremely powerful and importan[...] feature, so it bears some added attention.

What makes the hide-when conditions so important and useful is that they allow you to use a single form[...] for multiple purposes. Say you have an application where a document requires different kinds of input a[...] different times. For example, an originator makes a request to check out one of a number of different com[...] pany resources (say, a laptop computer, although she could request a company car, a cell phone, a portabl[...] overhead projector, and so on). She'll indicate the specific type of resource she wants and a date on whic[...] she'll need it. The request will go to a resource manager, who will indicate which specific laptop she get[...] (probably by entering a serial number) and the dates on which the laptop was checked out and returned[...] For the sake of convenience, you want all of this information in one document, but you don't want to giv[...] everybody the ability to change all of the data. The originator shouldn't record when she returns the com[...] puter, and the resource manager shouldn't be able to change the type of resource the originator requested[...]

So how do you manage this? You could use a variety of alternate forms plus some rather extensive machin[...] ery that tells the document which form to use at any given time. You could also use some of the advance[...] design elements we'll get to in the next chapter, such as subforms and controlled-access sections, to red[...] the look of the form.

But all of those alternatives hurt performance, and all the extra design is too much like real work. Th[...] smart way to do it is with hide-when conditions. You can put all the fields you need on a single form, the[...] use hide-when conditions to hide the ones you don't need. For example, let's say the form has a fiel[...] named Status. If the document is in the originator's hands, the Status is New. Once it goes to the resourc[...] manager, the status changes to Submitted. (How does the value change? See the section "Automatin[...] Using Actions" in the next chapter.) Select the area you want only the originator to see and give it this hide[...] when formula:

```
Status != "New"
```

When the value of the Status field isn't New, the selected text (and fields) will vanish. Likewise, you'l[...] select the section only the manager sees and give it this formula:

```
Status != "Submitted"
```

Your form now serves two different functions and all it cost you was two short lines of code.

You should know that hide-when conditions don't make the data *secure*. There are ways for determined user[...] to see and, if they have appropriate permission, edit data protected only by hide-when formulas. However[...] hide-when formulas make display *convenient*, and there's nothing users like more than convenience.

THE PARAGRAPH STYLES TAB

Styles allow you to predefine a specific set of text paragraph options and then save them (see F[...] ure 19.26). You can then apply these styles to various selections of text without having to redef[...] the paragraph options from the Text Properties Box. Depending on which options you ha[...] selected for a style, they may or may not render correctly for web applications. For our Reci[...] example, just leave the defaults.

FIGURE 19.26

Text Properties
Box, Paragraph
Styles tab

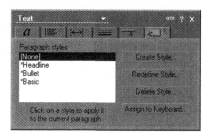

PASS-THRU HTML

When you view a Notes form via the Web, the Domino server takes the form and its contents and renders them into HTML. That is, text in bold face is passed along to the browser with <B> tags, the form title is in the <HEAD> section in <TITLE> tags, and so on. The translation from Notes' rich text to HTML is generally quite good, providing the web user with a close equivalent of what you design in Domino Designer. But sometimes it's not quite what you want. You may want to build a table to your exact specifications. You may want to custom-build certain kinds of links. You may, in a fit of poor judgment, decide to use <BLINK> tags. But how can you custom-build HTML on your forms?

The answer is pass-thru HTML, content that is passed directly to the browser without Notes trying to convert it into equivalent HTML first. There are several methods of creating pass-thru HTML; on a form, you'll do it by setting a text property. To have text passed directly to a browser without being rendered as HTML by the server, select the text (as well as fields and any other content you want marked), and then select Text ➤ Pass-Thru HTML. The text will appear highlighted in gray.

When text is marked as pass-thru HTML, the server makes no attempt to convert any styling on it into HTML. For example, if you have bold text on the form, it will not be marked with <B> tags when it is passed to the web browser. However, because the server isn't trying to convert the content into HTML that matches the appearance of the content on the form, anything already formatted in HTML on the form will be interpreted as HTML in the browser. For example, if you put text in <B> tags on your form, it will appear in boldface in the browser. Figure 19.27 shows a form with pass-thru HTML, and Figure 19.28 shows the same form in a web browser. All text on the form is pass-thru HTML; note that the bold text on the form is *not* bold on the Web.

The full power of pass-thru HTML may not be apparent to you now, but it should become so once you get to fields (see the next section) and computed text (see the next chapter). With data field and computed expressions, you can dynamically build finely tuned HTML on your web pages on the fly, giving you anything from elaborately formatted tables to automatically generated web links driven by human-readable keywords rather than the incomprehensible document IDs Notes uses when it generates links on its own.

FIGURE 19.27
A form with
pass-thru HTML

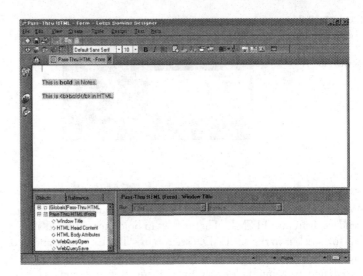

FIGURE 19.28
The same form
viewed through a
web browser

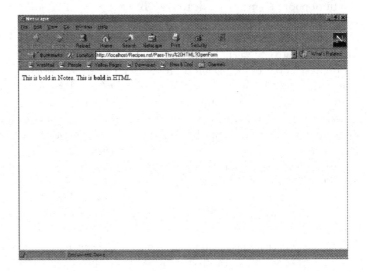

Creating Fields

So far, you've got a grasp of where to put overall instructions for how a form should act (in the fo
events), how to set its properties, and how to put text on it. The next step is to add all the compone
with which the user will actually interact.

When you've seen fields on forms so far, they've been represented by squared brackets or simp
open areas with a cursor. When you get into the form design, however, fields are represented by re
angular boxes bearing the field name and an icon representing the field type. For example, a text fi

has a T icon, a check box field has a check box, and a time zone field has an icon of the earth. Most of the icons should be fairly obvious.

To create a field, position the cursor on your form where you want the field to appear. You can then select Create ➤ Field, right-click the form and select Create Field, or click the Create Field toolbar button. The new field will appear where the cursor is.

When a field is added to a form, the Field Properties Box will automatically display because it is used to configure all fields. Each field has seven tabs for controlling its behavior: Field Info, Control, Advanced, Font, HTML Tag Attributes, Paragraph Alignment, and Hide-When.

All of the tabs except the Control tab are essentially the same for each type of field. The Control tab will be explained in more detail in "Selecting the Field Type" later in this chapter. Because the Font, Alignment, and Hide-When tabs are basically the same as the Font, Alignment, and Hide-When tabs for static text, we'll discuss only the Field Info, Advanced, and HTML Tag Attributes tabs in the following sections.

THE FIELD INFO TAB

The Field Info tab allows you to specify the field's name and type (see Figure 19.29). When a new field is created, the default name is Untitled (Untitled1 if there's already an Untitled, Untitled2 if there's already an Untitled and Untitled1, and so on) and the field type is Text and Editable. Just type in a new name to change it. The name must begin with a letter of the alphabet (but not a number), a period, the underscore symbol (_), or the dollar sign ($). The rest of the name can contain the letters A through Z, the numbers 0 through 9, and the underscore, period, and dollar signs. The name cannot contain any spaces and is limited to 32 characters.

FIGURE 19.29
Field Properties
Box, Field Info tab

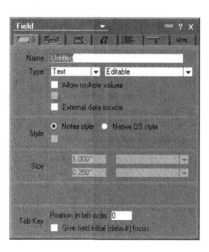

NOTE *You can use periods in field names, but that doesn't necessarily mean you should. If you're going to be programming with LotusScript or JavaScript, you'll be using a lot of periods to refer to object properties and methods anyway, so the additional periods might just be confusing.*

Field Type

To change the field type, select a type from the first drop-down list box (the field types will b
described in "Selecting the Field Type" later in this chapter). The second drop-down list box t
the right is a bit different. It determines if the field is editable by the user or automatically cal
lated by the Notes system. There are five different values for this field, although you'll usually or
see the first four:

Editable   When a field is marked as Editable on a form, the user can modify its contents. Th
are also three events you can use to help the user populate the data-entry field (the events are lis
in the Objects tab of the programmer's pane): Default Value, which provides an initial value (s
as the user's name) that the user can change; Input Translation, which modifies the contents of
field after the user is finished to aid in standardization (such as changing a name to the prop
case); and Input Validation, which checks the contents of the field to ensure that the data is in
correctly and issues an error message if it's not.

Computed   The data is automatically populated in a computed field. Each computed field
a Value event that can be populated by using a formula to supply a value. Computed fields a
recalculated when a document is created, refreshed, or saved.

Computed for Display   This is another type of computed field, but it is recalculated when a do
ment is opened or refreshed. The contents of fields of this type are never saved to the actual docum

Computed When Composed   This is also a computed field, but it is only calculated once w
a document is created. Unlike the Computed for Display field, the contents within this field t
are saved to the actual document and are not refreshed. Use this type of field to preserve the in
mation about a document when it is created (such as the author or the data and time the docum
was created). You can change the value of Computed When Composed fields with formulas a
other program code, so you can also use this type of field to store values that you want to chai
but that you don't want the user to be able to change directly.

Literalize Fields   This field type is only available for the Formula field, which is discussed :
more detail in "The Formula Field" later in this chapter

> **WARNING**   *Because the value for a Computed for Display field is not actually saved to the document, the field canne
> be used in a view.*

The next two options are Allow Multiple Values and Compute After Validation. If Allow Multi
Values is selected, a field can contain more than one value (this option may be automatically selected :
some types of fields and not allowed for others), and if Compute After Validation is selected, the va
of a computed field is recomputed after all the validation for a form is complete.

The External Data Source option allows you to use data from external databases for which yo
have set up Data Connection Resources. If you select this option, a section will appear at the botto
of the page, allowing you to link the field to a field in the external data source.

Style

You can also select the style for your fields on the Field Info tab. There are two choices available.

Notes Style   When this option is selected and a document is opened in editing mode, a field marked by brackets will appear on the form. The size of a field is not restricted with this style. As the user types, the field grows. If this option is selected, the Size option on the tab will be gray.

Native OS Style   This option allows you to create an outlined box for a field. You can select the height and width in the Size selection area. For Width, you can set an absolute width in inches, a width in characters, or a percentage of the document's width. For height, you can select a fixed height, Dynamic height (the field will expand up to three rows and show a vertical scroll bar thereafter), or Proportional (the field does not expand, but will show a vertical scroll bar if the content goes beyond the visible area). This option is not available for certain field types (dialog lists, check boxes, radio buttons, list boxes, combo boxes, and rich-text fields), and web applications ignore this option altogether. If you select this option, you may also chose to align the bottom of the control with the paragraph baseline.

You may notice that there is a gap on the tab between the Size and the Tab Key sections. If you select a field type of rich text, the Web Access section will appear. However, this doesn't mean that other fields cannot be accessed via the Web; they all can. Rich-text fields simply have different options. With this section, you can specify how a rich-text or rich-text lite field will be displayed on the Web. You have the option of using native HTML or a Java applet for editing a rich-text field within a web application or, with the Best Fit option, letting the Domino server decide which to use based on the client's operating system. The Java applet is a powerful feature that allows the user to create formatted text using the following properties:

- Bold, italics, underline
- Single-level indent
- Ordered and unordered lists
- Color selection
- Size and font selection
- URL link hotspots

Figure 19.30 displays an example of the Java applet in a web browser.

The last selection on the Field Info tab is the tabbing order for the fields and which field will get the default focus when a form is first displayed. By default, the field closest to the top-left of the form gets focus, and hitting the Tab key moves the cursor to the left. However, by setting tab order numbers, you can change that order. If you assign numbers, hitting the Tab key will move the cursor to the field with the next higher number, regardless of where it is on the form. You could use this to have Tab move the cursor down columns in a table layout rather than across rows or, if you're feeling perverse, start at the bottom of a form and move the cursor up toward the top. This option will translate to the Web.

FIGURE 19.30

The rich-text field
Java applet for the
Main Topic form
as shown in a web
browser

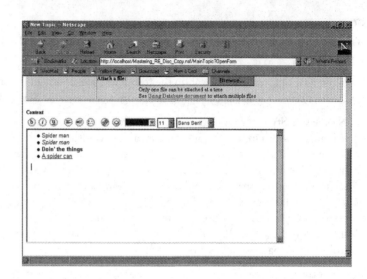

THE ADVANCED TAB

The Advanced tab allows you to specify a help message, field hint, multivalue field options, and se
rity options for the text data field, as shown in Figure 19.31. If a help message has been entered
the user, the message will display across the bottom of the screen when the user enters the field. T
field hint text pops up when the user moves the mouse over the field. For a multivalue field, you h
the option of deciding which data delimiters to use when data is input and displayed. Both the S
arate Values When User Enters and the Display Separate Values With options allow a space, com
semicolon, new line, or blank line to be used as a delimiter. The difference between the two selectic
is that multiple input delimiters can be selected, whereas only one output delimiter can be used. T
Security Options allow you to specify encryption options for the field. Selecting Security Options
entering a help message or field hint have no effect on a web application.

FIGURE 19.31

Field Properties
Box, Advanced tab

NOTE *The field hint text message will not be visible to users unless they are in editing mode and the Field Help option is selected from the View ➤ Show menu.*

THE HTML TAG ATTRIBUTES TAB

The HTML Tag Attributes tab (see Figure 19.32) allows you to assign various HTML tag values, which are then accessible via JavaScript or may provide hooks into HTML 4 specifications. The values for these tags only work when the application is viewed with a web browser. If you set these values and view the application in the Notes client, nothing will happen.

FIGURE 19.32
HTML Tag
Attributes Tab

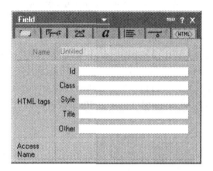

Name

With this option, you can assign the name used by JavaScript when referencing the field element. By default, any design element that already has a name, such as a field, will be automatically populated and cannot be changed. For design elements that do not have a name, such as an image, you can enter a name to be referenced in the JavaScript code.

ID

With this option, you can assign an ID attribute to an element. This can be used in conjunction with Cascading Style Sheets (CSS) and can be handy for use with CSS resources.

Class

With this option, you can classify an object. Again, this is intended for use with CSS.

Style

You can specify a specific style for the object. For example, if you want the text for a field to be blue, type **color:blue** in the Style field.

Title

The Title option allows you to store a prompt for the object.

You can type in additional HTML tag attributes for the object. These attributes must be valid HTML code, such as SIZE=10 and MAXLENGTH=8. You can also specify these attributes in the HT? Body Attributes event for a field.

Adding Fields to Your Form

Now that we have gone over the basics for a field, let's return to our Recipe form and see how it wo in practice. With the Recipe form open in Designer, we need to add a field for each one of the lal entered earlier in the chapter (except for the form title, of course). To add fields to the Recipe fo just follow these steps:

1. Place the cursor at the end of the Name of Recipe label. Press the spacebar once and se Create ➤ Field (there are a few other methods we'll be using through this example; it does actually matter which one you choose, but you should try all of them to see which one y find most convenient). This will automatically create an editable text field called Untitled. Basics tab should display by default. Change the name of the field by entering **NameOfRec** in the Name field.

2. Now create two more text fields. Place your cursor at the end of the Created By label. Pr the spacebar once, right-click, and select Create Field from the pop-up menu. Change the na of the field to **CreatedBy**. Change the type of field in the second drop-down list box fron Editable to Computed When Composed. Because this field is computed, you also need enter a value for the field to contain. To do so, select the Value event in the Objects tab of programmer's pane. In the script area, type **@Name([CN];@UserName)**. This will popul the CreatedBy field with the name of user who initially creates this document.

3. To create the next text field, place your cursor at the end of the Last Updated By label. Pre the spacebar once and click the Insert Field button on the toolbar. Change the name of tl field to **LastUpdatedBy**. Change the type of field in the second drop-down list box fron Editable to Computed for Display (we don't need to save this value because it is alrea saved in the $UpdatedBy field). Again, you will need to add a formula for the Value ever Enter **@Name([CN];@Subset($UpdatedBy;-1))** in the Value event of the script area f the field. The formula will grab the last entry in the $UpdatedBy field and place it in thi field (the $UpdatedBy field contains a list of all those who update the document).

4. We now need to add two date/time field types to the form. Place your cursor at the end of the C ated On label. Press the spacebar once and create a new field using whichever of the three metho with which you feel most comfortable. Change the name of the field to **CreatedDateTime**. Chan the field type to Date/Time in the first Type drop-down list box. In the second drop-down list b change the field type from Editable to Computed for Display; this is another value that we c already get by other means, so we don't need to make this a Computed or Computed When Cc posed. Add the formula **@Created** to the Value event for the field. This will place the date and ti the document was initially created in the CreatedDateTime field.

5. To create the next field, place your cursor at the end of the Last Updated On label. Press the spacebar once and create yet another field. Change the name of the field to **LastUpdatedOn**. Change the field type to Date/Time in the first Type drop-down list box. In the second drop-down list box, change the field type from Editable to Computed for Display. Add the formula **@Modified** to the Value event for the field. This will place the date and time that the document was last modified in the LastUpdatedOn field.

6. Place your cursor after Categories, press the spacebar, and create another field. Change the name of the field to Categories. Change the field type to Dialog List and check the Allow Multiple values option. Next, go to the Control tab and check the Allow Values Not in List option. Initially, there will be no categories available to assign to documents, but users can create categories as they go and reuse existing ones as they see fit.

7. The remaining two fields to be added are rich-text fields. Place your cursor at the end of the Recipe Instructions label. Press the Enter key so that your cursor ends up on the line underneath the label. Choose Create ➤ Field. Change the name of the field to **RecipeInstructions**. Change the field type to Rich Text in the first Type drop-down list box. In the Web Access section, select Using Java Applet from the Display drop-down list box. Select the Alignment tab. In the Spacing section, select 11/2 from the Below drop-down list box.

8. For the final field, place your cursor at the end of the Comments label. Press the Enter key so that your cursor ends up on the line underneath the label. Choose Create ➤ Field. Change the name of the field to **Comments**. Change the field type to Rich Text in the first Type drop-down list box. In the Web Access section, select Using Java Applet from the Display drop-down list box.

9. Place your cursor back on the same line as the Comments label. From the Alignment tab, select Single from the Below drop-down list box.

When you have finished adding all your fields, your form should look like the one shown in Figure 19.33. Make sure you save your new form and, if you want, preview it in the Notes client.

FIGURE 19.33
The Recipe form with fields

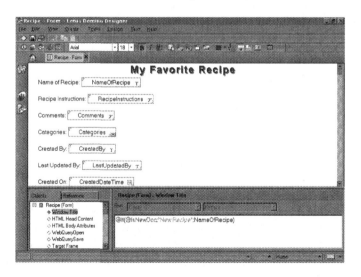

Selecting the Field Type

The preceding section explained the common properties available for a field. For each type of field there are also some unique properties, which we'll now explain in detail.

When you create a field on a form, you are defining the type of data a user can save to the document. As mentioned earlier, the form that contains the fields is nothing more than a *template* for data. If you use a text field called Birthdate on one form and then use a date/time field called Birthdate on another form, Notes will try to grab the data assigned to the Birthdate field when the document is opened. Depending on which form is used, the user may not get the results they expect. It's up to you, the developer, to ensure that the proper field type is used for each form.

THE TEXT FIELD

A user can type any letters, numbers, punctuation, and spaces into a text data field. End users can format data placed in a text field. Whatever you specify as the format will remain constant. In other words, if you specify bold, all the text will be bold when displayed in the form. However, formatting is not stored, only the text itself. If you format a field as bold in one form and as italic in another, text that will appear bold as you enter it in the first form will appear italic if you view it in the second. Each text field is also limited to only 64KB of data.

The text data field has one option if you've selected to display the field in Notes style: Show Field Delimiters. With this option selected, Notes will display the familiar squared brackets. If not, there will be no visible indication of where the field is on the form when the user goes to enter data. If you have chosen the Native OS Style, there are two options: Allow Multiple Lines, which determines whether multiple lines of data will be displayed simultaneously if the field is tall enough, and Border Style, which governs how the field is outlined.

THE DATE/TIME FIELD

The date/time field displays date and/or time information in many different formats. As you can with other fields, you can allow the user to enter the data into a date/time field or allow the field be computed (to show today's date, for example). Here are some of the various formats that can used in a date/time field:

- 1/31
- 1/31/98
- 1/31/1998
- Today
- 1/31/1998 11:00 PM
- 11:00 PM
- 11:00:01 PM

You use the Control tab to format the date/time field. There are an extremely large number of possibilities for formatting the data, as shown in Figure 19.34. One feature in the On Display section of the tab does help you determine the look and feel for your date/time field. The Use Preference From drop-down list box contains two choices: User Setting and Custom. The User Setting option will use the date/time format from the operating system on the user's machine for formatting. Selecting the Custom option will allow you to mix and match how you would like the date/time to display.

FIGURE 19.34

The various formats for a Notes date/time field

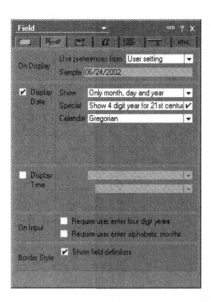

Directly beneath the Use Preferences From drop-down list box is the Sample field. This field directly reflects any changes you make to any of the options on the tab. For example, if you disable the Display Time option, the Sample field will change from displaying both the date and time to displaying just the date. This feature will help you quickly narrow down which options look best for your application.

Depending on how you want to use the date/time field, you can choose to show either a date or time or you can show both. If you display a date, you have the option of displaying a wide range of date information. For example, you could show day, month, and year; month and year; weekday; and a variety of other combinations. You can set a number of subsidiary options: Use a four-digit year for the 21st century, display *Today* for the current date, or show the year only if the date isn't for the current year. You can also choose between the Gregorian and Hijri calendars. If you display time information, you can choose between displaying various combinations of hours, minutes, and seconds, and you can choose how to treat the local time zone.

One important aspect to keep in mind when implementing a date/time field is whether to use the Notes style or Native OS Style for the field. If the Native OS Style is used, either a Date or Time Picker control element will be displayed next to the field. The former is a pop-up calendar; the latter is a slider allowing the user to pick a time. These tools allow the user to select the value instead of having to type it in. The Date and Time Pickers are not active for web applications.

THE NUMBER FIELD

The number field type is typically used for any type of numeric data. The field allows you quite a bit of flexibility in formatting your data; you can use decimal numbers, percentages, scientific display, and currency. Notes can store numbers from $2.225E-308$ to $1.798E-308$ with 14-digit accuracy.

The Control tab allows you to select the type of numeric data and the format to apply to th̶ numeric field. As shown in Figure 19.35, the formats allowed are Decimal, Percent, Scientific, a̶ Currency. Based on your selection, options on the tab may be grayed out. You can select the pr̶ ences to use for the decimal separator, the thousands separator, and currency symbols by selecti̶ Custom from the Use Preferences From drop-down list. You can select a fixed number of decir̶ places or allow it to vary for all the numeric types except Scientific. You can also use parentheses negative numbers and a thousands separator (the Scientific format does not use the latter). If y̶ select Currency, you have the option of defining the currency indicator. You can place the indica̶ before or after the numbers. You also have the option of putting a space between the indicator a̶ the numbers. All of the numeric types render on the Web.

FIGURE 19.35

The Control tab for
the number field

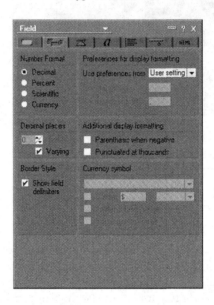

THE KEYWORD FIELDS

Keyword is a pre-Notes Release 5 term for a special field type that displays a list of choices to the us̶ Since Notes 5, the keyword field is gone and replaced by several different kinds of fields:

- Dialog list
- Check box
- Radio button
- List box
- Combo box

Notes regards these fields as separate field types, but they do have a great many things in comm̶ so we'll continue to refer to them under the keyword rubric. Each field type presents a text list of v̶ ues from which the user can select at least one entry. For many applications, it is much easier on t̶ user to select from a list rather than having to remember the value and type it in, and it can make the developer's task easier if she can be assured of a limited set of choices for a given field. Displaying a list will also eliminate a lot of potential data entry errors. In some cases, more than one entry can be selected from a keyword field, and sometimes the user can type in a value that is not in the selection list. Table 19.4 describes each keyword type.

TABLE 19.4: DESCRIPTION OF KEYWORD ENTRIES

FIELD TYPE	DESCRIPTION	ADD NEW VALUES?*	MULTIPLE VALUES?
Dialog list	Presents a list of choices in a dialog box. The user can display the list by clicking the helper button or by pressing the Enter key. To select an entry, the user can either click the entry or press the spacebar. The user can add new values by typing them in the space provided.	Yes	Yes
Check box	Presents a list of choices in the check box format. To select an entry, the user can click the entry or press the spacebar. Multiple items can be selected.	No	Yes
Radio button	Presents a list of choices in the radio button format. To select an entry, the user can click the entry or press the spacebar. Multiple items cannot be selected.	No	No
List box	Presents a list of choices in an expanded list box (shows more than one entry at a time). To select an entry, the user can either click the entry or press the spacebar.	No	Yes
Combo box	Presents a drop-down list box. To select an entry, the user can click the entry or scroll through the list until the desired entry is found.	Yes	No

This option does not work as expected when used in web applications.

One thing all the keyword fields have in common is their ability to display one or more entries. This can be accomplished in various ways, depending on the type of keyword field. There are essentially five different ways to display data in a keyword field (see Table 19.5). The data choice is an option displayed on the Control tab for the keyword field. The field types are dialog list (DL), check box (CH), radio button (R), list box (L), and combo box (C). Depending on the type of field, the choices available may vary.

TABLE 19.5: KEYWORD DATA CHOICES

DATA CHOICE	DESCRIPTION	DL	CH	R	L	
Enter Choices (One per Line)	Allows you to enter a fixed number of choices for selection. For example, you can enter Yes and No.	✓	✓	✓	✓	✓
Use Formula for Choices	Allows you to enter a formula to display a list of choices. This option will allow you to create a "dynamic" set of choices and is extremely useful. For example, use @DBColumn to display a list of values from a column in a view. Be careful when using this option because only 64KB of data can be returned from a function.	✓	✓	✓	✓	✓
Use Address Dialog for Choices	This selection displays the Address dialog box to the end user. This is similar to the dialog box that is used for addressing mail. Allows the user to select names and groups for the entry.	✓				✓
Use Access Control List for Choices	This selection displays a dialog box with the Access Control List entries from the current database.	✓				✓
Use View Dialog for Choices	This selection allows you to select a view to be used for the contents of the keyword field. You have the option of selecting which database, view, and column to be used for the data. This will display the entire view in a dialog box but only return the data from the column number you select.	✓				✓

Next, let's look at the Control tab in which you can select the various options for each field type. Keep in mind that certain options will be grayed out depending on the type of field selected. Also note that you don't have the option of selecting the style for the field. The Notes and Native OS Style options are not accessible on the Field Info tab.

NOTE   *When keyword fields are used in a web application, they do not render the same as in the Notes client. A combo box will display just like the dialog list field. One area to keep in mind is allowing values to be added in the list. When displayed on the Web, the field loses all the keyword features and becomes an entry field.*

The Control tabs for keyword-type fields are essentially identical. The biggest differences are that some have a few check box options not available to others. The Control tab allows you to control not only the contents of the keyword field but also its look and feel. From the Display section, you can select whether the field will have field delimiters. This section will change for both the check box and radio button fields and allow you to select the border style and number of columns to display. The Choices section allows you to decide what data to display to the user. You can select from the choices described in Table 19.5. The Options section allows you to fine-tune the field for the user. From this section, you can allow a user to add entries that aren't in the selection list, display the entry helper button, or refresh the values of the list. Each option is dependent on the field type, so you'll need to play around with them a bit.

THE RICH-TEXT AND RICH-TEXT LITE FIELDS

The rich-text field is similar to the text field type. The biggest difference is that a rich-text field will allow the user to format the data and input just about any type of data, including attachments and graphics. This free-form field is extremely useful because it allows users to type in as much data as they need. There is not a limit on the size of this type of field. The rich-text lite field is essentially the same as a rich-text field, except that it has a helper button, allowing the user to import nontext content easily.

Rich-text fields are somewhat more limited in how they can be computed. They may be either Editable or Computed, not Computed for Display or Computed When Composed. Rich-text lite fields may only be Editable.

The options are pretty limited for a rich-text field. You can specify whether the field will have delimiters and also whether pressing the Tab key will insert a tab or move the cursor to the next field (some users find inserting the tab annoying and would rather move to the next field). The Store Contents as HTML and MIME option allows you to store the data in native HTML or MIME format. In older releases of Notes, a rich-text field was always saved in a rich-text format composed of composite data (CD) records. You can select this option and, for example, have the bolded text *Hello World* saved as <B>Hello World</B>.

Rich-text lite fields have a slightly different set of options. You can select the list of helper buttons available with the Control tab (see Figure 19.36).

FIGURE 19.36

The Control tab
for a rich-text lite
field

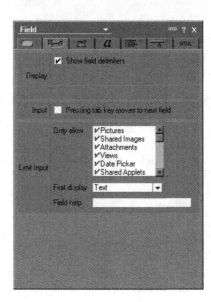

THE AUTHORS FIELD

The authors field identifies users, groups, and roles that have access to edit the document. This fie
is used in conjunction with other database security features. Author-level access to a database does
itself allow a user to edit documents. A user with Author-level access can only edit documents
which he is included in an authors field. To use an authors field, list those individuals who can e
the document in the field and grant them Author access to the database. Alternatively, you may
groups or roles in the field. If a user belongs to the group or has been assigned the role and F
Author-level access either individually or through group membership, he will be able to edit the d
ument. For those individuals with Editor access or greater, the authors field does not apply; anyc
with Editor-level access or better can edit any document. Likewise, users with Reader-level access
below will be unable to edit any document even if they appear in an authors field.

The Control tab for the authors field is similar to the Control tab for the keyword field. The ma
difference is in the Choices section. You have the option of allowing the user to select from an addr
book dialog box, an ACL dialog box, or a view dialog box. There is also a choice labeled None, b
that forces the user to type in the names, so you should avoid using it unless the authors field is cc
puted. If an authors field has a typo in it, it could block access to the original creator. Also note th
because an authors field can display a dialog box, the rules described for keyword fields also app
when an authors field is rendered for a web application. A dialog box will render correctly in th
Notes client, but it won't in a web application.

WARNING   *When you use authors fields, it is a good idea to always include the original authors' names or they won*
be able to edit the documents they created.

THE NAMES FIELD

The names field type is similar to the authors field type except a names field has nothing to do with a document's security. One other difference is how the name is displayed. The names field will convert the Notes hierarchical format to a more abbreviated form. For example, if a Notes name is CN=Hamid al-Hajj/OU=Admins/O=EasternOil, the names field would render it as Hamid al-Hajj/Admins/EasternOil. Other than that, all the options are the same. Why would you use this field type? There may be cases where you want a user to select a name or group of names for the application but not for security reasons. A good example would be for mailing a document. The user can select to whom the document should be sent.

THE READERS FIELD

A readers field identifies users, groups, and roles that have access to read the document. This field is also used in conjunction with the database security. List the individuals who can read the document in the readers field and grant them at least Reader access to the database. You can name each author individually, within a group, or through an ACL role. In either case, if the person with Reader ACL access is not listed in the field, they will not be able to read the document.

Don't get this field type confused with an authors field. Users who aren't defined in the readers field won't be able to read the document regardless of what level of access they have in the ACL. This includes servers and database managers. This is a major difference between the two field types and a source of a lot of confusion. It is important you make sure a role or group is always placed into the readers field. There is nothing worse than having Manager access to a database yet not being able to read a document.

WARNING   *Readers and authors fields work differently, so it's worth repeating: Authors fields control editing rights only for users with Author-level access to the database. Readers fields control the ability to read documents for everybody, no matter what level of access they have to the database.*

THE PASSWORD FIELD

The password field type is used for privacy. Whenever a character is typed into this field, an asterisk will be displayed. Typically, this field type is used for typing in a password. The data you enter is stored as plain text.

WARNING   *The contents of a password field are not inherently secure. Anyone can use the Document Properties Box to view the contents of the field. If you need the field contents to be secure, encrypt the field.*

THE FORMULA FIELD

The formula field type is specifically for populating a subscription list and is outside the scope of this book. For more information, refer to the Notes help database.

THE TIME ZONE FIELD

The time zone field provides a drop-down list, letting the user select a desired time zone.

THE COLOR FIELD

The color field allows the user to select a color. In the Notes client, the field provides a pop-up co
palette (which can be switched between a Notes palette and a web palette) and sliders that can be u
to set a custom RGB color, as shown in Figure 19.37. The color is saved as an eight-digit hexadeci
value.

FIGURE 19.37
The color field
palette

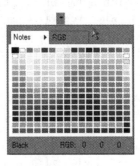

Testing Your Form

Once you've created your form, you need to test it to see if it actually does what you think it will.
see the various ways to test a form, open the Recipe form you created. Domino Designer includes a
options called *preview icons* in the upper-right corner of the window. Depending on your workstation c
figuration, you could have quite a few icons displayed, as shown here. In this case, we have Notes a
three web browsers: Notes as a web browser, Internet Explorer, and Netscape Navigator (the first t
ton, of course, displays the Properties box).

With the Recipe form displayed in Designer, click the Notes preview icon to display the Reci
form within the Notes client environment. You can interact and test the form to see how it looks a
performs. You can also test the form in the Notes client by choosing Design ➢ Preview in Note

Switch back to Domino Designer, and once there, click the Notes Browser preview icon. This v
render the Recipe document in the Notes browser unless you have configured your Location do
ment to use Notes with Internet Explorer. The remaining Internet Explorer and Navigator previ
icons will render the Recipe form in Internet Explorer and Navigator, respectively. Figure 19.3
shows the Recipe form displayed in Netscape Navigator. You can also test the form in a browser
choosing Design ➢ Preview in Web Browser and selecting the web browser of your choice.

As you can see, testing from Domino Designer is quite easy. You can now render the form in ea
environment to see how it looks and acts. Because Domino Designer can also act as a web server
a limited way, you can do all of your testing for both the Notes client and web applications from yo
local workstation.

WARNING *Designer can serve up Notes elements as web pages, but you won't be able to test security with it. For tha*
you'll need to test on a Domino server.

FIGURE 19.38

Testing the
Recipe form in the
Netscape browser

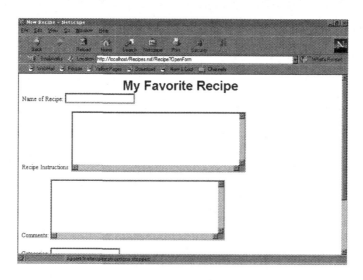

Summary

In this chapter, you learned how to create a form, which is the interface in which the end users create documents. A form is also used to create the document hierarchy, or parent-child relationship, commonly referred to as a response document. You learned about the form properties and also about all the events that make up a form. These events establish the backbone for developing a powerful Notes application for either the Notes client or the Web. You also learned about the types of data fields and when to use the properties for each field type. Finally, we discussed how to actually test a form in both the Notes client and web environments.

In the next chapter, we'll continue working with forms, but we'll take them a bit further by using more advanced design elements.

Chapter 20

Advanced Form Design

NOW THAT YOU KNOW how to put static text and fields on a form, it's time to get down to the really powerful stuff. In the preceding chapter, the forms were pretty straightforward, boring, and inflexible. You placed the fields on a form and that was about it. In this chapter, you'll learn how to jazz them up and make them a bit more flexible and user friendly.

All of the examples we'll use for this chapter are in the Recipe database. We'll enhance the basic forms you developed in Chapter 19, "Basic Form Design," by using some of the more advanced features, such as subforms, sections, layout regions, tables, actions hotspots, and graphics. We'll also explain how using each of these advanced features can affect a web-based application.

- ◆ Using tables
- ◆ Adding graphics
- ◆ Adding sections
- ◆ Creating layout regions
- ◆ Creating layers
- ◆ Using Actions and hotspots for automation

Working with Tables

Tables, as any web designer knows, are fundamentally important for arranging information on a page. Tables are typically used in Notes for aligning fields and labels or summarizing data. You can think of a table as a spreadsheet with a set number of rows and columns. You can place anything you want in any row or any column, such as text labels, fields, and even another table.

TIP *You can nest tables, putting a table inside a cell of another table, up to eight deep.*

The most common use of tables in Notes is aligning labels and fields on a form. Because you ▪ not place elements on a Notes form with pixel-precise layout you need to use a table to impose a ▪ inite starting position and ending position. Placing fields in a table column will also ensure that d stays within the boundaries of the table cell instead of wrapping over the width of the entire form (▪ only applies to Notes style fields because the operating system–style fields are fixed in nature).

Choosing a Table Type

Creating a table is a bit more involved than in previous Notes releases. You now have to choose the t ▪ of table you would like to create. There are five basic table designs/types: basic, tabbed, animated, ▪ tioned, and programmed. When you create a table, you choose the type via the Create Table dialog b ▪ as shown in Figure 20.1.

FIGURE 20.1

The Create Table dialog box, where you select the type of table to create

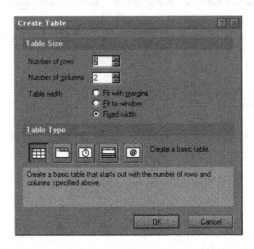

Click the buttons under Table Type to choose from one of the following:

Basic   The basic table has a typical row and column layout. You define the number of ro▪ and columns to display and a spreadsheet-like grid is created, allowing you to begin enterin▪ your information.

Tabbed   The tabbed table is also defined by rows and columns, but each row is translated to a t▪ This creates a more compact interface that allows groups of fields to be placed underneath a tab a▪ hidden from the user until that tab is selected.

Animated   The animated table is a special type of table that scrolls through each of its rows▪ based on some time interval.

Captioned   The captioned table allows the user to collapse and expand sections of the table ▪ clicking on captioned headers. Each row is a different section within the captioned structure.

Programmed   The programmed table allows you to display specific rows in a table based on t▪ value of a field. You also have the option of displaying each row with a tab (similar to the tabbed tab▪

When you create a table, you determine the number of rows and columns the table should contain, decide if you want to use a fixed width, and click the OK button. Don't worry if you make a mistake. Once the table is created, all the options can be changed after the fact using the Table Properties Box.

For all the table examples, we will again use the Recipe form we've been using so far. As we make modifications, we will make a copy of the existing form and start working from there. This will alleviate the need to create the fields, window title, and so on all over again. Every time the instructions ask you to make a copy of the Recipe form, follow these steps:

1. Click the form you want to copy.

2. Choose Edit ➢ Copy and then Edit ➢ Paste (you can also right-click, choose Copy, right-click again, and choose Paste). This will create a new copy of the form named Copy of Recipe (or, if there's already a Copy of Recipe form, Another Copy of Recipe).

Creating a Basic Table

We mentioned earlier that the Recipe form didn't look very good. The fields are staggered, which gives the form an unpolished look. To eliminate this problem, you are going to insert a basic table; each row in the table will contain one of the labels and its corresponding field. You will also create two columns and place the label into one column and the field into another to align them all on a common axis.

To add a table to the form, follow these steps:

1. Create a copy of the Recipe form.

2. Open the Recipe copy and change the name of the form to Recipe Using Basic Table | RecipeSTable. You can also update the comments in the Form Properties box to reflect this name change.

3. Place the cursor on the blank line between the form title and the first label/field.

4. Choose Create ➢ Table. Click the basic table button and make sure the value in the Rows field is 8 and the value in the Columns field is 2. Click the OK button and the table will be inserted on the form.

5. Cut and paste the text labels for each field into the first column of the table. Place them in order, each on a separate row. For example, *Name of Recipe:* should be in row 1, column 1. *Recipe Instructions:* should be in row 2, column 1. Do this for each text label.

6. Cut and paste the fields into the second column of the table, each on the same row as its corresponding text label. For example, the NameOfRecipe field should be on the same row as the *Name of Recipe:* text (but not the same column). When you complete all the fields, the form should look similar to Figure 20.2.

You may look at this form and think that it doesn't look much better than it did before, but we're not yet finished with the table. There are a lot of properties that can be associated to a table from the Table Properties Box—properties that will greatly influence how the table currently looks. Let's take a look at some of these properties. To open the Properties Box for a table, place the cursor inside the table and choose Table ➢ Table Properties (you can also right-click in the table and choose Table Properties).

FIGURE 20.2

The Recipe Using
Basic Table form with
the table inserted

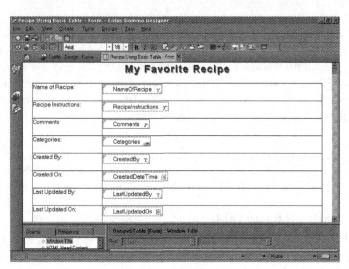

EXPLORING THE TABLE LAYOUT PROPERTIES

Select the Table Layout tab to customize the size and position of both the table and the cells with
the table. You can also position the text within each cell. The Table Layout tab allows you to size a
position the table and table cells (see Figure 20.3).

FIGURE 20.3

The Table Layout
tab in the Table
Properties Box

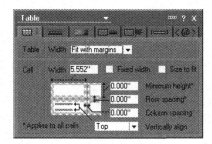

The Table Section

In the Table section, you can choose how to size your table. There are three possible selections in t
Width drop-down box:

Fit with Margins Selecting this option will automatically set the table width so the dimension
will fit *inside* the current size of the window. We prefer this option in most situations because you c
maximize the use of screen real estate and you don't have to worry about the user's screen resoluti

Fixed Width   The Fixed Width option allows you to set the size of the table. When you select this option, you will have the option of using the Position drop-down list box to set the table position (Left, Right, and Center).

Fit to Window   If you select the Fit to Window option, the table width will be automatically set so the dimensions will be the *same* as the current size of the window.

The Cell Section

The Cell section of the Table Layout tab allows you to set various properties for the cells within the table. The Width property allows you to set how wide an individual cell should be. If you have a fixed-width table, this will affect the overall width of the table. This setting only affects the selected cell. If you select either the Fit with Margins or Fit to Window option in the Table section, the Fixed Width check box will display. If you select it, you can have one or more cells that do not resize but remain fixed (even if other cells of the table change as the window size changes). The Size to Fit check box automatically makes the cell grow or shrink to fit any text it contains.

The remaining table cell size features—Minimum Height, Row Spacing, and Column Spacing—are self-explanatory. Note, however, the asterisk (*) next to each label. It signifies that a change to any three of these fields will affect *all* cells of the table. This is different from the other cell properties, which change on a cell-by-cell basis.

The last property, Vertically Align, affects the text contained within a cell. You can align the text vertically at the top, center, or bottom of each cell.

USING THE TABLE LAYOUT PROPERTIES

With the Recipe **Using Basic Table** form open in the Designer workspace, display the Table Properties Box and click the Table Layout tab. Then follow these steps to use some of the table layout options to clean up our table:

1. From the Table Width drop-down list box, select Fit with Margins.
2. With the cursor placed in the first column of the table, check the Fixed Width check box and adjust the Cell Width value to 1.5 inches. This will ensure that the first column of the table will always be 1.5 inches while the second column expands to fill the window.

WARNING   *If you decide to use a fixed-width column, make sure you select the Fixed Width check box before you adjust the cell width. Failure to do so will result in an incorrect cell width setting.*

3. Enter **0.050** for the Row Spacing option.
4. Enter **0.020** for the Column Spacing option.
5. Select all the cells in the first column from menu item **Table ➤ Table Select ➤ Columns especially if the table runs off the screen** and right-justify the text by choosing Text ➤ Align Paragraph ➤ Right.
6. Select the NameOfRecipe field, display the Field Properties Box, and change from the Native OS style to the Notes style (it will look better in this context).

When you have made the changes, your table should look similar to Figure 20.4. By using a sim table, you have been able to give your form a bit more structure. It's not perfect, but the text lab and fields form a nice even vertical line, which makes it easier for the end user to read the form. T technique works well for applications that are to be used in the Notes client and also on the W Now let's see if we can do something with those grid lines.

FIGURE 20.4
The Recipe Using
Basic Table form
after the table layout
properties are set

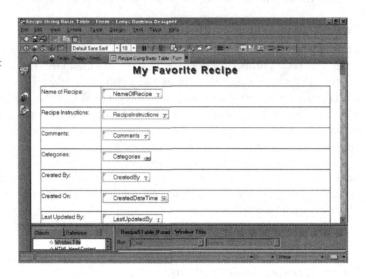

SETTING THE CELL BORDERS PROPERTIES

In the Cell Borders tab, you can select both the border style and the thickness for each cell in the ta (see Figure 20.5).

NOTE   *Web applications cannot display partial cell borders. If one cell has a border, all the cells and the entire table wi have borders.*

FIGURE 20.5
The Cell Borders
tab of the Table
Properties Box

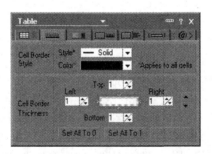

EXPLORING THE CELL BORDER STYLE SECTION

The Cell Border Style section allows you to select one of three styles of borders:

Solid   The Solid style is a plain simple line that surrounds the borders of the cell.

Ridge   The Ridge style gives a 3D appearance that simulates a wall being raised off the page.

Groove   The Groove style gives a 3D appearance that simulates a small trench being grooved into the page.

The Color property allows you to select the color for the line around the cells. The Style and Color properties both have an asterisk next to them, which means they affect every cell in the table. Neither variable has an effect on web applications; the Solid, Ridge, and Groove styles will all produce the same border, and the Color property is totally ignored.

EXPLORING THE CELL BORDER THICKNESS SECTION

The Cell Border Thickness section adjusts the thickness of the selected border style for an individual cell or group of table cells. You can adjust each border of a cell individually by using the Top, Left, Bottom, and Right arrows. If you would like to adjust all four settings at once, click the large set of up/down arrows on the far right. To remove all the borders, click the Set All to 0 option. To set the border back, click the Set All to 1 option. The last button, Outline, is used when more than one cell is selected. This option will only set a border on the outline of the selected cells. This eliminates the need to go to each cell individually and set the border to 0 or 1 just to create a border around the outskirts of the selected cells.

USING THE CELL BORDERS PROPERTIES

With the Recipe **Using Basic Table** form open, follow these steps to remove all the border entries from our example table:

1. Open the Table Properties Box.
2. Click the Cell Borders tab.
3. Select all the cells in the table by placing the cursor in the upper-left cell and swiping down to the lower-right cell while holding the left mouse button.
4. Click the Set All to 0 button.

Now the table looks more like a neatly laid-out form instead of a table (the users will never know it's a table).

EXPLORING THE TABLE/CELL BACKGROUND PROPERTIES

The Table/Cell Background tab allows you to set colors and even background images in various ways for both the entire table and individual cells (see Figure 20.6).

The first section, Table Color, is quite interesting. The Style drop-down list allows you to choose how to apply a color pattern to the entire table. There are eight different selections: Solid, Alternating Rows, Alternating Columns, Left and Top, Left, Right and Top, Right, and Top. Once you've selected a pattern, you'll be able to choose one (for the Solid option) or two (for all the rest) colors for backgrounds. When you select colors, you have the option of creating your own custom colors

using the color wheel in the upper-right corner of the Color box. When you use this option for a ⌐
application, make sure you only use colors from the web color palette. Otherwise, everything but
color will render correctly.

FIGURE 20.6

The Table/Cell
Background tab
of the Table
Properties Box

NOTE   *When you are using the Table/Cell Background options, be aware that some options take precedence over other⌐*
A cell image overrides the cell color, and the cell color overrides the table color.

In the next section, Cell Color, you can set color for an individual table cell or a group of select
table cells. Just select the cell or cells to which you want to apply the color and then select the desir
color from the Color drop-down list. An added bonus for cells is the ability to apply gradient col⌐
(a gradient color is a color that blends and fades into another color) by using one of three Style b⌐
tons. The gradient applies to each individual cell in the selection; that is, if you select multiple ce⌐
you'll see the gradient from one color to the other in each cell, not starting with one color at the beg⌐
ning of the selection and shading to the other at the end of the selection.

The first Style button uses a solid color (the default). The second Style option button creates
gradient from bottom to top. The third Style option button creates a gradient from left to right⌐

When a gradient is used, a second color selection box will display as a To option. One limitati⌐
of using a gradient color is that it will not render correctly for a web application.

TIP   *If you would like to apply your cell color selection to the entire table, click the Apply to All button.*

You can use the last section, Cell Image, to display an image in the background of one or more ce⌐
(like wallpaper). An image must be rendered from the image resources and therefore must already ⌐
a database image resource. Select the @ button to write a formula to evaluate to the name of an ex⌐
ing image resource. Select the folder button to select an existing image from the list of existing ima⌐
resources. You can also decide how you would like the image to appear in the cell. From the Repe⌐
drop-down list, you can choose Repeat Once, Repeat Vertically, Repeat Horizontally, Tile, Cent⌐
or Size to Fit.

TIP   *If you would like to apply your cell image selection to all the cells of the table, click the Apply to All button.*

WARNING *You cannot use the Cell Image property in a web application. If you would like to set a background image for a cell in a web application, you'll need to insert a reference to the image using the HTML tab of the Table Properties Box.*

USING THE TABLE/CELL BACKGROUND PROPERTIES

We are going to make a few changes to our sample application. Let's add a bit of color to the title of the form. With the Recipe **Using Basic Table** form open, follow these steps:

1. With the cursor at the top of the form, choose Create ➤ Table and select the basic table option with only one row and one column.

2. Display the Table Properties Box for the new table. From the Table Layout tab, select Fit with Margins from the Width option in the Table section. Also select Center from the Vertically Align option in the Cell section.

3. Select the Cell Borders tab. In the Cell Border Style section, select Groove from the Style drop-down list box. Select a dark blue from the Color option. All four values for the Thickness option should be left at 1.

4. Select the Table/Cell Background tab. In the Cell Color section, select the left-to-right gradient option button (the rightmost button) and choose light green as the primary color and deep green as the secondary color.

5. With the cursor placed in your newly created table, type in the title for the form, **My Favorite Recipe**.

6. Highlight all of the title text inside the table. With the Properties Box still visible, select Text from the Properties Box drop-down list box. From the Font tab, select Arial as the font, 18 as the point size, and dark blue as the color.

We have now completed all the changes to the Recipe form using a basic table. When rendered in the Notes client, the completed form should look like Figure 20.7.

FIGURE 20.7

The completed Recipe Using Basic Table form using a basic table

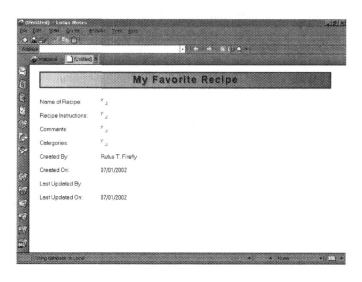

EXPLORING AND USING THE TABLE BORDER PROPERTIES

When you select the Table Border tab, the window shown in Figure 20.8 appears. The options this tab allow you to select the style, effect, and thickness of the border that surrounds your tab.

FIGURE 20.8

The Table Border tab of the Table Properties Box

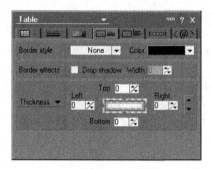

The Border Style section has options for the type of border for your table. Do not confuse th with the cell borders, although they are similar. The border style affects only the outer edge of t entire table. There are nine different styles to choose from: None, Solid, Double, Dotted, Dashe Ridge, Groove, Inset, and Outset. Depending on the style you select, you can also select a color. F our example, select the Outset style with a light gray color. If nothing visible changes on your tab do not fret. There are a few other options you need to set.

The Border Effects section only has one option, which allows you to set a drop shadow aroun the table. For our table, enable the Drop Shadow option and set a width of 10—a very nice effe indeed.

In the last section, Thickness, you can determine the thickness of your border style and adjust ea side of the border independently. These controls work in the same fashion that the controls for t cell borders work. The drop-down list on the left side of the dialog box also allows you to selec Inside and Outside as options. There are three parts to a table border, and you have full control o how thick each piece is. For our example, set the thickness to 2 all around. We are not going to fc with the dimensions for the Inset and Outset options.

NOTE   *Many of the table border options do not translate to a web application. This is not so much a limitation of Note as it is a limitation of Hypertext Markup Language (HTML).*

EXPLORING THE TABLE MARGIN PROPERTIES

The Table Margin tab allows you to set your table margins and set how the text will wrap (see Fi ure 20.9).

Now you have the option of setting the left and right margins for your table using an absolute po tion or a relative position. The Absolute option requires that you enter the number of inches to s the left or right margin, whereas the Relative option only requires a percentage. The percentage based on the actual window size.

The Table Wrap section allows you to decide how text is wrapped both inside and outside a tab Text is allowed to wrap only around a fixed-width table. The Inside Table setting allows you to crea a newspaper-style table by setting the height of a column; when the text fills one column, it will wrap into the beginning of the next column.

The last option, Compatibility, just resizes the table so it is equal to the size of tables in Notes Release 4.x. It seems that the tables in more recent versions of Notes are a bit smaller than they are in R4.x.

FIGURE 20.9
The Table Margin tab of the Table Properties Box

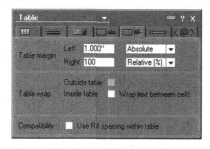

EXPLORING THE TABLE ROWS TAB

This tab lets you set up different kinds of tables: tabbed, programmed, animated, and caption. It has a broad range of options, many of which are dependent on one another, so we'll skip it to finish our discussion of the table properties first, but we'll come right back to it.

EXPLORING THE TABLE PROGRAMMING TAB

This tab bears a close resemblance to the Field Extra HTML tab in the Field Properties Box (see Figure 20.10). Not surprisingly, it serves much the same purpose. You can use this tab to specify HTML tags for such things as size and alignment for the table and even individual cells. The Name field under Row Tags will also be used for programmed tables.

FIGURE 20.10
The Table Programming tab of the Table Properties Box

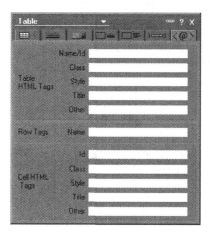

Creating a Tabbed Table

You've seen how you can use a table to improve a form's appearance. We've only covered some of options, however. We've skipped over the Table Rows tab of the Table Properties Box, which is w lets you create tabs and other interesting table effects.

In this section, we'll create a tabbed table. It won't be apparent to the user that the tabbed struct is a table, but it provides a user interface that is easy to use and understand.

To add a tabbed table to the form, follow these steps:

1. Create a copy of the Recipe Using Basic Table form (this is the form you just created).

2. Open the Recipe copy and change the name of the form to Recipe Using Tabbed Table RecipeTTable.

3. Place the cursor on the blank line between the form title table and the table with the labels fields.

4. Choose Create ➢ Table. Click the basic table button (yes, make sure it is the basic table; w going to change it later) and make sure the table has two rows and one column. Click the ◀ button and the table will be inserted on the form.

5. We are now going to nest a table within a table. Cut the first four rows from the original ta containing the labels and fields and paste them into the first row. You'll be asked "Do you w to paste across the cells of this existing table?" Click on the No button. Cut the remaining r and then paste them into the second row of the new table. When you have finished, you sho have a strange-looking form like the one in Figure 20.11.

FIGURE 20.11

An unattractive nested table

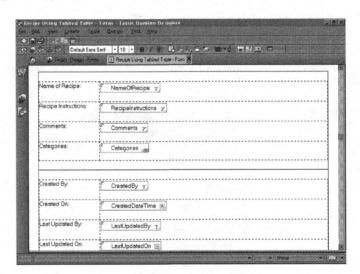

We could have created a tabbed table from the Create Table dialog box, but we created a basic t first to avoid confusion when copying the fields from one table to another. As stated in the defini of a tabbed table, each tab represents one row in the table. In this example, we'll have a tabbed table v two tabs. To create a tabbed table, we'll use the Table Rows tab of the Table Properties Box.

Open the Table Properties Box for the new table. You must be careful where you place the cursor. If you place the cursor inside the nested table, you will be using the incorrect Table Properties Box. To be safe, place the cursor just above the nested table in the first row of the new table and then choose Table ➢ Table Properties to open the Table Properties Box. To decide how to display the rows of your table, select the Table Row tab.

When the dialog box is first displayed, there will be only two radio buttons and the Show All Table Rows option will be selected. You need to select the Show Only One Row at a Time option; when you do so, a new list of properties will be displayed (see Figure 20.12). By default, the Users Pick Row via Tab Buttons option is selected, which is what transformed the flat table into a tabbed table. Ignore the other three options for now (they will be discussed for the other table types).

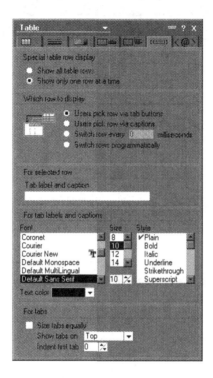

At the bottom of the dialog box is a For Selected Row section, which contains one field called Tab Label and Caption. Type the text you would like to see displayed on the individual tab. In our example, you have the first tab displayed, so type **Recipe Information**. Select the second tab of the table and type **Audit Trail** in the Tab Label and Caption field. Now you can start to see how the tabbed table is taking shape.

To make the tabbed table a bit easier to see, you can change each row to a different color. This is your choice. Any color will do. Just select the Table/Cell Background tab and change the cell color (don't forget to change the cell color for both rows).

The For Tabs section at the bottom of the Box allows you to adjust where and how the tabs app. By default, the tabs shrink or grow to fit their captions. However, if you check Size Tabs Equally, the all expand to the same size. The Show Tabs On menu allows you to move your tabs from the top to sides of the table or even the bottom. Finally, Indent First Tab allows you to move the tabs inward fr the edge of the table. It indents to the right if the tabs are on the top or bottom, or down if the tabs on the sides. We won't mess with any of these options right now, so your form should look similar Figure 20.13.

FIGURE 20.13

The Recipe Using
Tabbed Table form
using a tabbed table

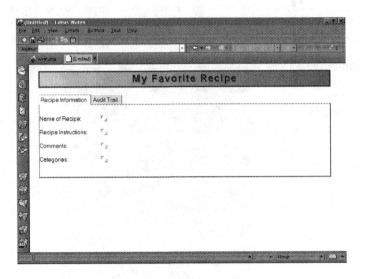

NOTE *A web application does not render the graphical tabbed pages in tabbed tables. There are still simulated pages the contain the same data displayed in the Notes client, but the look and feel is a bit different.*

TIP *If you want to put data-entry fields in a tabbed table on the Web, you'll probably want to check the form's General HTML for All Fields option. If you don't, any data entered in one tab will be lost if the user moves to another tab without saving the document first.*

Creating an Animated Table

In this section, we'll create an animated table. It is an animated table because the table rows can be s to display for a specific amount of time. This table type is typically used for graphical animation, b it can also be adapted to other needs. The first thing to do is create a copy of the tabbed table forr (both Recipe and Ingredient) and then change the table properties to create an animated table. Follc these steps to get the forms copied and converted:

1. Create a blank new form.

2. Create a regular table with three rows and one column.

3. In the first row, type the word **Eat.**

4. In the second row, type the word **At**. Center the text.

5. In the third row, type the word **Joe's**. Right-justify the text.

6. Select the table and increase the font size to something nice and visible, perhaps 18 point, and make it bold while you're at it.

7. Get the Table Properties Box and go to the Table Rows tab. As with the tabbed table, select Show Only One Row at a Time (see Figure 20.14).

FIGURE 20.14
Table Row
properties for an
animated table

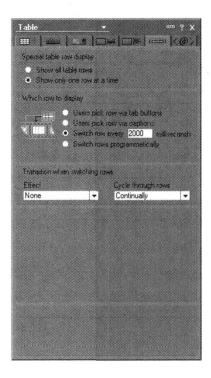

8. For which row to display, select Switch Row Every *n* Milliseconds. The value defaults to 2000, or two seconds. Enter a value of 750 (three-quarters of a second).

Now save your new form and test it in the Notes client. You should see the words *Eat At Joe's* appear to march across the screen. Now, an animated ad for a greasy-spoon diner may not be of much value in your employee manual or workflow database, but the effect can be put to good use. For example, if you have important instructions or reminders you want to put on a form but not much room in which to do so, you can use an animated table to scroll the information past the user, one bit at a time.

WARNING *The cycle for a continuous timed interval will stop once the document is placed into editing mode.*

There are some other options available for each row on the Table Rows tab of the Table Properties Box. A new section, Transition When Switching Rows, is only displayed for an animated table.

The Effect list allows you to select transitioning effects such as Wipe, Dissolve, Explode, and so
With these options, you can create all types of effects for text and graphics. Try applying some
them to the rows of the table you've just created and see if you like any of them. Many of the effe
will slow down the cycling a bit, as they take a little extra time to render. The Cycle through Ro
list lets you decide how many times the cycle will take place. You can select Continuous (the defau
Once When Opened, Advance on Click, or Once on Click. With this many options available, you
decide exactly how you would like your animated table to display to the end user.

NOTE *When using the animated table, keep in mind that the cycle options and effects will not work for a web applicatio*

Creating a Captioned Table

A captioned table is a lot like a tabbed table in that it presents the user with labeled areas indicat
different rows. If the user clicks the label, that row is displayed and others are hidden. The only
nificant difference is in the specific visual effect it uses to display the new row.

To see a captioned table, make a copy of the Recipe Using Tabbed Table form, open it, and
to the Table Rows tab of the Table Properties Box. Select the Users Pick Row via Captions opti
rather than Users Pick Row via Tab Buttons (see Figure 20.15). You'll see the tabs turn into ca
tioned bars, much like title bars of windows. You can save your changes and test the form in No

FIGURE 20.15

Properties of a
Pick Rows Via
Captions table
Properties of an
animated table

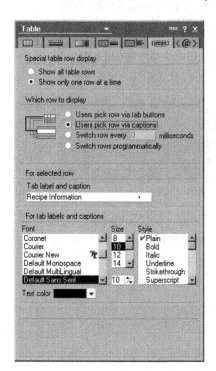

NOTE *If you access a captioned table via the Web, it will appear as a tabbed table.*

Creating a Programmed Table

A programmed table is similar to an animated table except the rows to be displayed are not based on a time interval or the click of the mouse button but rather on the contents of a special field, $table-name. Don't confuse this with the ability to create a table dynamically because that is not possible (in forms, anyway; with LotusScript, it is now possible to create tables in rich-text fields). What is possible is the ability to programmatically determine which row to display. This ability is similar to using the Hide-When option.

You set up a programmed table through the Table Row tab in the Table Properties Box. The first step is to create a copy of the forms and then change the table properties to create a programmed table. Follow these steps to copy and convert the form:

1. Create a copy of the Recipe Using Tabbed Table form.

2. Open the Recipe copy and change the name of the form to Recipe Using Programmed Table | RecipeDTable.

3. Display the Table Properties Box and select the Table Rows tab. In the Which Row to Display section, select the last option, Switch Rows Programmatically. This sets up the mechanism for looking at the $table-name field and causing the table to act dynamically.

Now the table is programmed, but what about this special field? There is one final tab in the Table Properties Box that allows you to define both a name for the table and a name for each row. The Table Programming tab displays the fields used for naming the table, rows, and cells for a table.

For our example, do the following:

1. Select the first tab on the table the Recipe Information page). In the Table HTML Tags section, enter **RecipeTable** in the Name/ID field. This is the name of the entire table.

2. In the Row Tags section, enter **RecipeInfo** in the Name field. This is the name of the row that contains the recipe information data.

3. Select the second tab on the table (the Audit Trail page). Enter **AuditTrail** in the Name field in the Row Tags section. This is the name of the row that contains the audit trail information data.

What we just did was name all the elements that make up the table. We gave the overall table a name and also named each row in the table. We must name each row uniquely so we can programmatically access each individual row of the table.

Now we need to set up the $table-name field. To do so, follow these steps:

1. Place the cursor in between the table and the page title. Type the following text: **Please select which information you would like to see.**

2. Create a new field at the end of this text. Name the field $RecipeTable, which is our $table-name (the $ followed by the actual name of the table).

3. Select Radio Button and Editable from the Type drop-down list boxes. Click the Control tab. Select Enter Choices (one per line), and in the Choices list box, enter the following entries on separate lines: **Recipe Information | RecipeInfo** and **Audit Trail | AuditTrail**. Note that the alias for each selection matches the name for each row in the table. This is how the table knows which row to display. The value of the $table-name field determines which row to display based on the user's selection.

4. Select the Refresh Fields on Keyword Change option. This will ensure that the table is refresh when a new choice is selected.

5. For the Default Value event for the field, enter **RecipeInfo**. This will ensure that the first r RecipeInfo, will display when the form is first opened.

When you have completed all of these changes, you should end up with a form similar to t one shown in Figure 20.16. Go ahead and test the new form. By selecting a different value for $RecipeTable field, either the recipe information or the audit trail data will display.

FIGURE 20.16

A programmed table with a field that allows the rows to change dynamically

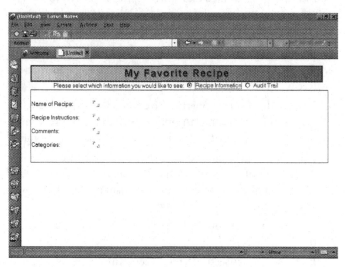

Adding Graphics

Having graphics in applications is becoming more of a requirement than a nice touch, especially with t popularity of web applications. In Notes, there are quite a few different ways graphics can be placed a form. You can insert an image resource, import a graphic, create a picture, or paste a graphic (regu and special). Whichever method you choose, the end result on the form will be the same—a Picture e ment containing the image you selected. We'll cover image resources in Chapter 23, when we deal w shared resources in general, but we'll deal with other methods of adding graphics now.

TIP Pasting a graphic is the least desirable of all the options. The main problem with this method is a loss of color clarity.

Importing a Graphic

The quickest way to get an image into a form is by importing it from an external graphic file. This w place the image directly on the form (such an image is known as an *inline image*), but the only way to ma changes to the image or to its position on the form would be to delete it and reimport the image aga This was typically the choice for versions of Notes previous to version 5. None of the image clarity lost when importing.

To import an image onto a form, place the cursor where you would like the image to be positioned. Choose File ➢ Import, which will open the Import dialog box (see Figure 20.17). Select the type of image you would like to import. You can choose from BMP, CGM, GIF, and JPEG. Once you have located the image file, highlight the filename and click the Import button. Once the file has been imported, you have the same capabilities for programming as you have for an image resource.

FIGURE 20.17
The Import
dialog box

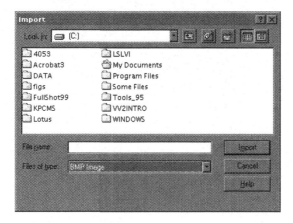

Creating a Picture

One other method for placing an image on a form is to create a picture. As importing does, creating a picture will place the image directly on the form. To create a picture, place the cursor where you would like the image to be positioned and choose Create ➢ Picture, which will open the Import dialog box. Select the type of image you would like to import. You can choose from BMP, CGM, GIF, JPEG, Lotus PIC, PCS, and TIFF 5. Once you have located the image file, highlight the filename and click the Import button.

Using the Picture Properties Box

Regardless of which method you use, placing a graphic directly on the form will result in the creation of a Picture element. If you would like to change any of the characteristics of the image, you'll need to open the Picture Properties Box.

The Picture element has the usual assortment of property tabs (Border, Alignment, Hide-When, and so on), but the one that is of interest is the Picture Info tab.

The Source field indicates where the image came from. If you have pasted, imported, or created a picture, the Source field for the image will not be editable; it will contain the text *[in-line image]*, as shown in Figure 20.18. Basically, unlike the image resource, the image is part of the form. If you used an image resource, the name of the resource, such as background.gif, will be displayed along with a formula icon (the @ symbol) and a folder icon. When the formula icon is clicked, a formula editor will be displayed in which you can write a formula to evaluate to the name of an existing image resource. If you click the folder icon, you can select an image from the image resources defined for the database.

FIGURE 20.18

The Picture
Properties Box for
an imported graphic

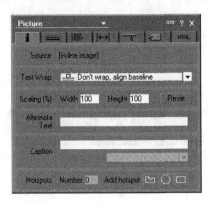

The next section, Text Wrap, allows you to specify how the text should be formatted with the ima
There are seven options to choose from; Don't Wrap, Align Baseline is the default. This option can
quite powerful and should not be overlooked.

The Scaling section allows you to resize the picture. If you click the Reset button, the image w
return to its original size.

In the Alternate Text section, you can supply text along with the image. For a web application, t
text will be displayed in place of the graphic if the user has elected not to display graphics. The te
will also be displayed while the web page is loading. If you enable the Show Alternate Text as Capti
option, the text will display underneath the image. This option only works in the Notes client a
has no effect on a web application.

The last section, HotSpots, allows you to add hotspots to the graphic. Hotspots are clickable are
within the graphic that perform actions or provide links to other Notes objects or even websites.
When a hotspot is created, you can program an action for the hotspot by using a Simple action, a f
mula, LotusScript, or JavaScript. This works in both the Notes client and a web application. Th
Number field tells you the number of hotspots the graphic contains. We'll discuss hotspots in mc
detail later in the "Automating Using Hotspots" section

Adding Computed Text

There are times when you'll want to put a bit of text on a form that changes in certain contexts. Yo
might, for example, want to put a personalized greeting on the form, an indication of the time, o
specially formulated link on a web page. A quick-and-dirty way to do this is to create a computed te
object.

To create a computed text object, click the form where you want the text to appear and sele
Create ➤ Computed Text. The computed text placeholder will appear on the form, as shown i
Figure 20.19.

When the computed text item is created, you'll also see a computed text entry appear on th
Objects tab of the programmer's pane. Much like a computed field, the entry has one event: Valu
Enter a formula in the Value event. The formula's result will be displayed when the form is opene
as shown in Figure 20.20. The value of the computed text is not saved and cannot be used by co
puted fields or other formulas.

FIGURE 20.19

A form with
computed text

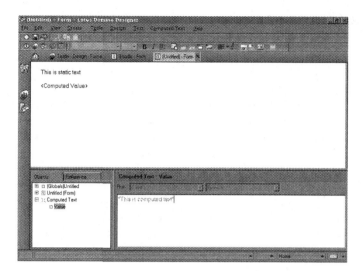

FIGURE 20.20

A form with the
computed text
formula's resultBox

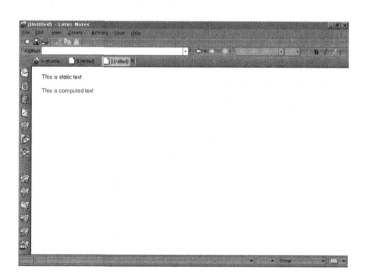

If you're observant, you may wonder what the difference is between computed *text* and a computed for display *field*, which we discussed in the previous chapter. Both perform a computation and display the results on screen without saving the data when the document is closed. In fact, there's little difference so far as forms are concerned, and so long as you don't have other formulas depending on it, it doesn't matter which one you use. The real importance of computed text will only become apparent when you start dealing with pages (the page is another Notes design element), which we'll present in Chapter 22, "Outlines, Pages, Framesets, and Navigators." You can't use fields on pages, but you can use computed text.

Adding a Section

If you look at the original Recipe form, you may notice there are quite a few new fields being d played. Making the audit trail information available to the user is a nice touch, but it takes away fr the actual recipe and ingredient fields and clutters the screen when it's always displayed. All of t fields seem to run together without some type of field separator. In addition, most users don't w. to see the audit trail information *all* the time because it really has nothing to do with the actual d ument contents. One way of dealing with that is with the tabbed table, but there are many other str. gies for hiding irrelevant data and making the form more navigable.

This is where *sections* come into play. Most designers have a tendency to place a lot of inform tion on one form, which can be quite confusing to the user. A section allows you to group li information together. These groupings can be displayed or hidden based on options selected b: you or by the end user. Moreover, unlike table rows, you also have the ability to limit access to the groups of information by assigning security rights.

There are two types of sections that you can define in Notes:

- Standard
- Controlled access

The major difference between these two types of sections is that, with a controlled access sectic you have the ability to limit who can access the contents of the section regardless of what a user's p missions to the document may be, while any user with appropriate access to the document can acc the contents of a Standard section.

Creating a Standard Section

You have two ways to create a section. Depending on your situation, you can have a selected gro of existing text and fields automatically placed into a new section, or you can create a new section a manually place the elements you want it to contain. For our example, we'll have the contents aut matically placed into the new section.

We mentioned earlier that it would be nice to have the ability to hide the audit trail fields wh the Recipe form is displayed. Using a section, you are going to hide the fields from the end user b also give the end user the ability to see the contents of those fields. To create a section containing the audit trail fields, follow these steps:

1. Make a copy of the Recipe form and name it Recipe with Sections.
2. Open the form and highlight the last four labels and fields.
3. Choose Create ➤ Section ➤ Standard. All of the labels and fields are immediately placed in a section. Note that the title for the section defaults to the first label that was selected, in th case, Created By. By default, the section is collapsed. To view the contents of the section, cli the twistie and all of the labels and fields within the section will be displayed, as shown in F ure 20.21.

Because you had Notes automatically populate the contents of the section, you may hav noticed that it also populated the title for the section. The Created By title is not very descr tive of the section contents, so you'll need to change it.

FIGURE 20.21

The Audit Trail
section

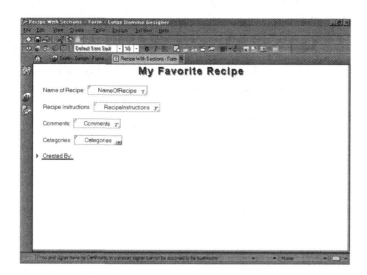

CHANGING THE SECTION TITLE

You can change the title for a section from the Section Properties Box. To display the Section Properties Box, click the section and choose Section ➤ Section Properties. The Section Properties Box, shown in Figure 20.22, appears (you can also right-click the section and choose Section Properties).

FIGURE 20.22

The Title and
Border tab of
the Section
Properties Box

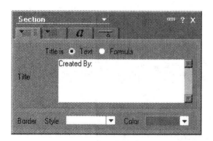

You may notice that the Title and Border tab contains a radio button with which you can choose to either enter a text section title or allow the section title to be generated via a formula. Keep the Text radio button selected (the default), highlight the text in the Title text box, and type **Audit Trail**. Let's also change the current default border style. Select the first entry from the Style drop-down list, which will box the section title. Keep the current color because it stands out a bit from the other parts of the form.

EXPANDING AND COLLAPSING SECTIONS

When you use sections, you can collapse or hide information from the user. In our example, the entire audit trail is placed into a section. When a Recipe With Sections form is viewed in the Notes client, the audit trail information is tucked neatly into a collapsed section, as shown in Figure 20.23. Temporarily hiding the audit trail information makes the screen less cluttered and easier to read.

FIGURE 20.23

The Recipe document with a collapsed Audit Trail section

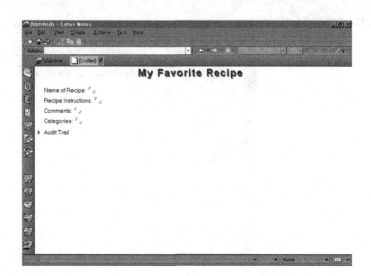

There are some additional properties for the section that allow you to control how it is present to the end user. In this example, we want to make sure the section is always collapsed. You have t ability to control the Expand/Collapse Action when a document is previewed, opened for reading editing, and printed. To set this property, follow these steps:

1. Click the section and choose Section ➤ Section Properties to open the Section Properties B

2. Select the Expand/Collapse tab, as shown in Figure 20.24.

3. Select the Auto-Collapse Section option from the Opened for Reading drop-down list.

FIGURE 20.24

The Expand/ Collapse tab of the Section Properties Box

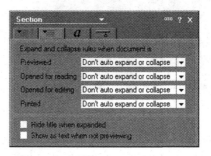

Now when a Recipe with Sections document is opened, the Audit Trail section will always be c lapsed, giving a cleaner look to the form. You can also choose the Auto-Collapse option from any the other drop-down lists on the Expand/Collapse tab.

Creating a Controlled Access Section

The difference between a standard section and a controlled access section is security rights. With controlled access section, you or the end user can choose who has access to edit particular section

This feature can be quite useful for a document that many different people or groups are allowed to edit. Using controlled access sections, you can group data based on who will have access to it. In the standard section, we grouped common data together. We can go a step further with the controlled access section by grouping common editable data.

You can create a controlled access section by choosing Create ➤ Section ➤ Controlled Access. Once the controlled access section is created, a new tab called Formula appears in the Section Properties Box. This tab allows you to enter an access formula, as shown in Figure 20.25. In this example three groups are allowed access to the section: the group LocalDomainServers, the document's creator (if the formula were Computed rather than Computed When Composed, it would let the current user, whoever that happened to be, edit the section!), and the role Admins.

FIGURE 20.25

The Formula tab of the Section Properties Box

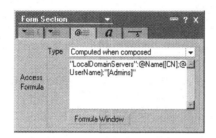

NOTE   *When you use a controlled access section in a web application, the security for the section will remain in effect. The end user will not have the ability to double-click the section title to add or remove section editors.*

It's critical that you understand the Type option (shown in Figure 20.25) of a controlled access section. If you select Editable from the drop-down list box, any user with the correct database and document security access can add and remove users from the controlled access list. When editing a document, the user only needs to double-click the section title and the Who May Edit This Section dialog box will appear (see Figure 20.26).

FIGURE 20.26

The Who May Edit This Section dialog box, which allows you to add or remove users

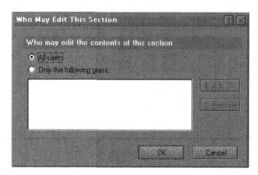

If you choose Computed from the Type drop-down list for the controlled access section, the list of users can be calculated via a formula each and every time the document is refreshed. The Computed

When Composed option will calculate the list of users only once (when the document is first create No changes can be made to this type of controlled access section.

Layout Regions

A *layout region* is a fixed-size design area that allows elements placed in the region to be easily mo around and resized for pixel-perfect placement. That is, instead of a page-of-text style of desig where layout is governed by such concepts as rows of text, tabs, and table columns, you can place ite in any way you desire, even to the point of overlapping them. This gives you extremely fine cont over layout, but you are somewhat limited in what you can place into a layout region.

Creating a Layout Region

In this section, you'll rearrange the audit trail fields yet again, except in this case, you'll use a layo region to contain the fields. Make yet another copy of the Recipe form (call it Recipe with Layo and open it. Once it's open, here's what to do:

1. Delete the last four fields and labels on the form and make sure the cursor is at the bottom the form.

2. Choose Create ➤ Layout Region ➤ New Layout Region.

3. Select the layout region (the black rectangle) and choose Design ➤ Layout Properties (right-click in the layout region and choose Layout Properties) to display the Layout Propert Box, shown in Figure 20.27.

FIGURE 20.27

The Properties Box for the layout region

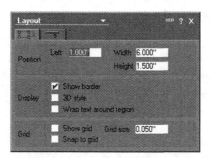

4. Select both the Show Grid and Snap to Grid options. Also make sure that the value in the Gr Size field is 0.050. These options will help align all the design elements within the layout regio You may also elect to enable the 3D Style option. This will give the layout region a dialog-b look (a gray background).

5. With the layout region still selected, choose Create ➤ Layout Region ➤ Text to insert a Cont object (a *text label* in layman's terms) within the layout region. Display the Object Properties B for the new object by choosing Design ➤ Object Properties (you can also just double-click t object). From the Static Text Info tab, you can enter the text to be displayed for the object. Th field will be the title for the layout region, so type **Audit Trail** in the Text field and center t text both horizontally and vertically. Select the Font tab, resize the text to 18, and change the color to dark blue. Next, size the field so that it is centered across the top of the layout regio

6. The next step is to add the four fields that make up the actual audit trail to the layout region. First, add the text labels to the layout region: Created By, Created On, Last Updated By, and Last Updated On.

7. Add the four fields to the layout region. To add a field, choose Create ➤ Field. To define the properties of each field, you must display the Field Properties Box, which does not display by default. To display the Field Properties Box, choose Design ➤ Field Properties (you can also double-click the field). Define the properties for each field. Also remember to type the formulas in the Value event for the computed fields. When you are finished, the layout region should be similar to Figure 20.28.

FIGURE 20.28

The completed layout region for the Audit Trail layout region

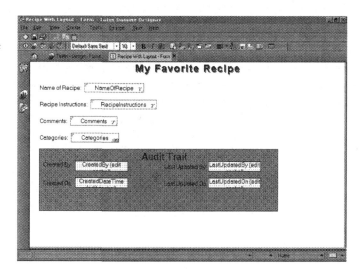

NOTE   *You cannot cut and paste fields from a non–layout region to a layout region and vice versa.*

Adding Graphics to Your Layout Region

You can also add graphics to your layout region. There are two options available: you can add a graphic, and you can create a graphic button. Neither option allows you to import a graphic directly or allow the use of the image. You must first copy the graphic to the Clipboard. You will need to use some type of graphics program—such as Adobe Photoshop or even a web browser—to display the image. Once you have selected the image and copied it to the Clipboard, it will be automatically pasted into the layout region when you insert a graphic or create a graphic button.

Once a graphic is added, you can move the image anywhere within the layout region. If you would like the graphic to be used as a background for the layout region, you can use the Design ➤ Send to Back command.

You can accomplish the same thing for a graphic button, although you'll probably want to use a smaller image. The name of this element implies a button with an embedded image, but in actuality, a copy of the image is just placed in the layout region. To create a graphic button, follow the steps for creating a graphic but choose Create ➤ Layout Region ➤ Graphic Button to actually place the graphic in

the layout region. Once the graphic button has been created, you can program specific events to oc̶
when the button is clicked. The language you decide to program with determines the events that can̶
programmed.

Advantages and Disadvantages of Layout Regions

You know what a layout region is; now it's time to discuss when and if you should actually use o̶
The biggest advantage to using a layout region is the ease with which you can place and move fiel̶
With pixel placement, you can arrange the layout in just about any shape, giving you considerat̶
artistic freedom. Although it is easy to move fields around, you still cannot move groups of field̶
around. The fields must be moved one at a time.

It's also nice to use a background graphic in a layout region. You can insert a graphic anywhere̶
the layout region and move it around freely. Another nice feature is that a layout region is fixed in si̶
so once you set everything up the way you like it, it will not be altered or changed when display̶
This will ensure that graphics do not get cut off from dynamic resizing.

There are, however, a number of drawbacks to using layout regions. For example, getting to do pi̶
by-pixel placement means having to do pixel-by-pixel placement. Being able to stagger fields and lab̶
and set distances precisely is nice, but most data entry forms don't require that sort of precision.

You may not be able to use the kinds of fields you want, either. When placing fields in the layo̶
region, you may have noticed that you do not have as many choices as you have with fields placed o̶
side a layout region. You cannot choose to display Notes delimited fields in a layout region, and y̶
cannot display the following types of fields:

- Dialog list
- Password
- Formula
- Rich text

You also cannot use the following elements:

- Attachments
- Hotspots
- Links
- Object linking and embedding (OLE) objects
- Pop up windows
- Sections
- Tables

Another major limitation is that layout regions will not display over the Web. If you plan to crea̶
a web-based application, refrain from using layout regions.

If you will have a lot of pop-up dialog boxes, layout regions help to create a nice-looking interfa̶
The 3D style is complementary for this style of dialog box. If you are going to develop a set a "ho̶
to" wizards, the layout regions will be extremely helpful.

Using Layers

Layers, a concept Release 6 has taken from the HTML 4 standard, are a bit like layout regions in that they are objects that can contain fields and other objects and they are treated as a unit. The difference is that although the items within the layer are laid out in the same rich-text way as a Notes form, the layer itself can be placed anywhere on the form, to the pixel.

You create a layer by clicking the form and selecting Create ➤ Layer. Two things will appear: a rectangle outlining the layer and a small two-page icon representing the layer anchor (see Figure 20.29). The anchor doesn't actually take up space. It just indicates the spot on the form from which the layer's position will be measured.

FIGURE 20.29

A layer and its anchor

Right-click the layer and select Layer Properties. You'll see the Layer Properties Box (see Figure 20.30). The first (Positioning) tab lets you set the size and position of the layer. Top and Left let you set the position relative to the anchor. Auto sets the appropriate coordinate to the anchor's position. You can set its coordinates in inches, pixels, or a number of other units of measure. Likewise, you can set the layer's size in pixels, inches, and so on. Z-Index sets the "altitude" of the layer. Layers appear on top of anything in their underlying form. However, you can make layers appear on top of or underneath one another. Layers with higher z-indexes appear over those with lower z-indexes.

FIGURE 20.30

Positioning tab of the Layer Properties Box

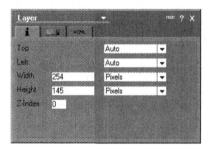

The Box also has Background and Extra HTML tabs, which operate pretty much as you'd expect by now. The important thing to know is that when created, a layer has a transparent background. Any text, fields, and other objects under it will still be visible, although they may be obscured by the contents of the layer. If you set a color, the layer will no longer be transparent.

By themselves, layers are, at best, mildly useful. Their real use is with advanced HTML and JavaScript techniques, which allow you to dynamically alter the z-index of individual layers, making areas filled with fields and controls appear and disappear quickly in response to user actions.

Automating Using Actions

Up to this point, everything has been accomplished by using the standard Notes client menu items and toolbars. This is deeply limiting. Your range of options is restricted to generic functions, and you can't reach them at all on the Web. To do more, you'll typically use *actions*, custom-built bits of code attached to the form. They generally appear as buttons conveniently located across the top of the form. Actions typically emulate items from the Notes menu or automate tasks such as creating a new document or running an agent. When building an action, you have the option of using a Simple Action, a formula, LotusScript, or JavaScript.

Defining Action Buttons

You can define an action for both a view and a form. Action buttons are not stored as part of an individual document; they are stored as part of the design for the view or form. Once defined, all Action buttons are displayed in a special area of the Notes client called *the Action bar*. The action bar is typically a horizontal button bar that is located at the top and that runs the width of the design element. Action buttons are usually the way to go when you want to automate an action, simple or complex. You use action buttons to perform trivial actions such as saving or closing documents as well as complex tasks such as simultaneously updating a brace of documents related to the current one and sending out e-mail notifications, all while saving and closing the current document and moving on to the next one. Even though some of the commands placed in an action button may be accessible from the Notes client menu, you will want to create action buttons for the more common tasks so the commands will be more readily available to the user.

Before creating an action button, you'll want to determine if the action to be performed is unique to the design element you're currently dealing with or if the action will be used in other forms or views in the same database. This is important because there are actually two types of action buttons: regular actions and shared actions. Regular actions are stored in a form or view, and shared actions are stored in their own design element and can be reused in different places. Both have the same properties and are virtually identical in every aspect except where they are stored and created. We'll come back to Shared Actions in Chapter 25.

To create an action, open the form or view and select Create ➤ Action. The submenu gives you three choices:

- Action
- Action with Subactions
- Insert System Actions

The first two options are actually fairly similar. The first option simply creates an action and brings up the Action Properties Box. The second does something similar but creates a more elaborate structure. It creates a placeholder that will appear in the action bar at the top of the page and the action itself, which appears beneath it—a bit like a cascading menu item. Indeed, when you click the placeholder in the form, the subaction will appear in a menu beneath it. You can take look at the New button in the mailbox database's Inbox to get an idea of what it will look like. If you click a subaction and then select Create ➤ Action ➤ Action, you'll create an additional subaction under the same heading (see Figure 20.31).

FIGURE 20.31

An action and two subactions

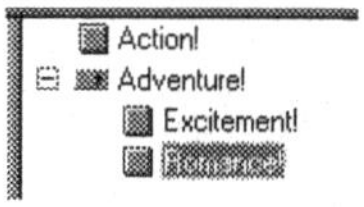

Insert System Actions does something a bit different. It creates action buttons for six very basic actions—so basic, in fact, that you don't even need formulas for them. They are Categorize, Edit Document, Send Document, Forward, Move to Folder, and Remove from Folder. If you look at Figure 20.32, you'll notice that they look slightly different; regular actions have a small square icon, and system actions have a square with a diamond in it. You can modify properties of the system action buttons, but you can't actually change what they do.

FIGURE 20.32

System Actions

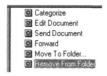

NOTE *If you're familiar with older versions of Notes, you'll remember the system actions as having been built into form design. Their presence has become optional in Release 6.*

You can also change the relative position of actions by clicking and dragging them up and down the list.

WARNING *If you plan to use one of the system commands (such as Edit Document) for an action button, be aware that these Actions will not be displayed for a web application. If you want to have an Action button that will allow a web user to edit a document, you will have to create one.*

However you decide to create your action button, the Action Properties Box is displayed (Figure 20.33).The options on the Action Info tab are responsible for the action button's look and feel. You can give the action both a name and a label. Why both? An action name is constant, so it's a good identifier, but it's possible to compute a label with a formula. That way, you can have a button itself prompt the user to press it or, in the words of the pointy-haired boss, "Click here, you fool!" The Target Frame field allows you to specify in which frame the action should take place (Chapter 22 covers frames in more detail).

The Type menu at the top of the Display section lets you determine the shape of the Action. By default, an Action appears as a button, which may have a label, a graphic, or both. If you choose Check Box instead, a small check box will appear next to the label, and you may not include a graphic. You can insert a formula that will determine whether the item appears checked. If you select Menu Separator, the action won't actually do anything. It won't even take up space on the Action bar. It only creates separators on the Actions menu, where actions can also appear.

FIGURE 20.33

Action Info tab
of the Action
Properties Box

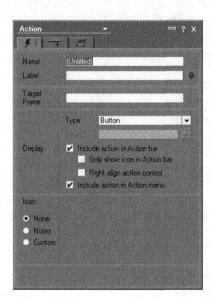

The other two options in the Display section let you determine if the Action button should only display on an Action bar, only display on the Action menu (the latter is only visible within a Notes client) or both. In some cases, you may want to place the less frequently used Actions on the Action menu the Action bar won't be cluttered. But don't worry if you have too many Action buttons. The Action bar allows scrolling to all buttons that aren't visible. The Icon section allows you to dress up the Action button. If you select either Notes or Custom, you can place a graphic alongside the Action button to to give your users another identifying characteristic. The Custom option allows you to pick an image resource. The Notes option gives you a quickly accessed list of images to use (see Figure 20.34). They aren't enormously attractive, but they're fairly generic and are useful if you don't have a lot of time create a custom graphic.

FIGURE 20.34

Notes Action icons

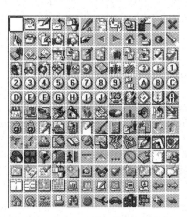

TIP   *To create an action button with only a graphic, just put an empty string ("") in the Label field.*

NOTE   *Don't worry about that ugly pink background. What appears pink in the Notes icons is transparent in the Notes client; the Action bar color will show through.*

Once you set the look and feel for the action button, you need to enter the action to be performed. In the script area of the programmer's pane, you can use a formula, a Simple action, JavaScript, or LotusScript.

We are going to add a few action buttons to make our form a bit easier to use. To do so, just follow these steps:

1. Create a copy of the Recipe Using Tabbed Table form.

2. Open the Recipe copy and change the name of the form to Recipe with Actions | RecipeActions. You can also update the comments in the Action Properties Box to reflect this name change.

3. The first action button to create will be a Close/Cancel button; this button will close the document without saving any changes. Open the Work pane in the programmer's pane for a shared Action. Choose Create ➤ Action and type **Cancel** in the Name field. In the Label field, enter this formula:

```
@If(@IsDocBeingEdited; "Cancel"; "Close")
```

This formula will change the button label depending on whether the document is in editing mode. If the document is being edited, the button will say Cancel. If it is just being read, it will say Close. Select the Notes Graphic radio button and choose the big red X as the graphic. In the script area for the action button, select Formula and enter the following program code:

```
FIELD SaveOptions := "0";
@Command([FileCloseWindow])
```

4. Next we'll create an Edit button; this button will put the document into editing mode. Choose Create ➤ Action and type **Edit** in the Name field. Select an appropriate Notes graphic (we use the red pencil). On the Hide-When tab, enable Opened for Editing because we don't want this option available once the document is in editing mode. In the script area of the programmer's pane, select Formula and enter the following program code:

```
@Command([EditDocument])
```

5. The next button will be a Save and Close button. Choose Create ➤ Action and type **Save and Close** in the Name field. Select an appropriate Notes graphic (we use the green check mark). On the Hide-When tab, enable all except Opened for Editing because we don't want this option available in reading mode. In the script area of the programmer's pane, select Formula and enter the following program code:

```
@Command([FileSave]);
@Command([FileCloseWindow])
```

6. Now we'll add a New\Recipe button. Choose Create ➤ Action with Subactions. Type **Rec** in the name field, then click the placeholder (which should still be labeled Untitled) and ty **New**. On the Hide-When tab, enable the Hide Action If Formula Is True option and enter formula **@IsNewDoc**. In the script area, select Formula and enter the following program co

```
@Command([Compose];"RecipeActions")
```

7. Finally, we'll create a New\Ingredient button; right now, the form this action points to does exist, but we'll create it in the next chapter when we get into view response hierarchies. Cl the Recipe action and select Create ➤ Action. Type **Ingredient** in the Name field. On t Hide-When tab, enable the Hide Action If Formula Is True option and enter the formu **@IsNewDoc**. In the script area, select Formula and enter the following program code:

```
@Command([Compose];"IngredientActions")
```

WARNING *When using a custom graphic for an Action button, the image must be the correct height and width or will not render correctly for a web application. When run in the Notes client, the image is automatically sized.*

Now that you have defined all the actions , give them a try in the Notes client. Create and sa a new document with the form, then reopen it and give the New\Recipe Action button a try. S Figure 20.35. If you look carefully, you will notice a graphical arrow on the button depicting th a submenu of options will be displayed when you mouse over the button.

FIGURE 20.35
The Recipe with Actions form with the actions added

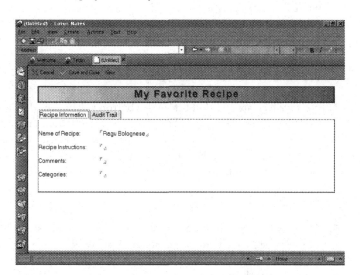

Customizing the Action Bar

You may not like how the action buttons look on the Action bar, but there is a solution. There is Properties Box for the Action bar that will allow you to customize its look and feel.

NOTE *The Action bar will automatically detect if there are more action buttons than can physically fit on one line across the screen. If there are more Action buttons to display, graphical arrows will display on the right and left side of the Action bar, allowing the user to scroll from left to right and vice versa. Although this option exists, it is easier to navigate if all the buttons are available on one screen. If you have more buttons than can fit on one screen, try grouping common functions together by creating Actions with subactions.*

To open the **Action Bar** Properties Box, select an action from the action pane and choose Design ➢ Action Bar Properties. There are six tabs that address the look and feel for both the Notes client and web application Action bar and buttons:

The Action Bar Info tab The Action Bar Info tab allows you to specify the alignment and web access information for the Action bar. For the Alignment section, you have only two choices for the actual buttons to be displayed: Buttons Start at Left (the default) or Buttons Start at Right. The Web Access section only applies to web applications and allows the Action bar to be displayed either as HTML or with a Java applet. For our example form, select the Using the Java Applet option because it looks a little better, even though it is slower to load.

The Action Bar Size tab This tab lets you set the height of the action bar (width, of course, is determined by the width of the screen and the space allowed to the form containing the Action bar). Your choices for height are Default, Exs, and Fixed. The Default option lets Notes determine the height of the action bar. Fixed allows you to set a size in pixels. Exs allows you to set a height base on the size of a font you've chosen. An *ex* is equal to the height of a lowercase letter in the font. If you choose Exs, you must then choose a font and size. Setting font and size here does *not* change the font and size of the button labels, nor will setting font and size on the Button Font tab later on change the height of the Action bar. Essentially, you must set the font and size twice.

The Button Background tab The Button Background tab allows you to set a background color or image for the Action button bar. You can either pick a color or pick an image and set options for tiling it. This should be familiar to you now because it's essentially the same dialog box you use for setting a form background.

The Action Bar Border tab This tab lets you set a border all around the Action bar. You can set a style, color, drop shadow, and thickness. This should look familiar, as well, because it's essentially the same as the Paragraph Border tab in the Text Properties Box.

The Button Properties tab This tab allows you to adjust the size and appearance of buttons on the form. The Height option gives you for options: Default, Minimum, Fixed, and Background. Default has Notes set the size, Minimum and Fixed are essentially indistinguishable, and Background sizes the button to the height of any background image you use. The Width drop-down list box allows you to select from three different options: Default, Fixed, and Background Size. Both of these options work exactly the same as they do for the Height option (except this option changes the width of the Action button). The Margin drop-down list box allows you to also select from two options: Default and Fixed Size. Changing this option will change the size of the border that surrounds each button. For our example, leave both the Height and Width options set to Default. Change the Margin option to Fixed Size and set the number of pixels to 5. None of these settings affect the display for Action buttons for a web application unless you use the Java applet. If you use the Java applet, the Action buttons work the same in both the client and the web application.

The Button Border section allows you to change, via the Button drop-down list box, how the but border will be displayed to the user. There are four selections available: On Mouse Over, Alwa Never, and Notes Style. It's nice to give the buttons a visual impact. If you select the On Mouse C option, the button appears to change, giving a more distinct but not excessively obtrusive preser tion. For our application, set the Display option to On Mouse Over.

The last section on this tab, Button Background, allows you to change the background that w be displayed for each button. You have the option of using the Color drop-down list box change the color, or you can specify a graphic. Selecting an image will override the Button Ba ground Color option. The Image option can produce some fascinating button faces. Try expe imenting with this option to see what combination works best for you.

The Button Font tab   The final tab, Button Font, allows you to change the font for the text played on the Action buttons. This should be yet another familiar tab; you should recognize from the Text Properties Box.

After setting all the Action bar properties, you should see a big difference in how your form loo By using the Action buttons, you can "guide" your users through your forms, saving them from h ing to look for the commands.

Automating Using Hotspots

Another mechanism that you as a developer can use to automate tasks is the *hotspot*. You can progra many different types of Actions to occur when the user clicks an area of the screen such as a block specially marked text, an image, or a button on the form itself. Most users will probably be quite fami with the idea of hotspots if they frequently use a web browser. Indeed, you can have your hotspots as hyperlinks to bring up web pages or Notes documents, but they can do far more. Notes provides y with several distinct types of hotspots:

- ◆ Text pop-up hotspot
- ◆ Formula pop-up hotspot
- ◆ Link hotspot
- ◆ Button hotspot
- ◆ Action hotspot

We're going to add quite a few hotspots to our example to demonstrate how they work (we'll a at least one of each type). Before we start, we need to create a new form on which to make our mc ifications. To do so, follow these steps:

1. Create a copy of the Recipe with Actions form.
2. Open the Recipe copy and change the name of the form to Recipe with HotSpot | RecipeHotSp

Creating a Text Pop-Up

The text pop-up hotspot is the simplest of hotspots. It will display a fixed bit of text information ir pop-up dialog box. It's a nice way to make supporting information and brief instructions unobtrusive available to users, but this option is only available for the Notes client. Web applications will ignore text pop-up hotspots. To create a text pop-up, follow these steps:

1. Open the Recipe with HotSpot form. On the Recipe Information tab, select the text *Name of Recipe*.

2. Choose Create ➢ HotSpot ➢ Text Pop-Up, which will automatically display the HotSpot Pop-Up Properties Box (see Figure 20.36).

FIGURE 20.36

The HotSpot Pop-Up Properties Box

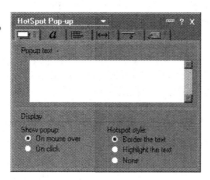

3. In the Popup Text field, type **Enter the name of the recipe**. This is the text that will be displayed in the pop-up dialog box.

4. For the Show Popup option, select the On Mouse Over radio button. When the user passes the mouse over the selected text, the dialog box will automatically appear.

5. For the Hotspot Style option, select the Highlight the Text radio button. This will highlight the text, giving a visual indication to the user that something will happen when the cursor is on the text.

6. Next, select the text *Recipe Instructions* and create another text pop-up hotspot. In the Popup Text field, type **Enter step-by-step instructions for making the recipe, but not a list of ingredients.**

7. For the Show Popup option, select the On Click radio button.

8. For the Hotspot Style option, select the None radio button.

9. Select the Font tab. Change the color of the text to a dark blue. Also select the underline style for the text. This will simulate a web link, so users should quickly grasp what it does.

If you need to display the HotSpot Pop-Up Properties Box, place the cursor in the hotspot and choose HotSpot ➢ HotSpot Properties.

TIP *You don't need to remove the text to remove a text hotspot. Instead, place the cursor in the hotspot and choose HotSpot ➢ Remove HotSpot.*

Creating a Formula Pop-Up

The formula pop-up hotspot is similar to the text pop-up hotspot. The only difference is, with a formula pop-up hotspot, a task using formulas can be executed and the results will be displayed in a pop-up box. Be careful because the formula cannot execute formulas that take Actions such a @OpenView. Again, this option is only available for the Notes client; web applications will igno formula pop-up hotspots. To create a formula pop-up, follow these steps:

1. Open the Recipe with HotSpot form. On the Recipe Information tab, select the text Comm
2. Choose Create ➤ HotSpot ➤ Formula Pop-up, which will automatically display the HotS Pop-Up Properties Box.
3. Select "None" for the Show Border around HotSpot option on the Basics tab.
4. Select the Font tab. Change the color of the text to a dark blue. Also select the underline st for the text.
5. To enter a formula for the pop-up, expand the HotSpot event from the Object tab in the p grammer's pane and select the Click event (you can also place the cursor in the hotspot direc on the form). Enter the following formula:

```
@Name([CN];@UserName) + ", we look forward to your comments."
```

When the hotspot is displayed, the formula will be evaluated and display a message with the use name. Although this example is not that practical, this is another place to customize your output, p haps providing different instructions at different times for the same field.

Creating a Link Hotspot

The link hotspot will link to a Uniform Resource Locator (URL), to a link (a database, view, d ument, or anchor), or to a named element (a page, form, frameset, view, folder, or Navigator). T option works in both the Notes client and a web application.

In our example form, we'll create links to a URL, a link, and a named element. The HotSp Resource Link Properties Box is the key to setting different types of links. As shown in Figure 20.3 you can choose the type of link from the Content section of the Info tab. This selection drives t remaining fields for the section.

FIGURE 20.37
The HotSpot Resource Link Properties Box for the link hotspot

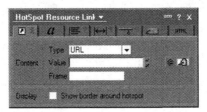

For a link to a URL, you only need to type URL in the Value field or use a formula to formula the URL. For a link to a link, you must first use the Copy Link command to copy either a database, vie document, or anchor link to the Clipboard. Once the link is on the Clipboard, click the paste icon place the link in the link hotspot and fill in the remaining Content fields. For a link type to a named e ment, you have a few choices. You can select the element type from the list box and enter the name the element. You can select the folder icon and, from the Locate Object dialog box, select the eleme type, the database, and the element name. You can also select the element type and enter a formula compute the correct element name.

For this example, we'll need to set up the form to allow the creation of the three various types of links. In the next series of steps, we'll guide you through both the form setup and the actual link hotspot creation. To get started, follow these steps:

1. Open the Recipe with HotSpot form. Place the cursor at the bottom of the Info tab (place it after the table). Enter the words **Hey, juice!**

2. Highlight the text and choose Create ➢ HotSpot ➢ Link HotSpot. Select URL from the Type drop-down list and enter **www.buffy.com** in the Value field.

3. Place the cursor at the top of the form and type **- View Categorized Recipes -**. Highlight the text and choose Create ➢ HotSpot ➢ Link HotSpot. Select Named Element from the Type drop-down list and click the folder icon. Select View from the Kind of Object drop-down list. Leave the Database field on Current Database, and for the View field, select Recipes By Category. Notice that the text is already set to blue. Notes knows that it is going to be a link and sets up font styles for you accordingly.

4. Open the About **Database** document for the database by choosing Help ➢ About This Database. Once the About document is displayed, choose Edit ➢ Copy as Link ➢ Document Link. This will store the document on the Clipboard. Close the About document.

5. Place the cursor just above the table in the Recipe Information tab. Type **Need Help?** and then select the text. Choose Create ➢ HotSpot ➢ Link HotSpot. Because you already have a document on the Clipboard, Link and the correct values will be preselected in the Type option. Notes already sets the font color to something that stands out a bit, but we want this to be a little more prominent. Select the Font tab and set the color to red and the style to Underline.

Now you have completed all the links for the form. When you are finished, the form should look similar to Figure 20.38. All three links should work flawlessly in either the Notes client or a web browser.

FIGURE 20.38

The completed form with all three types of link hotspots

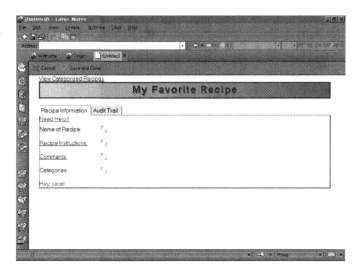

Creating a Button HotSpot

The button hotspot is similar to an Action button. The main difference is that the button is placed within the contents of the form, whereas an Action button always displays on the Action bar. You would typically place a button hotspot next to a field where a process needs to occur; for actions that seem more related to the document as a whole rather than a specific field (save and/or close document, approve or decline, create response, and so on), you're better off using the Action bar. You can place a button anywhere you want, and you can also use a Simple action, a formula, LotusScript, or JavaScript to program the button to execute a specific task.

NOTE *To remove a button, simply highlight the button and press the Delete key. This type of hotspot is different from all the others.*

NOTE *LotusScript button hotspots will not work on the Web.*

In the Button Properties Box, you can type in text that will display in the button, which is the only real difference between the Button Properties Box and the other Properties Boxes. The button itself looks just like any other button and cannot be altered. The button's Action lies in the script area for the hotspot. You can have the button do anything you want, from setting field values to running Agents. To create a button hotspot, follow these steps:

1. Open the Recipe with HotSpot form. Select the Audit Trail tab. Place the cursor next to the Last Updated On field.

2. Choose Create ➤ HotSpot ➤ Button, which will automatically display the Button Properties Box.

3. In the Button Label field, type **Show All Edit Times**.

4. Let's enter a formula for the hotspot. You will need to expand the Button event from the Objects tab in the programmer's pane and select the Click event (you can also place the cursor in the hotspot directly on the form). Type in the following formula:

```
EditTimes := @Implode($Revisions; @Newline);
@Prompt([OK]; "Revision date/times"; EditTimes)
```

Now you can test the button hotspot. When the button is clicked, the user is shown a dialog box indicating when the document has been updated before.

If you need to redisplay the Button Properties Box for a button hotspot, select the button on the form and choose Button ➤ Button Properties (or right-click the button and select Button Properties). To remove the button, just select it and delete it.

Creating an Action HotSpot

There is only one major difference between the Action hotspot and the button hotspot: how they look. Other than that, they are identical. You can create an Action hotspot on text or on a graphic (similar to the other hotspots mentioned previously). To create an Action hotspot, follow these steps:

1. Open the Recipe with HotSpot form. Select the Audit Trail tab and place the cursor to the right of the button. Press Enter to create a new line underneath the button.

2. Type **Show All Edit Times**. Highlight this text and choose Create ➢ HotSpot ➢ Action HotSpot, which will automatically display the Action HotSpot Properties Box.

3. Enter the same formula you entered for the button hotspot.

We created two hotspots which perform the same action to prove they both can accomplish the same tasks and also to point out how different from one another they look. When you have inserted these last two hotspots on the form, your form should be similar to Figure 20.39.

FIGURE 20.39

The completed form with the button and Action hotspots

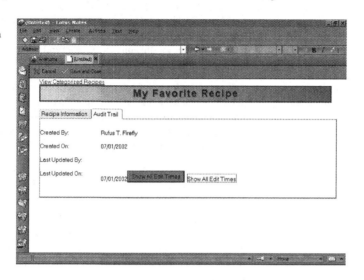

Embedding Elements

Embedded elements are objects that can be embedded on a form (and also on a document and a page). Table 20.1 describes all the elements that can embedded. To insert an embedded element on a form, choose Create ➢ Embedded Element and then select the element from the list.

TABLE 20.1: EMBEDDED ELEMENTS FOR A FORM

ELEMENT	DESCRIPTION
Outline	If you choose to embed an outline, you will be prompted to select from a list of outlines currently defined for the database. Once selected, the outline will be embedded on the form. If you want to be able to use an outline you have created, you *must* embed it. You have the option of embedding an outline in either a form or a page. An outline is typically used as a navigation menu for switching views, creating documents, or anything else you can think to create. Because you, the developer, create the outline, you can decide how and where to use it. Once an outline is embedded, you can use the Outline Properties Box to format it. You can embed more than one outline on a form or a page. Please refer to Chapter 22, "Outlines, Pages, Framesets, and Navigators," for more information about outlines.

Continued on next page

ELEMENT	DESCRIPTION
View	An embedded view will produce the same results in either the Notes client or a web browser. Therefore, you won't have to worry about how the documents will display in either environment. To embed a view, select from a list of views currently defined for the database. You have the option of selecting a specific view or using a formula to evaluate to the name of the view to use. Once the view is embedded, you can use the Embedded View Properties Box to change the look and feel of the display for both the Notes client and a web browser. Only one view can be embedded on a form (once a view is selected the option is no longer available on the menu).
Navigator	This option will prompt you to select from a list of Navigators currently defined for the database. You have the option of selecting a specific Navigator or using a formula to evaluate to the name of the Navigator to use. When using this type of Navigator, do not use the Hide-When property to hide the Navigator from web browsers, or the form will *not* display. You can embed a Navigator as many times as you like.
Import Navigator	This option will prompt you to select from a list of Navigators currently defined for the database. Once this option is selected, a "snapshot" of the Navigator will be taken and placed into a Picture object on the form. You can use the events and properties associated with a Picture object. You can import a Navigator as many times as you like.
Date Picker	If you embed a Date Picker, you can easily create a custom calendar application. The Date Picker displays a graphical monthly calendar in which a user can scroll from month to month and select a day. You can use it in conjunction with a frameset and place the Date Picker in one frame and a Calendar view in another. When the user clicks a day, a message is automatically broadcast. This message will be acknowledged by the Calendar view and that day will be displayed (this feature is only supported for a Notes client application).
Group Scheduler	The Group Scheduler control allows you to display the schedules of specific users. By default, the display is set to the one-day format, but it can be set to two-, five-, six-, and seven-day formats. When you design the form, the scheduling information will not be displayed. Only one Group Scheduler control can be embedded on a form (once a Group Scheduler control is embedded, the option is no longer available).
Editor	An Editor control lets you open a form inside a form. The form appears in a fixed-size window (the size can be adjusted in the form design, but not by the window. When you save a form containing an Editor element, the contents of the main form and the contents of the contained form are saved as separate documents.
Folder pane	In the Notes client, the database will display a default navigational pane that shows a list of all the views to which the user has access. The Folder pane is a control that displays the same list of views, but it's only used for a web application. Instead of having to manually code a list of views to which the user has access, you only need to embed this element. Only one Folder pane can be embedded on a form (once it's embedded, the option is no longer available).

Continued on next page

TABLE 20.1: EMBEDDED ELEMENTS FOR A FORM *(continued)*

ELEMENT	DESCRIPTION
File Upload control	If you want to attach a file to a document in the Notes client, you use the File Attachment menu option. For a web user, this menu option is not available and requires special handling. When embedded on a form and rendered on the Web, this control will display a field and a Browse button that will display a File Open dialog box on the end user's machine. When the user selects a file and submits the form, the file will automatically be sent over the Web and attached directly to the document. Only one File Upload control can be embedded on a form (once it's embedded, the option is no longer available).

The main reason for using an embedded element is to maintain a consistent look and feel across both the Notes client and the web browser. As you have probably noticed by now, there are some significant differences in elements—the differences depend on the environment in which the elements are displayed. When you embed elements in a web application, your application's functionality will more closely resemble what happens in the Notes client.

Summary

This chapter has dealt with quite a few advanced form features, including sections, layout regions, and tables. We also discussed how automation through Action buttons and hotspots can increase an application's functionality. Finally, we showed you various ways to place images and graphics into your application so that forms are a bit easier to understand.

In the next chapter, you'll begin to see how all of the work you put on your forms can benefit the end user. What good is information if the user can't find what he is looking for? Using views to sort and display the contents of your data is an integral part of any well-planned application.

Chapter 21

Using Views and Folders

ONE OF THE BIGGEST challenges facing workers today is *finding* information, not using it. Views and their cousins, folders, provide a mechanism for summarizing the data in documents, which makes the database easier to navigate. A database can contain one or more views, each displaying the data in a slightly different way.

- ◆ The definition of a view
- ◆ Creating a view
- ◆ Using view lookup tables
- ◆ Understanding folders
- ◆ The document response hierarchy

What Is a View?

In Notes, all data is stored in documents. A *view* can be thought of as a table of contents for those documents. In a book, a table of contents is used to navigate to a specific piece of information. Each entry in the table of contents contains a brief description or summary for a chapter or subsection in the book. You look through the table of contents for the information you want, find the page number, and turn to that page to see the information. A view is similar (except you don't have to turn pages). You select the view, look through the list of documents until you find what you want, and open the document. That's all there is to it.

One of the primary goals of a view is to help you find the information you need. Without views, finding information within each document would be extremely tedious. All the documents would be presented in some unpredictable and unstructured layout (which is, presumably, suitable to the data but not necessarily appropriate for high-level navigation) that you would have to decipher. A view provides a structure for the process of finding your information, and it can display that information in a variety of ways. Unlike a static table of contents, a view can show documents sorted by their contents (alphabetically or numerically), grouped in categories, or grouped in the order in which they were created. Also, they can often be resorted to suit the user's whim. Finally, views can have actions that allow you to work with documents without even opening them.

How does a document relate to a view? That's a good question, so let's take a look at a view a see. First, there are two styles you can use for views in Notes: the standard outline style and the endar style. They are visually quite different, even though they are created in exactly the same way standard outline view is commonly referred to as a *table view* because the information is laid out i row/column fashion. The calendar view, on the other hand, is laid out like a calendar, visually r resenting the days, weeks, and months. For the examples in this chapter, we'll continue to use the R ipe database.

The Standard Outline View Style

You can think of the *standard outline view* as a table of contents for the documents in the database (see I ure 20.1). This is probably the more common style of view. The contents of this view are grouped rows and columns as they would be on a relational database report, with each row of data in the datab query corresponding to a document in the Notes database. Each row (depicted in alternating colors a representation of a document and displays selected pieces of information from that document. To useful, each row should contain enough information for the user to easily identify the document. F example, look at the highlighted document (the document on the bottom) in Figure 21.1. The u would have difficulty identifying the document if we showed only the date the document was creat instead of the recipe name. By using the recipe name as one of the row values, the user can easily ident each specific document.

FIGURE 21.1

A standard outline view displayed in the Notes client

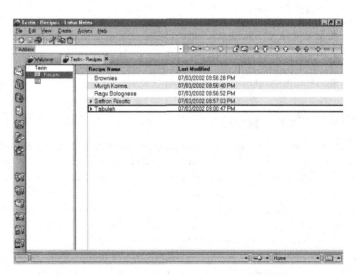

TIP What are those triangles to the left of some of the rows in Figure 21.1? In Notes-speak, they are known as twisties A twistie indicates there is more information relating to that row, which you can see by clicking the twistie to expand it These are quite common in views that use the Response document hierarchy and views that group documents into categories

NOTE *Each database must have at least one view. When you create a database, it contains a view named (Untitled).*

Not so obvious are the columns that make up a view. Each column displays a specific type of information about a document. The designer decides which element from a document should be displayed or used in computations. One or more columns in the view are usually identified as organizing elements. In Figure 21.1, the documents are arranged alphabetically by the name of the recipe. The column containing the name of each recipe can be considered the organizing column. Columns can also be a bit deceiving. In our example view, it looks as if there are only two columns, Recipe Name and Last Modified. There are actually three, but you cannot tell from looking at the view in the Notes client. To see all of the columns and the column definitions, you need to use Domino Designer to examine the Recipes view, as shown in Figure 21.2. In addition to the two labeled columns, there's a third, very narrow column to the left of Recipe Name; it's the selected column in the figure.

FIGURE 21.2

A standard outline view, Recipes, shown in Domino Designer

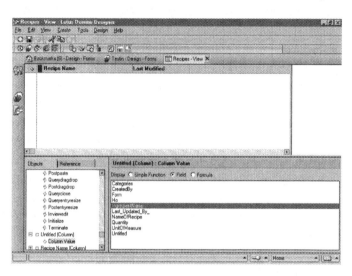

You can display information in a column by declaring a field or formula for it. In most cases, the column will reference a field in the document. This doesn't mean the column *must* reference a field, however. You can write a formula to display today's date or a number indicating the document's position in the view if you so desire. You also have the option of using a simple function, referencing a document field, or writing a formula to display a column value. In our example, we used the field IngredientName to generate what is displayed in the column.

USING SIMPLE FUNCTIONS

A simple function isn't quite an @function from the formula language. It's a shortcut to some of the more common functions used in a view column. There is nothing special about using a simple function; each selection has an @function counterpart, as shown in Table 21.1.

TABLE 21.1: SIMPLE FUNCTIONS

SIMPLE FUNCTION	@FUNCTION	DESCRIPTION
Attachment Lengths	@AttachmentLengths	Lengths of the attachments in the docume
Attachment Names	@AttachmentNames	Filenames of the attachments
Attachments	@Attachments	The number of attachments
Author(s) (Distinguished Name)	@Author	The name from the authors fields (Edwar Plunkett/Dunsany/Meath)
Author(s) (Simple Name)	@Name([CN];@Author)	The name from the authors fields (Edwar Plunkett)
Collapse/Expand (+/-)	@IsExpandable	Returns a plus sign if a row is expandable a minus sign if it is not
Creation Date	@Created	The date and time the document was created
Last Modified	@Modified	The date and time the document was last modified
Last Read or Edited	@Accessed	The date and time the document was last accessed
Size (bytes)	@DocLength	The size of the document in bytes
# in View (eg 2.1.2)	@DocNumber	A string representing the entry number o the document (2.3 represents the third ent below the second entry)
# of Responses (1 Level)	@DocChildren	The number of child documents for the current document
# of Responses (All Levels)	@DocDescendents	The total number of descendant documen for the current document

The Calendar View Style

The second style of view is called a *calendar view*. This view style organizes documents by date and tim Figure 21.3 shows an example of a calendar view style, called the Create Date view, viewed from t Notes client. As you can see, the layout is quite different from the layout for the standard outline vie Instead of the typical row/column layout, the view looks like a calendar. You can use this view f grouping and displaying information that is based around some date/time information (for examp the date a document was created). One point to keep in mind when using this view style is that t first column in the view definition *must* be a field that evaluates to a date and time. That date/tim information governs where the document falls in the calendar grid.

FIGURE 21.3

A seven-day calendar
view displayed in the
Notes client

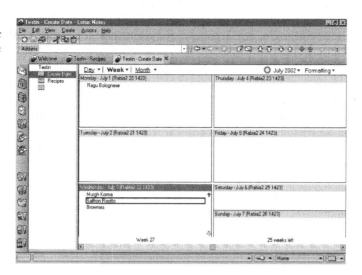

NOTE *You cannot select the view style when you create a view. By default, all new views use the standard outline style. If you want to create a calendar-style view, first create the view and then change the style via the View Properties box.*

TIP *The first column of a calendar view must be sorted, must contain a time-date value, and should be hidden (we'll show you how to hide columns later). You must also specify a second column that evaluates to the duration in minutes. If the duration does not apply, leave it set to 0. This column should be hidden as well.*

If you look at the view from Domino Designer, you'll notice that it is similar to the basic Recipes view. The only difference is that the first column is using the document creation date (and of course, the view is a calendar-style view), and the second column specifies the duration in minutes (because our example identifies a single point in time, we set it to 0). The organization of the entire view is based on the first two columns so each entry can be associated with a specific date and time on the calendar. The calendar-style view can be quite useful when it is used in the correct application. For an excellent example, open your Notes mail and select the calendar option.

Navigating Views: Client vs. Web

Before we get into the details of creating views and view properties, let's examine a view from both the Notes client and the web perspective. It's important to understand how a user navigates a view and how a view will display in each environment. This knowledge will be handy when you design views for your databases. For the examples, we'll use the Recipes view

You've seen how the Notes client displays a view. The default Notes database will have a Navigation pane (the pane on the left), which displays all the currently defined views and folders, and a View pane (the pane on the right), which shows the currently selected view. Figure 21.4 shows the standard outline view within the Notes client environment, with the twisties expanded this time.

To navigate the view, the user can use the typical navigation keys, select documents by clicking them or clicking in the margin area, and so on. Review Chapter 3, "Working with Databases," if you need to refresh your memory.

Figure 21.5 shows the same view Figure 21.4 shows, except it is shown in a web browser. Nothing has been done to the view properties, so Notes is using a default navigational bar across the top and rendering the entire contents of the view as HTML. The web implementation is much simpler than the Notes implementation, but the basic functions are still there. Because it's a web application, the familiar buttons of the Notes client are replaced with links to open individual documents, to expand and collapse sections, and to page back and forth between pages of the view (if it contains a lot of documents, a web view may not show all results at once; users will need to click the Previous and Next links to see slices of the view). Like any other web application, every time the user wants to see different data—like when she navigates to another time period or expands/collapses documents—a request must be made to the server and then the results are returned to the browser, which can mean poorer performance than using a Notes client. Another drawback is that you cannot easily select, delete, or otherwise manipulate groups of documents from a view listing.

TIP *Although it's true you can't directly manipulate groups of documents from the Web using HTML display, there is a setting in the view preferences that allows you to select groups of documents using check boxes. You can then submit that information to the Domino server, where you can write program code that processes the documents. This is several steps more complex than you'll need for basic applications, but it opens up a wide range of possibilities for processing documents through the Web.*

FIGURE 21.4

The standard outline view accessed via a Notes client

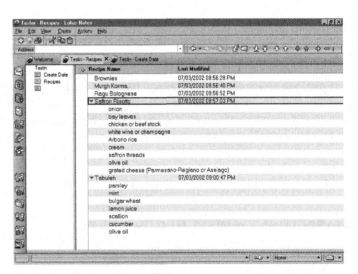

There is an alternative to using the HTML view: the view applet (see Figure 21.6). By selecting a property on the view, you can change the view so that it is a Java view applet instead of HTML (see "Setting the View Properties" later in this chapter). This view resembles the Notes client more closely, both in the way it looks and in the way it functions. A user can page up and down using the navigational keys just as in the Notes client. The only difference is that you cannot open a document by using the Enter key or by right-clicking the document. To open a document, you only need to double-click one of the rows. You can select documents and also delete documents from the view applet. Because the view applet uses caching for the documents, navigating the view and expanding/collapsing rows is just as quick as it is when you use the Notes client. The drawback, of course, is that the view applet requires the Domino server to send more information to the web browser than the HTML option does, which likewise slows performance.

FIGURE 21.5

The standard HTML view accessed via a web browser

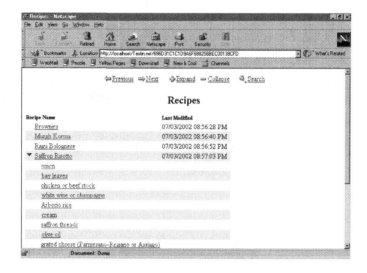

FIGURE 21.6

The standard view applet accessed via a web browser

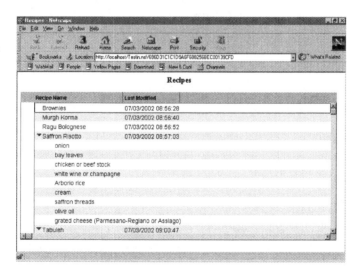

Creating a New View

Using the example Recipes database, let's create a new view that will categorize the recipes by ty~~pe~~ (whether it is an appetizer or a dessert, the ethnicity of the cuisine, and so on). As you may recall, ~~the~~ Recipe form has a Categories field. We'll use its contents to subdivide the contents of the view. ~~To~~ create the view, follow these steps:

1. Open the database in Domino Designer.

2. Choose Create ➢ Design ➢ View. The Create View dialog box appears (see Figure 21.7)

FIGURE 21.7

The Create View dialog box

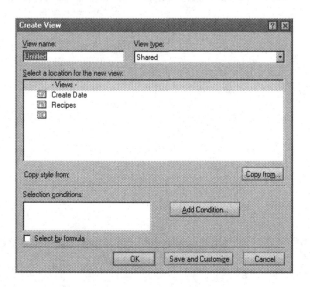

3. Type **Recipes by Category** in the View Name field.

4. Select Shared from the View Type drop-down list (we'll discuss all six types in the next section).

5. Leave the Select a Location for the New View list box as it is. If you select a view from this list, the selected view becomes a parent and the new view will appear under it. In other words, it will create a cascaded view.

6. Click the Copy From button to display the Copy From dialog box (see Figure 21.8). The default is to use the default database view's layout when a new view is created. If you want to create a blank view, select Blank in the Copy Style From list box. (This feature is also a handy way to quickly create new views. If you're creating a new view that is similar to an existing view, copy from the existing view and save yourself a bit of work.) For our example, we'll create a blank view, so select Blank and click OK. The Copy From dialog box disappears, and you are taken back to the Create View dialog box (see Figure 21.9).

TIP *If you want to create a view similar to an existing one (or, for that matter, any design element similar to an existing one), you can skip this entire dialog box. When you have a list of views displayed in the Work pane, you can click on the view you want to work from, copy, and paste it.*

NOTE *If you are unsure which view will be used or copied when you create your new view, look at the text next to Copy Style From in the Create View dialog box. If a view is specified, such as Recipes View in Figure 21.7, that will be the view that is used as the starting point.*

FIGURE 21.8

The Copy From dialog box allows you to select a view on which to base your new view.

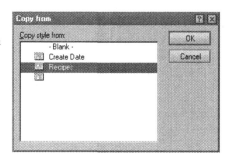

7. The last item to consider is the document selection criteria. The default is to select all the documents in the database. You can override this selection formula by enabling the Select by Formula option and entering a formula in the Selection Conditions text box. For our example, we'll use the default SELECT @All formula. You can easily change the selection conditions after you create the view (see "Selecting Your Documents" later in this chapter).

TIP *If you leave the Selection Conditions text box empty, it will default to SELECT @All. This formula tells the view to display all documents in the database.*

FIGURE 21.9
The Create View
dialog with all the
data filled in

8. You have now entered all the criteria and are ready to generate the new view. If you click t
OK button, the new view will be generated and displayed in the list of views. Another alte
native is to click the Save and Customize button. This will also create the view and open t
new view in the Designer workspace to allow you to customize it (basically, this option ope
the view for you so you don't have to open it yourself). In this case, click the OK button (v
have a few more sections to cover before we actually design the contents of the view).

NOTE   *When you create a Shared, Contains Documents Not in Any Folders view or a Shared, Contains Deleted Doc*
uments view, you don't need to enter a selection criterion because it is predetermined. (The predetermined criterion for
Shared, Contains Documents Not in Any Folders view is, as its name implies, if a document is not in a folder. The pre-
determined selection criterion for a Shared, Contains Deleted Documents view is if a document is deleted).

NOTE   *You should always make sure that a database has a default view specified. Only one view can be set as the default*
and will be shown in the Work pane with a dark blue arrow (those with a light gray arrow are hidden views).

Understanding View Types

When we created the Recipes by Category view, we selected the Shared view type. There are six d
ferent types of views that fall under two main classifications:

- ♦ Shared
- ♦ Private

The only difference between these two main types is that a Shared view can be accessed by mar
different people, whereas a Private view can only be accessed by a single person.

SHARED VIEWS

A Shared view can used by anyone who has at least Reader access to the database. Almost all the views you will create will be Shared views because it is the most common type. There are five types of shared views that can be created for a Notes database.

Shared

The Shared view is the generic and most common type of view. It is also the default for any new views that are created.

Shared, Contains Documents Not in Any Folders

This is a special type of view in that it will only show those documents that are not in any folders.

Shared, Contains Deleted Documents

The Shared, Contains Deleted Documents view is another special type of view that will only show those documents that have been deleted. This view is only effective when the Allow Soft Deletions option in the Database Properties InfoBox has been activated.

Shared, Private on First Use

The Shared, Private on First Use view can be initially declared as shared to all the users. Once a user accesses the view, it immediately becomes a private view for that user. The actual private view is stored in the database.

Shared, Desktop Private on First Use

The Shared, Desktop Private on First Use view is exactly the same as the Shared, Private on First Use view with one exception: The view is not stored in the database but in the user's `Desktop.dsk` file.

WARNING   *Once the user has accessed the Shared, Private on First Use or Shared, Desktop Private on First Use view and the private copy has been saved, design changes you make will never be reflected in the user's private copy. The only way for a user to see new design changes is to remove the Private view and access the Shared view again (which will create a Private view once again).*

PRIVATE VIEWS

A Private view is no different from its counterpart, the Shared view, except that an individual user is responsible for creating it. There is only one type of Private view that can be created by a user: Private.

Just as the name suggests, the view is private and will only pertain to the person who actually creates it. No other person will ever see or have access to use this view. If the person creating the view has access rights to create a view or folder, the Private view will be stored in the database. If the person does not have the access to create a view or folder, the Private view will be stored in the user's `Desktop.dsk` file.

NOTE   *Private views and Shared views are visually the same. So you can tell them apart, a Private view will display a different icon than a Shared view icon in the Navigation pane in the Notes client. In Designer, a Private view will have a key icon. For a Shared, Private view, the icon will be the key with blue marking.*

Selecting Your Documents

One of the main purposes of a view is to make sure the correct documents are being displayed. In [ ] view created earlier in the chapter, we did not change the default selection criteria (we left it blan[ ] By default, a view will use the SELECT @All formula, which "selects" all the documents in the datab[ ]. This may be fine for some views, but you may also want to restrict a view to a subset of docume[ ]

When you create a view, you can determine the selection criteria that will be applied for the se[ ] tion of documents. When we created the view earlier, you had the option of typing in a formula[ ] using the Add Condition button. For an existing view, you have the same two choices. You can en[ ] the selection criteria before a view is created, or you can modify the criteria after the view is crea[ ]

SETTING THE SELECTION CRITERIA

To change the selection criteria after a view is created, you need to select the View Selection eve[ ] This is actually quite easy because this event is automatically displayed when a view is first open[ ] Let's go over the steps for displaying the View Selection event:

1. From Domino Designer, highlight the View element in the Design list. This will display all [ ] views for the current database in the Work pane.

2. From the Work pane, double-click the Recipes by Category view (you can also right-click t[ ] view and select Edit). Now the View Selection event shows up in the script area of the pr[ ] grammer's pane, but it is not displayed in the Objects list.

3. Expand the Recipes by Category (View) entry in the Objects list. By default, this entry will [ ] highlighted.

4. Select the View Selection event and the programmer's pane will display, as shown in Figure 21.[ ]

FIGURE 21.10

The document
selection criteria
event (View
Selection)

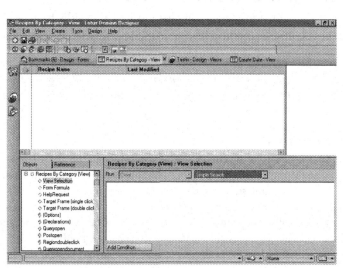

You'll notice that, in the script area, there is a drop-down list box with the entry Simple Searc[ ] already selected. There are two possible selections: Simple Search and Formula.

Because the selection criterion uses a formula, you may be wondering what the Simple Search option is all about. When the Simple Search option is selected, the Add Condition button is displayed. You don't have to know how to program a formula, yet you can create the selection criteria.

So you don't have to manually code a formula for selecting records, the button will display a dialog box that will allow you to "point and click" to the selection criteria. When you click the Add Condition button, the dialog box shown in Figure 21.11 displays. There are seven choices in the Condition drop-down box.

FIGURE 21.11

The Add Condition dialog box, which is used to select the criteria for searching for documents

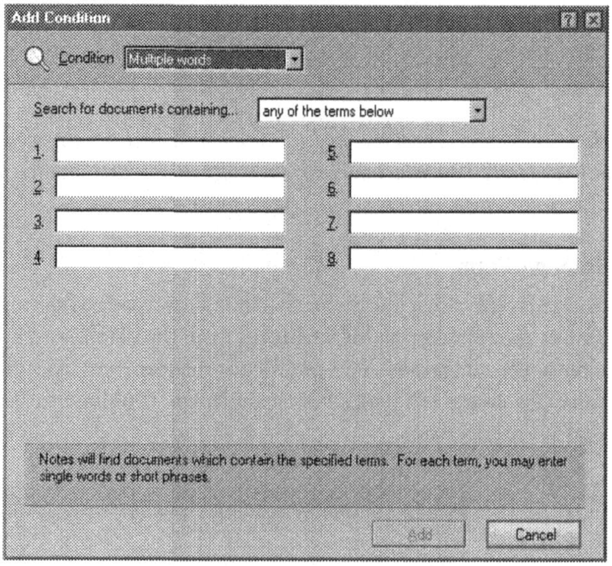

By Author

The By Author option is similar to the By Field option except Notes will search the authors fields on each document to find a match. The difference between this option and the By Field option is that *all* authors fields will be searched (you can have more than one on a document). This option is useful if a user wants to see a list of all the documents she created.

By Date

The By Date option allows you to select documents based on the creation or modification date of the document. It is important you understand that the creation and modification dates are the only choices available with this option. One nice feature of using this criterion is the vast number of comparison operators. You can search between two date values, before a specified date, on a specified date, and so on.

By Field

The By Field option allows you to base the selection criterion on the values of a specific field. All you need to do is select a field from the Search for Documents Containing drop-down list and enter the value of the field. For example, if you want to list only those recipes that contain the word *beef* in the title, select the Recipe field, select the Contains condition, and type **beef** in the text box. Only documents that have *beef* in the Recipe field will be returned.

By Form

The By Form option is probably the easiest and most widely used. You can select documents based on the form that was used to create them. For example, if we want to show recipes grouped by the food type and we only want the recipe documents that were created with the Recipe form, we would select the Recipe form from the form list (by placing a check mark next to it). In this case, because we may have created recipes using a number of different forms, we'll want *all* of the recipe-related forms, so check all of them.

NOTE   *If one or more of your forms do not show up in the By Form list, make sure the Search Builder option on the Basics tab of each form's Properties InfoBox is enabled. This tells Notes that this form can be used in the Search Builder process.*

Fill Out Example Form

This option starts out much like By Form, but it allows you to fine-tune the selection (see Figure 21.12). In the menu at the top, you can select a form from the database. That form will appear in the window in the center of the dialog box. You can fill out the form with specific data. It even allows you to fill in desired values for computed fields. For example, you could use this option to select Recipe documents created by a specific person.

FIGURE 21.12
The Fill Out
Example Form
condition

In Folder

This option allows you to grab the same documents as appearing on other views. This is not terribly useful in itself, but it can be helpful if you want to base your selection criteria on another view but also want to add additional conditions.

Multiple Words

This option allows you to enter a number of words and see documents with any or all of them, regardless of where in the document they appear. You might, for example, select all Recipe documents mentioning the word *chocolate*.

SETTING THE SELECTION CRITERIA WITH THE FORMULA OPTION

It's a bit more difficult to create the view selection criteria with the Formula option, but you have a commensurate increase in power and flexibility. From the Run drop-down list in the script area (see Figure 21.10), select Formula. Notice that there is already a formula typed in for you. You'll see a long formula selecting documents where there's a value associated with the recipe-related form names and their aliases in the Form field. Doesn't that sound familiar?

When you enter a Search Builder selection, Notes will automatically translate that selection to a formula. This is an excellent way to learn how to use selection formulas. You use the Add Condition button to add different scenarios and then switch to the formula to see how to write it.

We've covered most of the basic elements of a view that need to be defined (except for the data columns). As it is currently defined, our example view will select the correct documents, but it is still not perfect. Before deciding what data to actually display in the view, let's go over the view properties.

Setting the View Properties

A view also has a set of properties that control its look and feel; that is, they control how the view will behave when a user accesses it. One important factor to keep in mind when developing an application is how the user will access the data. Because views display various pieces of data contained within the documents, it's especially important to sketch out the different ways a user will want the data displayed. We cannot stress this point enough. Also, depending on the style of view (standard outline or calendar), the number of view option tabs will vary. With that in mind, let's go over the properties.

To open the Properties box for a view, just follow these steps:

1. Open the Recipes database.
2. Open the Recipes by Category view.

TIP   If you would like to see the current contents of the view, press the F9 key to refresh it.

3. Open the View Properties box by choosing Design ➢ View Properties (you can also right-click the view and choose View Properties).

The View Properties box contains the following five tabs:

◆ View Info
◆ Options

- ◆ Style
- ◆ Advanced
- ◆ Security

THE VIEW INFO TAB

The View Info tab (see Figure 21.13) allows you to specify four basic parameters for the view:

- ◆ Name
- ◆ Alias
- ◆ Comment
- ◆ Style

FIGURE 21.13
The View Info tab of the View Properties box

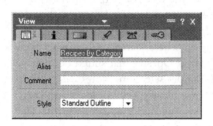

The Name field contains the name used when we originally created the view, Recipes by Catego
The view is one of the few design elements that has a separate Alias field. You have the option of ty
ing the alias in the Alias field or using the vertical bar (|) and appending the alias to the view nam
For this example, give the view an alias by typing **RBC** in the Alias field. The Comment field allo
you to enter some comments about the view. A brief explanation of what the view is used for is ty
ically enough. The comments will be displayed in the Work pane underneath the View element. T
last field determines the style of the view. As mentioned earlier in the chapter, a view can be eithe
standard outline or calendar view style. By default, all new views are standard outline. If you want
create a calendar view, you only need to change this parameter.

TIP   Remember to always use an alias for a view and reference that element by its alias name. As with forms, you ca
create different versions of views for Notes, web, and mobile device use, and if your user community doesn't like your vie
name, you can change it without breaking anything.

THE OPTIONS TAB

The Options tab, shown in Figure 21.14, allows you to specify the overall behavior of the view. The
are ten different options that can be selected.

FIGURE 21.14

The View Options
Properties tab of the
View Properties box

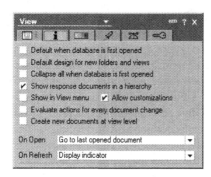

Default When Database Is First Opened

Default When Database Is First Opened allows you to decide which view will automatically display the first time the database is opened. You can only specify this option for one view (Designer will automatically disable any other view when you enable this option and save the view). For our example, deselect this option if it is enabled. This option has no effect on a web application.

Default Design for New Folders and Views

Default Design for New Folders and Views allows you to select which folder or view should be used as the default when a new folder or view is created. You may remember that, when we initially created this view, you could specify which view to copy (using the Copy From button). Using this option, you can specify that all new views automatically inherit the design from a specific view. For our example, deselect this option if it is enabled.

NOTE *When creating a new view, it's sometimes hard to determine the design on which a view was based. If no view has been selected as the default view and no view has been selected as the default design, the view will use the default design view, which shows a single column displaying the document number and selects all the documents in a database. If a default view has been selected but no view has been selected as the default design, the new view will inherit the design from the default view. If a view has been selected as the default design, the new view will inherit the design from the default design view.*

Collapse All When Database Is First Opened

The Collapse All When Database Is First Opened option only applies to views that have expandable rows. When it is selected, all of the rows will be collapsed. There is an exception, however, and it applies only to the Notes client. If the user is positioned on a specific document, the expandable category will not be collapsed. This option is helpful for large views with many categories. It's not available for calendar-style views, which cannot be categorized. For our example, deselect this option if it is enabled. This option also applies to web applications.

Show Response Documents in a Hierarchy

If your database contains forms for both a Main document and Response documents, the Show Respo
Documents in a Hierarchy option is important for maintaining and displaying the document relationsh
Enabling this option will allow the view to automatically maintain the parent-child document relationsl
You don't need to worry about how to include Response documents in the view. Notes automatically d
it. We'll discuss this in detail in "Understanding the Response Hierarchy." This option is not available
calendar-style views. For our example, deselect this option if it is enabled. This option also applies to v
applications.

Show in View Menu

When the Show in View Menu option is selected, the view displays as an option in the View me
of the Notes client (because there is no menu for the Web, this only applies to the Notes client). T
option can be useful when you are not using the default view Navigator and want to give the use
another way to access the view. For our example, deselect this option if it is enabled.

Allow Customizations

This option allows the user to modify the view and have those changes stick without changing tl
underlying design. For example, users can re-sort the view or change the widths of columns.

Evaluate Actions for Every Document Change

Views may have various actions associated with them that are evaluated when a user opens the vie
If you check this option, those actions will run every time a document changes. This makes yo
view more responsive to user actions, but it will give you a performance hit because the formul
execute more frequently.

Create New Documents at View Level

This option creates a new entry at the bottom of the view. If you Ctrl+click, you can create a new d
ument. If you select this option, you'll also have to program the view's InViewEdit event. There
actually a pretty complex sequence of events connected to this process, which is beyond the scope
this chapter. If you're curious, search the Domino Designer help for *Display Options for Views.*

On Open

The On Open option allows you to specify which document to highlight when the view is first
opened. There are three choices in the drop-down list. Go to Last Opened Document takes the use
to the same document they were viewing when they left the database. This is the most commo
option to use because it lets users keep their position within the view. Go to Top Row and Go to
Bottom Row will position the user either on the first row of the view or on the last row of the view.
For our example, select Go to Last Opened Document. This option is not available for calenda
style views and also has no effect on a web application.

On Refresh

The last option, On Refresh, determines how the user will see changes to a view. There are four choices in the drop-down list. Display Indicator will not show view changes automatically but displays the refresh indicator in the left corner of the view. The user must click the icon to see the changes. Refresh Display will automatically refresh the view before displaying it to the users. Refresh Display from Top Row updates the view from the top down. This is handy for reversed chronological views so the user will see the most recent changes first. Refresh Display from Bottom Row updates the view from the bottom up. This is handy when the user expects to see changes at the bottom of the view. For our example, select Refresh Display. This option has no effect on a web application.

THE STYLE TAB: STANDARD OUTLINE

The Style tab for the standard outline view, shown in Figure 21.15, allows you to control how the view will look to the end user. The Body section controls the view background. The Rows menu allows you to set an overall background color for the view, while the Alternating Rows menu lets you set up a secondary color. If you select an Alternating Rows color, every second row in the view will be in that color. If you want a more nuanced background, the Image field lets you select an image resource to use as a background image. You can also set up a formula that selects an image resource. If you use an image, you have several options for how the image is tiled. Your choices are as follows:

- ◆ Repeat Once
- ◆ Repeat Vertically
- ◆ Repeat Horizontally
- ◆ Tile
- ◆ Size to Fit
- ◆ Center

If you think this list sounds familiar, you're right. It's similar to the list of options you have for manipulating the background image on a form.

Color is one of the most important aspects of the view. Too much color can make the view difficult to read, but too little color can make it difficult to track down individual pieces of information. (That goes double for the use of background images.) You should give the user just enough color to make information easily identifiable. Alternating row colors are extremely useful. They make it much easier for users to distinguish between rows of otherwise undistinguished text, particularly if the view is especially wide. Try to use subtle colors and subdued graphics; a bright red background color or a full-color image of Carnival in Rio de Janeiro can be distracting and make the information on the page hard to read. Likewise, use a color that contrasts with the color of the view text. A pastel color makes a good background, but not if you're using pastel-colored text.

The Grid, Header, and Rows sections allow you to further distinguish between rows and columns. The Grid section lets you put lines (or some combination of dashed, dotted, and sold lines) between individual "cells" in the row/column format, much like cells in a spreadsheet. This is can be a useful tool for distinguishing between tightly packed columns, something that alternating row colors doesn't do.

FIGURE 21.15

The Style tab for a standard outline view

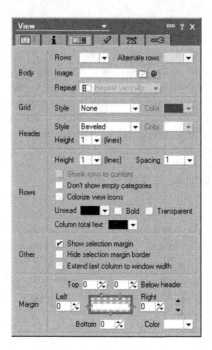

The Header section lets you adjust the background color, height, and style of column headers Style, in this context, means how the columns are distinguished from one another. By default, head have a shaded, "beveled" style. The Simple style is marked off by black lines, and the Flat style h no visible dividing lines at all. If you select None, no header will be visible.

The Rows section sets some display options for the row text. The most important options he are row Height and Spacing. If you intend to include columns with a great deal of data, you can a single row take up several lines. If you select this option, you can also have rows "shrink to fit," ti ing up no more lines than the data requires. There are several options for rows containing unread di uments here. You can, for example, make them appear in boldface or in a particular color. The Do Show Categories Having Zero Documents option prevents categories from being displayed in a vie if there aren't any documents to be displayed for that category. This may sound silly. How can a ca gory display with no documents? Simple. The documents may have a readers field (which preven some users from seeing the document), yet the category for the document will still display.

The Other section lets you show or display the selection margin. If it is displayed, you can choose n to display a dividing line between the view proper and the selection margin. You can also have the fin row extend to the far right of the screen regardless of what the individual column's properties are.

Finally, the Margin section lets you set up a colored border around the view. You can set the thic ness of the margin individually for the top, bottom, left, and right sides, as well as a separate marg for the line between header and view body.

THE ADVANCED TAB

The Advanced tab, shown in Figure 21.16, contains a set of the more complex view options. Two of the options, Refresh and Discard, have a direct impact on the speed of your database. There are four selections available for refreshing the index:

Auto, after First Use   Updates the view every time a user opens it after the first time it is opened (slow).

Automatic   Updates the view whether or not the user opens it (faster).

Manual   The view is not updated unless the user indexes it manually (fastest).

Auto, at Most Every   Updates the view index at a specified hourly interval (good for large databases).

When trying to determine which option to select, keep in mind how volatile the data is and also how quickly it changes. There are many options that need to be considered, and each situation is a bit different. For our example, set the Refresh option to Automatic.

FIGURE 21.16

The Advanced tab for a view

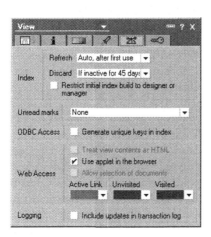

The Discard Index also has a direct impact on speed. There are three options available:

If Inactive for 45 Days   The view index is retained, using more disk space but speeding up access time for opening a view. However, if the view is not accessed for 45 days, the index will be discarded, freeing up disk space.

After Each Use   Saves a lot of disk space but may cause long delays because the view index needs to be rebuilt each time the user opens the view.

If Inactive For   This option is essentially the same as If Inactive for 45 Days, except that it allows you to set an interval of your own.

The tradeoffs with these Discard properties is either speed or disk space. If you always discard the index, the user will need to wait every time the view is opened and the index is rebuilding. If you keep

the index for a long time, you take up disk space. For our example, keep the default value of If Inact
for 45 Days.

The Unread Marks property is only useful within the Notes client (it doesn't work on the We
Don't overlook how important this option is to many users. Unread marks allow users to open a d.
base and quickly see which documents they have not read (or documents they have read that have be
modified). This is one of the more useful options within a Notes database. There are three optic
available for unread marks:

None   Does not track unread marks

Unread Documents Only   Displays an asterisk next to unread documents

Standard (Compute in Hierarchy)   Displays an asterisk next to unread documents and any
lapsed category containing unread documents

For our example, set the Unread Marks option to Standard (Compute in Hierarchy).

NOTE   *If you set the Unread Marks option to Unread Documents Only or Standard (Compute in Hierarchy) an
unread marks are still not showing up, remember that there is a database property that can be enabled that prevents main
taining unread marks.*

The option in the ODBC Access section can be used if you're going to access your Notes apr
cation via ODBC. With the "Generate unique keys in index" option checked, the view will crea
unique key values by the Draconian expedient of suppressing documents which display the same v
ues in the view as other documents. Imagine a view listing documents containing employee first a
last names. For whatever reason, there are two documents for employees named Charles Darna
With this option selected, only one of those documents will appear in the view.

The Web Access area lets you set a number of web-specific options. If you select Use Applet
the Browser, the view will be rendered as a Java applet when viewed through the Web (this option
not available for calendar views). If you select Treat View Contents as HTML, the Domino serv
goes to the extreme other end of complexity. Rather than rendering the view as a complex progra
matic object, the server won't render it at all. It will simply pass on the text content of the view to t
browser, assuming it already has whatever HTML formatting it needs. This may sound useless, b
it can come in handy if you want to add your own HTML to achieve particular special effects. If yo
select Allow Selection of Documents, when the server renders the view into HTML, it generate
check box fields for each document that carry the document ID numbers of the documents to whi
they correspond. By themselves, these check boxes do nothing, but you can use these fields to identi
individual documents to the server over the Web and process the data with agents on the backen
Finally, like a form, you can set the colors of links.

The "Include updates in transaction log" option causes Notes to record in the system log (the da
base log.nsf) whenever the view index is updated. This can be useful if you want to closely monitor vie
usage and performance, but otherwise is a waste of time and space in the log.

THE SECURITY TAB

The Security tab, shown in Figure 21.17, should already be familiar to you. You can select who h
access to use the view and who does not. For our example, select All Readers and Above.

FIGURE 21.17

The Security tab

THE STYLE TAB: CALENDAR

The Style tab for the calendar-style view, shown in Figure 21.18, allows you to control how the view will look to the end user. Many of the options are similar to, but not quite the same as, those for the standard outline view.

FIGURE 21.18

The Style tab for a calendar view

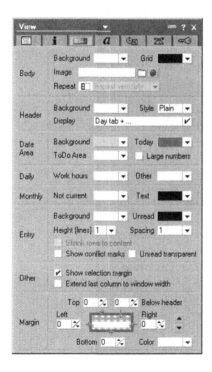

The Body section is quite similar, but instead of alternating row colors, it lets you pick a color the calendar grid. The Header area lets you choose between plain (unlined), tabbed, and no head row. It also allows you to select any combination of header items and controls: separate tabs for ferent periods of time, formatting buttons, a Go to Today button, and so on. The Entry section essentially the same as the Rows section in a standard outline view, but it applies to individual c endar entries within a day. The Other and Margin sections are also nearly identical to their stand outline counterparts.

A calendar view also has sections that are not available to standard outline views. The Date A section sets options for the backgrounds of individual days. By default, for example, the current c is outlined in red. The Daily area sets background options for one-day and two-day views. You c set separate background colors for during-work and after-work hours. The Monthly area lets you text and background colors for days that may be visible in the view but are not part of the select month.

THE FONT TAB: CALENDAR

The Font tab, shown in Figure 21.19, is only used for the calendar-style view. There is really nothi special about the font selection boxes, but you can select which elements of the calendar view change from the drop-down list at the top. Your choices are as follows:

Time/Slots Grouping   The time slots displayed for a calendar day

Header   The month, day, and weeks/days remaining displayed in the header and footer for t entire calendar

Day and Date   The date and day of the week displayed in the header for a calendar day

FIGURE 21.19
The Font tab for a
calendar-style view

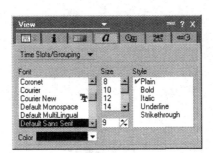

THE DATE AND TIME FORMAT TAB: CALENDAR

The Date and Time Format tab, shown in Figure 21.20, includes options for formatting the displ of a calendar-style view. There are quite a number of options that allow you to completely control t display for this type of view. You can enable and disable specific time periods available to the use and set one of them as a default value for when the view is first opened. You can also enable daily tin slots, specifying the start time, end time, and duration increments (from as little as 1 minute to as much as 2 hours) and determine whether users can override those settings with their own persona preferences.

FIGURE 21.20

The Date and
Time tab for a
calendar-style view

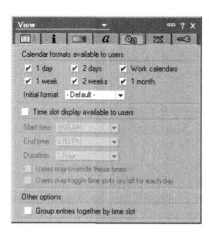

Defining the View Column Data

The next step is to actually put data into a view. As mentioned earlier in this chapter, each row in a view is actually a small representation of the contents of an actual document. Without this information, a view is meaningless. These columns of data allow a user to identify which document is actually being represented.

By default, when a new view is created (assuming you did not create the view based on an existing view definition), only one column of data is created, as shown in Figure 21.21. This column has a number sign (#) as the column title and displays the document number for each document. As you can see, this is meaningless to an end user. A user is not going to be able to identify a specific document using 1, 2, and so on. To remedy this situation, we are going to add a few columns to identify a document uniquely.

FIGURE 21.21

The default
definition for a
new view

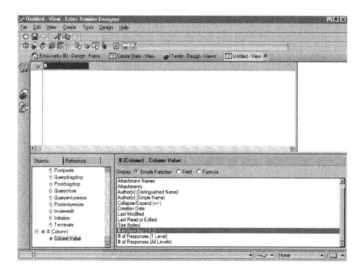

Creating and Moving Columns

By default, a view has a single column. This is rarely enough. You'll usually want multiple columto display a number of different values. You can add columns to a view in a number of ways:

- ◆ Select Create ➢ Insert New Column. This inserts a column to the left of the currently seleccolumn.
- ◆ Select Create ➢ Append New Column. This adds a new column to the far right end of the vie
- ◆ Right-click in the Work pane. Append New Column and Insert New Column will both
  appear on the contextual menu.

Once you've gotten a column in your view, you may decide to move it from its current positic
You can move a column simply by clicking the column header and dragging it to a new positic
Because we based the Recipes by Category view on the existing Recipes view, we're already most
the way there, but we need to add another column at the beginning of the view. To do that, click tleftmost column in the view. Next, select Create ➢ Insert New Column. The new column will appeto the left of the selected column. Now that it's in place, we can change it.

Setting the Column Value and Properties

In our example, we want to change the value that the column is going to display. To do so, just clithe column header. This will display the value or formula for the column selected in the script arof the programmer's pane. The selected column's value is a simple function of # in View (eg 2.1.
If you select the Formula radio button in the script area, you'll see that the simple function is actuausing the @formula @DocNumber, which in turn displays the number for each document in the vie

For our view to be a bit more meaningful, we want to change the value of this column so that ttype of recipe will be displayed (this value is contained in the Categories field). You have two optiofor setting this value. One would be to just type **Categories** (the name of the field) over the formu
@DocNumber. In some cases (for example, if you've got a large database with a long, long list of fieldyou may find this quicker. The second option is a bit easier in that you don't have to worry aboumaking a typographical error because you can select the field from a list.

To display a list of fields, select the Field radio button in the script area (see Figure 21.22). Juclick the name of the field you want to use. In this case, select Categories. That is all there is to it. Ncthe column will show the contents of the Categories field for each document in the view.

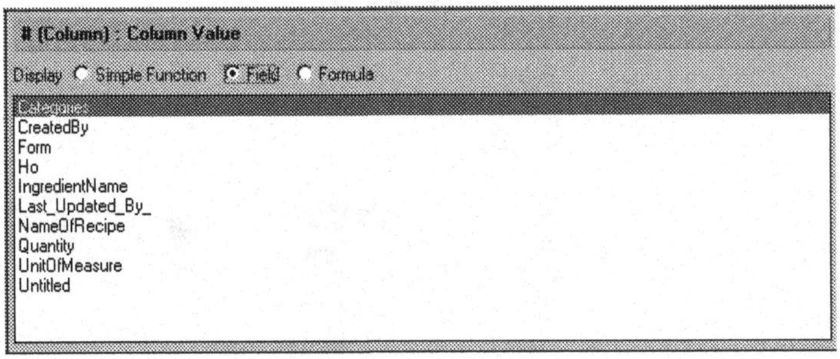

FIGURE 21.22

Selecting a column
value from a list of
defined fields for the
database

```
# (Column) : Column Value

Display  ○ Simple Function  ● Field  ○ Formula

Categories
CreatedBy
Form
Ho
IngredientName
Last_Updated_By_
NameOfRecipe
Quantity
UnitOfMeasure
Untitled
```

The next step in the process of setting up a column in a view is to change the column title or header. This requires you to open the Column Properties InfoBox for the column. To open the Column Properties box, follow these steps:

1. Select the column for which you want to display the properties by clicking the column heading.

2. Open the Column Properties InfoBox by choosing Design ➤ Column Properties (you can also right-click the column header and choose Column Properties or just double-click the heading).

The Column Properties InfoBox contains the following seven tabs:

◆ Column Info

◆ Sorting

◆ Font

◆ Numbers

◆ Date and Time Format

◆ Title

◆ Advanced

THE COLUMN INFO TAB

The Column Info tab, shown in Figure 21.23, allows you to specify the following:

Title   This value is the title displayed in the column heading. For our example, enter **Category**.

Width   This number determines the actual width for the column. If you make it too short, values in the column will be cut off. If you make it too long, you'll waste valuable screen real estate. For our example, enter a value of **3**. (You may think that this value is too low, but when we get to the Sorting tab, you'll see that this column is actually going to be categorized, and a categorized column is handled a bit differently.)

Multi-Value Separator   If a field contains multiple values, this option allows you to set how the values will be separated (None, Space, Comma, Semicolon, or New Line).

Resizable   Enabling this option will allow the user to change the width of the column.

Show Responses Only   Determines whether this column will display values for Response documents only. This will be explained in more detail in "Understanding the Response Hierarchy" later in this chapter.

Display Values as Icons   One handy feature of a view is that you can display an icon. If you select this option, make sure the column width is set to 1 (you're only going to display a small icon). Also, the value for the column must evaluate to an integer ranging in value from 1 to 172 (use 0 to signify no icon or blank). Each number represents an icon. For example, if you wanted to show the paperclip icon to represent a document that contains an attachment, use the formula @If(@Attachment;5;0). Figure 21.24 shows a list of all the possible graphics (this table is also contained in the help database; search for *displaying an icon in a column*).

FIGURE 21.23
The Column Info tab for the column

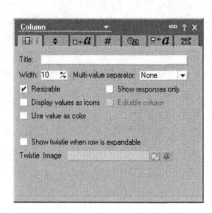

FIGURE 21.24
The column icons and their respective numbers

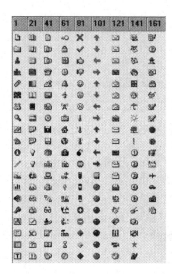

ADDING VIEW ICONS

Although Notes Help states that you cannot add to the list of built-in view icons, that is not entirely true. It's difficult, but possible. The list of view icons is located in the Domino\Icons directory (look under the Notes root data directory). A view icon is named vnicnXXX.gif, where XXX is a three-digit number (for example, 021 or 130). This number matches the value for the icon. If you want to add a specific icon and it's not listed, or if you want to change an existing icon, you can do so by manipulating these graphic files. There are two major limitations here. First, you'll need to manipulate files on every machine where you want the change to take place. Second, if you change or replace existing icons, you may have to change or replace them again after every time you upgrade your Notes or Domino software. There seem to be an awful lot of people who want to do this (in order, say, to use their own set of priority icons), but it's probably best left alone.

Editable Column If this option is checked, the column is editable. That is, the column can be used to edit data in the underlying document without having to open the document itself. To edit an item in an editable column, click the document to select it, and then click the column to get it into an editing mode. To edit a column value, the user must have permission to edit the underlying document.

Use Value as Color This option allows you to set the color of the text and the background of the column and the rest of the row programmatically. If this option is selected, you can provide colors in the form of a three-item list expressed in red, green, and blue values from 0 to 255. For example, green would be 0:255:0. If you use one color expression, color for the text in the rest of the row will be that color. If you use two color expressions separated by a colon (that is, a six-member list), the first color value will be used as for the background of the row, and the second will be used as the text color. For example, if the value of the column is 200:0:200, the text in the rest of the row will be a fairly deep purple. If the value in the column is 200:0:200:200:200:10, the remainder of the row will have a purple background and bright yellow text (if you actually use those values, Sybex takes no responsibility for how ugly your view is).

Show Twistie When Row Is Expandable This option is used for a categorized row (see the following section, "The Sorting Tab") and also for Response documents (see "Understanding the Response Hierarchy" later in this chapter). A categorized row eliminates duplication of the value on every row of the view. Instead, the value is shown next to a twistie (an arrowhead), and when it's clicked, all the rows are either expanded (all the rows are shown for the value) or collapsed (none of the rows are shown for the value). Think of a categorized value as a "header" for all the "like" rows. For our example, enable this option. If you choose to use a twistie, you can use an image resource to serve as a twistie rather than use the default green triangle. As with view and form backgrounds, you can either set a single image resource for the view, or you can use a formula to select one.

THE SORTING TAB

The Sorting tab, shown in Figure 21.25, allows you to control whether the data in the view should appear in a specific sorted order.

FIGURE 21.25

The Sorting tab for a column

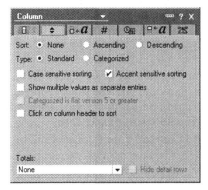

The following options appear on this tab:

Sort   This option sets the sorting rule (or sort order) for the column. You have the choice None, Ascending, or Descending. For our example, select Ascending.

Type   You can choose either a standard or categorized sorting type. If you select Categoriz you must specify a sorting rule (however, if you forget, the Ascending sort rule will automatica be selected for you). For a group of documents to be grouped under one category, the docume need to be sorted by that same value. For our example, select the Categorized option. You'll not that Sort is immediately switched to Ascending.

Case Sensitive Sorting and Accent Sensitive Sorting   These options allow you to decide if case and accents should be taken into account when the data is sorted.

Show Multiple Values as Separate Entries   By default, a categorized column will display multivalue field as a separate entry. This can be a major factor when you create documents beca it allows a single document to be classified under many different categories.

Categorized Is Flat Version 5 or Greater   This option is typically used for hidden categoriz views. It creates one entry for each category; it doesn't look good, but because the view is hidd how it looks should not matter. Use this type of view for a performance improvement when acce ing categorized views using features such as `@DBColumn` and `@Dblookup`.

Click on Column Header to Sort   You can specify that the column header can be used for alter the sort. The column can be sorted in ascending order, descending order, or both. This will appe to the user as up or down arrows in the column header. When an arrow is clicked, the sorting or for the column will change. Another handy feature is the ability to switch views when the user clic the column header. Instead of actually changing the sort for the view, the user is quickly transferr to another view.

WARNING   *If you allow the user to change the sorting order for views that contain categorized columns, the results may not be what you would expect. If a sorting order is changed, the documents won't be grouped together by the categorize column, hence the category is no longer valid. Because the categorized column is not really displaying the data for each doc ument, it will just disappear. If the category is an important piece of information for distinguishing different documents the results may confuse the user.*

Totals   This may be a bit of a stretch, but you do have the ability to add some statistics abo the documents within the view. You can sum the contents of a view, display averages, and displ percentages. It's not anything like the kind of summary functions you'll get out of a spreadshe or a true reporting program, but it can give you some simple numbers.

THE FONT, NUMBERS, AND DATE AND TIME FORMAT TABS

The Font tab, Numbers tab, and Date and Time Format tab allow you to control how the values f the column are actually formatted. The Font tab allows you to control the size, color, and justificatic for text values. The Number tab allows you to control the display format for numeric data. You ca select General, Fixed, Scientific, or Currency. You also have the option of selecting the number of decimal places, percentage values, negative numbers, or punctuation for numbers greater than 1,000. The Date and Time Format tab allows you to control how date and time values should be displayed. You have the option of displaying both date and time, date only, or time only. You also have various options available to format each of these types. This should all look familiar to rich-text formatting and form design. For our example, the value is always text. Select the Font tab and change the size to 12, the style to bold, and the text color to navy.

TIP   *One handy feature for time values is the built-in ability to adjust the value for local time zones. You can have the time automatically adjust to the user's local time zone, always show the time zone, and show the time zone only if it is not local.*

THE TITLE TAB

The Title tab is used for formatting the title in the header column. The options are the same as the options on the Font tab. The only difference is that this tab will only apply the formatting to the title of the column. For our example, just keep the default values.

THE ADVANCED TAB

The Advanced tab does not have many values from which to choose. The Name property is used and generated internally, and our advice is to never change this value. The only other parameter is for views that will be used on the Web. Selecting the Show Values in This Column as Links option allows you to select which column should be a link to the document when viewed in a web browser. By default, the first column of a view is automatically the web link. In some cases, this may not be your choice, so you have the ability to change it. You can also select more than one column to be used as a document link. Also, this option is only meaningful for views that will be rendered as HTML (remember that a view can also be displayed using a Java applet).

The most interesting options are probably the Hide Column options. These are handy for sorting the documents in a view without having to show the actual data for the column. For example, you may want to sort the view based on the 32-character document universal identifier (UNID), but you don't want to display this value to the end user.

TIP   *If you don't want any of the columns to be links to documents (such as when you are generating an online report), the solution is a bit tricky. First, select any column and enable the Show Values in This Column as Links option. Close and save the view. Now open the view and disable the option on the column. Close and save the view again. Now none of the columns will contain a document link.*

At this point, you should save the changes you've made to Recipes by Category. If you open the database in the Notes client, your view should look like Figure 21.26. You'll notice that only the Recipe documents are being displayed, not the actual ingredients for the recipe. Remember that the view selection limits the document selection to those documents that were created using the Recipe form. You'll also notice that some of the documents appear repeatedly. The Categories field is a multivalue field, so each document appears under each category under which it falls.

FIGURE 21.26

The Recipes by
Category view
displayed in the
Notes client

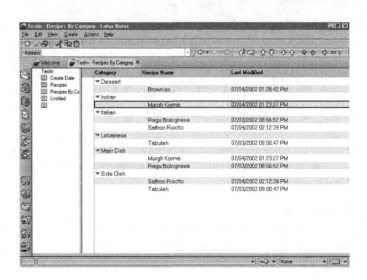

VIEWS AND ACTIONS

As you recall from the previous chapter, forms can have *actions*, buttons attached to the form that can perform complex, useful tasks such as updating document values, saving the current document, opening a form, and so on. Views can have actions as well. The actions you've already seen in the mailbox and personal address book databases are typical of what you'll find in view actions. You'll usually use them to create new documents or configure the database. You can use view actions to set document values. For example, an action with this formula would set the value of a field named Status to Complete in a view just as it would in a form:

```
FIELD Status := "Complete";
```

Something to be aware of, though, is that a field-setting view action will only set values for the currently highlighted document. That is, you could select a batch of documents and run the Action, but the value of the Status field would only be changed for one document. The way to get view Actions to update batches of documents is by using an *agent*, a design element we'll be discussing in Chapter 25, "Shared Code Objects." Your view action will contain a command that runs the agent, probably @ToolsRunmacro("*agentname*"). The agent itself will contain the code that does all the work.

Understanding the Response Hierarchy

One of the more confusing aspects of creating views is understanding how Notes interprets the document response hierarchy. In the preceding section, you saw how to display documents in a view, but you didn't learn how Response documents are displayed.

Creating Response Documents

Before we get into displaying them in views, you'll need to create forms capable of supporting responses and some response documents:

1. Create a new form.

2. In the Form properties, name it Ingredient | IngredientActions and make it a Response. On the Defaults pane, select Formulas Inherit Values from Selected Document.

3. Give it four fields: IngredientName (editable text field), Quantity (editable numeric field), UnitOfMeasure (editable text field), and Recipe (computed when composed text field). The Value formula for Recipe should be simply NameOfRecipe. Because the form inherits values from the parent document when the response is created, the new document will inherit the name of the parent recipe into the NameOfRecipe field. Label and arrange the fields as you see fit.

4. Open the Recipe with Actions form, click the Cancel action, and copy it. Go back to the Ingredient form and paste it. Repeat with the Edit action and the Save and Close actions.

5. Save and close the form.

When you're done, you should have something like the form shown in Figure 21.27. The New Ingredient action you created on the Recipe form should work now. Create a new Recipe with Actions document if you haven't already, then create a few Ingredient documents for it using the New Ingredients action.

FIGURE 21.27

The Ingredient form

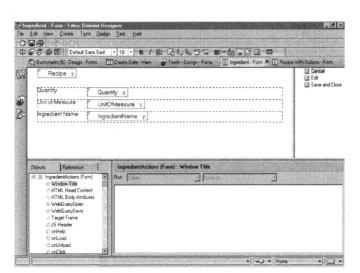

Displaying a Response Document

As you may recall from Chapter 19, "Basic Form Design," there are three types of documents that can be created in Notes. The Main document (or parent), the Response document (or child), and

the Response to Response document (child of the child). When you use these special docume
types, Notes automatically displays the documents in a view using a document response hierarc
Although Notes understands the document response hierarchy, it doesn't display these types c
documents automatically; you must understand how to set up a view so that responses will
indented properly.

It is useful to indent Response documents beneath the Main document when a user wants to s
the progression of a discussion. The indentation scheme for responses is limited to 32 levels, an
each response is indented three spaces beneath its predecessor. To set up a view that supports th
type of structure, you must first make sure you have designed the database to use Response ar
Response to Response documents. You must also make sure the Show Response Documents i
Hierarchy option is enabled in the View Properties Options tab. Otherwise, you may end up wit
a column in the view that displays Response documents only, which is what we'll cover next.

Using the Response Only Column

You can tell there is a response column defined in the view in Figure 21.28 because the Response d
uments are displaying. For a Notes view to display this hierarchy, you need to define a column s
cifically designed for Response documents (enable this option from the Column Info tab of th
Column Properties InfoBox). If you open the Basic view in Designer, you'll see that there are only t
columns defined for the view. The first column is the Response Only column, and the second colu
displays the recipe name.

FIGURE 21.28

An example of the
document hierarchy
in a view

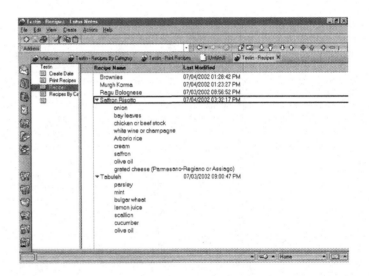

Although it doesn't make much sense, the Response Only column must be placed to the *left* of t
column under which the responses are to be indented. You should also leave the Title field blank ar
set the width to 1. The most important factor is to enable the Show Responses Only option. If it
not enabled, the Response Only column will not work correctly.

Once you have set up the column properties, you must also specify a value for the column. Whatever value you decide to place in this column will be shown for every Response document in the hierarchy; it doesn't matter how many other columns are defined for the view. In most cases, a Response Only column shows the subject, author, and creation time (you can find a good example of this in the discussion database template included with Notes).

In the Recipe example, the formula for the response column is simply this:

```
IngredientName
```

The column displays the name of the ingredient. This could be a problem if there were multiple types of responses. For example, if there were also response documents containing other user comments, we'd want a formula that could distinguish between them, showing ingredients for Ingredient documents and something else for comment documents.

TIP *If you are creating a view that will show documents in a response hierarchy, make sure the View Selection formula does not exclude the Response documents.*

Using View Form Formulas

One handy feature of views is that they give you the ability to change which form is used to display the document. In Chapter 19, we mentioned how Notes determines the form to use. Within a view, you can actually change this process by using a view property called a Form formula. When a document is opened from a view that has a Form formula defined, the Form formula will be evaluated, and the data will be presented based on the result; that is, it will be presented in the form the Form formula returned. Remember that the default form to use when displaying a document is usually saved within the document in the Form field. Using a Form formula does not necessarily alter this value. When you open the document, the data is displayed using another form. However, if you save and close the document after opening it, the document will be saved using the new form.

WARNING *If you use a form formula for a view, don't use the Form field as a criterion for your view selection formula.*

Now at first glance, it may not be readily apparent how this property may prove useful, so here's an example. Open the view called Print Recipes (this view has already been provided for you) in the Designer client. In the programmer's pane, select the Form Formula event. You'll notice that the script area contains the text *"Recipe Printing"*, as shown in Figure 21.29 (this form has been supplied for you as well). Although this is not really a formula, the result is the same: the name of a form.

Because the name of the form Recipe Printing is in the Form Formula event in the Print Recipes view, whenever a document is opened using the Print Recipes view, the Recipe Printing form will be used. One reason for having this type of view is to provide a black and white, graphic-free form used primarily for printing. If you look at the Recipe form, you'll see there are a lot of colors, graphics, and so on that really do not need to be there if all you want to do is print the recipe.

To try out the Form formula, open the Recipes database in the Notes client and select the Print Recipes view. This view will display the documents categorized by type (just as the Recipes by Category view does). At first glance, these two views look identical, but go ahead and open one of the documents. You'll see that the form looks completely different, as shown in Figure 21.30. The form being used is the Recipe Printing form and not the Recipe form. If you look at the Document Properties InfoBox for the current document, you'll see that the contents of the Form field are unchanged.

The document has not been altered in any way except in how it is displayed to the user. This fo displays all the recipe information, including the ingredients (we'll show you how the ingredients displayed in the next section).

FIGURE 21.29
Using the Form Formula event inside a view to display a document with an alternate form

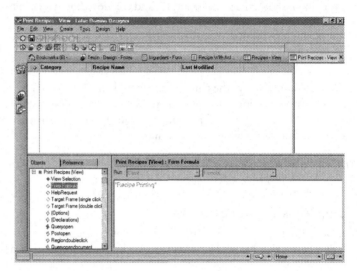

FIGURE 21.30
Displaying the contents of a recipe with an alternate form that shows all the recipe information and the ingredients listing

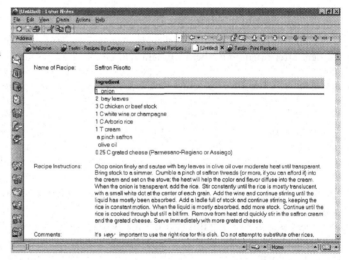

Using this technique, you have now given the users a quick way to print all the information abo a recipe. The user could have just opened the Basic view and printed the contents of the view. Th would have given them the name of the recipe and the ingredients, but it would not give them bo the instructions and comments. Using an alternate form, you can give the user the best of both worl

This is a minimalist example; you could use an intricate formula as well to calculate which form to use. For example, say you were building a product catalog containing products belonging to product lines, each with a distinctive logo or color scheme. You could create documents containing descriptive material and a field containing the name of the product line and a number of display forms with different colors or graphics. You could then use a form formula to take advantage of the product line name field to pick an appropriately decorated form automatically.

Embedding Views and Displaying Categories

Something that may have struck you about the Recipe Printing form is that it included a list of ingredients, even though ingredients are contained in separate documents, not the main recipe document. How did we do that? We used an embedded view. We took a view containing ingredients, put it on the form, and told it to display only those ingredients related to the recipe.

You'll find a view named (IngredientsCategorized) in the example database. It's a fairly simple categorized view. The only thing unusual about the view properties is that we've unchecked the Show Response Documents in a Hierarchy option. If this option were selected, it would only show the ingredient documents grouped with their parent recipe documents; because the recipe documents won't appear in the view, neither would the ingredients. The selection criteria pick ingredient documents. The first column simply shows the contents of the recipe field. The second column uses this formula to display complete ingredient information:

```
@Text(Quantity) + " " + UnitOfMeasure + " " + IngredientName
```

The completed (IngredientsCategorized) has as many categories as there are recipes with ingredients, but in the Recipe Printing form, the categories from the lookup view are not being displayed. This is because we are using a Show Single Category feature. This option is only available for an embedded view and allows you to specify a key for a category to display. In our example, because all the ingredients are categorized by the recipe name, we'll set the key to the name of the recipe and only those ingredients will be displayed.

To see how this works, we can examine the Recipe Printing form. Open this form. You will see that the list of ingredients is showing up on it. Click the list of ingredients in the form and a box will be displayed around the list of ingredients, as shown in Figure 21.31. This list of ingredients is actually an embedded view. Looking at the Objects tab, you will notice that there are two events for the embedded view: Embedded Selection (the view to embed) and Show Single Category. We are interested in the latter. The formula for the Show Single Category event is the field NameOfRecipe. This field is actually used as the title for the form as well. Because the contents of this field contain the name of the recipe and the embedded view is categorized by the recipe name, the embedded view is smart enough to only display those documents for the selected recipe.

This type of embedded view can be extremely powerful. It allows you to limit the scope of a view to only those records pertinent to the record being displayed. This could be useful in situations such as when you only want to show items for a particular order in an invoice application. The implementation of this type of view is endless. Although the view is not really dynamic (a dynamic view would only select those records using the selection formula), it is pretty close.

FIGURE 21.31

Using the
Show Single
Category event
to limit the scope
of an embedded view

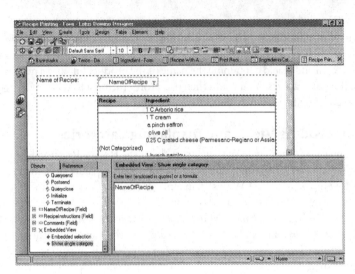

Using Folders

You can think of a folder as another type of a view. It has the same design elements as a view and
created in a similar manner: by choosing Create ➤ Folder (instead of Create ➤ View). The only r
difference between a folder and a view is that a folder does *not* have a selection formula. Rememb
for documents to show up in a view, the selection formula determines the criteria to collect the d
uments. A folder remains empty until a user adds documents to it (you can also add documents to
folder programmatically).

So how can a user add documents to folder? All a user needs to do is drag a document from a vi
and place it on top of a folder. The document is not actually copied to the folder; instead, the fold
references the document like a pointer. You can distinguish folders from views by the different ic
used in the Navigation pane of the Notes client. A folder is represented by a file folder icon, where
a view is represented by a table-like printed page icon. We've said this before, but it bears repeatir
If you decide to remove a document from a folder, do not use the Delete key. Doing so will dele
the document permanently from the database. To remove a document from a folder, use the Remo
from Folder option within the Actions menu.

NOTE *When moving Response documents to a folder, you must also move the parent document. The same is true wher
removing Response documents from a folder. In other words, the parent and child documents must all move in unison.*

NOTE *Web users cannot drag documents into folders.*

Summary

By now, you've learned the majority of the basics of building a Notes database. This chapter showed you how to give users access to the documents they create while also giving them a graphical interface in which to navigate. Views are an important aspect in Notes. Using a view, you can display documents in various ways that allow users quick access to the information they need. Using sorting techniques and the built-in response document hierarchy, you can display the data in an easy-to-use format similar to a table of contents for a book.

In the next chapter, we'll look at some design elements used to create a visually appealing application for both the Notes client and the Web. Although pages, outlines, and framesets sound like purely web objects, they can allow you to create an application that looks and works the same in both web and Notes environments.

Chapter 22

Outlines, Pages, Framesets, and Navigators

ALL OF THE DESIGN elements discussed in this chapter—outlines, pages, framesets, and navigators—draw inspiration from web design concepts but may be used in Notes applications as well. These new design elements have been engineered so they can be used in both the Notes client and web applications. The best part about them is that they virtually look and perform the same way in both environments.

Outlines, pages, framesets, and navigators have been designed to give your applications a more cohesive look and feel. In fact, if you've been using your Release 6 mail database, you've already been exposed to them without even knowing it.

All of the examples in this chapter are in the Recipe database.

Each one of these design elements builds upon everything you have learned thus far. After reading this chapter, you should have a good understanding of how each one can enhance the quality of your application and of when to use them.

- ◆ Creating an outline for your database navigation
- ◆ Creating pages for views and help documents
- ◆ Tying all of your design elements into a complete frameset
- ◆ Creating navigators

What Is an Outline?

You may be familiar with the Navigation pane, particularly if you've used earlier versions of Notes (also known as the *Folder pane*), shown in Figure 22.1. This is the default navigation structure for a database. There's not much you can do to customize the look and feel of the default Navigation pane.

FIGURE 22.1

The default
Navigation pane for
the Recipe database
(so far, anyway)

This is where *outlines* come into play. An outline is also a navigational element, but it is easily a broadly customizable. With outlines, you are no longer limited to displaying just views and folders the Navigation pane; you can easily construct a similar hierarchical structure. Think of the outline a hierarchical tree structure of all the links and elements you want to direct users to in your applicatic You can place links to views, pages, forms, websites, or anything else you need for your application. Y can think of the outline design element as a high-level site map for your database. If you are familiar w web programming, this concept should be quite familiar to you; most websites these days have a bar buttons across the top, bottom, or side of a page providing navigation through the site. Outlines perfoi the same function. The outline will help you structure your entire database, which in turn becomes t navigational structure for your application.

One major advantage to using an outline is that this design element is quickly built and easily cu tomized. You can control when and how the various items in the tree appear and where they will ta users. With the default display of views and folders in the Navigation pane, items appear in alph betical order whether you like it or not. You have to rename each view or folder if you want it to sho up in a particular place in the order. In an outline, you can put views and folders in any order you want. An outline is also not limited to navigating to just views and folders. You can create an ent that links directly to any Notes element (such as a page or a form) and to elements not contained within your application (such as a website). You also have some control over the outline's look. Yo can change the fonts and colors and add graphics for the entries, and you can make the entries appe either vertically or horizontally.

TIP You can use an outline to lay out and plan your application. You can create an outline entry prior to creating each design element. This will allow you to create a blueprint of your entire application.

Another major advantage is the ability to program each outline entry individually. As you will see later in the chapter, there is a wide range of features available in the Outline Entry Properties Box. You can use one set of features to display an outline in the Notes client and another to display it in a web application. In addition, you're not limited to one outline per application. You can create as many outlines as you need. Because an outline can be embedded on just about any design element, you have enough freedom and flexibility to create quite a powerful application.

NOTE   *Keep in mind that an outline cannot be used by itself. It must be embedded within some other type of element, such as a page or form. Outlines can even be embedded in tables.*

Using the Outline Designer

Before creating a new outline for our example database, let's first go over the components of the Outline Designer. To display the Outline Designer, follow these steps:

1. Open the Recipe database in Domino Designer.

2. Expand the Shared Code entry and select the Outlines element in the Design list. All the outlines for the current database will be displayed in the Work pane.

3. To display the Outline Designer (see Figure 22.2), choose Create ➤ Design ➤ Outline (you can also right-click in the Work pane and select New or click the New Outline Action button).

FIGURE 22.2

A new outline as it appears in the Outline Designer

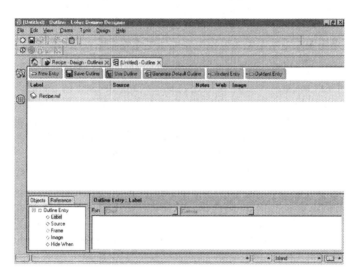

The Outline Designer consists of three main areas:

◆ Design Action buttons

◆ The Outline pane (work area)

◆ The programmer's pane

OUTLINE DESIGN ACTION BUTTONS

Across the top of the work area are six Action buttons, which can provide the important functic for creating a new outline.

New Entry   Use the New Entry button to create a new entry for your outline (you can also cho Create ➤ Outline Entry). When you click it, a new entry named Untitled will be created within outline, and the Outline Entry Properties Box will automatically display (see Figure 22.3).

FIGURE 22.3

The Outline Entry Properties Box automatically displays when a new outline entry is created.

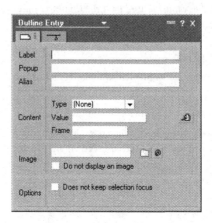

Save Outline   The Save Outline button saves the current outline. You can also choose File ➤ Sa

Use Outline   As we've said, outlines can't be used by themselves. They must be embedded i other objects. The Use Outline button lets you jump immediately to a place where your outli is available in a usable context. It automatically creates a new page and embeds your outline in Outlines are typically embedded in pages (although they can also be placed on forms), so this b ton can save you from having to create a new page and embed the outline yourself.

Generate Default Outline   The Generate Default Outline button automatically generates default outline based on the contents of the current database. The outline will contain an entry f all the views and folders currently defined. This option also creates entries for all of your hidd views and four additional outline entries: Other Views, Other Folders, Other Private Views, a Other Private Folders (the last four entries are primarily placeholders for additional entries). I default, the automatically generated entries for hidden views are hidden from both the Notes clie and web applications.

TIP   The Generate Default Outline button is a great time-saver when you are creating a new outline. If you select it you won't have to add each view and folder to the outline manually. However, generating the default outline will remove any entries already in the view, so if you're going to create the default outline, it should be the first thing you do.

Indent Entry   Use the Indent Entry button to indent the current outline entry. This feature creates a hierarchy of top-level and sublevel entries. You can indent more than one entry at a time by selecting all the entries you want to indent and clicking the Indent Entry button (you can also use the Tab key as a shortcut for indenting entries). This is a great feature for an outline that contains long lists of entries. You can also group logical entries under a heading.

Outdent Entry   The Outdent Entry button reverses the indented entry, or "outdents" it. Again, this creates a hierarchy for your outline. You can outdent more than one entry at a time by selecting all the entries you want to outdent and clicking the Outdent Entry button (you can also use the Shift+Tab key combination as a shortcut for outdenting entries).

THE OUTLINE PANE

The Outline pane is where you can modify your actual outline. You can use the drag-and-drop technique to change the sequence of the entries. To move an entry higher or lower in the hierarchy, click and hold down the mouse button on the entry you want to move, drag the entry to its new location in the outline, and drop it (let go of the mouse button). When you use this technique, Designer will display a thick black bar showing you where the entry will be placed in the outline as you move the mouse along. From the Outline pane, you can open either the Outline Properties Box or the Outline Entry Properties Box (these will be discussed in more detail in "The Outline Properties Box").

THE PROGRAMMER'S PANE

The programmer's pane for the outline is similar to the programmer's pane for other design elements in Designer. The Objects tab will only display one object at a time, which is always the outline entry (whereas all the objects for other design elements are shown). The events for the outline entry are always Label, Source, Frame, Image, and Hide When; they contain the values you typed into the Outline Entry Properties Box.

Creating an Outline

You now have a basic understanding of outlines, so let's create a new outline for the example database. The goal of our outline is twofold: to create a layout or site map for the application and to give the users an easy and intuitive interface with which to interact. To create a new outline, follow these steps:

1. Open the Recipes database in Domino Designer.
2. Select the Outlines element in the Design list. This will display all the outlines for the current database in the Work pane.
3. Choose Create ➤ Design ➤ Outline (you can also right-click in the Work pane and select New or click the New Outline Design Action button). The Outline Designer displays (refer to Figure 22.2; if you haven't closed the example under "Using the Outline Designer," you're already here).
4. Click the Generate Default Outline Design Action button.

You are now looking at a new outline that contains all the views and folders for the Recipes database, as shown in Figure 22.4. By default, a new outline is always called Untitled, which is not very descriptive, so the first thing we'll do is change the name.

FIGURE 22.4

The default outline
for the example
database

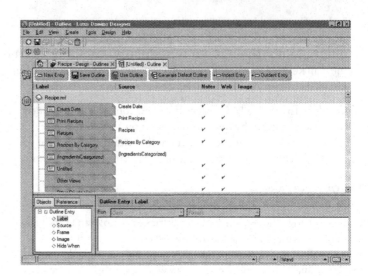

Using the Outline Properties Box

To change the name of the outline, you need to open the Box for the outline properties. Choose Design ➤ Outline Properties (you can also right-click in the Work pane and select Outline Properties) and the Box will display (see Figure 22.5). As you can see, there are not many properties for outline. You can specify the name of the outline in the Name field and give the outline as alias in the Alias field. There is also a Comment field in which you can add a description for the outline. The Available to Public Access Users option allows users with no access (except public access) to use the outline as well, and the Read Only option prevents users from altering the outline.

FIGURE 22.5

The Outline
Properties Box

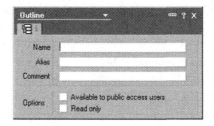

For our example, let's fill in the fields and save the outline by following these steps:

1. Enter **Master Recipe Outline** in the Name field.

2. In the Alias field, enter **RecipeOutline**.

3. In the Comment field, enter a short yet descriptive title for the outline, such as **The recipe database navigation outline**.

4. Leave Available to Public Access Users unchecked.

5. Choose File ➤ Save to save your outline.

That's all there is to it. You have created a basic navigational outline for the database. If you would like to take a quick peek at what the outline would look like, click the Use Outline Design Action button. A new untitled page containing your outline will be generated (see Figure 22.6). When you've finished looking at your outline, just close the page. When you're prompted to save the page, click the No button (remember that the Use Outline option actually creates a new page with your outline embedded on it; we don't want to save it yet because we're not finished with the outline).

FIGURE 22.6

Click the Use Outline Design Action button to display your outline on a page.

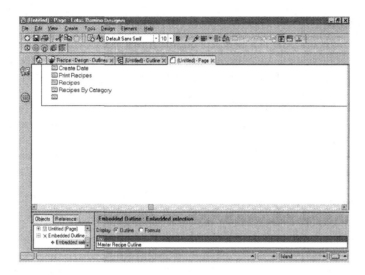

Removing Outline Entries

The default outline may or may not contain the entries you want to use in your application. As stated earlier, the default outline contains an entry for all the hidden views and also inserts four other entries (or placeholders). The first thing we'll do is remove all the unwanted entries. In our example, we'll remove some entries we don't want available to the users. These include (IngredientsCategorized), the Untitled folder, Other Views, Other Folders, Other Private Views, and Other Private Folders. We'll show you how to delete one entry, then a group of entries.

To remove the unwanted entries, follows these steps:

1. Open the Master Recipe Outline example outline in the Domino Designer.

2. Select the hidden view, (IngredientsCategorized), by clicking the entry.

3. Press the Delete key.

4. When prompted to confirm that you really want to delete the selected entries, click the Yes button.

5. Now click the entry for the folder Untitled.

6. Hold down the Shift key and select the last outline entry, Other Private Folders.

7. Press the Delete key again.

8. When prompted to confirm that you really want to delete all of the selected entries, click Yes button.

Now all the unwanted entries are gone. You should be left with only these four entries: Crea Date, Print Recipes, Recipes, and Recipes by Category. All of these views were displayed in t default Navigation pane, but we want to change how they are displayed to the end user. To do s we'll need to look at each entry's Outline Entry Properties Box.

Changing the Outline Entry Properties

As with any design element, the outline entry has its own Properties Box. If you want to change t text or an image, you must open the Outline Entry Properties Box and modify the properties for ea entry (unless you want to reorder or indent/outdent the entries).

USING THE OUTLINE ENTRY PROPERTIES BOX

We'll start with modifying the third entry, which points to the basic Recipes view. To open the B for the entry, select Recipes and choose Design ➤ Outline Entry Properties (you can also just dout click the entry). The Outline Entry Properties Box only contains two tabs: Outline Entry Basics a Entry Hide-When.

The Outline Entry Info Tab

The Outline Entry Info tab, shown in Figure 22.7, allows you to specify the characteristics for yo outline entry. Both the Label and Alias fields are used for naming your entry. The purpose of th Label field is twofold. It contains the name of your entry, which is also the text the end user will s when viewing your outline. *Recipes* is somewhat descriptive, but it could be better, so type **All My R ipes** in the Label field. Then type **Recipes** in the Alias field. The Popup field is used if the Labe too wide for the window in which the outline appears. When the user mouses over the entry, the po up text will appear. Type **All My Recipes** there as well.

FIGURE 22.7

The Outline Entry Info tab of the Outline Entry Properties Box for the Recipes entry, before any changes are made

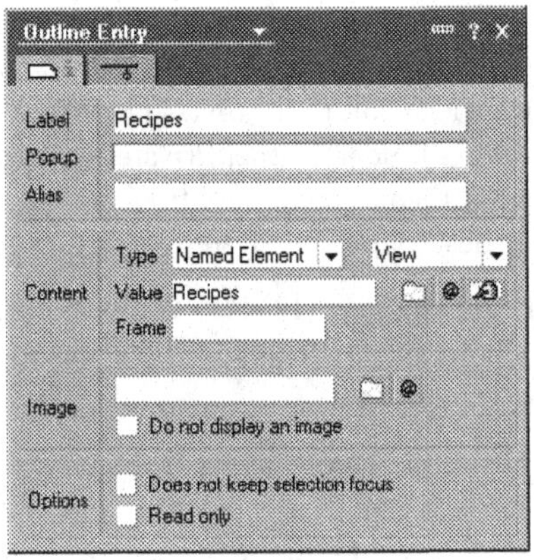

The Content section is the brains behind the entry. Your selections here allow you to specify what will happen when the user selects the outline entry All My Recipes. This section is quite dynamic in that your selection for the Type field will determine what other options are available for the remaining Content fields. The Type drop-down list box has five selections:

(None)   Specifies that the outline entry does nothing. The label is nothing more than that, a text label. When you create an outline for a database that does not yet contain any design elements, leave the Type field set to this option. You can also use this option if you want to create a heading for a series of subentries. This is the default selection for a new entry. No other field is available in the Content section when you select this option.

Action   Specifies a formula or Action to be performed when the outline entry is selected. Selecting the function icon will display the Edit Formula dialog box, where you can enter the formula for the Action. You can use this option to open forms, run agents, and so on.

Link   Specifies a link to a specific database element to open. There are easier ways to create links to views, pages, and other design elements, so the most common use for this option is to create links to specific documents. You can also specify the target frame where the link should be opened by entering the name of the frame in the Frame field. To use this option, copy the item you want as a link, then come to the Outline Entry Properties Box. Click the Paste icon, and the link currently on the Clipboard will be automatically entered in the second Type drop-down list box and the Value field.

Named Element   When you select Named Element, you can select the type of named element you want to use from the second drop-down list box. You can select Page (the default), Form, Frameset, View, Folder, or Navigator. If you click the folder icon, you can select to link to a different database. Once you've selected a kind of object and a database, the menu at the bottom will show a list of objects of the designated type in the selected database (see Figure 22.8).

Alternatively, you can click the @ icon to enter formulas calculating the link location. You can create separate formulas for the type of element, the database, and the name of the element (see Figure 22.9). As with the Link selection, you can also specify the target frame in which the link should be opened by entering the name of the frame in the Frame field.

URL   Specifies a URL to link to when the outline entry is selected. You can either type in the URL or paste it in by clicking the link icon. You can also specify the target frame in which the link should be opened by entering the name of the frame in the Frame field.

In our example, Named Element was chosen for the Type field because the outline entry is based on a view. You don't need to change any of these options except for the Frame field. Although we have not covered framesets yet (they will be covered later in this chapter under "What are Framesets?"), go ahead and type **NotesView** into the Frame field (it's not case-sensitive, but since we'll be entering the name in a few different places, the presence or absence of a space will make a difference; consistency is key).

The Image section allows you to specify whether to use an image for each of your outline entries. By default, the View icon will be used for each view, and the file folder icons will be used for each folder.

These are the same images used on the default Navigation pane. You also have two other options available. You can select the Do Not Display an Image option, which will prevent an image from being played next to the text, or you can specify a custom image of your own. To specify a custom image, you must place the images to use in the Image Repository for the database.

The Options section only has one selection available. You can enable Does Not Keep Selection Focus to prevent an outline entry from being selected when selected. By default, when an outline is selected, it will also retain the focus.

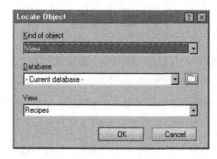

FIGURE 22.8
The Locate Object
dialog box

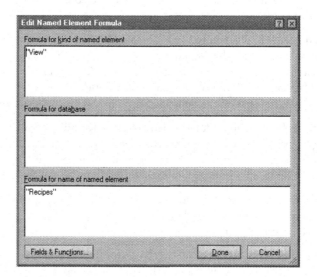

FIGURE 22.9
The Named
Element Formula
dialog box

The Entry Hide-When Tab

You've seen Hide-When tabs for other design elements, but this one is slightly different (see Figure 22.10). You only have three options available for hiding an outline entry. In the Hide Outline

Entry From section, you can select to hide an entry from a Notes client, a web application, or both; there is no check box to hide individual outline entries from mobile devices. You can also specify a formula for hiding the outline entry by enabling the Hide Outline Entry If Formula Is True option and entering a formula for evaluation. This is an extremely powerful tool. You have the ability to hide entries from a user based on anything that can be evaluated in a formula.

FIGURE 22.10

The Entry Hide-When tab of the Outline Entry Properties Box

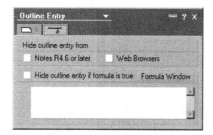

Updating the Outline Entries

We have edited the properties for the Recipes outline entry. Now we need to update the remaining entries so they have the same look. To change the remaining entries, follow these steps:

1. Select the Recipes by Category outline entry in the Work pane. Choose Design ➤ Outline Entry Properties (you can also right-click the selected entry and choose Outline Entry Properties or just double-click the outline entry).

2. With the Outline Entry Properties Box open to the Outline Entry Info tab, change the Label field to **By Categories** and the Alias field to **RecipesByCategory**. In the Frame field of the Content section, type **NotesView**.

3. Select the Create Date outline entry. If the Box is still displayed, it will display the properties for the newly selected entry (if you closed the Box, open it again for this entry).

4. On the Outline Entry Info tab, enter **By Date Created** in the Label field, **CreateDate** in the Alias field, and **NotesView** in the Frame field.

5. Select the Print Recipes outline entry and display the Box.

6. On the Outline Entry Info tab, enter **Print My Recipes** in the Label field, **PrintRecipes** in the Alias field, and **NotesView** in the Frame field.

7. Now save the changes to the outline by clicking the Save Outline Design Action button.

When you have completed all your changes, the outline should look like the outline in Figure 22.11.

FIGURE 22.11

The Master Recipe
Outline example

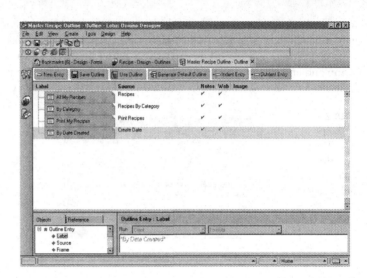

Adding a New Outline Entry

To show off some of the other functions of outline entries, we'll add some entries to the outline. Fir
let's set up a grouping (or hierarchy) to separate the views used for looking at and printing the Reci
documents.

We need to add a new entry to use as a parent or top level. Once the new entry is added, we'll ne
to indent the outline entries to create a hierarchical tree for the outline. To add a new entry, follc
these steps:

1. Open the Master Recipe Outline example in Designer.

2. Choose Create ➢ Outline Entry (you can also just click the New Entry Design Action bu
   ton). This will automatically display the Outline Entry Properties Box for the new entry
   called Untitled.

3. In the Label and Popup fields, type **Recipe Views**. You can also enter **RecipeView** in the Al
   field.

4. In the Content section, leave Type set to (None); we don't want this entry to do anything
   except be the top-level outline entry.

5. Close the Box. Next, depending on where your cursor was positioned when you created th
   outline entry, you may need to move the outline entry so it is positioned at the top of the li
   To do so, click the Recipe Views outline entry and drag it to the top of the outline. We wa
   this to be the first entry in the list.

We also want to arrange the remaining outline entries in a specific order (if they aren't already
Drag and drop the remaining outline entries one at a time so they are in the following order:

   ◆ Recipe Views

- All My Recipes
- By Category
- By Date Created
- Print My Recipes

Once the entries are rearranged, we'll indent them to create the hierarchy for the outline. All My Recipes, By Category, and By Date Created will be indented under Recipe Views. To accomplish this, select the All My Recipes outline entry. Hold the Shift key down and click on By Date Created so that all three outline entries are selected. Now click the Indent Design Action button (you can also just press the Tab key), and all three entries will be cascaded underneath the Recipe Views entry, as shown in Figure 22.12.

TIP   *You can cut and paste outline entries from other outlines.*

FIGURE 22.12

Creating a
hierarchical
outline

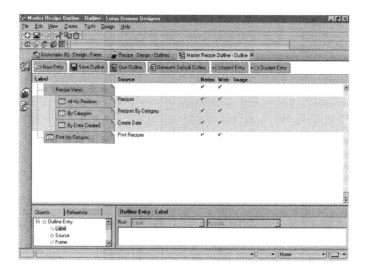

You've seen how an outline entry can link to views. Let's add a few new outline entries that will allow the user to create Recipe documents and navigate to related websites. To do so, follow these steps:

1. Open the Master Recipe Outline example.

2. Append a new outline entry by selecting the Print My Recipes outline entry and clicking the New Entry Design Action button.

3. This new entry will be used as a spacer. To leave the label blank, press the spacebar once. Select the Do Not Display an Image option in the Image section and the Does Not Keep the Focus option in the Options section.

4. Click the New Entry Design Action button again. Enter **Create Recipe** in the Label field and **CreateRecipe** in the Alias field. In the Type drop-down list box, select Named Element and click the folder icon to display the Locate Object dialog box.

5. In the Locate Object dialog box, select Form from the Kind of Object drop-down list box Recipe with Actions from the Form drop-down list box (this will be the last drop-down box whose name changes based on the kind of object you select). Click the OK button.

6. Enter **_blank** in the Frame field.

7. Append another blank outline entry as shown in step 3.

8. Add one last outline entry. Enter **Gourmet Website** in the Label and Popup fields and **GourmetWebsite** in the Alias field. From the Type drop-down list box, select URL and type **www.epicurious.com** in the Value field. Enter **NotesView** in the Frame field.

9. Save your outline by clicking the Save Outline Design Action button.

When you have finished, the outline should look similar to Figure 22.13. Now that you have outline, you need to create a page in which to display it.

FIGURE 22.13
The finished Master Recipe Outline for the Recipe example database

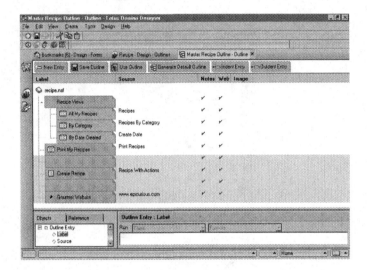

What Is a Page?

A *page* is a hybrid design element in that it is a cross between a standard form and the special Hel About and Help Using forms. A page acts a bit like a form (it can have Action buttons and events but it cannot have any fields. Most of the capabilities of a form (images, hotspots, and attachment are fully functional. Pages are stored as a separate design element, too. You can refer to a page eith by its name or by its alias.

If pages are so much like a form, why not just use a form? The main reason is that a form is use for gathering and manipulating information, whereas a page is used purely for *displaying* informatio Pages are also unique, whereas forms represent a class of documents. For example, a product catalo may have a number of similar product pages but only one Contact Us page with its own design, front page with yet another unique design, and so on. Those uniquely designed documents would b implemented as pages in Notes, whereas the individual item documents would use forms. You can use pages for help screens, home pages, splash screens—the list goes on. The major point to keep in mind when you're trying to decide between a form and a page is whether you need to gather information from the end user. If you do, don't use a page.

Another major reason for using pages is to replace the $$ViewTemplate field typically used in early versions of Notes for displaying embedded views. You can also launch a specific page when a database is opened so you don't have to use the About Database form (in earlier releases of Notes, one of the database launch options was to display the About This Database form). Because pages have more options than the About This Database form has, you as a designer have more flexibility in designing your application.

A page is another type of design element that can be used anywhere in your application, and it can in turn contain the following types of design elements:

- Text
- Computed text
- Horizontal rules
- Tables
- Sections
- Links
- Graphics
- Image maps
- Attachments
- Actions
- Applets
- Embedded views, folders, navigators, outlines, and Date Picker controls
- Hypertext Markup Language (HTML)
- Object linking and embedding (OLE) objects

A page cannot contain the following design elements:

- Fields
- Layout regions
- Subforms
- Embedded group schedules and File Upload controls

As you can see, any design element that allows a user to enter data is prohibited, but all the design elements that simply display data are allowed. Now that you have a basic understanding of this design element, let's go ahead and create one.

Creating a Page

The process for creating a page is similar to the process for creating a form. We'll start with something simple. On the Recipe with Actions form, there is a Need Help? hotspot; we'll create a page that

will be displayed when the user clicks it. The page won't have anything on it except text and som
graphics. To create the new page, follow these steps:

1. Open the Recipe database in Domino Designer.

2. Select the Pages element in the Design list. This will display all the pages for the current d
base in the Work pane.

3. Choose Create ➤ Design ➤ Page (you can also right-click in the Work pane and select N
or click the New Page Design Action button).

You won't see much of a difference between the new page and a new form. The only major d
ference is in the Create menu. If you choose Create, you'll notice that some of the menu options th
are available for a form are not present for a page. You may also notice that the toolbar buttons f
creating fields are grayed out and cannot be used.

The first thing we need to do is give the page a name. To open the Box for the page, choos
Design ➤ Page Properties (see Figure 22.14). This tab lets you set up basic identification info
mation for the page and lets you set some web access options that should be familiar from for
design.

FIGURE 22.14

Page Properties Box

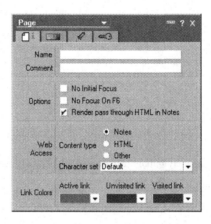

On the Page Info tab, type **HelpRecipe** in the Name field and **Help page for the recipe form**
the Comment field. The remaining tabs in the Box are similar to those that have been covered for p
vious design elements, so we won't spend any time reviewing them here.

For the Recipe help page, you can type in anything you want. We have included a sample help pa
named SampleHelp (which admittedly, will not be very helpful). To save time, you can copy and pas
the contents of this page into the new page. Once you have copied the text and graphics to the new pag
feel free to add anything else that you want. Once you are finished, just save and close the page.

Embedding an Outline on a Page

You've created a page, now let's get back to the outline. As stated earlier, you must place an outli
on some other design element in order to use it. A page is the perfect place because it is only used
display information to the user (as opposed to having the user enter or update information).

NOTE *You can embed more than one outline on a page.*

Now you need to create another page to hold the outline. Following the steps in the preceding section, create a new page and enter **dspOutline** for the name. Starting with a blank page, choose Create ➢ Embedded Element ➢ Outline. The Insert Embedded Outline dialog box will automatically display (see Figure 22.15). We have only one outline for the database, so select it in the list, Master Recipe Outline (if you have more than one, all of them would show up in the list). The outline will be automatically placed on the page, and the default properties will be set. Don't be alarmed if some of the outline entries you entered do not automatically display. They're hidden from view based on the properties for the embedded view. To rectify this problem, you need to change some of the properties, so you'll use the Embedded Outline Properties Box.

FIGURE 22.15

The Insert Embedded Outline dialog box

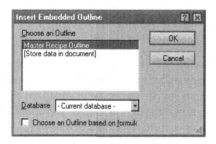

TIP *Once an outline is embedded on a page, you don't need to worry about reinserting or modifying the current page if you make any modifications to the outline. What the page really contains is a pointer to the outline, so changes made to the outline are reflected immediately when you open the page.*

Using the Embedded Outline Properties Box

You may recall that, when you were creating your outline, there were not a lot of properties to choose from for the outline or the outline entries. Most of the options for the outline are actually contained in the Embedded Outline Properties Box. You can use many different combinations to create various effects. The Embedded Outline Properties Box has seven tabs: Info, Font, Background, Border, Paragraph Margins, and Paragraph Hide-When.

To open the Box, first select the embedded outline and choose Element ➢ Outline Properties (you can also right-click the embedded outline and choose Outline Properties). By default, the first tab to display is the Info tab.

THE INFO TAB

The Info tab, shown in Figure 22.16, allows you to identify your outline and set the properties that control how the outline will be displayed to the user. The Info tab is made up of many different properties:

Name This option allows you to identify your outline by name. It is a good habit to name all of your outlines because you can embed more than one on any given design element. For this example, type in **MainOutline**.

Type   This drop-down list box has only two options—Tree Style and Flat Style. The Tree Style option displays the entire hierarchical structure of the outline at once. When this option is selected, the Show Twisties option is also displayed. You can use it to display the triangular icon that allows a user to expand and collapse the view. The Image field allows you to pick your own image resource to replace the standard twistie. The Flat Style option only displays one level of the hierarchy at a time. If you click an entry that has subentries, you'll move to that level of the hierarchy. You should use this in conjunction with the Title Style Simple option. When Flat Style is selected, another drop-down list displays, allowing you to choose whether the outline entries should be listed horizontally or vertically. You can use this option to create a horizontal menu bar across the top or bottom of a page. For this example, select both the Tree Style option and the Show Twisties option.

Title Style   This drop-down list has only two options—Hide and Simple. Use the Simple option in conjunction with the Flat Style option to display the parent of the current hierarchical level so the user can navigate to upper levels. The Hide option will prevent the database title from displaying. For this example, select the Hide option.

Target Frame   This option allows you to specify the frame for the results of an action in the outline entry. (For example, you may have an outline that contains a link to a specific page on a web site. This option allows you to specify the frame in which the web page should appear when the link is clicked.) When you created the outline entries, you specified a target frame for each one in the Outline Entry Properties Box. That target frame takes precedence over the target frame specified here. For this example, because you've provided target frames for all of your entries, leave this field blank. The next time around, though, it would be more efficient to set a target frame here rather than setting target frames for all of the entries individually.

Root Entry   This is another handy feature for hierarchical outlines. You can place the alias of an outline entry in this field, and only the sublevels of that entry will initially be displayed in the outline (if no sublevels exist, the outline will be blank). You can use this in combination with the Title field's Simple Title option and your users will have a way to navigate to upper levels of the outline. For this example, leave this field blank.

Display As   This option doesn't have a label, but the drop-down list box is just to the right of the Root Entry field. There are four options—Expand All, Expand First, Display as Saved, and Collapse All (note that if you have selected Flat Style from the Type option, there is only one option available, Collapse All). This setting is extremely useful for hierarchical outlines because you can force the outline to display a certain way the first time it is displayed. For this example, set this option to Expand All.

Outline Size   The Outline Size section allows you to specify both the horizontal and vertical dimensions for your outline. Fit to Content is available for both dimensions and will automatically size your outline to fit its contents. The Fixed option is also available for both dimensions, and when selected, it will open a field in which you can specify the exact size of each dimension in inches. The Fit to Window (%) option is only available for the horizontal dimension; it allows you to specify the size based on a percentage of the actual window size. The Show Scroll Bar option will automatically display a scroll bar within the confines of the embedded outline. If you have quite a number of outline entries that extend beyond the height of the page, you should enable this option. This will allow the user to use the scroll bar to see the options that aren't currently visible. Also, you can deselect this option because we don't have many outline entries. Select Fit to Content for both dimensions.

Web Access   As the name implies, this option only applies to web applications. It allows you to specify whether to use the Java applet or HTML. The HTML option is perfectly serviceable for a basic outline, but many of the more colorful display options won't work in a web application unless you use the applet. So that the example page will look similar in both the web application and the Notes client, select the Use Java Applet option.

Special   This section gives you a single check box: Show Folder Unread Information. If this option is checked, folders with unread documents will appear in boldface type, and the number of unread documents they contain will appear in parentheses next to the name. This tiny but useful feature lets users determine by a glance at the outline where new documents may have appeared. For our example, we'll leave it alone.

FIGURE 22.16

The Info tab of the Embedded Outline Properties Box

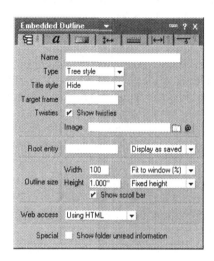

THE FONT TAB

The Font tab, shown in Figure 22.17, is similar to the Font tabs for other design elements. The major difference is the addition of a few drop-down list boxes in the upper-left corner and along the bottom. The first drop-down list box allows you to choose separate font and text styles for top-level and sublevel entries. This selection determines whether the remaining font selections apply to the top-level outline entries or the sublevel outline entries. The Normal, On Select, and On Mouse drop-down list boxes allow you to change the color of the outline entry based on its state. Normal means no action has been taken yet. On Select means the entry has been selected. On Mouse means the mouse is hovering over the entry. For this example, select the Top-Level Font option and make the font bold. For Selected, choose dark blue, and for Moused, choose red. Select Sub-Level Font and make the same color selections, but don't change the font size or style.

FIGURE 22.17

The Font tab of the Embedded Outline Properties Box

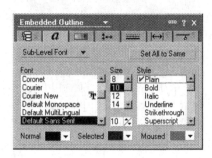

THE BACKGROUND TAB

The Background tab, shown in Figure 22.18, allows you to control the background colors or ba
ground graphics not only for the entire outline, but also for top-level and sublevel entries. In the
upper-left corner, there is a drop-down list box that allows you to choose between three options: C
trol Background, Top-Level Background, and Sub-Level Background. The selected option det
mines the effect of the remaining options. Control Background determines the background color
the overall outline. If you use an image, you can use the Repeat option to determine how it will
displayed. The options available here (Repeat Once, Repeat Vertically, and so on) should be famil
by now. The Top-Level Background and Sub-Level Background options give you additional bac
ground color options. As you can on the Font tab, you can elect to have a different color based
state (Normal, On Select, or On Mouse). You've already made the font colors dance when th
change state, so you won't be altering the background color properties in this example.

FIGURE 22.18

The Background tab of the Embedded Outline Properties Box

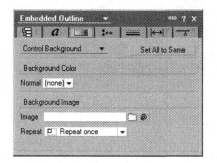

THE LAYOUT TAB

The Layout tab, shown in Figure 22.19, allows you to control the offsets for each entry in the outlir
From the drop-down list box, you can select either Top-Level Layout or Sub-Level Layout. You
selection determines which entries are affected by the options displayed. There are three sections
this tab: Entry, Entry Label, and Entry Image. The Entry section allows you to specify the vertical
horizontal offset for the overall entry. Think of it as margin settings for an entry. The Entry Lab
section allows you to specify the vertical and horizontal offsets for the text label. If you don't speci

an offset and you are using images, the text will overlay the image. For this reason, by default, an entry with an image is automatically offset horizontally. The Entry Image section allows you to specify the vertical and horizontal offsets for just the image. In both the Entry Label and Entry Image sections, you can also specify an Alignment option. You can choose from Top-Left, Top-Center, Top-Right, Middle-Left, Middle-Center, Middle-Right, Bottom-Left, Bottom-Center, or Bottom-Right. Using this option along with the offsets, you can create a wide array of visual effects, such as placing the entry image above the text label or to the right of the text label. For this example, just use the defaults that have been preset by Notes.

FIGURE 22.19

The Layout tab of the Embedded Outline Properties Box

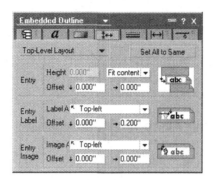

THE BORDER, MARGIN, AND HIDE-WHEN TABS

The Border, Paragraph Margin, and Hide-When tabs are no different than they are for any other design element. The most useful is probably the Hide-When tab. You can hide various outline entries by entering a formula. You could, for example, enter a formula that would hide an entry from users who don't belong to the appropriate group or role.

What Is a Frameset?

Now that you have all of these pages and the outline, you can start tying them all together. This is where *framesets* come into play.

Framesets originated in web applications. You can use them to divide the screen into areas known as *frames*. The virtue of framesets is that they allow you to display more than one design element at a time. For example, you can show a view and a document at the same time, using the view to navigate between documents. With a big enough screen area, you could display multiple view and document windows, pages for navigational control and database help, and so on, all at the same time. If you are familiar with the Web, you know what a frameset looks like. In rather older releases of Notes, a pseudo-frameset design was possible with the Navigator pane, the View pane, and the Preview pane. The major stumbling block with the earlier design was that the programmer didn't really have any control over what displayed in each frame.

That changed with Release 5, the previous release of Notes. By default, a Notes database still uses the original default Navigation/content pane design. However, you can create framesets to use in addition to or instead of the default layout. Each frame is an independent section of the frameset

design element and thus can be controlled independently. You can also create frames that are sc
lable. With the prevalence of web browsers, users won't have any trouble grasping the idea of in
pendent areas of content in your application.

Creating a Frameset

Domino Designer has really taken the drudgery out of creating frames. Hand-coding a frameset
be tedious and prone to errors because you can't view the results. Framesets have their own spec
design components, which we will show you shortly. To create a new frameset, follow these step

1. Open the Recipe database in Domino Designer.

2. Select the Frameset element in the Design list. This will display all the framesets for the curr
   database in the Work pane.

3. Choose Create ➤ Design ➤ Frameset (you can also right-click in the Work pane and sele
   New or click the New Frameset Design Action button). The Create New Frameset dialog b
   will display (see Figure 22.20).

FIGURE 22.20

The Create New
Frameset dialog box

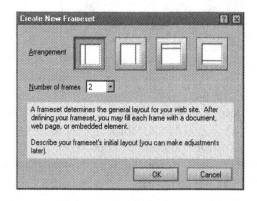

The first thing you must consider when creating a frameset is how many frames you want to u.
There are many schools of thought on this subject, but not many surefire answers. It boils down
what information you need to display to the user. Once you've decided how many frames to use, y
must decide how to arrange them.

Setting Frameset Arrangement and Frames

When the Create New Frameset dialog box appears, two frames are selected in the Number of Fram
drop-down list by default. You can choose between two, three, or four frames. This does not me
you cannot have more than four frames; it just means that you will start with only two, three, or fou
Once in the Frameset Designer, you can add and remove frames at will (although using more tha
four frames is probably too many to usefully put on the screen).

Using the number of frames you've selected, the Arrangement option will display four differer
basic options. Figure 22.20 shows the possible arrangements for two frames, Figure 22.21 shows tl
possible arrangements for three frames, and Figure 22.22 shows the possible arrangements for fo

frames. Once you have decided on the number of frames, just select the arrangement that best fits your needs by clicking the button. Then click the OK button and your new frameset will be displayed.

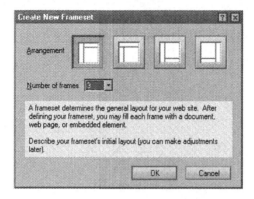

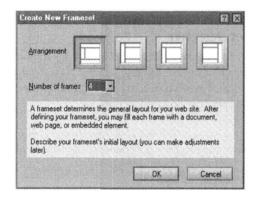

For the example database, you need to use four frames. To generate the frameset, follow these steps:

1. From the Number of Frames drop-down list box, select 2 (you'll add more later, but this is where you'll start).
2. In the Arrangement section, select the icon on the far left.
3. After selecting the arrangement, click the OK button and the frameset will be automatically displayed in the Frameset Designer, as shown in Figure 22.23.

NOTE *The options available in the Create New Frameset dialog box are not the only options available for frames. You can make any number of adjustments in the Frameset Designer once the frameset has been generated.*

Now that the general structure for the frameset has been generated, let's manipulate the structure to fit the needs of the example database.

FIGURE 22.23

The generated
frameset with
two frames in the
Frameset Designer

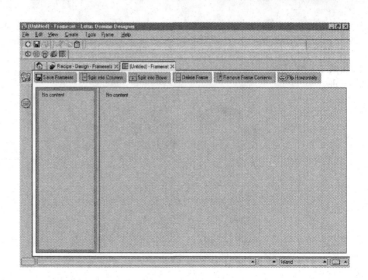

Using the Frameset Designer

Once the frameset is generated, you can add, remove, and manipulate the existing frames to furth
refine the interface. The layout shown in Figure 22.23 is close to what we need, but not exactly. W
need to add a frame, and we may need to resize it a bit. But first we need to name the frameset. A
to do that, we need to display the Box for the frameset.

NOTE   Do not confuse the frameset with the frame. Each frame is a unit of the frameset. The frameset defines the enti
page; all frames are defined in the frameset. Think of the frameset as the outside walls of a house and each frame as a roon

USING THE FRAMESET PROPERTIES BOX

The Frameset Properties Box refines some of the options for the frameset and frames. This Box has t
tabs, Basics and HTML, but now you are only concerned with the first one. To name the frameset, ty
MasterFrameset in both the Name and Alias fields. You can also type a comment in the Commen
field. The frameset title is the name that will appear in the title bar of your application in the Notes cli
and the web browser. For this example application, type **My Recipe Database.**

MODIFYING YOUR FRAMES

In addition to the ubiquitous Save button, the Frameset Designer has five Action buttons to help y
design your frames:

- Split into Columns
- Split into Rows
- Delete Frame
- Remove Frame Contents
- Flip Horizontally

You can select the frame to modify and click one of the Action buttons. Depending on which button you clicked, the frame will break into two columns or two rows, it will disappear, or the contents will be removed. Flip Horizontally will flip the entire frameset horizontally, not just selected frames. In this example, you'll need to split up the left-side frame. Click in the left pane and click the Split into Rows button, dividing it into upper and lower frames.

There are two options for resizing frames. One option is to place your cursor over one of the frame split bars and resize each frame by holding the mouse button and dragging the bar. This is a good way to get an idea of what you want, but it is better to actually size your frames individually using the Frame Properties Box.

USING THE FRAME PROPERTIES BOX

The Frame Properties Box is important because it determines the characteristics of each individual frame. It contains the following tabs:

- Basics
- Frame Size
- Frame Border
- Advanced
- Additional HTML

For this example, you are only concerned with the first three tabs because they contain the name, content, and border information.

The Basics Tab

The Basics tab contains two sections: Name and Content (see Figure 22.24). With frames, the Name section is important. In the other Properties Boxes discussed in this chapter, there was a field called Target Frame. The name you placed in the Target Frame field must match one of names in the frameset. You can tell your application which frame to *target* when information is to be displayed (such as a specific frame to display a view). This is how the various pieces of your application communicate in a framed environment. For example, if you have a Navigation frame that includes only links, you don't want the linked documents to appear in the Navigation frame when a user clicks the link; you want the document to appear in the document frame (unless, of course, you want the navigation element to change). In this example, the document frame would be the target frame of the navigator frame.

NOTE *When you name a frame, it is important that the name matches the contents of any Target Frame field previously defined for other elements.*

The other important part of the Box is the Content section. You can choose what is to be displayed initially in each frame (remember that you can use the Target Frame field to change the contents of a frame). Selecting what to display in a frame is similar to selecting what to display in an outline. Just select what you want from the drop-down list boxes. The remaining option in the Content section is the Default Target for Links in This Frame option. You can set this field at a frame level, thereby eliminating the need for specifying it on components that make up the frame.

FIGURE 22.24

The Basics tab
of the Frame
Properties Box

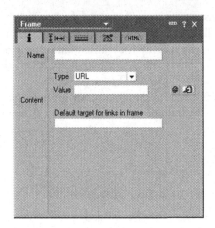

*TIP If a frame is specified as the target frame for a lower component, and another frame is specified as the target fram
in the Properties Box for the lower component, the properties for the lower component are used. For example, the conten
of the Target Frame field for an outline overrides the contents of the Default Target for Links in This Frame field fo
the frame.*

So let's start modifying the frames by setting the fields on the Basics tab. You should still have
new, blank frameset displayed in Designer. To change the values for each frame, follow these ste

1. Open the Box for the upper-left frame by first selecting the frame and then choosing Frame
   Frame Properties (you can also right-click the frame and choose Frame Properties).

2. Enter **topLeft** in the Name field. For the Type fields in the Content section, select Named E
   ment from the first drop-down list box and Page from the second drop-down list box. Ty
   TitlePage in the Value field (this page has already been created for you).

3. Next, select the middle, left frame with the Box still showing. Type **left** in the Name fie
   In the Content section, select Named Element and Page. Type **dspOutline** in the Value fie
   (this is the outline you created earlier in the chapter). Also type **NotesView** in the Defau
   Target for Links in This Frame field. This will ensure that, if you forgot to place a targe
   frame on any elements contained in the outline, they will automatically be displayed in th
   NotesView frame.

4. Select the last remaining frame. Type **NotesView** in the Name field, and in the Content s
   tion, select Named Element and Page. Type **dspWelcome** in the Value field (this page ha
   already been created for you).

5. Save the frameset and continue with the next tab.

The Frame Size Tab

As its name implies, the Frame Size tab allows you to resize each frame (see Figure 22.25). You c
resize each frame manually by dragging the frame borders around. You can use the Frame Size tab
you want to be more exact.

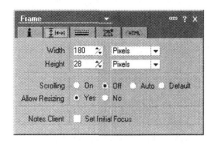

FIGURE 22.25

The Frame Size tab of the Frame Properties Box

When sizing the frame, you have a few variations for the Height and Width fields. You can size a field based on a percentage, by the number of pixels, or relative to the other frames. You also have the option of setting a frame as scrollable and choosing whether the end users can resize the frame.

To adjust the sizing for the example database frameset, follow these steps:

1. With the Box still open, select the Frame Size tab.

2. Select the topLeft frame and set Width to 180 Pixels and Height to 28 Pixels. You're using pixels in this frame because you don't want the size to change. When a view is displayed, the bottom border for this frame needs to match the border for the Action buttons in the NotesView frame exactly. Also set Scrolling to Off and Allow Resizing to On.

3. Select the left frame and set Width to 180 Pixels (this should already be set for you because all three left frames have to be the same width) and Height to 100 Relative. Set Scrolling to Off and Allow Resizing to On.

4. Select the NotesView frame and set both Width to 100 Relative. Set Scrolling to Default and Allow Resizing to On. Because this frame will contain various types of information that may extend beyond the bottom of the frame, we will allow scrolling if necessary. There's no frame above or below NotesView, so you can't set a height.

5. Save the frameset and continue with the next tab.

The Frame Border Tab

In the Frame Border tab, you can determine just how the frame borders should be displayed (see Figure 22.26). By default, the borders are set to On, have a width of 7 pixels, and use the system color. We want to keep the borders but change them slightly so they look a bit more two dimensional. Change the properties in each frame as follows and then save the frameset:

◆ Set the Border field to On.

◆ Make sure the Border Width Default option is not selected and the size is set to 3 pixels.

◆ Set the Border Color option to Black.

One other thing you can do on this tab is to create a caption for a frame. The caption will appear at the top or bottom of the frame outside of the content area. You can only create a caption for frames that have another frame neighboring them to the top or bottom. If a frame only has neighbors to the left or right, Notes won't let you use a frame caption.

FIGURE 22.26

The Frame Border tab of the Frame Properties Box

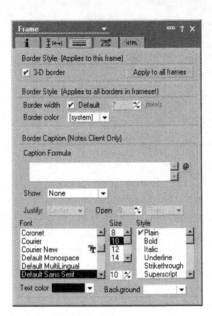

Looking at the Finished Product

There is one last change you need to make before testing the application. Open the Database Properties Box and select the Launch tab. Because you have spent so much time setting up the application to use a frameset, you'll set the database launch option so the new frameset will be used when the database is opened. When the Box is displayed, set the options as shown in Figure 22.27.

FIGURE 22.27

Setting the database launch options to use the frameset when the database is opened

To test the application, open the database in the Notes client. When the database is first displayed it should look Figure 22.28. Figure 22.29 shows the application in a web browser.

You can see how the frames have separated the various parts of the application. The upper-left frame displays a reference title, and the lower-left frame displays the title for the database. The middle, left frame is where the user will perform all the navigation, and the right frame will display the application data.

Select All My Recipes. Notice how the color of the text changes to give the user a visual cue to what is happening. Also, the All My Recipes view is automatically displayed in the right frame. This is accomplished through the use of the Target Frame field in the outline (remember that, on the outline entry, you specified that the target frame would be NotesView; the right frame is named NotesView). Navigate around the application and try viewing and adding new documents.

FIGURE 22.28
The finished application using the Notes client

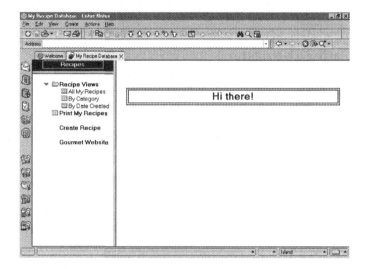

FIGURE 22.29
The finished application using a web browser

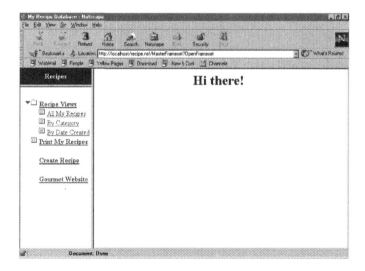

What Is a Navigator?

The last of the major navigational elements is called, appropriately enough, the navigator. A navig
is similar to an outline in that it consists of links and places to click that perform actions. Howe
where an outline is text oriented, perhaps incorporating some graphics, navigators are graphic o
ented, perhaps incorporating some text. Navigators are a lot like image maps on the Web. In fact,
thing you can do with navigators is convert them into image maps for web use.

A navigator is not just one object but a combination of many different types of objects. By c
bining these objects, you can create a myriad of dazzling designs. Most navigators begin with a ba
ground image, and then various types of buttons, hotspots, and text are added. Lotus appears to
trying to de-emphasize navigators, and they're best used sparingly, but we'll briefly cover how to
ate and use them.

Creating a Navigator

In this section, you'll see how to create a simple navigator. We have already done some of the wo
for you. This will eliminate the need for you to create the graphics; you can just copy an existing r
igator. Although you can create a full-screen navigator, you are going to create a navigator that v
be used in conjunction with the views.

To create a navigator, follow these steps:

1. Open the Recipes database in Designer and select Navigators from the Design list.

2. Normally, you would choose Create ➤ Design ➤ Navigator (you can also just select the N
   Navigator button), which will display a new blank navigator. But we have already provide
   navigator that contains several graphic images. Right-click the navigator called Start and sel
   Copy from the pop-up menu. Now right-click again and select Paste.

3. Open the newly copied navigator called Copy of Start. The navigator should look like the o
   in Figure 22.30. If you want to create a background, there are two options. The first is to co
   the background graphic to the Clipboard and then choose Create ➤ Graphic Background
   automatically paste the graphic to the background. The second way is to choose File ➤ Imp
   and then select the file to use as the graphic background.

*TIP   Always try to use the File Import method to create a background because better color fidelity will be retained whe
the graphic is displayed.*

*NOTE   You can only have one background graphic for a navigator. The background graphic cannot be moved once it ha
been pasted. Keep this in mind when you create the graphic; the size really does matter.*

FIGURE 22.30

The starting point
for the Navigator for
the database

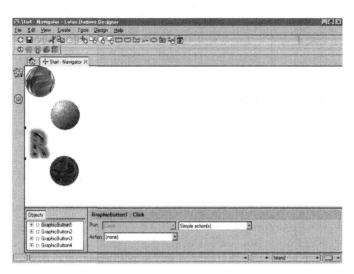

SETTING THE NAVIGATOR PROPERTIES

The next step is to set the properties for the Navigator. Choose Design ➢ Navigator Properties to
display the Navigator Properties Box (shown in Figure 22.31). Change the name to All Recipes
because this navigator will be used to display the All Recipes view. You can type in comments about
this navigator as well.

FIGURE 22.31

The Navigator
Properties Box

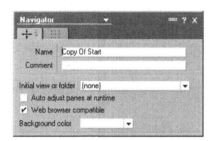

The Initial View or Folder option is very important. We were going to create a navigator, which
will display along with the view. You can use the Initial View or Folder option to have a view or folder
automatically open along with the All Recipes navigator. For this example, select Recipes from the
drop-down list box. This will cause Notes to automatically display the Recipes view when the navigator is opened. Also enable the Auto Adjust Panes at Runtime option. This option will automatically adjust the split-screen bar, which separates the navigator and the view so that only the minimum
amount of the screen will be used for the navigator.

One of the really interesting properties here is Web Browser Compatible. If this option is checked you'll be able to use it in web applications. What the Domino server will do is to turn the entire navigator into a single graphic and an image map. When you click areas of the image, the navigator will perform whatever action the buttons you created are supposed to perform.

ADDING ACTIONS TO THE NAVIGATOR OBJECTS

Now you have a navigator that, when opened, will automatically display a view containing a list of all the recipes. The only problem is that the user does not have any other options available for navigating to the rest of the views in the database. To alleviate this problem, we'll add some options to the navigator that will allow the user to do so.

You have the option of adding text, buttons, graphical buttons, and other types of hotspots. In our example, we'll keep it simple and just play with some buttons. To add buttons to a navigator, choose Create ➤ Button. This will change the cursor to a plus sign. Hold down the left mouse button and draw the button. Once you have the correct size and placement, let go of the mouse button. The Button Properties Box will be displayed automatically (see Figure 22.32). You can use the Box to name the button, adjust its font properties, have it highlight when touched, and so on. Create a button on the All Recipes navigator and nudge it toward the left edge, as shown in Figure 22.33.

FIGURE 22.32
The Button
Properties Box

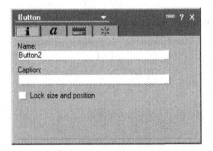

FIGURE 22.33
All Recipes with
a button

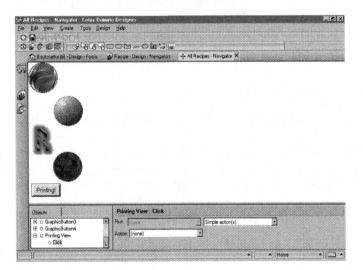

The more interesting thing to do, though, is to use graphic buttons. You can import graphic images, as with our Start navigator. You can copy and paste graphics or import them as you would import a graphic into any other Notes design element. The important thing here is that when Notes gives you a choice between bringing in the graphic as a button or a background, select button.

You have created your navigator, but there is still one more step you need to perform. You created some nifty buttons, but nothing happens when you click them. We need to add some type of Action to each button.

To add an Action to a button, you first need to select the button object. Click the "swirly" red button at the top of the navigator. In the script area of the programmer's pane, you'll notice that there are some options available for the Click event of the button. By default, the Simple Action option is selected. You can also code either a formula or LotusScript, but for our example, the Simple action will do.

In the Action drop-down box, select the Open a View or Folder option (you will notice that there are quite a few other options available). When this option is enabled, a second list box appears. From this second list box, you can select which view or folder you want to open when the button is selected. Let's go with Create Date for now. The script area should now look similar to the script area in Figure 22.34.

FIGURE 22.34

The action
selection criteria
for a navigator
object

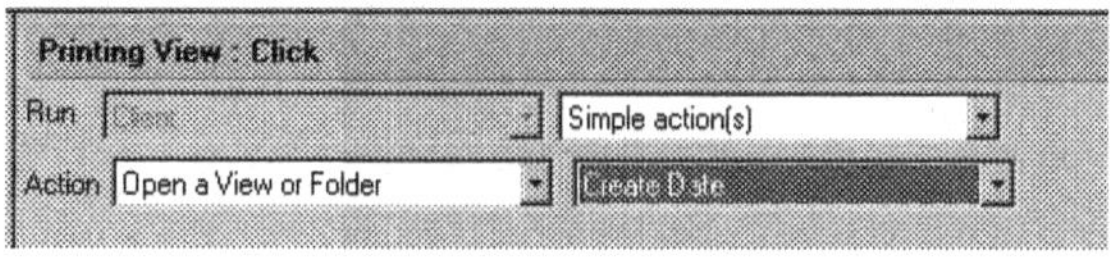

Now do the same thing for the remaining three buttons, pointing the orange ball to Recipes, the capital R to Recipes by Category, the blue ball to (IngredientsCategorized), and the Printing button to Print Recipes.

This still isn't much good. Your graphic buttons can perform actions, but how is the user to know what they do? Create some text labels. You can create Text from the Create menu, or you can click the toolbar button. Either way, create a text label; like a button, you can draw a text area, enter a name and caption in the Properties Box, set font and size, and so on. Name the label Recipes by Date and make the text white. Now you can drag it over the red button. Yes, just like layout regions in forms, you can overlap items in a navigator. Create similar labels for the other buttons and assign them actions as you did for the buttons they overlap.

Using Navigators

There is one last step that you need to perform. How does the navigator get displayed in the first place? Using the Database Launch option, you can tell the database to open a specific Navigator whenever the database is opened. We'll set this option to open the All Recipes Navigator.

Open the Database Properties Box and select the Launch tab. From the Launch tab, select Open Designated Navigator from the On Database Open option. From the Type of Navigator option, select Standard Navigator. This will display a third list box from which you should select All Recipes. Now we are ready to give your navigator a try.

Open the database in the Notes client. When the database is opened, the All Recipes navigator the Recipes view should be automatically launched and look like Figure 22.35.

FIGURE 22.35
Displaying our
All Recipes view
and the Basic view
in the Notes client

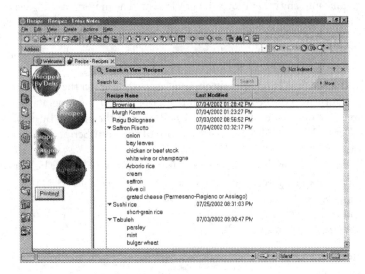

Summary

In this chapter, you were introduced to some useful navigational tools. The basic tools are simple, they can be used together in a wide variety of ways. Outlines provide you with a flexible, easily constructed, and potentially attractive navigational tool. Using pages, you can combine the various elements Designer has to offer to create a vast array of text and graphics. Navigators give you a flexible graphic way of navigating your database. The frameset is the glue that ties all of the design element pieces together. Using a combination of outlines, pages, and framesets, you are well on your way creating some interesting applications.

In the next chapter, we'll look at shared resources and other designer capabilities. Notes gives y the ability to store supporting files and objects that you can centrally manage and reuse among oth design elements, greatly reducing the burden on both the designer and database administrators.

Chapter 23

Shared Resources and Other Features

A RECURRING PROBLEM WITH Notes development has been managing non-Notes files that are important to the application. For example, an application might have some standard company logos or graphic navigation buttons on the form. The developer would dutifully put the common graphic elements on every form where they are needed. But what happens if the company changes its logo or wants to give the application a facelift by changing the boring old graphics to something new or exciting? The developer would have to go through the forms again and replace each occurrence of each image, quite possibly missing some in the process. Similarly, a web application could incorporate Cascading Style Sheets (CSS) or links to downloadable files. But what if the application moves from one server to another? How can the developer be sure that the files come along for the ride? Or what if the developer needs to change the Hypertext Markup Language (HTML) style sheet but doesn't have access to the server directories where the style sheet file lives?

Lotus's answer has been to create shared resources, giving these formerly separate files a home inside the database. It started with images and Java applets in Release 5. However, the feature proved so useful that it has been expanded in R6 to include a number of other kinds of data.

- ◆ Image Resources
- ◆ Files and Style Sheets
- ◆ Applets
- ◆ Style Sheets
- ◆ Data Connections
- ◆ Database Resources
- ◆ Database Synopsis

Image Resources

Image resources are where it all began, and they'll probably be the most used kind of resource Release 6. You can use image resources for many different design elements, such as pages, fo tables, hotspots, action buttons, and backgrounds, to name a few. Wherever you can insert an im you will usually have the option of calling on image resources. You can even draw in the ima resources of other databases, so you can create serverwide repositories of images from which all your applications can draw.

It's easy to create an image resource. First you must display the Work pane for the images. To ac the images, expand the Shared Resources design element in the Design list. Select Images from the and the Work pane will list all the images currently saved for the database. To add a new image, c the New Image Resource button and the File Open dialog box will display. Just find the image to ins highlight the filename, and click the Open button. You image will be saved with the original filena (you can change the name later).

Once an image resource has been created, you can use the Image Resource Properties Box change its name, assign an alias, or change the number of images the resource represents (we' come back to this later in detail; it's a remarkably powerful feature). Select an image and cho Resource ➤ Resource Properties or simply double-click to open the Image Resource Propert Box for the image (see Figure 23.1).

FIGURE 23.1

The Image Resource Properties Box

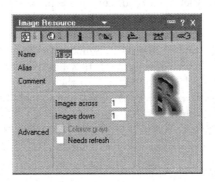

By default, the Name field contains the name of the original graphic file (including the file ty extension). You can change it to anything you want, but you shouldn't delete the extension becau it is used for filtering images in the Insert Image Resource dialog box, which is displayed when a image is selected. You can also enter an alias and a comment for the image file. In the Advanced s tion, you can enter the number of images contained in the file, colorize grays (this option match grays in your image with colors in the Notes palette, making your image blend with your operati system's background), and mark it as needing to be refreshed (checking this box delays changes ur you manually commit them).

The Images Across property may sound a bit odd, but it's a very useful feature. Using the fie in conjunction with specially constructed images will give you images that change as you roll yo mouse over them. How does this work? Start by creating a single image that consists of up to fou equally sized parts, each separated by a single pixel. For example, our example in the Recipe d base, rolling.gif, is 63 by 22 pixels. It has been constructed by taking one 15 ×22 image, leav a column one-pixel wide next to it, inserting another 15 × 22 image, leaving another blank column one-pixel wide, inserting a third 15 × 22 image, leaving a third blank column, and inserting a final 15 × 22 image. We want the image to be treated as four separate images, so we've also set the Images Across property to 4.

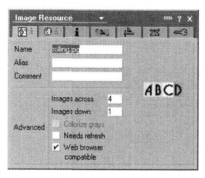

What happens when we use this image depends on how many images there are. The image in the first (leftmost) position is the default state. The image in the second position, if any, appears when the mouse rolls over the image. The image in the third position appears when the image has been selected (that is, after it has been clicked). The fourth image appears when the mouse is being clicked. What all this means is that you can create image rollovers with a little graphic manipulation but no JavaScript programming. Neat, isn't it? Image rollovers work in the Notes client and in web contexts that employ Java applets (for example, outlines rendered as Java). Unfortunately, they don't work in web contexts rendered as HTML (as, for example, most forms are).

NOTE *Images Down does something a little similar to Images Across but not nearly as interesting. It provides up to three sizes of database icons for the bookmark bar.*

Image resources are also useful for managing changes. If you want to update an image, you do not have to delete the resource. Instead, highlight the Image element in the Work pane and click the Refresh button or choose Resource ➤ Refresh. The Open File dialog box will display and you can select the updated image on your computer. When you update an image here, the updated version will appear everywhere that image resource is used in your database.

The Work pane has three buttons other than New Image Resource and Refresh. Open File will launch the image file using whatever external application is registered to open that file type (for example, Photoshop or Painter). Open With will also launch an external application and display the file, but you can choose which application to use. Export saves an external copy of the image resource.

TIP *Once an image has been inserted as an image resource, do not change its name because there is no easy way to determine which forms are using a copy of it. When an image resource is placed on a form, the source for the picture is the name of the image.*

There are three ways to insert an image resource into a form. If you want to insert an image where the cursor lies, choose Create ➤ Image Resource. The Insert Image Resource dialog box will then display (see Figure 23.2). You can select an image from this dialog box and it will be placed directly on the form, page, or whatever you happen to be editing at the time. The dialog box defaults to the current database, but you can, optionally, select a different database to draw the image resource from.

FIGURE 23.2

The Insert Image Resource dialog box

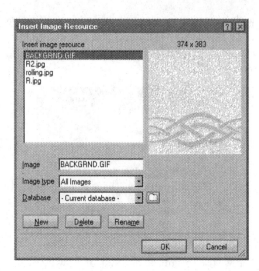

A similar method is to select Create ➤ Insert Resource. This brings up the Insert Resource dia. box (see Figure 23.3). Under Resource Type, click Images. You can select a database to draw th image from, then select from the Available Resources list. The selected image will appear at the tom of the dialog box.

FIGURE 23.3

The Insert Resource dialog box

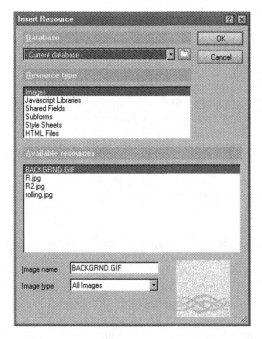

The third method involves the properties of a specific design element. If you think back to the section on tables in Chapter 20, you will recall a Table Property tab called Table/Cell Background. On this tab is a folder icon that displays the Insert Image Resource dialog box. If you select an image from this dialog box, a copy of it will be placed in the background for the selected table cell.

If you have inserted an image resource directly on the form, you may notice that the image is actually a Picture object. You can scale the image, add captions and borders, and even program the Picture object using JavaScript. You can see the available events by selecting the Picture object and looking in the Object tab window.

File and Style Sheet Resources

File and style sheet resources are two comparable kinds of shared resources. They're created, maintained, and used similarly, so we'll deal with them together. Style sheet resources are a way of including CSS files, part of the HTML 4 specification, in your Notes database rather than having to keep track of them as external files. File resources are a way to collect any and all external files you want to use in your database and keep them inside the Notes database. You can bring in any kind of file you want as a file resource: graphics, sounds, multimedia files, PDF files, word processor and spreadsheet documents, executable programs, compressed archives, and even, if you're so inclined, other databases. However, the file resource object is best suited to dealing with HTML files.

You construct file and style sheet resources in much the same way as image resources. Navigate to the database's shared resources, then click Files or Style Sheets to bring up a list of shared files. Click the New File Resource or New Style Sheet Resource button to bring up the Open dialog box. Select the file you want and click OK. You can select any file for a file resource, but only style sheet (.css) files for a style sheet resource.

The File Resource Properties Box is much simpler for file resources and style sheets than for image resources (see Figure 23.4). It just has a name, alias, comment, a Needs Refresh check box, and an optional drop-down menu for character set.

FIGURE 23.4

File Resource
Properties Box

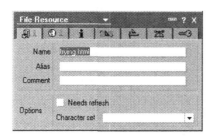

You can open, refresh, and export file and style sheet resources in the same way you can perform those operations on image resources.

It's relatively easy to use style sheet resources on a form or page. Call up the Insert Resource dialog box, click Style Sheets, and select the style sheet you want from the Available Resources list. A small icon will appear on your form or page. You can then use the styles in the style sheet as you would use styles in any other web page, only here you can rest assured that you won't have to figure out a path to the style sheet file.

Shared files are another matter. Although it's nice to be able to bundle all kinds of files into yo Notes database, it's not easy to use most of them. As of this release of Notes, you can't actua include most types of file resources on forms and pages as you can images, applets, and most ot shared resources. There are really only two things you can do with a shared resource. One is access it from the Web. The uniform resource locator (URL) to open a file resource looks like t.

```
http://server/pathtodatabase/databasename.nsf/resourcename?OpenFileResource
```

pathtodatabase is the path to the database relative to the server's Data directory. To get to the bigfile.zip in the database mymail in the mail subdirectory of the data directory on a server nam www.fake.com, for example, the URL would be as follows:

```
http://www.fake.com/mail/mymail.nsf/bigfile.zip?OpenFileResource
```

If you want to create links to file resources in your Notes database, you'll have to do so by ha and use Passthru HTML.

The other way is an exception to not being able to insert a shared file resource in a form or pa You *can* insert a shared file, but only if it's an HTML file. In the Insert Resource dialog box, the an option for HTML files. If you select this option, you can select from among the file resources t the database recognizes as HTML files. In the Designer client, you'll see the inserted file resource o as a small icon (see Figure 23.5). However, if you open the form on the Web or in the Notes clie you'll see the inserted HTML fully rendered (see Figure 23.6). What this allows you to do is to cre HTML files with other tools of your choice (say, Dreamweaver or GoLive) but keep those page inside your Notes database file.

FIGURE 23.5

A shared HTML
file in the form
design

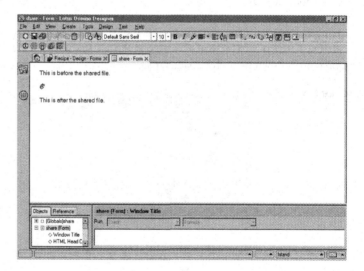

FIGURE 23.6

The form viewed through a web browser

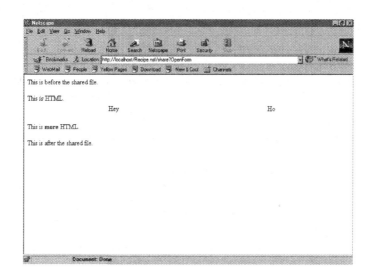

URL COMMANDS

We've ignored the issue so far, but because we've brought it up with file resources, we may as well discuss the idea of URL commands in general. As we've said several times, Domino lets you access Notes databases through a web browser. There must, therefore, be a way to construct URLs to address specific database elements. Domino has specific language for doing that, and if you're going to build web-enabled databases, it's a language you'll need to understand. The basic URL for getting to a database is, as we've implied, the server name, the path to the database, and the database filename, thus:

```
http://server/path/database.nsf
```

To open many types of design element, such as pages and views, you can simply append the name of the element. This URL opens an object named AllDocs:

```
http://server/path/database.nsf/AllDocs
```

However, that URL will only work if there's one object named AllDocs. You might have several objects with the same name. It's best to be specific by appending a question mark (the traditional punctuation dividing a URL path to an object from data to be passed to it) and a command to open a specific type of object. The commands are pretty easy. For example, use OpenView to open a view, OpenForm to open a form, or OpenPage to open a page. Here's that URL again, this time specifically opening a view:

```
http://server/path/database.nsf/AllDocs?OpenView
```

Some objects can take additional parameters. For example, a view can have a Count parameter, telling the server how many documents to display, and a Start parameter, indicating how many documents into the view to start. Domino parameters use standard URL syntax for parameters (parameters are separated with ampersands and formatted as name=value), so this URL will open AllDocs, displaying 50 documents starting with the 20th document in the view:

```
http://server/path/database.nsf/AllDocs?OpenView&Count=50&Start=20
```

Continued on next page

Documents are a little different. First, you must go through a view or folder to get to a document. Second, specifying a document in the view can be tricky. If you're using a sorted view, you can use a value. Domino will bring up the first document with that value in the first sorted column in the view. This URL opens the first document that has the value MyDoc in the first sorted column of AllDocs:

```
http://server/path/database.nsf/AllDocs/MyDoc
```

Strictly speaking, you should use MyDoc?OpenDocument, or even MyDoc?EditDocument (to bring the document up in editing mode), instead of just MyDoc.

One other thing to be aware of is the use of Universal IDs (UNIDs). It's certainly possible but prohibitively difficult to use an object's 32-digit ID number when constructing a URL on your own. However, that's exactly what Domino will do when it creates URLs on its own. Rather than the simple, human-readable URL to the MyDoc document we've provided above, a Domino-generated URL for the document might look something like this:

```
http://server/path/database.nsf/8fk3f551gs9m2uvj29xn3rh4nd7265c3/
nx734g20cm5j2z19gyp4ma7v41hc15mg?OpenDocument
```

The name of the view and the "index" value for the document have been replaced by their UNIDs. As inconvenient as this may be, it's an equally valid way of building a URL, and although you won't be doing it yourself, the Domino server will, so be aware.

For more detailed information on opening database objects via the Web, search the Designer help for *URL commands*.

Applets

Applets, like image resources, are a type of shared resource that has been around since the previous release. Applet resources shouldn't be confused with Java agents. With applet resources, you can store independent Java applets in your Notes database and deploy them on forms and pages.

To create an applet resource, navigate to Shared Resources and click Applets to get to the list shared applets. Click New Applet Resource to bring up the Locate Java Applet Files dialog box (Figure 23.7). You can look for various kinds of Java-related file types (classes, Java source, and so on select the ones you want, and import them into file resources.

To put an applet on a form, select Create Java Applet, which opens a Create Java Applet dialog box You'd use this dialog box to include a Java applet on the form from your computer's file system. However, you'll bypass it by clicking the Locate button, bringing up the dialog box shown in Figure 23. From the Browse menu, select Shared Resources, which brings up a list of shared Java applets. Click C buttons until you get back to the form.

Once you've got the applet on the form, you can do a great deal with it. If you call up the Java Applet properties box, you can review the names and locations of the source files (see Figure 23.8 You can also adjust the size of the applet and note whether the applet uses Common Object Request Broker Architecture (CORBA) classes. CORBA classes allow the Java applet to interact directly with the Domino server. It's a powerful technology, but it's complex and requires specific server settings that are beyond the scope of this book. Search the Designer help for *CORBA* for more information.

FIGURE 23.7

The Locate Java Applet Files dialog box

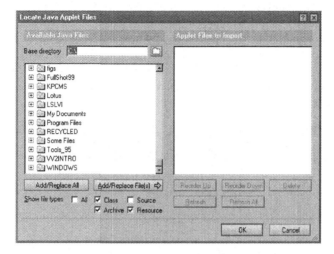

FIGURE 23.8

A form with an applet

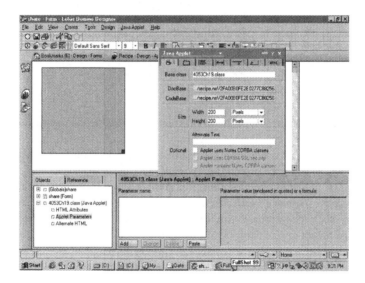

You can also provide the applet with parameters by using the programmer's pane (the bottom of Figure 23.8). For example, an applet running on the Web may pay attention to fields set in an HTML form, such as the time or information provided by the user. To add a parameter, click the Add button. It will add a parameter name to a list, then allow you to enter a value for the parameter or a formula for computing the value. When the agent starts running, the value of the parameter will be computed.

Data Connections

Data Connection resources are a powerful new database resource. They define a connection to an ex:
nal database, allowing you to share information with other systems. A Data Connection resource def:
a connection to a specific object in an external database, generally a table or table-like object. You
use a data connection in conjunction with forms and fields to share data with the external database.
of data connections requires specific configuration information that depends on the specific typ
external database. That is beyond the scope of this book, but we'll cover the basics here.

To create a new data connection, navigate to Shared Resources and click Data Connections. C
the New Data Connection Resource button to create a new connection (see Figure 23.9).

FIGURE 23.9

A new data
connection

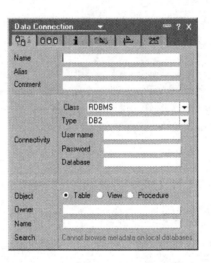

As with other design elements, you may assign the connection a name, alias, and comment. T
Connectivity section sets up important identifying information. The first two fields define the type
of database. At the moment, you can choose from four specific types of database (DB2, Orac
Oracle 8, and Sybase) and two types of generic database connection (ODBC and OLE DB). On
you've chosen a type of database, you'll need to provide at least a username and password. You
also have to provide sufficient information to connect to the desired target database. For exampl
for an Oracle database, you'll need to enter a host string, whereas for an ODBC database, you
enter a data source name (DSN). Finally, you'll choose a specific object to connect to: a table, vi
(not a Notes view, but a stored SQL statement that produces table-like results; some databases ca
this a *query*), or procedure. You'll also need to provide an object name and, if necessary, an own
The Options tab lets you fine-tune the database connection; the specifics depend on the type o
database to which you're attempting to connect.

This is where things get complex. First, when you start creating Data Connection resources, yo
have to enable data connections in the database properties (look back at Chapter 17, "Database C
ation and Properties"). Second, you'll have to make sure that Domino Enterprise Connection Servic
(DECS) is enabled on the Domino server where you expect the application to be used. DECS is a s
cial service of the Domino server that mediates connections to external databases. It is not enabled

default, so check with your Domino administrator before you go any further. Data connections will only work if the database is on a server with DECS running; they will not work on local copies of a database on a Notes client.

Once you've created and enabled Data Connections, you'll need to attach forms and individual fields on them to specific data connections (review Chapter 19, "Basic Form Design"). If everything has been configured correctly, each Notes document made with the form in question will correspond to a row in the associated relational database object. Changes you make in your Notes database will push changes back to the external database and vice versa. Making sure you're addressing the external database will require a deep understanding of how the external database works, but for more information on the Notes side, search the Designer help file for *Overview of Data Connection Resources*.

NOTE *If you're familiar with DECS from earlier releases of Notes, you'll see that this arrangement is more flexible, in that you don't have to define the complete relationship between a form and a set of fields.*

Database Resources

Despite the name, Database Resources have nothing to do with Shared Resources. Rather, they're a separate set of database elements that every database contains. To find them, navigate to Other and select Database Resources. This will bring up a list of the four database resources: Icon, Using Database document, About Database document, and Database Script. They're not particularly powerful and can't be reused through the database, but they can be useful.

Icon

The database icon appears by default for the database's bookmarks and will appear if you use the old Workspace view. Double-clicking the Icon entry under Database Resources will bring up the Design Icon dialog box (see Figure 23.10). This dialog box is a special image editor. The first four buttons down the left are drawing tools: pixel-by-pixel drawing, two area-painting tools, and a straight-line painting tool. The next two switch modes between painting and erasing. Along the bottom is a palette of the 16 available colors. The buttons on the right allow you to copy, paste, and save the icon. You can copy icons from other databases or from any other graphic source, but when you paste it into the icon editor, your image will be reduced to the available 16 colors.

FIGURE 23.10
Design Icon
dialog box

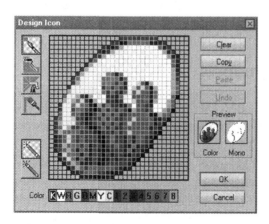

Using Database and About Database Documents

These elements are a holdover from earlier versions of Notes, but they're still useful. They are essentially pages, but they have a special property: the Notes client and Domino server make them particularly easy to reach. Under the Help menu, the Notes client has About This Database and Using This Database entries. The entries bring up the About and Using documents, respectively. Likewise, there are special URL commands to bring up a database's About and Using documents via the Web with a Domino server (`filename.nsf/$about` and `filename.nsf/$help`, respectively). Pages are great for creating elaborate customized help and instruction, but you should always put something in your About and Using documents. They're too convenient to your users not to use.

Database Script

You've already seen that forms, views, and other design elements have events that trigger code. The same is true of the database as a whole. You can attach code to those events in the Database Script area (see Figure 23.11). You can, for example, use this area to run a script when the database is opened or closed. Database scripts can use either LotusScript or the formula language.

FIGURE 23.11

Database
Script area

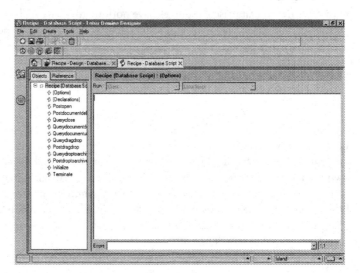

Database Synopsis

Design Synopsis is the last element under Other. The database synopsis isn't a design element so much as it is a tool, and it's not likely to help you build your database, but it will help you make sense of it after you're done. The design synopsis builds a plain-text description of the design of your database. The design synopsis has four tabs:

Choose Design Elements   This screen lets you choose which elements you want information about. Select a type of design element you want information from, use the add and remove buttons to select which specific design elements you'd like to see summarized, and move on to the next type of element.

Choose DB Info   This tab lets you determine what database-level information you want included in your summary, such as access control lists and replication settings.

Define Content   This tab controls what information you'll see on each type of design element. You can selectively control whether the synopsis includes such things as aliases, security information, and program code.

Format Output   This tab determines the form the output will take. You can choose from page breaks vs. blank lines for internal formatting and document vs. database for overall output format.

When you've selected your design elements and decided what information you want about them, click the OK button. Notes will quickly prepare a summary document containing the database information, which will look something like Figure 23.12. The design synopsis won't give you any information on the appearance of individual design elements, but it will give you enough information on the underlying technical aspects of the database that you can use it to help debug problems and figure out where to repair damage.

FIGURE 23.12

A database synopsis

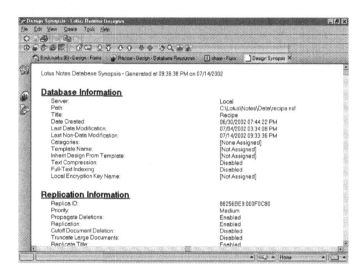

Summary

This chapter has shown you a number of resources your database can contain. Although they mostly cannot be accessed individually, they can be a great help in the design of other elements, such as forms and views. They range from simple conveniences, such as shared files, to powerful data tools, such as Data Connections.

The next chapter covers our most advanced topics: LotusScript, Java, and how to use them in a Notes database.

Chapter 24

Language Extensions and the Object Model

IF YOU'VE MASTERED THE material presented so far, you can already produce completely functional Notes databases that will allow you to create and maintain hierarchies of documents, make your content secure, perform all manner of calculations, send mail, and display summary data. But you can do even more than that. Any decent database development platform allows you to use a fully featured programming language to manipulate your data. Notes gives you a choice of two: LotusScript and Java (the other languages you can use with Notes don't quite qualify as fully featured for these purposes; the formula language still has limited flow control and JavaScript, which can be used in some contexts, is more richly featured but can't address most Notes objects). Most users and even some developers will never see either of them, and not all developers will use both, but they're available.

This chapter discusses where and how to use scripts, the basic rules of LotusScript syntax, and how to navigate the Notes/Domino object model. Although Java and JavaScript are part of the Notes programming environment as well, this is *not* the place to learn the basics. Java is a wildly popular, cross-platform language, so there are any number of other places to learn it in greater depth than would be feasible here. For more in-depth coverage, you might be interested in *Mastering Java 2, J2SE 1.4* by John Zukowski (Sybex, 2002) and *Mastering JavaScript Premium Edition* by James Jaworski (Sybex, 2001). This chapter may appear to concentrate on LotusScript, but when we get to the heart of programming for Notes and Domino, the object model, we'll present LotusScript and Java examples in parallel so you can see how things are done in both languages.

- ◆ Adding scripts to your databases
- ◆ Basic LotusScript programming techniques
- ◆ The object model
- ◆ JavaScript

The Languages

Java, of course, is a widely used language introduced by Sun in the mid-1990s. It was once touted a universal programming platform that could make operating systems obsolete. It hasn't lived up that promise, but it has established itself as a useful language and a viable, somewhat easier to use c petitor to C. LotusScript is a complete object-oriented programming language and an nth generati proprietary descendent of BASIC, one of the first programming languages (and still one of the m influential) developed for entry-level programmers. LotusScript is used by several Lotus progra such as the spreadsheet program 1-2-3.

NOTE *There's yet another language you can use in Notes: JavaScript. JavaScript, which bears only a vague, superfici resemblance to Java, was created to allow developers to include programming on web pages without having to send da back to the server. JavaScript is a somewhat more bare-bones language than LotusScript and Java. More importantly, doesn't have the extensions into Notes objects that the other two have, so we won't be covering it in any depth, but we w be going over where it can be used, both on the Web and inside Notes.*

Which language you choose depends on a number of factors, such as the context in which t script runs, what your developed code base is in, and which language you know better. One thing t doesn't matter much, though, is on which operating system your script is supposed to run. As lo as your script doesn't deal with certain system-specific features such as directory structures, it will whether your database happens to be on a Linux server, a Mac, or a Windows computer.

Although Java is being used in more and more places in Notes, LotusScript still has a privile place in Notes databases. LotusScript programs, known informally as *scripts*, lurk behind agents, l tons, and events that happen invisibly when a user does things with documents, views, databases, even individual fields. In fact, scripts run every time you open or close a document in your mailbc At the moment, you can't use Java in those contexts. As a result, this chapter will lean more towa LotusScript than Java, but we'll cover both where possible.

When you use either language, you can create applications that give the programmer tremendc control over databases, documents, and even external files, including:

- ◆ Extremely complex manipulation of and access to documents. For example, you can u LotusScript and Java to move large groups of documents into and out of folders and vie with just a few instructions or to base workflow on the number and attributes of docume already awaiting a user's approval.

- ◆ Access to and control over database properties. You can write your own maintenance utility p grams to keep track of database size and utilization or even control access control lists (ACl

- ◆ Access to external files. With the ability to manipulate text files and Open Database Conn tivity (ODBC) data sets, you can integrate your Notes databases with your relational databa and with applications that can output structured text files.

Because these languages are powerful and versatile, they are also complex and have the potential be dangerous if used carelessly. They are also very different tools from what you've seen so far. W fields, forms, views, and folders, you've been seeing a visual development environment, and you' never been far away from the objects in question. With scripts, you'll be writing a lot of instructio without much in the way of ready-made lists of fields or forms to help you.

Nevertheless, LotusScript is relatively easy to learn as programming languages go, and there's a wealth of resources for Java code. If you already know another scripting language, such as Perl or Visual Basic, you're already well on your way to understanding the languages you can use in Notes. If you haven't done any programming before, hang tight. You'll need to pick up some new techniques early on, but when you get to the section "Understanding the Object Model", things will start to look familiar again.

NOTE   *LotusScript syntax is particularly close to Visual Basic, which is not surprising because they evolved from a common source. In fact, they're so similar that it's possible to copy and paste some kinds of simple code between them.*

Why, When, and How to Use Scripts

If you've mastered formulas, you may wonder why you would want to bother with another, completely different and far more complex language. The reason is simple: raw power. You can do things with a script that you simply can't do with formulas. For example, the Out of Office agent cycles through new messages, compares the senders' addresses to several different lists (addresses to receive a special reply, addresses to receive no reply, and addresses to which a reply has already been sent), composes appropriate messages from several different parts, sends them on their way, and modifies lists as appropriate. The Out of Office agent's tasks would be difficult if not impossible to do with formulas. LotusScript and Java provide numerous benefits:

◆ Fine control over complex data types to which formulas have no access. For example, you can use LotusScript and Java to manipulate ACLs and ODBC data sets.

◆ The ability to read and write external files.

◆ The ability to deal with errors that would cause formulas to stop dead in their tracks.

◆ Superior access to other database objects. Although you can make a formula agent run on a set of documents, the formula itself can only affect the database object on which it is running at the moment.

◆ Superior branching and flow control. Formulas have some ability to make choices and repeat tasks, but you have much greater control over the behavior of LotusScript and Java routines.

NOTE   *If you use Java, you have the additional benefit of using a language with a well-developed set of existing code. You can include just about any Java classes you want in the Java code you write in Notes.*

Of course, just because you can use a script doesn't mean you must. There are often instances where you can do the same things with a script and a formula. For example, the following script (don't worry about what it means, you'll find out later) is for a button:

```
Dim ws As NotesUIWorkspace
Dim uidoc As NotesUIDocument
Set ws = new NotesUIWorkspace
Set uidoc = ws.UIDocument
Call uidoc.Print
```

This formula does the same thing:

```
@Command([FilePrint])
```

For a simple task like this, it's clearly a better idea to use the formula. Formulas and Simple Acti
also run slightly faster than scripts of comparable size. Given the choice, if a script and a formula
perform exactly the same function and the formula isn't terribly hard to write, you'll probably w
to go with the formula.

In some cases, the choice is made for you. For example, a field's Input Validation and Input Tr
lation events will only take a formula, whereas the field's Entering and Exiting events can only t
scripts (rich-text fields don't have Validation and Translation, so if you want to validate them, yo
have to use a script and the Exiting event).

Beyond that, it's your choice. If you're a novice programmer, you're less comfortable with scri
and you can make formulas work, use them. If you're a more experienced programmer, use scrip
Some professional developers reach the point where they hardly use formulas at all.

And where, exactly, do scripts go? Agents, buttons, view and form actions, form and view eve
and just about anything else that can take a formula can take a script instead. You've already s
form, view, and other design element events that can take LotusScript, and we'll be going into de
about where to put both LotusScript and Java in the next chapter.

Basic LotusScript Programming

The following sections address basic programming terms and techniques for LotusScript. If you'i
programmer, you might want to skim this section or just skip ahead to the "Understanding the Obj
Model" section on using the Notes object model. If you're not a programmer, or you've never p
grammed in a BASIC-compatible language before, read on.

So What Is a Script, Anyway?

You've dealt with formulas (you have done that, haven't you?), so you've already gotten close to w
you'll be doing with scripts in LotusScript. Like a complex formula, a script consists of a sequer
of instructions the computer executes when you press the related button, when the agent trigger
when you enter or leave a field, and so on. A script, however, can have a far more complex structu

A script in LotusScript consists of one or more *subroutines*, which are blocks of instructions me:
to perform particular tasks; you'll see the script's component subroutines listed separately instead
like in some programming languages and development platforms, as one great big block of co
Dividing a long script into subroutines has a number of advantages. First, it's much easier to organ
and modify large programs if you can write smaller blocks of code (each with its own special fui
tion) and arrange them into a larger structure. Second, you can reuse code by going back to speci
subroutines as many times as necessary. Formulas always execute from the top down, but you ca
write a script that repeats code or decides whether to use parts of itself while it runs. Imagine a p
gram that, at various times, needs to calculate the sales tax on an item depending on the state in whi
it's being sold. Using formulas, you'll need to rewrite (or at least copy and paste) a huge formula eve
time you need to calculate the tax, resulting in a much larger block of formulas and making it diffic
to update if a state's sales tax ever changes. With the more advanced languages, you write the co
once and, when you need it, refer to the subroutine by name. If something changes, you only have
modify it once.

You also know, more or less, where to write scripts. Scripts are written in the same programmer's pane where you write formulas, although a script editor will look a little different from a formula editor. Create an agent, name it, and tell it to run LotusScript instead of a Simple Action (for more information on this topic, see Chapter 25). Figure 24.1 shows what you'll get. Instead of the diamond you've seen in the lower-left pane, there's a list of items marked with scrolls. If it were JavaScript, you would see circles. If there's code in any of those places, the scroll will be shaded. You may want to go back to chapter 19 and review table 19.1 to keep all the symbols straight. In addition to the familiar Design pane features, a LotusScript programmer's pane has a number of other features, visible and otherwise, to help you write scripts. The interface you use to write scripts has enough going on in it that it has a name of its own: the *integrated development environment*, more commonly called the IDE. The IDE gives you a place to write scripts and helps you debug them.

FIGURE 24.1

An agent using LotusScript

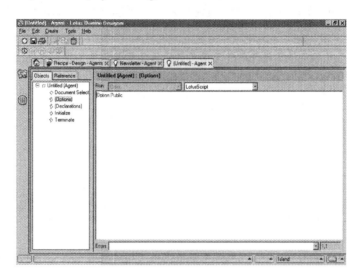

The IDE's left pane displays a list of objects, events, and LotusScript subroutines (or, in the case of Java agents and script libraries, Java routines) associated with them. The right pane, where you've already written Simple Actions and formulas, is where you'll write the script. An additional feature of the script editor is the Errors bar across the bottom of the screen. If you make an illegal statement in your script, Notes will flag the error and define it in the bar. Finally, in the bottom-right field, Notes displays the current position of the cursor in the format *line number, position*. For example, if it says 1,1, as it does in Figure 24.1, the cursor will be at the first character of the first line of the script.

As you may recall from Chapter 16, "Introducing Domino Designer," the script editor will help you keep track of what the words mean by coloring them. By default, identifiers (the names of variables and other user-defined objects) are black, keywords (commands, operators, and other words reserved by LotusScript) are blue, comments are green, errors are red, and constants are a sort of magenta. However, you can change the colors from the Properties Box for the programmer's pane. You can take advantage of the full range of colors, so if you want your variables to be a specific shade of lime green, you can make it happen. You can also change the font and size from a readable but unexciting default of 9-point default sans serif.

Commenting

You can insert a comment into a script by typing a single quote (') or the word *REM* (short for *rem* a holdover from ancient versions of BASIC). A comment can start anywhere in a line, and everyth after the comment marker is part of the comment. You can't start a comment partway into a line then end it and enter more commands on the same line. After the comment marker, you can write thing you want: a description of what the following code will do, a warning about possible error history of changes, or even snide comments about the script's development process. When the sc: runs, Notes will completely ignore comments, even if they happen to contain legal commands.

"Why," you may ask, "would anybody want to write something in a script that the program ignore?" The answer is that comments aren't for the computer. They're for you and anybody else v might have to look at the script. Try as you may to indent lines properly and give your variables nar that make immediate sense, you'll still write scripts that are long, convoluted, and incomprehensi on first glance. Even if your scripts are short and to the point, it won't be immediately obvious w they're supposed to do or, more important, why they were written. It's a good idea to insert hea information in your scripts before the executable code starts; the header information can describe script's purpose and perhaps contain other useful information such as the programmer's name (you'll know who to contact in an emergency, or at least who to hold accountable) or a list of m fications. A typical header might look like this:

```
' Script name: PeaceAndLove
'
' Author: Marion Morrison
'
' Last Modified: 2/3/99
'
' Description: Spread peace, love, and understanding
' among all mankind, using a Domino server.
```

In addition to any "header" comments, you should put internal comments into your script to ke the reader posted on what's happening. Even if you can keep track of what a large script does wh you're writing it, you won't remember in six months, and if somebody else has to look at your scr they won't have any idea how it works. Eventually, you may be able to read through the script a figure out how it works, but you'll save a lot of time if you just write a few brief comments describ what's happening. In fact, comment lavishly. It will take an extra few minutes while you're writir but it will save you hours later.

One particularly useful thing to comment is where your loops and If and Case statements end you can keep better track of where nested bits of code begin and end. The automatic indenting p vided by the IDE is nice, but it's pretty easy to write code that ends up several layers deep, and it c be a long way between the beginning and end of a loop or an if or case statement. It's easy to fin where multiline statements begin, but not so hard to find where they end. Making comments like t following can help you figure out where things are:

```
If (x = y) then
   While not (doc is nothing)
     If doc.SomeField(0) = "Safe" Then
       Set doc = vw.GetNextDocument(doc)
```

```
      End If ' Check of SomeField ends
   Loop ' getting documents from vw ends
 End if ' x = y comparison ends
```

Subroutines

Go back to the list of scrolls on the left side of the LotusScript programmer's pane in the agent you created and click Initialize. Each item in the list represents a subroutine. Clicking the Initialize subroutine brings up a few lines of code. The `Sub Initialize` and `End Sub` are what make the subroutine exist. The `(Button as Source)` bit in the `Sub` line is declaring a variable in a way that makes it easy for the script to refer back to the button. Certain form events come with other built-in variables. For example, events related to opening and closing a form, such as PostOpen and QueryClose, have built-in variables that make it easy to refer to the document being opened. That's not important right now, but it can be a useful tool, and we'll get back to it later in the "Scope" section.

To create a subroutine, just add another `Sub` statement *after* the `End Sub` line. In the example from the preceding paragraph, go to the `End Sub` line in the `Initialize` subroutine, press Enter to go to the next line, type **Sub Main**, and press Enter again. That will create an empty subroutine named `Main` (the `End Sub` line is created automatically) and put you in it. Those subroutines form the structure in which programs are written.

To use a subroutine in a program, just type the name. When a subroutine finishes running, the script will return to where it started. For example, the following script runs three subroutines (`Firstroutine`, `Secondroutine`, and `Lastscript`) in order; then it runs `Firstroutine` a second time:

```
Sub Initialize
' This calls a series of other routines
   Firstroutine
   Secondroutine
   Lastscript
   Firstroutine
End Sub
```

Now you should be able to construct the skeleton of a LotusScript program. However, a batch of subroutines won't do you any good if they don't do anything individually.

Variables and Data Types

If you've dealt with Notes formulas or taken an algebra class, you know what a *variable* is: an expression that stands for a value. However, unlike in an algebraic expression, a variable in LotusScript doesn't just stand for a number. It can stand for a string (that is, text), numbers (both integers and floating-point numbers), dates and times, and Notes native objects such as databases, documents, views, and fields.

DECLARING VARIABLES

It's a good idea, if not always necessary, to declare a variable before using it. When you declare a variable, you're telling Notes what its name will be and what type of data it will hold. Variables are declared with the `Dim` statement, like this:

```
Dim variablename as type
```

In the early days of programming, *dim* was short for *dimension*, setting up a space in memory for variable's value. The old terminology is long gone, but the function stays the same. When you dec a variable, Notes sets up a space in memory large enough to hold the information for the type of able you declare.

You can declare several data types, each of which can have values that fall into a given ra (see Table 24.1).

TABLE 24.1: LotusScript Data Types

TYPE	VALUES	SIZE
Boolean	True (-1) or False (0)	2 bytes
Byte	Integers from 0 to 255	1 byte
Integer	Integers (whole numbers) from –32,768 to 32,767.	2 bytes
Long	Integers from –2,147,483,648 to 2,147,483,647.	4 bytes
Single	Any number from –3.402823E+38 to 3.402823E+38.	4 bytes
Double	Any number from –1.7976931348623158E+308 to 1.7976931348623158E+308.	8 bytes
Currency	Any number from –922,337,203,685,411.5807 to 922,337,203,685,411.5807. Currency variables may have, at most, four decimal places.	8 bytes
String	Any plain-text value.	2 bytes pe character
Variant	Any value.	16 bytes

The data types listed in Table 24.1 are all for *scalar* variables, simple variables that hold a single va of a simple type. You may also declare a variable as an array (a set of values of the same type, discuss in "Lists and Arrays" later in this chapter) or as a Notes object class, but those follow slightly differe rules (we'll get to that later). Although you might be tempted to declare everything as an easy-to-han variant, don't. A variant takes up from two to eight times as much space in memory as any other ki of variable. Any one variable will take up a nearly trivial amount of space, but a big script that juggle lot of variables can be slowed down if it takes up too much room.

A variable name must start with a letter and can contain any combination of numbers, letters, a underscores up to 40 characters. These are valid:

```
Dim MyText As String
Dim time1 As Double
Dim some_money As Currency
Dim anunreasonablylongbutlegalvariablename As Long
```

These are not:

```
Dim 1variable As Integer
Dim my text As String
Dim avariablenamesoamazinglylongthatitisntalegealnameanymore As Long
```

Variable names aren't case sensitive. Both `ItemName` and `Itemname` name the same variable.

It's tempting to give your variables simple, one-letter names like we all remember from high-school algebra (x, y, a, b, and so on), but don't do that either. Near-meaningless variable names are barely acceptable for counters (that is, variables you use to count the number of times a process has happened, the number of times through a loop, and so on) and other "throwaway" variables that are used once or twice and ignored for the rest of the script, but it's a good idea to give your variables meaningful names. For example, `docA` and `docB` for a pair of documents that you want to compare or `fullprice` for an undiscounted price would be reasonable variable names. You'll notice that, in the examples later dealing with Notes objects, a fairly regular set of variable names is being used: `vw` for a view, `doc` for a Notes document, `db` for a Notes database, and so on. LotusScript reserves a number of words, mostly commands and statements, which should not be used as variable names. It might be tempting to use `notesdocument` as the name of a variable representing a Notes document, but `notesdocument` happens to have a meaning. You should avoid using the names of objects, properties, and variables to avoid confusing both yourself and Notes.

SETTING VALUES

Once a variable has been declared, you can assign a value to it with an equation, like this:

```
Dim x As Integer
x = 2
```

These two lines create a variable named x and set its value to 2. Notice that you just use the $=$ sign, not $:=$ like you would in a formula. In LotusScript, $=$ is used for both comparison and assignment. The variable you want to assign the value to goes on the left side of the equal sign, and the value you want to assign goes on the right. You can put any valid expression on the right side. This code sets x equal to four:

```
y = 2
x = y*2
```

If you want to concatenate strings, use the $+$ or $\&$ sign, and be sure everything you want to concatenate is a string.

This code sets `thirdstring` equal to "Hello world!":

```
firststring = "Hello "
secondstring = "world!"
thirdstring = firststring + secondstring
```

If you concatenate a string with a number or some other non-text variable, use the `Cstr()` command to turn the variable into a string. For example:

```
x = 4
thestring = "There are " + Cstr(x) + " lights!"
```

After this code, the value of the variable `thestring` is "There are 4 lights!"

LISTS AND ARRAYS

In addition to scalar variables, LotusScript provides for some more complex data types: *lists* *arrays*, which are variables that hold sets of values of the same type. You declare a list by adding List operator to the Dim statement. For example, you would declare a Currency list, which migh used to hold a list of prices, like this:

```
Dim priceList List As Currency
```

Members of a list are named. You can use a string or a string variable. The following code cre two entries (named Apples and Oranges) for the Currency list and assigns values to them, usin string to name the first item and a string variable to name the second:

```
Dim priceList List As Currency
Dim itemName As String
PriceList("Apples") = 1.05
ItemName = "Oranges"
PriceList(itemname) = 0.85
```

Like a list, an array can hold a number of values, but it can be far more complex. Unlike lists, arr have a set number of members (although it's possible to change those bounds) in a set order. Th is, an array has a first member, a second member, and so on. An array is declared with a range (defin the number of values it can have) in parentheses, thus:

```
Dim valArray (5) As Integer
```

Arrays start counting at zero, so the preceding array can hold up to six values, and those values c be referred to using the numbers 0 to 5 as indexes. That is, the first member of the array is valArray(the second valArray(1), and so on. You can also name the lower bound of the array. This defines array identical to valArray:

```
Dim otherArray (0 to 5) As Integer
```

Any given item in the array is addressed by using the variable name and the appropriate index nu ber in parentheses. A value could be assigned to the last member of the array like this:

```
valArray(5) = 2
```

You can, of course, use any values you want to assign the upper and lower bounds. The array defin by Dim valArray(10 to 15) as Integer also holds six values, but the last member of the array wot be valArray(15).

So far, an array is hardly different from a list. But one of the advantages of an array is that, becau the "names" of the items in the array are numbers, the values of an array are arranged in a meaning order. It's easy to set up a loop (see the "Forall" section on looping later in this chapter) to cycl through the list of values. One of the other advantages is that an array can be multidimensional. Y can think of valArray as a table with one row and six columns. However, we could create a table multiple rows with multiple columns by giving the array a second range:

```
Dim twoDArray(1 to 5, 1 to 4) As Integer
```

In this code, `twoDArray` has two dimensions, not just one. It could be considered a table with five columns and four rows. The value of the second column, third row would be set like this:

```
twoDArray(2,3) = 1
```

In LotusScript, an array can have as many as eight dimensions.

You may think it strange that arrays start counting at zero instead of one. The reason comes from that multidimensional capability. Think back to high-school algebra and geometry again. All of those grids you graphed parabolas on had an origin point at 0 on the x-axis and 0 on the y-axis. That kind of geometric thinking has carried over into programming, so the first value of an array is not at one, but at ground zero, both virtually and literally. This makes particular sense when you consider that arrays are built to deal with multidimensional grids, where starting from a zero point is essential.

USING OPTION BASE

If your brain can comfortably change gears to start counting at zero rather than at one when it comes to arrays, it shouldn't be a problem to refer to `arrayname(0)` whenever you want to retrieve a value. But if it annoys you, you can take steps to change the way LotusScript acts. If you go to the (Options) routine, you can add the line `Option Base n`, where *n* is the default lower boundary of an array. Adding `Option Base 1` will make the default lower bound 1, which would make `arrayname(1)` the first member of an array. However, be careful using `Option Base` if you're going to use multidimensional arrays. `Option Base 1` would move the "center" of a three-dimensional array from (0,0,0) to (1,1,1), which can lead to some exciting math.

LotusScript gives you the ability to resize arrays, so you can declare an array even if you have no idea how big it needs to be when the script begins. Use the `ReDim` command to resize the array like this:

```
Dim valArray(2) As Integer
ReDim valArray(4) As Integer
```

`valArray` has gone from having three members (0 through 2) to five members (0 through 4). In this particular case, `valArray` was declared with members, but it would be possible to declare an array with no members at all (`Dim valArray () as Integer`) and use the `ReDim` command later. If you already have values in an array and want to keep them, use the `PRESERVE` keyword to keep the values from being erased when you resize the array. Here's an example:

```
Dim valArray(1) As Integer
valArray (0) = 1
valArray (1) = 5
ReDim Preserve valArray (2) As Integer
```

After this code, `valArray` has three members, the last of which, `valArray(2)`, is null.

Two invaluable functions for dealing with arrays are `Ubound` and `Lbound`. These functions return the upper and lower boundaries of an array. You might use them like this:

```
' assume that valArray has been declared as an integer and has had
' values set elsewhere
x = Ubound (valArray)
```

```
ReDim Preserve valArray (x + 1) As Integer
valArray (x+1) = 1
```

This code finds out the upper bound of `valArray` and uses it to add another member the arr

WHEN AND WHERE TO DECLARE

In certain cases, you must declare variables before you use them. Arrays must be declared, althou
you can reset their bounds. If you put `Option Declare` in the `Options` section of a script, you m
declare all variables no matter what kind they are.

If you don't use `Option Declare`, you can create variables implicitly, which is to say, witho
declaring them first. Just use a name that has not previously been used as a variable and Notes v
create it with a null value. For example, if x and y haven't previously been declared, the following st
ment will return the value 0 for x and 2 (2+0) for y:

```
y = x + 2
```

The use of `Option Declare` (`Option Explicit`, the syntax that some other dialects of BASIC use, v
also work) is worth a little attention here. Often, LotusScript programmers will go to the Options
tion of their scripts and put in the line `Option Declare`. This option prohibits creating variables im
citly, forcing programmers to declare any variables they intend to use. The advantage of not using `Opt`
`Declare` is that it's a little faster for the experienced programmer to create variables at will. Not hav
the `Dim` statements makes the script a bit shorter, and more important, a programmer who knows exa
what she's doing can write operational code without having to type an extra line for every single varia

However, there is a downside—several downsides, actually. First, if you don't declare a variab
Notes won't know what kind of data you're about to drop into it. Therefore, it creates a variant, wh
takes up more room in memory than other data types.

Second, if you have complete freedom to create new variables on the fly, you have complete freed
to get them wrong. Consider this code:

```
Firstvar = 1
Secondvar = 2
Thirdvar = Fristvar + Secondvar
```

The inattentive programmer might expect `Thirdvar` to equal 3, not realizing that he's sudden
creating the variable `Fristvar` instead of using the variable `Firstvar`. If you use `Option Decla`
Notes will let you know about any misspelled variable names immediately. It may not sound li
much on the surface, but half of debugging is cleaning up punctuation and spelling errors. Usir
`Option Declare` can save a lot of time and hair-pulling trying to find a well-hidden mystery varia

SCOPE

It's not enough just to declare your variables. You've also got to know where to declare them. Wh
a variable is declared determines what parts of a script can know about it; in techno-speak, this
called *scope*. A variable's scope is the range of subroutines in which it can be used. If you declare a va
able within a subroutine, it can only be used within that subroutine. If your script moves to anoth
subroutine, that variable (and its value) will go away. If you're not declaring variables before you u
them, your script will lose them as well.

LotusScript gives you several methods to give variables a wider scope. You can build variables into the definition of the subroutine or into a function by declaring it with parameters. In addition to the built-in LotusScript functions (type conversion functions that perform much the same tasks as @functions such as @Text, mathematical functions such as tangents and cosines, and so on), LotusScript allows you to write your own special-purpose functions. For example, you might want to create a convenient means for calculating sales tax for different states or for computing the check digit for a UPC code.

You create a function much like you create a subroutine, but functions require a more complex syntax. Use the FUNCTION keyword rather than Sub, give the function a name, provide parameters, and give the function a data type. For example, this line creates a function named volume that requires three parameters and returns a single-precision floating-point number:

```
Function volume (height,width,length) As Single
```

At some point in the function, you must set the function name equal to some value. This will be the value returned by the function. Our volume function might look something like this:

```
Function volume (height,width,length) As Single
  volume = height * width * length
End Function
```

To use a function you wrote yourself, simply use it as you would any of LotusScript's built-in functions, plugging in values as necessary. The following line sets x equal to the value of the volume function with a height of 2 and width and length equal to the variables firstnumber and secondnumber:

```
x = volume (2, firstnumber, secondnumber)
```

The values you plug into the function will become the values of the variable names you use in the parameters you used to create the function.

Just as you can define parameters for a function, you can define them for a subroutine. For example, if you created a subroutine with the line Sub myroutine (myvar as String), you would invoke it not just by using the name of the subroutine, but with a line like this:

```
myroutine(some_string_value)
```

By plugging a value into the subroutine call, you can pass the value of a variable from one subroutine to another.

Most of the time, that isn't good enough. You may need to pass a great many values from one subroutine to another, making it tedious to create the whole list of parameters, or you may not be able to fill in all of the parameters with values. Fortunately, you can also give variables a broader scope by declaring them in a special place. Most objects and events that can take LotusScript have a special subroutine labled (Declarations). The Declarations subroutine can only take Dim statements, but any variable declared there has a scope of the entire script. You can use the variable in any subroutine, and it will keep its value as you move from one subroutine to another. Although the Declarations subroutine is probably the best place to declare your variables, don't try to instantiate them with As New. You'll have to put Dim objectname as objecttype in the Declarations subroutine and put Set objectname = New objecttype in the subroutine where you actually start using it. Forms have a

Globals section with a `Declarations` subroutine that may be used to declare variables valid in a script used in the form.

Looping and Branching

Two vitally important tasks that a full programming language needs to perform are *looping* and *branching*. Looping, also called *iteration*, is when a program repeats a block of instructions, usually until a particular condition is met. Branching, also called *flow control*, is when a program is presented with a set of choices, selects one, and executes a related set of instructions.

CONDITIONS

Looping and branching techniques depend on *conditions*, expressions that will allow them to determine what they should do. A condition can be any function or equation that will return a Boolean value (that is to say, any statement the computer can evaluate as being true or false). For example, a line of code might have the condition (x > 1). If x is 1 or less, the expression is false. If x is greater than 1, it is true. Although equations may be more familiar, Notes also has a number of functions that will return Boolean values. For example, the `IsNumeric` function examines a string variable. If the string can be converted to a number, the function is true. If not, it is false. The expression `IsNumeric(mystring)` is true if `mystring` is, say, `"123"`, but the expression is false if `mystring` is `"onetwothree"`.

A condition can even be an expression that can be evaluated as a number. If the expression evaluates to 0, the condition is false; otherwise it is taken as true. For example, (x + 1) is a valid condition. If x is –1, the expression becomes (–1 + 1), which becomes 0 and is therefore false. Any other value would make the condition true.

Complex conditions can be built by connecting them with Boolean operators, usually the key words AND, OR, and NOT. For example, ((x > 1) and IsNumeric(mystring)) is true so long as x is greater than one or `mystring` can be converted into a number.

Conditional expressions should always involve variables. It's certainly possible to have (2 + 2= as a condition, but unless something goes terribly wrong with your computer, it will always be true.

BRANCHING

Branching, though a standard term, may not be the best word to describe what it does. It implies that the program goes down one path or another, never rejoining the main "trunk." Nothing could be further from the truth. Most "branches" are of the character, "If some condition is true, set this value and continue; if not, just continue" or at most, "If this is true, perform these instructions, then come back here and go on to the next line." The two important branching methods in LotusScript are the `If...Then` statement and the `Select Case` statement.

If...Then

The most straightforward and commonly used branching method is the `If...Then` block. It checks a condition and, if it's true, executes the code. The end of the block is marked by an `End If`, thus:

```
x = Inputbox("Type in a number")
y = Cdbl(x)
If y < 1 Then
  Msgbox("The number is less than 1")
End If
```

The preceding code brings up a dialog box asking for a number (the input is a string, so we convert it to a double-precision floating-point number with the `Cdbl()` function). If the number is less than one, it brings up a message saying so. Otherwise, it does nothing. With the `Else` statement, you can set up two different bits of code. If the condition is true, the code after the `If` statement is true. If not, the code after the `Else` statement runs. This code does almost the same thing as the preceding code, but it will also put up a message if the number is one or more:

```
x = Inputbox("Type in a number")
y = Cdbl(x)
If y < 1 Then
  Msgbox("The number is less than 1")
Else
  Msgbox("The number is greater than or equal to 1")
End If
```

An `If...Then` block can actually get much more complex, turning into an `If...Then...ElseIf...Else` block. In this kind of block, each `ElseIf` gets its own condition, setting up as many different possibilities as the programmer wants. The program will run through the conditions until it finds one that is true and executes the associated instructions. Once that code is executed, the program will skip down to the next line after the `End If`. Consider this example:

```
x = Inputbox("Type in a number")
y = Cdbl(x)
If y < 1 Then
  Msgbox("The number is less than 1")
Elseif (y >= 1) Then
  Msgbox("The number is greater than or equal to 1")
Elseif (y >= 2) Then
  Msgbox("The number is greater than or equal to 2")
End If
```

If someone were to type in a 2, the resulting message box would say "Y is greater than or equal to 1" because the first condition that is true is y >= 1.

There are several methods you can use if you want to fill multiple conditions. For example, you can check the values of two variables in a single `If` statement like this:

```
If x > 1 And y = "a" Then
' ...some instructions here
End If
```

Or you can check them by nesting two statements, putting one inside the other, like this:

```
If x > 1 Then
  If y = "a" Then
' ...some instructions here
  End If
End If
```

If the first instruction is true, Notes will look at the second `If` statement. If it's not true, Notes will skip over it.

You may have noticed that statements within the If...Then block are indented. That's no accid-
Another nice thing the script editor does for you is automatically indent the contents of conditic
statements and loops. That makes it a lot easier to tell where a block of instructions begins and er
It's purely for display; you can add and remove spaces all you want without affecting the operat
of the script. However, if you don't want your code indented, you can turn that feature off.

Select Case

A Select block is like an If...Then...ElseIf block. The block starts with a Select Case variablen
statement, which tells the block which variable to examine. It is followed by a number of Case st
ments. Each Case statement takes a possible value of the variable. If the variable chosen in the Sel
Case line is equal to the value in the Case line, Notes will execute the block of code associated w
that value. The block can also take a Case Else statement for code to execute if none of the other c
ditions are true, and it always ends with an End Select statement. Select Case statements are usu:
used when the programmer expects a limited range of input, like this:

```
x = Inputbox("Type in the number 1, 2, or 3")
Select Case x
Case 1
 Msgbox("You chose 1")
Case 2
 Msgbox("You chose 2")
Case 3
 Msgbox("You chose 3")
Case Else
 Msgbox("You chose something not on the list")
End Select
```

If you type 1, 2, or 3, you'll get a message box telling you the number. In this example, the Case E
block will tell you that you typed in something not on the list. However, if you want nothing to hapf
if the variable isn't one of the choices, simply omit the Case Else statement and go directly to Ee
Select.

Select Case statements are best used when you know that you'll have a limited range of inpu
For example, a routine like this might be used to translate an abbreviation (stateabbr) into the na:
of a state (statename):

```
Select Case stateabbr
Case "AL"
 Statename = "Alabama"
Case "AK"
 Statename = "Alaska"
Case "AR"
 Statename = "Arkansas"
 ' ...and so on, forty seven more times.
Case Else
 Statename = "(no state)"
End Select
```

LOOPING

Branching may not be the best word to describe what branching does, but *looping* is the best possible word for what it is used to describe. A loop goes around and around, running the same code repeatedly until it decides or is told when to stop. However, rather than doing the exact same thing over and over again, loops can be smart enough to do slightly different things on each loop. A loop might perform the same set of actions on a different document each time through or perform a calculation with a different number. Among the most commonly used looping commands are For...Next, Do...Loop, and Forall.

For...Next

A For...Next loop executes a block of code a set number of times. It needs a variable to act as the counter, a beginning value, and a final value, and the block ends with a Next statement. For example, this code will print the numbers from 1 to 10:

```
For x = 1 to 10
   Print x
Next
```

You can, of course, begin and end with any value. This code prints the numbers from 18 to 34:

```
For x = 18 to 34
   Print x
Next
```

You can also control the pace and direction of a For...Next loop by qualifying the For line with a Step statement. This code counts down from 10 to 0:

```
For x = 10 to 0 Step -1
   Print x
Next
```

This counts from 0 to 10 by twos. It will print 0, 2, 4, 6, 8, and 10:

```
For x = 0 to 10 Step 2
   Print x
Next
```

Do...While/Until...Loop

Unlike a For...Next loop, which runs its code a given number of times, a Do...Loop repeats the code while a condition is true (for a Do...While...Loop) or until it becomes true (for a Do...Until...Loop). This code comes up with a random number and asks the user to guess what it is until he guesses right:

```
' This line uses the rnd() statement to come up with
' a random number between 0 and .999..., multiplies it
' by ten to turn it into a number between 0 and
' 9.999..., turns it into an integer (rounding down) and
' adds one, ending up with a random number between 1
' and 10
```

```
X = cint(rnd()*10)+1
Guess = Inputbox("Guess a number from 1 to 10")
Do Until X = Guess
 Guess = Inputbox("Guess a number from 1 to 10")
Loop
Msgbox("Right!")
```

A useful feature of Do...Loop statements is that you can put the condition either at the beginn▪ (right after the Do statement) or at the end (right before the Loop statement), as illustrated in the lowing code. This makes a difference in the number of times the code will execute:

```
Do While X > 1
' ...some code goes here
Loop
Do
' ...more code here
Loop While X > 1
```

The difference between these two examples is that in the first loop, if x is less than or equal to the code in the loop won't execute. Putting the condition in the Do line tells the script to run the co if the condition is met. In the second example, the code will run at least once. The Do statement unqualified, so the following code gets executed. Putting the condition in the Loop line tells the co go back and do it *again* if the condition is met.

When you use Do...Loop statements, you'll need to keep an eye out for infinite loops. An infin▪ loop is a set of instructions that will repeat over and over again because the condition under whi▪ the loop ends never comes true. Often, a loop becomes infinite when the programmer forgets to wr▪ instructions that affect the condition. Do not try this one at home:

```
x = 1
Do While x < 2
 ' The Beep statement tells the computer to make a
 ' single beep sound.
 Beep
Loop
x = x + 1
```

If the x = x + 1 statement were before the Loop statement, the script would beep once, x wou▪ go from 1 to 2, and you'd be on your way. Here, however, there's nothing inside the loop to chan▪ the value of x. The loop will repeat over and over, beeping incessantly until you do violence to th▪ computer.

Forall

Forall is a looping command that you can use with lists, arrays, and object collections. The Forall sta▪ ment takes the name of a variable to stand for values and the name of a container (Forall variablena in containername) and ends with an End Forall statement. In the loop, the variable name stands f▪ the value of the object in the collection. For example, this script sets all of the values in the array to

```
Dim shortarray(1 to 5) As Integer
```

```
Forall x In shortarray
   x = 1
End Forall
```

Forall is particularly useful when you want to perform an operation on every document in a collection.

Colorless Green Ideas Sleep Furiously: Debugging

In order to demonstrate the contention that you could follow all the rules of a language and still produce something meaningless, the linguist Noam Chomsky composed the famous sentence which serves as the title to this section. As it happens, the same is just as true of computer languages as of natural languages. Just because you write legal code doesn't mean that it will do what you want it to.

When you start writing scripts, rest assured that you *will* get things wrong. The Notes programming environment provides some help as you write your script. When you save a script, it gets compiled; that is, it gets translated from the more-or-less English language commands of LotusScript into fast-running machine code. If you type in a flatly impossible or nonexistent command (say, you try to declare a variable but type in *Din* instead of *Dim*, or you leave the second set of quotation marks off of a string), the compiler will catch the error. Notes will stop and flag the error in the Errors bar at the bottom of the LotusScript programmer's pane. Notes won't be able to tell you exactly what you should have written. After all, it doesn't really know what you're trying to do. However, it can give you some idea of what's missing.

But more often, you'll make errors that are far more subtle. The instant error checking provided by the compiler only ensures that individual lines of code are legally structured. The most common cause of errors, however, is that you will write a script with instructions that are each perfectly legal individually but, once assembled and run, don't work. For example, a line such as myarray(10) = 1 is fine by itself. It simply sets an element of an array to a particular value. The script editor won't flag it as an error, but when you actually run the script, you will get an error if you haven't defined the array myarray() as having enough elements or if you have defined it as a string rather than as a numeric value. There are many other ways for your script to go wrong. You may try to compare string variables with integers, call subroutines that don't exist, forget to increment counters, add instead of subtract, or make an expression true when you want it to be false. You won't know that you did anything wrong until you run a script that does nothing or does something but does it very, very wrong. Sometimes, the only way to tell why your script doesn't work is to follow it through every step of the way to see where it goes wrong. Fortunately, Notes lets you do just that.

If your LotusScript code isn't working, you can turn on the debugger. The debugger will allow you to run through a script line by line or jump through or over chunks of functional code to get to problematic areas while monitoring the values of variables and the contents of Notes objects. If you write scripts, you'll be using it a lot, so it's a good idea to familiarize yourself with it early.

To turn on debugging, select File ➤ Tools ➤ Debug LotusScript. While that option is checked, the debugger will appear whenever a script runs (see Figure 24.2). The upper pane of the debugging window displays the script being run. It starts with the first line in the first subroutine that contains instructions. For most scripts, it starts at the first line of the Initialize subroutine, although it will start with the appropriately named subroutine for the event-related scripts. Statements in the (Options) and (Declarations) subroutines will be executed, but the debugger will not put them on screen.

The buttons across the top of the upper pane allow you to move through the script, processing in chunks, going through it one line at a time, or even skipping over parts of it. The buttons you probably be using most are Step Into and Continue. Step Into runs the program one line at a tim When you click it, Notes will execute the line of code and move on to the next, stopping there wi out executing it. Don't confuse the Step Into button with the Step Over button, which will exec the next line of code but not take you into any subroutines or functions called by that line.

FIGURE 24.2
The debugger

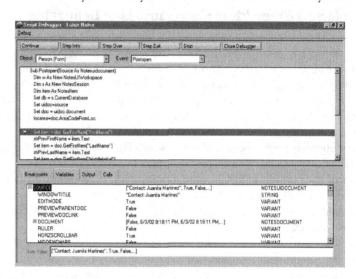

The Continue button tells the script to continue running as it would normally unless it hits a *bre point*. A breakpoint is a line in the script at which the debugger will pause until told to continue. set a breakpoint, simply double-click a line in the script. A red "stop sign" will appear next to the li alerting you to the fact that there's a breakpoint there. Double-clicking again will put a yellow sla next to the breakpoint. The breakpoint is still marked for you, but it has been disabled; the debugg won't stop there, but it does show you where you set the breakpoint earlier. Double-clicking one mo time will remove the breakpoint. You can set as many breakpoints in a script as you want. The debu ger will stop at each one before executing it, and you can use Continue, Step Into, or any of the oth buttons.

The upper pane of the debugging window shows you the program, but it's the lower pane that w show you what you actually get out of it. There are four tabs on the lower pane: Breakpoints, Variabl Output, and Calls. All are useful, but you'll probably be spending most of your time looking at the Va ables tab. This tab shows the values of all variables the script knows about in a three-column forma variable name, value, and type (string, variant, notesdocument, and so on). Complex data types, such arrays and documents, don't have a single value. Instead, they are displayed with a plus sign icon next them. You can expand them to see what's in them. Figure 24.2 shows a Variables tab displaying the v ues contained by a variable named Source. Source happens to be a Notes document, so it contains oth complex variables. The values in the Variables tab change as the variables themselves change during t execution of the script. When you step through a script with the Variables tab selected, you can s exactly what your script is doing.

Debugging for Java isn't as detailed for LotusScript, but there are some tools. To debug Java in the Notes client, select File ➤ Tools ➤ Show Java Debug Console. This will bring up a debugging messages window (see Figure 24.3). You can then use code such as `system.out.println` statements to indicate the state of your code as it runs.

FIGURE 24.3

Java debugging console window

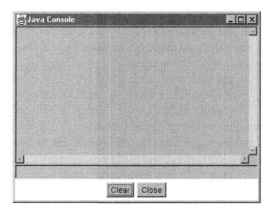

Debugging, by the way, is one of the big advantages LotusScript and Java have over formulas. If your script doesn't work, you can walk through it in the debugger and find out fairly quickly where it's going wrong. Formulas either execute or they don't. If they don't do exactly what you want them to, it's much harder to find out where they are going wrong.

WARNING   *The debugger only runs in the Notes client. If you're running code on the Web, you'll need to resort to other debugging methods as you would for formulas.*

Understanding the Object Model

This is where the experienced programmers should come back into the room. The techniques and syntax we've been discussing are unremarkable and aren't too different from similar structures in other languages, but getting into Notes objects requires specific commands not found in other languages. It takes a little more code to deal with Notes objects than it does to deal with other variables, but with a few extra lines of code, you can manipulate entire Notes databases and their contents.

NOTE   *As with Chapter 18, "Understanding the Formula Language," we'll only scratch the surface of the object model for LotusScript and Java. This section will get you oriented, but if you want to do serious LotusScript or Java programming in Notes, read the Designer help file. Once you understand the core classes, they'll make a lot more sense to you than they do now, and they'll be an invaluable aid.*

LotusScript, Java, and Object-Oriented Languages

Java and LotusScript are object-oriented languages. With the rise in popularity of Java and mass-market, application-conscious languages such as LotusScript and VBA, *object-oriented* is one of the buzzwords of the day. If you're new to the game, you may wonder just what it means. In addition to doing all of the other things you'd expect a programming language to do (count, do math, loc for files, beep, throw messages on the screen...), an object-oriented language has *objects*, comp data constructs that have specific attributes and on which specific operations can be performe

All explanations of object-oriented languages include an extended metaphor using a real-wor object, so here you go: Consider, for example, a book. Every book has a number of characteristics t other objects (say, an ice cream cone) won't necessarily have: number of pages, binding (hardcover paperback), Library of Congress number, and so on. Likewise, there are a number of operations y might perform on a book that you might not perform on other objects (if you do any of these to ice cream cone, we don't want to know about it): take off shelf, flip through pages, put in bookma smash annoying insect, put back on shelf. In an object-oriented language, the type of object (in example, a book) is called a *class*. Bits of data contained by the object (number of pages) are called *p erties*, and the things you can do to or with the object (flip through pages) are called *methods*. Ratl than doing complex operations to collect and modify data, classes, properties, and methods give y a convenient shorthand way to perform specific operations.

Another powerful aspect of object-oriented languages is that many properties are actually obje themselves. To return to the metaphor, the pages of the book are themselves objects, with propert such as page number and the text each page contains. Likewise, a set of books may be contained another object, such as a bookshelf, and a bookshelf might be contained by a library object.

The way this plays out in Notes is that just about every object you're used to dealing with in Notes database has a programming counterpart you can use in a script. For example, a databa object has (as properties) views and documents, and many common Notes actions (such as printi documents or changing ACL entries) can be performed by using methods with LotusScript an Java classes. The scheme of programming objects and how they relate to one another is the *ob model*. For reasons we'll get to later, there are some small differences between the Notes obje model for LotusScript and the Notes object model for Java. However, they're both based on th familiar structure of Notes databases, for obvious reasons, so they're nearly identical, and we'll able to present them together.

Some things you'll be seeing a lot in this section are references to objects and their methods and pr erties. You can refer to any property of any object by using the name of the object, a period, and the na of the property. For example, every Notes database has a title, which means that a Notes database obj has a `Title` property. If a script in LotusScript has a variable `db` representing a database, the expressi that would return the database's title would be `db.Title`.

You can invoke object methods in a similar way. In general, you'll use the variable name, a peric and the method. The method may be followed by parentheses containing parameters. In LotusScri you may need to precede the statement with the keywords `SET` or `CALL`. `CALL` is used for methods tl perform an action, and `SET` is used as part of an equation with methods that return another objec For example, a document represented by the variable `doc` could be sent as an e-mail message with t line `Call doc.Send`. The equivalent Java method is `send`, which doesn't use a `CALL` statement. Th equivalent Java line would be simply `doc.send();`. Getting the first document in a view represent by the variable `vw` might be performed with the line `Set doc = vw.GetFirstDocument`. The Java equ alent, again, doesn't need a `Set` statement: `doc = vw.getFirstDocument();`. The big, complex class such as databases and documents have a lot of useful properties. It's well worth the time to look the classes in the Designer help files and read about the possibilities.

Fundamental Classes

LotusScript and Java allow you to read and manipulate just about any Notes object or Notes native property, from ACLs to time zones. However, most of your programming will be done with an eye toward dealing with documents and their contents. Therefore, we'll concentrate most of our attention on the classes you'll use to get to documents and fields.

You probably already think of Notes objects as existing in a hierarchy. For example, a database holds documents, documents hold fields, and fields may, in the case of multivalue fields, hold a set of values. Databases also contain views and folders, which in turn hold documents. The object model thinks the same way. You'll need to start at the top of the hierarchy to get to the specific parts, but depending on what you're trying to accomplish, you can use different hierarchies. If your script works on the currently open database or document, you'll be starting with the frontend classes, but scripts that deal with databases and documents that aren't open will work with backend classes.

Things get a little weird here, so hang on. When you write code that acts on an open document or an open database, you're actually dealing with two different versions of it. First, there's what appears on your screen. That's what is called the *front end*. The LotusScript classes are called, not surprisingly, *frontend classes*. The frontend classes all have *UI*, short for *user interface*, at the beginning. The most important frontend classes are NotesUIWorkspace, which refers to the currently open Notes workspace window; NotesUIDatabase, which refers to the currently open database; and NotesUIDocument, which refers to the currently open document. NotesUIWorkspace is the big container here. The NotesUIWorkspace contains all of the other UI classes, so you must address it first to get to the other frontend classes. A significant limitation here is that if you want to deal with frontend objects, you're limited to using LotusScript. Java can't use the frontend classes.

Backend classes, on the other hand, refer to a copy of a database or document that is held in memory and not necessarily displayed on the screen. NotesUIDatabase and NotesUIDocument are directly related to two backend classes, NotesDatabase and NotesDocument. NotesUIWorkspace doesn't have a direct correspondent among the backend classes, but there's an equally important backend class: NotesSession in LotusScript, or simply Session in Java. Just as NotesUIWorkspace contains all of the other frontend objects, a NotesSession/Session contains all backend objects. When you get to the back end, you'll be able to use Java.

Using Frontend Classes

Let's return to the short programming example from the beginning of the chapter. Remember this? Now we can explain how it works:

```
Dim ws As NotesUIWorkspace
Dim uidoc As NotesUIDocument
Set ws = new NotesUIWorkspace
Set uidoc = ws.CurrentDocument
Call uidoc.Print
```

First, we set up some variables. Objects are a little trickier than scalar variables. Although it is ⟨no⟩ longer absolutely necessary to initialize an object variable with a `Dim` statement (unlike in earlier ⟨ver⟩sions of LotusScript), you do have to *instantiate* some classes with the `NEW` keyword before you can ⟨use⟩ them. Instantiation is object-oriented terminology for getting down to cases. The `Dim` statement ⟨just⟩ sets up a space in memory big enough to hold the object. However, objects have properties that n⟨eed⟩ to be filled in (for example, the creation date). That's what the `Set` statement does. It takes the m⟨em⟩ory space you've set aside and tells Notes to fill in all of the properties necessary to make it an obj⟨ect⟩ of the desired type. Remember the book metaphor used earlier to explain objects? `Dim` clears a sp⟨ace⟩ on the bookshelf; `Set` fills the space with a cover and some (possibly blank) pages.

We could save a line with the `NotesUIWorkspace` by declaring and instantiating it at the same ti⟨me⟩ `Dim ws as New NotesUIWorkspace` would do the same thing as the `Dim` and `Set` lines together, and ⟨in⟩ this script, it might be a good idea just for compactness. However, be aware that you can't use `D⟨im⟩ variablename as New type` in the (Declarations) routine. The `as New` makes the line an execu⟨table⟩ instruction, not just a `Dim` statement, and thereby a line you can't use in (Declarations).

The lines that set up `uidoc` do something similar. A `NotesUIWorkspace` has a number of proper⟨ties⟩ (that is, objects and attributes associated with it), including the document that happens to ⟨be⟩ open at the moment. First, the `Dim` statement sets up a space for the `NotesUIDocument`, then t⟨he⟩ `Set` statement goes into the hierarchy of the `NotesUIWorkspace` to get the currently open doc⟨u⟩ment, a *property* of the `NotesUIWorkspace`. Finally, the `Call` line calls a *method* that can be perform⟨ed⟩ on a `NotesUIDocument`, namely, telling it to print to a printer. Essentially, what this script does ⟨is⟩ tell Notes, "Look at the copy of Notes I'm running, get the document that's open in front, a⟨nd⟩ act like I selected File ➤ Print."

CODE TO REMEMBER

Bookmark this page or type the code in somewhere to copy and paste. Almost every script you write that⟨?⟩ deals with frontend objects will use this code or something like it. These six lines give your script access to⟨?⟩ the workspace and the current document:

```
Dim ws As NotesUIWorkspace
Dim uidoc As NotesUIDocument
Dim doc As NotesDocument
Set ws = new NotesUIWorkspace
Set uidoc = ws.CurrentDocument
Set doc = uidoc.Document
```

What's the `NotesDocument` for? Read on...

Using Backend Classes

If you're writing scripts for your own use, you may tend to think in terms of using the frontend class⟨es⟩ After all, you'll probably be working with the objects that happen to be open at the moment. Ho⟨w⟩ever, sooner or later you'll need to go into the backend classes. The frontend classes can't be used ⟨on⟩ databases, views, and documents that *aren't* currently open and at the front of the Notes client wo⟨rk⟩space. This means, among other things, that scheduled agents and agents that you want to run on⟨?⟩

server can't use frontend classes. Although the agents may select and act on Notes documents, those documents aren't actually open. The same goes for programming for the Web. Documents open on the Web aren't *really* open so far as Notes is concerned; if it isn't open in your Notes client, you can't use the frontend classes on it. Most importantly, though, although the frontend classes only let you get at the currently open document, the backend classes can manipulate *every* document in the database and even other databases on the same computer. If you want to work with groups of documents, or just a single document that doesn't happen to be the one you're currently looking at, you must use backend classes.

The first thing to create when you're using backend classes is a new session. In LotusScript, the relevant object is called a `NotesSession`; in Java, it's a `Session`. The session is the environment the script is running in, giving the script access to a broad range of data, including information about the current user, the version of Notes being used, environment variables, and access to address books. It's also the first step in getting to objects in the database running the script or even other databases on the same computer or on a connected Domino server.

TIP *If you know the LotusScript classes, you can usually figure out the names of the Java classes, and vice versa. Notes classes have the word Notes at the beginning (`NotesDatabase`, `NotesDocument`, and so on); Java classes have the same name without Notes at the beginning (`Database`, `Document`, and so on). One other common difference is that you can address properties in LotusScript directly; in Java, you'll use a method to get a property value.*

For the most part, Java code inside Notes must take one additional step before it can get to familiar Notes objects. Although LotusScript simply needs a `NotesSession` object, a Java agent needs both a `Session` object, representing the total environment of the Notes client or Domino server, and one of its properties, the `AgentContext` object, which represents the context in which the agent runs. That context includes such things as the name of the agent and the name of the database in which it runs. It's also possible to create applets using the Java class files installed with the Notes client and Domino server. They'll need an object of the `NotesAppletContext` class instead.

NOTE *As long as you don't want to interact with specific Notes objects, Java applets you include in forms and pages don't need `AppletContext`, or any other Notes-specific code for that matter. They don't run inside Notes. They can be carried by Notes objects, but the context they really run in is the client's web browser.*

In LotusScript, there are two commonly used ways to get from the `NotesSession` to a database. First, there's the `GetDatabase` method. `GetDatabase` takes as parameters the name of the server that the desired database is on and the path to it. For example, to get the database `mydb.nsf` on the server Sales, you might use the following line:

```
Set db = session.GetDatabase ("Sales", "mydb.nsf")
```

More often, however, a script will want to address the database from which it's running. To get the database the script is in, use the `CurrentDatabase` property, which needs no parameters, thus: `Set db = session.CurrentDatabase`. The Java syntax for getting to a specific database is similar. Use the `getDatabase()` method of the `AgentContext` object (which, like its LotusScript counterpart, uses a server name and database filename) to get a database, or use the `getCurrentDatabase()` method of the `AgentContext` (which needs no parameters) to get the database in which the agent is running.

Just as most of your frontend scripts will start with the code given in the "Code to Remember" sidebar most of your backend scripts will start out with a standard bit of code. Here's something to drop into any script that will use backend objects. It starts from the most fundamental objects and grabs the database in which the agent runs:

```
Dim s As NotesSesson
Dim db As NotesDatabase
Set s = New NotesSession
Set db = s.CurrentDatabase
```

Here's a corresponding bit of code for Java agents:

```
Session s = getSession();
AgentContext ac = s.getAgentContext();
Database db = ac.getCurrentDatabase();
```

But you probably won't need to actually type that code. When you create a Java agent, Notes fills in the first two lines of code creating the Session and AgentContext objects (albeit with slightly different names), as shown in Figure 24.4.

FIGURE 24.4

Code provided for you in a Java agent

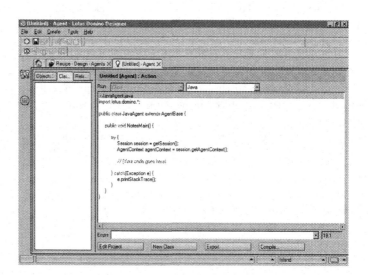

Getting from database to individual documents can be trickier. You usually can't jump directly documents; rather, you often have to use an intermediate object that contains a number of objects One such object is a *document collection*. As the name implies, a document collection is simply a batch of Notes documents. One way to create a document collection is to use the Search method on a database object. The Search method takes three parameters: a formula, a date, and a maximum number of documents. The formula can be any valid formula that could be used to provide conditions for view. The date, in a `NotesDateTime` variable, provides a creation date after which the document was created (if you want to search through all the documents in the database, provide a date before the database was created). The search will return no more than the maximum number you provide unless you use 0, which imposes no maximum number. Using the `Search` method creates a document collection object, so you'll need to declare a `DocumentCollection` variable and, to create the collection, use a line like this:

```
Set dc = db.Search("Duedate > @Now", SomeDateVariable, 0)
```

The corresponding line in Java looks like this (the second and third parameters are optional in Java; we've chosen to omit the third):

```
DocumentCollection dc = db.search("Duedate > @Now", SomeDateVariable);
```

These lines of code will populate a document collection named `dc` with all the documents where the value of the `Duedate` field is later than the current time and the document was created after the date provided in the variable `SomeDateVariable`.

However, you might find it easier to let existing database objects do some of the work for you. If you have an agent that you want to run on some or all documents in a view or folder that already exists, you can get the view to gain easy access to the documents. All you need to do to use the `GetView` method and the name of the view or folder. For example, to get a To Process view, you'd use a line such as `Set vw = db.GetView("To Process")`. In Java, the line would be `View vw = db.getView("To Process");`.

Once you have the view or document collection, you can navigate through the documents. You can use the `GetFirstDocument` and `GetLastDocument` methods to get the first and last documents (particularly useful if you're dealing with the contents of a sorted view) and the `GetNextDocument` and `GetPrevDocument` methods to move from one document to the next. For `GetNextDocument` and `GetPrevDocument`, you must refer to a Notes document you have set elsewhere. The following script gets the contents of a view, loops through its documents, and counts the number of documents:

```
' Get the declarations out of the way

Dim s As NotesSession
Dim db As NotesDatabase
Dim vw As NotesView
Dim doc As NotesDocument
Dim CreateTime As Variant
Dim doccount As Integer
' Create a Notes session and drill down to the view MyView

Set s = New NotesSession
Set db = s.CurrentDatabase
Set vw = db.GetView("MyView")
' Get the first document in the view
Set doc = vw.GetFirstDocument

' Perform the loop until there are no documents left
' and get the creation date of each
```

```
Do Until doc Is Nothing
   doccount = doccount + 1
   ' Make the document that the variable doc refers to equal
   ' to the next document relative to the current one

   Set doc = vw.GetNextDocument(doc)
Loop
```

And here's how to do it in Java:

```
Session s = getSession();
AgentContext ac = s.getAgentContext();
Database db = ac.getCurrentDatabase();

// create an integer variable to hold the count
int doccount = 0;

// get the view and then its first document
View vw = db.getView("MyView");
Document doc = vw.getFirstDocument();

// while there's a document in the view...
while (doc != null) {
   doccount = doccount + 1;

   // get the next document in the view
   doc = vw.getNextDocument(doc);
}
```

If you're programming for the Web, there's yet another way of getting to a document: DocumentConte▪
DocumentContext is a property of the Session object in LotusScript and the AgentContext object in Ja▪
This object is a document. Specifically, it's a document containing whatever information is submitted fro▪
the Web. If you use a QuerySaveAgent, use DocumentContext to refer to the document being submitte▪
One of the really useful aspects of DocumentContext is that it doesn't actually need a Notes document.▪
you submit a Hypertext Markup Language (HTML) form whose action is a Notes agent (something l▪
this: `<form action="http://server/path/database.nsf/agentname">`, the Domino server will create▪
document in memory containing the data sent along by the form. You can then dissect the document a▪
work with its data.

Of course, getting access to a document will only help you if you can read and manipulate its co▪
tents. Just as there are many ways to get Notes documents, there are several ways to get to field value▪
In LotusScript, the easiest way to get to most values in a Notes document is by treating the field ▪
question like an array. Consider the following code:

```
Dim s As NotesSesson
Dim db As NotesDatabase
Dim vw As NotesView
Dim doc As NotesDocument
Dim status as String
```

```
Set s = new NotesSession
Set db = s.CurrentDatabase
Set vw = db.OpenView("MyView")
Set doc = vw.GetFirstDocument
status = doc.Status(0)
```

This code goes to the database in which the code is running, opens the view MyView, takes the first document, and sets the value of the variable **status** to the first item in the Status field. Fields are treated as properties of documents, so they can be referred to with the *object.property* notation, but if they're referred to that way, they are themselves arrays, so they need an index. Remember that if you use `Option Base 1`, the first value in a field is `document.fieldname(1)`.

That method, useful though it is, is a shortcut. If you want to be a bit more rigorous, you can use the `GetItemValue` method on the document. This method gets the values in the field you name and puts them in an array. You might use it like this:

```
Dim s As NotesSesson
Dim db As NotesDatabase
Dim vw As NotesView
Dim doc As NotesDocument
Dim statuslist as Variant
Dim status as String
Set s = new NotesSession
Set db = s.CurrentDatabase
Set vw = db.OpenView("MyView")
Set doc = vw.GetFirstDocument
statuslist = doc.GetItemValue("Status")
status = statuslist(0)
```

We mention the `GetItemValue` method specifically because it's the LotusScript analog of the important Java method for getting item values, `getItemValue`. This code is the Java equivalent of the previous LotusScript:

```
Session s = getSession();
AgentContext ac = s.getAgentContext();
Database db = ac.getCurrentDatabase();
View vw = db.getView("MyView");
Document doc = vw.getFirstDocument();
Vector statuslist = doc.getItemValue("Status");
String status = statuslist(0);
```

In LotusScript, you can set document values like this:

```
doc.Status = "Approved"
```

Setting a property of the document (which happens to be a field name) to a value is simple. There is, again, a more rigorous method using a `NotesItem` object, which represents a field and its attributes (for example, whether it's an Authors or Readers field). To set a field value with a `NotesItem`, you'll use the `ReplaceItemValue` method of the `NotesDocument` and provide it with a field name and a value.

This code gets the familiar first document from MyView and sets the value of the status field t
Approved via a NotesItem object:

```
Dim s As NotesSesson
Dim db As NotesDatabase
Dim vw As NotesView
Dim doc As NotesDocument
Dim status as String
Dim itm as NotesItem
Set s = new NotesSession
Set db = s.CurrentDatabase
Set vw = db.OpenView("MyView")
Set doc = vw.GetFirstDocument
Set itm = doc.ReplaceItemValue("Status", "Approved")
```

Again, we bring this up because that's also what you'll do to set item values in Java:

```
Session s = getSession();
AgentContext ac = s.getAgentContext();
Database db = ac.getCurrentDatabase();
View vw = db.getView("MyView");
Document doc = vw.getFirstDocument();
Item itm = doc.replaceItemValue("Status", "Approved");
```

If you want to save a changed value, you must use the Save method on the document. Up to tha
point, changes are made on a copy of the document held in memory. Changes are only saved to disk
you actively save the document. To save the changes in the LotusScript, you'd append a line like th

```
Call doc.Save(false, false)
```

The two parameters are required in LotusScript. They determine whether the save is forced, p
haps creating a save conflict, and whether the document is saved as a Response document. The Ja
method can take the same parameters, but they're optional, so the corresponding line in Java can
as simple as this:

```
doc.save();
```

Seeing LotusScript in Action

So what's a useful thing you can do with all this complex code? For the moment, we'll content ou
selves with a small example of LotusScript (we'll have some Java in the next chapter when we d
cuss agents). You'll find this code in the Postopen event of the Recipe with Event form in th
Recipes database. The script runs after the form opens and displays helpful messages. When
runs, it checks to see if the just-opened document has been saved, using the IsNewNote property c
the NotesDocument object. If it's a new document, the script will mention that the document mus
be saved before Ingredient documents can be created. If it's a previously saved document, the scrip
gathers responses (the Responses property of the NotesDocument object is a document collectio
containing all direct responses to the document). If there are no responses (the Count property c

the NotesDocumentCollection object is the number of documents in the collection), the script gives a different message, pointing out that there are no ingredients:

```
Sub Postopen(Source As Notesuidocument)
  Dim s As notessession
  Dim uiws As notesuiworkspace
  Dim db As notesdatabase
  Dim dc As notesdocumentcollection
  Dim doc As notesdocument
  Dim is_new As Boolean

  ' Get the current database and document
  Set uiws = New notesuiworkspace
  Set s = New notessession
  Set source = uiws.CurrentDocument
  Set doc = source.Document

  ' see if it's a new document
  is_new = doc.IsNewNote
  If is_new Then
   ' if it's a new document, point out that you can't create ingredients yet
   Msgbox("You won't be able to create ingredient documents until
   this document has been saved.")
  Else
   ' check the number of responses (that is, ingredient documents)
   Set dc = doc.Responses
   If (dc.Count = 0) Then
     ' if there aren't any responses, ask for some
     Msgbox("This recipe has no ingredients; you may want to add some.")
   End If
  End If

End Sub
```

Using JavaScript

In earlier versions of Notes, programmers could use JavaScript in a limited fashion, putting Java-Script routines in the $$HTMLHead field and adding a few small instructions to field or button HTML attributes. Use of JavaScript was limited to web applications. More recent versions of Notes have expanded the use of JavaScript considerably. As you've seen, you can build JavaScript programs directly into button and field events.

More importantly, you can use JavaScript in Notes as well as on the Web. Still, JavaScript within Notes faces several restrictions:

◆ You can use JavaScript only with some objects (form fields, actions, and buttons). You cannot use it in form and view events or in agents.

- For JavaScript to run on a Notes client, the user must first enable JavaScript in the User Preferences (under Advanced Preferences). If JavaScript is not enabled on the client, objects that run JavaScript will do nothing.

- JavaScript on a Notes client runs a limited set of commands. You can, for example, use the form object hierarchy to retrieve and set the values of fields, but you can't use the form Submit method to save a Notes document. You may need to create duplicate buttons for some operations (example, save and submit buttons), using JavaScript for one and hiding it from Notes clients and using formulas or LotusScript for the other and hiding it from web browsers.

With those limitations in mind, you can use JavaScript to write some portable commands into buttons and actions. For example, the following code takes the values of the fields First and Second, adds them together, puts up an alert box informing you of the new value, and sets the field Third to that value. This code will work equally well on the Web and in a Notes client:

```
var firstvar = this.form.First.value
var secondvar = this.form.Second.value
var thirdvar = firstvar + secondvar

alert ("The field will be set to " & thirdvar)
this.form.Third.value = thirdvar
history.go(0)
```

Summary

This chapter has dealt with the basic elements of high-level programming in Notes. LotusScript and Java can use an elaborate language to manipulate Notes databases and documents. You can reach documents through familiar processes related to Notes objects and Notes conventions, such as views and searches. The next chapter covers the last few design elements, shared code elements.

Chapter 25

Shared Code Objects

IN THIS LAST CHAPTER, we'll discuss shared code design elements. What this means, really, is that we'll discuss shared objects that are likely to carry program code with them. We've already covered one shared code element, the outline, because it's an important navigational element as well as something that can carry program code. However, whereas outlines can easily be free of program code (for example, a default outline or a simple list of links), the other elements are of little use if they don't contain at least some program code. In fact, three of the elements—agents, shared actions, and script libraries—are nothing but vehicles for program code.

- ◆ Agents
- ◆ Subforms
- ◆ Shared fields
- ◆ Shared actions
- ◆ Script libraries

Using Agents

You've already seen how you can perform a wide range of operations on documents and document fields with various kinds of program code. So far, you've had to make those actions happen in two ways:

- ◆ By using hotspots in forms, by adding actions to views and forms, and otherwise by constructing buttons to press
- ◆ By using formulas in Form, Field, and View events, which are executed when a user opens a form, leaves a field, or performs an operation on a specific document or field, usually in a specific context

The limitation of those devices is that a user has to take a specific action to trigger the code. The program code will execute every time a user presses the button, exits the field, and so on. But what if, for example, you want to send out daily summaries listing the documents that have been approved in a particular database? You could build the necessary formulas into a button somewhere, but someone would have to remember to press that button every day, and the summary might not go out if the person who job it is to press the button didn't come in one day or left for another job. You could also put it into Field, Form, or View event, but then the summary would be sent out every time someone performed action that triggers the formula. That could potentially mean that your "daily" summary could go many, many times daily if several people take the appropriate action, or not at all if nobody happens take the appropriate action. This is where agents come in. With agents, many actions can be complet automated, running themselves so that you don't have to lift a finger.

An *agent* is a database object that will perform actions for you. Like an action button, it holds anyth from a set of Simple Actions to a complex LotusScript or Java program (in fact, agents are one of t few, and most useful, places you can put Java). What makes agents so powerful, however, is the cont you have over when and how they run. You can set an agent to run periodically (every day, every ho and so on) to perform regular housekeeping or informative tasks, at certain events (when mail arriv when documents are created, and so on) to automatically process data, or even manually, just like action hotspot or button. Agents act on documents, or at least in relation to them. Although they c sometimes use folders and views as organizational devices, they ultimately operate by gathering a co lection of documents and performing actions either on them or based on the data in them.

Why Use an Agent?

Before you dive into using agents, it might be a good idea to know what they're good for and ho you can use them in your applications. Like form actions and action hotspots, agents can perforr complex tasks for you. However, agents give you more flexibility when those actions are performe The circumstances under which agents run can be divided into four broad categories:

- ◆ Manual operation
- ◆ Document events
- ◆ Scheduled operation
- ◆ Web access

MANUAL OPERATION

You can set an agent to run when you select it from a menu or press a button. The manual operatic options are most useful when you want to make the agent's function widely available through yo database. If an agent is always available from a menu, you can use it anywhere in the database at ar time, saving you the trouble of putting an action button with the same set of instructions on ever form, view, and folder. For example, if you have a database in which employees are supposed to no which documents they have read, you can use an agent to let users mark each document with thei name in a hidden People Who Have Read This Document field. Because Notes lets you create share actions, the various manual operation options may not be used as widely as they have in earlier ve sions, but they're still useful at times.

You have a few different ways to run an agent manually. You can run some agents from a menu (see "Action Menu Selection" later in this chapter). However, you can make any agent rt with an action button or hotspot. If you want to use a Simple Action, the Run Agent option le you select the agent to run. You can also run an agent with the functions @Command([RunAgent] and @Command([ToolsRunMacro]). The syntax is @Command([RunAgent]; "agentname") and @Command([ToolsRunMacro]; "agentname").

DOCUMENT EVENTS

When we say *document events* here, we're making up a term as a general description, not using an actual technical term from Lotus. Document events are *not* the same thing as the Form and View events discussed in earlier chapters. Rather, it's possible to make agents run when certain events related to the creation and modification of documents take place, regardless of which forms are used. For example, you can make an agent run automatically when new mail arrives or when documents are created. You might have an agent in a mail-in order database dismantle an original document sent from another database, sending order and shipping information to a warehouse and credit and payment information to sales personnel for processing. The agent would do all of this without user intervention. More importantly, it could perform these tasks as soon as the document comes in rather than waiting for a user to act on the new order.

SCHEDULED OPERATION

Like the document event agents, scheduled agents run themselves (that is, the user does not have to choose a menu item or press a button). However, scheduled agents run not after certain events, but at set intervals. Unlike event agents, which require a user or another automatic process to perform an action with a document, a scheduled agent depends on nothing but time. Scheduled agents can run as frequently as every five minutes or as infrequently as once a month. Like the document event agents, scheduled agents can be used for automatic document processing. However, because they operate at specific intervals, they will process documents in batches rather than one at a time, and they won't run until a specific time, regardless of whether or not it might be more efficient for them to run at other times.

You usually use scheduled agents to perform tasks that can or should wait to be performed at regular intervals. For example, a scheduled agent could be used to send out daily reminders to perform regular tasks (say, filling out a time card) or to distribute weekly summaries of documents in a database. With a scheduled agent, you could automatically send reminder messages to users of a workflow database, providing them with the titles of documents they need to approve. Or you could send out a weekly list of changes in a documentation database, informing users of documents that have been added or modified since last week.

Use document event and scheduled agents (the more frequently scheduled ones, at least) with some caution. Users and designers see manually triggered agents operate, so they quickly come to appreciate how long they take to run, and manually triggered agents tend to use the client's "brainpower," so they have little impact on the server. Scheduled agents, however, usually run on the server. A large, complex agent can use a lot of the server's memory and processor time, slowing down server access for everyone. The same is true of agents that operate on a large number of documents. In general, the more complex an agent is and the more documents it runs on, the less frequently it should run on a server.

Finally, if you're designing a Notes application with an eye toward using it over a web browser inste[ad] of through a Notes client, you can invoke agents through a web browser in several ways. You can r[un] an agent on a Notes document on the Web by using a `ToolsRunMacro` command in the WebQueryO[pen] form event (for opening the document) or the WebQuerySave event (for submitting the document[).] The agent will automatically run on the document. If you're using LotusScript (which was discusse[d in] Chapter 24, "Language Extensions and the Object Model"), use the `DocumentContext` property of t[he] agent's `CurrentDatabase` object to get the document.

You can also run an agent directly without going through a document. The syntax to run an ag[ent] is as follows:

```
http://servername/pathtodatabase/dbname.nsf/agentname?OpenAgent
```

Many formula commands can't be used over the Web (they're all listed in Designer help), so [be] careful of which ones you use on your web-enabled agents.

Creating an Agent

You can find agents, like other shared code objects, in their own listing in the Design pane, jus[t] as images and other elements under Shared Elements. However, the list of agents is a bit differe[nt] from other design lists, as shown in Figure 25.1. Agents have their own special properties, inclu[d]-ing a trigger (we addressed types of triggering events in the previous section) and whether they'r[e] shared or private. Scheduled agents can be enabled or disabled (hence the Enable and Disable bu[t]-tons); if a scheduled agent is enabled, a check mark will appear to the left of the agent name.

FIGURE 25.1

A list of agents

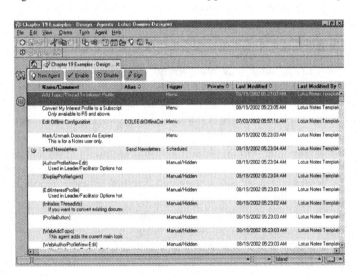

To create an agent, select Create ➤ Agent in any database or click the New Agent button in th[e] Agents view in Designer. This gives you a nearly blank canvas on which to create your agent, as show[n] in Figure 25.2.

FIGURE 25.2

A new agent

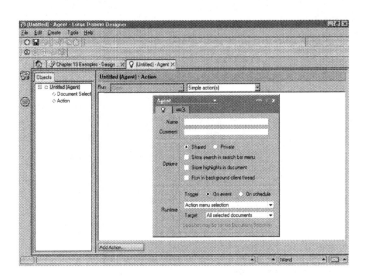

Once you have created the new agent, you'll need to decide four big things:

◆ What it's called (and who can use it)

◆ When it runs

◆ What documents it runs on

◆ What it does

You can also modify the agent's properties for running on the Web and modify some security properties. Most of these settings are controlled in the agent properties box, so we'll start there.

NOTE   Developers familiar with earlier versions of Notes will be happy to know that everything but the agent code now appears in the Agent Properties Box.

BASICS TAB

The Basics tab, shown in Figure 25.3, controls many important aspects of an agent's behavior. As you can see at the top of the Agent Properties Box, you can name agents just like any other database design element, and you can give them an alias and comments as well.

The most important item in the Options section is the Shared/Private selection. Any user with appropriate permission to the database can see and run shared agents. Only the user who marks an agent as private can run that agent. Agents default to Shared, but you can change them at any time. This fixes an irritating problem in earlier releases. Before Release 6, this setting was fixed the first time the agent was saved and could not be changed thereafter.

The next two options only come into play if the agent involves a search and runs in the client (agents can involve a selection formula; we'll return to this later). If you check the Store Search in Search Bar Menu option, the search criteria will appear in the search bar menu. If you select the Store Highlights in Document option, documents found by the search will have search terms highlighted when the documents are opened.

FIGURE 25.3

Agent Properties
Box, Basics tab

The Runtime section determines when the agent will run and the documents, theoretically, on which it will run. There are two options: On Event and On Schedule.

On Event

If you select this option, the agent will run when a specific event takes place, such as a document being pasted into the database or an item being chosen from a menu. There are six events from which to choose, discussed in the following sections.

Action Menu Selection   Choosing the Action Menu Selection option puts the agent on the Actions menu.

When you select this option, as when you select any scheduling option, you need to pick target options as well, indicating the documents on which the agent will run. You have a number of options ranging from every document in the database to no documents at all, and you can refine those choices by adding search conditions elsewhere in the agent. For the Action Menu Selection option, these are your search options:

All Documents in Database   The agent will examine and can potentially alter every document in the database, or at least all documents that the user running the agent can see and edit.

All New and Modified Documents Since Last Run   The first time an agent with this target condition runs, it runs on all documents. The agent has never run on them, so it considers them new. It will also run on all documents the first time it is run after you change the agent in any way.

All Unread Documents in View   With this target condition, you must run the agent in a view. If you don't, the agent will fail to run.

All Documents in View   An agent with this target condition must also be run in a view.

All Selected Documents   If this option is selected, the agent must again be run in a view.

None   The agent has no designated target document. This option should be used for @commands which already act on a specific document or set of documents.

Agent List Selection   The Agent List Selection option, inherited from earlier versions of Notes, doesn't run an agent so much as hides it. When the agent is saved, Notes puts parentheses around its name. You'll probably recognize that as the way Notes hides a database object. In Notes 4.6 and earlier, Designer wasn't a separate client. Instead, there was a special view that showed all the agents in the database: the Agent list. Users could go to the Agent list just as they could go to any other view and run agents manually from there. This option is retained in the current version, although the way to get to the Agent list is much less obvious in versions 5 and 6 (select View ➤ Agents in the Notes client). You can run an agent from the Agent list by right-clicking to bring up a menu and selecting Run. This is also a good place to put agents you want to use with `@Command([ToolsRunMacro])`, but be sure to include the parentheses around the agent name if you do.

The Agent List Selection option has the same list of options for documents to run on as the Action Menu Selection option does.

Before New Mail Arrives   Before New Mail Arrives is the first truly automatic agent option. This agent runs as mail is delivered to a database. The most obvious use of this option is to create mail-processing agents for your mail database. Rules (presented in Chapter 5, "Communicating with Notes Mail") can shuffle documents between folders, but if you use an agent, you can use far more powerful and flexible tools, such as the @formula language or LotusScript. You can, for example, use an agent to automatically respond to incoming mail or change the values of fields (such as, for example, the subject line) in incoming mail to make the affected documents easier to spot and sort. You can also use this option in applications that share data by mailing documents to one another. For example, you could have a set of databases mail documents to a central data "reservoir." Using a new mail agent, the central database could give documents produced with different forms a set of standard fields, modifying the documents to fit into its own organizational scheme.

Your choice of documents on which to run the agent is far more limited. A Before New Mail Arrives agent can run only on arriving mail. It will not run on other documents.

After New Mail Arrives   An agent with the After New Mail Arrives option, another holdover from earlier versions of Notes, runs once mail is delivered and appears in a database. There is usually a brief delay, usually a minute or two, between the time a new document appears and the time the agent runs. This option is also good for automatically processing documents coming into your mailbox. As with the Before New Mail Arrives option, this kind of agent runs only on newly delivered documents.

After Documents Are Created or Modified   An agent with the After Documents Are Created or Modified option runs when any new or existing document is saved. When you select this setting, you'll have to click the Edit Settings button to determine when and where the agent runs. Clicking the button brings up the Agent Schedule dialog box (see Figure 25.4). As the message says, the agent won't run immediately when documents are modified. More importantly, though, you can limit the dates when the agent runs. By checking the appropriate boxes and entering date information, you can limit the agent to running on certain days and even skipping weekends. The Which Server the Agent Runs On section lets you determine on which server the agent will run. You can pick a specific server, pick the local machine (only select this option if the database will exist on client machines; otherwise, the agent won't run), or check the box and have the user choose when the agent is enabled.

FIGURE 25.4

Agent Schedule
dialog box

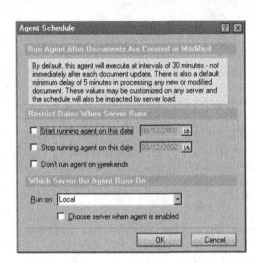

When Documents Are Pasted   If you choose the When Documents Are Pasted option, the agent w
run when documents are pasted into the database. As you may have guessed, it runs on the pasted d
uments. An agent with this option can be an excellent tool for ensuring that all documents in yo
database follow the rules you set down for them. Because documents that are copied and pasted i
from another database are not mailed in, nor are they created with a Save operation that would trig
an After Documents Are Created or Modified agent, pasting would otherwise be a hole in the ru
governing documents in your database. You could use a When Documents Are Pasted agent to a
or modify important fields, marking the documents as having been pasted in for later review. If y
want to be draconian about it, you could even delete them immediately.

On Schedule

If you choose this option, the agent will run on a regular schedule, from every few minutes to eve
few months. Choose from the first drop-down menu to determine how often it runs.

More Than Once a Day   With this option selected, the agent runs several times a day. As with th
other kinds of scheduled agents, you'll want to click the Schedule button. Clicking the button wi
bring up the Agent Schedule dialog box, as shown in Figure 25.5. You'll use this dialog box to fi
tune the schedule.

The top section holds information on the interval at which the agent should run. For More Tha
Once a Day Agents, you can choose a number of hours and a number of minutes. This kind of age
defaults to running once every hour (that is, every 1 hour and 0 minutes), but you can choose anythir
from every 5 minutes to every 11 hours and 55 minutes. If you check the Between Times radio bu
ton, you can restrict the agent so that it runs at particular times during the day. For example, yo
might have an agent that sends alerts only during regular business hours because there's no point i
having it run when nobody is likely to be around. Conversely, you might have the agent run outsic
of business hours so it won't slow down other processes on the server when people are likely to b
using it. If you don't care to restrict the times, click the All Day option.

You've already seen the other two entries of the Agent Schedule dialog box for the When Documents Are Pasted option for On Event agents. Like those agents, you can restrict the dates on which scheduled agents run and determine on which computer they run.

To let your Notes client run scheduled agents locally, select File ➢ Preferences ➢ User Preferences. In the Startup Options section of the Basics tab, make sure Enable Scheduled Local Agents is checked.

There's a more subtle permissions issue here as well. You should be aware that, for scheduled agents, the Local option doesn't really mean the local machine (that is, the computer on which you're currently working). What it really means in this context is the local *identity*. A local scheduled agent has to run on a computer with a Notes client running, but the Notes client must be running under a specific identity, which means a specific ID. If someone switches to another ID, the agent won't have permission to run. If you choose to make the agent run on a server, be sure you have permission. Your Domino administrator can assign various levels of permission to Notes users. You can be prohibited from running certain types of agents or from running agents altogether.

You have two choices for documents on which to run any kind of On Schedule agent:

♦ All Documents in Database

♦ All New and Modified Documents Since Last Run

SCHEDULED JAVA AND LOTUSSCRIPT AGENTS

The other major permissions issue for agents has to do with agents using LotusScript and Java. Domino servers distinguish between *restricted* and *unrestricted* agents. Unrestricted agents can use every command in the LotusScript and Java languages. Restricted agents can use most of the language but are prohibited from using some of the commands that are most susceptible to abuse. Among the commands that restricted agents cannot use are those related to manipulating external files. An unrestricted LotusScript agent could, theoretically, navigate through folders, read text files, and mail documents as attachments; a restricted LotusScript agent could not. Before you start writing agents, check with your Domino administrator to see whether you can write unrestricted agents. You can also be prohibited from writing LotusScript and Java agents on a database-by-database basis.

Daily An agent for which you've chosen the Daily option is in all ways identical to a More Th[an] Once a Day agent except for its scheduling (see Figure 25.6). Instead of selecting an interval, you g[ive] the agent a time during the day to run. It will run once a day at that time.

FIGURE 25.6
Agent Schedule
dialog box for a
Daily agent

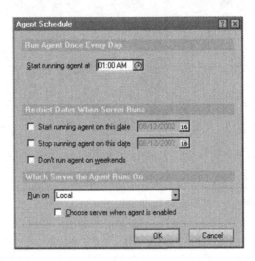

Weekly If you choose the Weekly option, the agent is also identical to a More Than Once a D[ay] agent except for scheduling. A Weekly agent takes both a day of the week (Sunday through Saturda[y]) and a time of day. Also, the Don't Run Agent on Weekends check box is absent. After all, if you choose a day from Monday through Friday, it will never run on a weekend, and if you were to choo[se] Saturday or Sunday and not let it run on weekends, it would never run at all.

Monthly A Monthly agent is identical to a Weekly agent except that it takes a day of the mont[h] (1 through 31) instead of a day of the week. Like the Weekly agent, it cannot be turned off for wee[k]ends. Unfortunately, it only counts forward (day 1, day 2...), so you can't easily make it run on t[he] last day of the month.

Never A Never agent will never run. At least, it won't run on a schedule or on any other behind-th[e] scenes event. The purpose of having an agent like this is to allow a designer to temporarily disable [a] scheduled agent without losing the All Documents/All New and Modified Documents since the La[st] Run setting. Like all other agents, it can still be run through `@Command([ToolsRunMacro])` and all t[he] other methods of running an agent manually.

SECURITY TAB

This tab, shown in Figure 25.7, is more detailed than the security tabs you've seen for other object[s]. The new settings mostly concern web operation or restricted agent code.

FIGURE 25.7

Agent Properties
Box, Security tab

The Run as Web User causes the agent to run in the name of the logged-in user if it is invoked via the Web. Without this setting checked, the agent runs under the name (and therefore the permissions) of the last person to save the agent. This is useful for a number of reasons. It limits agent operations to the permission of the person running the agent rather than the agent's designer, who probably has much greater permissions in the database, and any documents created or modified by the agent will show the web user's name in $UpdatedBy and other automatically maintained fields. You may instead put a name in Run On Behalf Of, specifying a username to run as. There are, though, some safeguards on how this field operates. If the agent is saved by someone who cannot run restricted agents, the agent will not run restricted commands regardless of whose name is entered. Allow Remote Debugging lets the developer debug the agent with remote debugging tools. The Restricted Operations menu allows the designer to limit the agent to running with restricted rights even if he has unrestricted rights.

PROGRAMMER'S PANE

The agent programmer's pane is where the meat of the agent, the program code, goes (see Figure 25.8). At the top center of the pane is a drop-down menu that allows you to pick a programming language. This is fairly similar to the menu you've seen for selecting a language for form events, but there's a different list of choices: formula, Simple Actions, LotusScript, Java, and Imported Java. Regardless of which language you choose, the programmer's pane actually gives you two places to put code: the Document Selection formula and the agent code itself.

The target document option you select in the Agent Properties Box is actually fairly coarse. It is quite likely, for example, that you'll want the agent to run on all documents created with a particular form or all documents that fit a specific category instead of on all documents. The Document Selection lets you refine the list of documents presented by the agent's target selection criteria. The agent will run on the documents that fit both the agent's target selection and the formula entered there. The machinery for creating a Document Selection is identical to that used for a Simple Search view selection formula.

FIGURE 25.8

Agent
programmer's pane

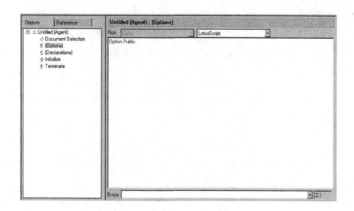

Finally, you get to tell your agent to do something. The programmer's pane for an agent works
it does for any other programmer's pane for the language in question. The agent code you provi
if it's a Simple Action or a formula, will act on every document returned by the selection criteria. T
is a place to be careful when writing agents and making a target selection. Simple Actions and for
mulas can't "remember" data between documents, and they can't perform a single aggregate actio
using the sum total of the documents on which the agent runs. For example, suppose you wanted
report on the number of documents in a view on demand. To do so, you use formulas such as the f
lowing to set up an agent run from the Actions menu that runs on all documents in the view:

```
ListOfItems := @DBColumn("":"";"":"MyDB.nsf";"ReportingView";1);
Listcount := @Elements(ListOfItems);
Messagetext := "There are " + @Text(Listcount) + " documents in
ReportingView."
@mailsend("MailingGroup";"";"";"ReportingView Contents";Messagetext;
"")
```

This code uses the @DBColumn formula to get a list of everything in the first column of the view a
@Elements to count the elements in the list. If ReportingView is uncategorized, the number of ele
ments returned by @Elements is the same as the number of documents in the view. That number ge
tossed into a string that is sent out with @Mailsend. Mission accomplished? Yes, but only too we
Because a formula agent acts on every document, you'll send out this message once *for every docume*
in the view. If there are 100 documents in the view, that's 100 separate but identical mail messages. Us
ally, you'll want to do the same thing 10 or 100 times, but this isn't one of those times. If you wa
an agent to work on an aggregate of documents, select the None option. The code will run once, ta
ing values from no one document, and be done.

Often, though, an operation on a batch of documents is exactly what you want. Imagine a view
of documents pending a supervisor's approval. Typically, the supervisor can determine at a glance
which documents should be approved and which denied. The code to approve a document is simpl
something such as FIELD Status := "Approved", but how many times will the supervisor have to pre
a button? Using a form action, the supervisor would have to open each document in turn and pres
the button. With a view action, the supervisor would have to select each document in turn in the vie

and press the button. Not quite as tedious, but still bad. But with an agent with All Selected Documents as its target selection, the supervisor needs to select only a batch of documents to be approved and select a menu item (if it's an Action Menu Selection agent) or press a button (if you use an @command to trigger the agent) and it's done.

For LotusScript and Java agents, however, target selection is a mere suggestion. You can, as shown in the previous chapter, run searches within the database, use views and folders as devices to get documents, and so on. However, if you do want to work with the documents provided by the agent's target criteria, use the UnprocessedDocuments property of a database object. UnprocessedDocuments is a document collection containing the documents selected by the agent's target selection and Document Selection formula. So how does this all work in practice? We've created two sample Java agents in the Recipes database. Open the database, go to Agents in Shared Code, and open NewsletterAgent and ViewNewsletterAgent. Both agents are set to trigger on agent menu selection, targeting all selected documents. However, the target selection doesn't actually matter for NewsletterAgent. It selects its own set of documents. Here's NewsletterAgent:

```
import lotus.domino.*;

public class JavaAgent extends AgentBase {

  public void NotesMain() {

   try {
     int int_count = 0;
     Session session = getSession();
     AgentContext agentContext = session.getAgentContext();

     // (Your code goes here)
     Database db = agentContext.getCurrentDatabase();
     // Create a search string and use it to find all
     // of the recipe documents
     String thestr = "@Contains(Form; \"Recipe\")";
     DocumentCollection dc = db.search (thestr);

     // If there are any documents...
    if (dc.getCount() > 0) {
     // Create a newsletter object
    Newsletter news = session.createNewsletter(dc);
     // These lines pick a field from the documents
     // to serve as a "subject" for each item in the
     // newsletter. The contents of the field will appear
     // next to the link to its document
    news.setSubjectItemName("NameOfRecipe");
    news.setDoSubject(true);
     // Take the object and turn it into a document
    Document doc = news.formatMsgWithDoclinks(db);
     // Set some field values; appendItemValue is
     // similar to replaceItemValue
    doc.appendItemValue("Form", "Memo");
```

```
        doc.appendItemValue("Subject", "All recipes");
        // The send method mails the document to anybody
        // named in the second parameter
        doc.send(false, session.getUserName());
    }


    } catch(Exception e) {
        e.printStackTrace();
    }
  }
}
```

NOTE   *In addition to working with Java, we're also introducing a new kind of object: the newsletter. A newsletter*
a special kind of mail message that takes a batch of documents and creates a list of links to them. It's a useful way of pro-
viding pointers to a set of documents.

Here's the code for `ViewNewsletterAgent`. Notice that the only significant difference in the co
is how the document collection is obtained:

```
import lotus.domino.*;

public class JavaAgent extends AgentBase {

  public void NotesMain() {

    try {
      int int_count = 0;
      Session session = getSession();
      AgentContext agentContext = session.getAgentContext();

      // (Your code goes here)
      Database db = agentContext.getCurrentDatabase();
      DocumentCollection dc = agentContext.getUnprocessedDocuments();
    if (dc.getCount() > 0) {
      Newsletter news = session.createNewsletter(dc);
      news.setSubjectItemName("NameOfRecipe");
      news.setDoSubject(true);
      Document doc = news.formatMsgWithDoclinks(db);
      doc.appendItemValue("Form", "Memo");
      doc.appendItemValue("Subject", "All docs in the view");
      doc.send(false, session.getUserName());
    }


    } catch(Exception e) {
      e.printStackTrace();
    }
  }
}
```

Both of these agents do pretty much the same thing. They get a batch of documents out of the database, create a newsletter containing links to those objects, and mail it to the user triggering the agent. The difference is in the documents selected. NewsletterAgent uses the Search method, always obtaining the same set of documents (specifically, everything using a form whose name contains the word *Recipe*). ViewNewsletterAgent, however, uses the unprocessedDocuments collection, so it gets whatever documents are selected. Although NewsletterAgent will always produce a list of the same documents, ViewNewsletterAgent will return a different list depending on which documents are selected.

Implementing Subforms

Back in Chapter 19, "Basic Form Design," and Chapter 20, "Advanced Form Design," you learned what a form is and how it is used. A *subform* is similar to a form except that it cannot be used by itself. A subform must be embedded within a form to be displayed to the user. This may not sound like an advantage at first, but because the contents of a subform are separate from the form, you can reuse the subform in many different forms. Any change you make to the subform will be automatically reflected in every form in which the subform is embedded. This allows you to make changes from a central location, which means less work for you. You can also have Notes select a subform with a formula, so you can swap out large chunks of form design as you desire.

Creating a Subform

Creating a subform is similar to creating a regular form. In our Recipes database, you'll create a subform that contains an audit trail. The subform will display information about who created the document and when it was created plus who last modified the document and when it was last modified. To create a blank subform, choose Create ➤ Design ➤ Subform or call up the Subform pane and click the New Subform button. This will display the Design workspace with a blank subform, as shown in Figure 25.9.

FIGURE 25.9

A blank subform ready for designing

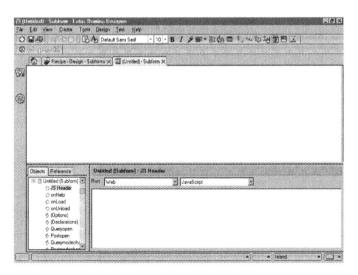

The Audit Trail subform will contain fields for username, dates, and times. To add these fields to the newly created subform, perform the following steps:

1. Type **Created By:** on the first line.

2. With the cursor just to the right of the text, choose Create ➤ Design ➤ Field, which displays the Field Properties Box. Type **CreatedBy** in the Name field and make sure Text and Computed When Composed are selected from the drop-down list boxes. Because this is a computed field, in the Value event for the field, type the formula **@Name([CN];@UserName)**, which will store the current username in the field.

3. On the next line, type **Created On:**.

4. With the cursor just to the right of the text, add a field named **CreatedDateTime** and select Date/Time and Computed for Display from the drop-down list boxes and give it a value **@Created**. You should have something like the subform displayed in Figure 25.10.

FIGURE 25.10

The Audit Trail subform

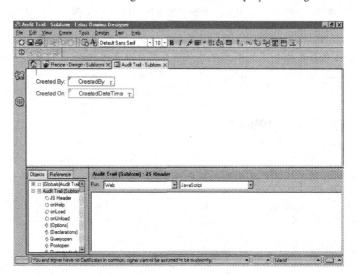

Using the Subform

To use the subform, you must place it on a form, which is easy to do. The only prerequisite is that you must have a form open on which to place the subform. You'll place the Audit Trail subform on the Recipe and Ingredient forms in the Recipes database.

There are two ways a subform can be displayed on a form:

◆ Standard

◆ Computed

If you use the standard subform method, you designate a specific subform to use. If you use the computed subform method, you give the form a formula that returns the name of a subform.

DISPLAYING THE STANDARD SUBFORM

To insert a standard subform on a form, just follow these steps:

1. Open the Recipe form in the Recipes database.
2. Delete all the table rows after the Categories field.
3. Choose Create ➤ Insert Subform. The Insert Subform dialog box appears.
4. Select Audit Trail from the Insert Subform list box and click the OK button (see Figure 25.11).

FIGURE 25.11

Selecting the Audit Trail subform from the Insert Subform dialog box

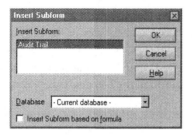

Because you inserted a standard subform, its contents will display within the context of the Recipe form, as shown in Figure 25.12. Although you can see the individual subform fields and labels, you cannot change them within the context of the form. You must open the subform using the Design list in the Design pane. There is, however, a more convenient way to open it; you may notice that, in the script area of the programmer's pane for the selected subform, there is a reminder that you can double-click the subform to edit the contents.

FIGURE 25.12

The Recipe form with a standard subform placed on it

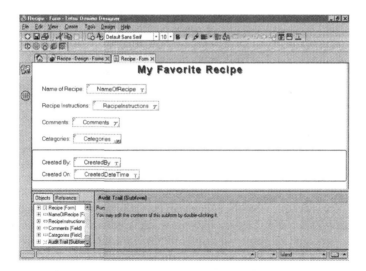

DISPLAYING THE COMPUTED SUBFORM

To insert a computed subform on a form, follow these steps:

1. Open the Ingredient form in the Recipes database.

2. Place the cursor at the bottom of the form after the Description field.

3. Choose Create ➤ Insert Subform.

4. Select the Insert Subform Based on Formula option in the Insert Subform dialog box and click the OK button. This will place a Computed Subform marker on the form. Notice th although the Formula option is enabled, you cannot select a subform from the list.

5. From the Objects tab in the programmer's pane, select the Computed Subform object (you c also select the Computed Subform object directly on the form).

6. Type the formula **"Audit Trail"** in the script area of the programmer's pane, which will ev uate to the name of the subform in the Default Value event, as shown in Figure 25.13.

FIGURE 25.13

Entering a formula to calculate the name of the subform to display

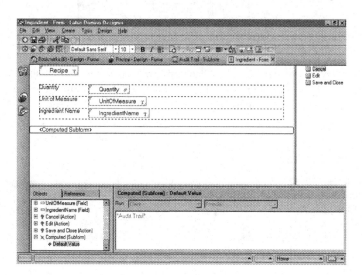

NOTE *"Audit Trail" is just barely a formula, but you can write a complex formula that will evaluate to the name of any subform you want. Using this idea, you could display different subforms based on the user's name, the time of day, or the security access level.*

You will notice that the contents of the subform are not displayed on the form; instead, a box th contains the text *<Computed Subform>* is displayed. You elected to *compute* the name of the subform use; hence, no subform will display until the form is actually used.

One of the nice features of using the computed subform is the ability to decide at runtime whic subform to use. In this example, the Audit Trail subform is always used, but there is no reason yo couldn't enter a formula that returns a different subform name based on certain criteria. One drav back to using this type of subform is not being able to actually view the subform contents on the forr

If you want to see what the subform contains, you must open it from the Design list of the Design pane (unlike with the standard subform, there is no shortcut to open the computed subform).

USING THE SUBFORM PROPERTIES BOX

There are a few options that are only enabled and disabled through the Subform Properties InfoBox (see Figure 25.14). To display the Subform Properties Box, you must first open the subform in Domino Designer. Double-click the embedded subform and it will automatically open. To open the Subform Properties Box, choose Design ➤ Subform Properties.

FIGURE 25.14

The Subform Properties Box

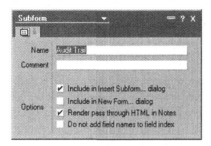

As with all the other design elements, you can assign your subform a name and an alias.

The next check box limits the subform's availability for use in forms. When you are trying to insert a subform on a form, you are prompted with a list of subforms via the Insert Subform dialog box. If this box is unchecked, the subform will not appear there. However, you can still invoke the subform if you use the computed subform method.

You can also have the Insert Subform dialog box automatically display when you are creating a new form. The Include in New Form... Dialog option is disabled by default, which will prevent the dialog box from automatically popping up every time you create a new form. When it's enabled, this option can be a bit irritating, so you may want to leave it disabled. However, it's very useful if you want a standard subform (for, say, workflow or audit trails) on every form in your database.

Finally, the Render Pass Through HTML and Do Not Add Field Names to Field Index options are identical to those settings in the Form Properties InfoBox.

Creating Shared Fields

If you find yourself creating the same field for use on different forms, it may be time to create a *shared field*. A shared field is *not* an object that allows you to share a piece of data between forms or documents. Rather, it is a shared field *definition*. Say, for example, that you have a number of forms on which you want users to enter a product number that must use one of two or three formats (say, three digits, a hyphen, and two letters; four digits, a hyphen, and two digits; or four letters, a hyphen, and two digits). You can write an input validation formula to check the format, but each time the organization adds a new format for product numbers, you'll have to go back and revise the formula in every form where it occurs. Using a shared field, you can manage that change centrally, doing it just once and having it update everywhere.

The process for creating a shared field from scratch is quite simple:

1. Choose Create ➤ Design ➤ Shared Field or click the New Shared Field button in the Shared Fields work pane.
2. Enter a name for the field.
3. Assign all the field types, properties, and events.
4. Close and save the field.

You can also create a shared field from an existing field definition. If you have a field that would make a good candidate for a shared field, do the following:

1. Open the form in which the field resides.
2. Click the field to be shared.
3. Choose Design ➤ Share This Field.

Once this process has been completed, you'll notice that a dark border appears around the field. The border indicates that the field is actually a shared field. It is a subtle difference that makes it easy to tell which fields are single-use fields and which are shared fields.

Converting a single-use field to a shared field eliminates the need to create a shared field from scratch. To insert an existing single-use field into a shared field, follow these steps:

1. Open the form and place the cursor where you want the field.
2. Choose Create ➤ Insert Shared Field.
3. From the Insert Shared Field dialog box that appears, select the field you want to use from the Insert Shared Field list box (once a shared field has been placed on the form, it will no longer appear in the Insert Shared Field list box).

If you want to convert a shared field back to a single-use field, just do the following:

1. Open the form.
2. Select the shared field.
3. Choose Edit ➤ Cut.
4. Display the list of shared fields for the database. To access the shared fields, expand the Resources object in the Design list and select Shared Field.
5. Highlight the shared field you want to remove in the Work pane and press the Delete key.
6. Switch back to the form and choose Edit ➤ Paste.

Creating Shared Actions

Just as you can create shared field definitions, you can create shared action buttons. As you can see in Figure 25.15, the Work pane listing of shared actions is, like the listing of agents, a bit different from other object listings. The listing indicates whether each action is displayed in the Action bar, or the menu, what kind of graphic it uses, and which language it uses, as well as its appearance in Notes on the Web, and for mobile devices.

FIGURE 25.15

Shared actions
listing

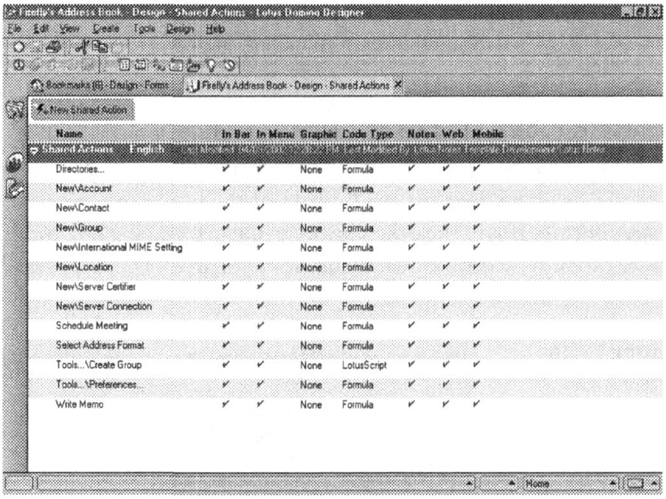

If you want to use an existing shared action button on your form or view, choose Create ➤ Insert Shared Action and a dialog box will appear allowing you to select the shared action you would like to insert (assuming that at least one action has been defined). When an action button in placed on a form or view, you may notice that the Action pane automatically slides open. It lists all the current actions defined for the element in the order they will appear to the end user on the Action bar.

Using Script Libraries

Script libraries are, in a way, the purest shared code object. They are simply central repositories of program code. They allow you to create libraries of functions, subroutines, and custom classes that you can then use anywhere in your database.

Script libraries may be created from the Create menu. The Script Library option gives you a sub-menu allowing you to create a LotusScript, JavaScript, or Java library. Likewise, if you call up the list of script libraries, there are separate creation buttons for LotusScript, JavaScript, and Java libraries. Just how you use a library depends on what language you use.

Accessing LotusScript Libraries

You can call a LotusScript library from inside any LotusScript action, agent, or event. As you may recall, every script has a routine named (Options). You can put a statement here telling the script to include the code in the script library. The command is Use "libraryname". For example, if you had a database with several agents that processed web input, you might want to create a library of functions to process data coming in through the Web. If you named the library *CGI Functions*, you'd put the line Use "CGI Functions" in the (Options) section of each script. You can include multiple code libraries in any script. Simply put a different Use command in the (Options) section for each library you want to include.

NOTE *You can even use LotusScript libraries in other LotusScript libraries. Likewise, you can use Java libraries in other Java libraries.*

Accessing Java Libraries

Just as you can call LotusScript libraries from any script, you can call Java libraries from any object in Notes that runs Java. At the bottom of the programmer's pane of every Java object is an Edit Project button. If you click the button, you'll get a dialog box for organizing files (see Figure 25.16). Under the Browse drop-down menu, select Shared Java Libraries. This will let you include any Java libraries in your own Java code.

FIGURE 25.16

Organize Java Agent Files dialog box

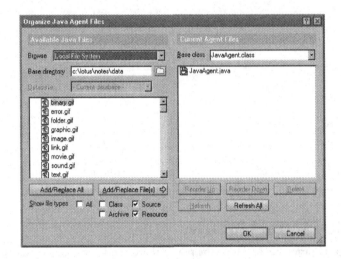

Accessing JavaScript Libraries

JavaScript libraries are a little different from the other code libraries. Because everything in JavaScript happens at the client end, you don't include the JavaScript library in a particular chunk of JavaScript. Rather, you include it on a form. This makes the JavaScript functions in the library available to other functions and events on the form. To put a JavaScript library on a form, insert it as you would any other resource. Select Create ➤ Insert Resource and select JavaScript Libraries from the list. You'll be able to select a JavaScript library to include on the form.

Summary

This chapter has covered the use of shared code objects. Like shared resources, shared code objects give you a way of centrally maintaining objects shared through your database, but shared code objects let you share program code, not just pictures and files. Most of the objects (subforms, shared fields, and shared actions) are used in form design, and code libraries are used in the design of other code-bearing objects. However, agents can operate independently of individual design elements or, indeed, independently of user activity altogether.

Appendix A

Installing IBM Lotus Notes and Domino 6 Clients

IBM HAS UPDATED THE Notes and Domino installation process for the new release, focusing on a simple and commonly used process. This appendix will cover the installation process for the clients. Depending on whether you're a Notes user, programmer, or administrator, you can choose to install just one client or all three. All three clients are included in the same installation program. The software available to you during installation will depend on the type of license you purchased. The single Notes client installs just the software needed to work with Lotus Notes Domino databases. The Designer client installs the Lotus Notes client and all the software needed to create and code Domino databases. The Administration client installs the software needed to remotely administer a Domino server.

You can perform two types of installations: a new clean install (use this if you don't have Notes on your current machine) and an upgrade. Though the process for both types of installations is the same, there are a few minor differences, which we'll discuss as they occur. The Notes installation process has three components to it:

1. Using the Installation Wizard to load the software on your computer
2. Using the Lotus Notes Client Configuration wizard to customize the installed software for your personal use
3. Using the Lotus Notes Welcome Page setup to tailor your Notes workspace

You may be installing the software from a CD or from an Internet download from the www.lotus.com website. In either case, double-click the setup.exe program icon to start the process. With a CD, the installation process will begin automatically through an autorun program, or you can browse the contents of the CD and run the setup.exe program manually.

If you're one of those ambitious souls who played with the beta releases of Notes and Domino, you've already seen in-progress versions of many of the features discussed here. Your computer has seen it, too, and that can be a problem. Previous installations of Notes, including the early betas, can leave traces in your system. Usually, that's OK. In fact, it's usually exactly what you want. If you're upgrading an existing installation of Notes, you probably want your Notes client to talk to the same server, keep using the same ID file, and so on. Lotus's installers have historically been good about keeping the settings you probably want while getting rid of obsolete DLL files and executables, and if you're coming to the current version of Notes from one of the Gold versions like 5 or 4, you don't have to worry. However, if you're upgrading from a beta release of Notes, there may be problems in your notes.ini file, which isn't replaced when you upgrade.

If you're installing Notes over a beta release, it's a good idea to completely uninstall the beta version and throw away the notes.ini file.

Starting the Installation Wizard

After initiating the setup program, the Installation Wizard will take over, as shown in Figure A.1.

FIGURE A.1

Starting the Installation Wizard

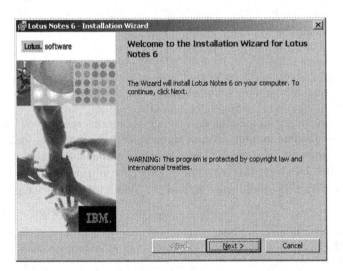

One of the requirements of any software installation is accepting the licensing agreement. You'll see a screen where you need to accept or reject the terms outlined by IBM; rejecting the terms halts the installation process. Next, you'll be asked to type two pieces of customer information: your name and your organization. After supplying the customer information, you'll see a screen to choose the installation directories on your computer for Lotus to place its files, as shown in Figure A.2.

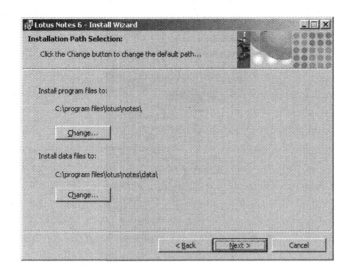

You need to specify two directories: one stores the Lotus Notes and Domino software, and the other stores all the Notes databases on your machine. These two directories have traditionally separated executable code from stored data to protect the data from crashes or reinstalls of software. With this release of Lotus Notes and Domino, the Windows client installation directories have changed from prior releases; client software and databases are now stored under the \Program Files\Lotus directory by default. In prior releases, the directory path was \Lotus\Notes with no reference to the Program Files directory. You can accept the default (recommended) or use the Change button to specify a different directory (including the old \Lotus\Notes directory).

NOTE   *If you already have a copy of the Notes client software on your computer, the default folders will reflect where the current installation of Notes resides. Before overwriting your current installation of Notes, it is a good idea to back up your current* Data *folder just in case something goes wrong.*

After specifying the directories in which to place the client files, you need to determine which Lotus Notes or Domino clients to install on your machine. The Installation Wizard allows you to perform a custom setup to select one, two, or all of the clients. With this dialog box, you can choose the clients and the components within the clients by double-clicking an option; when the red X is *not* present, that software component is selected for installation. Figure A.3 shows the Lotus Notes client and four of six of its components selected for installation; the Domino Designer and Domino Administrator clients are not selected and will not be installed. Table A.1 describes the options available for each of the types of clients.

FIGURE A.3

Custom Setup
components

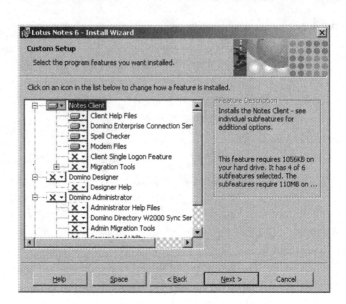

TABLE A.1: Custom Setup Component Options

CLIENT TYPE	OPTION	DESCRIPTION
Notes Client	Client Help Files	Help file for end users showing how to use the Lotus Notes user interface and all of its feature
Notes Client	Domino Enterprise Connection Services	Files necessary to use Domino Enterprise Connection Services (DECS) to interact with relational databases
Notes Client	Spell Checker	Spell-check support for Notes documents
Notes Client	Modem Files	Files for configuring a wide variety of modems in Notes
Notes Client	Client Single Logon Feature	Synchronize Notes password with Windows X 2000, and NT
Notes Client	Migration Tools	Migrate mail to Notes from ccMail, Exchange, MSMail, and Outlook Express
Domino Designer	Designer Help	Help file for Domino programmers showing hov to use the features of Domino Designer

Continued on next pag

CLIENT TYPE	OPTION	DESCRIPTION
Domino Administrator	Administrator Help Files	Help file for Domino administrators showing how to use the Domino Administrator user interface and all of its features
Domino Administrator	Domino Directory W2000 Sync Services	Adds entries to the Domino Directory using Windows 2000 (W2000)
Domino Administrator	Admin Migration Tools	Tools to assist administrators in migrating users from other mail systems to Domino
Domino Administrator	Server Load Utility	Capacity planning tool
Domino Administrator	Remote Server Setup	Installs Domino server software on a remote machine
All Clients	Symbol Files for Support	Installs symbolic files to help in debugging Notes problems

After making all your client and component choices, the Installation Wizard is ready to install the software you've chosen. Figure A.4 displays and gives you a chance to go back and make any needed changes; Figure A.5 shows you the progress of the installation process. When the Installation Wizard completes its tasks, Figure A.6 displays.

FIGURE A.4

Ready to install

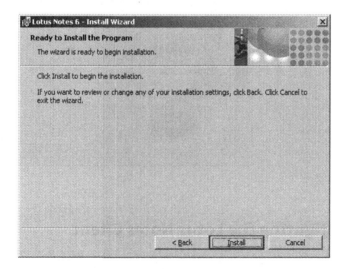

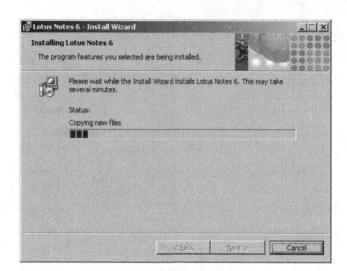

Configuring the Lotus Notes Client

Once the software has been installed on your computer, the next phase of the process configures th
client for your use. In this phase, you'll be asked questions about how you want to use the Notes clier
and, if you'll be connecting to a Domino server, how that connection will be made. Figure A.7 show
the first screen you'll see as the Lotus Notes Client Configuration phase of the installation begins

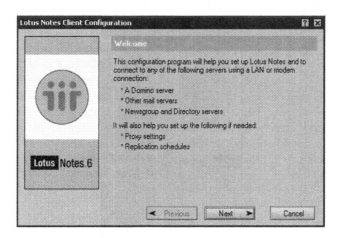

FIGURE A.7

Lotus Notes Client Configuration

NOTE *Before beginning this part of the installation, you'll need to know your Lotus Notes Domino username and password. If you have an existing locally stored Notes user ID, it will be used during this process. If you do not have a Notes user ID but have been told by your Domino administrator that you have a username and you know your password, you can continue without a user ID; the user ID will be placed on your machine during the installation.*

The questions asked during this phase help define your Notes environment. Whether you're upgrading or installing from scratch, a series of screens will present questions for you, and if you don't know the answer to a question, just skip it (or answer No); you can come back to it later (you can also change your answers).

Connecting to a Domino Server

On the User Information dialog box, shown in Figure A.8, you'll provide the following pieces of information:

◆ The first name and last name of your registered Lotus Notes username

◆ The name of the Domino server to connect to in `Server Name/Organization Name` format

NOTE *Your Domino administrator can supply the exact server name and organization name for you to use.*

At the bottom of the screen is a check box to mark if you want to connect to a Domino server. If you have a network or other type of connection to the Domino server at this point, enable the check box and click the Next button. If you don't have access to the server at this point, leave the check box unmarked and proceed with the installation by clicking the Next button.

If you have network access or another type of access to a Domino server and you've enabled the check box in Figure A.8, the next screen lets choose the type of connection to configure for accessing the Domino server. There are two options available, as shown in Figure A.9. You can connect to the server using either a local area network (LAN) connection or a phone connection.

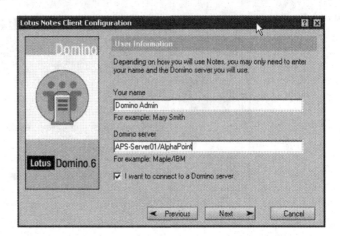

FIGURE A.9
How will you
connect to the
Domino server?

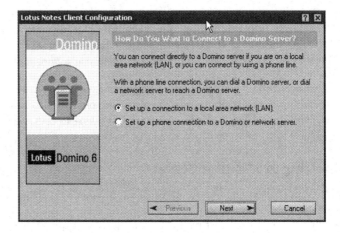

If you will be using a phone connection, a screen will appear asking for the type of phone connection (directly to the Domino server, through a network server, or both).

Specifying Who You Are

In this step of the installation process, you'll be challenged to enter a password that can be used to unlock your Notes user ID file. If you are upgrading from a previous version of Notes, your current Notes ID will most likely be stored locally on your computer. Select the location of your Notes ID (typically, your Notes ID is in the Notes Data folder). If this is your first installation of Notes and you don't have a user ID file, it will be stored for you during this installation process. The first time you connect to the Domino server, you will be prompted to enter your Notes password, and your username is used to match against the password. Figure A.10 shows the dialog box you'll see if you're installing Notes for the first time and connecting to a Domino server. If you elected to not connect to a Domino server at this time, you'll see one more screen asking if you want to set up a remote connection to a remote network server.

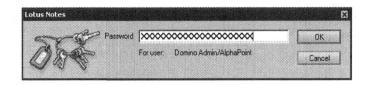

At this point, the Domino-related installation information is complete.

Installing Internet Access

You can use the Notes client for Internet mail and newsgroup access, and configuration for this purpose is built in to the Lotus Notes client setup configuration. For the Notes client to send and retrieve mail and also allow you to browse Internet newsgroups, you'll need to supply some basic information.

INTERNET MAIL

If you have an Internet mail account, you can use the Notes client for both your Domino (Notes) mail and your Internet mail. To configure Internet mail, three configuration screens are required to collect three different types of information:

◆ Post Office Protocol (POP) information for outing Internet mail

◆ Account name and password

◆ Simple Mail Transfer Protocol (SMTP) server name for incoming Internet mail

To set up the Notes client properly for Internet mail, you need your e-mail address, your Internet mail provider's SMTP server name, your Internet mail provider's POP or Internet Message Access Protocol (IMAP) server name, and your Internet mail account username and password. If you're not sure what the answers to these questions are, you can get them from your Internet service provider (ISP). Figure A.11 shows a configuration for a POP server. Figure A.12 uses an account name and password for the POP Internet account. Figure A.13 shows a configuration for an SMTP server.

FIGURE A.11

POP information

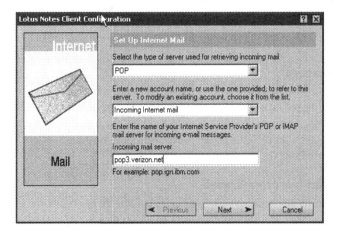

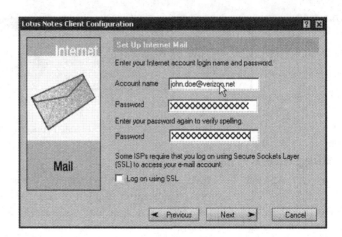

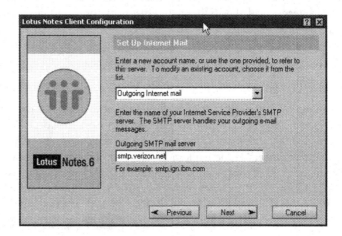

NEWSGROUPS

After you've entered the information on the Internet mail installation screens, you'll be asked if yo
would like to access newsgroups via a news server. If you decide that you would like to set up acce.
to a newsgroup server, you will need to know the name of the server. You can get that informatio
from either your ISP or, in some cases, your Domino administrator. You can also come back later an
configure Notes to access newsgroups.

INTERNET DIRECTORY SERVER

Another option you can install will give you the ability to use the Lightweight Directory Access Pr
tocol (LDAP) to search for people. The address book within the Notes client supports LDAP, whic
allows you to search other Internet directory services. By default, the Notes installation routine wi

add a few of the more common LDAP servers automatically, such as Bigfoot and Verisign. You can get the LDAP server names from either your ISP or your Domino administrator.

After you've finished answering questions tailored to your needs, your client is configured and ready to use. With the process complete, a message box telling you that the Notes setup has completed will display, as shown in Figure A.14.

FIGURE A.14
Setup is complete.

Setting Up the Lotus Notes Welcome Page

You're almost ready to start using the Notes client! With the Installation Wizard and the Client Configuration behind you, the last step of the process places you inside the Lotus Notes client to customize the Welcome page. The Welcome page is your starting point for all activity when you open Lotus Notes. Figure A.15 shows the screen that will let you customize a personal Welcome page, see what's new in Lotus Notes 6, or set up your Welcome page with standard defaults. Figure A.16 shows the standard Welcome page. Enjoy!

FIGURE A.15
Welcome page
setup options

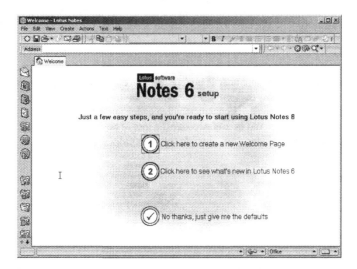

FIGURE A.16

The Notes Client
Welcome page

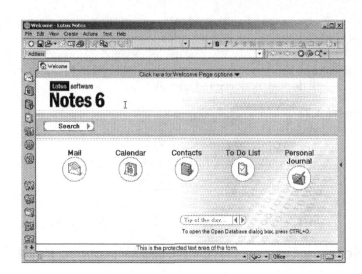

UPGRADING NOTES

For those of you who are upgrading from previous versions of Notes, we would like to mention what entries the installation process has affected. Most importantly, your notes.ini file has been changed and potentially moved. The installation process also upgrades the Notes program and the Notes templates in the Notes Data folder.

When Notes is initially launched and you have completed answering all of the installation questions, the final portion of the upgrade takes place. Release 4 desktop.dsk files are converted to a desktop5.dsk. The bookmarks.nsf and headlines.nsf files are also automatically created. The bookmarks.nsf file is configured based on the contents of your desktop5.dsk file. The names.nsf design is automatically updated for the new template. Both the mail.box and smtp.box databases are also replaced. The upgrade process is seamless and occurs without the loss of any of your settings. Your mail database design is not automatically upgraded. You must do this manually.

to the Reader: Throughout this index **boldfaced** page numbers indicate primary discussions of a topic. *Italicized* page numbers indicate illustrations.

S

Master These Fundamentals

Master These Advanced Topics